Birding Florida

Over 200 Prime Birding Sites at 54 Locations

Brian Rapoza

FALCONGUIDES ®

GUILFORD, CONNECTICUT
HELENA, MONTANA
AN IMPRINT OF THE GLOBE PEQUOT PRESS

FALCONGUIDES®

Falcon and FalconGuides are registered trademarks of
Morris Book Publishing, LLC.

Text design by Eileen Hine
Overview and site maps by Melissa Baker, range maps by
Brian Rapoza © Morris Book Publishing, LLC.

Library of Congress Cataloging-in-Publication Data is
available
ISBN: 978-0-7627-3914-1

Manufactured in the United States of America
First Edition/Third Printing

This book is dedicated to my father, who instilled in me a work ethic and attention to detail that influence everything I do, and to my dear friends Jill Rosenfield and Dick Cunningham, both of whom deeply influenced my passion for birds and birding. I wish all of you could have seen the completion of this book.

Osprey. PHOTO: NANCY MORELAND

Contents

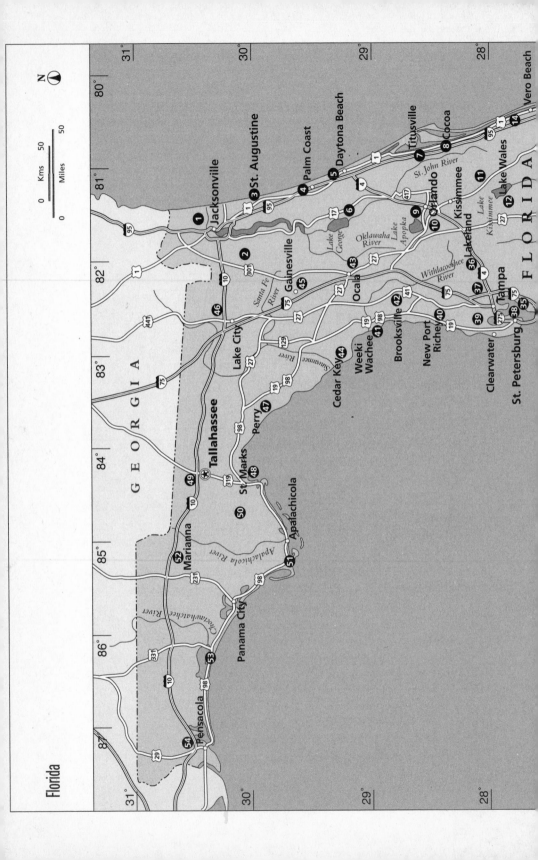

Florida

N

Kms 0 50
Miles 0 50

GEORGIA

FLORIDA

Jacksonville

St. Augustine

Palm Coast

Daytona Beach

Titusville

Cocoa

Vero Beach

St. John River

Orlando

Kissimmee

Lake Wales

Lakeland

Gainesville

Ocala

Lake
Apopka

Oklawaha
River

Lake George

Withlacoochee
River

Lake City

Santa Fe River

Suwannee River

Cedar Key

Weeki
Wachee

Brooksville

New Port
Richey

Clearwater

St. Petersburg

Tampa

Lake
Kissimmee

Tallahassee

Perry

St. Marks

Apalachicola

Apalachicola River

Marianna

Choctawhatchee River

Panama City

Pensacola

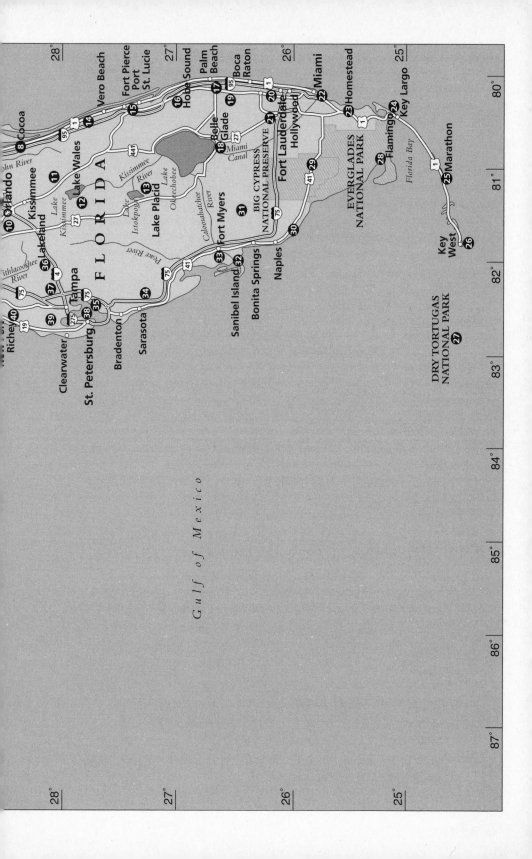

Southeast

Florida Keys/The Everglades

Southwest

West-central

Northwest

The Panhandle

Help Us Keep This Guide Up to Date

Every effort has been made by the author and editors to make this guide as accurate and useful as possible. However, many things can change after a guide is published—trails are rerouted, regulations change, techniques evolve, facilities come under new management, etc.

We would love to hear from you concerning your experiences with this guide and how you feel it could be improved and kept up to date. While we may not be able to respond to all comments and suggestions, we'll take them to heart, and we'll also make certain to share them with the authors. Please send your comments and suggestions to the following address:

The Globe Pequot Press
Reader Response/Editorial Department
P.O. Box 480
Guilford, CT 06437

Or you may e-mail us at:

editorial@GlobePequot.com

Thanks for your input, and happy trails!

Foreword

Florida has long been considered a premier location for the serious birder to seek an abundance of avian specialties. Whether a birder is visiting the state on a business trip, for a family vacation, or as an avid lister hoping to add a rarity to his or her life list, a current guide to birding hot spots is essential to maximize opportunities for finding target birds.

FalconGuides searched for an author who is familiar with this bird-rich state from the far reaches of the Panhandle to the Florida Keys and Dry Tortugas. Fortunately, my dear friend, Brian Rapoza, was up to the task. As field trip coordinator for the Tropical Audubon Society and an environmental field trip coordinator for Miami-Dade County Public Schools, he has introduced thousands of birders and school-children alike to the flora and fauna unique to South Florida. His passion for birding and tireless effort to share his vast knowledge of Florida birding locales will become self-evident when the reader first opens this book. His attention to detail and collaboration with birders across the state will ensure that directions and species accounts are accurate and up to date. As a bonus, his guide also offers DeLorme grids and information on hazards, nearby food, gas, and lodging, camping, and contacts.

Unfortunately, Florida's population explosion invites rampant development. The results: urban sprawl reaching outside of urban development boundary lines, destruction of buffer zones with national forests and parks, and threats to the very survival of the Everglades. As a Miami native, I have personally witnessed many birding hot spots become "here one day and gone the next!"

As a longtime board member of the Tropical Audubon Society, Brian is committed to preserving the many native ecosystems and environmentally endangered lands of our great state. Our future generations need to enjoy and marvel at seeing native Wood Storks, Snail Kites, Florida Scrub-Jays, and "Cape Sable" Seaside Sparrows. This guide is invaluable to both beginner and advanced birders when planning their birding trips to see these wonderful Florida specialties.

Birding across Florida in the footprints of William Bartram, John James Audubon, Harold H. Bailey, Samuel Grimes, Alexander Sprunt Jr., Herbert Kale, William B. Robertson Jr., Glen E. Woolfenden, Henry M. Stevenson, and Bruce H. Anderson . . . life is good.

Paul Bithorn
Tropical Audubon Society
Virginia Gardens, Florida

Acknowledgments

I'd first like to thank Cynthia Guerra, Executive Director of the Tropical Audubon Society, who brought to my attention the opportunity to write *Birding Florida*. Thanks also to Roger Hammer, director of Castellow Hammock Nature Center, Tropical Audubon Society board member, and author of three titles in the FalconGuides series, for his helpful suggestions and advice during the early stages of the writing process.

Several research expeditions were needed to create this birding guide, providing me with a unique opportunity to explore every corner of this beautiful and bird-rich state. Unexpected challenges were faced, especially during the summer and fall of 2005, when I had to deal with several hurricanes during my travels. In spite of the obstacles, I'm proud to say that I managed to personally visit every site included in this guide. Of course, there was no way I could have visited every location at the optimal time of year or even the most favorable time of day, hiked every trail in its entirety, or seen during my visit even a significant fraction of the birds listed for each site. I couldn't always locate an adequate checklist for a particular site, or I would discover after a visit that I neglected to collect certain mileage information. As a result, I needed the assistance of a number of individuals to help fill in the blanks.

I am indebted to birders from throughout the state (and a few no longer in Florida), as well as to several federal and state wildlife biologists, foresters, and others, who generously responded to my requests for information or provided advice and encouragement. These individuals include (in alphabetical order): Lyn Atherton, Helder Balladares, Paul Bithorn, Bill Boeringer, John Boyd, Jim Cox, Dick Cunningham, Thomas Dunkerton, Brad Ellis, John Epler, Susan Epps, Brian Ettlino, Nancy Freedman, Wally George, Liz Golden, Bev Hanson, Alex Harper, Mark Heddon, John Huchinson, Linda Humphries, Deborah Jansen, Patrick Leary, Vince Lucas, Larry Manfredi, Phyllis Mansfield, Roberta Martin, Linda McCandless, Nancy and Bruce Moreland, Brennan Mulrooney, Jill Rosenfield, Rex Rowan, Conrad Sankpill, David Simpson, Arthur Sissman, Roberto Torres, Ken Tracey, Mickey Wheeler, and Meret Wilson. To all of the unacknowledged individuals, including many national and state park and forest personnel who offered assistance along the way, my apologies for failing to record your names and my heartfelt thanks.

I am forever grateful for the assistance provided by my good friend Robin Diaz, who reviewed every word of the submitted manuscript. Robin spent untold hours grammatically overhauling or fine-tuning much of my original writing. I simply couldn't have written this without her. I'd also like to thank my friends Larry Manfredi and Trey Mitchell, as well as Nancy Moreland, my friend and colleague at MAST Academy, for generously providing photographs for this guide. I also wish to thank several other colleagues at MAST Academy, my place of employment since 1991, including Craig Kirk and Diane Garcia, who assisted with range maps, Melissa Fernandez and Grace Iudica, who provided technical assistance, and Lisa Fischer, who provided useful suggestions as the completed manuscript became ready for submission. Finally, I thank my principal, Dr. Consuelo Dominguez, for her support during this project.

Of course, I need to thank my editors at FalconGuides for their assistance throughout this endeavor. Bill Schneider, acquisitions editor, along with project editor Russ Schneider, guided me from the first chapter submission through editing of the final draft. Map coordinator Steven Stringall and art coordinator Gina Grasso helped with maps and photographs, respectively. Finally, associate editor Julie Marsh provided assistance and support during the final rounds of editing as the manuscript was prepared for printing.

CHAPTER ONE

Introduction

Ever since John James Audubon's legendary visits to the state in the early 1830s, Florida has been a dream destination for anyone fascinated by birds. Visitors from around the world travel here to view the state's spectacular assortment of wading birds, subtropical specialties, migrants, and introduced species, not to mention the occasional Caribbean rarity. Unfortunately, considerable loss of habitat for birds and other wildlife results from our ever-expanding population, especially along our coasts. However, many areas within the state remain protected and attractive to birds and accessible to birders. Federally protected areas include three national parks and 28 national wildlife refuges. Protected areas under state jurisdiction include 33 state forests, 154 state parks, and 152 wildlife management areas, and wildlife and environmental areas. Various counties, cities, and towns manage other public lands. These areas protect a wide variety of habitats, from sandy beaches to salt marsh, pinelands, scrub, sawgrass marsh, cypress swamp, mangrove forest, and hardwood hammock, each with a unique avian assemblage.

Though most of Florida's resident birds, as well as Florida's many migrant hot spots, can be found throughout the state, subtropical specialties are generally restricted to the southern peninsula and Keys. If introduced species such as White-winged Parakeet, Red-whiskered Bulbul, and Spot-breasted Oriole are on your must-see list, the Miami area will be included in your itinerary. Your best bet for Mangrove Cuckoo, Antillean Nighthawk, Black-whiskered Vireo, and other Caribbean species is a trip to the Florida Keys. A cruise to the Dry Tortugas is required to find seabirds such as Brown and Masked Booby, Sooty Tern, and Brown Noddy. On the other hand, resident South Florida birders, hoping to expand their state lists, must at some point travel to the Panhandle for White-breasted Nuthatch, Winter Wren, Brown Creeper, Purple Finch, and other species more typical of areas north of Florida. It was along the Choctawhatchee River in the western Panhandle that evidence was collected in 2005 strongly suggesting that Ivory-billed Woodpecker, that rarest of all birds, continues to survive in the state.

Whether you are a resident or a visitor, novice, or hard-core lister, hoping to see a few birds while visiting the theme parks or traveling to the state expressly for birding, it is the aim of this guide to provide the information needed to find the birds you seek.

How to Use This Guide

Fifty-four site descriptions are included in "Florida's Best Birding Areas," chapter 5 of this guide. Almost every site description includes two or more neighboring locations. As a result, titles for most site descriptions describe the general area (for example, Walt Disney World area) rather than specific locations within that area. The site descriptions are grouped into eight geographic regions, beginning in the northeast corner of the state and ending in

Masked Booby. PHOTO: LARRY MANFREDI

the western Panhandle. Maps showing site locations are provided for each region. The site descriptions are also arranged so that locations are geographically contiguous with locations within the site descriptions that precede and follow them. In general, the sites are ordered to proceed in a clockwise fashion around the periphery of the state, with several forays to inland locations and a side trip through the Florida Keys.

Each site description includes the following information:

- A list of major **habitats** found at the site. Refer to chapter 3 for descriptions of, and birds typically found in, each of these habitats.

- A list of **specialty birds** for the site. This list may include Florida specialties (those species found nowhere else in the United States except Florida), Southeastern specialties (those species generally restricted to the southeastern United States), endangered or threatened species, or other birds likely to be sought by birders. For the most part, only specialties considered common for that location are listed. Uncommon, rare, or restricted range species are listed only in key locations for finding that specialty. For site descriptions containing more than one location, keep in mind that due to habitat differences, some species may be found in one location but not others. All specialties are categorized as resident, summer, winter, and migrant, based on the season in which they are most likely to be found. Residents are birds that breed in the area and are present year-round. Summer species breed in the area during spring and summer but usually leave after breeding. Winter species breed elsewhere and generally arrive in the area during fall and depart during spring. Migrant species pass through the area during spring and/or fall but do not stay for the winter. Remember that some species that breed in, or migrate through, the northern part of the state may winter in the southern part.

- The **best times to bird** at that location. Considerations used to determine the optimal season to visit include the likelihood of seeing specialties and other key birds, weather conditions, and the presence or absence of mosquitoes and other biting insects.

- **Directions** to the site, usually from an interstate exit or highway intersection. Interstate exits in Florida are numbered based on mileage, with exit numbers increasing from west to east and south to north. All turns are described as either "left" or "right" and direction of travel is described using compass points (north, south, east, west, etc.). If more than one birding location is included in the site description, directions to a starting point or primary birding location are given in this section. Directions to secondary birding locations may also be included here or in the birding section of the site description. Note that all distances in this book have been rounded to the nearest tenth of a mile. Regional maps are also included for all locations. These maps should be used for trip planning and not for navigation. All of the sites in this guide can be located in the *DeLorme Florida Atlas and Gazetteer* (available at most Florida bookstores or from P.O. Box 298, Yarmouth, ME 04096; (207) 846–7000; www.delorme.com), using grid coordinates provided in the DeLorme grid section of each site description.

- **The birding,** which provides an account of the birding potential for the site, describing points of interest, where to hike or drive, and the birds you may see during your visit.

- **General information,** which includes days and hours of operation, entrance fee requirements, trail conditions, procedures, and precautions for locations where seasonal hunting is permitted, and the location of restrooms and other on-site amenities.

Each site description also includes a section that provides the following information:

- **DeLorme grid** provides the pages and grid coordinates to find the site in the *DeLorme Florida Atlas and Gazetteer* (2003).

- **Hazards** describes any poisonous plants or venomous snakes, biting insects, traffic issues, crime concerns, or anything else about the birding site that requires your attention. All of these hazards can be avoided with the use of common sense and should in no way discourage you from visiting the site.

- **Nearest food, gas, lodging** names the nearest city or town where a reasonable selection of these amenities may be found.

- **Camping** provides the name and number of sites for nearby campgrounds. Contact information is usually included under For more information. In almost all cases, campgrounds listed are located in state, county, or municipal parks, and are often located at sites described in The Birding section. For campgrounds located at nonbirding sites, directions to the campgrounds are provided.

- **For more information** provides mailing addresses, phone numbers, and Web sites (when available) for each location mentioned in the site description. For locations without on-site offices or staff, such as areas managed by the Florida Fish and Wildlife Conservation Commission or by water management districts, agency contact information is provided.

CHAPTER TWO
Florida's Birds

In Florida almost everyone seems to be from somewhere else. "Snowbirds" is a term often used to describe the hordes of northerners who, seeking Florida's world-renown sun, sand, and surf, invade the state every fall. Many others pass through the state on their way to exotic Caribbean ports of call. Still others immigrate here seeking opportunity and a better life. As a result, in some parts of the state (particularly the Miami area), it has become increasingly difficult to find someone who can claim to be a native Floridian. I, myself, am not a native, having moved to South Florida in 1988 for many of the reasons described above. Florida's bird life is much the same: many visitors but a surprisingly small number of natives. Of the 500 species of birds whose occurrence has been verified within the state by the Florida Ornithological Society Records Committee, slightly over 125 are native species present year-round. The rest are here only during the breeding season or they winter here, migrate through, are here accidentally, or are introduced species that have established and maintained stable populations within the state. Following is a breakdown of Florida's incredibly diverse avifauna.

Resident Birds

Of Florida's 151 resident birds—defined as native species that breed annually in the state—127 can be found in Florida year-round (on their breeding grounds, as migrants or winter visitors), while 24 are present in the state only part of the year (on their breeding grounds or as migrants). As described in chapter 1, only "specialty birds" are listed in the chapter 5 site descriptions. The specialty birds listed as residents include 37 sought-after species present in Florida year-round: Black-bellied Whistling-Duck, Fulvous Whistling-Duck, Mottled Duck, Masked Booby, Magnificent Frigatebird, Least Bittern, Reddish Egret, Roseate Spoonbill, Wood Stork, White-tailed Kite, Snail Kite, Bald Eagle, Short-tailed Hawk, Crested Caracara, Black Rail, Clapper Rail, King Rail, Purple Gallinule, Limpkin, Sandhill Crane, Snowy Plover, Wilson's Plover, American Oystercatcher, American Woodcock, White-crowned Pigeon, Mangrove Cuckoo, Smooth-billed Ani, Burrowing Owl, Red-cockaded Woodpecker, Florida Scrub-Jay, "West Indian" Cave Swallow, White-breasted Nuthatch, Brown-headed Nuthatch, "Cuban" Yellow Warbler, Bachman's Sparrow, "Florida" Grasshopper Sparrow, and Seaside Sparrow (including "Cape Sable" Seaside Sparrow). Great White Heron, the white morph of Great Blue Heron, is also listed as a specialty bird.

Another 52 resident species are not listed as specialties but may be mentioned in site description narratives. These species are present in Florida year-round but are also widespread in occurrence outside Florida: Wood Duck, Wild Turkey, Northern Bobwhite, Pied-billed Grebe, Brown Pelican, Anhinga, Black-crowned Night-Heron, Yellow-crowned

Night-Heron, Glossy Ibis, Black Vulture, Osprey, Cooper's Hawk, Red-shouldered Hawk, Red-tailed Hawk, American Kestrel, Willet, Laughing Gull, Caspian Tern, Royal Tern, Sandwich Tern, Black Skimmer, Common Ground-Dove, Barn Owl, Eastern Screech-Owl, Great Horned Owl, Barred Owl, Ruby-throated Hummingbird, Belted Kingfisher, Red-headed Woodpecker, Downy Woodpecker, Hairy Woodpecker, Northern Flicker, Pileated Woodpecker, Great Crested Flycatcher, Loggerhead Shrike, White-eyed Vireo, American Crow, Fish Crow, Northern Rough-winged Swallow, Carolina Chickadee, Tufted Titmouse, Carolina Wren, Marsh Wren, Blue-gray Gnatcatcher, Eastern Bluebird, Brown Thrasher, Yellow-throated Warbler, Pine Warbler, Prairie Warbler, Eastern Towhee, Field Sparrow, and Eastern Meadowlark.

Rarely listed in the site descriptions are 24 native year-round residents with widespread distributions within the state, as well as species that may not be especially sought by birders: Double-crested Cormorant, Great Blue Heron, Great Egret, Snowy Egret, Little Blue Heron, Tricolored Heron, Cattle Egret, Green Heron, White Ibis, Turkey Vulture, Common Moorhen, American Coot, Killdeer, Mourning Dove, Red-bellied Woodpecker, Blue Jay, Gray Catbird, Northern Mockingbird, Common Yellowthroat, Northern Cardinal, Red-winged Blackbird, Common Grackle, Boat-tailed Grackle, and Brown-headed Cowbird.

Specialty birds listed in site descriptions as summer species are resident at that particular site only during the spring and summer breeding season. Of the 25 species listed primarily as such, 16 typically do not winter in the state: Swallow-tailed Kite, Mississippi Kite, Roseate Tern, Least Tern, Bridled Tern, Sooty Tern, Brown Noddy, Antillean Nighthawk, Acadian Flycatcher, Gray Kingbird, Black-whiskered Vireo, Wood Thrush, Swainson's Warbler, Kentucky Warbler, Hooded Warbler. and Orchard Oriole. The other 9 specialty birds listed as summer species are also common-to-occasional winter visitors (in the southern peninsula and Florida Keys) and may be listed as winter species for those sites: Gull-billed Tern, Chuck-will's-widow, Yellow-throated Vireo, Prothonotary Warbler, Louisiana Waterthrush, Yellow-breasted Chat, Summer Tanager, Blue Grosbeak, and Painted Bunting. Another 13 summer species may be mentioned in site description narratives; of these, 7 typically do not winter in the state: Yellow-billed Cuckoo, Common Nighthawk, Chimney Swift, Eastern Wood-Pewee, Eastern Kingbird, Red-eyed Vireo, and Purple Martin. The other 6 are common-to-occasional winter visitors: Broad-winged Hawk, Black-necked Stilt, American Robin, Barn Swallow, Northern Parula, and Indigo Bunting.

Visitors

Visiting birds are defined as those species that regularly spend all or part of the year in Florida but do not breed in the state. Brown Booby and Greater Flamingo are both year-round visitors in the Dry Tortugas and Florida Bay, respectively, but neither currently breeds in Florida. Both are listed in site descriptions as "resident specialty" birds. The majority of birds regularly visiting Florida are wintering species, usually arriving during fall migration and departing during spring migration. For some species, wintering birds may arrive as early as July, while other wintering species may not arrive until November. For certain species, shorebirds in particular, nonbreeding individuals may remain in the state year-round. The wintering behavior of some species is irruptive in nature, meaning that their movement into or within Florida is determined by the availability of food in that species' wintering range north of the state. Four species are widespread and common-to-abundant in Florida during winter and as such, are not usually mentioned in site descriptions: American Coot, Gray Catbird, Yellow-rumped Warbler (irruptive in the southern peninsula), and Palm Warbler.

Specialty birds listed primarily as winter visitors include the following 33 species: Snow Goose, American Black Duck, Greater Scaup, Surf Scoter, White-winged Scoter, Black Scoter, Common Goldeneye, Red-throated Loon, Yellow Rail, Virginia Rail, Piping Plover, Whimbrel, Purple Sandpiper, Lesser Black-backed Gull, Whip-poor-will, Western Kingbird, Scissor-tailed Flycatcher, Red-breasted Nuthatch (irruptive), Brown Creeper, Winter Wren, Golden-crowned Kinglet (irruptive), American Pipit, Henslow's Sparrow, Le Conte's Sparrow, Nelson's Sharp-tailed Sparrow, Saltmarsh Sharp-tailed Sparrow, Fox Sparrow, Lincoln's Sparrow, Dark-eyed Junco, Rusty Blackbird, Brewer's Blackbird, Purple Finch (irruptive), and Pine Siskin (irruptive).

Another 67 winter visitors may be mentioned in site description narratives: Gadwall, American Wigeon, Blue-winged Teal, Northern Shoveler, Northern Pintail, Green-winged Teal, Canvasback, Redhead, Ring-necked Duck, Lesser Scaup, Bufflehead, Hooded Merganser, Red-breasted Merganser, Ruddy Duck, Common Loon, Horned Grebe, Northern Gannet, American White Pelican, American Bittern, Northern Harrier, Sharp-shinned Hawk, American Kestrel, Sora, Black-bellied Plover, Semipalmated Plover, Greater Yellowlegs, Lesser Yellowlegs, Spotted Sandpiper, Marbled Godwit, Ruddy Turnstone, Red Knot, Sanderling, Western Sandpiper, Least Sandpiper, Dunlin, Short-billed Dowitcher, Long-billed Dowitcher, Wilson's Snipe, Bonaparte's Gull, Ring-billed Gull, Herring Gull, Great Black-backed Gull, Forster's Tern, Belted Kingfisher, Yellow-bellied Sapsucker, Eastern Phoebe, Blue-headed Vireo, Tree Swallow, House Wren, Sedge Wren, Ruby-crowned Kinglet, Hermit Thrush, American Robin (irruptive in the southern peninsula), Cedar Waxwing (irruptive in the southern peninsula), Orange-crowned Warbler, Black-and-white Warbler, Chipping Sparrow, Field Sparrow, Vesper Sparrow, Savannah Sparrow, Grasshopper Sparrow, Song Sparrow, Swamp Sparrow, White-throated Sparrow, White-crowned Sparrow, Baltimore Oriole, and American Goldfinch (irruptive).

Migrants

Spring and fall migrants may include species that breed or winter in Florida, as well as birds that breed to the north or winter to the south of the state. Spring migrants returning north via islands in the Caribbean are typically more common along the Atlantic coast of the peninsula, while trans-Gulf migrants, those species flying directly over the Gulf of Mexico, are more common along the Gulf coast of the peninsula and Panhandle. Circum-Gulf migrants, who fly around the Gulf of Mexico rather than across it, are most likely to be seen in the Panhandle. Fall migrants returning from northern breeding grounds are likely at both coastal and inland locations. Hardwood hammocks and other woodland habitats are most attractive to migrant land birds. Flooded agricultural fields often attract migrant shorebirds, especially in fall. Weather is a major factor during both seasons and determines where migrant birds make landfall. Migrants are often scarce in locations experiencing fair weather and favorable tailwinds, while headwinds, stormy weather, or the passage of fronts may force birds to land, producing local fallouts. Strong onshore winds may also redirect migrants to the opposite coast, especially during spring. For example, strong easterly winds may result in increased sightings of Caribbean migrants on the Gulf coast. Conversely, strong westerly winds increase sightings of trans-Gulf migrants on the Atlantic coast.

Specialty birds listed as migrants in the site descriptions include the following 27 species: Peregrine Falcon, American Golden-Plover, American Avocet, Upland Sandpiper, White-rumped Sandpiper, Buff-breasted Sandpiper, Wilson's Phalarope, Black Tern, Chuck-will's-widow, Acadian Flycatcher, Blue-winged Warbler, Golden-winged Warbler, Chestnut-sided Warbler, Bay-breasted Warbler, Cerulean Warbler, Prothonotary Warbler, Swainson's Warbler, Louisiana Waterthrush, Kentucky Warbler, Hooded Warbler, Canada Warbler, Summer Tanager, Scarlet Tanager, Rose-breasted Grosbeak, Blue Grosbeak, Painted Bunting, and Orchard Oriole.

Another 35 migrant species are likely to be mentioned in site description narratives: Cooper's Hawk, Sharp-shinned Hawk, Broad-winged Hawk, Merlin, Solitary Sandpiper, Semipalmated Sandpiper, Pectoral Sandpiper, Stilt Sandpiper, Common Tern, Yellow-billed Cuckoo, Chimney Swift, Eastern Wood-Pewee, Least Flycatcher, Bank Swallow, Blue-gray Gnatcatcher, Veery, Gray-cheeked Thrush, Swainson's Thrush, Tennessee Warbler, Northern Parula, Yellow Warbler, Magnolia Warbler, Cape May Warbler, Black-throated Blue Warbler, Black-throated Green Warbler, Blackburnian Warbler, Blackpoll Warbler, Black-and-white Warbler, American Redstart, Worm-eating Warbler, Ovenbird, Northern Waterthrush, Indigo Bunting, Bobolink, and Baltimore Oriole. Gray Catbird is a common and widespread migrant and is not usually listed in site descriptions.

Vagrants and Other Rarities

Vagrants can be defined as birds whose natural range does not include Florida but who accidentally find their way to the state. Species from as far away as Europe and Asia have appeared in Florida, including Eurasian Kestrel, Northern Lapwing, Lesser Sand Plover, Long-billed Murrelet, and White Wagtail. Eurasian vagrants that are found annually or almost annually in Florida include Eurasian Wigeon, Ruff, and Black-headed Gull. Of interest primarily to Florida birders are western vagrants, those species from the western United States that, for a number of possible reasons, become misdirected from their usual migration route and end up here. Western vagrants expected annually or almost annually in

Roseate Spoonbill in flight. PHOTO: LARRY MANFREDI

Florida include Greater White-fronted Goose, Ross's Goose, Cinnamon Teal, Pacific Loon, Eared Grebe, White-faced Ibis, Groove-billed Ani, Lesser Nighthawk, Buff-bellied Hummingbird, Black-chinned Hummingbird, Rufous Hummingbird, Vermilion Flycatcher, Ash-throated Flycatcher, Brown-crested Flycatcher, Tropical Kingbird, Bell's Vireo, Sprague's Pipit, Black-throated Gray Warbler, Wilson's Warbler, Western Tanager, Lark Sparrow, Black-headed Grosbeak, and Bronzed Cowbird.

Of interest to Florida and visiting birders alike are Caribbean vagrants, usually birds that find their way to Florida from the Bahamas or Cuba. Caribbean vagrants found annually or almost annually in Florida (most often in the southern peninsula and Florida Keys) include "Antillean" Short-eared Owl, La Sagra's Flycatcher, Bahama Mockingbird, and Western Spindalis. Less frequently or rarely seen are White-cheeked Pintail, Masked Duck, Least Grebe, Zenaida Dove, Key West Quail-Dove, Ruddy Quail-Dove, Bahama Woodstar, Cuban Pewee, Thick-billed Vireo, Bahama Swallow, Kirtland's Warbler (winters in the Bahamas), Bananaquit, Yellow-faced Grassquit, and Black-faced Grassquit. Some sightings of Caribbean and Central and South American vagrants in Florida have provided the only record for that species in the United States! These mega-rarities include Scaly-naped Pigeon, Cuban Pewee, Loggerhead Kingbird, Antillean Palm-Swift, Cuban Martin, Southern Martin, Mangrove Swallow, and Tawny-shouldered Blackbird. Red-legged Honeycreeper has been sighted on several occasions in the past few years; all sightings have been of males. Due to the possibility that these beautiful birds may be escapees, the Florida Ornithological Society Records Committee has not accepted sightings for this species.

Introduced Birds

Over 200 non-native bird species have been introduced to Florida, either intentionally or accidentally. Over 75 parrot species have been reported in the state. Many of these birds are able to survive, especially in residential areas in the southern peninsula, due to the combination of hospitable climate and the availability of exotic subtropical vegetation. While almost 70 species of these exotics are now believed to be breeding here, only 12 have populations acknowledged as established by the Florida Ornithological Society Records Committee: Muscovy Duck, Rock Pigeon, Eurasian Collared-Dove, Budgerigar, Monk Parakeet, Black-hooded Parakeet, White-winged Parakeet, European Starling, Red-whiskered Bulbul, Spot-breasted Oriole, House Finch, and House Sparrow. In addition, wild birds that seasonally migrate into the state supplement populations of introduced and established species like Canada Goose, Mallard, and White-winged Dove.

Over 20 species of parrots that have bred or are breeding in Florida currently do not have populations considered established, including Rose-ringed Parakeet, Blue-crowned Parakeet, Green Parakeet, Mitred Parakeet, Red-masked Parakeet, White-eyed Parakeet, Dusky-headed Parakeet, Chestnut-fronted Macaw, Blue-and-yellow Macaw, Yellow-chevroned Parakeet, White-fronted Parrot, Red-crowned Parrot, Lilac-crowned Parrot, Blue-fronted Parrot, Orange-winged Parrot, Yellow-headed Parrot, Yellow-crowned Parrot, and Yellow-naped Parrot. Other introduced species with breeding populations not yet considered established include Purple Swamphen (originally found in western Broward County, now apparently spreading throughout the southern peninsula), Common Myna (found in shopping-center parking lots throughout the southern peninsula and Florida Keys, and spreading), and Hill Myna (locally common in tropical hardwood hammocks and suburban residential areas in Miami-Dade and Broward Counties).

Whooping Crane is a historically resident and winter visitor to Florida. In an effort to ensure its survival, two populations of this highly endangered species have been introduced to the state. A permanent, nonmigratory population, now numbering almost 90 birds, has been established in the Lake Kissimmee area. In 2002 a juvenile crane from this population successfully fledged, a first for the United States. A second, migratory population now winters at Chassahowitzka National Wildlife Refuge; its migration from breeding areas in Wisconsin is assisted by ultralight aircraft.

Pelagic Birds

Pelagic birds are those species that spend the majority of their lives at sea. Surrounded by the Atlantic Ocean and Gulf of Mexico and with over 1,100 miles of coastline, one would think that the pelagic possibilities in Florida are extraordinary. Unfortunately, except for the occasional deepwater fishing trip involving alert birders, Florida's offshore waters have, for the most part, remained relatively unexplored. Trips to the Dry Tortugas provide birders with one of the few opportunities for organized pelagic birding. In recent years, offshore excursions have been arranged by local birding guides or as part of birding festivals in an effort to expand our understanding of pelagic bird life in Florida.

Multiday spring birding trips to the Dry Tortugas, especially those that include exploration of the Gulf Stream, provide opportunities to view a number of pelagic species, including Audubon's Shearwater and Bridled Tern. Within Dry Tortugas National Park, nesting Magnificent Frigatebird, Sooty Tern, and Brown Noddy are guaranteed during their nesting season. Nesting Masked Booby can be viewed (from a distance) on Hospital Key, while Brown Booby and Roseate Tern are possible on channel markers. Tortugas rarities always possible include White-tailed Tropicbird, Red-footed Booby, and Black Noddy. Some of these species may also be seen on boat trips to Islamorada or Marathon Humps, areas of upwelling located south of the Florida Keys. Also possible from spring through fall are Black-capped Petrel, Cory's, Greater, and Sooty Shearwater, and Wilson's and Band-rumped Storm-Petrel. More likely from fall through spring are Northern Gannet, Red-necked and Red Phalarope, and Pomerine and Parasitic Jaeger.

To explore the Gulf Stream off the Atlantic coast, trips are periodically arranged out of Port Canaveral, Ponce Inlet, and other locations, often in conjunction with birding festivals. From fall through spring, deepwater areas of the Atlantic off the northern coast of the peninsula are the most likely locations to search for Manx Shearwater, South Polar Skua, Long-tailed Jaeger, Black-legged Kittiwake, and even alcids such as Dovekie and Razorbill. Pelagic trips in the Gulf of Mexico are rare, though excursions out of Destin (in the Panhandle) are occasionally arranged. For those who prefer to avoid the queasy side effects of boat-based birding, persistent onshore winds provide opportunities to search for pelagics from the relative comfort of shore. Turtle Mound, at Canaveral National Seashore, provides an excellent vantage point to scan for shearwaters, storm petrels, jaegers, and most reliably, Northern Gannet. Other locations offering land-based pelagic opportunities include Ft. Clinch State Park, Ponce, Sebastian, and Boynton Inlets, Jetty Park at Port Canaveral, and John U. Lloyd State Park. Other species recorded from these locations include South Polar Skua, Sabine's Gull, and Arctic Tern.

CHAPTER THREE
Florida's Environment

Habitats

Visitors to Florida cannot help noticing the state's overall flat terrain. Much of the state is only a few feet above sea level, with elevations above 200 feet found only in the Panhandle and the Lake Wales Ridge of the central peninsula. The porous limestone bedrock that underlies the peninsula is covered in many areas by a thin layer of quickly draining and often-infertile soil. With such a narrow range of topography, generally poor soil, and limited surface water, one would expect low habitat diversity. In reality, biodiversity in Florida exceeds that of any state east of the Mississippi. More than 3,500 species of plants have been identified in the state. In many areas of the state, especially in the southern peninsula, elevation changes of even a few inches lead to dramatic habitat variation.

Several factors contribute to Florida's amazing array of plant (and associated animal) assemblages, including climate, geographic location, and geological history. The state has a humid climate and abundant rainfall, encouraging the proliferation of a wide variety of plant species. Florida's position at the edge of the tropics allows for both temperate and tropical species to coexist. Much of the state is located on a long, narrow peninsula surrounded by water, with no point of land located much more than 60 miles from the coast. This helps moderate climate and minimize temperature extremes that impede diversity. Over the course of geological time, areas of Florida were periodically submerged and exposed by rising and falling sea levels, altering topography and soil composition and further encouraging habitat diversity.

Florida's natural habitats fall into three general categories: coastal, inland aquatic, and upland. Some habitats such as scrub, pine flatwoods, and hardwood hammock may be found at both coastal and inland locations. Man-altered habitat includes agricultural and urban areas. Following are brief descriptions of habitats found within the state, including characteristic plants and associated bird species. For more detailed descriptions, see *Ecosystems of Florida,* edited by Ronald L. Myers and John J. Ewel, University of Central Florida Press (1990).

Coastal Habitats

Pelagic areas include offshore waters of the Atlantic Ocean, Gulf of Mexico, and Florida Straits. Typical birds in summer include Cory's, Greater, and Audubon's Shearwater, Wilson's Storm-Petrel, and Bridled Tern. Pomarine and Parasitic Jaeger can be found during winter. Many of these species approach the Atlantic coast during periods of persistent onshore winds. Northern Gannet is often seen along both coasts during winter, feeding just offshore. Around the **tropical islands** of the Dry Tortugas, look for Masked and Brown Booby, Magnificent Frigatebird, Sooty Tern, and Brown Noddy.

Over 700 of Florida's 1,100 miles of coastline are **sandy beaches,** mostly found on the ocean side of barrier islands. Typical birds seen on the beach year-round include Brown Pelican, Double-crested Cormorant, Willet, Laughing Gull, Royal Tern, and Black Skimmer. Reddish Egret, American Oystercatcher, and Wilson's and Snowy Plover are more local in occurrence. Least Tern is widespread during summer, while Ruddy Turnstone, Sanderling, Ring-billed and Herring Gull, and Sandwich and Forster's Tern can be found in winter. Many of these species, as well as migrant and wintering shorebirds, are attracted to **coastal mudflats.** Black-bellied, Semipalmated, and Piping Plover, Marbled Godwit, Red Knot, Western and Least Sandpiper, Dunlin, and Short-billed Dowitcher visit these intertidal areas, which are exposed at low tide. Common Loon and Horned Grebe can be found beyond the surf line during winter, though most frequently in the Panhandle and northern peninsula.

Coastal dunes are home to sea oats, morning glory, and other wind- and salt-tolerant plants. American Kestrel and Savannah Sparrow are found here during winter. Wading birds and wintering ducks are attracted to coastal dune lakes, most common in the Panhandle. **Coastal scrub** or **strand,** located between the dunes, is characterized by saw palmetto with a mixture (depending on location) of sand pine, oaks, cabbage palm, prickly pear cactus, and other plants adapted to dry, sandy soils and often stunted by salt spray. Birds seen year-round in this severely fragmented habitat include Common Ground-Dove, White-eyed Vireo, Florida Scrub-Jay (local, central peninsula), and Eastern Towhee. Painted Bunting is found during summer in coastal strand along the Atlantic coast of the extreme northern peninsula. **Maritime hammock** occupies the most stable dunes and is attractive to a variety of migrant land birds. Though live oak is most typical of this hardwood habitat, tropical species such as sea grape, gumbo limbo, and strangler fig may also be found in maritime hammock in the central and southern peninsula.

Salt marsh is found in sheltered bays and river mouths, on the backside of barrier islands, and in other areas protected from significant wave action. This coastal habitat is dominated by cordgrass and needlerush, plants adapted to significant salinity changes and tidal fluctuations. These areas are most extensive on the Gulf coast of the eastern Panhandle and northern and central peninsula. Salt marsh is an essential nursery for marine fish and invertebrates, attracting a variety of wading birds including Great Blue, Little Blue, Tricolored, and Green Heron, Great and Snowy Egret, Black-crowned and Yellow-crowned Night-Heron, White Ibis, and Wood Stork. Other year-round residents include Bald Eagle, Clapper Rail, Marsh Wren, Seaside Sparrow, and Red-winged Blackbird. Gray Kingbird breeds in the vicinity of salt marsh during summer. Sedge Wren, Common Yellowthroat, and Saltmarsh Sharp-tailed and Nelson's Sharp-tailed Sparrow visit during winter. Many of these same species also inhabit **coastal prairie,** found primarily along the coast of the extreme southern peninsula in areas above the high-water mark. Buttonwood trees and salt-tolerant succulents such as glasswort and saltwort are characteristic of this habitat. **Estuaries,** areas of open water usually near river mouths where salt and fresh water mix, are attractive to wintering waterfowl.

Mangrove forest is a tropical marine habitat restricted to the coasts of the southern and central peninsula and Keys. Like salt marsh, mangrove forests are found in areas protected from substantial wave action. Mangroves help stabilize shorelines and, like salt marsh, act as nurseries for marine fish and invertebrates. Of the four trees associated with this habitat, red mangrove, with its distinctive appendage-like prop roots, is the most salt-tolerant and usually inhabits the edges of tidal creeks and bays. Black mangrove, with pencil-like roots, is more cold-tolerant but prefers areas with less tidal fluctuation, usually behind the red mangrove zone. White mangrove and buttonwood can be found in areas least affected by tides. All of Florida's wading birds, including Roseate Spoonbill, are year-round residents of mangrove forests and surrounding estuaries. Other mangrove-associated species include Magnificent Frigatebird, Brown Pelican, Double-crested Cormorant, Osprey, Clapper Rail, and Prairie Warbler. Caribbean species that breed in mangrove habitat in the southern peninsula and Keys include White-crowned Pigeon, Mangrove Cuckoo, Gray Kingbird, Black-whiskered Vireo, and the Cuban race of Yellow Warbler.

Inland Aquatic Habitats

Freshwater marshes, most widespread in the southern peninsula, are shallow-water wetlands dominated by sawgrass and other sedges and grasses. Cattails, fire flag, pickerelweed, and water lilies grow in areas of deeper water. Brushy thickets or stands of willow occupy higher ground around the marsh periphery. Resident birds may include Mottled Duck, Pied-billed Grebe, Anhinga, Least Bittern, various herons and egrets, White and Glossy Ibis, Wood Stork, Snail Kite, Red-shouldered Hawk, King Rail, Common Moorhen, Purple Gallinule, Limpkin, Common Yellowthroat, Red-winged Blackbird, and Boat-tailed Grackle. Winter visitors include several species of ducks plus American Bittern, Northern Harrier, Sora, American Coot, Greater and Lesser Yellowlegs, Wilson's Snipe, Belted King-fisher, Eastern Phoebe, Marsh Wren, and Swamp Sparrow. Many of these same species, plus Black-bellied and Fulvous Whistling-Duck and migrant shorebirds are attracted to **seasonally flooded agricultural fields, freshwater impoundments, spray fields,** and any of the thousands of **freshwater ponds** and **lakes** scattered throughout the peninsula.

Pitcher plant savannahs, unique to the Panhandle, are characterized by grasses and insectivorous plants adapted to acidic soils. Winter visitors to this habitat may include Yellow Rail, Sedge Wren, and Henslow's and Le Conte's Sparrow. Seasonally wet grasslands called **wet prairie** are attractive to wading birds such as Sandhill Crane and small land birds including Common Yellowthroat and Swamp Sparrow. Most of the Everglades area between Lake Okeechobee and Florida Bay was once an endless expanse of seasonally wet **sawgrass prairie.** Water flow and nutrient levels throughout this area have been significantly altered by decades of shortsighted water control and agricultural practices. The original "river of grass" is now restricted to Everglades National Park, Big Cypress National Preserve, and impounded water-conservation areas. The immense populations of wading birds that once inhabited this region have been greatly reduced by habitat loss. It is hoped that the comprehensive Everglades restoration project now under way will assist in the recovery of these unique wetlands.

Cypress swamps are wetlands dominated by bald cypress (a deciduous conifer) and are usually found along rivers and lakeshores. In the southern peninsula, cypress domes and strands and **dwarf cypress forests** are surrounded by sawgrass prairie. Extensive tracts of cypress swamp have been heavily logged, particularly in the northern peninsula and Panhandle. Year-round residents of cypress swamp may include Wood Duck, Wild Turkey, Anhinga, various herons and egrets, Red-shouldered Hawk, Limpkin, Barred Owl, Red-bellied, Downy, and Pileated Woodpecker, White-eyed Vireo, Carolina Chickadee, Tufted Titmouse, Carolina Wren, Blue-gray Gnatcatcher, and Common Grackle. Summer breeders may include Swallow-tailed and Mississippi Kite, Great Crested Flycatcher, and Prothonotary Warbler. Winter visitors may include Yellow-bellied Sapsucker, Blue-headed Vireo, Ruby-crowned Kinglet, Gray Catbird, Yellow-rumped, Yellow-throated, and Black-and-white Warbler, Rusty Blackbird, and American Goldfinch.

Hardwood swamps are wet forests characterized by a variety of deciduous trees including (depending on location) bald cypress, red maple, swamp tupelo, magnolia, sweet gum, and water oak. These habitats, sometimes referred to as floodplain or bottomland forest, are found around lakes, rivers, and springs with seasonal water-level fluctuations. Though scattered throughout the state, hardwood swamps are most widespread in the northern peninsula and Panhandle. Ivory-billed Woodpeckers may continue to survive in bottomland forest along the Choctawhatchee River in the western Panhandle. **Oak/cabbage palm hammocks** are seasonally wet forests more typical of the central and southern peninsula. Year-round residents and winter visitors to hardwood swamps are similar to that of cypress swamps. Summer breeders may include Swallow-tailed Kite, Broad-winged Hawk, Yellow-billed Cuckoo, Acadian and Great Crested Flycatcher, Red-eyed Vireo, Northern Parula, and Hooded Warbler.

Upland Habitats

Once Florida's most widespread upland habitat, **pine flatwoods** are dominated by slash or longleaf pine with an understory of saw palmetto and wire grass and are maintained by periodic fires. As the name implies, this habitat, located in both coastal and inland locations, is found on relatively level terrain that may flood seasonally. Much of the state's flatwoods have been converted to residential developments, farmlands, and commercial pine plantations. **Pine rocklands,** a flatwood community unique to the southeastern peninsula, is extremely endangered. Plants in this habitat, including tropical species such as poisonwood, have adapted to a thin layer of nutrient-poor soil that barely covers the underlying limestone bedrock. Year-round residents of pine flatwoods may include Northern Bobwhite, Great Horned Owl, Red-bellied, Red-headed, Downy, Red-cockaded, and Pileated Woodpecker, Northern Flicker, American Crow, Brown-headed Nuthatch, Eastern Bluebird, Yellow-throated and Pine Warbler, Eastern Towhee, and Bachman's Sparrow. Summer breeders may include Common Nighthawk, Chuck-will's-widow, Great Crested Flycatcher, Eastern Kingbird, and Summer Tanager. Winter visitors are similar to that of cypress swamps.

Sandhills are pinelands found on rolling, sandy hills and are dominated by longleaf pine with an open understory of wire grass and scattered patches of turkey oak. Periodic fires also maintain this habitat, sometimes called high pines. Where clay soils are found, such as the Red Hills area around Tallahassee, sandhills are more accurately called **clayhills.** Year-round residents of sandhill habitat may include Common Ground-Dove, Red-headed and Red-cockaded Woodpecker, Brown-headed Nuthatch, Eastern Bluebird, Pine Warbler, and Bachman's Sparrow. Summer breeders and winter visitors are similar to that of pine flatwoods.

Oak/sand pine scrub, a desertlike upland habitat, is characterized by sand pine with an understory of scrub oak, saw palmetto, prickly pear cactus, and other plants adapted to dry, sandy soil. Like other upland habitats, the frequency of fires determines the composition of plant communities. Areas that frequently burn are maintained as **oak scrub,** dominated by oaks and other understory plants and with scattered sand pines. Year-round residents of oak scrub are similar to that of coastal scrub and may include Northern Bobwhite, White-eyed Vireo, Florida Scrub-Jay, and Eastern Towhee. Much of this habitat, once widespread on the Lake Wales Ridge in the central peninsula, has been converted to citrus groves and residential and commercial developments. Areas that rarely burn become **sand pine scrub,** forests of sand pine with little understory. In scrub that becomes dominated by sand pine, oak scrub residents are replaced by species typical of other pineland habitats, including Great Crested Flycatcher and Pine Warbler.

Found north and west of Lake Okeechobee, **dry prairie** is a mostly treeless, fire-maintained habitat dominated by saw palmetto, wire grass, and broomsedge. Much of this habitat has been converted to cattle pasture, citrus groves, and other uses. Several of the birds associated with dry prairie have adapted to its conversion to pasture. Year-round residents include relic populations of three species found in grasslands in the southwestern United States: Crested Caracara, Burrowing Owl, and Grasshopper Sparrow. Other residents may include Sandhill Crane, Loggerhead Shrike, and Eastern Meadowlark. Summer breeders may include Common Nighthawk and Eastern Kingbird. Winter visitors may include Northern Harrier, American Kestrel, Sedge Wren, and Savannah Sparrow.

Hardwood hammocks are usually composed of fire-tolerant trees growing in upland areas not prone to flooding. In northern Florida, trees found in this temperate habitat may include live oak, beech, hickory, tulip poplar, dogwood, and magnolia. **Slope forest,** also found in north Florida, is a mixture of hardwoods and pines growing in ravines and other rugged terrain. Year-round residents of temperate hardwood hammocks include Eastern Screech-Owl, Red-bellied and Downy Woodpecker, Blue Jay, Tufted Titmouse, Carolina Chickadee, Carolina Wren, Brown Thrasher, and Northern Cardinal. Summer breeders may include Mississippi Kite, Broad-winged Hawk, Yellow-billed Cuckoo, Great Crested Flycatcher, Yellow-throated and Red-eyed Vireo, Northern Parula, and Summer Tanager. In the southern peninsula, trees with a distinctly Caribbean influence, such as gumbo limbo, pigeon plum, poisonwood, and strangler fig, inhabit **tropical hardwood hammock.** Resident species are similar to that of northern hammocks (with the exception of Tufted Titmouse and Carolina Chickadee). Summer breeders in tropical hardwood hammock include White-crowned Pigeon, Mangrove Cuckoo, and Black-whiskered Vireo. Migrant and wintering land birds are attracted to hardwood hammock habitat throughout the state.

Human-altered Habitat

Native birds common to **residential areas** throughout the state include Mourning Dove, Red-bellied Woodpecker, Blue Jay, Northern Mockingbird, and Northern Cardinal. Cattle Egret and Boat-tailed Grackle are commonly seen in **agricultural areas, pastures,** and **sod farms,** mostly on the peninsula. Muscovy Duck, Rock Pigeon, Eurasian Collared-Dove, European Starling, and House Sparrow are introduced species that are common-to-abundant in residential areas. A wide variety of introduced parrot species have adapted to urban life in scattered locations throughout the peninsula, but especially in southeastern Florida. Other non-native species found in parks and residential areas in southern Florida include Red-whiskered Bulbul, Common and Hill Myna, and Spot-breasted Oriole.

Climate

Climate refers to the persistence of weather patterns at a particular location over an extended period of time. Except for the Panhandle, Florida experiences a subtropical climate. Warm, humid, and rainy conditions prevail from mid-May through October and milder, drier weather remains in place from November to mid-May. Seasonal rainfall amounts are more pronounced in the southern peninsula, and average daytime temperatures are typically 5 to 15 degrees F warmer than those in the northern peninsula. Overnight temperatures in the north may average 10 to 20 degrees cooler than in the south, especially during winter. Due to ocean breezes, temperatures along the coast tend to be cooler in summer and warmer during winter than those at inland locations. Climate in the Panhandle is similar to that of neighboring southeastern states, with hot summers and cool winters. This area has an increased likelihood of passing fronts, so rainfall occurs most frequently during late winter and early spring.

In late fall and winter, temperatures throughout the state are generally mild and humidity is low. Winter is the most comfortable time to visit the southern peninsula; numbers of mosquitoes and other biting insects tend to be low during this period. Persistent high pressure typically prevents the buildup of clouds that produce rainstorms, though the passage of cold fronts may result in brief periods of rain and cooler temperatures. Occasionally, strong cold fronts may bring near-freezing temperatures to all but the Keys, threatening subtropical plants, citrus groves, and winter vegetables. Overnight temperatures in the Panhandle often fall near, or even below, freezing during winter, but snow is rare.

Warmer weather and mostly clear skies characterize spring, though the passage of fronts may cause temperatures to briefly drop. Lack of substantial rainfall sometimes leads to drought conditions, especially in the southern peninsula, stressing vegetation and increasing the chance for brush fires. By mid-May, high pressure weakens, temperature and humidity increase significantly, and afternoon thunderstorms begin, signaling the onset of the rainy season. Sea breezes and the direction of prevailing winds determine whether summer rainstorms affect coastal or inland locations. For example, along the east coast, southwesterly winds tend to confine storms to coastal areas, while southeasterly winds combined with sea breezes push thunderstorms into the interior. Thunderstorms often build quickly but cover relatively small areas. Lightning strikes are common; anyone outdoors should seek shelter immediately should a thunderstorm approach.

And then there are hurricanes! These tropical low-pressure systems, which can produce devastating winds and storm surge, may form in the Caribbean, Gulf of Mexico, or as far away as off the western coast of Africa. Though the hurricane season stretches from June through November, the peak of activity tends to be in August and September. For much of the last half of the 20th century, Florida escaped hurricane seasons relatively unscathed. Two exceptions were Hurricane Donna, which struck the state in 1960, and Hurricane Andrew, which in 1992 caused locally extensive damage in the extreme southeastern peninsula. Beginning in 2004, Florida's long stretch of good fortune apparently ran out. In that year the state was affected by a number of tropical systems, including four major hurricanes: Charley, Frances, Ivan, and Jeanne. By the end of the 2005 hurricane season, the most active and destructive in recorded history, several more storms tore through the state, including Katrina and Wilma. From Pensacola to the Dry Tortugas, virtually the entire state was affected. A number of popular birding locations did not escape the storm damage. Some meteorologists believe that changes in global climate make active hurricane seasons increasingly likely in coming years.

CHAPTER FOUR

Planning a Birding Trip to Florida

When to Go

Three factors determine which time of year is best to visit Florida: which species you most want to see, when you are available to see them, and the local conditions at the time of your visit. Most birders prefer to avoid visiting during the summer months, when oppressive temperatures and humidity, afternoon thunderstorms, and hordes of biting insects are a daily fact of life throughout much of the state. Bird diversity is also lowest during the summer months. If you plan a birding excursion as part of a family summer vacation to a beach resort or the Central Florida theme parks, your experience may result in limited success under uncomfortable conditions. By far, the most popular months to visit are during winter and spring.

During a winter visit to the state, you should experience mostly moderate temperatures and humidity, little rain, and few mosquitoes and other biting insects. This is the best season to visit Everglades National Park, when lower water levels concentrate wading birds in viewing areas such as Anhinga Trail. Specialties such as Short-tailed Hawk are most likely, and up to 20 species of wintering warblers may be found during a full day of birding. Snail Kite is actively hunting along Tamiami Trail, and by late winter, Swallow-tailed Kite can be seen soaring over hammocks and cypress swamps. Winter is also an excellent time to visit Merritt Island and St. Marks National Wildlife Refuges, when waterfowl concentrations are highest. The major downside to a winter visit is the often-horrendous traffic in urban areas, as residents and "snowbirds" combine to clog local roads and highways during rush hour, which can sometimes last the entire day.

Spring is a great season to find both local specialties and migrant species, with mid- to late April typically the peak of spring migration. Though temperatures begin to climb during this period, rain is infrequent, and humidity and insect concentrations remain bearable at migrant hot spots such as Ft. De Soto and Bill Baggs Cape Florida State Park. Early morning is usually the most productive time to venture out, when birds are singing and temperatures are tolerable. Specialties such as Mangrove Cuckoo are somewhat easier to find in the Florida Keys during this season, and White-crowned Pigeon, Gray Kingbird, Antillean Nighthawk, and Black-whiskered Vireo are all nesting. Caribbean vagrants such as La Sagra's Flycatcher, Thick-billed Vireo, Bahama Mockingbird, and Western Spindalis are also possible during this period. Trips to the Dry Tortugas are most popular in late

April and early May, when all the pelagic specialties are present and the greatest potential exists for spectacular fallouts of trans-Gulf migrants. By late spring, North Florida nesting species such as Mississippi Kite, Acadian Flycatcher, and Swainson's, Kentucky, and Hooded Warbler are all on their breeding territories.

Fall migration can also be exciting and is much more protracted, with the first migrant shorebirds arriving in July and the last neotropical migrants passing through in November. Both Caribbean and western vagrants are possible during this season. From late July to early September, local birders often head to flooded fields around Lake Apopka and the Everglades Agricultural Area, staging areas for tremendous flocks of wading birds and southbound shorebirds. Unfortunately, this is also the season when hurricanes are most likely to occur. Raptor migration extends from September through early November. Birders flock to favorite hawk-watch sites, such as Guana River Preserve, Curry Hammock State Park, and St. Joseph Peninsula, to witness the river of migrant accipiters, buteos, and falcons. Relief from late summer and early fall's often unbearably sticky weather eventually arrives, and cooler temperatures and fewer mosquitoes become the norm by the beginning of November. This is often a good time to hike Snake Bight Trail in Everglades National Park in search of Florida Bay's flock of Greater Flamingo.

What to Bring

Lightweight and breathable clothing is highly recommended when birding in Florida during the warmer months, which is most of the year in the southern peninsula and Florida Keys. Long pants and long-sleeved shirts are suggested to protect against the unrelenting sun and are especially beneficial where biting insects are a problem. In areas and during seasons when pesky insects are especially bothersome, a mesh fabric shirt with a zippered hood can be a godsend. Other clothing essentials include a wide-brimmed hat, comfortable socks, and a sturdy pair of hiking shoes, preferably waterproof. Water shoes (not flipflops!) are suggested if birding on sandy beaches, especially where broken shells and other debris are common. A poncho or umbrella can come in handy during the rainy season. A lightweight jacket may be useful for early-morning birding during the cooler winter months. Prepare for occasional subfreezing temperatures if birding in North Florida during winter. Dressing in layers allows you to remove clothing as temperatures increase over the course of the day.

Other travel essentials include sunscreen, sunglasses, insect repellent, a water bottle, toilet paper, a *Florida Atlas and Gazetteer,* a North American field guide, binoculars, a spotting scope (for waterfowl and shorebirds), a journal for field notes, travel money, and snacks for the road. Finally, don't forget this birding guide.

How to Get Here and Where to Stay

Florida has international airports in most major cities, including Jacksonville, Daytona Beach, Orlando, Melbourne, Palm Beach, Fort Lauderdale, Miami, Key West, Fort Myers, Sarasota, Tampa, St. Petersburg, and Panama City. Regional airports are located in Tallahassee and Pensacola. Public transportation will not provide access to most birding locations in this guide, but rental vehicles are available at all major airports and cities. Rent accordingly if you plan to visit one of the few locations described in this guide where a highclearance or four-wheel-drive vehicle is recommended. If driving into the state, visitor centers are located on interstates near state lines. Speed limits on major highways are usually 65 to 70 miles per hour. Seat belts are mandatory for drivers, front-seat passengers, and children ages 4 to 18. It is wise to avoid urban areas such as Orlando, Miami, and Tampa during weekday rush hours.

Since Florida is a major tourist destination, it should come as no surprise that overnight accommodations are readily available virtually everywhere in the state. Check the section at the end of each site description for nearby locations where lodging, food, and gas are available. Nearby campgrounds are also included in this section. Specific information is available online or from auto clubs such as AAA. During peak seasons in major tourist areas and when special events are taking place (such as the Daytona 500 or other major sporting events), advance reservations are essential.

Hazards

Alligators and crocodiles: The American alligator is a common-to-abundant resident of fresh- and brackish-water habitats throughout the state and is one of Florida's most popular natural tourist attractions. Adult alligators average 6 to 8 feet in length, though some grow larger. These reptiles are often seen sunbathing on the banks of rivers, lakes, canals, and other bodies of water. They may appear lethargic but are capable of running very quickly for short distances. Though attacks on humans are rare, they do occur, so always view alligators from a safe distance. Though seasonal hunting of alligators is once again legal, it is illegal to harass or feed them. Hand-fed alligators usually lose their natural fear of humans and become dangerous. These alligators must often be exterminated.

The American crocodile is a rare and endangered resident of saltwater habitats in the extreme southern peninsula and Upper Keys. Crocodiles can be differentiated from alligators by, among other things, their pointed rather than rounded snout. Population expansion in recent years has led to crocodile sightings in more-developed areas of the southern peninsula. The most reliable location to view American crocodiles is the Flamingo area of Everglades National Park, especially around the marina. Though wary of humans, crocodiles are unpredictable and, like alligators, should be viewed from a safe distance.

Snakes: Of the 70 species of snakes found in Florida, 6 are venomous: eastern coral snake, southern copperhead, cottonmouth (also known as water moccasin), dusky pygmy rattlesnake, timber rattlesnake (known in Florida as canebrake rattlesnake), and eastern diamondback rattlesnake. Except for cottonmouth, you are unlikely to encounter any of these snakes while birding. View any venomous snake from a safe distance, and if bitten, seek medical attention immediately.

Eastern coral snakes are common residents of woodlands throughout the state, including suburban areas, and average 27 to 35 inches in length. Similar to the nonvenomous scarlet snake and scarlet kingsnake, coral snakes have a black snout and wide black and red bands, each separated by narrow yellow bands. The two nonvenomous snakes have red snouts and wide red and narrow yellow bands, each separated by narrow black bands (if confused, remember "red touches yellow, kills a fellow; red touches black, venom lack"). Coral snakes are the only venomous snake in Florida whose head is not wedge-shaped.

Southern copperheads are restricted in Florida to the north-central Panhandle, where they are fairly common residents of woodlands and suburban areas. Averaging 24 to 36 inches in length, copperheads have tan bodies with darker brown, hourglass-shaped bands. Cottonmouths are very common residents of fresh, brackish, and saltwater habitats throughout the state. Averaging 38 inches in length (though the record is almost 75 inches!), cottonmouths generally have dark gray-brown bodies with paler bands. Florida's eight species of water snakes are often confused with cottonmouths but can be identified by their round eyes, as opposed to the cottonmouth's slit-shaped eyes. When in the defensive strike position, cottonmouths will widely open their jaws, revealing the white interior that gives them their name.

Dusky pygmy rattlesnakes are common-to-abundant residents of a variety of aquatic and upland habitats throughout the state. A small snake, usually not more than 20 inches long, dusky pygmy rattlesnakes have gray bodies with small reddish splotches on their backs surrounded by large blackish splotches on their backs and sides. Canebrake rattlesnakes are restricted in Florida to the area in and around Osceola National Forest, in the northern peninsula, where they are uncommon residents of moist forests. Averaging 30 to 48 inches in length, canebrake rattlesnakes have creamy bodies with black stripes, a reddish back, and a black tail. Adults tend to darken in color with age. Eastern diamondback rattlesnakes are uncommon (and declining, due to habitat destruction) residents of pinelands and hammocks throughout the state. Once averaging 60 inches in length, the declining population of eastern diamondback rattlesnakes now averages 32 to 48 inches in length. The backs of their grayish brown bodies are lined with black-outlined diamonds, each in turn outlined in white.

Insects and arachnids: Mosquitoes are by far the most widespread insect pest you will encounter in Florida. Present year-round but most common during the rainy season, these annoying insects can be found along the coast as well as at inland locations and in both aquatic and upland habitats. Mosquitoes can be especially abundant in Everglades National Park and in the Florida Keys. Under these often-unbearable conditions, insect repellent or a mesh shirt with hood are indispensable. Mosquitoes are usually less of a concern in urban areas, thanks to costly eradication programs. Keep in mind that West Nile virus, carried by mosquitoes, has now spread almost statewide, so it is necessary to protect yourself. Use care if applying an insect repellent containing DEET, which can damage rubber-coated binoculars.

Other bothersome insects present in Florida include horse, deer, and sand flies, fire ants, bees, wasps, and lovebugs. Horse flies are large, black-bodied flies that can inflict a painful bite. Deer flies are smaller, come in a variety of colors, and are often more numerous (and thus more annoying) than horse flies. Sand flies, also known as no-see-ums, are tiny flies abundant in coastal areas and most conspicuous at dawn and dusk. Horse and deer flies are most common in spring and summer while sand-fly populations peak during fall. Fire ants are small, red, non-native ants that build sandy mounds, usually in open, disturbed areas. If the mounds are disturbed, the ants will inflict a painful sting that leaves itchy welts and may produce allergic reactions in some people. Some bees and wasps may also sting if disturbed. Lovebugs are harmless to people but, when mating in spring and fall, are inexplicably attracted to automobile fumes. They tend to swarm in large numbers along grassy roadsides and are crushed by passing vehicles by the thousands. Damage to your vehicle's paint may result if the bodies of these insects are not removed promptly.

Arachnids found in Florida include spiders, scorpions, chiggers, and ticks. Spiders are common in woodland areas throughout the state. Look ahead as you walk woodland trails to avoid the unpleasant experience of walking into the web of a golden orb weaver or other harmless spider. Only four species of spider found in Florida are poisonous to humans: brown recluse and black, brown, and red widows, but all four are rarely seen. Scorpions can be found throughout the state, usually hidden in leaf litter and rarely observed, but can inflict a painful sting if encountered. Chiggers are tiny mites that live in areas of tall grass and are found statewide. When they bite, usually where socks or other tight-fitting clothing meets skin, they leave itchy welts. Ticks are most likely in grassy or brushy areas in North Florida and occasionally carry Lyme disease. To avoid both chiggers and ticks, stay away from grassy and brushy areas or treat clothing beforehand with a permethrin-based repellent.

Poisonous plants: Three members of the poisonous cashew family, all of which produce an itchy rash when contacted, can be found in Florida. Poison ivy, a vine best recognized by red stems and shiny leaves in groups of three, is common throughout the state. Poison sumac, an uncommon shrub found in wet woodlands and swamps in northern Florida, is recognized by its red stems and compound leaves. Poisonwood is widespread in South Florida and the Keys, growing into a full-size tree in tropical hardwood hammocks but remaining a sapling in frequently burned pine rocklands. The poisonous sap is visible as black splotches on the reddish brown bark of the trunk. The shiny leaves, in groups of three to seven, usually have black spots.

Manchineel, or poison guava, is a highly poisonous tree found at the edge of mangrove forests in the extreme southern peninsula and Keys. The bright white sap can produce burnlike sores on the skin if contacted and the fruit is extremely poisonous if ingested. This tree is now difficult to find in developed areas due to eradication efforts, but it can still be found in the Flamingo area of Everglades National Park. Brazilian pepper is an introduced shrub now considered a pest plant throughout much of central and southern Florida. This plant is most easily recognized by the clusters of bright red berries that may appear throughout the year. Contact with the plant causes a rash similar to poison ivy in some people. When in bloom, Brazilian pepper causes respiratory distress in some people. A massive effort to eradicate this plant from Everglades National Park is currently ongoing.

Other hazards: As mentioned in chapter 3, lightning strikes are a distinct possibility during summer thunderstorms, which occur almost daily and often develop quickly. If thunderstorms are in the area, seek shelter quickly, either in a building or your vehicle.

A few of the birding locations in this guide, in particular wildlife management areas and state forests, are also used seasonally by hunters. Refer to regulations-summary brochures, updated annually and usually available at check stations or online, for hunt dates and locations in the area you plan to visit. If birding on foot in these areas during hunting season, wear a blaze orange vest or cap. If unsure of the safety of an area being used by hunters, it's best to simply not enter that area.

In large urban areas such as Miami and Tampa, crime is unfortunately always a possibility. To avoid becoming a victim of crime, simple common sense should be exercised. It is never a good idea to bird alone anywhere, but particularly in unfamiliar urban areas. This is especially true when searching for parrots at dusk in urban Miami or Ft. Lauderdale. Always lock your vehicle and keep valuables out of sight, in urban and rural areas alike. Break-ins are much more likely to occur if valuables are visible from the outside.

The overwhelming majority of birders never experience the hazards just listed (the mosquitoes will be the most difficult hazard to avoid). As you will soon discover, Florida is an outstanding birding destination. By being adequately prepared and taking a few simple precautions, your visit here is guaranteed to be a memorable one.

Ethics

Readers of this guide are expected to follow the American Birding Association's Code of Birding Ethics, which is listed below.

Everyone who enjoys birds and birding must always respect wildlife, its environment, and the rights of others. In any conflict of interest between birds and birders, the welfare of the birds and their environment comes first.

Code of Birding Ethics

1. Promote the welfare of birds and their environment.

(a) Support the protection of important bird habitat.

(b) To avoid stressing birds or exposing them to danger, exercise restraint and caution during observation, photography, sound recording, or filming.

Limit the use of recordings and other methods of attracting birds, and never use such methods in heavily birded areas, or for attracting any species that is Threatened, Endangered, or of Special Concern, or is rare in your local area.

Keep well back from nests and nesting colonies, roosts, display areas, and important feeding sites. In such sensitive areas, if there is a need for extended observation, photography, filming, or recording, try to use a blind or hide, and take advantage of natural cover.

Use artificial light sparingly for filming or photography, especially for close-ups.

(c) Before advertising the presence of a rare bird, evaluate the potential for disturbance to the bird, its surroundings, and other people in the area, and proceed only if access can be controlled, disturbance minimized, and permission has been obtained from private landowners. The sites of rare nesting birds should be divulged only to the proper conservation authorities.

(d) Stay on roads, trails, and paths where they exist; otherwise keep habitat disturbance to a minimum.

2. Respect the law and the rights of others.

(a) Do not enter private property without the owner's explicit permission.

(b) Follow all laws, rules, and regulations governing use of roads and public areas, both at home and abroad.

(c) Practice common courtesy in contacts with other people. Your exemplary behavior will generate goodwill with birders and nonbirders alike.

3. Ensure that feeders, nest structures, and other artificial bird environments are safe.

(a) Keep dispensers, water, and food clean and free of decay or disease. It is important to feed birds continually during harsh weather.

(b) Maintain and clean nest structures regularly.

(c) If you are attracting birds to an area, ensure the birds are not exposed to predation from cats and other domestic animals, or dangers posed by artificial hazards.

4. Group birding, whether organized or impromptu, requires special care. Each individual in the group, in addition to the obligations spelled out in item nos. 1 and 2, has responsibilities as a group member.

(a) Respect the interests, rights, and skills of fellow birders, as well as people participating in other legitimate outdoor activities. Freely share your knowledge and experience, except where code 1(c) applies. Be especially helpful to beginning birders.

(b) If you witness unethical birding behavior, assess the situation, and intervene if you think it prudent. When interceding, inform the person(s) of the inappropriate action, and attempt, within reason, to have it stopped. If the behavior continues, document it, and notify appropriate individuals or organizations.

Group leader responsibilities (amateur and professional trips and tours).

(c) Be an exemplary ethical role model for the group. Teach through word and example.

(d) Keep groups to a size that limits impact on the environment and does not interfere with others using the same area.

(e) Ensure everyone in the group knows of and practices this code.

(f) Learn and inform the group of any special circumstances applicable to the areas being visited (for example, no tape recorders allowed).

(g) Acknowledge that professional tour companies bear a special responsibility to place the welfare of birds and the benefits of public knowledge ahead of the company's commercial interests. Ideally, leaders should keep track of tour sightings, document unusual occurrences, and submit records to appropriate organizations.

Please follow this code and distribute and teach it to others.

The American Birding Association's Code of Birding Ethics may be freely reproduced for distribution/dissemination. Please visit the ABA Web site at http://americanbirding.org. Thank you.

CHAPTER FIVE

Florida's Best Birding Areas

NORTHEAST

 Jacksonville Area

Habitats: Sandy beach, coastal strand, salt marsh, freshwater ponds, maritime hammock.

Specialty birds: *Resident:* Wood Stork, Bald Eagle, Clapper Rail, Wilson's Plover, American Oystercatcher, Seaside Sparrow. *Summer:* Reddish Egret, Roseate Spoonbill, Gull-billed Tern, Least Tern, Chuck-will's-widow, Yellow-throated Vireo, Summer Tanager, Painted Bunting, Orchard Oriole.

Winter: Black Scoter, Red-throated Loon, Piping Plover, Long-billed Curlew, Purple Sandpiper, Lesser Black-backed Gull, Winter Wren, Saltmarsh Sharp-tailed Sparrow. *Migrant:* Peregrine Falcon, Whimbrel, Black Tern, Wood Thrush, Prothonotary Warbler, Louisiana Waterthrush, Hooded Warbler.

Best times to bird: September through April.

Directions: *Ft. Clinch State Park:* From Interstate 95 north of Jacksonville, exit at State Road A1A (exit 373). Drive east 14.3 miles to Atlantic Avenue in Fernandina Beach (SR A1A turns north and becomes Eighth Street within the town limits of Fernandina Beach). Turn right and drive east 1.4 miles to the park entrance. *Huguenot Memorial Park:* From I-95, exit at State Road 9A (exit 362). Drive south 6.4 miles to the State Road 105 (Heckscher Drive) exit. You may also access SR 105 directly from I-95 at exit 358. Drive east 6 miles to the intersection with SR 9A. Continue east 10.2 miles on SR 105 to the park entrance. (SR 105 becomes SR A1A at the ferry terminal, 1.5 miles west of the park entrance). *Little Talbot Island State Park:* Continue east, then north 3.6 miles on SR A1A. If coming from Ft. Clinch State Park, you can reach Little Talbot Island State Park by driving east 0.1 mile on Atlantic Avenue, turning right at SR A1A, and driving south 15 miles to the park entrance. *Ft. George Island Cultural State Park:* Backtrack to Huguenot Memorial Park and continue west 0.7 mile on SR A1A to the entrance. *Ft. Caroline National Monument:* Return to SR 9A. Drive south 5 miles to Monument Road. Turn left and drive north 4 miles to Ft. Caroline Road. Turn right and drive east 0.3 mile to the intersection with Mount Pleasant Road. Turn left and drive north 0.3 mile on Ft. Caroline Road to the visitor center entrance.

The Birding

Ft. Clinch State Park is located at the northern tip of Amelia Island, Florida's northernmost barrier island, and at the mouth of the St. Mary's River, which separates Florida from Georgia. The main park road leads 2.8 miles to the fort and visitor center. On the western border of the park is Egan's Creek Marsh. Access the marsh from the Amelia Island Light-

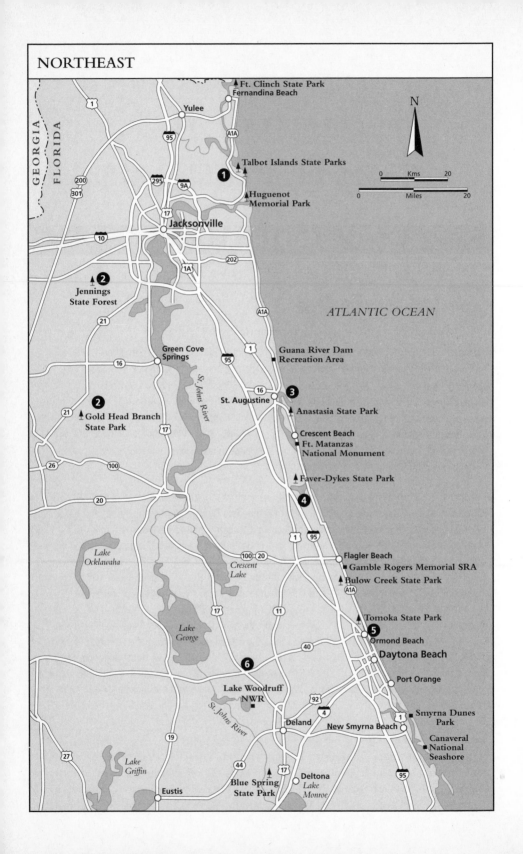

NORTHEAST

GEORGIA
FLORIDA

Ft. Clinch State Park
Fernandina Beach

Yulee

1

Talbot Islands State Parks

Huguenot
Memorial Park

Jacksonville

2
Jennings
State Forest

ATLANTIC OCEAN

Green Cove
Springs

St. Johns River

Guana River Dam
Recreation Area

2
Gold Head Branch
State Park

St. Augustine **3**

Anastasia State Park

Crescent Beach
Ft. Matanzas
National Monument

Faver-Dykes State Park

4

Lake
Ocklawaha

Crescent
Lake

Flagler Beach
Gamble Rogers Memorial SRA
Bulow Creek State Park

Lake
George

Tomoka State Park

5
Ormond Beach
Daytona Beach

6

Port Orange

Lake Woodruff
NWR

Smyrna Dunes
Park

St. Johns River

Deland

New Smyrna Beach

Canaveral
National
Seashore

Lake
Griffin

Deltona
Lake
Monroe

Eustis

Blue Spring
State Park

N

0   Kms   20

0   Miles   20

house overlook, on the main park road 0.3 mile from the entrance station. Clapper Rail is common here year-round. Look in winter for Seaside and Saltmarsh Sharp-tailed Sparrow. Roseate Spoonbill and Gull-billed Tern can be found here during the summer months. The marsh may also be viewed from **Egan's Creek Greenway.** A 3.4-mile trail system begins behind the Atlantic Avenue Recreation Center, 0.1 mile west of the state park entrance. To reach the ocean side of the state park, turn right 1.8 miles from the entrance station. Drive 0.3 mile and turn right, continuing another 0.3 mile to the beach parking area (continuing straight leads to the beach campground). At the north end of the parking area, a feeding station has been installed as part of a kiosk promoting the Great Florida Birding Trail. A large glass window separates the feeders from viewers. Painted Bunting, which breeds in the surrounding dunes, is among the many species attracted to the feeders. Beyond the kiosk is a boardwalk that leads to a fishing pier extending 0.5 mile into the Atlantic. During winter a few Purple Sandpipers can reliably be found with Ruddy Turnstone on the rock jetty that parallels the pier. Beaches on both sides of the pier attract an assortment of shorebirds, gulls, and terns. Least Tern nests here in summer. Migrant Black Tern can often be found on the beach beginning in midsummer. Franklin's, Iceland, and Glaucous Gull have all been recorded from this location in winter. Scan offshore during the winter months for Common Loon, Northern Gannet, and Black Scoter. Sea-watches from this location have on occasion produced sightings of Red-throated Loon, White-winged and Surf Scoter, Long-tailed Duck, and both Pomarine and Parasitic Jaeger.

The Willow Pond Trail begins at a parking area on the main park road 0.4 mile from the beach turnoff. Two loop trails encircle a series of freshwater ponds. The surrounding hammock is attractive to migrant and wintering land birds as well as resident species such as Barred Owl, Pileated and Downy Woodpecker, White-eyed Vireo, Carolina Chickadee, Tufted Titmouse, and Carolina Wren. Continue another 0.6 mile to reach the fort parking area. The fort, though never fully completed, was used as a military post from the Civil War through World War II. During winter check grassy areas surrounding the fort for Savannah, White-throated, Song, and Vesper Sparrow. Watch overhead during summer for Chimney Swift. A hiking trail begins at the fort parking area and parallels the main park road for about 2 miles before crossing the road and returning to the fort on the opposite side. Much of the trail passes through maritime hammock where Yellow-billed Cuckoo, Painted Bunting, and other breeding species can be found.

Throughout the year, thousands of resident and migrant shorebirds, gulls, and terns can be found roosting on beaches and mudflats in Ft. George Inlet, north of Jacksonville near the mouth of the St. Johns River. **Huguenot Memorial Park,** on Ft. George Island, provides the best access to this area. After entering the park, drive east 1 mile to the end of the paved road, beyond the campground and picnic shelters. The St. Johns River will be on your right and Ft. George Inlet on your left. Turn left, then right, and drive east over hard-packed sand to an opening in the dunes. Though vehicles are allowed to drive through this opening onto the beach, it is best to park on the inlet side of the dunes and walk to the beach. During some winters Lapland Longspur can be found along these dunes. Snow Bunting has been found here as well, but not in recent years. To the south of this opening is a rock jetty that in winter occasionally attracts Purple Sandpiper. This can also be a good location during winter to watch for loons, grebes, jaegers, and sea ducks offshore. To the north is Ward's Bank, a spit of land separating Ft. George Inlet from the Atlantic. At low tide you may drive north between the inlet and the dunes. Shorebirds and wading birds may be found anywhere along the inlet. Look for Reddish Egret, American Oystercatcher,

Wilson's Plover, and Willet year-round. Migration and winter bring Black-bellied, Semipalmated, and Piping Plover, Red Knot, Sanderling, Dunlin, Semipalmated, Western, and Least Sandpiper, and Short-billed Dowitcher. Both Whimbrel and Long-billed Curlew are regular during fall and winter. A Bar-tailed Godwit was discovered here in October 1999. Gulls and terns tend to congregate at the northern end of the spit. Laughing Gull, Royal Tern, and Black Skimmer are all common year-round. Gull-billed and Least Tern are here in summer, and Black Tern passes through during late summer and fall. In winter expect Great and Lesser Black-backed, Herring, Ring-billed, and Bonaparte's Gull and Caspian, Sandwich, and Forster's Tern. A thorough search of the gull flocks in winter may produce a Glaucous, Iceland, or Franklin's Gull.

Many of these same species may be found on the beaches and mudflats at the southern end of **Little Talbot Island State Park.** A parking area at the end of the park road provides access to this area. A 3.8-mile nature trail begins at the entrance station and winds through maritime hammock to the beach at the north end of the island. Look for Painted Bunting along this section of the trail during summer and migrant land birds in spring and fall. If you walk to the northern tip of the island, you can reach Big Bird Island, where thousands of gulls and terns roost and Black Skimmer nests. A Curlew Sandpiper was sighted here in July 2004. The nature trail returns south along the beach before crossing the dunes via a boardwalk leading to a picnic area. From here it is a short walk back to the entrance station. As you drive north from Little Talbot Island to Big Talbot Island, SR A1A passes through salt marsh habitat good for Clapper Rail and Seaside Sparrow year-round and Saltmarsh Sharp-tailed Sparrow during winter. At the north end of **Big Talbot Island State Park** (4.6 miles north of the Little Talbot Island State Park entrance), just before the bridge that crosses Nassau Sound to Amelia Island, look on the east side of SR A1A for a marsh called Sawpit Pond. The pond (sometimes referred to as Spoonbill Pond) attracts a variety of wading birds, including Roseate Spoonbill in summer. Wintering ducks and migrant shorebirds, including American Avocet, Whimbrel, and Wilson's Phalarope have been reported from this location. Peregrine Falcon and other migrant raptors have occasionally been seen attacking the shorebird flocks. Don't park along the roadside. Instead, park in the Sawpit Creek boat-ramp parking area on the opposite side of the road.

Kingsley Plantation, a 19th-century cotton plantation, is located at the north end of Ft. George Island. The ruins are managed by the National Park Service as part of **Timucuan Ecological and Historic Preserve.** A 1920s-era golf course once occupied most of the surrounding uplands in what is now **Ft. George Island Cultural State Park.** Oak hammock, attractive to migrant and wintering land birds, has reclaimed much of this area. Saturiwa Trail, a 4.3-mile driving loop, provides access to the plantation and surrounding hammock. From SR A1A, drive north, then east 0.5 mile to the trail entrance. Turn left and drive north 2 miles to the plantation. A feeder set up on the plantation grounds attracts Painted Bunting, which nests in the vicinity. Winter visitors recorded here include Bell's Vireo, Red-breasted Nuthatch, and Winter Wren. From the plantation, drive east, then south 0.4 mile to a small parking area for a hiking trail through the hammock. The trail can also be accessed from the parking area for Ribault Club, the golf course clubhouse now used as a visitor center. To reach Ribault Club, which houses interactive exhibits depicting the natural and cultural history of the island, continue south 0.6 mile on Saturiwa Trail. The driving loop returns to its starting point in another 1.3 miles.

On the south side of the St. Johns River is **Ft. Caroline National Monument,** also a part of Timucuan Ecological and Historic Preserve. Begin your exploration of this area at the **Timucuan Preserve Visitor Center,** where maps and a bird checklist are available. The fort, built in 1564, was part of the first French colony in what is now the United States. The fort was built with the assistance of the Timucua, the original inhabitants of northeast Florida. A 1.5-mile trail winds through maritime hammock in the vicinity of the fort. This trail can be productive for migrant and wintering land birds. Across Ft. Caroline Road from the visitor center entrance is Spanish Pond Trailhead, one of two access points into the **Theodore Roosevelt Area.** This property, originally owned by the Browne family, was donated to The Nature Conservancy in 1969 by Willie Browne, the last surviving member of the Browne family and an admirer of the conservation efforts of Theodore Roosevelt. The 600-acre property was acquired by the National Park Service and incorporated into the preserve in 1990. From Spanish Pond Trailhead, the 1-mile Spanish Pond Trail passes through coastal scrub habitat and along two freshwater ponds. Along this trail, watch in summer for Painted Bunting and for migrant land birds during spring and fall. To reach the second access point into the area, Willie Browne Trailhead, backtrack on Ft. Caroline Road 0.3 mile to the stop sign, turn left onto Mt. Pleasant Road, and drive east, then south 1 mile to the trailhead parking area. The 2-mile Willie Browne Trail leads through maritime hammock to ruins of the rustic cabin where Willie Browne lived until his death in 1970 and to the family cemetery where he is buried. The Spanish Pond and Willie Browne Trails are connected by the 0.8-mile Timucuan Trail. This trail leads to oyster shell middens left by the Timucua, and to an observation platform overlooking Round Marsh. Year-round residents of this salt marsh habitat include Wood Stork, Clapper Rail, Bald Eagle, and Seaside Sparrow. Look for Roseate Spoonbill in summer and Saltmarsh Sharp-tailed Sparrow during winter.

General information: Ft. Clinch and Talbot Islands State Parks (entrance fees) are open daily from 8:00 A.M. until sunset. The fort (additional entrance fee) and visitor center at Ft. Clinch are open daily from 9:00 A.M. to 4:30 P.M. Restrooms are available at the visitor center and on the fishing-pier boardwalk. Restrooms at Little Talbot Island State Park are located in the campground and at beach pavilion areas. Huguenot Memorial Park (entrance fee) is open daily from 8:00 A.M. to 6:00 P.M. (extended to 8:00 P.M. during the summer). Restrooms are located near the campground. Timucuan Preserve Visitor Center (no entrance fee) is open from 9:00 A.M. to 5:00 P.M. (except Thanksgiving, Christmas, and New Year's Day). Restrooms are located at the visitor center. Theodore Roosevelt Area trails (no entrance fee) are open daily from 8:00 A.M. until sunset. Restrooms are located at the Willie Browne Trail parking area.

DeLorme grid: Page 41, C-3; page 58, A-1, B-1.

Hazards: Keep a safe distance from alligators (Willow Pond Trail, salt marsh areas). Eastern diamondback rattlesnakes are present but rarely encountered. Mosquitoes are common in salt marsh and maritime hammock areas during summer.

Nearest food, gas, lodging: In Fernandina Beach, Jacksonville.

Camping: Ft. Clinch State Park: 62 sites in two campgrounds. Huguenot Memorial Park: 88 sites. Little Talbot Island State Park: 40 sites.

For more information: *Ft. Clinch State Park,* 2601 Atlantic Ave., Fernandina Beach, FL 32024; (904) 277-7274; www.floridastateparks.org/fort clinch. *Huguenot Memorial Park,* 10980 Heckscher Dr., Jacksonville, FL 32226; (904) 251-3335; www.coj.net/Departments/Parks+

and+Recreation/Recreation+Activities/Huguenot +Memorial+Park.htm. *Talbot Islands State Parks,* 12157 Heckscher Dr., Jacksonville, FL 32226; (904) 251-2320; www.floridastateparks.org/

littletalbotisland. *Timucuan Ecological and Historic Preserve,* 12713 Ft. Caroline Rd., Jacksonville, FL 32225; (904) 641-7155; www.nps.gov/timu.

Jennings State Forest/Gold Head Branch State Park

Habitats: Pine flatwoods, sandhills, slope forest, hardwood/cypress swamp, freshwater ponds.

Specialty birds: *Resident:* Wood Stork, Bald Eagle, King Rail, Limpkin, Red-cockaded Woodpecker, Brown-headed Nuthatch, Yellow-breasted Chat, Bachman's Sparrow. *Summer:* Least Bittern, Swallow-tailed Kite, Purple Gallinule, Chuck-will's-widow, Acadian Flycatcher, Yellow-throated Vireo, Wood Thrush, Hooded Warbler, Summer Tanager, Blue Grosbeak, Painted Bunting, Orchard Oriole. *Winter:* Peregrine Falcon, Sandhill Crane, American Woodcock, Winter Wren, Golden-crowned Kinglet, American Pipit, Henslow's Sparrow.

Best times to bird: October through April.

Directions: *Jennings State Forest:* From Interstate 295 in Orange Park, exit at State Road 21 (exit 12). Drive south 7.8 miles to Old Jennings Road (County Road 220A). Turn right and drive west 4 miles to Live Oak Lane (unpaved). Turn right and drive north 0.5 mile to the Old Jennings Recreation Area trailhead. Continue north 1 mile to the Fire and Water parking area. *Gold Head Branch State Park:* Return to SR 21. Drive south 22.2 miles to the park entrance. From Interstate 75 in Gainesville, exit at State Road 26 (exit 387). Drive east 23.8 miles to SR 21. Turn left and drive north 12.7 miles to the park entrance.

The Birding

Jennings State Forest, located southwest of Jacksonville, contains more than 15 natural communities within its almost 24,000 acres. A recent addition to Florida's state forest system, little is known about the birding potential here. Two hiking trails on Live Oak Lane provide access to the forest. The North Fork Black Creek Trail begins at the Old Jennings Recreation Area trailhead. This 5-mile loop trail leads through restored longleaf-pine forest to a primitive campground along Black Creek. Two shorter trails also begin at this trailhead: the 0.6-mile Bird Blind Loop and 1.5-mile Long Leaf Pine Loop. Maps and bird checklists are available at the trailhead. Most of the original longleaf pines in this forest were harvested in the late 19th and early 20th centuries. Red-cockaded Woodpecker, which nests in mature longleaf pines, is now a rare breeder in the state forest. The Fire and Water Nature Trail begins at a parking area 1 mile north on Live Oak Lane. This 1.5-mile trail winds through pine sandhills and also includes a short spur trail leading to an observation blind with bird feeders. Look along this trail for Wild Turkey, Northern Bobwhite, Chuck-will's-widow, Red-headed Woodpecker, Brown-headed Nuthatch, Pine Warbler, Summer Tanager, and Bachman's Sparrow. The trail also passes through a seepage slope community inhabited by insect-eating pitcher plants, and by slope forest and the Wheeler Branch of Black Creek. Species to watch for in this area during summer include Acadian Flycatcher and Hooded Warbler. In winter Golden-crowned Kinglet and Winter Wren are possible. From the Fire and Water parking area, continue north 1.2 miles on Live Oak Lane to its intersection with Powerline Road. Turn right and follow Powerline Road 0.6 mile to an observation platform. Along this road watch for American Kestrel, Eastern Bluebird, and Bachman's Sparrow. In winter look for other sparrow species in grassy or brushy areas, including Field, Vesper, Song, and White-throated. Swamp Sparrow and possibly Henslow's Sparrow may winter in wet areas along this road. The observation tower overlooks a marsh where Wood Duck may be found.

Officially dedicated in 1939, **Gold Head Branch State Park** is among the oldest in the Florida state park system. Many of the buildings constructed by the Civilian Conservation Corps in the 1930s are still being used today. Most of the 2,100-acre park consists of pine sandhills, with old stands of longleaf pine, turkey oak, and wire grass. A ravine system cuts through the sandhills. Freshwater springs along the sides of the ravine form a stream called Gold Head Branch, which flows into Little Lake Johnson. The stream was once panned for gold, though little was found. Unlike the surrounding sandhills, the ravine is characterized by hardwoods such as hickory, magnolia, and live oak, with a lush understory of ferns. Access to the ravine is via a stairway that begins on the main park road 0.7 mile from the entrance station. Two trails begin at the base of the stairway. The Fern Trail is a short trail leading to the head spring of Gold Head Branch. The Ravine Ridge Trail winds for 1 mile along the upper ridges of the ravine and leads to the site of an old mill. Watch for resident species such as Barred Owl, Downy Woodpecker, and Carolina Wren, joined in summer by Yellow-billed Cuckoo, Acadian Flycatcher, Yellow-throated Vireo, Wood Thrush, and Northern Parula. House and Winter Wren as well as Ruby-crowned and Golden-crowned Kinglet are possible during the winter months. On the opposite side of the main park road about 0.1 mile beyond the ravine stairway parking area is a short trail leading through sandhill habitat to Sheelar Lake, actually a small freshwater pond. Here or anywhere along the main park road for the next mile or so, look for sandhill residents including Wild Turkey, Northern Bobwhite, Red-headed Woodpecker, Carolina Chickadee, and Tufted Titmouse. In summer expect to hear or see Chuck-will's-widow, Common Nighthawk, Chimney Swift, Great Crested Flycatcher, and Summer Tanager. Watch overhead during the summer months for Swallow-tailed Kite and for Bald Eagle year-round. To reach Little Lake Johnson, turn left 1 mile beyond the ravine stairway parking area (continuing straight on the main park road leads to Big Lake Johnson) onto a 1.3-mile one-way loop road. The lake will be on your right 0.2 mile after the loop-road turnoff. Wintering waterfowl may be found on this or any of the lakes in the park. Continue 0.5 mile to the Mill Site parking area. The 0.5-mile Loblolly Trail begins here and leads to the old mill, as well as to the southern terminus of the Ravine Ridge Trail. The trail is named after the loblolly pine, which, unlike the longleaf pine, typically grows in wet areas such as the ravine (habitats such as this were called a "loblolly" by early settlers). Many of the largest loblolly pines in the park are found along this trail.

General information: Jennings State Forest (daily-use fee) is open daily from sunrise to sunset. No restrooms are available. Seasonal hunting is permitted in designated areas. Refer to regulations-summary brochures, updated annually and available at check stations, for hunt dates and locations. Wear blaze orange if hiking during hunting season. Gold Head Branch State Park (entrance fee) is open daily from 8:00 A.M. until sunset. Restrooms are located at Little Lake Johnson.

DeLorme grid: Page 57, C-1; page 66, B-3.

Hazards: Keep a safe distance from alligators. Venomous snakes are present but rarely encountered. Mosquitoes are common in summer. Trails may be flooded during the summer months.

Nearest food, gas, lodging: In Orange Park.

Camping: Gold Head Branch State Park: 74 sites, plus 14 rental cottages. Primitive camping in the state forest requires a State Forest Use Permit.

For more information: *Jennings State Forest,* c/o Florida Division of Forestry, 1337 Long Horn Rd., Middleberg, FL 32068; (904) 291-5530; http://www.fl-dof.com. *Gold Head Branch State Park,* 6239 SR 21, Keystone Heights, FL 32656; (352) 473-4701; www.floridastateparks.org/goldhead.

 # St. Augustine Area

Habitats: Salt marsh, sandy beach, coastal scrub, maritime hammock, pine flatwoods.

Specialty birds: *Resident:* Wood Stork, Bald Eagle, Clapper Rail, Wilson's Plover, American Oystercatcher, Monk Parakeet, Black-hooded Parakeet, Seaside Sparrow. *Summer:* Least Bittern, Reddish Egret, Roseate Spoonbill, Swallow-tailed Kite, Least Tern, Chuck-will's-widow, Gray Kingbird, Summer Tanager, Painted Bunting. *Winter:* Whimbrel, Saltmarsh Sharp-tailed Sparrow. *Migrant:* Peregrine Falcon, Black Tern, Prothonotary Warbler.

Best times to bird: October through March.

Directions: *Guana River Dam Recreation Area:* From I-95 west of St. Augustine, exit at State Road 16 (exit 318). Drive east 5.3 miles to U.S. Highway 1. Turn right and drive south 0.5 mile to SR A1A. Turn left and drive east, then north 9.4 miles to the state park entrance. *Anastasia State Park:* From the intersection of SR A1A and US 1, follow SR A1A south 3 miles to the park entrance.

The Birding

The **Guana Tolomato Matanzas National Estuarine Research Reserve (GTMN-ERR)** encompasses 60,000 acres of salt marsh and other coastal habitats on barrier islands both north and south of the historic city of St. Augustine. Access to the northern section of GTMNERR is via **Guana River Dam Recreation Area,** formerly known as Guana River State Park. A state-of-the-art environmental education center has recently been constructed at the entrance, and maps and checklists are available there. Beyond the entrance station is a dam across the Guana River. Salt marsh lines the banks of the river south of the dam—good Clapper Rail habitat year-round. During low tide, migrant shorebirds feed on exposed mudflats. Watch for Seaside and Saltmarsh Sharp-tailed Sparrow in the marsh during winter. North of the dam is the artificially created Guana Lake (also known as Lake Ponte Vedra). American White Pelican and a variety of waterfowl can be found on the lake during the winter months. Roseate Spoonbill, Swallow-tailed Kite, Least Tern, and Gray Kingbird have all been seen in the area around the dam in summer. Watch overhead for Bald Eagle any time of year. Guana River Dam Recreation Area has several miles of trails through maritime forest, coastal scrub, and pine flatwoods. From the parking area on the dam, drive west 0.2 mile down a dirt road to the trailhead parking area. Check grassy areas on both sides of the road for Bobolink during migration. The area around the trailhead can be excellent for migrant warblers, vireos, buntings, and other land birds. Beyond the trailhead, several hiking options are available. Continuing west, the road leads 1 mile to Shell Bluff on the Tolomato River, which separates the barrier island from the mainland.

Heading south, the 3-mile Timucuan Loop Trail connects with the 2.8-mile South Point Loop Trail, providing opportunities to explore a cross section of habitats within the tract. The trail ends near where the Guana River dumps into the Tolomato. Hiking north from the trailhead, the Guana Loop reconnects after 1.9 miles with Shell Bluff Road. A spur trail from Guana Loop provides access to the 9,800-acre **Guana River Wildlife Management Area** farther north. A short hike leads to an interpretive kiosk and observation platform at Big Savannah Pond, an excellent location to observe an assortment of wading birds, including Roseate Spoonbill in summer. Other observation

Roseate Spoonbill. PHOTO: BRIAN RAPOZA

platforms are located at Capo Creek and along Lake Guana, but they require longer hikes. These platforms can be superb locations to observe raptor migration. Sightings of dozens of Peregrine Falcons moving up or down the coast are not uncommon in late March and early October. Much of the wildlife management area trail system is only open to birders on days when hunting is not allowed. Three parking areas, located 3.4, 4.2, and 6.4 miles north of the reserve entrance, provide access to beach overlooks. These locations offer excellent vantage points for sea-watching in winter, where Northern Gannet, loons, and sea ducks can often be seen offshore. Reddish Egret is occasionally seen feeding along the water's edge somewhere along this beach. Expect shorebirds such as Willet and Sanderling, plus a variety of gulls and terns.

Just south of the historic forts and monuments, not to mention the kitschy museums and tourist traps of downtown St. Augustine, is one of Florida's busiest recreation areas, **Anastasia State Park.** After the founding of St. Augustine in 1565, Spanish settlers quarried coquina rock, the porous limestone found in what is now the park, to build the Castillo de San Marcos, which is the nation's oldest stone fort, and many other buildings in the city. One of these quarries, just south of the park entrance on SR A1A, is now used as the St. Augustine Amphitheatre. While driving through the city, listen for Monk and Black-hooded Parakeet; both species nest locally. Once inside the park, drive east 0.8 mile on the main park road to a picnic area on the left, near a windsurf concession. The road here skirts the southern edge of Salt Run, a salt-marsh-fringed tidal lagoon. The picnic area provides access to the marsh's edge. Look and listen year-round for Clapper Rail and an assortment of wading birds, including Wood Stork year-round and Roseate Spoonbill in summer. Both Seaside and Saltmarsh Sharp-tailed Sparrow winter in the marsh. To reach the Ancient Dunes Nature Trail, located in the park's campground, turn right 0.4 mile east of the windsurf concession. Drive south 0.2 mile to the trailhead parking area. During spring and fall a variety of warblers and other land birds can be found within this maritime hammock. Return to the main park road and continue east 0.1 mile to the beach parking area. In summer watch for Painted Bunting around the adjacent Hill Top Picnic Area. A boardwalk begins at the beach parking area and crosses over the marsh and dunes, providing access to the park's 4 miles of white-sand beaches. Look for Wilson's Plover, Willet, Laughing Gull, Royal Tern, and Black Skimmer throughout the year. Least Tern is common here in summer and Reddish Egret is occasionally seen. Several species of gulls, terns, and shorebirds can be found on the beach during the winter months, while Northern Gannet feeds offshore.

General information: Guana River Dam Recreation Area and Anastasia State Park (entrance fees) are open daily from 8:00 A.M. until sunset. The environmental education center (separate entrance fee) is open daily from 9:00 A.M. to 4:00 P.M. Restrooms at Guana River Dam Recreation Area are located in the environmental education center, near the entrance station, and at the trailhead on the west side of the dam. Restrooms at Anastasia State Park are located at picnic areas. Seasonal hunting is permitted in the Guana River Wildlife Management Area. Refer to regulations–summary brochures, updated annually and available at check stations, for hunt dates and locations. Wear blaze orange if hiking during hunting season.

DeLorme grid: Page 58, D-1; page 68, B-2.

Hazards: Keep a safe distance from alligators. Eastern diamondback rattlesnakes are present and occasionally encountered. Ticks and chiggers are present in grassy areas. Mosquitoes and other biting insects are common in summer and fall.

Nearest food, gas, lodging: In St. Augustine.

Camping: Anastasia State Park: 139 sites.

For more information: *Guana Tolomato Matanzas National Estuarine Research Reserve,* 505 Guana River Rd., Ponte Vedra Beach, FL 32082; (904) 823-4500; www.dep.state.fl.us/coastal/sites/gtm/guana_river.htm. *Anastasia State Park,* 1340 SR A1A S., St. Augustine, FL 32080; (904) 461-2033; www.floridastateparks.org/anastasia.

 # Matanzas River/Pellicer Creek Area

Habitats: Sandy beach, coastal scrub, maritime hammock, salt marsh, freshwater marsh, hardwood hammock, pine flatwoods.

Specialty birds: *Resident:* Wood Stork, Bald Eagle, Clapper Rail, Wilson's Plover, Florida Scrub-Jay, Brown-headed Nuthatch. *Summer:* Reddish Egret, Roseate Spoonbill, Least Tern, Chuck-will's-widow, Summer Tanager, Painted Bunting.

Best times to bird: September through April.

Directions: *Ft. Matanzas National Monument:* From I-95 west of Crescent Beach, exit at State Road 206 (exit 305). Drive east 6 miles to SR A1A. Turn right and drive south 4 miles to the monument entrance on the right and beach access on the left. *River to Sea Preserve:* Continue south 4 miles on SR A1A to the parking area. *Washington Oaks Gardens State Park:* Continue south 2 miles on SR A1A to the park entrance. *Faver-Dykes State Park:* From I-95 south of St. Augustine, exit at US 1 (exit 298). Drive north 0.2 mile to Faver-Dykes Road. Turn right and drive east 1.5 miles to the park entrance.

Princess Place Preserve: Return to the intersection of US 1 and I-95. Drive south 1.5 miles on US 1 to Old King Road (dirt road). Turn left and drive east 1.5 miles to Princess Place Road (dirt road). Turn left and drive north 2 miles to the preserve entrance.

The Birding

Ft. Matanzas National Monument is located at the southern tip of Anastasia Island. The fort itself is located on Rattlesnake Island, near the mouth of the Matanzas River, which separates Anastasia Island from the mainland. Completed by the Spanish in 1742, the fort was built to defend St. Augustine against a rear attack. A passenger ferry leaves from behind the visitor center and provides access to the fort. Watch overhead for Osprey and Bald Eagle during the crossing. A 0.6-mile boardwalk through maritime hammock begins near the visitor center. Check the hammock in spring and fall for migrant land birds. The boardwalk leads to an overlook of the salt marshes lining the Matanzas River. Clapper Rail and a variety of wading birds can be found in these marshes, including Wood Stork year-round and Roseate Spoonbill during summer. Directly across SR A1A from the entrance to the visitor center parking area is a road leading through coastal scrub to the beach. Florida Scrub-Jay is occasionally seen in this area or on the wires along SR A1A. During summer look for Gray Kingbird on these same wires. From the beach, scan off-shore in winter for Northern Gannet, loons, jaegers, and flocks of sea ducks moving up or down the coast. This is also a good place in spring and fall to watch for Peregrine Falcon and other migrating birds of prey. Matanzas Inlet is 1 mile south of the visitor center parking area. In summer Least Tern nests on the beach on the north side of the inlet. Good numbers of shorebirds, gulls, terns, and skimmers can be found on sandbars here year-round at low tide. During winter Purple Sandpiper has been seen on rocks on the south side of the inlet. Reddish Egret may occasionally be spotted feeding along the shore. The best vantage points to scope the beach are from the bridge that crosses the inlet or from an observation platform on the north side of the inlet. Use the parking area on the east side of SR A1A, just north of the bridge, to access both areas. Continue south on SR A1A 3 miles to Marineland (home of the world's first oceanarium). Just south of the oceanarium is **River to Sea Preserve.** This 90-acre property includes a boardwalk on the ocean side of SR A1A. A walking trail on the west side of the highway leads through coastal scrub and maritime hammock to the Matanzas River. Watch for Florida Scrub-Jay on the wires along this stretch of SR A1A.

The 425-acre **Washington Oaks Gardens State Park** was once part of a plantation owned by a Spanish general. The property was purchased in 1936 by Owen D. Young, then chairman of the board of General Electric. He expanded the plantation's gardens to include plants from around the world. The gardens, donated to the state in 1964, overlook the Matanzas River and are adjacent to the Owen D. Young Visitor Center. Several trails in the park lead through maritime hammock. Search for Pileated Woodpecker, migrant warblers, and other land birds along these trails. The 0.5-mile Mala Compra Trail begins near the visitor center, while the 0.7-mile Jungle Road Trail and 1-mile Timucuan Trail begin at a parking area between the park entrance and the gardens, where the main park road turns left (south). Across SR A1A from the park entrance is a road leading through coastal scrub to a beach parking area. Florida Scrub-Jay is sometimes seen in this area.

Surrounding the 505 submerged acres of **Pellicer Creek Aquatic Preserve** are 3,865 acres of pristine salt marsh, pinelands, and hardwood forest in **Pellicer Creek Conservation Area.** The creek, whose waters flow into the Matanzas River, forms a section of the border between St. Johns and Flagler Counties. Access to the St. Johns County side of the preserve is via **Faver-Dykes State Park.** This 6,000-acre park was once a Spanish plantation and became a state park in 1950. The park has two short nature trails. The loop trail beginning at the picnic area leads through pine flatwoods. Species possible here include Wild Turkey, Northern Bobwhite, Brown-headed Nuthatch, and Summer Tanager. The trail that starts at the campground winds through oak hammock that's good for migrant and wintering land birds. This trail also leads to an observation platform overlooking salt marsh along the creek. Look and listen here for Clapper Rail. A variety of wading birds feed in and around the creek, including Roseate Spoonbill in summer. A boat ramp provides canoe or kayak access to the aquatic preserve. Explore the Flagler County side of the creek by visiting **Princess Place Preserve.** This 1,505-acre property, once the home of an exiled Russian prince and his American wife, is situated at the confluence of the creek with the Matanzas River. A lodge at the preserve includes Florida's first in-ground swimming pool. Several color-coded trails provide hiking and birding opportunities. The 2-mile Red Trail, 1.5-mile Orange Trail, and 1.4-mile Yellow Trail begin at The Hill parking area near the preserve entrance and pass through pine flatwoods. The 0.6-mile Blue Trail begins near the lodge and is the only paved, wheelchair-accessible trail in the preserve. This trail winds through an oak hammock good for Barred Owl, Pileated Woodpecker, and migrant and wintering land birds. An observation platform at the midpoint of the trail provides an overlook of the creek. A 1.4-mile driving loop that also begins near the lodge leads, via a 0.2-mile spur road, to the Green Trail, which loops through salt marsh habitat along the Matanzas River.

General information: Ft. Matanzas National Monument (no entrance fee) is open daily from 9:00 A.M. to 5:30 P.M. (except Christmas). The visitor center is open daily from 9:00 A.M. to 4:30 P.M. Restrooms are located near the nature trail. Free ferry service to Ft. Matanzas is available daily, weather permitting, from 9:30 A.M. to 4:30 P.M. River to Sea Preserve (no entrance fee) is open daily from 7:00 A.M. to 6:00 P.M. No restrooms are available. Washington Oaks Gardens and Faver-Dykes State Parks (entrance fees) are open daily from 8:00 A.M. until sunset. Restrooms at Washington Oak Gardens are located at the visitor center. Restrooms at Favor-Dykes are located in the picnic area. Princess Place Preserve (no entrance fee) is open Wednesday through Sunday from 7:00 A.M. to 6:00 P.M. Restrooms are located near the lodge.

DeLorme grid: Page 68, C-2.

Hazards: Keep a safe distance from alligators. Prepare for mosquitoes in summer. Areas of tall grass may have ticks and chiggers.

Nearest food, gas, lodging: In Crescent Beach, St. Augustine, and Palm Coast.

Camping: Faver-Dykes State Park: 30 sites. Anastasia State Park: 139 sites, 1340A SR A1A S., St. Augustine, FL 32080; (904) 461-2033.

For more information: *Fort Matanzas National Monument*, 8635 SR A1A S., St. Augustine, FL 32080; (904) 471-0116; www.nps.gov/foma.

River to Sea Preserve, SR A1A, Marineland, FL 32080; (386) 437-7490; www.flagleronline .com/local/whattodo/rivertoseapreserve.asp. *Washington Oaks Gardens State Park*, 6400 N. Oceanshore Blvd., Palm Coast, FL 32137; (386) 446-6780; www.floridastateparks.org/ washingtonoaks. *Faver-Dykes State Park*, 1000 Faver-Dykes Rd., St. Augustine, FL 32086; (904) 794-0997; www.floridastateparks.org/ faver-dykes. *Princess Place Preserve*, c/o Flagler County Parks and Recreation, 160 Sawgrass Rd., Bunnell, FL 32110; (386) 437-7490; www.flagler parks.com/princess/preserve.htm.

5 Daytona Beach Area

Habitats: Sandy beach, coastal dunes, coastal scrub, maritime hammock, salt marsh.

Specialty birds: *Resident:* Wood Stork, Bald Eagle, Clapper Rail, American Oystercatcher, Florida Scrub-Jay. *Summer:* Magnificent Frigatebird, Reddish Egret, Roseate Spoonbill, Swallow-tailed Kite, Least Tern, Chuck-will's-widow, Painted Bunting. *Winter:* Piping Plover, Purple Sandpiper, Lesser Black-backed Gull, Saltmarsh Sharp-tailed Sandpiper. *Migrant:* Peregrine Falcon, American Avocet.

Best times to bird: October through April.

Directions: *Gamble Rogers Memorial State Recreation Area:* From I-95 west of Flagler Beach, exit at State Road 100 (exit 284). Drive east 3.4 miles to SR A1A. Turn right and drive south 3 miles to the park entrance. *North Peninsula State Park:* Continue south 2 miles on SR A1A to Highbridge Road. Turn right and drive west 0.3 mile to the Smith Creek Landing Trail parking area. *Bulow Creek State Park:* Continue west, then north 1.6 miles on Highbridge Road to Walter Boardman Lane. Turn left and drive west 1 mile to West Dixie Highway (County Road 5A). Turn left and drive south 1 mile to the Fairchild Oak parking area. To reach this area from I-95, exit at West Dixie Highway (exit 278). Drive east 1 mile to where West Dixie Highway curves south at Walter Boardman Lane. Continue south on West Dixie Highway 1 mile to the Fairchild Oak parking area. *Tomoka State Park:* Continue south on West Dixie Highway 4.7 miles to the park entrance. To reach the park from I-95 in Ormond Beach, exit at State Road 40 (exit 268). Drive east 4.3 miles to North Beach Street (CR 5A). Turn left and drive north 4 miles to the park entrance. *Smyrna Dunes Park:* From I-95 west of New Smyrna Beach, exit at State Road 44 (exit 249). Drive east 4 miles to where the road becomes SR A1A. Continue east 1.3 miles on SR A1A to Peninsula Avenue. Turn left and drive north 2.6 miles to the park entrance. *Canaveral National Seashore:* Return to SR A1A, turn left and drive east, then south 8 miles to the entrance station.

The Birding

Though much of the coastal scrub habitat along the Atlantic coast of Florida has been lost to development, scattered patches remain. Two locations in the Daytona Beach area where coastal scrub has been preserved are south of the town of Flagler Beach, on SR A1A. At **Gamble Rogers Memorial State Recreation Area,** access is via the 0.8-mile Joe Kenner Nature Trail, which begins near the picnic area. In this community of sand live oak, red bay, and saw palmetto, Florida Scrub-Jay may be found throughout the year. During summer look and listen for Painted Bunting. At **North Peninsula State Park,** Florida Scrub-Jay is easiest to find when perched on wires along SR A1A, both north and south of Highbridge Road. The Smith Creek Landing Trail, on Highbridge Road just west of SR A1A, provides the only access to the interior of this relatively new addition to the Florida park system. A pull-off near the intersection of SR A1A and Highbridge Road provides opportunities to check the beach for shorebirds, gulls, and terns. Scan offshore from this location during the winter months for Northern Gannet, loons, jaegers, and sea ducks. Magnificent Frigatebird is occasionally seen offshore in summer.

Bulow Creek State Park provides access to salt marsh along the creek and to one of the largest remaining stands of southern live oak forest on Florida's east coast. To scan Bulow Creek for shorebirds and ducks in winter, or to listen for Clapper Rail year-round, park at the west end of the bridge on Walter Boardman Lane and walk up onto the bridge. The 6.8-mile Bulow Woods Trail crosses the road 0.1 mile west of the bridge. North of the road, the trail parallels the creek before ending at Bulow Plantation Ruins, a 19th-century sugar mill. Look for ducks and shorebirds, including American Avocet, from vantage points along the trail. South of the road, the trail winds through live oak hammock and ends at Fairchild Oak Trailhead. The parking area for this trailhead is on West Dixie Highway, 1 mile south of Walter Boardman Lane. The massive Fairchild Oak, visible from the parking area, is one of the largest live oak trees in the southern United States. The Wahlin Trail also begins here, looping 1.6 miles around a groundwater spring. Watch for Wild Turkey, Barred Owl, Pileated Woodpecker, and migrant land birds. Live oak forest stretches south several miles to **Tomoka State Park,** located on a peninsula between the Tomoka and Halifax Rivers. This 2,000-acre park was, until the 15th century, the site of a Timucuan Indian village called Nocoroco. The park is home to an impressive 40-foot sculpture created by artist Fred Dana Marsh, depicting the imaginary Chief Tomokie. A 0.5-mile nature trail winding through the live oak forest leads from the Fred Dana Marsh Museum to the sculpture. The museum is on the main park road, 0.5 mile from the entrance station. In spring and fall look for migrant land birds along the trail or the main park road. Watch for resident Bald Eagle overhead.

South of Daytona Beach, **Smyrna Dunes Park** preserves 255 acres of beach, coastal dune, and salt marsh habitats on the south side of Ponce de Leon Inlet. More than 1.5 miles of wheelchair-accessible boardwalk provides access to these areas. The boardwalk begins and ends at the parking area and may be walked in either direction. Maritime hammock in the vicinity of the parking area should be checked for migrant and wintering land birds and for resident species such as Brown Thrasher and Eastern Towhee. Hiking the boardwalk in a clockwise direction leads to a spur trail providing access to the park's salt marsh habitat. Look and listen here year-round for Clapper Rail. During winter search the marsh for Sedge Wren and Saltmarsh Sharp-tailed Sparrow and for Bald Eagle overhead. Beyond the salt marsh spur trail, the boardwalk becomes elevated as it passes over dune habitat. Watch for Loggerhead Shrike throughout the year and American Kestrel and Savannah Sparrow in winter. On more than one occasion, Lapland Longspur has been discovered in winter along this stretch. Several spur trails lead over the dunes to provide beach access. Walk the beach to reach the rock jetty at the mouth of Ponce de Leon Inlet. The jetty is a reliable place in winter to find Purple Sandpiper, usually seen feeding with Ruddy Turnstone. In April 2004 a Surfbird was spotted on the jetty. The beach on either side of the jetty attracts Reddish Egret and an assortment of shorebirds, gulls, and terns. Both Least Tern and Black Skimmer nest on the beach. Franklin's, Lesser Black-backed, and Thayer's Gull are among the larids recorded from this area. Northern Gannet feed offshore in winter. In April 2003 a Red-footed Booby was spotted on the north jetty. A Masked Booby was found near the inlet in December 2005, and both Masked and Brown Booby were seen in this area in September 2006. During periods of persistent easterly winds, storm-petrels, shearwaters, jaegers, and other pelagic species may be driven close to the inlet. To drive directly to the jetty area, exit the park and backtrack 1.2 miles on Peninsula Avenue to Beachway Road. Turn left and drive east 0.1 mile to the beach entrance station. Once you are on the beach, turn left and drive north to the jetty. Avoid areas of soft sand. Park in any area above the high tide line but don't park beyond the dune-conservation-zone markers.

The north entrance to **Canaveral National Seashore** provides access via SR A1A to Apollo Beach and several short trails. The **Turtle Mound** Trail, a boardwalk located 0.5

mile south of the entrance station and 0.2 mile north of the visitor center, leads to a shell midden left by Timucuan Indians. Turtle Mound is the highest point in the area and can be an excellent location for sea- or hawk-watching, especially in fall. From the visitor center, continue south 0.6 mile to Eldora Road, a one-way loop road. Turn right and drive south 0.8 mile to the parking area for Eldora Hammock Trail. This 0.5-mile trail loops through maritime hammock that is attractive to migrant and wintering land birds. Continue south another 0.3 mile to return to SR A1A. Turn right and drive south 0.8 mile to Apollo Beach Parking Area 3. The Castle Windy Trail begins across the road from the parking area. Follow this trail 0.5 mile through maritime hammock to Mosquito Lagoon, which in winter may have American White Pelican and other waterbirds. SR A1A ends in 3.2 miles, at a parking area that, like Turtle Mound, provides first-rate opportunities for sea-watching.

General information: Gamble Rogers Memorial State Recreation Area and Tomoka State Park (entrance fees), and Bulow Creek and North Peninsula State Parks (no entrance fees), are open daily from 8:00 A.M. until sunset. The Fred Dana Marsh Museum at Tomoka State Park is open daily from 9:30 A.M. to 4:30 P.M. At Gamble Rogers, restrooms are located at the trailhead for the Joe Kenner Nature Trail. At North Peninsula, restrooms are located at the parking area for the Smith Creek Landing Trail. At Bulow Creek, restrooms are located at the Fairchild Oak parking area. At Tomoka, restrooms are located at the museum and in the campground. Smyrna Dunes Park (entrance fee) is open daily from sunrise to sunset. Restrooms are available at the parking area. Driving on New Smyrna Beach (entrance fee) is allowed from 8:00 A.M. to 7:00 P.M. Canaveral National Seashore (entrance fee) is open daily from 6:00 A.M. to 6:00 P.M. November through March and from 6:00 A.M. to 8:00 P.M. April through October. The visitor center is open from 8:00 A.M. to 4:00 P.M. November through March and 9:00 A.M. to 5:00 P.M. April through October. Restrooms are available in the visitor center, at the Eldora House parking area, and at Apollo Beach parking areas.

DeLorme grid: Page 75, B-1, D-2; page 81, A-3.

Hazards: Keep a safe distance from alligators. Eastern diamondback rattlesnakes are present but rarely encountered. Mosquitoes are common in summer. If driving on New Smyrna Beach, only drive or park on the seaward side of dune-conservation-zone markers. Citations are issued to violators.

Nearest food, gas, lodging: In Flagler Beach, Ormond Beach, and New Smyrna Beach.

Camping: Gamble Rogers Memorial State Recreation Area: 34 sites. Tomoka State Park: 100 sites. Private campgrounds are located in New Smyrna Beach.

For more information: *Gamble Rogers Memorial State Recreation Area,* 3100 SR A1A, Flagler Beach, FL 32174; (386) 517-2086; www.florida stateparks.org/gamblerogers. *North Peninsula State Park,* c/o Gamble Rogers Memorial State Recreation Area; www.floridastateparks.org/north peninsula. *Tomoka State Park,* 2099 North Beach St., Ormond Beach, FL 32174; (386) 676-4050; www.floridastateparks.org/tomoka. *Bulow Creek State Park,* c/o Tomoka State Park; www.florida stateparks.org/bulowcreek. *Smyrna Dunes Park,* 2995 N. Peninsula Dr., New Smyrna Beach, FL 32169; (386) 424-2935; http://volusia.org/ parks/smyrnadunes.htm. *Canaveral National Seashore,* 308 Julia St., Titusville, FL 32796; (321) 267-1110; www.nps.gov/cana.

6 Deland Area

Habitats: Freshwater marsh, freshwater lake, hardwood/cypress swamp, oak/cabbage palm hammock, pine flatwoods, sand pine scrub.

Specialty birds: *Resident:* Mottled Duck, Wood Stork, Bald Eagle, King Rail, Black Rail, Purple Gallinule, Limpkin, Sandhill Crane, Brown-headed Nuthatch, Bachman's Sparrow. *Summer:* Least Bittern, Swallow-tailed Kite, Chuck-will's-widow, Yellow-throated Vireo, Prothonotary Warbler, Summer Tanager. *Winter:* Fulvous Whistling-Duck, American Woodcock, Golden-crowned Kinglet. *Migrant:* Black Tern, Swainson's Warbler, Louisiana Waterthrush, Hooded Warbler.

Best times to bird: October through April.

Directions: *Lake Woodruff National Wildlife Refuge:* From I-95 west of Ormond Beach, exit at SR 40 (exit 268). Drive west 19.7 miles to State Road 17. Turn left and drive south 6.7 miles to Retta Avenue. Turn right and drive west 0.1 mile to Grand Avenue. Turn left and drive south 0.6 mile to Mud Lake Road. Turn right and drive west 0.1 mile to the refuge headquarters. From Interstate 4 in Deltona, exit at State Road 472 (exit 114). Drive west 3 miles to the SR 17 exit. Drive north 10.7 miles on SR 17 to Retta Avenue. Turn left and proceed as above. *DeLeon Springs State Park:* Return to SR 17 and drive north 0.4 mile to Ponce de Leon Boulevard. Turn left and drive west 0.8 mile to the entrance. *Blue Spring State Park:* Return to the intersection of SR 17 and SR 472. Drive south 1.5 miles on SR 17 to West French Avenue. Turn right and drive west 2 miles to the entrance. *Lyonia Preserve:* Return to the intersection of SR 472 and I-4. Continue east 2.5 miles on SR 472 to Providence Boulevard (County Road 4155). Turn right and drive south 0.6 mile to Eustace Avenue. Turn left, then immediately right into the library parking area.

The Birding

Begin your tour of the 21,574-acre **Lake Woodruff National Wildlife Refuge** at the refuge headquarters on Mud Lake Road. Pick up a refuge map and bird checklist. Continue east 0.6 mile on Mud Lake Road. The road passes through wet hammock that should be checked in summer for Prothonotary Warbler. After crossing a railroad track, you will reach a parking area for the refuge trailhead. A trail leads through hammock to three freshwater marsh impoundments. Along this trail look for breeding species such as Yellow-billed Cuckoo, Barred Owl, Chuck-will's-widow, Great Crested Flycatcher, Red-eyed Vireo, and Northern Parula. Occasionally in winter Golden-crowned Kinglet joins flocks of Ruby-crowned Kinglet, Tufted Titmouse, and other land birds in this habitat. American Woodcock is sometimes present in winter, though you may have to go off-trail to find one. An observation tower at the intersection of the three impoundments provides an overlook of the impoundments and surrounding marsh. Spring Garden Lake, outside the refuge, is visible to the north. From the parking area, it's a 0.8-mile hike to the tower. It's a 1.5-mile hike around Impoundment 1 and 2.5-mile hikes around both Impoundments 2 and 3. Beyond the impoundments is Jones Island, a large area of hammock and pine flatwoods. Look for nesting species such as Summer Tanager and Bachman's Sparrow in the flatwoods. Listen for Brown-headed Nuthatch, which can occasionally be found here. A trail leads through Jones Island to Spring Garden Creek, which connects Spring Garden

Lake to Lake Woodruff. It is a 6-mile round-trip hike from the parking area to Spring Garden Creek.

Water levels within the impoundments are seasonally managed for wading birds and wintering waterfowl. Over 20 species of waterfowl have been recorded on the refuge. Mottled and Wood Duck are resident. During winter Blue-winged Teal and Ring-necked Duck are most common. Seen in fewer numbers in winter are Northern Pintail, American Wigeon, Green-winged Teal, Northern Shoveler, Lesser Scaup, Hooded Merganser, and Ruddy Duck. Occasional are Fulvous Whistling-Duck, Mallard, American Black Duck, Gadwall, Canvasback, Redhead, Bufflehead, and Red-breasted Merganser. Both Canada and Snow Goose have been recorded on the refuge. Look for marsh birds along canal or impoundment edges. King Rail, Purple Gallinule, Limpkin, and Sandhill Crane are possible year-round. Winter brings American Bittern, Glossy Ibis, Wilson's Snipe, Sora, and occasionally Virginia Rail. Also watch for Marsh and Sedge Wren and Swamp Sparrow. Large flocks of Tree Swallow often roost in the marsh during this season. Migration attracts shorebirds to pools of shallow water. Look for Black-necked Stilt, Greater and Lesser Yellowlegs, and Least, Pectoral, and Solitary Sandpiper. A few Black-necked Stilts may stay to breed. Least Bittern is most likely in summer. Look for it in cattails or other dense emergent vegetation. Early or late in the day during summer, listen for the distinctive "keekeedrrr" of Black Rail. You are more likely to hear than see this elusive species. Watch overhead for Osprey, Bald Eagle, and Red-shouldered Hawk year-round. Short-tailed Hawk has been seen in the refuge in winter, though Northern Harrier and Sharp-shinned Hawk are much more likely. Large numbers of Black Vulture roost in the refuge during the winter months. The refuge also hosts the second-largest premigration roosting colony of Swallow-tailed Kite in the southeastern United States. From late July through early August, about 500 of these beautiful raptors forage on the refuge in preparation for their journey to their wintering grounds in South America. They roost in cypress swamps and wet hammocks along Spring Garden Creek and Lake Woodruff.

DeLeon Springs State Park is adjacent to Lake Woodruff National Wildlife Refuge. The 603-acre park features a spring producing a flow of 14 million gallons of water per day. Local folklore claims that Ponce de Leon discovered the Fountain of Youth here. Before the state purchased the property in 1982, the area was a resort and the winter home of

Red-shouldered Hawk. PHOTO: NANCY MORELAND

the Clyde Beatty Circus. In the 1950s and 1960s, the resort featured a campground, jungle cruises, and a water circus that included a waterskiing elephant! Today the spring is artificially maintained as a swimming pool. The waters of the spring flow into Spring Garden Lake. Canoes may be rented at the state park concession for exploration of this area. Snail Kite, though rare this far north, has been seen on more than one occasion around the lake and reportedly has nested here. A 0.5-mile paved nature trail begins near the spring and loops through wet hammock. Typical species found here include Tufted Titmouse, Carolina Wren, and Northern Parula. A short spur trail leads to "Old Methuselah," a bald cypress believed to be over 500 years old. The 5.2-mile Wild Persimmon Hiking Trail provides opportunities for further exploration of the park but may be flooded in summer.

Blue Spring State Park is home to the largest spring on the St. Johns River. In winter large numbers of West Indian manatee are attracted to the relatively warm waters of the spring. During the warmer months the manatees disperse to the St. Johns River. When present, these gentle mammals may be viewed from an observation platform along Blue Spring Run. Swimming and scuba diving is allowed in the spring but not with the manatees. The parking area for the spring is 1 mile from the entrance; an elevated boardwalk through oak hammock leads to the spring. Watch along Blue Spring Run for resident species such as Eastern Screech-Owl, Downy Woodpecker, Tufted Titmouse, and Carolina Wren. This area is best during spring and fall when a variety of warblers and other migrant land birds are moving through. Great Crested Flycatcher, Red-eyed Vireo, and Northern Parula stay to breed. A 4-mile (one-way) nature trail passes through sand pine scrub, pine flatwoods, and oak hammock and around freshwater marsh and cypress swamp. The trail begins at the entrance to the parking area, opposite the historic Thursby House, and ends at a primitive campground. Look for Florida Scrub-Jay as you pass through sand pine scrub habitat. In the pine flatwoods you may find Wild Turkey, Northern Bobwhite, Eastern Bluebird, Yellow-throated Warbler, Pine Warbler, Eastern Towhee, and Bachman's Sparrow. Summer Tanager breeds here in summer. Watch along marsh or river edges for Wood Stork, Mottled and Wood Duck, King Rail, Purple Gallinule, Limpkin, and Sandhill Crane. In cypress swamp, look and listen for Barred Owl, Pileated Woodpecker, and Prothonotary Warbler. On summer evenings listen for Chuck-will's-widow along the park road. Marsh and cypress swamp habitat along the St. Johns River may be explored via a two-hour nature cruise or by canoe. While on the river, watch overhead year-round for Osprey and Bald Eagle. Swallow-tailed Kite may be seen in spring and summer.

A restored 380-acre parcel of scrub habitat can be found at **Lyonia Preserve,** behind the Deltona Regional Library. A series of loop trails provides access to the preserve. A trail guide as well as animal and plant checklists are available at the information desk in the library. Florida Scrub-Jay has been introduced to the preserve and is usually easy to locate, especially early in the day. Other species to watch for include Northern Bobwhite, Great Horned Owl, Red-headed Woodpecker, Great Crested Flycatcher, and Eastern Towhee. Wood Duck and Sandhill Crane are attracted to seasonally wet areas.

General information: Lake Woodruff National Wildlife Refuge (no entrance fee) is open daily from sunrise to sunset. Restrooms are available at refuge headquarters. DeLeon Springs and Blue Spring State Parks (entrance fees) are open daily from 8:00 A.M. until sunset. Restrooms are available at both locations. Lyonia Preserve (no entrance fee) is open daily from 6:00 A.M. to 8:00 P.M. Restrooms are located in the library.

DeLorme grid: Page 74, D-1; page 80, A-2.

Hazards: Trails may be flooded in summer. Keep a safe distance from alligators. Cottonmouths and eastern diamondback rattlesnakes are present but rarely encountered. Mosquitoes and other biting insects are common in summer.

Nearest food, gas, lodging: In Deland, Orange City, and Deltona.

Camping: Blue Spring State Park: 51 sites.

For more information: *Lake Woodruff National Wildlife Refuge,* P.O. Box 488, DeLeon Springs, FL 32130; (386) 985-0926; http://lakewoodruff .fws.gov. *DeLeon Springs State Park,* P.O. Box 1338, DeLeon Springs, FL 32130; (386) 985-4212; www.floridastateparks.org/deleonsprings. *Blue Spring State Park,* 2100 W. French Ave., Orange City, FL 32763; (386) 775-3663; www .floridastateparks.org/bluespring. *Lyonia Preserve,* c/o Volusia County Land Acquisition and Management, 123 W. Indiana Ave., DeLand, FL 32720; (386) 736-5927; http://volusia.org/ environmental/.

EAST-CENTRAL

 # Merritt Island Area

Habitats: Fresh and brackish water impoundments, salt marsh, mangrove forest, coastal scrub, sandy beach, hardwood hammock, pine flatwoods, wet prairie, cypress swamp.

Specialty birds: *Resident:* Black-bellied Whistling-Duck, Mottled Duck, Least Bittern, Roseate Spoonbill, Wood Stork, Snail Kite, Bald Eagle, Short-tailed Hawk, King Rail, Clapper Rail, Black Rail, Purple Gallinule, Limpkin, Sandhill Crane, Florida Scrub-Jay, Brown-headed Nuthatch, Bachman's Sparrow. *Summer:* Swallow-tailed Kite, Least Tern, Chuck-will's-widow, Gray Kingbird, Acadian Flycatcher, Prothonotary Warbler, Summer Tanager, Painted Bunting. *Winter:* Eurasian Wigeon, Reddish Egret, Peregrine Falcon, Virginia Rail, Bonaparte's Gull, Nelson's Sharp-tailed Sparrow, Saltmarsh Sharp-tailed Sparrow.

Best times to bird: September through April.

Directions: *Merritt Island National Wildlife Refuge:* From I-95 west of Titusville, exit at State Road 406 (exit 220). Drive east 4.3 miles to the refuge entrance. *Orlando Wetlands Park:* From I-95, exit at State Road 50 (exit 215). Drive west 10.2 miles to Ft. Christmas Road. Turn right and drive north 2.2 miles to Wheeler Road. Turn right and drive east 1.5 miles to the parking area. *Tosohatchee State Reserve:* Backtrack to SR 50 and turn left. Drive east 0.3 mile to Taylor Creek Road. Turn right and drive south 2.8 miles to the check station.

The Birding

Merritt Island is a 43-mile-long barrier island that since the 1960s has been home to the Kennedy Space Center. After completion of the space center, those lands not included within the space center were designated **Merritt Island National Wildlife Refuge** and **Canaveral National Seashore.** The 140,000-acre refuge provides habitat for more federal and state listed threatened and endangered species than any other national wildlife refuge in the continental United States. Over 300 species of birds have been recorded in the refuge. As you cross the Indian River on SR 406, watch in winter for Bonaparte's Gull roosting or feeding in the vicinity of the bridge. The causeway between the bridge and the

EAST–CENTRAL

Wekiwa Springs
State Park

Lake
Harney

Canaveral
National Seashore
Merritt Island NWR

4   17   417

Apopka

9

Lake
Apopka

441

Mead Garden

Orlando
Wetlands Park

91

Oakland

Tibet-Butler
Preserve

10

Orlando

436

Lake Buena Vista

Walt Disney
World

192

Kissimmee

27   4   17

St. Cloud

Lake
Tohopekaliga

Haines
City

542

Disney
Wilderness Preserve

Lake Kissimmee
State Park

Lake Wales

12

60

Frostproof

Lake Wales
Ridge State
Forest

Avon Park
Air Force
Range

Avon Park

27

Highlands
Hammock
State Park

Sebring Lake

Sebring

66

Lake June in Winter

Lake
Istokpoga

13

Lake Placid

Lake Placid

70

N

Archbold
Biological Station

Platt Branch
WEA

27

Kms   20

Miles   20

Fisheating Creek WMA

Christmas

50

Tosohatchee
State Reserve

528

520

7

Titusville

46

1

95

St. Johns River

3

405

401   Jetty Park

Cocoa

8

95   1

Merritt Island

Cocoa Beach

A1A

Viera
Wetlands

Satellite Beach

518

192

192

Melbourne

Melbourne Beach

Palm Bay

95

441

11

Three Lakes
Wildlife
Management
Area

Kenansville

Lake
Kissimmee

60

91

Turkey Creek
Sanctuary

1

14

T.M. Goodwin
WMA

Sebastian Inlet
State Park

Sebastian

Pelican
Island
NWR

Yeehaw
Junction

Kissimmee
Prairie Preserve
State Park

60

Florida Turnpike

Vero
Beach

A1A

95   1

Kissimmee River

98

441

91

Fort Pierce

15

70

Savannas Preserve
State Park

Port
St. Lucie

Okeechobee

70

95

78

98   710

441

Lake
Okeechobee

ATLANTIC
OCEAN

refuge entrance is a good place to scope the river during winter. Watch on both sides of the causeway for Common Loon and occasionally Red-throated Loon, Horned Grebe, and Lesser Scaup. Long-tailed Duck is recorded here during some winters. Along the water's edge you can usually find Laughing and Ring-billed Gull, Black Skimmer, Willet, Sanderling, and Ruddy Turnstone. Once in a while something more unusual, such as American Oystercatcher, will be found on the causeway. About 1 mile east of the bridge, stop at an information kiosk on the south side of SR 406 to pick up refuge and seashore brochures and a bird checklist. An observation platform here overlooks the first of many impoundments you will pass as you head into the refuge. The impoundments within the refuge were originally created to control the salt marsh mosquito population. A variety of wading birds, including Reddish Egret and Roseate Spoonbill, feed in the impoundments year-round. During winter American Coot congregates in huge rafts. Other waterfowl can usually be found in scattered flocks in the impoundments. Species vary from winter to winter, but most common are Blue and Green-winged Teal, Northern Pintail, Northern Shoveler, and American Wigeon. Other species to look for include Mottled Duck, Gadwall, Ring-necked Duck, Lesser Scaup, Hooded Merganser, and Ruddy Duck. Osprey is common along this road; watch for them perched on utility poles. Bald Eagle is most common during the winter months, when prey is abundant. Look for Belted Kingfisher on electrical wires along the road in winter. Gray Kingbird can sometimes be seen perched on wires during the summer months.

If you wish to stop first at the refuge visitor center, drive east 1.5 miles to County Road 402, bear right, and drive east 2 miles to the visitor center entrance. The visitor center has a gift shop and interpretive displays; be sure to check the sightings log at the main desk. Exit through a back door to an observation deck that overlooks a small pond. A 0.3-mile wheelchair-accessible boardwalk leads over the pond to an oak hammock that may harbor migrant and wintering land birds. From the visitor center, continue east 0.4 mile on CR 402 and turn right onto Peacocks Pocket Road, a bumpy, unmanaged dirt road (high-clearance vehicles recommended) that leads to an area of the refuge heavily used by hunters but still attractive to waterfowl and shorebirds. This loop road leads for 8 miles through impoundments and skirts the Indian River before connecting with East Gator Creek Road. Turn left on East Gator Creek Road and drive west 0.6 mile to return to SR 406, or turn right and drive northeast 1 mile (high-clearance vehicles also recommended) to return to CR 402. This intersection is 0.2 mile east of SR 406 and 1.8 miles west of the visitor center. In November 1996 three Greater White-fronted Geese were found along this road. In May 1996 a White-cheeked Pintail of unknown origin was found in the impoundment between East Gator Creek Road and SR 406, but was later shot by a hunter. Opposite the intersection of East Gator Creek Road and SR 406 is Pumphouse Road, a dirt road that leads to impoundments that are off-limits to hunters, attractive to shorebirds, and thus frequently visited by birders. Depending on water levels, shorebirds may be found in the impoundment between Pumphouse Road and SR 406 or in impoundments north of Pumphouse Road. Species typically seen here during migration and in winter include Black-bellied and Semipalmated Plover, American Avocet, Greater and Lesser Yellowlegs, Marbled Godwit, Semipalmated, Western, and Least Sandpiper, Dunlin, and Short-billed Dowitcher. Rarities found here include Long-billed Curlew, Ruff, and White-rumped Sandpiper. Watch for Clapper Rail as you drive on Pumphouse Road or hike the dikes between impoundments. In 0.8 mile Pumphouse Road rejoins SR

406. Turn left and drive east 1.2 miles to reach Black Point Wildlife Drive (described later), or turn right and drive west 0.1 mile to the intersection with CR 402.

The Hammock Trails parking area is on the north side of CR 402, 1.2 miles east of the visitor center. From the trailhead, turn right to hike the 0.5-mile Oak Hammock Trail or left for the 2-mile Palm Hammock Trail. Sulphur-bellied Flycatcher and Townsend's Warbler are among rarities that have been found along these trails. Continue east 1 mile on CR 402 to the intersection with SR 3. Continue east 0.8 mile to the Canaveral National Seashore south access entrance station. You are now passing through coastal scrub, prime habitat for Florida Scrub-Jay. An estimated 2,500 of this endangered species reside in the refuge. Drive slowly in this area, since the jays are often seen searching for food along the road. Farther east, mangrove-fringed lagoons on both sides of the road may hold wading birds or wintering waterfowl. Diving ducks such as Canvasback and Redhead are more likely here. Use the pull-offs to check these ponds. In the distance to the south, you can't help but notice NASA's massive Vehicle Assembly Building; closer to the beach is Space Shuttle Launch Complex 39B. The road curves north 3.4 miles past the entrance station and parallels Playalinda Beach for the next several miles. Numerous parking areas are available on the right; boardwalks cross the dunes to the beach. Incredibly, Snow Bunting has been found on at least two occasions in the parking areas! The dune boardwalks are a good place to scan the ocean for sea ducks winging down the beach in winter, Northern Gannet feeding offshore, or pelagic species pushed close to land during periods of persistent onshore winds. Turn around and scope Mosquito Lagoon to the west. During winter large flocks of American White Pelican are often on the lagoon. Brown Pelicans are likely to be flying overhead. Return to SR 3 and turn right. For several miles, you should watch for Florida Scrub-Jay. To hike the 1-mile Scrub Ridge Trail through coastal scrub, drive north 3.8 miles and turn right. Follow this dirt road 0.4 mile to the trailhead. In addition to Florida Scrub-Jay, look for Painted Bunting, which may nest in this area. From the parking area, you can also scan a narrow lagoon to the east for wading birds, waterfowl, and shorebirds. Biolab Road, which passes between this narrow lagoon and the much larger Mosquito Lagoon, begins 0.8 mile north of the entrance road to Scrub Ridge Trail. Turn right after 0.3 mile (continuing straight 0.1 mile leads to a boat ramp). This dirt road exits at CR 402 in another 5.5 miles. Roseate Spoonbill, Reddish Egret, and a wide variety of migrant and wintering shorebirds feed in the narrow lagoon. A Ruff was seen here in August 2005. Scan Mosquito Lagoon during winter for Common Loon and American White Pelican. Once at CR 402, turn right and drive west 2.2 miles to return to the intersection with SR 3.

To reach **Black Point Wildlife Drive,** turn right and drive north 3.2 miles on SR 3 to SR 406. Turn left and drive west 2.6 miles to the wildlife drive entrance. Black Point Wildlife Drive provides some of the most spectacular birding opportunities in the refuge. This 6.2-mile one-way dirt road passes through impoundments teeming with wading birds, shorebirds, and wintering waterfowl. Pick up an interpretive brochure just beyond the entrance. Be sure to observe posted speed limits and pull completely off the roadway when stopped to allow others to pass. The first mile of the wildlife drive passes through salt marsh habitat that should be checked for Clapper Rail and, in winter, Sora. This habitat was once the home of the "Dusky" race of Seaside Sparrow, sadly now extinct due to mosquito control efforts during the last century. The next 2 miles of the drive have impoundments on both sides of the road. Impoundments on the left side are open year-round to the Indian River Lagoon. Tidal flow results in fluctuating water levels, making

Merritt Island NWR. PHOTO: TREY MITCHELL

these impoundments attractive to wading birds, shorebirds, and puddle ducks. Impoundments on the right side are not open to tidal flow, making them attractive to a greater variety of waterfowl. During winter coots and ducks using these impoundments can number in the tens or even hundreds of thousands! Most abundant are Blue-winged Teal, Northern Pintail, and American Wigeon. Green-winged Teal, Northern Shoveler, Gadwall, and Hooded Merganser are usually well represented. Occasionally a rare-for-Florida species such as Common Goldeneye will be found. Carefully scan all flocks of wigeon. Almost every winter Eurasian Wigeon is found among these flocks. Snow and Canada Goose seem to find their way to the refuge every few winters. All of the refuge shorebirds previously mentioned may be found in the left-side impoundments during the appropriate season. Large numbers of gulls often roost here, occasionally including Bonaparte's and Lesser Black-backed Gull. Gull-billed, Least, Royal, and Caspian Tern and Black Skimmer all breed in the refuge. Forster's Tern is common during winter. Wood Stork can be seen year-round, Reddish Egret is most often sighted in fall and winter, and Roseate Spoonbill numbers increase during spring and summer. Least Bittern is present throughout the year, while American Bittern can be found only in winter. Feel free to hike gated roads on berms separating the impoundments, but be prepared for mosquitoes and other biting insects in summer and fall. The Cruickshank Trail, named for the wildlife photographer and naturalist instrumental in establishing the refuge, is a 5-mile loop trail located 3.3 miles from the wildlife drive entrance. An observation platform close to the trailhead parking area provides opportunities to scope the impoundment enclosed within the loop trail. The next mile of the wildlife drive passes through restored salt marsh. In winter this habitat can be good for both Nelson's and Saltmarsh Sharp-tailed Sparrow. Black Rail has also been heard in this area. When you reach the end of the wildlife drive, you will have returned to SR 406, about 1.3 miles east of the entrance.

Between Merritt Island and Orlando is **Orlando Wetlands Park,** a 1,650-acre artificial wetland that filters water from an Orlando water-treatment facility before it is discharged into the St. Johns River. Consisting of a series of impoundments separated by 18 miles of raised berms, the park not only effectively cleans wastewater but has also become a refuge for a wide variety of birds and other wildlife. Though avian diversity is at its peak in winter, the park is closed from October through late January due to an agreement between the city of Orlando and the property's original landowners. As a result, plan to visit during late winter or early spring. Before venturing out into the wetland, check the interpretive displays and pick up a bird checklist and map at the entrance. Though the park includes a 2.5-mile birding route, feel free to explore other areas of the wetland by hiking any of the berm roads. The Florida National Scenic Trail skirts the perimeter of the wetland, connecting the park with the 29,000-acre Seminole Ranch Conservation Area on the park's eastern border.

A wide variety of herons, egrets, and other wading birds can be found in the marshes, including Anhinga, both night-herons, Glossy Ibis, Wood Stork, Roseate Spoonbill, Limpkin, and Sandhill Crane. Least Bittern can be found here during summer, while American Bittern is here during winter. Common Moorhen is, as the name suggests, common in open areas of the marsh and joined in winter by large numbers of American Coot. Search for the more secretive Purple Gallinule by scanning areas of emergent vegetation. During early morning, King Rail may be found along marsh edges or even scurrying across the berm roads. In winter Sora, Wilson's Snipe, and occasionally Virginia Rail may be found in similar habitat. Black-necked Stilt is the only shorebird that breeds in the park. Greater and Lesser Yellowlegs, Least, Semipalmated, Solitary, and Spotted Sandpiper, Short and Long-billed Dowitcher (best discerned by call), and occasionally other shorebirds are attracted to the marsh during winter and migration, depending on water levels. Black-bellied Whistling-Duck is a recent nesting species in the park, joining resident Mottled and Wood Duck. The whistling-ducks will often perch on trunks of dead cabbage palms in the marsh. Blue-winged Teal is the most common waterfowl in winter, though other duck species such as Green-winged Teal, Mallard, Northern Pintail, Northern Shoveler, Gadwall, American Wigeon, Ring-necked Duck, Lesser Scaup, Hooded Merganser, and Ruddy Duck are occasionally seen, usually in impoundments with deeper water. Rare waterfowl recorded in the park include Cinnamon Teal and Masked Duck. Six species of raptors have nested in the park: Swallow-tailed Kite, Snail Kite, Bald Eagle, Osprey, Red-shouldered Hawk, and Red-tailed Hawk. During winter you may also see Northern Harrier, Sharp-shinned and Cooper's Hawk, American Kestrel, Merlin, and Peregrine Falcon. Both Turkey and Black Vulture are common year-round. Look for these species perched on dead cabbage palms and other trees scattered throughout the marsh. These trees, killed when the property was flooded during the creation of the marsh, have also become excellent nesting habitat for woodpeckers. Northern Flicker and Red-bellied, Downy, and Pileated Woodpecker all breed in the park, and Red-headed Woodpecker nests nearby. This species is occasionally seen in the wetland but more often along roads outside the park. Pockets of hammock scattered throughout the wetland, along with a larger area of forest along the park's eastern edge, provide nesting habitat for Yellow-billed Cuckoo, Barred Owl, Chuck-will's-widow, Great Crested Flycatcher, Carolina Wren, Blue-gray Gnatcatcher, and Northern Parula. Check these areas during migration and winter for warblers, vireos, thrushes, and other land birds. Search grassy areas for Bobolink, sparrows, and buntings. Check the marsh edge for Marsh and occasionally Sedge Wren, Common Yellowthroat, and Swamp Sparrow.

Tosohatchee State Reserve, located south of Orlando Wetlands Park, provides access to extensive pine flatwoods as well as the St. Johns River. Before entering the reserve, check along the creek that crosses the road just north of the entrance. Park under the power lines north of a single-lane bridge that crosses the creek and walk to the bridge. Acadian Flycatcher and Prothonotary Warbler may nest along this creek. Scan the open area under the power lines for Wild Turkey. Turn left into the reserve and pick up maps and brochures at the check station. Drive east on Beehead Road 1 mile to St. Nicholas Road, listening in spring for singing Bachman's Sparrow. This sparrow has often been found in an open area of saw palmetto near the intersection with St. Nicholas Road. Check adjacent pinelands for Hairy and Pileated Woodpecker, Brown-headed Nuthatch, and Pine Warbler. Turn left on St. Nicholas Road and drive north 0.3 mile to Powerline Road. Continue north 0.3 mile, through oak hammock good for small land birds including Carolina Chickadee, Tufted Titmouse, and Blue-gray Gnatcatcher. In winter look for Blue-headed Vireo and Ruby-crowned Kinglet. The road ends at a parking area along Tootoosohatchee Creek. A short trail loops through this area. Watch for Hermit Thrush, Louisiana Waterthrush, and other wintering and migrant land birds. Return to Powerline Road and turn left, watching along this stretch for Eastern Bluebird. Trail-access parking areas are located at various points along this road. Drive east 3 miles to Jim Creek Slough. Where two narrow bridges cross the slough, look for Wood Stork, Limpkin, and other wading birds. Continue east 2.6 miles to the St. Johns River. Marsh habitat along the road and at the river can be good for rails, Purple Gallinule, and wintering waterfowl. Watch overhead for Bald Eagle year-round and Swallow-tailed Kite during spring and summer. Backtrack 0.3 mile to Long Bluff Road. To explore pine flatwoods and oak/cabbage palm hammock along roads south of Powerline Road, turn left and drive southwest 6.5 miles to Fish Hole Road. Turn right and drive north 4 miles to Beehead Road. Turn left and drive west 1.7 miles to return to St. Nicholas Road.

General information: Merritt Island National Wildlife Refuge (no entrance fee) is open daily from sunrise to sunset. The refuge closes during launches at Kennedy Space Center. The visitor center is open Monday through Friday from 8:00 A.M. to 4:30 P.M., Saturday and Sunday from 9:00 A.M. to 5:00 P.M. The visitor center is closed Sundays from April through October and on federal holidays. Restrooms are available at the visitor center. Orlando Wetlands Park (no entrance fee) is open daily from sunrise to sunset. The park is closed October 1 through January 20. Restrooms are located near the parking area. Tosohatchee State Reserve (entrance fee) is open from 8:00 A.M. until sunset. A primitive restroom is located at the check station. Canaveral National Seashore (entrance fee) is open daily from 6:00 A.M. to 6:00 P.M. November through March and from 6:00 A.M. to 8:00 P.M. April through October. Restrooms are available at beach parking areas. Seasonal hunting is permitted in designated areas of Merritt Island National Wildlife Refuge and Tosohatchee State Reserve. Refer to regulations-summary brochures, updated annually and available at check stations, for hunt dates and locations. Wear blaze orange if hiking during hunting season.

DeLorme grid: Page 81, D-1; page 82, C-1.

Hazards: Keep a safe distance from alligators. Cottonmouths are present but rarely encountered. Mosquitoes and other biting insects are most abundant during the summer months. Trails at all locations may be seasonally flooded. Use caution when driving roads in Tosohatchee State Reserve, especially if conditions are wet.

Nearest food, gas, lodging: In Titusville.

Camping: Private campgrounds are in Titusville.

For more information: *Merritt Island National Wildlife Refuge*, P.O. Box 6504, Titusville, FL 32782; (321) 861-0667; www.nbbd.com/godo/minwr. *Canaveral National Seashore*, 308 Julia St., Titusville, FL 32796; (321) 267-1110; www.nps.gov/cana. *Orlando Wetlands Park*, 25155 Wheeler Rd., Christmas, FL 32709; (407) 568-1706. *Tosohatchee State Reserve*, 3365 Taylor Creek Rd., Christmas, FL 32709; (407) 568-5893.

8 Cocoa Area

Habitats: Sandy beach, maritime hammock, freshwater impoundments, pasture, sod farms.

Specialty birds: *Resident:* Black-bellied Whistling-Duck, Fulvous Whistling-Duck, Mottled Duck, Magnificent Frigatebird, Least Bittern, Reddish Egret, Wood Stork, Bald Eagle, Crested Caracara, Purple Gallinule, Limpkin, Sandhill Crane. *Summer:* Swallow-tailed Kite, Least Tern.

Winter: Black Scoter, Purple Sandpiper, Lesser Black-backed Gull, American Pipit. *Migrant:* Peregrine Falcon, Upland Sandpiper, White-rumped Sandpiper, Painted Bunting.

Best times to bird: October through March at Jetty Park. April and September through mid-October at Lori Wilson Park. September through April at Viera Wetlands.

Directions: *Jetty Park:* From I-95 west of Cocoa Beach, exit at State Road 528 (exit 205). Drive east 12 miles to George King Boulevard (Terminal B exit for Port Canaveral). Drive east 1 mile to the park entrance. *Lori Wilson Park:* Return to SR 528. Drive east as SR 528 curves south and becomes SR A1A. Continue south 4.4 miles to the park entrance. *Viera Wetlands:* From I-95 in Viera, exit at Wickham Road (exit 191). Drive west 2 miles to the entrance.

The Birding

Jetty Park is a 35-acre park on the south side of Port Canaveral Inlet. A fishing pier at the inlet extends 1,200 feet into the Atlantic and provides excellent opportunities for sea-watching. Magnificent Frigatebird is possible in summer. In winter Northern Gannet feeds offshore but sometimes flies into the inlet or directly over the pier. During periods of persistent easterly winds, storm-petrels, shearwaters, and other pelagic species are possible here. Jaegers occasionally follow fishing boats into the inlet. Inexplicably, Common Eider has been reported at the port on several occasions, either near the inlet or around turning basins farther inland. From the pier, watch in winter for flocks of Black Scoter or other waterfowl streaming up or down the coastline. Purple Sandpiper is sometimes seen in winter among the Ruddy Turnstone feeding on the rock jetty below the pier. Common Loon is often seen around the jetty or within the inlet. The adjacent beach attracts Reddish Egret, Black Skimmer, and an assortment of gulls and terns. Willet, Sanderling, and Ruddy Turnstone are the common shorebirds, though Black-bellied, Semipalmated, and sometimes Piping Plover can also be found here. This beach has attracted its share of rare gulls including Franklin's, Iceland, and Glaucous. A wetland area near Canaveral Lock is attractive to wading birds and migrant shorebirds, especially at low tide. To reach this area, backtrack on George King Boulevard 0.9 mile to Dave Nesbit Drive. Turn right and drive north 0.2 mile to Mullet Drive. Turn left and drive west 1.4 miles, past Port's End Park and under a bridge to the parking area for Canaveral Lock. The wetlands are to the east, surrounded by Brazilian pepper. Species recorded here have included Roseate Spoonbill, American Avocet, Black-necked Stilt, Black-bellied and Semipalmated Plover, Red Knot, Sanderling, Ruddy Turnstone, Short-billed Dowitcher, and Stilt, Western, Semipalmated, Least, and White-rumped Sandpiper. Wood Stork and other wading birds sometimes congregate on grassy areas around the lock.

Lori Wilson Park is a 32-acre county park in Cocoa Beach, 4.4 miles south of Port Canaveral. The Johnnie Johnson Nature Center is located in the park. A 0.3-mile boardwalk winds through maritime hammock adjacent to the nature center. In spring and fall look for warblers, vireos, tanagers, buntings, and other migrant land birds. Florida Scrub-Jay once resided in the park but has not been seen in recent years.

The Brevard County South Central Wetlands, better known to birders as **Viera Wetlands,** is maintained by the Brevard County Water Resources Department as part of its water-treatment facility. As you drive west on Wickham Road toward the facility, watch for raptors such as Bald Eagle, Red-tailed Hawk, and Crested Caracara perched on utility poles or in fields on the south side of the road. In April and again in August, scan the sod fields on the south side of the road for migrating Upland Sandpiper. In August 2000 a Fork-tailed Flycatcher spent several days in an area just north of Wickham Road that has since been developed. At the end of Wickham Road jog left, drive through the water-treatment facility gate, then jog right. Stop first at the Operations Building, where you must sign in before proceeding to the wetland. A map is available in the office. The wetland consists of five impoundments divided by berms. The Berm Trail is a 2.3-mile-long roadway around the perimeter of the wetland. Another 1.4 miles of roadway are on berms separating the five impoundments. The inner roadway provides access to two observation platforms. All berm roads are one-way and are indicated as such on the wetland map. Drive only on these roads, observe posted speed limits, and do not block the roadway. You may also hike the berm roadway.

Year-round residents of the wetland include Black-bellied Whistling-Duck, Mottled Duck, Pied-billed Grebe, Anhinga, Great Blue, Tricolored, Little Blue, and Green Heron, Great, Snowy, and Cattle Egret, Black-crowned Night-Heron, Least Bittern, White and Glossy Ibis, Wood Stork, Red-shouldered Hawk, Purple Gallinule, Common Moorhen, Limpkin, and Sandhill Crane. The cranes may also be seen in surrounding pasture. Fulvous Whistling-Duck and Roseate Spoonbill are seen occasionally in the impoundments. Look for Loggerhead Shrike and Eastern Meadowlark perched on fences surrounding the facility and Northern Bobwhite along grassy edges. Watch overhead in spring and summer for Swallow-tailed Kite. During winter look for American Bittern, Northern Harrier, Wilson's Snipe, Belted Kingfisher, Eastern Phoebe, and several species of waterfowl, including Blue and Green-winged Teal, Ring-necked Duck, and Hooded Merganser. Rare waterfowl recorded here has included Greater White-fronted Goose, Snow Goose, Ross's Goose, Eurasian Wigeon, and Masked Duck. Swallows are commonly seen feeding over the wetland in all seasons. Tree and Northern Rough-winged Swallow are here in winter, while Purple Martin and Barn Swallow can be seen in spring and summer. Cliff, Cave, and Bank Swallow have been recorded during migration. In November 2002 a flock of Mexican race Cave Swallow spent several days at the wetland. Also seen (and photographed) during that period was an unusual swallow with a white rump patch. After much discussion, this bird was identified as a Mangrove Swallow, a Central American species and the first ever recorded in the United States!

Two large rectangular settling ponds just outside the water-treatment facility attract large numbers of migrant shorebirds and wintering waterfowl. To reach this area, backtrack to Wickham Road then take your first left onto a dirt road. Take an immediate left, then turn right, through an open metal gate (continuing straight instead of turning right leads to River Lakes Conservation Area, which opened to the public in 2006). Grassy berms encircle these impoundments, known to local birders as the "Click Ponds." Waterfowl seen here in winter include all the species listed for the wetland plus American Wigeon, Gadwall, Northern Shoveler, Northern Pintail, Canvasback, Redhead, Lesser, and Greater Scaup, and Ruddy Duck. Two White-cheeked Pintails of unknown origin were discovered here in July 2000, and Eared Grebe has been recorded here on more than one occasion. Also in winter, the grassy berms and impoundment edges attract flocks of Savannah Sparrow and American Pipit. Lapland Longspur has occasionally been seen with these flocks. During migration shorebirds are attracted to impoundment edges, especially if the water has been drawn down to expose mudflats. Regular are Black-bellied and Semipalmated Plover, Black-necked Stilt, Greater and Lesser Yellowlegs, Solitary, Spotted, Semipalmated, Western, Least, Pectoral, and Stilt Sandpiper, Dunlin, and both Short-billed and Long-billed Dowitcher (best discerned by call). Occasional are American Avocet, Willet, Ruddy Turnstone, White-rumped Sandpiper, and Wilson's Phalarope. Ruff has also been recorded here. Swirling flocks of shorebirds may mean a Merlin or Peregrine Falcon is in the area. Bonaparte's Gull is occasionally seen here in winter, while Least Tern is regular in summer. Both Black and Gull-billed Tern have been recorded during migration. Incredibly, a Sooty Tern was once found here after a Gulf storm!

General information: Jetty Park (entrance fee) is open daily from 7:00 A.M. to 10:00 P.M. Lori Wilson Park (no entrance fee) is open daily from sunrise to sunset. Canaveral Lock Observation Area (no entrance fee) is open daily from 7:00 A.M. to 9:00 P.M. Hours at Johnnie Johnson Nature Center (no entrance fee) vary by season. Restrooms are available at all locations. The Brevard County South Central Wetlands (no entrance fee) is open daily from 7:00 A.M. until sunset. Sign in at the Operations Building before entering, even if only visiting the Click Ponds. Speed limit on the Berm Trail is 15 miles per hour. Restrooms are available in the Operations Building.

DeLorme grid: Page 88, B-2, C-1.

Hazards: Keep a safe distance from alligators. Cottonmouths are present at Viera Wetlands but are rarely encountered. Seek shelter should thunderstorms threaten.

Nearest food, gas, lodging: In Cocoa Beach, Viera, and Melbourne.

Camping: Jetty Park: 150 sites. Wickham Park, in Melbourne: 88 sites, 2500 Parkway Dr., Melbourne, FL 32935; (321) 255-4307. From I-95, drive east 6 miles on Wickham Road to Parkway Drive. Turn left and drive 0.5 mile to the park entrance.

For more information: *Jetty Park,* 400 E. Jetty Park Rd., Cape Canaveral, FL 32920; (321) 783-7111; www.portcanaveral.org/funport/recreation .htm. *Lori Wilson Park,* 1500 N. Atlantic Ave., Cocoa Beach, FL 32931; (321) 868-1123; www.brevardparks.com/nature. *Brevard County Water Resources Department,* (321) 255-4328; http://countygovt.brevard.fl.us/usd/documents/ Wetlands%20Map.pdf.

⑨ Orlando Area

Habitats: Lakes, freshwater marsh, seasonally flooded agricultural fields, cypress swamp, hardwood hammock, pine flatwoods, sandhills, sand pine scrub.

Specialty birds: *Resident:* Black-bellied Whistling-Duck, Fulvous Whistling-Duck, Mottled Duck, Wood Stork, Bald Eagle, King Rail, Purple Gallinule, Limpkin, Sandhill Crane, Florida Scrub-Jay. *Summer:* Least Bittern, Swallow-tailed Kite, Chuck-will's-widow, Yellow-throated Vireo, Prothonotary Warbler, Yellow-breasted Chat, Summer Tanager, Bachman's Sparrow, Blue Grosbeak, Dickcissel, Orchard Oriole. *Winter:* Virginia Rail, American Woodcock, Short-eared Owl, Ash-throated Flycatcher, Western Kingbird, Scissor-tailed Flycatcher, American Pipit, Clay-colored Sparrow, Le Conte's Sparrow, Lincoln's Sparrow, Painted Bunting. *Migrant:* Black Tern, Chestnut-sided Warbler, Hooded Warbler.

Best times to bird: September through April.

Directions: *Wekiwa Springs State Park:* From Interstate 4, exit at State Road 434 (exit 94). Drive west 0.8 mile to Wekiwa Springs Road. Turn right and drive north, then west 4.2 miles to the park entrance. *Lake Apopka:* Turn right on Wekiwa Springs Road and drive west, then south 2.7 miles to State Road 436. Turn right and drive west 1.7 miles to U.S. Highway 441. Turn right and drive northwest 2 miles to State Road 429. Turn left and drive south 6.2 miles to West Road. Turn right and drive west 0.5 mile to Ocoee-Apopka Road. Turn right and drive north 2 miles to County Road 437 (Binion Road). Turn left and drive east 0.6 mile to Magnolia Park, on the eastern shore of the lake. From Florida's Turnpike, exit at SR 429 (exit 267). Drive north 4.2 miles to West Road (exit 26, toll). Turn left and proceed as above. *Mead Garden:* From I-4, exit at Fairbanks Avenue (exit 87). Drive east 1.2 miles to Denning Drive. Turn right and drive south 0.5 mile to the park entrance.

The Birding

Wekiwa Springs State Park is located north of Orlando, at the headwaters of the Wekiva River. Native Americans lived in the area around the springs for thousands of years. In the Creek language, *wekiva* means "flowing water," while *wekiwa* means "spring of water." Today Wekiwa Springs is a popular place to swim or snorkel, while the Wekiva River offers excellent opportunities for canoeing. Watch along the river for Wood Duck, Limpkin, Barred Owl, Pileated Woodpecker, and Prothonotary Warbler. A 2-mile trail links the springs and Sand Lake, though you may also access the Sand Lake trailhead via the park road. During summer evenings listen for Chuck-will's-widow along the road. The 7,800-acre park contains an additional 13 miles of hiking trails, 8 miles of equestrian trails, and 9 miles of multiuse trails. These trails, which wind through pine flatwoods and sand pine scrub, crisscross each other at several points, and can be very confusing (I learned this fact the hard way several years ago). Ask for a trail map at the ranger station.

For many years, Lake Apopka, specifically the Zellwood area at the north end of the lake, was a birding destination primarily during late summer when large numbers of southbound shorebirds would stop to feed in flooded vegetable fields. Nearby sod farms would attract sought-after species such as American Golden Plover and Upland and Buff-breasted Sandpiper. Because of agricultural, wastewater, and citrus-processing-plant discharges, lake water quality severely declined during the past few decades. St. Johns River Water Management District stepped in and purchased more than 19,000 acres of these farmlands in the mid-1990s. The conversion of the farms to filtration marshes resulted in significant improvements in water clarity in the lake. Since the conversion from farmlands to wetlands began, an astounding variety of bird life has been attracted to the area. In 1998 34 birders participating in the area's revived Christmas Bird Count tallied 174 species, an inland CBC record! Over 270 species have now been recorded within or near the restoration area, including such rarities as Rough-legged Hawk, Eurasian Kestrel, Curlew Sandpiper, Groove-billed Ani, Tropical Kingbird, and Fork-tailed Flycatcher. In late 1998 and early 1999, though, hundreds of birds, mostly American White Pelican, Wood Stork, and Great Blue Heron, died on the former farmlands, evidently as the result of consuming fish contaminated with residual pesticides. Though the restoration of the farmlands now known as **Lake Apopka Restoration Area** continues, this setback forced the water management district to close most of the property to the public.

Begin your exploration of public-accessible areas at **Magnolia Park,** a county park on the eastern shore of the lake. If low water levels expose mudflats, check the lakeshore near the park's boat ramp for migrant shorebirds. Occasionally appearing here are rarities including Buff-breasted Sandpiper and Wilson's Phalarope. Watch for Bobolink moving through this area during migration. Scan the lake in winter for American White Pelican and Bonaparte's Gull. Cross the road and check the oak hammock for migrant and wintering land birds. Drive north 1.6 miles on CR 437 to the intersection with Hooper Farms Road. During winter Western Kingbird roosts on wires here, sometimes in large numbers. A few Scissor-tailed Flycatchers often join them. Study the kingbirds carefully, since both Cassin's and Tropical Kingbird have been reported from this area. A Fork-tailed Flycatcher was seen here in December 2005. Weedy fields near this intersection often hold an assortment of wintering sparrows. Continue north 1 mile to Lust Road. Turn left and drive west 0.6 mile to the locked gate. Though the area beyond the gate is within Lake Apopka Restoration Area and currently closed to the public, the brushy and weedy areas outside the gate can be very productive in winter. Flycatchers seen along this road have included Least, Ash-throated, and Brown-crested. Several Groove-billed Anis were discovered here in January 2005. Also possible here in winter are Yellow-breasted Chat, Painted and Indigo Bunting, Blue Grosbeak, Dickcissel, and a variety of sparrows. Indigo Bunting, Blue Grosbeak, Dickcissel, and Orchard Oriole all breed in the area. When rarities such as Rough-legged Hawk, Eurasian Kestrel, and Fork-tailed Flycatcher were discovered in the fields beyond the gate, the water management district arranged for birders to enter.

Return to CR 437, turn left, and drive north 2.2 miles to US 441. Turn left and drive east, then north 4 miles to Jones Avenue. Turn left and drive west 0.2 mile to Laughlin Road. Turn left to reach another restoration area gate. Birders used this entrance to access the farmlands prior to their designation as a restoration area. Weedy fields outside this gate also attract wintering sparrows. Expect Chipping, Vesper, Savannah, Grasshopper, Swamp, and White-crowned. Occasionally in the mix are Clay-colored, Field, Lark, Le Conte's, Song, Lincoln's, and White-throated. Also scan plowed fields for flocks of American Pipit and watch overhead for Bald Eagle. Return to Jones Avenue, turn left, and drive west 3.5 miles to County Road 448A. Turn left and drive south 0.5 mile to County Road 48. Continue south 1.5 miles on CR 448A to the Duda gate of the restoration area, another location to search for flycatchers, sparrows, and other wintering species. Vermilion Flycatcher has been recorded here on more than one occasion. Backtrack to CR 48, turn left, and drive west 3 miles to Ranch Road. Along the way you will cross the Apopka-Beauclair Canal, through which water flows from Lake Apopka to a chain of lakes farther north. The water eventually flows to the Ocklawaha River, then to the St. Johns River before reaching the Atlantic. Turn left on Ranch Road and drive south 1 mile. The road curves east and becomes unpaved. In another mile the road passes through a patch of scrub where Florida Scrub-Jay can be found. Ranch Road then curves south and continues 0.7 mile to Peebles Road. Turn right and drive west 0.1 mile to Carolyn Road. Turn left and drive south 0.1 mile to the Clay Island entrance to the restoration area. This is currently the only entrance that allows access by foot, via a 5.7-mile loop trail. An observation tower overlooking Lake Apopka is 2.4 miles from the trailhead. The trail follows levees through a series of wetland impoundments. Look throughout the year for both types of whistling-duck, Mottled Duck, King Rail, Purple Gallinule, Limpkin, Sandhill Crane, and other wading birds. Least Bittern and Black-necked Stilt are here during summer. In winter watch for American Bittern, Virginia Rail, Sora, Wilson's Snipe, and a variety of waterfowl. Check surrounding forest for migrant and wintering land birds. To visit **Trimble Park,** return to the intersection of CR 448A and Jones Avenue, and then continue north 0.8 mile to Sadler Road. Turn right and drive east 1.2 miles to Dora Drive. Turn left and drive north 1 mile to Earlwood Drive. Turn left on Earlwood Drive and drive west 0.4 mile to Trimble Park Road. Turn right and drive north 0.1 mile, passing the first park entrance on your right. Bear left and drive west 0.5 mile, through the park's main entrance, to the picnic area. This 71-acre county park is located on the south shore of Lake Beauclair. Look for migrant and wintering land birds in oak hammock around the picnic area. A trail and boardwalk begins behind the picnic area and winds along the lake to the campground. Look for Limpkin and other wading birds along the lake. Watch overhead for Bald Eagle year-round and Swallow-tailed Kite in spring and summer.

Mead Garden, located just north of downtown Orlando, was founded in 1937 to honor the memory of world-renowned horticulturist Theodore L. Mead. Now a city park, the property consists of 55 acres of upland hammock and freshwater wetlands, ponds, and streams. From a birder's perspective, the park is most popular as a migration hot spot. Almost 30 species of warblers have been recorded in the park, along with an assortment of flycatchers, vireos, thrushes, and buntings. Unfortunately, the park was hit hard by the series of hurricanes that crisscrossed the state in 2004. Damage was especially severe in wetland areas. After entering the park, drive straight ahead to the parking area for the gardens. In the surrounding hammock and around the pond beyond the parking area, migrant land birds and resident species are possible, including Red-shouldered Hawk, Barred Owl, Pileated Woodpecker, Tufted Titmouse, and Yellow-throated Warbler. To the left of the parking area is a trail sign and path to the butterfly garden. Ruby-throated Hummingbird can be found here from fall through spring. In spring and summer watch overhead for Chimney Swift and Purple Martin. A wetland boardwalk loop begins beyond the butterfly garden. During periods of high water, sections of the boardwalk may be impassable. Wood Duck is frequently sighted in the wetland, as is a variety of wading birds, including Wood Stork. During migration look for water-associated warblers such as Prothonotary, Hooded, and Northern Waterthrush. Brushy areas may conceal Painted and Indigo Bunting and other migrant land birds. In winter expect to see Eastern Phoebe and Belted Kingfisher. Watch overhead for the occasional Bald Eagle.

General information: Wekiwa Springs State Park (entrance fee) and Mead Garden (no entrance fee) are open daily from 8:00 A.M. until sunset. Clay Island Trail at Lake Apopka Restorafion Area (no entrance fee) is open daily from sunrise to sunset. Magnolia Park and Trimble Park (no entrance fees) are open daily from 8:00 A.M. to 6:00 P.M. (until 8:00 P.M. in summer). Restrooms are available at Wekiwa Springs State Park, Magnolia and Trimble Parks, and Mead Garden. Do not trespass into any gated section of Lake Apopka Restoration Area.

DeLorme grid: Page 79, C-2; page 80, C-1, D-2.

Hazards: Keep a safe distance from alligators. Cottonmouths and eastern diamondback rattlesnakes are present but rarely encountered. Be prepared for thunderstorms during summer. As is the case when visiting any large metropolitan area, common sense is essential. Birding alone is not recommended. Lock car doors and secure all valuables out of sight.

Nearest food, gas, lodging: In Orlando.

Camping: Wekiwa Springs State Park: 60 sites. Magnolia Park: 18 sites. Trimble Park: 15 sites.

For more information: *Wekiwa Springs State Park,* c/o Wekiva Basin Geo Park, 1800 Wekiwa

Circle, Apopka, FL 32712; (407) 884-2008; www.floridastateparks.org/wekiwasprings. *Lake Apopka Restoration Area,* c/o St. Johns River Water Management District, P.O. Box 1429, Palatka, FL 32178; (386) 329-4404; www .sjrwmd.com. *Magnolia Park,* 2929 Binion Rd.,

Apopka, FL 32703; (407) 886-4214. *Trimble Park,* 5802 Trimble Park Rd., Mt. Dora, FL 32757; (352) 383-1993. *Mead Garden,* 1300 S. Denning Dr., Winter Park, FL 32789; (407) 262-2049; www.meadgarden.org.

10 Walt Disney World Area

Habitats: Pine flatwoods, oak scrub, freshwater marsh, cypress swamp, freshwater lakes.

Specialty birds: *Resident:* Mottled Duck, Least Bittern, Wood Stork, Snail Kite, Bald Eagle, Crested Caracara, King Rail, Limpkin, Sandhill Crane, Florida Scrub-Jay, Brown-headed Nuthatch, Bachman's Sparrow. *Summer:* Roseate Spoonbill, Swallow-tailed Kite, Purple Gallinule, Chuck-will's-widow, Prothonotary Warbler, Summer Tanager. *Winter:* American Woodcock, Whip-poor-will. *Migrant:* Hooded Warbler, Painted Bunting.

Best times to bird: October through April.

Directions: *Tibet-Butler Preserve:* From I-4 in Lake Buena Vista, exit at State Road 535 (exit 68). Drive north 0.5 mile and turn left. Continue west, then north on SR 535 (Winter Garden Vineland Road) for another 5.3 miles to the entrance. *Lake Louisa State Park:* From I-4 in Kissimmee, exit at U.S. Highway 192 (exit 64). Drive west 8 miles to U.S. Highway 27. Turn right and drive north 8.5 miles to the entrance. *Osceola County Schools Environmental Study Center:* Return to the intersection of US 192 and I-4. Drive east 3 miles on US 192 to Poinciana Boulevard. Turn right and drive south 13 miles to the entrance. *Disney Wilderness Preserve:* Continue south, then east on Poinciana Boulevard another 1 mile to Pleasant Hill Road. Turn right and drive south 0.5 mile to Old Pleasant Hill Road. Turn left and drive east, then south 0.6 mile to the entrance.

The Birding

You've been at Walt Disney World for a week and so far the only avian species you've checked off is Donald Duck. What's a visiting birder to do? Fortunately there are several locations nearby where you can relieve your birding frustrations and experience a little of the "real" Florida. At **Tibet-Butler Preserve,** just north of the Disney theme park, 4 miles of trails wind through 438 acres of pine flatwoods, wetlands, and scrub along Lake Tibet-Butler. Trails begin behind the Vera Carter Environmental Center, which contains a variety of interpretive displays. Interpretive trail guides are available here. Bird feeders set up outside the environmental center attract titmice, cardinals, and other common species. The Pine Circle Trail passes through pine flatwoods surrounding the environmental center. Look for Wild Turkey, Northern Bobwhite, Common Ground-Dove, Great Horned Owl, Pileated Woodpecker, Pine Warbler, Eastern Towhee, and other resident species. Watch overhead in spring and summer for Swallow-tailed Kite. Patches of oak hammock along this trail may attract migrant and wintering land birds. Fallen Log Crossing is a boardwalk trail passing through a bayhead swamp. Tarflower Loop circles through an area of oak scrub, while Osprey Overlook passes through a freshwater marsh before ending at an over-look along Lake Tibet-Butler. **Lake Louisa State Park** is located at the northeast edge of a vast wetland system known as Green Swamp. Several lakes and ponds, including Lake

Louisa, are found in the park, part of a chain of 13 lakes connected by the Palatlakaha River. A 0.4-mile nature trail begins at the Lake Louisa parking lot, 3 miles from the park entrance. Search here for migrant and wintering land birds. Over 20 miles of hiking and equestrian trails are available for a more extensive exploration of the park.

Osceola County Schools Environmental Study Center is used by local schoolchildren during the week but is open to the public on weekends. An 1,800-foot elevated boardwalk leads through Reedy Creek Swamp, a mixed hardwood and cypress wetland. An assortment of wading birds can be viewed from the boardwalk. Also watch for Barred Owl and Bald Eagle, which nests nearby. Look for Prothonotary Warbler and Summer Tanager in spring and summer. Just south is the 12,000-acre **Disney Wilderness Preserve,** owned and managed by The Nature Conservancy. The preserve was created to mitigate Kissimmee area wetlands damaged by Disney and other developers. About 700 acres is open to the public. The 1.8-mile preserve road winds through freshwater wetlands where Sandhill Crane, Wood Stork, and other wading birds may be feeding, including Roseate Spoonbill during the summer months. A closer inspection of these seasonally wet areas may reveal Least Bittern, Wood Duck, King Rail, Purple Gallinule, and Limpkin. Areas that remain wet during the winter months may attract Sora, Wilson's Snipe, and other shorebirds. The road ends at the preserve's educational center, where two trails provide opportunities for further exploration. The 0.5-mile John C. Sawhill Interpretive Trail leads through open grasslands to cypress swamp along Lake Russell. A short boardwalk leads through the swamp to an overlook of the lake. Scan for raptors such as Osprey, Snail Kite, and Bald Eagle. In winter waterfowl such as Blue-winged Teal, Ring-necked Duck, and Hooded Merganser may be on the lake. The 3-mile Wilderness Trail leads through a variety of habitats including wet and dry prairie, pine flatwoods, and oak scrub. Look for Crested Caracara in dry prairie. Several families of Florida Scrub-Jay reside in the preserve's scrub habitat. In the pine flatwoods watch for Red-headed Woodpecker, Brown-headed Nuthatch, Eastern Bluebird, Summer Tanager, and Bachman's Sparrow. Other sparrows, including Vesper, Savannah, and Grasshopper inhabit prairie grasslands in winter. From November through January it's also possible to flush American Woodcock along woodland edges.

General information: Tibet-Butler Preserve (no entrance fee) is open Wednesday through Sunday from 8:00 A.M. to 6:00 P.M. Restrooms are available near the environmental center. Lake Louisa State Park (entrance fee) is open daily from 8:00 A.M. until sunset. Restrooms are available at the beach bathhouse. Osceola County Schools Environmental Study Center (no entrance fee) is open Saturdays from 10:00 A.M. to 5:00 P.M. and Sundays from noon to 5:00 P.M. Restrooms are available in the environmental center. Disney Wilderness Preserve (entrance fee) is open daily from October through May, from 9:00 A.M. to 5:00 P.M. From June through September, it's open Monday through Friday only and closed on major holidays. Restrooms are available at the Conservation Learning Center.

DeLorme grid: Page 85, A-2, 3; page 86, C-1.

Hazards: Keep a safe distance from alligators. Venomous snakes are present but rarely encountered. Mosquitoes are common during wet periods. Trails may be flooded in summer.

Nearest food, gas, lodging: In Kissimmee and Lake Buena Vista.

Camping: Lake Louisa State Park: 75 sites, 20 cabins.

For more information: *Tibet-Butler Preserve,* 8777 CR 535, Orlando, FL 32836; (407) 876-6696. *Lake Louisa State Park,* 7305 US Hwy. 27, Clermont, FL 34714; (352) 394-3969; www .floridastateparks.org/lakelouisa. *Osceola County*

Schools Environmental Study Center, 4300 Poinciana Blvd., Kissimmee, FL 34758; (407) 870-0551. *Disney Wilderness Preserve, 2700 Scrub* Jay Trail, Kissimmee, FL 34759; (407) 935-0005; www.nature.org/florida.

 # Three Lakes Wildlife Management Area

Habitats: Pine flatwoods, cypress swamp, wet prairie, dry prairie, pasture, oak/cabbage palm hammock, oak scrub, freshwater marsh, freshwater lakes.

Specialty birds: *Resident:* Mottled Duck, Least Bittern, Wood Stork, White-tailed Kite, Snail Kite, Bald Eagle, Short-tailed Hawk, Crested Caracara, King Rail, Purple Gallinule, Limpkin, Sandhill Crane, Whooping Crane, Burrowing Owl, Red-cockaded Woodpecker, Brown-headed Nuthatch, Bachman's Sparrow, Grasshopper Sparrow (Florida race). *Summer:* Swallow-tailed Kite, Chuck-will's-widow, Summer Tanager. *Winter:* Roseate Spoonbill, American Pipit.

Best times to bird: October through April.

Directions: From the Florida Turnpike in Kissimmee/St. Cloud, exit at US 192. Drive east 4.5 miles to County Road 523 (Vermont Avenue/Canoe Creek Road). Turn right and drive south 19 miles to the Whooping Crane viewing location at the Double C Bar Ranch. From the Florida Turnpike in Yeehaw Junction, exit at State Road 60. Drive west 0.4 mile to US 441. Turn right and drive north 14 miles to CR 523 (Canoe Creek Road). Turn left and drive west 3.3 miles to Arnold Road, the access road to Lake Marion viewing locations. At Arnold Road, CR 523 curves north. From this point to the Double C Bar Ranch is 12.3 miles.

The Birding

Three Lakes Wildlife Management Area is located south of the now heavily developed Kissimmee/St. Cloud area. Though altered by years of cattle ranching and logging, this wildlife management area still contains within its 62,000 acres a wide range of central Florida habitats. Named for three lakes that border the area (Kissimmee, Jackson, and Marion), the wildlife management area and surrounding ranchland are now home to captive-raised Whooping Crane, released in the hope of creating a nonmigratory population of this highly endangered species. One of the most reliable locations to view these magnificent birds is at the Double C Bar Ranch on Canoe Creek Road. Since you must view the birds from the road, a spotting scope is helpful. Sandhill Crane is also likely at the ranch and in pastures or marshy spots throughout the area. Whooping Crane is also possible along **Joe Overstreet Road,** especially at its terminus at Lake Kissimmee. This dirt road begins at Canoe Creek Road, 0.7 mile south of the Double C Bar Ranch. As you drive west toward Lake Kissimmee, scan pastures on both sides of the road for cranes. Other species likely on this drive at any time of year include Bald Eagle, Black and Turkey Vulture, Red-shouldered Hawk, Crested Caracara, Wild Turkey (often in large flocks!), Northern Bobwhite, American Crow, and Eastern Meadowlark. Nesting Burrowing Owl is also possible along this road. Wet areas may attract Glossy Ibis, Wood Stork, Greater and Lesser Yellowlegs, and other shorebirds. Watch fence lines in winter for sparrows. Among the abundant Savannah Sparrow may be a few Grasshopper Sparrows. Occasionally other species such as White-crowned Sparrow join the mix. American Robin is common in the pastures during winter, sometimes joined by flocks of American Pipit. After 5.3 miles you will reach a fishing camp and boat launch on the shores of Lake Kissimmee. Fish Crow is common around the camp. Scan the wet area along the lakeshore both north and south of the boat launch for cranes, wading birds, and Bald Eagle. Gulls and, occasionally, Black Skimmer roost north of the boat launch in winter. In winter Forster's Tern often perches along the boat dock or on posts farther out in the lake. Snail Kite also uses these posts as perches. Winter brings a variety of ducks to the lake, joining the resident Mottled Duck. Most will be far out in the lake, and a spotting scope is a must if you hope to identify any of them.

Return to Canoe Creek Road, turn right, and drive south. In 3.6 miles you will reach the first entrance to Three Lakes Wildlife Management Area. A hunter camp at the entrance is the most reliable location in the WMA for Red-cockaded Woodpecker. Nest trees are marked with white rings. Those nest trees within the hunter camp itself are also enclosed in a wooden fence. Dawn and dusk are the best times to view this species. At other times of day, they usually forage a considerable distance from the nest area. Other species likely in the vicinity of the hunter camp are Common Ground-Dove, Brown-headed Nuthatch, Eastern Bluebird, and Eastern Meadowlark. Bachman's Sparrow is possible, especially in spring when males are singing, in open areas of saw palmetto beyond the hunter camp fence line. A daily-use permit is required to enter the wildlife management area beyond the hunter camp. A 5-mile self-guided driving tour begins at the Prairie Lakes Unit entrance on Canoe Creek Road, 2 miles south of the hunter camp. The driving tour follows Road 16 for 1.2 miles then turns right onto Road 19, becoming Road 5 after 2.8 miles. The tour ends in another 1 mile at the Road 5 entrance in the hunter camp. Daily-use permits, maps, and hunting schedules are available at kiosks by both entrances to the driving tour. The roads may be driven in either direction. If you enter by Road 16, suitable saw palmetto habitat for Bachman's Sparrow can be found just beyond the entrance. Look or listen for Wild Turkey, Northern Bobwhite, Brown-headed Nuthatch, Eastern Bluebird, Pine Warbler, and Eastern Towhee in longleaf pine flatwoods along Road 16. You may explore the area between Lake Jackson and Lake Marion by continuing south on Road 16, beyond the driving tour turnoff onto Road 19. In 0.4 mile you will reach a parking area at Parker Slough, which connects the two lakes. The trailhead for two spur loops of the Florida Trail is located here. Both loop trails, one 5 miles and the other 5.5 miles, first pass through oak hammock and cypress swamp that should be checked for migrant and wintering land birds. Occasionally a Short-tailed Hawk can be seen overhead. In summer watch for Swallow-tailed Kite, Chuck-will's-widow, Northern Parula, and Summer Tanager. Barred Owl and Pileated Woodpecker are here year-round. The north loop doubles back through pine flatwoods while the south loop travels through oak hammock surrounding saw palmetto scrub.

Another 0.3 mile beyond Parker Slough on Road 16 is Boat Ramp Road, which leads in 1 mile to Lake Jackson. Road 16 ends in 3.4 miles at the Jackson-Kissimmee Canal, which connects Lake Kissimmee to Lake Jackson. An observation tower overlooking Lake Jackson is a 10-minute walk from the parking area at the end of Road 16. The tower provides opportunities to scope the lake for Bald Eagle and wintering waterfowl. Scan the marshy edges of the lake year-round for Least Bittern, Wood Duck, King Rail, Purple Gallinule, Limpkin, and Sandhill Crane. American Bittern, Roseate Spoonbill, and Virginia Rail are possible here in winter. To return to the driving tour, backtrack to Road 19 and turn left. This road passes through pine flatwoods and patches of oak hammock, all worth exploring. White-tailed Kite can occasionally be seen over recently burned areas. An area of dry prairie habitat can be accessed by turning left on Road 5 B, 2.8 miles from Road 16. This 1-mile road is rough and may be seasonally wet; a four-wheel-drive vehicle is recommended. The Florida race of Grasshopper Sparrow breeds here in small numbers. Other species to watch for here include Crested Caracara, Sandhill Crane, and Burrowing Owl. The last mile of the driving tour passes through longleaf pine flatwoods containing several Red-cockaded Woodpecker nest trees, all marked with white rings. Return to Canoe Creek Road and turn right. Pass the Prairie Lakes Unit entrance and continue south another 2.2 miles to the parking area for Sunset Ranch Interpretive Trail. A short distance from the trailhead is a viewing blind beside an abandoned pasture. This is an excellent location to find Wild Turkey. Check the surrounding oak hammock for migrant and wintering land birds, in addition to common residents such as Tufted Titmouse and Carolina Wren. A short boardwalk leads through a cypress slough that may shelter nesting Wood Duck. In about 1 mile the trail reaches Lake Marion. Watch for Bald Eagle and Red-tailed Hawk soaring overhead. This area was used for captive-raised Whooping Cranes before their release into the wild. Occasionally one of these birds is seen along the lakeshore. An easier way to explore Lake Marion is to return to Canoe Creek Road and continue south. In 3.8 miles turn right onto Arnold Road. Lake Marion can be reached by continuing 0.5 mile to the end of Arnold Road, or turning right in 0.2 mile onto Lakeside Boulevard, then 0.3 mile to the lake. At both locations look for Bald Eagle and Osprey overhead and Wood Stork and Limpkin along the shore. During winter American White Pelican and occasionally Bonaparte's Gull may be seen on the lake.

General information: Three Lakes Wildlife Management Area (entrance fee for Three Lakes WMA wildlife drive) is open 24 hours a day. Seasonal hunting is permitted. Refer to regulations-summary brochures, updated annually and available at check stations, for hunt dates and locations. Wear blaze orange if hiking during hunting season. Primitive restrooms are located at check stations and at the fishing camp at the end of Joe Overstreet Road.

DeLorme grid: Page 94, A-3.

Hazards: Keep a safe distance from alligators. Rattlesnakes and cottonmouths are present but rarely encountered. Only drive on named and numbered roads. Four-wheel-drive vehicles are strongly recommended on sandy roads or when conditions are wet. Trails may be seasonally flooded.

Nearest food, gas, lodging: In St. Cloud.

Camping: Primitive camping is allowed at designated campsites within Three Lakes Wildlife Management Area except during established hunting seasons for the area. No drinking water is available.

For more information: *Three Lakes Wildlife Management Area,* c/o Florida Fish and Wildlife Conservation Commission, 620 S. Meridian St., Tallahassee, FL 32399; (800) 955-8771; www .floridaconservation.org.

 # Lake Wales/Sebring Area

Habitats: Oak/sand pine scrub, pine flatwoods, sandhills, dry prairie, oak/cabbage palm hammock, cypress swamp, freshwater lakes.

Specialty birds: *Resident:* Mottled Duck, Least Bittern, Wood Stork, Snail Kite, Bald Eagle, Short-tailed Hawk, Crested Caracara, King Rail, Purple

Gallinule, Limpkin, Sandhill Crane, Whooping Crane, Burrowing Owl, Red-cockaded Woodpecker, Florida Scrub-Jay, Brown-headed Nuthatch, Grasshopper Sparrow (Florida race), Bachman's Sparrow. *Summer:* Swallow-tailed Kite, Chuck-will's-widow, Summer Tanager. *Winter:* Whip-poor-will, Henslow's Sparrow. *Migrant:* Prothonotary Warbler, Louisiana Waterthrush.

Best times to bird: September through May.

Directions: *Lake Kissimmee State Park:* From the Florida Turnpike in Yeehaw Junction, exit at SR 60. Drive west 37.2 miles to Boy Scout Road. Turn right and drive north 3.5 miles to Camp Mack Road. (Note for the return trip: At this intersection, Boy Scout Road is called Barney Keen Road.) Turn right and drive east 5.3 miles to the park entrance. From the intersection of US 27 and SR 60 in Lake Wales, drive east 9.3 miles on SR 60 to Boy Scout Road. Turn left and proceed as above. *Lake Wales Ridge State Forest:* Return to the intersection of Boy Scout Road and SR 60. South of this intersection, Boy Scout Road becomes Walk in Water Road. Drive south 7 miles to Walk in Water Campground. *Avon Park Air Force Range:* From the intersection of US 27 and State Road 64 in Avon Park, drive east 10.2 miles on SR 64 to the entrance gate. *Highlands Hammock State Park:* From US 27 in Sebring, drive west 2.6 miles on Hammock Road (County Road 634) to the park entrance.

The Birding

Lake Kissimmee State Park consists of 5,930 acres along the western shore of Florida's third-largest lake. Two smaller lakes, Tiger Lake and Lake Rosalie, are to the south and east. Check scrub habitat near the entrance station for Florida Scrub-Jay, Northern Bobwhite, and Eastern Towhee. Drive south, then east 3.3 miles on the park drive to the parking area at its terminus. Walk east through the picnic area to an observation tower overlooking Lake Kissimmee. When water levels are low, the shoreline may recede a considerable distance east, requiring the use of a spotting scope. Sandhill Crane is common along the lake and is often seen around the picnic area. Whooping Crane from the nonmigratory population introduced to Three Lakes Wildlife Management Area, on the east side of the lake, will occasionally fly over to the west side and may be visible from the tower. Wood Stork, Limpkin, and other wading birds may also be seen feeding along the shoreline. Watch for raptors over or along the edges of the lake including Snail Kite, Bald Eagle, and Crested Caracara. A short nature trail begins at the west end of the parking area, on the north side of the road. The trail leads through hardwood hammock where Downy Woodpecker, Tufted Titmouse, Carolina Wren, Brown Thrasher, and other resident species can be found. Watch overhead during spring and summer for Swallow-tailed Kite. Check this trail in spring and fall for migrant land birds. Summer breeders include Yellow-billed Cuckoo and Northern Parula. During winter look for Blue-headed Vireo, Hermit Thrush, American Robin, and Yellow-throated and Black-and-white Warbler. Two longer trails begin on the opposite side of the road. The 6-mile North Loop Trail winds through pine flatwoods on both sides of the park drive. Numerous snags along the trail attract Red-headed, Hairy, and Pileated Woodpecker and Northern Flicker. Other residents in this habitat include Wild Turkey, Common Ground-Dove, Eastern Bluebird, Pine Warbler, and Bachman's Sparrow. Summer breeders include Great Crested Flycatcher, Eastern Kingbird, and Summer Tanager. Listen at dawn and dusk during the summer months for Chuck-will's-widow. If walking this trail counterclockwise, you will reach a spur trail after 0.9 mile. This 1.1-mile trail leads to Gobbler Ridge, a live oak hammock along Lake Kissimmee. The 6.7-mile Buster Island Loop Trail passes through hardwood hammock in the southern half of the park.

At 300 feet above sea level, the Lake Wales Ridge is the highest point in the Florida peninsula. An ancient sand dune, formed when higher sea levels covered most of the state, the ridge is home to plants and animals found nowhere else on earth. Tragically, most of this unique desertlike habitat has been converted to citrus groves or residential and commercial developments. A patchwork of protected areas on the ridge is now managed by federal, state, and nonprofit agencies. Federally controlled parcels comprise Lake Wales Ridge National Wildlife Refuge. Areas under state jurisdiction include Lake Wales Ridge State Forest, Lake June in Winter Scrub State Park (see next chapter), and Lake Wales Ridge Wildlife and Environmental Area. In order to protect this distinctive ecosystem, many of these areas have restricted public access. One area accessible to birders and where Florida Scrub-Jay may be found is the Walk in Water Tract of **Lake Wales Ridge State Forest.** Search for scrub-jays around the Walk in Water Campground or along a trail that begins 1.5 miles south of the campground, near the intersection of Walk in Water Road and County Road 630. Other trails begin west of this intersection. South of this intersection, Walk in Water Road becomes Blue Jordan Road. To reach the Arbuckle Tract of the state forest, drive southwest 1.6 miles on Blue Jordan Road to Lake Reedy Boulevard. Turn left and drive south 1.6 miles to Lake Arbuckle Road. Turn left and drive east 1.5 miles to Rucks Dairy Road. Turn right and drive south 0.8 mile to the check station. Two overlapping loop trails, each about 11 miles in length and part of the Florida Trail system, wind through the forest and provide access to the western side of Lake Arbuckle. The trails may be accessed at several locations, including Reedy Creek Campground, Lake Godwin, and McClean Cabin. From the check station, turn right to reach Reedy Creek Campground. Watch overhead in spring and summer for Short-tailed Hawk, which nests in the vicinity of Reedy Creek. Return to the check station and turn left on School Bus Road. Drive southeast 1 mile to Lake Godwin Road. Turn right and drive south 0.8 mile to tiny Lake Godwin. Brown-headed Nuthatch and Bachman's Sparrow can be found in pine flatwoods along this road. Return to School Bus Road and continue southeast 1.5 miles to McClean Cabin. In addition to the Florida Trail, a short nature trail loops through the forest here.

School Bus Road continues southeast to SR 64, intersecting 1 mile west of the entrance gate to **Avon Park Air Force Range.** Inconveniently, this end of the road is gated and locked. To reach the base from the Arbuckle Tract, return to Lake Reedy Boulevard and turn left. Drive west 3.6 miles (Lake Reedy Boulevard becomes Wilson Road after 1.7 miles) to U.S. Highway 17. Turn left and drive south, then west 3.4 miles to US 27. Turn left and drive south 6.3 miles to SR 64. Turn left and drive east 10.2 miles to the entrance gate. Of the 106,000 acres within the base, 78,000 are within a Public Recreation Area, open to visitors for a variety of recreational opportunities including hunting, fishing, and birding. All visitors must first register at the Outdoor Recreation Office, located at the intersection of Frostproof and Jennings Roads, 1.5 miles east of the entrance gate. You will receive a map indicating the location of 17 management units within the Public Recreation Area, as well as all closed and restricted areas. Except for a 0.3-mile grassy road to Sandy Point Wildlife

Short-tailed Hawk. PHOTO: TREY MITCHELL

Refuge, all routes described below are on stabilized roads normally passable with two-wheel-drive vehicles.

From the Outdoor Recreation Office, drive north 1 mile on Frostproof Road to the Lake Arbuckle Nature Trail. Turn left and drive west 0.3 mile to the trailhead. A boardwalk leads to an observation tower on the east side of Lake Arbuckle. Migrant and wintering land birds can be found in oak hammock and cypress swamp anywhere along the boardwalk. From the observation tower, scope the lake for wintering waterfowl. Scan vegetation along the lakeshore for Least Bittern, Wood Duck, Purple Gallinule, Limpkin, and other waterbirds. Watch overhead for Bald Eagle and Cooper's Hawk throughout the year. Swallow-tailed Kite and Short-tailed Hawk are possible in spring and summer. Return to Frostproof Road and continue north 0.6 mile to Bravo Road. Turn right and drive east 1.7 miles to Billig Road. Bravo Road first passes through scrub habitat where Florida Scrub-Jay may be found. As you enter pine flatwoods, watch for trees painted with white rings, indicating Red-cockaded Woodpecker nest cavities. You will also notice that nest boxes have been installed for Eastern Bluebird along this and many other roads on the base. As a result of the nest box program, Eastern Bluebird is common throughout. Other species to watch for in the pinelands include Wild Turkey, Northern Bobwhite, Common Ground-Dove, Great Horned Owl, Red-headed and Hairy Woodpecker, Eastern Kingbird, Brown-headed Nuthatch, Pine Warbler, Summer Tanager, Eastern Towhee, and Bachman's Sparrow. Listen at dawn and dusk for Chuck-will's-widow during summer and Whip-poor-will in winter. Turn left on Billig Road and drive north 3 miles to Degagne Road. Red-cockaded Woodpecker nest cavities are common along this road. The woodpeckers often forage elsewhere during the day and are most likely to be seen around their nest cavities at dawn and dusk. Turn left on Degagne Road and drive west, then south 4.3 miles to return to Frostproof Road. Degagne Road passes through the Deadins Pine Swamp. Watch for wading birds, including Wood Stork, in wet areas along both sides of this road. The Willingham Campground is at the intersection of Degagne Road and Frostproof Road. In this oak hammock, look for migrant and wintering land birds as well as Barred Owl, Tufted Titmouse, Carolina Wren, and other resident species. The Lake Arbuckle Scenic Trail begins at the campground. This 16-mile loop trail winds through habitat just explored by road. Drive south 0.7 mile on Frostproof Road to return to the intersection with Bravo Road.

Return to the Outdoor Recreation Office and turn left on Jennings Road to reach birding areas south and east of the main base. Drive east, then south 0.9 mile on Jennings Road to UTES Road (unmarked at the east end). Turn right and drive west 0.7 mile (along the edge of base runways) to South Road. Turn left and drive south 1.6 miles to the intersection of Ebersbach and Kissimmee Roads. Turn right and drive south 0.2 mile to a grassy path on the west side of the road. This path is usually passable even in two-wheel-drive vehicles. Turn right and drive west 0.3 mile to Austin Hammock Group Camp. The 6.5-mile Sandy Point Wildlife Refuge Trail begins at the campground entrance and winds south to Arbuckle Marsh, a large area of freshwater marsh. This trail is composed of several loops, allowing for shorter hikes. To drive to Arbuckle Marsh, return to Ebersbach Road and continue south another mile or so (depending on grass height and water levels). An assortment of waterbirds, including Least Bittern, American Bittern (in winter), Wood Stork, and King Rail, can be found in the marsh. Waterproof footwear is essential for exploration of this area. Backtrack to the intersection of Ebersbach Road with South and Kissimmee Roads. Turn right and drive east on Kissimmee Road through dry prairie, preferred nesting habitat for the Florida race of Grasshopper Sparrow. Search for this species only along designated roads. Do not enter the bombing range on the south side of the road! Also watch for Crested Caracara and Burrowing Owl in this habitat. Henslow's Sparrow can be found here during winter in patches of moist wire grass. These wet areas may attract Sandhill Crane and other wading birds throughout the year. After 3.5 miles you will cross Morgan Hole Creek. Oak hammock in the campground along this creek should be checked for migrant and wintering land birds. To reach Tick Island Slough, another area of freshwater marsh attractive to waterbirds, continue east 4.4 miles to Bubba Road. Turn left and drive north 1.3 miles to Wood Road. Turn right and drive east into the marsh. Return to Kissimmee Road and drive east another 5 miles to reach Ft. Kissimmee Campground. Driving this section of road is only allowed when the gate is open at the western entrance to Charlie Range, a restricted access area. From Ft. Kissimmee Campground, one may hike either north or south along the 12-mile stretch of Florida National Scenic Trail that passes through the base. The trail winds through oak hammock, pinelands, and freshwater marsh along the Kissimmee River, which forms the eastern border of the base. Heading north, the trail leads to Kicco Wildlife Management Area. Southbound, the trail follows the western edge of Kissimmee Marsh.

Highlands Hammock State Park, in Sebring, is one of Florida's original state parks, first opened to the public in 1931. With recent acquisitions, the park has grown to over 9,000 acres, including 500 acres of old-growth hammock. Before their apparent rediscovery in the Florida Panhandle in 2005, the state's last sighting of Ivory-billed Woodpecker, in 1967–69, was in a wilderness area now within this park. Eight different nature trails provide access to old-growth habitat along the park's 3-mile loop drive. A ninth trail, the 0.6-mile Allen Altvater Trail, begins at the family campground (just beyond the entrance station) and winds through adjacent pine flatwoods. Look here for Great Horned Owl, Wild Turkey, Northern Bobwhite, Red-headed Woodpecker, Pine Warbler, Summer Tanager, Eastern Towhee, and Bachman's Sparrow. If camping during summer, listen for Chuck-will's-widow at dawn or dusk. A dirt road opposite the family-campground entrance leads through pine flatwoods to a primitive campground. Florida Scrub-Jay is occasionally seen in oak scrub surrounding this campground. Scrub-jays may also be found in oak scrub habitat along the eastern border of the park. To reach this area, return to the park entrance and turn right onto County Road 635. Drive south 2.3 miles to a parking area on the east side of the road. Sandhill Crane is often attracted to a marsh beyond the parking area. The park's Scrub Trail begins at a small picnic area on the opposite side of the road.

From the family campground, drive west 0.2 mile, beyond the Civilian Conservation Corps Museum and Hammock Inn camp store on the south side of the road, to where CR 634 veers north from the main park road. Drive 1.6 miles on CR 634, now a dirt road, to a bridge over Charlie Bowlegs Creek. Check along the creek for migrant land birds, including Prothonotary Warbler and Louisiana Waterthrush. Return to the main park road and continue west to the aforementioned trails along the loop drive. Two trails begin before the road becomes one-way. On the north side is the 0.2-mile Alexander Blair Big Oak Trail. One live oak on this trail is over 1,000 years old, with a circumference of 36 feet! On the south side is the 0.6-mile Wild Orange Grove Trail, which passes through hammock, pine flatwoods, and a grove of wild orange trees before returning to the camp store and museum. Once the road becomes one-way, parking areas along the loop provide access to the remaining nature trails. Among the most popular is the 0.5-mile Cypress Swamp Trail, at the midpoint of the loop drive. A section of this boardwalk trail along Charlie Bowlegs Creek is a "catwalk," a narrow boardwalk with railings on only one side.

Look for migrant and wintering land birds along this trail, as well as resident species including Red-shouldered Hawk, Limpkin, Barred Owl, Pileated Woodpecker, Tufted Titmouse, and Carolina Wren. In summer watch overhead for Swallow-tailed Kite and Short-tailed Hawk. Alligators are commonly seen along this trail, so watch your step! Two other trails include boardwalks through hardwood swamp: the 0.3-mile Richard Leiber Memorial Trail and 0.3-mile Fern Garden Trail. Additional trails worth checking include the 0.4-mile Hickory Trail, which connects with the Big Oak Trail, the 0.6-mile Young Hammock Trail, and the 0.6-mile Ancient Hammock Trail.

General information: Lake Kissimmee and Highlands Hammock State Parks (entrance fees) are open daily from 8:00 A.M. until sunset. Restrooms at Lake Kissimmee State Park are located in the picnic area. Restrooms at Highlands Hammock State Park are located at the CCC Museum. Ranger-led canoe and kayak tours of Lakes Kissimmee and Rosalie, Tiger Lake, and other park waterways are available at Lake Kissimmee State Park. Rental canoes and kayaks are not available for unguided exploration. More than 200 acres of the park are used to maintain a herd of scrub cows and horses. A "Cow Camp" is located a short walk from the picnic area and is staffed by park rangers, who vividly re-create living and working conditions on an 1870s Florida cattle ranch. This living-history site is open weekends and holidays from 9:30 A.M. to 4:30 P.M.

Lake Wales Ridge State Forest (entrance fee) is open daily from sunrise to sunset. Primitive restrooms are located at McClean Cabin Nature Trail and Walk in Water Campground. Avon Park Air Force Range is an active military installation and bombing range. The Public Recreation Area is open from noon on Thursday through 8:00 P.M. on Monday except when superseded by announcements posted at the entrance and information stations, on the Web site (www.avonparkafr.com), or in recorded messages (863–452–4119, ext. 5). Weekend Outdoor Recreation Permits ($8.00) are required and are available at the Outdoor Recreation Office. Permits must be returned to the Outdoor Recreation Office before leaving. Primitive restrooms are located at Willingham, Morgan Hole, and Ft. Kissimmee Campgrounds. Seasonal hunting is permitted on the Air Force Range and in the state forest. Refer to regulations-summary brochures, updated annually and available at check stations, for hunt dates and locations. Wear blaze orange if hiking during hunting season.

DeLorme grid: Page 94, A-2, C-1, C-2; page 99, A-3.

Hazards: Keep a safe distance from alligators. Cottonmouths are present in cypress swamp habitat, eastern diamondback rattlesnakes in pinelands, scrub, and hammock. Contact with poison ivy may result in a severe rash. Mosquitoes and other biting insects are common in summer. Trails may be flooded in summer. At Avon Park Air Force Range, only enter open management units and remain on designated roads and trails. Do not stop in restricted access areas or enter any bombing range. Do not approach unexploded ordnance!

Nearest food, gas, lodging: In Lake Wales, Avon Park, and Sebring.

Camping: Lake Kissimmee State Park: 60 sites. Highlands Hammock State Park: 159 sites.

For more information: *Lake Kissimmee State Park,* 14248 Camp Mack Rd., Lake Wales, FL 33898; (863) 696-1112; www.floridastateparks .org/lakekissimmee. *Lake Wales Ridge State Forest,* 452 School Bus Rd., Frostproof, FL 33843; (863) 635-7801; www.fl-dof.com. *Avon Park Air Force Range Outdoor Recreation Program,* 29 South Blvd., Avon Park AFR, FL 33825; (863) 452-4119, ext. 5; www.avonparkafr.com. *Highlands Hammock State Park,* 5931 Hammock Rd., Sebring, FL 33872; (863) 386-6094; www .floridastateparks.org/highlandshammock.

ⓘ⃝ Lake Placid Area

Habitats: Oak/sand pine scrub, sandhills, pine flatwoods, freshwater marsh, ponds and lakes, dry prairie, pasture, oak/cabbage palm hammock, cypress swamp.

Specialty birds: *Resident:* Mottled Duck, Wood Stork, Bald Eagle, White-tailed Kite, Short-tailed Hawk, Crested Caracara, King Rail, Purple Gallinule, Limpkin, Sandhill Crane, Burrowing Owl, Red-cockaded Woodpecker, Florida Scrub-Jay, Brown-headed Nuthatch, Bachman's Sparrow, Grasshopper Sparrow (Florida race). *Summer:* Swallow-tailed Kite, Chuck-will's-widow, Prothonotary Warbler, Summer Tanager. *Winter:* Henslow's Sparrow.

Best times to bird: October through April.

Directions: *Archbold Biological Station:* From the intersection of US 27 and State Road 70 in Lake Placid, turn right and drive west 1 mile on SR 70 to Old State Road 8. Turn left and drive south 1.8 miles to the entrance. *Venus Flatwoods Preserve:* Continue south 8.2 miles on Old SR 8, then turn right on Sheppard Road. The preserve begins in 0.2 mile on the south side of Sheppard Road. *Platt Branch Wildlife and Environmental Area:* Return to Old SR 8 and drive south 1 mile to County Road 731. Turn left and drive east 2.3 miles to Detjens Dairy Road (County Road 17). Turn right and drive south 1.3 miles to the entrance gate. *Fisheating Creek Wildlife Management Area:* Continue south, then east 2.2 miles on Detjens Dairy Road to US 27. Turn right and drive south 6.4 miles to Fisheating Creek State Campground. The campground is 27 miles south of the intersection of US 27 and SR 70. *Lake June in Winter Scrub State Park:* From the intersection of US 27 and SR 70, drive north 8 miles on US 27 to County Road 621 (Lake June Road). Turn left and drive west 4.2 miles to Daffodil Road. Turn left and drive south 2 miles to the park entrance. *Istokpoga Park:* Return to US 27 and continue north 8.5 miles to U.S. Highway 98. Turn right and drive east 8 miles to the park entrance. *Kissimmee Prairie Preserve State Park:* Continue east 20 miles on US 98 to County Road 700A. Turn left and drive north 5.5 miles to County Road 724 (Eagle Island Road). Turn left and drive west 6 miles to the park entrance. From SR 70 in Okeechobee, drive west 14 miles on US 98 to CR 700A. Turn right and proceed as above. From the Florida Turnpike in Yeehaw Junction, exit at SR 60. Drive west 0.4 mile to US 441. Turn left and drive south 17.5 miles to CR 724. Turn right and drive west 18 miles to the park entrance. From I-95 in Ft. Pierce, exit at State Road 68 (exit 131). Drive west 25.4 miles to US 441. Turn right and drive north 1 mile to CR 724. Turn left and proceed as above.

The Birding

Archbold Biological Station is an environmental research facility located south of Lake Placid on a 5,193-acre preserve. Most of the preserve and surrounding property, a mixture of oak and sand pine scrub, pine flatwoods, and seasonal ponds, is off-limits to the public. A 0.5-mile nature trail beginning beyond the research buildings provides the only access. Several species of woodpecker, including Hairy, Red-headed, and Pileated, can be found along this trail. Look for Florida Scrub-Jay on the preserve, as well as in patches of scrub farther south on Old SR 8. Also watch for Crested Caracara and Sandhill Crane in pastures along this road. **Venus Flatwoods Preserve** is a 40-acre Nature Conservancy property consisting of virgin longleaf-pine flatwoods near the southern limit of its range. This property is now closed to the public but may be birded from Sheppard Road. Red-cockaded Woodpeckers previously nested in trees adjacent to the road but apparently have abandoned these nest cavities in recent years. Bachman's Sparrow continues to nest here.

Listen for males in spring, singing from saw palmettos or other low perches. Brown-headed Nuthatch also nests here, though sporadically. Other species to watch for in the pinewoods or in pasture on the north side of Sheppard Road include Northern Bobwhite, Sandhill Crane, Great Horned Owl, Red-headed Woodpecker, Eastern Bluebird, Pine Warbler, Eastern Towhee, and Eastern Meadowlark. **Platt Branch Wildlife and Environmental Area,** formerly a cattle ranch, contains 1,972 acres of old-growth longleaf-pine flatwoods, oak and sand pine scrub, pasture, seasonal wetlands, oak hammock, and cypress swamp near the southern end of Lake Wales Ridge. A 3.5-mile loop trail through many of these habitats can be reached by driving west 0.8

Crested Caracara. PHOTO: TREY MITCHELL

mile on a service road through open pasture. If the service road gate is locked, park at the gate and walk through the pedestrian entrance to the trailhead. Several families of Florida Scrub-Jay reside in sand pine scrub along the first part of the trail. Seasonal wetlands attract Wood Stork, Sandhill Crane, and other wading birds. Wild Turkey, Summer Tanager, and other pine-associated species may be found in the flatwoods. From the trailhead, a service road continues west to oak hammock and cypress swamp along Fisheating Creek, on the western border of the park. The road also passes longleaf pines where several active Red-cockaded Woodpecker nest cavities may be found. Nest trees are marked with white paint.

Fisheating Creek Wildlife Management Area is just south of Lake Wales Ridge. This WMA consists of 18,272 acres of cypress swamp and oak hammock along 40 miles of Fisheating Creek, which flows into Lake Okeechobee. Both Swallow-tailed Kite and Short-tailed Hawk nest in the vicinity of the creek. As much as 50 percent of the U.S. population of Swallow-tailed Kite may roost during fall migration on a section of the creek between US 27 and Lake Okeechobee. Though this area is currently off-limits to the public in order to protect the kites, a proposed observation platform may one day allow distant views of the roost. The creek is most easily explored by canoe, which may be rented at Fisheating Creek State Campground on US 27 in Palmdale. Check water levels, which vary seasonally, before disembarking. Watch for Prothonotary Warbler (in summer), Wild Turkey, Barred Owl, Pileated Woodpecker, Limpkin, and other wading birds along the creek. A few families of Florida Scrub-Jay can be found in scrub habitat southwest of Fisheating Creek. To reach this area from the campground, drive south on US 27, then east 0.8 mile to State Road 29. Turn right and drive south 0.7 mile to County Road 74. Turn right and drive west 1.2 miles to where scrub begins on the south side of the road. The jays will often perch on the fence or trees along the road. Watch for Crested Caracara in surrounding dry prairie.

Lake June in Winter Scrub State Park, which opened to the public in 1999, consists of 845 acres of scrub and pine flatwoods along 3,500-acre Lake June in Winter, located north of Lake Placid. The lake was originally called Lake Stearns but was renamed in 1927 at the request of Dr. Melvil Dewey (inventor of the Dewey decimal system for cataloging library books), who built a resort in the area for his wealthy and winter-weary friends. Watch for Osprey and Bald Eagle over the lake. Florida Scrub-Jay is a common resident in the park and is often seen perched on wires along Daffodil Road, near the park entrance. A nature trail begins at the parking area and leads through scrub and along a blackwater creek. Lake Istokpoga, located east of Lake Placid, is, at 27,692 acres, the fifth-largest natural lake in Florida. The lake attracts waterfowl in winter and wading birds, including Limpkin, year-round. In December 1997 a Northern Lapwing was discovered in a wet pasture on the east side of the lake. **Istokpoga Park,** a 38-acre county park on the north side of the lake, provides public access. A boardwalk parallels the boat-launch area and provides views of the lake. Check live oak and cypress trees between the parking area and the lake for migrant and wintering land birds.

At 54,000 acres bordering the east side of the Kissimmee River, **Kissimmee Prairie Preserve State Park,** located north of Lake Okeechobee and east of Avon Park Air Force Range, is the largest tract of unaltered dry prairie remaining in Florida. This habitat, a seemingly endless sea of grasses and saw palmettos with occasional patches of freshwater wetlands, cabbage palm islands, and oak hammocks, once stretched from Lake Okeechobee to Orlando. Florida's dry prairies have now been converted almost entirely to cattle ranches and citrus groves. To simulate lightning fires that for thousands of years have naturally maintained dry prairie habitat, ranchers use controlled burns to maintain pastureland for cattle. Fortunately, these prescribed burns also ensure that this habitat remains suitable for native species. As you drive past ranches outside the park, watch at any time of year for Crested Caracara perched on snags or fence posts, Sandhill Crane in wet areas, and Bald Eagle overhead. In winter Northern Harrier can often be found coursing over pastureland. Burrowing Owl nests in a pasture on the west side of the road just before the park entrance.

After entering the park, drive north on the main park road, here called Peavine Trail. Species likely along this road include Wild Turkey, Northern Bobwhite, Common Ground-Dove, Loggerhead Shrike, Eastern Towhee, and Eastern Meadowlark. After 2.7 miles the road bends and becomes Military Grade. Vehicles are not allowed any farther north on Peavine Trail. Park on the right and walk a short distance to where the road crosses Seven-mile Slough, the most easily accessible wetland area in the park. A variety of wading birds can often be found here, including Black-crowned Night-Heron and Wood Stork. Watch for King Rail and Wilson's Snipe along the edges of the slough. Search for wintering and migrant land birds in the surrounding oaks. White-tailed Kite has been spotted along Sevenmile Slough, albeit in an area that requires a hike through the prairie. A trail that begins near the office at the park entrance provides access to this area. White-tailed Kite has nested in other areas of the park. Reaching these areas usually involves a lengthy hike. Call the park to request information on nest sites before you visit. Beyond Sevenmile Slough, Peavine Trail continues north for several miles. A side trail about 1 mile north of Sevenmile

Slough provides access to the northern interior of the park. Burrowing Owl can occasionally be found along the first mile or so of this trail. Bachman's Sparrow and the federally endangered Florida race of Grasshopper Sparrow can be found in suitable habitat along both Peavine Trail and Military Grade. Bachman's Sparrow prefers open areas of saw palmetto and is most easily found in spring when males sing from exposed perches. The Florida race of Grasshopper Sparrow favors dry, undisturbed areas of wire grass. Its high-pitched, buzzy song and secretive nature may make finding this species more of a challenge. Early morning is best. Keep in mind that the eastern race of Grasshopper Sparrow can be found here in winter, though these birds are just as likely to be found in disturbed areas such as pastures and along roadsides. During winter Henslow's Sparrow inhabits flooded areas of wire grass. Le Conte's Sparrow has also been recorded in similar habitat within the park. The park campground is in an oak hammock on Military Grade, 1.5 miles west of Peavine Trail. Check the hammock for Barred Owl as well as wintering and migrant land birds. A trail that begins at the campground leads through the southern interior of the park. Sections of this trail may be underwater through much of the year. Beyond the campground Military Grade is closed to vehicles, but it may be hiked several miles to the Kissimmee River along the western border of the park. In April 2003 a Short-eared Owl was seen west of the campground and south of Military Grade.

General information: Archbold Biological Station (no entrance fee) is open daily from 8:00 A.M. to 5:00 P.M. Complete a visitor application form in the main office. Restrooms are located in the main office. Lake June in Winter Scrub (entrance fee) and Kissimmee Prairie Preserve (no entrance fee) State Parks are open daily from 8:00 A.M. until sunset. A primitive restroom at Lake June in Winter Scrub is located in the picnic area. Restrooms at Kissimmee Prairie Preserve are located near the campground. Istokpoga Park and Platt Branch Wildlife and Environmental Area (no entrance fees) and Fisheating Creek Wildlife Management Area (entrance fee at campground) are open daily from sunrise to sunset. Restrooms at Istokpoga Park are located near the parking area. No restrooms are available at Platt Branch. Restrooms at Fisheating Creek are located in the campground.

DeLorme grid: Page 95, D-2; page 100, C-2, D-2; page 106, A-2.

Hazards: Keep a safe distance from alligators. Venomous snakes are present but rarely encountered. Trails may be flooded in summer. Kissimmee Prairie Preserve was used during World War II for bomber pilot training. Unexploded bombs are still a possibility! Do not touch any suspicious object. You are unlikely to encounter ordnance if you stay on trails. Avoid dehydration, sunburn, and other sun-related hazards in this very open habitat.

Nearest food, gas, lodging: In Lake Placid and Okeechobee.

Camping: Fisheating Creek State Campground: 250 sites. Kissimmee Prairie Preserve State Park: 35 sites. Private campgrounds are in Lake Placid.

For more information: Archbold Biological Station, P.O. Box 2057, Lake Placid, FL 33862; (863) 465-2571; www.archbold-station.org. Platt Branch Wildlife and Environmental Area and Fisheating Creek Wildlife Management Area, c/o Florida Fish and Wildlife Conservation Commission, 620 S. Meridian St., Tallahassee, FL 32399; (800) 955-8771; www.floridaconservation.org. Lake June in Winter Scrub State Park, 5931 Hammock Rd., Sebring, FL 33872; (863) 386-6099; www.floridastateparks.org/lakejunein winter. Kissimmee Prairie Preserve State Park, 33104 NW 192nd Ave., Okeechobee, FL 34972; (863) 462-5360; www.floridastateparks.org/kissimmeeprairie.

14 Palm Bay/Sebastian Area

Habitats: Hardwood swamp, pine flatwoods, sand-hills, oak/sand pine scrub, cypress swamp, wet prairie, freshwater impoundments, salt marsh, mangrove forest, maritime hammock, sandy beach.

Specialty birds: *Resident:* Black-bellied Whistling-Duck, Fulvous Whistling-Duck, Mottled Duck, Magnificent Frigatebird, Reddish Egret, Wood Stork, Snail Kite, Bald Eagle, King Rail, Purple Gallinule, Limpkin, Sandhill Crane, American Oystercatcher, Red-cockaded Woodpecker, Florida Scrub-Jay, Brown-headed Nuthatch, Bachman's Sparrow. *Summer:* Roseate Spoonbill, Swallow-tailed Kite, Least Tern, Chuck-will's-widow. *Winter:* Painted Bunting. *Migrant:* Yellow-throated Vireo, Prothonotary Warbler.

Best times to bird: April, late August to mid-October at Turkey Creek; November through March elsewhere.

Directions: *Turkey Creek Sanctuary:* From I-95 west of Palm Bay, exit at County Road 514 (Malabar Road, exit 173). Drive east 0.5 mile to Babcock Street. Turn left and drive north 1.4 miles to Port Malabar Boulevard. Turn right and drive east 1 mile to Santiago Road. Turn right and drive south to the parking area opposite the sanctuary entrance. *Malabar Scrub Sanctuary:* Backtrack to Malabar Road, turn left, and drive east 2.3 miles to the entrance. *St. Sebastian River Preserve State Park:* Return to Babcock Street, turn left, and drive south 13.6 miles to the park entrance at Buffer Preserve Drive. From I-95 west of Sebastian, exit at County Road 512 (Fellsmere Road, exit 156). Drive west 2.8 miles to County Road 507 (Broadway Street) in Fellsmere. Turn right and drive north 4.3 miles to the entrance. *Pelican Island National Wildlife Refuge:* From I-95 west of Sebastian, exit at CR 512. Drive east 2.4 miles to County Road 510. Turn right and drive south, then east 8.5 miles to SR A1A. Turn left and drive north 3.7 miles to the refuge entrance. *Sebastian Inlet State Park:* Continue north 3.3 miles on State Road A1A to the park entrance.

The Birding

Turkey Creek Sanctuary is one of the most heavily birded migrant traps on the east coast of Florida. And with good reason: The sanctuary includes within its 113 acres a variety of habitats, all easily accessible by an extensive boardwalk and trail system. Well over 30 species of warblers have been recorded in the sanctuary, including Blue-winged, Golden-winged, Tennessee, Chestnut-sided, Bay-breasted, Cerulean, Prothonotary, Swainson's, Kentucky, Connecticut, Hooded, and Wilson's. Fall migration, which usually peaks in early October, brings the greatest warbler diversity. Begin your visit at the Margaret Hames Nature Center, just inside the sanctuary entrance. From the nature center, a trail leads east to a gate that is locked at dusk. Beyond the gate the trail splits off in several directions. To the right is a 0.8-mile jogging trail through mostly open, weedy, and brushy terrain. To the left is the Sand Pine Ridge Trail, which passes through pineland habitat. Continue straight onto a 1.3-mile boardwalk that winds through wet hammock and along Turkey Creek. The boardwalk splits in two directions just past a gazebo. To the left the 0.7-mile Creek Overlook Trail continues east along Turkey Creek before connecting with the Sand Pine Ridge Trail. To the right the 0.4-mile Hammock Loop Trail leads south along the creek through wet and transitional hammock. A dirt path at the southern end of the loop leads to the McKinnons Way Nature Trail, which in turn connects with the southern end of the jogging trail.

As you explore the sanctuary, search year-round in the vicinity of Turkey Creek for Wood Duck, Red-shouldered Hawk, Eastern Screech-Owl, Barred Owl, Pileated, Downy, and occasionally Hairy Woodpecker, Great Crested Flycatcher, White-eyed Vireo, and Carolina Wren. Watch overhead for Osprey and Bald Eagle. Check this area in winter for Belted Kingfisher, Yellow-bellied Sapsucker, Ruby-crowned Kinglet, Blue-headed Vireo, and Black-and-white Warbler. Scan the creek itself for telltale bubbles of wintering West Indian manatees. Flocks of wintering Pine Warbler can often be observed while hiking the Sand Pine Ridge Trail. Search weedy and brushy areas where the jogging trail meets the McKinnons Way Nature Trail for Eastern Phoebe, House Wren, Painted Bunting, and wintering sparrows including Chipping, Field, White-throated, and White-crowned. Wild Turkey has been seen on occasion in this area. A Black-headed Grosbeak was found here in October 2002. Though birds could be found anywhere during migration, including around the nature center, concentrate on areas along Turkey Creek, the McKinnons Way Nature Trail, and the aforementioned weedy and brushy area at the end of the jogging trail. In addition to warblers, search for Chuck-will's-widow, a variety of flycatchers, including any of the eastern Empidonax flycatchers, plus vireos, thrushes, tanagers, grosbeaks, buntings, and orioles. Migrating birds of prey to watch for include Sharp-shinned, Cooper's, and Broad-winged Hawk. During spring and summer look for Swallow-tailed Kite soaring overhead.

The neighboring **Malabar Scrub Sanctuary** has an extensive trail system through 395 acres of oak and sand pine scrub, pine flatwoods, and wet prairie. Trail maps are available at a kiosk near the entrance. Florida Scrub-Jay is resident and can be found in scrub along the east side of a paved road that bisects the sanctuary. Northern Bobwhite, Common Ground-Dove, Great Horned Owl, Northern Flicker, Eastern Towhee, and other pineland species may be seen by hiking trails through pine flatwoods farther east. A series of ponds on the west side of the sanctuary should be checked for wading birds, waterfowl, and Sandhill Crane.

St. Sebastian River Preserve State Park provides opportunities to search for Red-cockaded Woodpecker and other sought-after pineland species in a location surprisingly close to the interstate. Begin your tour at the visitor center on Buffer Preserve Drive, 0.6 mile east of the entrance. Maps of the park and trail information are available at a kiosk outside the visitor center. Trails leading to Red-cockaded Woodpecker colonies can be found at several locations along Buffer Preserve Drive. Nest trees are marked with white rings. In the northwest section of the park, trails begin at the entrance gate near CR 507, behind the visitor center, and at Scrub-Jay Road, 1.5 miles east of the visitor center. Another mile east, beyond the I–95 overpass, are more trails leading through the northeast section of the park. Several Red-cockaded Woodpecker nest trees within sight of Buffer Preserve Drive can be found between the road to

Snail Kite. PHOTO: LARRY MANFREDI

Horseman's Headquarters, 0.2 mile east of I–95, and Stumper Flat Road, 1 mile farther east. The 2.3-mile Green Trail, which begins at the road to Horseman's Headquarters, passes through these pine flatwoods. Bald Eagle, Wild Turkey, Northern Bobwhite, Brown-headed Nuthatch, Pine Warbler, and Bachman's Sparrow can all be found in this habitat. Areas of oak and sand pine scrub are home to family groups of Florida Scrub-Jay. The 4.3-mile Blue Trail, 1-mile Red Spur Trail, and 1.2-mile Green Spur Trail, all of which begin at Stumper Flat Road, pass through scrub habitat. Both spur trails lead to the north fork of the St. Sebastian River. The 5.3-mile Red Trail and 4.9-mile Yellow Trail also begin on Buffer Preserve Drive and lead deep into the northeast section of the park, through extensive wet prairie, cypress swamp, and wet hammock habitat. Search year-round in wet prairie for Wood Stork and Sandhill Crane. Roseate Spoonbill can be found there in summer. Pileated Woodpecker is resident in cypress swamp, while Swallow-tailed Kite can be seen there during spring and summer. Migrant warblers and other land birds prefer wet hammock. While hiking the Red or Green Trails, also watch for remnants of the elevated railway system built in the early 1900s when these pinelands were being logged.

Buffer Preserve Drive parallels the C-54 Canal, which divides the park into northern and southern sections. Manatees can often be observed in the canal, especially during winter. A manatee observation area is available near Stumper Flat Road. Also in winter watch for American White Pelican in the canal. The southern section of the park can only be accessed from entrances on CR 512. The 11-mile Blue Loop Trail and 12.8-mile Red Loop Trail provide access to the park's southwest quadrant. These trails begin at an entrance 0.8 mile west of I–95. The 9.5-mile White Loop Trail winds through the southeast quadrant. To reach this trail, return to I–95 and continue east 1.8 miles to the entrance. Turn left and drive north 0.8 mile to a kiosk at the trailhead. Biking and horseback riding are also allowed on this trail. Open prairie in this part of the park provides suitable habitat for a variety of raptors. Several spur trails from the White Loop Trail lead east to the south fork of the St. Sebastian River.

West of CR 507, several wetland areas are managed for resident and wintering waterfowl. To reach this area, return to the intersection of CR 507 with the C-54 Canal. Drive west on Fellsmere Grade Road, which begins on the south side of the canal. Watch along the way for Crested Caracara and in summer for Swallow-tailed Kite. The road ends after 6 miles at Fellsmere Grade Recreation Area. To the southwest are Stick Marsh and Blue Cypress Conservation Area, while to the northwest are **T. M. Goodwin Waterfowl Management Area** and Three Forks Marsh Conservation Area. From Fellsmere Grade Recreation Area, only T. M. Goodwin WMA (developed in cooperation with Ducks Unlimited) is accessible to birders. It is open to birders only on days when hunting is not allowed. On select days you may drive the dikes surrounding the impoundments. On other days, only hiking is allowed. Both Black-bellied and Fulvous Whistling-Duck may be found here, joined in winter by a wide variety of ducks and other waterfowl. Additional wintering species include American Bittern, Sora, and Wilson's Snipe. Numerous shorebirds and raptors pass through during migration. Birds to watch for year-round include Least Bittern, Snail Kite, Northern Bobwhite, King Rail, Purple Gallinule, Limpkin, and Sandhill Crane.

On March 14, 1903, President Theodore Roosevelt created the nation's first national wildlife refuge at **Pelican Island.** The refuge was created to safeguard the last rookery for Brown Pelican on the east coast of Florida as well as to protect other wading birds from being slaughtered by plume hunters. This act led to the creation of the national wildlife refuge system, which has since grown to over 500 refuges protecting more than 93 million acres. Only in recent years has this historic refuge become accessible to the public via a 4.5-mile road called Jungle Trail. To view Pelican Island itself, drive 0.6 mile to the Viewing Area parking lot. A paved 0.8-mile path leads to an information kiosk and the Centennial Trail. This elevated wheelchair-accessible boardwalk leads to an observation platform overlooking Indian River Lagoon. Along the boardwalk is a chronological list of every national wildlife refuge created in the last 100 years. From the observation platform, Pelican Island can be seen in the distance. Scan the island for roosting Brown Pelican, Wood Stork, and other wading birds. American Oystercatcher may be seen feeding on nearby oyster bars. Roseate Spoonbill and Reddish Egret can occasionally be found in the vicinity, mostly during the summer months. Wintering species in the lagoon include Common Loon, American White Pelican, Lesser Scaup, and Red-breasted Merganser. Three Brants spent the winter here in 2003. A pond near the Viewing Area parking lot may attract wintering waterfowl, including Hooded Merganser. Pete's Impoundment Foot Trail also begins at the parking lot. Two 2.5-mile loop trails encircle mangrove-fringed salt marsh impoundments. Watch for wading birds and wintering waterfowl in the impoundments, with Least Tern present during summer. Land birds may be in the mangroves during migration and winter. Migrants may also be found in patches of maritime hammock farther along Jungle Trail, which continues south another 4 miles to CR 510. Much of this habitat sustained heavy damage as a result of the hurricanes of 2004. Once on CR 510, turn left and drive east 0.5 mile to return to SR A1A.

Sebastian Inlet State Park is on SR A1A, 3.3 miles north of the entrance to Jungle Trail. The entrance on the south side of the inlet leads to the campground and a boat launch on the Indian River. A Kirtland's Warbler was found in the campground in May 2007, and a Black-headed Gull was discovered near the boat launch in February 2002. A Purple Sandpiper was found along the inlet in January 2006. The entrance on the north side of the inlet provides access to both the Indian River Lagoon and the beach. A nature trail through maritime hammock begins on the lagoon side and should be checked for wintering and migrant land birds. A fishing jetty on the north side of the inlet extends into the Atlantic and provides excellent opportunities for sea-watching. Magnificent Frigatebird is most likely during the summer months. Northern Gannet is a common sight feeding offshore in winter. During periods of persistent easterly winds, watch for other pelagic species, including Sooty, Cory's, and Audubon's Shearwater, Wilson's, Leach's and Band-rumped Storm-Petrel, and Pomarine and Parasitic Jaeger.

General information: Turkey Creek and Malabar Scrub Sanctuaries (no entrance fees) are open daily from 7:00 A.M. until sunset. The Margaret Hames Nature Center is open daily from 9:00 A.M. to 4:00 P.M. Restrooms are available at the nature center and in the public library adjacent to the sanctuary entrance. At Malabar Scrub restrooms are available at the community park adjacent to the sanctuary entrance. St. Sebastian River Preserve State Park (no entrance fee) is open daily from 8:00 A.M. until sunset. The visitor center is open Monday through Friday from 8:00 A.M. to 5:00 P.M. Restrooms are available at the visitor center. Trails may be seasonally flooded. General-public access (by foot, bicycle, horseback, or boat) to T. M. Goodwin Waterfowl Management Area (no entrance fee) is permitted from one hour before sunrise to one hour after sunset on all days when hunting is not allowed. Vehicle access and parking is permitted on Mondays and Thursdays (excluding state holidays) from 9:00 A.M. to 4:00 P.M. Call (321) 726–2862 or visit www.myfwc.com/duck for updated hunting schedules. Restrooms are available at Fellsmere Grade Recreation Area.

Pelican Island National Wildlife Refuge (no entrance fee) is open daily from 7:30 A.M. until sunset. Restrooms are available at the entrance on Jungle Trail. Sebastian Inlet State Park (entrance fee) is open 24 hours a day. Restrooms are available at several locations.

DeLorme grid: Page 88, D-1; page 96, B-2, B-3.

Hazards: Keep a safe distance from alligators. Poison ivy is present on trails in Turkey Creek Sanctuary. Watch for fire ants on impoundment dikes at T. M. Goodwin Waterfowl Management Area.

Nearest food, gas, lodging: In Palm Bay and Sebastian.

Camping: Sebastian Inlet State Park: 51 sites. Primitive campsites are available in St. Sebastian River Preserve State Park. Private campgrounds are in Palm Bay and Sebastian.

For more information: *Turkey Creek Sanctuary,* P.O. Box 060175, Palm Bay, FL 32906; (321) 952-3433. *St. Sebastian River Preserve State Park,* 1000 Buffer Preserve Dr., Fellsmere, FL 32948; (321) 953-5004; www.floridastateparks .org/stsebastian. *T. M. Goodwin Waterfowl Management Area,* c/o Florida Fish and Wildlife Conservation Commission, 620 S. Meridian St., Tallahassee, FL 32399; (800) 955-8771; www .floridaconservation.org. *Pelican Island National Wildlife Refuge,* 1339 20th St., Vero Beach, FL 32960; (561) 562-3909; www.fws.gov/pelican island. *Sebastian Inlet State Park,* 9700 S. SR A1A, Melbourne Beach, FL 32951; (321) 984-4852; www.floridastateparks.org/sebastianinlet.

⑮ Vero Beach/Ft. Pierce Area

Habitats: Freshwater marsh, pine flatwoods, oak/sand pine scrub, oak/cabbage palm hammock, maritime hammock, mangrove forest, sandy beach.

Specialty birds: *Resident:* Mottled Duck, Magnificent Frigatebird, Least Bittern, Reddish Egret, Wood Stork, Bald Eagle, Clapper Rail, King Rail, Purple Gallinule, Sandhill Crane, Florida Scrub-Jay, Brown-headed Nuthatch. *Summer:* Roseate Spoonbill, Least Tern, Chuck-will's-widow, Gray Kingbird.

Best times to bird: October through April.

Directions: *Indian River County Wetlands Treatment Facility:* From I-95 west of Vero Beach, exit at SR 60 (exit 147). Drive east 0.3 mile to 90th Avenue. Turn right and drive south 1.4 miles to Eighth Street. Turn left and drive east 0.6 mile to the entrance. *Oslo Riverfront Conservation Area:* Return to Eighth Street, turn right, and drive east 0.4 mile to 82nd Avenue. Turn left and drive north 1.4 miles to SR 60. Turn right and drive east 7.4 miles to U.S. Highway 1. Turn right and drive south 3.6 miles to Oslo Road. Turn left and drive east 0.1 mile to the parking area. *Indrio Savannahs Natural Area:* Continue south 40 miles on US 1 to Tozour Road. Turn right and drive 0.1 mile to the parking area. From I-95, exit at Indrio Road (exit 138). Drive east 5.8 miles to US 1. Turn left and drive north 0.6 mile to Tozour Road. Turn left and proceed as above. *Ft. Pierce Inlet State Park:* Continue south 4.4 miles on US 1 to SR A1A North. Turn left and drive east 2.2 miles to the park entrance. From I-95 in Ft. Pierce, exit at SR 70 (exit 129). Drive east 4 miles to US 1. Turn left and drive north 3 miles to SR A1A North. Turn right and proceed as above. *Jack Island Preserve State Park:* Continue east, then north 1.4 miles on SR A1A to the park entrance. *Savannas Preserve State Park:* From I-95 west of Port St. Lucie, exit at Midway Road (exit 126). Drive east 5 miles to US 1. Turn right and drive south 5.5 miles to Walton Road. Turn left and drive east 1.8 miles to the park entrance. From the Florida Turnpike, exit at Port St. Lucie Boulevard (State Road 716). Drive east 4 miles to US 1. Turn left and drive north 2 miles to Walton Road. Turn right and proceed as above. *Savannas Recreation Area:* Return to the intersection of US 1 and Midway Road. Drive east 1.3 miles on Midway Road to the entrance.

The Birding

Indian River County Wetlands Treatment Facility, just off I–95 in Vero Beach, is an excellent location for viewing resident wading birds, migrant shorebirds, and wintering waterfowl. From the entrance, drive 0.3 mile to the facility's office. After checking in, drive to the parking area on the south side of the facility buildings and walk west to reach the impoundments. The pond near the parking area usually has a few wintering coots and ducks. A boardwalk and observation platform is located in an impoundment at the southern end of the wetland. Hiking the surrounding levees allows access to other impoundments within the 227-acre facility. Look for Glossy Ibis, Wood Stork, Limpkin, and other wading birds year-round. Sandhill Crane may be seen on the levees or other grassy areas. Check emergent vegetation for Least Bittern, King Rail, and Purple Gallinule. Watch during winter for American Bittern, Sora, and Wilson's Snipe. Scan areas of open water, where resident Mottled Duck is joined in winter by Blue and Green-winged Teal, American Wigeon, Northern Pintail, Northern Shoveler, Hooded Merganser, and other duck species. Exposed mudflats may attract shorebirds, including Black-necked Stilt, American Avocet, yellowlegs, peeps, and dowitchers. Be sure to check out at the office before departing.

At **Oslo Riverfront Conservation Area,** south of downtown Vero Beach, trails meander through 336 acres of oak/cabbage palm hammock and impounded mangrove forest along Indian River Lagoon. The property was home to a slash pine said to be the world's largest. Sadly, this magnificent tree was toppled by a recent hurricane. Search the hammock for Pileated Woodpecker and other resident species, as well as migrant and wintering land birds. From observation platforms accessed along the coastal wetlands trail, scan open areas of the mangrove impoundments for wading birds including Wood Stork and Roseate Spoonbill. Check exposed mudflats for migrant shorebirds and deeper areas for wintering waterfowl. Watch overhead for Osprey and Bald Eagle. Gray Kingbird may be found along this trail during summer. An extensive trail system also provides access to 423-acre **Indrio Savannas Natural Area,** 4 miles south between Vero Beach and Ft. Pierce. Look for wintering waterfowl on the lake near the parking area. Surrounding freshwater wetlands attract a variety of wading birds. Check upland areas for Northern Bobwhite, Pine Warbler, Eastern Towhee, and other pineland species. Florida Scrub-Jay may be found in the few remaining patches of scrub.

Add coastal species to your trip list with a visit to 340-acre **Ft. Pierce Inlet State Park.** From the entrance, drive 1 mile to the beach parking area. Check the beach in any season for Reddish Egret, shorebirds, gulls, and terns. Scan in winter for Northern Gannet feeding offshore. Maritime hammock within the park was heavily damaged by recent hurricanes but may still attract migrant land birds. Access to one section of hammock is via the Coastal Hammock Trail, which begins at the parking area. Mangrove habitat can be explored at nearby **Jack Island Preserve State Park,** consisting of 1,342 submerged and upland acres. From the parking area, cross a footbridge over Ft. Pierce Cut to reach the island, watching for Clapper Rail along mangrove edges. The Marsh Rabbit Run Trail crosses the island, leading to an observation tower overlooking Indian River Lagoon.

With over 5,100 acres, **Savannas Preserve State Park** stretches more than 10 miles from Ft. Pierce to Jensen Beach and contains the largest remaining freshwater marsh in southeast Florida. Begin your visit at the Education Center on Walton Road. A hiking trail that begins here provides access to the western side of the marsh and surrounding pine flatwoods. The trail may also be reached from Sandhill Crane Park, on Scenic Park Drive 0.2 mile west of the Education Center. The marsh may also be explored by canoe, as part of a ranger-led canoe trip or on your own. The canoe-launching area is reached by driving 0.5 mile on a dirt road that begins left of the state park entrance. Marsh residents to watch for include Least Bittern, Wood Stork, King Rail, Purple Gallinule, Sandhill Crane, and Mottled Duck. Bald Eagle is more common in winter, as is a greater variety of waterfowl. In the pine flatwoods watch or listen for Northern Bobwhite, Brown-headed Nuthatch, Pine Warbler, and Eastern Towhee. Pine flatwoods in the southern portion of the park may be accessed from a parking area on Jensen Beach Boulevard. To reach this area, return to US 1. Turn left and drive south 4 miles to Jensen Beach Boulevard. Turn left and drive east 1.3 miles to the parking area. A 1.5-mile hiking trail begins here. Florida Scrub-Jay may be found in oak and sand pine scrub habitat in the southeastern section of the park. The Hawks Bluff Nature Trail provides access. To reach this area, continue east on Jensen Beach Boulevard 0.8 mile to Savanna Road. Turn left and drive north 1.2 miles to the trailhead. There is currently no parking area, though you may park across the street from the trailhead. This trail also provides access to the eastern side of the marsh. **Savannas Recreation Area** allows access to the northern section of the marsh. A hiking trail begins beyond the campground. Look for marsh species listed previously, with Least Bittern usually easier to find here. Canoes may be rented at this location.

General information: Indian River County Wetlands Treatment Facility (no entrance fee) is open Monday through Friday from 7:00 A.M. to 3:30 P.M. and weekends by appointment only. No restrooms are available. Oslo Riverfront Conservation Area and Indrio Savannas Natural Area (no entrance fees) and Savannas Recreation Area (entrance fee) are open daily from sunrise to sunset. Restrooms are only available in the Savannas Recreation Area campground. Ft. Pierce Inlet, Savannas Preserve (entrance fees), and Jack Island Preserve (no entrance fee) State Parks are open daily from 8:00 A.M. until sunset. The Savannas Preserve Education Center is open Wednesday through Sunday from 9:00 A.M. until 5:00 P.M. Restrooms are available at the Education Center, the canoe-launching area, and the Jensen Beach Boulevard parking area. Restrooms at Ft. Pierce Inlet are located in the picnic area and on beach-access boardwalks. No restrooms are available at Jack Island Preserve.

DeLorme grid: Page 96, D-3; page 103, A-1, B-1.

Hazards: Keep a safe distance from alligators. Mosquitoes are present, especially in summer. Trails at all locations may be seasonally flooded.

Nearest food, gas, lodging: In Vero Beach, Ft. Pierce, Jenson Beach, and Port St. Lucie.

Camping: Savannas Recreation Area: 48 sites.

For more information: *Indian River County Wetlands Treatment Facility,* c/o Indian River County Department of Utility Services, 1840 25th St., Vero Beach, FL 32960; (772) 770-5045. *Oslo Riverfront Conservation Area,* c/o St. Johns River Water Management District, P.O. Box 1429, Palatka, FL 32178; (386) 329-4500. *Indrio Savannas Natural Area,* c/o St. Lucie County Environmental Resources Department, 6120 Glades Cutoff Rd., Ft. Pierce, FL 34981; (772) 462-2526; www.co.st-lucie.fl.us/erd. *Ft. Pierce Inlet and Jack Island Preserve State Parks,* 905 Shorewinds Dr., Ft. Pierce, FL 34949; (772) 468-3985; www.floridastateparks.org/fort pierceinlet. *Savannas Preserve State Park,* 9551 Gumbo Limbo Lane, Jensen Beach, FL 34957; (772) 340-7530; www.floridastateparks.org/ savannas. *Savannas Recreation Area,* 1400 E. Midway Rd., Ft. Pierce, FL 34982; (800) 789-5776.

16 Hobe Sound Area

Habitats: Freshwater marsh, cypress swamp, pine flatwoods, oak/cabbage palm hammock, coastal scrub, mangrove forest.

Specialty birds: *Resident:* Mottled Duck, Least Bittern, Wood Stork, Snail Kite, Bald Eagle, Purple Gallinule, Limpkin, Sandhill Crane, Red-cockaded Woodpecker, Florida Scrub-Jay, Bachman's Sparrow. *Summer:* Roseate Spoonbill, Swallow-tailed Kite, Least Tern, Chuck-will's-widow, Gray Kingbird. *Winter:* Short-tailed Hawk, Virginia Rail, Painted Bunting.

Best times to bird: October through April.

Directions: *Jonathan Dickinson State Park:* From Interstate 95 in Hobe Sound, exit at County Road 708 (exit 96). Drive east 6.3 miles to U.S. Highway 1. Turn right and drive south 4.5 miles to the park entrance. From I-95 in Jupiter, exit at Indiantown Road (exit 87), drive east 4 miles to US 1, turn left, and drive north 5 miles to the park entrance. *Hobe Sound National Wildlife Refuge:* Headquarters is 2.3 miles north of the state park entrance on US 1. To reach the beach area, continue north on US 1 another 2.2 miles to CR 708. Turn right and drive east 1.7 miles to the parking area. *Peck Lake Park:* Return to US 1, turn right, and drive north 3 miles to Osprey Street. Turn right and drive east 0.6 mile to Gomez Avenue. Turn left and drive north 0.2 mile to the park entrance. *DuPuis Management Area:* From I-95 in Hobe Sound, exit at CR 708. Drive west 4.8 miles to State Road 76. Turn left and drive west 15 miles to Gate 1, the entrance to the auto tour road. Continue west 1 mile on SR 76 to Gate 2, the trailhead for the preserve's hiking trails. Another 1.5 miles west is the visitor center, at Gate 5. From I-95 in Stuart, exit at SR 76 (Kanner Highway, exit 101). Drive west 19.5 miles to Gate 1. *J. W. Corbett Wildlife Management Area:* From Gate 1, backtrack 5.5 miles on SR 76 to State Road 710. Turn right and drive south 7.6 miles to the north check station entrance, on the west side of the road just before reaching County Road 706. *Grassy Waters Preserve:* Continue south 15.2 miles on SR 710 to Northlake Boulevard. Turn right and drive west 1 mile to the main (south) entrance. The north entrance is 0.2 mile farther west. From I-95 in Palm Beach Gardens, exit at Northlake Boulevard (exit 77). Drive west 5.4 miles to the main entrance. *Hungryland Boardwalk and Trail:* Continue west 7.3 miles on Northlake Boulevard to Pratt Whitney Road. Turn right and drive north 2.8 miles (the pavement ends after 1 mile). Turn left and drive west 0.8 mile, past the J. W. Corbett WMA south check station on the left and Everglades Youth Camp on the right, to the trailhead parking area.

The Birding

Jonathan Dickinson State Park is named after a Quaker merchant who shipwrecked off the Hobe Sound coast in 1696. The park consists of over 11,500 acres, much of it along the Loxahatchee River, Florida's first federally designated Wild and Scenic River. Coastal sand pine scrub, a preferred habitat of the Florida Scrub-Jay, predominates at higher elevations in the eastern section of the park. Trails through this habitat begin at a parking area near the entrance station. The hurricanes of 2004 severely damaged many of the pines in this already rare and endangered habitat. At the T intersection 0.1 mile beyond the entrance station, turn left to reach the Pine Grove Campground. The Australian pines that predominated here were all toppled by the 2004 hurricanes, providing the park with

SOUTHEAST

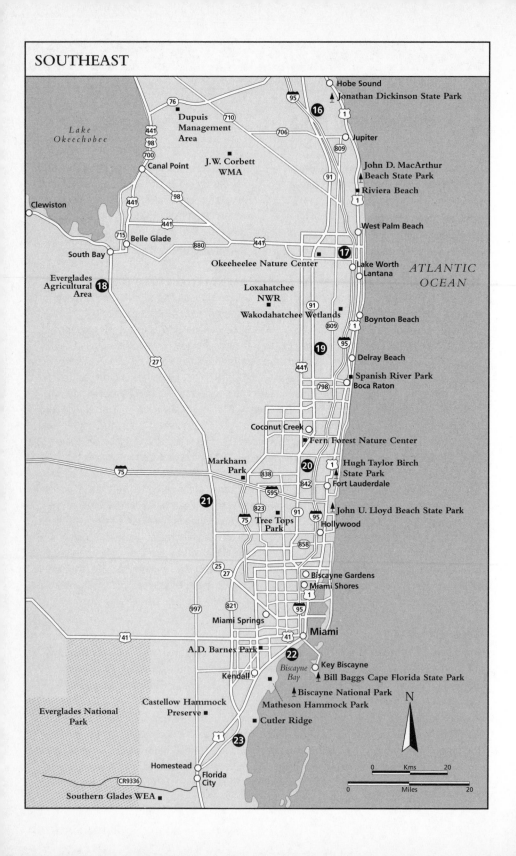

Lake Okeechobee

Clewiston

76

Dupuis Management Area

710

441
98
700

Canal Point

J.W. Corbett WMA

441

98

441

715

Belle Glade

South Bay

880

441

Everglades Agricultural Area **18**

Okeeheelee Nature Center

Loxahatchee NWR

Wakodahatchee Wetlands

91

809

19

27

441

798

Coconut Creek

Fern Forest Nature Center

Markham Park

75

838

21

595

823

75

Tree Tops Park

91

95

858

25
27

Biscayne Gardens
Miami Shores

1

997

821

95

Miami Springs

41

A.D. Barnes Park

Kendall

41

22

Everglades National Park

Castellow Hammock Preserve

Cutler Ridge

1

23

Homestead

CR9336

Florida City

Southern Glades WEA

Hobe Sound

95

Jonathan Dickinson State Park

16

1

706

Jupiter

809

91

John D. MacArthur Beach State Park

1

Riviera Beach

West Palm Beach

17

Lake Worth
Lantana

ATLANTIC OCEAN

809

1

Boynton Beach

95

Delray Beach

Spanish River Park
Boca Raton

Hugh Taylor Birch State Park

1

842

Fort Lauderdale

John U. Lloyd Beach State Park

Hollywood

20

Key Biscayne

Biscayne Bay

Bill Baggs Cape Florida State Park

Biscayne National Park

Matheson Hammock Park

Miami

N

Kms
0   20

Miles
0   20

an opportunity to restore this area to a more natural state. A wetland area on the right just before the campground may attract wading birds. A mountain-bike trail system winds through the scrub on the west side of the main park road. One access point is near the T intersection. To reach another access point, turn right at the T intersection and drive 0.8 mile to a parking area just before a railroad crossing. A walk on any of these trails may produce Florida Scrub-Jay, Eastern Towhee, and other scrub species. Halfway between the T intersection and the railroad crossing, a spur road to the north leads 0.5 mile to an observation tower atop Hobe Mountain. A boardwalk leads through coastal sand pine scrub to the tower. A climb to the top provides dramatic views of the entire park, the Intracoastal Waterway, and the Atlantic Ocean. Watch for raptors including Bald Eagle soaring over the park. Actually an ancient sand dune, Hobe Mountain rises 86 feet above sea level, one of the highest points of land in South Florida! Along this road you may also see evidence of Camp Murphy, the radar-training school built here during World War II.

Return to the main park road and continue west 1 mile beyond the railroad tracks. The road bisects a narrow cypress strand here, and a short boardwalk paralleling the road provides access. Check for migrant land birds in the cypress and alligators in areas of deeper water. Beyond this point the road passes through pine flatwoods and marshy areas. After 1.7 miles turn left to reach the River Campground. Continue on the main park road 0.1 mile to reach the picnic area along the Loxahatchee River. Mangroves predominate at this brackish-water section of the river. Explore the cypress swamp farther upriver on the 44-passenger *Loxahatchee Queen II* or by rented canoe. Traveling by boat is the only way to reach the Trapper Nelson Interpretive Site, the restored homestead of a 1930s trapper who became known as the "Wildman of the Loxahatchee." Park staff provides tours of the site, once known as "Trapper's Jungle Gardens and Wildlife Zoo." Watch for Limpkin and Pileated Woodpecker along the way. The Wilson Creek and Kitching Creek Trails begin at the picnic area parking lot. These loop trails pass through pine flatwoods and cypress strands along two tributaries of the Loxahatchee River. The longer Kitching Creek Trail, named in honor of the family who bought the surrounding land in 1886, begins after crossing Wilson Creek. Look for Bachman's Sparrow in open pinelands with an understory of saw palmetto. Other pineland species to watch for include Northern Bobwhite, Northern Flicker, Pine Warbler, and Eastern Towhee. Red-cockaded Woodpecker was last observed in this area in the early 1980s.

The headquarters of **Hobe Sound National Wildlife Refuge** is north of the state park entrance on the east side of US 1. The 0.4-mile Sand Pine Scrub Oak Trail begins opposite the Interpretive Museum. Look for Florida Scrub-Jay and other scrub species here year-round. Gray Kingbird may be found here during summer. The refuge includes a public-access beach area; look here for Least Tern in summer and a variety of shorebirds during the winter months. Refuge beaches also provide nesting habitat for leatherback, green, and loggerhead turtles. **Peck Lake Park** is a small county park north of the refuge. A boardwalk leads from pine flatwoods through mangrove swamp to the Intracoastal Waterway, here known as Peck Lake. In October 2004 a Red-breasted Nuthatch was found with Pine Warbler in the pinelands adjacent to the parking area.

The site of a former livestock ranch, **DuPuis Management Area** is almost 22,000 acres of pine flatwoods, wet prairies, marshes, and cypress swamps. Access is provided via a 7.5-mile auto tour road that begins at Gate 1. Twenty-two miles of hiking trails begin at the Gate 2 trailhead. Forty miles of horse trails begin at the Gate 3 equestrian center. The visitor center at Gate 5 has indoor and outdoor interpretive displays, a butterfly garden, and a constructed wetland. Habitat along the auto tour road is primarily pine flatwoods and restored marsh. An interpretive brochure is available at the entrance. A spur of the Florida Trail leading to J. W. Corbett Wildlife Management Area can be accessed from auto tour stop 8. The road ends at a fishing pier on the L-8 Canal. Typical species seen along this route are Wild Turkey, Northern Bobwhite, Downy Woodpecker, Carolina Wren, Pine Warbler, and Eastern Towhee. Several pairs of Bald Eagle nest in the area. The open pine flatwoods around auto tour stop 3 are being managed for the reintroduction of Red-cockaded Woodpecker, which still breeds in the adjacent Corbett Wildlife Management Area. In addition to prescribed burns and vegetation removal to restore this habitat, nest-cavity boxes have been inserted into select pine trees (marked with white bands) in preparation for relocation of breeding pairs to this site. The 60,000-acre **J. W. Corbett Wildlife Management Area** is heavily used by hunters. Except for the Hungryland Boardwalk and Trail area, which is off-limits to hunters, birders should avoid this area during hunting season. In addition to Red-cockaded Woodpecker, species known to breed here include Least Bittern, Bald Eagle, Wild Turkey, Northern Bobwhite, King Rail, Purple Gallinule, Sandhill Crane, Eastern Kingbird, Eastern Bluebird, and Bachman's Sparrow. The 1.2-mile **Hungryland Boardwalk and Trail** passes through pine flatwoods, sawgrass marsh, oak/cabbage palm hammock, and cypress swamp. Species typically seen or heard here include Barred and Eastern Screech-Owl, Pileated Woodpecker, Tufted Titmouse, and Carolina Wren. Watch overhead for Swallow-tailed Kite in summer and Short-tailed Hawk almost any time of year. This area can be excellent for land birds during migration.

The 20-square-mile West Palm Beach Water Catchment Area is now accessible to the public as **Grassy Waters Preserve.** In addition to providing drinking water to over 130,000 people in the West Palm Beach area, the marsh, cypress swamp, and wet pine flatwoods of Grassy Waters provide excellent habitat for wildlife. The main entrance, on the south side of Northlake Boulevard, has a visitor center and 0.6-mile wheelchair-accessible boardwalk. Canoes may be rented for further exploration of the preserve. Hiking trails are available at the north entrance. Resident species to watch for in the preserve include Least Bittern, Wood Stork, Snail Kite, Bald Eagle, Purple Gallinule, Limpkin, and Sandhill Crane. Least Tern feeds here during the summer months.

General information: Jonathan Dickinson State Park (entrance fee) is open daily from 8:00 A.M. until sunset. Hobe Sound National Wildlife Refuge (entrance fee at Beach Area, no entrance fee at Headquarters Area) is open daily from sunrise to sunset. The Interpretive Museum at Headquarters Area is open Monday through Friday from 9:00 A.M. to 3:00 P.M. Peck Lake Park (no entrance fee) is open daily from sunrise to sunset. Restrooms are available at all locations. The auto tour road and hiking trails at DuPuis Management Area (no entrance fee) are open 24 hours a day. The visitor center is open Tuesday through Friday from 8:00 A.M. to 4:00 P.M. Restrooms are available at the visitor center. A daily-use permit ($3.00, available at check stations) is required to enter J. W. Corbett Wildlife Management Area, except for Hungryland Boardwalk and through-hiking the Florida Trail. No restrooms are available. Seasonal hunting is permitted at DuPuis Management Area and J. W. Corbett WMA. Refer to regulations-summary brochures, updated annually and available at check stations, for hunt dates and locations. Wear blaze orange if hiking during hunting season. Trails at both locations may be seasonally flooded. Grassy Waters Preserve (no entrance fee) is open Monday through Saturday from 8:00 A.M. to 4:00 P.M. and Sunday from 9:00 A.M. to 5:00 P.M. The nature center is closed on Monday. Restrooms are available in the parking area and visitor center.

DeLorme grid: Page 103, D-2; page 109, B-1.

Hazards: Keep a safe distance from alligators. Eastern diamondback rattlesnakes and cotton-mouths are present but rarely encountered. Mosquitoes can be bothersome in summer.

Nearest food, gas, lodging: In Hobe Sound, Jupiter, and Palm Beach Gardens.

Camping: Jonathan Dickinson State Park: 135 sites at two campgrounds. Private campgrounds are in Palm Beach Gardens and West Palm Beach.

For more information: *Jonathan Dickinson State Park,* 16450 SE Federal Hwy., Hobe Sound, FL 33455; (800) 326–3521; www.floridastateparks .org/jonathandickinson. *Hobe Sound National Wildlife Refuge,* 13640 SE Federal Hwy., Hobe Sound, FL 33455; (772) 546–6141; www.fws .gov/hobesound. *DuPuis Management Area,* 23505 SW Kanner Hwy., Canal Point, FL 33438; (561) 924–5310. *J. W. Corbett Wildlife Management Area,* c/o Florida Fish and Wildlife Conservation Commission, 620 S. Meridian St., Tallahassee, FL 32399; (800) 955–8771; www.floridaconservation.org. *Grassy Waters Preserve,* 8264 Northlake Blvd., West Palm Beach, FL 33412; (561) 627–8831; www.grassywaters preserve.com.

 # West Palm Beach Area

Habitats: Sandy beach, coastal dunes, coastal scrub, mangrove forest, maritime hammock, pine flatwoods, freshwater marsh.

Specialty birds: *Resident:* Mottled Duck, Least Bittern, Wood Stork, Limpkin, Purple Gallinule, Sandhill Crane, Florida Scrub-Jay. *Summer:* Magnificent Frigatebird, Roseate Spoonbill, Swallow-tailed Kite, Least Tern, Chuck-will's-widow. *Winter:* Painted Bunting. *Migrant:* Peregrine Falcon.

Best times to bird: All year.

Directions: *Jupiter Ridge Natural Area:* From I-95 in Jupiter, exit at Indiantown Road (exit 87). Drive east 4 miles to US 1. Turn right and drive south 1.3 miles to the parking area. *Juno Dunes Natural Area:* Continue south 2.2 miles on US 1 to the parking area. *Frenchman's Forest Natural Area:* Continue south 2.8 miles on US 1 to PGA Boulevard. Turn right and drive west 0.6 mile to Prosperity Farms Road. Turn right and drive north 0.7 mile to the parking area. From I-95 in Palm Beach Gardens, exit at PGA Boulevard (exit 79). Drive east 2 miles to Prosperity Farms Road. Turn left and proceed as above. *John D. MacArthur Beach State Park:* Return to the intersection of PGA Boulevard and US 1. East of US 1, PGA Boulevard becomes State Road A1A and curves south. Drive south 2 miles on SR A1A to the park entrance. From I-95 in Riviera Beach, exit at Blue Heron Boulevard (exit 76). Drive east 2.8 miles to US 1, where Blue Heron Boulevard becomes SR A1A. Continue east, then north 4 miles to the park entrance. *Okeeheelee Nature Center:* From I-95 in West Palm Beach, exit at Forest Hill Boulevard (exit 66). Drive west 5.5 miles to the park entrance. Drive north on the park road 2 miles to the nature center. *John Prince Park:* From I-95 in Lake Worth, exit at South 6th Street (exit 63). Drive west 1.3 miles to Congress Avenue, turn left, and drive south 0.3 mile to the park entrance. *Hypoluxo Scrub Natural Area:* From I-95 in Lantana, exit at Hypoluxo Road (exit 60). Drive east 0.7 mile to the entrance. *Boynton Inlet:* Continue east on Hypoluxo Road 0.1 mile to US 1, turn left and drive north 0.9 mile to East Ocean Avenue. Turn right and drive east 0.7 mile to SR A1A. Turn right and drive south 2.8 miles to the inlet. Parking is available at Ocean Inlet Park, just south of the inlet on the west side of SR A1A. From I-95 in Boynton Beach, exit at Woolbright Road (exit 56). Drive east 1 mile to SR A1A. Turn left and drive north 2 miles to the inlet. *Seacrest Scrub Natural Area:* From I-95 in Boynton Beach, exit at Woolbright Road. Drive east 0.5 mile to Seacrest Boulevard, turn right, and drive south 1.5 miles to the entrance.

The Birding

Two areas on US 1 in northeastern Palm Peach County contain coastal scrub habitat suitable for Florida Scrub-Jay. At both **Jupiter Ridge** and **Juno Dunes Natural Areas,** wheelchair-accessible nature trails and longer dirt paths provide opportunities for exploration. At Juno Dunes the 1,100-foot Sawgrass Nature Trail and the 1.3-mile Scrub Oak Hiking Trail provide access to scrub and depression marsh habitat. On the east side of US 1, the 1,800-foot Sea Grape Nature Trail crosses over the dunes, passing through maritime hammock, coastal strand, and scrub habitat. At Jupiter Ridge the 1,020-foot Little Blue Heron Nature Trail leads to a mangrove swamp. The 1.7-mile Scrub Lizard Hiking Trail passes through scrub and pine flatwoods habitat. In addition to Florida Scrub-Jay, look for Eastern Towhee year-round at both locations and Painted Bunting in winter. In March 2004 a Black-faced Grassquit was found along the nature trail at Jupiter Ridge. A variety of habitats can be found at **Frenchman's Forest Natural Area,** including pine flatwoods, cypress strand, scrub, freshwater marsh, and tidal marsh. The Blazing Star Trail, a 2,100-foot wheelchair-accessible nature trail, passes through many of these habitats along the southern border of the property. The Saw Palmetto Hiking Trail, a 1.3-mile dirt path, provides access to the remainder of the preserve. Look for a variety of warblers, vireos, and other land birds during migration and in winter. Wild Turkey has also been seen in the area.

John D. MacArthur Beach State Park preserves 174 acres of coastal dune, mangrove, and maritime hammock habitat on Singer Island, a barrier island in North Palm Beach. The Satinleaf Nature Trail begins at the north end of the parking area and loops through maritime hammock, which is attractive to migrant land birds. Caribbean vagrants seen here have included La Sagra's Flycatcher and Western Spindalis. The nature center at the south end of the parking area houses interpretive exhibits describing the park's plant and animal communities. A 1,600-foot wheelchair-accessible boardwalk begins at the nature center and spans mangrove-fringed Lake Worth Cove. At low tide a variety of wading birds, occasionally including Reddish Egret, can be found feeding on exposed mudflats. Roseate Spoonbill and Least Tern are common here during summer. On the beach side of the boardwalk, a trail winds through maritime hammock on the backside of the dunes. Several short boardwalks over the dunes provide access to the beach. Look for gulls, terns, and beach shorebirds year-round and Northern Gannet offshore in winter.

Built on over 900 acres of reclaimed strip mine, Okeeheelee Park has become one of the most popular recreational destinations in the city of West Palm Beach. Only about 90 acres of pine flatwoods in the northern section of the property remained in its original state when the park was acquired in 1973. This area is now the home of the **Okeeheelee Nature Center.** Inside the nature center are interpretive displays, live-animal exhibits, and a gift shop. Behind the facility are feeders that in winter consistently attract Painted and Indigo Bunting. Over 2 miles of trails allow exploration of the surrounding pine flatwoods and wetland areas. A paved, wheelchair-accessible trail leads through the pinelands to viewing areas at two small ponds. Unpaved trails lead to marsh areas good for Wood Duck and other waterfowl. Other species to watch for in the wetland areas include Least Bittern,

Limpkin, and Sandhill Crane. Great Horned Owl and Chuck-will's-widow have nested in the pine flatwoods.

Several areas in the suburbs south of West Palm Beach may be worth a quick stop. **John Prince Park,** just west of I–95 in Lake Worth, is a reliable location for Limpkin. Check the wetland area between the park entrance and Lake Osborne, or the canal along the road leading to the campground. A nature trail through disturbed scrub habitat begins near the campground entrance. Undeveloped patches of scrub habitat can be found just east of I–95 in Boynton Beach. A few families of Florida Scrub-Jay inhabit **Hypoluxo Scrub Natural Area.** The birds will often perch on wires along the western edge of the property. A paved wheelchair-accessible path loops through the preserve. Pine flatwoods attractive to flocks of Pine Warbler and other wintering warblers can be found at **Seacrest Scrub Natural Area.** A Black-throated Gray Warbler was found among a wintering warbler flock in 2005.

Boynton Inlet can be an excellent sea-watch location. A fishing pier on the north side of the inlet provides the best vantage point. In winter watch for flocks of scoters and other waterfowl streaming up or down the coast. Northern Gannet often feed just offshore. During periods of strong easterly winds, scan offshore for Pomarine and Parasitic Jaeger, Cory's and Audubon's Shearwater, Wilson's Storm-Petrel, and possibly Leach's and Band-rumped Storm-Petrel. In recent years a number of rarities have turned up in this location. In November 2001 two immature Sabine's Gulls were spotted in the vicinity of the inlet, while a Purple Sandpiper was found feeding with Ruddy Turnstone along the inlet seawall. In November 2003 a Red-footed Booby was discovered perched on a light pole at the end of the fishing pier. In January 2005 a Razorbill was seen briefly near the mouth of the inlet.

General information: John Prince Park, Ocean Inlet Park and Jupiter Ridge, Juno Dunes, Frenchman's Forest, Hypoluxo Scrub, and Seacrest Scrub Natural Areas (no entrance fees) are open daily from sunrise to sunset. Restrooms are available at John Prince and Ocean Inlet Parks. Portable restrooms are available at Jupiter Ridge. John D. MacArthur Beach State Park (entrance fee) is open daily from 8:00 A.M. to sunset. Restrooms are available at the nature center and at the beach end of the boardwalk. Okeeheelee Nature Center is open Tuesday through Friday from 1:00 to 4:30 P.M., Saturday from 8:15 A.M. to 4:30 P.M., and Sunday from 1:00 to 4:30 P.M. (except Memorial Day through Labor Day). The nature center is closed on Monday. The nature trails at the nature center are open daily from sunrise to sunset. Restrooms are available at the nature center or at picnic areas throughout the park.

DeLorme grid: Page 109, B-3, C-2.

Hazards: Contact with poisonwood or poison ivy may result in a severe rash. Fire ants inflict a painful bite. As is the case when visiting any large metropolitan area, common sense is essential. Birding alone is not recommended. Lock car doors and secure all valuables out of sight.

Nearest food, gas, lodging: In West Palm Beach.

Camping: John Prince Park: 265 sites. Jonathan Dickinson State Park, in Hobe Sound: 135 sites at two campgrounds, 16450 SE Federal Hwy., Hobe Sound, FL 33455; (800) 326-3521. From Jupiter Ridge Natural Area, drive north 6.3 miles on US 1.

For more information: *Jupiter Ridge Natural Area,* 1800 S. US 1, Jupiter, FL 33410; www.pbcgov .com/erm/stewardship/jridge.asp. *Juno Dunes Natural Area,* 14200 US 1, Juno Beach, FL 33408; www.pbcgov.com/erm/stewardship/jdunes.asp. *Frenchman's Forest Natural Area,* 12201 Prosperity Farms Rd., Palm Beach Gardens, FL 33477; www.pbcgov.com/erm/stewardship/french.asp. *John D. MacArthur Beach State Park,* 10900 SR 703 (SR A1A), North Palm Beach, FL 33408;

(561) 624–6950; www.floridastateparks.org/mac arthurbeach. *Okeeheelee Nature Center,* 7715 Forest Hill Blvd., West Palm Beach, FL 33413; (561) 233–1400; www.pbcgov.com/parks. *John Prince Park,* 2700 S. 6th Ave., Lake Worth, FL 33461; (561) 582–7992; www.co.palm-beach .fl.us/parks/locations/johnprince.htm. *Seacrest* *Scrub Natural Area,* 3400 S. Seacrest Blvd., Boynton Beach, FL 33435; www.pbcgov.com/ erm/stewardship/seascrub.asp. *Ocean Inlet Park,* 6990 N. Ocean Blvd., Boynton Beach, FL 33435; (561) 966–6600; www.co.palm-beach.fl.us/ parks/locations/oceaninlet.htm.

18 Everglades Agricultural Area

Habitats: Seasonally flooded agricultural fields, sod farms, freshwater marsh, lakes.

Specialty birds: *Resident:* Black-bellied Whistling-Duck, Fulvous Whistling-Duck, Mottled Duck, Least Bittern, Wood Stork, White-tailed Kite, Snail Kite, Crested Caracara, King Rail, Purple Gallinule, Purple Swamphen, Limpkin, Sandhill Crane, Smooth-billed Ani, Barn Owl. *Summer:* Roseate Spoonbill, Swallow-tailed Kite, Least Tern. *Winter:* Painted Bunting. *Migrant:* America Avocet, Upland Sandpiper, Buff-breasted Sandpiper, Wilson's Phalarope, Gull-billed Tern, Black Tern.

Best times to bird: Late July to early September.

Directions: From I-95 in West Palm Beach, exit at Southern Boulevard (exit 68). Drive west 8.2 miles to U.S. Highway 441. Continue west 11.4 miles on US 441, turning left onto County Road 880, an area known as Twenty Mile Bend, where this tour begins.

The Birding

On the south side of CR 880, beginning 0.8 mile west of the intersection with US 441, is **Stormwater Treatment Area 1W.** Managed by the South Florida Water Management District (SFWMD), this is one of several Stormwater Treatment Areas (STAs) constructed as part of the multibillion-dollar Comprehensive Everglades Restoration Project. These artificial wetlands serve to clean high-nutrient runoff from surrounding sugarcane fields before it enters South Florida's water conservation areas and Everglades National Park. Large numbers of wading birds, waterfowl, and migrating shorebirds are attracted to the wetlands. The STA impoundments are currently open to birders only during regularly scheduled SFWMD-sponsored tours. Flooded areas between CR 880 and the impoundments often attract smaller numbers of the same species. These areas may be viewed from the roadside. Beginning about 7 miles farther west on CR 880, sod farms on the south side of the road should be checked in August and September for Upland Sandpiper and other grass-loving shorebirds, occasionally including Buff-breasted Sandpiper. Puddles in these fields usually attract Pectoral and Stilt Sandpiper and both Greater and Lesser Yellowlegs. Nesting Black-necked Stilt is ubiquitous in summer. Scan rice fields in the area for Fulvous and Black-bellied Whistling-Duck. If time permits, drive side roads in the area, such as Sam Senter Road (near Nine Mile Bend, on the right about 11 miles from the intersection with US 441) and Brown's Farm Road (at Six Mile Bend, on the left 3.7 miles farther west). While most of the agricultural fields will still be planted in sugarcane in August and September, a few will have been harvested then flooded to control nematodes. Any of these flooded fields may attract wading birds, waterfowl, and migrant shorebirds. Several species of tern, including Least, Gull-billed, Black, and Caspian, can be found here in late summer. Scan wires along these roads for Common Nighthawk and swallows, mostly Barn but also including Tree, Bank, Cliff, Northern Rough-winged, and Purple Martin. Rarities reported from this area have included White-tailed Kite, Hudsonian Godwit, Ruff, Wilson's Phalarope, and Couch's/Tropical Kingbird. Be sure to check for NO TRESPASSING signs before driving or walking on any unpaved farm road.

To explore the southern end of Lake Okeechobee, Florida's largest lake, continue west on CR 880 to the town of Belle Glade. In 5.8 miles, bear right onto County Road 717. In 0.5 mile turn right on State Road 80, cross the canal, and turn left onto West Canal Street North. Drive west 3.6 miles to the **Belle Glade Marina and Campground.** The marshes surrounding the campground provide good habitat for Fulvous Whistling-Duck, Least Bittern, and Purple Gallinule. In July 2001 a Black Rail was heard calling from these marshes in the middle of the day! During winter check surrounding shrubby areas for Painted and Indigo Bunting, Blue Grosbeak, and Orchard Oriole. A Vermilion Flycatcher wintered here in 2002. To continue your search for flooded agricultural fields, return to SR 80 and turn right. Drive south 1.3 miles to where the road curves west. Turn right onto County Road 827A and drive south 3.6 miles to where this road curves west and becomes CR 827. Continue west 2.4 miles to U.S. Highway 27. Cross this divided highway and continue west on CR 827, searching for flooded fields on the north side of the road. Look for Limpkin along the canal bordering the south side of the road. Smooth-billed Ani has been seen in brushy areas along both CR 827 and 827A. Other breeding land birds to watch for include Common Ground-Dove, Yellow-billed Cuckoo, Eastern Kingbird, Common Yellowthroat, and Eastern Towhee. Yellow Warbler may be found in this habitat during migration. The pavement ends after 4.7 miles, but this road continues another 3 miles to the Miami Canal. Across the canal is a stand of cypress that Barn Owl uses as a roosting site. A dozen or more owls may be present here during the day. To cross the canal, turn right and drive north to a bridge, then backtrack along Miami Canal Road to the cypress stand. Search for the owls from the dike along the canal. Black-crowned Night-Heron also uses this stand as a day roost. Stay out of the stand to avoid disturbing the owls and other birds. In summer watch for Swallow-tailed Kite soaring over the surrounding fields. White-tailed Kite is also possible here. Additional flooded fields may be found south of CR 827 on both sides of the Miami Canal.

Stormwater Treatment Area 5 is located west of the Miami Canal. To reach this area from the Barn Owl site, drive north 2.8 miles on Miami Canal Road to Rogers Road. Turn left and drive west 4.7 miles to County Road 835. Turn left and drive south 3 miles to where the road curves west. Turn left here onto Blumberg Road. Watch for Crested Caracara and Sandhill Crane in this area. Drive south 11 miles (the pavement ends after 9 miles) to a locked gate. Large flocks of Fulvous and Black-bellied Whistling-Duck have been seen in the impoundments here, along with Wood Duck and several species of wintering waterfowl. Purple Swamphen, accidentally introduced to western Broward County (see "Western Broward County") seems to be spreading to this area. Migrant shorebirds also use the impoundments when flooded. Rarities found here include Ruff and Cinnamon Teal. As is the case with STA 1W, this area is currently open to birders only during regularly scheduled SFWMD-sponsored tours. Flooded fields and sod farms can also be found on US 27 south of CR 827. Drive south on US 27, watching for flooded fields on both sides of the highway. At 7.5 miles scan the sod fields surrounding a radio tower on the west side of the highway. More sod fields can be found on the opposite side of the

Smooth-billed Ani. PHOTO: LARRY MANFREDI

highway. Upland Sandpiper is regular here in August and early September, along with Pectoral and Stilt Sandpiper, both yellowlegs, and other shorebirds and wading birds. Also look for American White Pelican, King Rail, and both whistling-ducks. A pair of Hudsonian Godwit was found here in September 2004. Continue south 14.4 miles to Holey Land Road, on the border of Palm Beach and Broward Counties. Turn right to access **Holey Land Wildlife Management Area.** Much of this marsh habitat can only be accessed by hiking the numerous levees that crisscross the WMA. Black Rail has been found on the north side of Holey Land Road for the first mile or so. As much of this habitat is being converted into a storm-water-treatment area, it has apparently become less suitable for this elusive species.

Drive west along this road, searching in brushy areas for Smooth-billed Ani and other breeding land birds. The pavement ends after 5.5 miles. You will reach the Miami Canal in another 9 miles. Cross over the canal at this point via a water-control structure to access **Rotenberger Wildlife Management Area.** You may drive north 20 miles on Miami Canal Road to return to the Barn Owl site, or backtrack to US 27. If you turn right and drive south on US 27, in 14.7 miles you will reach Interstate 75. Drive east to reach Ft. Lauderdale and Miami, or west to reach Naples.

General information: The Everglades Agricultural Area is mostly privately owned agricultural fields planted in sugarcane, sod, and vegetables. Do not enter any posted or gated areas. Trucks and other vehicles move at a high rate of speed on CR 880 and US 27. Pull completely off the road if birding in these areas. STA 1W tours are arranged through Pine Jog Environmental Education Center in West Palm Beach. For reservations, call (561) 686–6600. STA 5 tours are arranged through Audubon Society of Hendry-Glades. For reservations, call (863) 517–0202 or e-mail sta5birding@earthlink.net. Seasonal hunting is allowed in the Stormwater Treatment Areas and in Holey Land and Rotenberger Wildlife Management Areas (no entrance fee). Restrooms are available only at fast-food restaurants in Belle Glade.

DeLorme grid: Page 107, D-2; page 108, C-1, C-2, C-3; page 114, A-1.

Hazards: Mosquitoes can be bothersome in summer. Keep a safe distance from alligators. Be watchful for sudden thunderstorms in summer.

Nearest food, gas, lodging: In Belle Glade.

Camping: Belle Glade Campground: 350 sites. 110 Dr. Martin Luther King Jr. Blvd. W., Belle Glade, FL 33430; (877) 630-0060.

For more information: *Stormwater Treatment Areas 1W and 5,* c/o South Florida Water Management District; (561) 682-6640; www.sfwmd .gov. *Holey Land and Rotenberger Wildlife Management Areas,* c/o Florida Fish and Wildlife Conservation Commission, 620 S. Meridian St., Tallahassee, FL 32399; (800) 955-8771; www .floridaconservation.org.

 # Delray Beach/Boca Raton Area

Habitats: Sawgrass prairie, freshwater marsh, cypress swamp, maritime hammock, mangrove forest, sandy beach.

Specialty birds: *Resident:* Black-bellied Whistling-Duck, Fulvous Whistling-Duck, Mottled Duck, Least Bittern, Wood Stork, Roseate Spoonbill, Snail Kite, King Rail, Purple Gallinule, Limpkin, Smooth-billed Ani, Chuck-will's-widow, Spot-breasted Oriole.

Summer: Swallow-tailed Kite, Least Tern, Gray Kingbird. *Winter:* Short-tailed Hawk, Virginia Rail, Lesser Nighthawk, Painted Bunting. *Migrant:* Peregrine Falcon, Black-whiskered Vireo, Prothonotary Warbler, Swainson's Warbler, Hooded Warbler.

Best times to bird: October through March for wintering birds, April and September for migrants.

Directions: *Arthur R. Marshall Loxahatchee National Wildlife Refuge:* From Boynton Beach, exit I-95 at Boynton Beach Boulevard (exit 57). Drive west 8.5 miles to US 441. Turn left and drive south 2 miles to Lee Road. Turn right and drive west 0.3 mile to the entrance station. From the Florida Turnpike, exit at Boynton Beach Boulevard (exit 86) and drive west 2 miles to US 441. Turn left and proceed as above. From I-95 in Delray Beach, exit at Atlantic Avenue (exit 52). Drive west 7.2 miles to US 441. Turn right and drive north 3 miles to Lee Road. Turn left and proceed as above. From the Florida Turnpike, exit at Atlantic Avenue (exit 81) and drive west 1.8 miles to US 441. Turn right and proceed as above. To reach the Hillsboro Recreation Area entrance to the refuge from Lee Road, drive south 11.7 miles on US 441 to Loxahatchee Road. Turn right and drive west 6.2 miles to the parking area at the end of the road. *Daggerwing Nature Center (South County Regional Park):* From Loxahatchee Road, return to US 441 and drive north 4.7 miles to Yamato Road. Turn left and drive west 1 mile to the park entrance. Turn left and drive south 1.5 miles to the nature center. From Lee Road, drive south 7 miles on US 441 to Yamato Road. Turn right and drive west 1 mile to the park entrance. *Green Cay Wetlands:* From the Florida Turnpike in Delray Beach, exit at Atlantic Avenue (exit 81). Drive east on Atlantic Avenue 0.7 mile to Hagen Ranch Road. Turn left and drive north 2.2 miles to the entrance. *Wakodahatchee Wetlands:* Backtrack south 1.2 miles to Lake Ida Road. Turn left and drive east 1 mile to Jog Road. Turn left and drive north 0.5 mile to the entrance. From I-95, exit at Atlantic Avenue (exit 52). Drive west 3.7 miles to Jog Road. Turn right and drive north 1.5 miles to the entrance. *Spanish River Park:* From I-95 in Boca Raton, exit at Yamato Road (exit 48). Drive east 1 mile to US 1. Turn right and drive south 0.6 mile to Spanish River Boulevard. Turn left and drive east 0.5 mile to SR A1A. Turn right and drive south 0.3 mile to the park entrance. *Gumbo Limbo Nature Center:* Continue south 1 mile on SR A1A to the entrance. From I-95, exit at Palmetto Park Road (exit 44). Drive east 3 miles to SR A1A. Turn left and drive north 0.8 mile to the entrance.

The Birding

Arthur R. Marshall Loxahatchee National Wildlife Refuge was established in 1951 and renamed to honor South Florida conservationist Arthur R. Marshall in 1986. Most of the refuge is within Water Conservation Area 1, the northernmost of three water-conservation areas in southern Florida maintained to provide water storage and flood control, as well as to provide a habitat for wildlife. Along with Everglades National Park, these water-conservation areas are all that remain of the original Everglades. The Head-quarters Area covers only a small portion of this 147,368-acre refuge and is the only area in the northern half of the refuge that is open for public use. Turn right immediately after the entrance station to reach the visitor center. Inside are interpretive displays and a book-store. Ask for a map and bird checklist at the information desk and check the log for the latest bird sightings. Behind the visitor center is a 400-acre cypress swamp, the largest remaining section of a cypress strand that once separated sawgrass marsh to the west from pine flatwoods to the east. The 0.4-mile wheelchair-accessible Cypress Swamp Boardwalk circles through a small portion of the swamp. Look or listen for Great Horned, Barred, and Eastern Screech-Owl, Pileated Woodpecker, Great Crested Flycatcher, and Carolina Wren. In winter watch for Yellow-bellied Sapsucker, Blue-headed Vireo, and possibly Ruby-crowned Kinglet. The area around the visitor center parking lot should be checked for wintering and migrant land birds.

Return to Lee Road, turn right, then immediately left to reach Compartment C and the Marsh Trail parking area. Compartment C consists of 10 numbered impoundments surrounded by levees. The 0.8-mile Marsh Trail encircles Compartment C-7. An observa-tion tower at the southwest corner of C-7 provides a bird's-eye view of the surrounding impoundments. This trail consists of hard-packed dirt that should be accessible to wheel-chair users with strong upper-body strength. The other nine impoundments are all accessi-ble by foot. Before entering the parking area, check the wires along Lee Road in summer for Gray Kingbird. Flocks of swallows may perch on the wires, mostly Tree, Barn, and Northern Rough-winged but also including Bank in late summer and Cave during win-ter. The water levels, vegetation, and soil in Compartment C impoundments are manipu-lated seasonally to provide feeding and nesting habitat for waterbirds. As you walk the levees, check weedy areas in winter for Painted Bunting and sparrows, mostly Savannah but occasionally Grasshopper and other species. Search areas of emergent vegetation for Purple Gallinule throughout the year. Scan areas of taller marsh grass for Least Bittern, especially in summer, and King Rail year-round. Look here for Marsh Wren and Swamp Sparrow in winter. Also during winter Sora may be seen scurrying between clumps of marsh vegetation. Watch for Wilson's Snipe feeding on exposed patches of mud. These mudflats may attract other shorebirds during migration, including Black-bellied and Semi-palmated Plover, Greater and Lesser Yellowlegs, both Short and Long-billed Dowitcher (best discerned by call), and Solitary, Spotted, Semipalmated, Western, Least, Pectoral, and Stilt Sandpiper. Black-necked Stilt will stay to nest.

In areas of open water, look for Common Moorhen, Mottled Duck, and a variety of wading birds including Wood Stork and occasionally Roseate Spoonbill. Impoundment C-6, adjacent to the parking area, has been a reliable location to find Limpkin. Large num-bers of ducks used to winter in the impoundments. In recent winters only Blue-winged and Green-winged Teal and Ringed-necked Duck have been seen consistently. Still occa-sionally reported are Black-bellied Whistling-Duck, Wood Duck, American Wigeon, Northern Shoveler, Northern Pintail, and Hooded Merganser. A Snow Goose was discovered in Impoundment C-7 in January 2005. Fulvous Whistling-Duck used to be a common sight in the impoundments but has now become scarce. The rare and secretive Masked Duck could once be found here in winter, with nine being seen in February 1977. This species was last reported from the refuge in 1984. Another species once reliably seen in Compartment C but now infrequently reported is Smooth-billed Ani. Small flocks of this strange-looking member of the cuckoo family were once a common sight in areas of tall marsh grass within the impoundments. It's possible that numbers of anis remain in the northern part of the refuge, but in areas closed to public use. Sightings of Snail Kite in Compartment C are also less frequent than in the past. As always, the presence of this beautiful raptor depends on the availability of apple snails upon which they feed. Evening roosts of the kites have been reported in recent years, in particular in the northeast corner of Impoundment C-8. Red-shouldered Hawk is the most common raptor seen in the refuge throughout the year. During winter birders should look for Northern Harrier coursing over the marsh or Short-tailed Hawk soaring overhead. Watch for Swallow-tailed Kite in spring and summer. This heavily birded refuge has had its share of vagrants over the years, notably flycatchers. A Fork-tailed Flycatcher was found here in July 1992. La Sagra's Flycatcher, Cassin's Kingbird, and Couch's/Tropical Kingbird have all been seen in or just outside the refuge. Lesser Nighthawk has wintered in the Headquarters Area in recent years. The nighthawks are best seen at dusk, a risky proposition since you may find yourself locked in by the refuge's automatic gate and facing a hefty fine! Check with refuge personnel before attempting to see these birds.

The southern half of the refuge is accessed from the end of Loxahatchee Road, 12 miles south of the Headquarters Area. Known as the Hillsboro Recreation Area entrance, this area is also a boat-access point for anglers and hunters. A hike on Levee 39, which extends west from the end of Loxahatchee Road and parallels the Hillsboro Canal, may produce Smooth-billed Ani and Snail Kite. Levee 40 forms the eastern border of the refuge and may be hiked or biked the 12 miles north to the Headquarters Area. If in this area in winter or during migration, **Daggerwing Nature Center** in South County Regional Park may be worth a stop. A boardwalk behind the nature center leads through a wet hardwood hammock that attracts a variety of migrant warblers and other land birds. Watch in winter for Painted and Indigo Bunting in weedy areas near the beginning of the boardwalk, and Yellow-bellied Sapsucker, Black-and-white Warbler, and Black-throated Green Warbler within the hammock.

Located adjacent to Palm Beach County's water-reclamation facility in Delray Beach, **Wakodahatchee Wetlands** consists of 50 acres of artificially created freshwater marsh. Every day about one million gallons of highly treated water are pumped into the wetlands, which act as a natural filter for nutrients remaining in the water. Since it opened to the public in 1996, Wakodahatchee has attracted a wide variety of wildlife, including over 150 species of birds. A 0.8-mile wheelchair-accessible boardwalk provides access to the marsh. The boardwalk has become very popular with local residents who use the facility for power walking and jogging. The birds seem to have become accustomed to the crowds and can usually be viewed at close range. Anhingas and herons often perch on the boardwalk railings and allow for outstanding photographic opportunities. Common Moorhen is abundant year-round, joined in winter by American Coot. Purple Gallinule is also common and surprisingly conspicuous. Black-crowned Night-Heron, Glossy Ibis, Wood Stork, and Limpkin are seen consistently here, along with all the common wading birds. Typical land birds include Red-winged Blackbird and Boat-tailed Grackle. An unexpected resident for such a habitat is Spot-breasted Oriole. Usually found in suburban residential areas, the orioles here can sometimes be found perched in vegetation surrounding the parking area, in trees planted along upland sections of the boardwalk, or even on plants in the marsh itself.

During winter a variety of ducks join resident Mottled Duck. Blue-winged Teal is most common and a few Green-winged Teal are usually present. Less frequently seen are Northern Pintail, Northern Shoveler, American Wigeon, and Ring-necked Duck. In recent years a small flock of Black-bellied Whistling-Duck has been spotted regularly. Other wintering species to look for include American Bittern, Sora (often common here), Wilson's Snipe, and occasionally Virginia Rail. Tree and Northern Rough-winged Swallow will be soaring overhead, joined in late winter by Purple Martin and by Barn Swallow during migration. The martins nest in a colorful collection of houses erected for them adjacent to the boardwalk. Swallows often perch on the wires in the parking area. Look for an occasional Cave or Bank Swallow mixed in with the regulars. During the spring and summer months, Least Bittern becomes common and conspicuous, especially after nesting. Common Moorhen chicks will seem to be everywhere you look. Both Anhinga and Great Blue Heron nest in pond apple trees close to the boardwalk. A few Black-necked Stilt have also nested in the wetland in recent years. Migration will bring a greater variety of shorebirds, including Greater and Lesser Yellowlegs and Solitary Sandpiper. A few warblers and other migrant land birds may be found in the trees planted along the upland sections of the boardwalk.

Just west of Wakodahatchee is the significantly larger **Green Cay Wetlands,** which opened to the public in 2005. Originally open prairie and wetlands, this area had been farmed for winter vegetables during the past several decades. About 175 acres have now been transformed to wetlands that, like Wakodahatchee, are helping to filter water from the nearby water-reclamation facility. The Green Cay Nature Center has interpretive displays demonstrating how the wetland plays a part in the area's water purification cycle. Exhibits including an alligator hole and a turtle pond illustrate the marsh's role as a habitat for wildlife. Wheelchair-accessible boardwalks begin at the visitor center and loop through the artificially created wetland. Areas of shallow freshwater marsh have been planted with emergent vegetation attractive to Least Bittern, Limpkin, Common Moorhen, Purple Gallinule, and Sora. Deeper zones of open water appeal to waterfowl, including Mottled Duck, Blue-winged and Green-winged Teal, and Northern Shoveler. Occasionally spotted are Black-bellied Whistling-Duck and Wood Duck. An Eared Grebe wintered here in 2006–7. Exposed mudflats attract migrant shorebirds including Black-necked Stilt, Greater and Lesser Yellowlegs, Pectoral Sandpiper, and Short-billed and Long-billed Dowitcher. Huge numbers of swallows, mostly Tree and Northern Rough-winged, feed over the wetlands in winter. The boardwalks pass through tree islands planted in bald cypress, cabbage palm, and tropical hardwoods that attract migrant and wintering land birds, including Painted Bunting.

Throughout much of the year, birders visiting **Spanish River Park** in Boca Raton can usually find Fish Crow, Red-bellied Woodpecker, Blue Jay, Cardinal, and other common species, but not much else. During spring and fall, though, this small coastal park comes alive with migrant land birds. Over 30 species of warblers have been recorded here in recent years, including Blue-winged, Golden-winged, Chestnut-sided, Blackburnian, Bay-breasted, Cerulean, Swainson's, Kentucky, Connecticut, Mourning, and Wilson's. Black-whiskered Vireo is a regular migrant in spring. Other unusual vireos seen in the park have included Bell's, Warbling, and Philadelphia. On good days expect a wide assortment of flycatchers, thrushes, tanagers, and buntings. Peregrine Falcon and other raptors are often spotted soaring over the park during migration. Its close proximity to the ocean also makes the park an attractive destination for Caribbean vagrants. North America's first record of Cuban Pewee was from this park in March 1995. Other Caribbean birds found here in recent years include Bahama Mockingbird, Bananaquit, and Western Spindalis. Though Australian pines dominate the park landscape, some native vegetation is still present, especially along the park's nature trail. The trail, which runs between the picnic areas and the Intracoastal Waterway, begins a short distance south of the entrance road and ends near the southernmost picnic area. A spur trail leads to an observation platform overlooking a lagoon, which may attract wading birds. Yellow-crowned Night-Heron has nested in the park. Check fruiting trees along the nature trail for flocks of warblers and other migrants. Areas with leaf litter will attract ground-feeding migrants. Other native trees attractive to migrants can be found scattered beside the park roads. A tunnel under SR A1A provides access to the beach, where you can expect to see Sanderling, Ruddy Turnstone, Laughing Gull, and Royal Tern.

Gumbo Limbo Nature Center is in Red Reef Park, 1 mile south of Spanish River Park on SR A1A. The complex includes a nature center with interpretive displays and four large saltwater tanks filled with sea turtles, stingrays, and other marine creatures. On the south side of the complex, a wheelchair-accessible boardwalk winds through maritime hammock and mangrove forest. On the north side a short trail passes through a butterfly garden, then loops through maritime hammock and areas of non-native vegetation. Rarities reported on these trails include Cuban Pewee and Ash-throated Flycatcher. Another 0.2 mile south is the beachside entrance to Red Reef Park. Gazebos built on the steep coastal dunes offer an excellent vantage point for sea-birding. Possible during periods of strong easterly winds are Pomarine and Parasitic Jaeger as well as Audubon's and Cory's Shearwater. Watch in winter for lines of sea ducks streaming past the dunes. Black Scoter is most likely, but Surf and White-winged Scoter are also possible. Northern Gannet should be just offshore throughout the winter.

General information: Loxahatchee National Wildlife Refuge (entrance fee) is open daily from sunrise to sunset. Hiking and wildlife observation are only allowed in Public Use Areas and on designated trails. Hunting (waterfowl only) is permitted in designated areas. Restrooms are adjacent to the visitor center. Portable restroom facilities are located at the Marsh Trail parking area, at the western end of Lee Road, and at the Hillsboro Recreation Area entrance. South County Regional Park (no entrance fee) and the boardwalk at Daggerwing Nature Center are open daily from sunrise to sunset. Restrooms are available in the nature center. The boardwalks at both Wakodahatchee and Green Cay Wetlands (no entrance fee) are open daily from sunrise to sunset. The nature center at Green Cay is open Tuesday through Friday from 1:00 to 4:30 P.M., Saturday from 8:15 A.M. to 4:30 P.M., and Sunday from 1:00 to 4:30 P.M. The nature center is closed on Sundays from Memorial Day through Labor Day. Modern restroom facilities are available in the nature center at Green Cay and adjacent to the parking area at Wakodahatchee.

Spanish River Park is open daily from 8:00 A.M. until sunset. Admission is $16 per vehicle on weekdays and $18 per vehicle on weekends. Only birders unaware of the steep admission prices, or for whom money is no object, drive their cars into this park. Budget-conscious birders try to find a parking space along Spanish River Boulevard on the north side of the park. Arriving early is the key to competing with beachgoers for these prized parking spaces. An unmarked path leads from Spanish River Boulevard into the park (look for the trailhead near the second trash receptacle from SR A1A). Gumbo Limbo Nature Center (donation requested) is open Monday through Saturday from 9:00 A.M. to 4:00 P.M. and Sunday from noon to 4:00 P.M. Red Reef Park (entrance fee) is open daily from 8:00 A.M. to 10:00 P.M. Restrooms are available at all locations.

DeLorme grid: Page 115, A-2, A-3.

Hazards: Keep a safe distance from alligators. Mosquitoes are widespread in summer and fall. Fire ants inflict a painful bite. Ant mounds are common on the Marsh Trail impoundment dikes.

Nearest food, gas, lodging: In Boynton Beach, Delray Beach, and Boca Raton.

Camping: A private campground is located in Delray Beach.

For more information: *Arthur R. Marshall Loxa-hatchee National Wildlife Refuge,* 10216 Lee Rd., Boynton Beach, FL 33437; (561) 732-3684; www.fws.gov.loxahatchee. *Daggerwing Nature Center,* 11200 Park Access Rd., Boca Raton, FL 33498; (561) 488-9953; www.co.palm-beach

.fl.us/parks/specfac/daggerwing_nc. *Wakoda-hatchee Wetlands,* 13026 Jog Rd., Delray Beach, FL 33446; (561) 493-6000; www.pbcwater .com/wakodahatchee. *Green Cay Wetlands and Nature Center,* 12800 Hagen Ranch Rd., Boynton Beach, FL 33437; (561) 966-7000; www.pbc water.com/green_cay.htm. *Spanish River Park,* 3001 N. SR A1A, Boca Raton, FL 33429; (561) 393-7815; www.ci.boca-raton.fl.us/parks/ spanishriver.cfm. *Gumbo Limbo Environmental Complex,* 1801 N. SR A1A, Boca Raton, FL 33432; (561) 338-1473; www.gumbolimbo.org. *Red Reef Park,* 1400 N. SR A1A, Boca Raton, FL 33432; (561) 393-7974; www.ci.boca-raton.fl .us/parks/redreef.cfm.

20 Ft. Lauderdale Area

Habitats: Sandy beach, mangrove forest, maritime hammock, oak/cabbage palm hammock, hardwood swamp, freshwater lakes.

Specialty birds: *Resident:* Mottled Duck, Magnificent Frigatebird, Reddish Egret, Roseate Spoonbill, Limpkin, Monk Parakeet, Smooth-billed Ani, Spot-breasted Oriole. *Summer:* Swallow-tailed

Kite, Least Tern, Gray Kingbird. *Winter:* Short-tailed Hawk. Lesser Black-backed Gull, Painted Bunting. *Migrant:* Chuck-will's-widow, Swainson's Warbler, Black-whiskered Vireo.

Best times to bird: September through April. Early morning, late afternoon, or at dusk throughout the year for parrots.

Directions: *Crystal Lakes Area:* From I-95, exit at Sample Road (exit 39). Drive west 2.2 miles to Powerline Road. Turn right and drive north to access Crystal Lakes. From the Florida Turnpike, exit at Sample Road (exit 69). Drive east 0.8 mile to Powerline Road. Turn left and drive north to Crystal Lakes. *Tradewinds Park:* Return to Sample Road, turn right, and drive west 1.3 miles to the park entrance. From the Florida Turnpike, drive west 0.5 mile on Sample Road to the park entrance. *Windmill Park:* Continue west 0.7 mile on Sample Road to Lyons Road. Turn left and drive south 2.4 miles to the park entrance. From the Florida Turnpike, exit at Atlantic Boulevard (exit 66). Drive west 0.6 mile to Lyons Road. Turn right and drive north 0.4 mile to the entrance. *Fern Forest Nature Center:* Backtrack south 0.6 mile on Lyons Road. Fern Forest is 0.2 mile south of Atlantic Boulevard. To reach southbound Lyons Road from westbound Atlantic Boulevard, exit on the right after the Lyons Road intersection. *Hugh Taylor Birch State Park:* From I-95 in Ft. Lauderdale exit at Sunrise Boulevard (exit 29). Drive east 4 miles to the park entrance. *Secret Woods Nature Center:* Exit I-95 at State Road 84 (exit 25). Drive west 0.5 mile. Turn right into the nature center. *Greenbelt Park:* Exit I-95 at Griffin Road (exit 23). Drive east 0.6 mile to NW 10th Street. Turn left and drive 0.3 mile to the parking area. *Anne Kolb Nature Center:* Exit I-95 at Sheridan Street (exit 21). Drive east 2.5 miles. Turn left into the nature center. *John U. Lloyd Beach State Park:* Continue east 0.3 mile on Sheridan Street to SR A1A. Turn left and drive north 1.5 miles to the park entrance.

The Birding

Patches of cypress/maple swamp can be found at two urban parks in Coconut Creek, north of Ft. Lauderdale in northern Broward County. **Tradewinds Park** has the largest stand of such habitat. A 3,000-foot boardwalk winds through the swamp. To reach the trailhead, drive 1.2 miles to the parking area at the southern end of the park road. Resident species include Eastern Screech-Owl, Pileated Woodpecker, Great Crested Flycatcher, and Carolina Wren. In summer watch for Yellow-billed Cuckoo and Chuck-will's-widow. Passing through during migration are Eastern Kingbird, Yellow-throated Vireo, and a variety of warblers. Lakes in the park may attract wading birds including Glossy Ibis, Roseate Spoonbill, and Limpkin. Least Tern and Black-necked Stilt are found here in summer. A variety of shorebirds may be present during the winter months. Both Monk Parakeet and Spotbreasted Oriole have been seen in the park. Tradewinds Park is also the home of Butterfly World (fee). Walk through their 8,000-square-foot Tropical Rain Forest Aviary (the world's largest) for up-close and personal looks at over 5,000 butterflies. The Jewels of the Sky Aviary houses an impressive variety of tropical hummingbirds.

At **Fern Forest Nature Center,** a series of trails and boardwalks provide access to cypress/maple swamp and oak/cabbage palm and tropical hardwood hammock. All trails begin at or near the nature center building. Park residents include Limpkin, Eastern Screech-Owl, Great Horned Owl, and Barred Owl. The Cypress Creek Trail, a 0.5-mile wheelchair-accessible boardwalk, passes through habitat attractive to migrant and wintering land birds. Painted Bunting can be expected in winter. Uncommon species seen here have included Blue-winged and Nashville Warbler. A MacGillivray's Warbler was found in the park in February 2001. Two other locations in Coconut Creek may be worth a stop during winter. **Windmill Park,** 0.6 mile north of Fern Forest, has a lake that is attractive to wintering waterfowl including Mottled Duck, American Wigeon, Ring-necked Duck, Lesser Scaup, and Ruddy Duck. A Bufflehead was seen here in January 2006. Limpkin can usually be found year-round. You may also view the lake from Coconut Creek Community Center, 0.3 mile farther north. A variety of win-

La Sagra's Flycatcher. PHOTO: TREY MITCHELL

tering gulls congregate on lakes surrounding the Broward County Landfill, on Powerline Road north of Sample Road. These freshwater ponds, collectively known as **Crystal Lakes,** have in the past attracted good numbers of Lesser Black-backed Gull. Other rare gulls seen here have included Thayer's, Iceland, and Glaucous Gull. Waterfowl may also use these lakes in winter. The lakes are surrounded by business parks and residential areas, with very limited public access. The large lake on the west side of Powerline Road, 1.2 miles north of Sample Road, can be scoped from the road. The series of lakes east of Powerline Road may be viewed from the parking lots of surrounding business parks, though access to some of these parking areas may be prohibited. Check for NO TRESPASSING signs before entering.

Ft. Lauderdale Beach is legendary in song and story as the home of sun, sand, surf, and spring-break insanity. Though a crackdown on the craziness in recent years has driven most of the spring-breakers elsewhere, this beach can still be packed with sunbathers, especially on weekends. Directly across SR A1A from the beach is **Hugh Taylor Birch State Park.** While the beach may no longer be "where the boys are," during spring and fall migration, this park is definitely where the birds are! The park has been a magnet for Caribbean vagrants including Key West and Ruddy Quail-Dove, La Sagra's Flycatcher, Bahama Mockingbird, Bananaquit, and Western Spindalis. After passing the entrance station, turn right into the parking area for the Beach Hammock Trail. A Bananaquit was found in this parking area in October 1999. The trail through maritime hammock first passes along the southern portion of "Lake Helen," a freshwater lagoon system that extends to the northern end of the park. Look for waders and shorebirds in the lagoon including Roseate Spoonbill and Black-necked Stilt. Migrant land birds can be found in the hardwood hammock. In winter watch overhead for Short-tailed Hawk.

Exit the parking area and turn right to reach the Terramar Visitor Center. This is the former home of Hugh Taylor Birch, the Chicago attorney who settled in Ft. Lauderdale in 1893 and who donated his estate for use as a state park in the 1940s. As a visitor center, it offers a park orientation video as well as exhibits interpreting the natural and cultural history of the park and surrounding area. Near the visitor center is an underpass to reach Ft. Lauderdale Beach, where Brown Pelican, Ruddy Turnstone, Sanderling, Black Skimmer, Laughing Gull, and Royal Tern may be seen. Return to the main park road and turn right. This one-way road runs along the west side of the lagoon system. It then loops back through mangrove habitat along the Intracoastal Waterway before returning to the entrance station. Shortly after turning right, a parking area is available on the left side of the road. Check fruiting trees on both sides of the road for migrant land birds or possibly Caribbean vagrants such as La Sagra's Flycatcher, Bahama Mockingbird, and Western Spindalis. Gray Kingbird should be easy to find in summer. A series of unmarked trails passes through hardwood hammock on the left side of the road and along the lagoon on the right side. At the northern end of the parking area is the entrance to the Exotic Trail. Markers along the trail point out the many ornamentals planted by Mr. Birch when the property was his estate. All of these trails can be excellent for migrant land birds. The extensive leaf litter occasionally attracts ground-feeding migrants such as Kentucky, Hooded, and Swainson's Warbler. This is also the most likely location for vagrant Key West and Ruddy Quail-Dove.

If in the area late in the day, listen for parrots returning to their evening roosts. A well-known location is on NE 18th Avenue, just north of Sunrise Boulevard and about 1 mile west of the entrance to the state park. To reach this location from Sunrise Boulevard, turn right onto US 1 (Federal Highway) and drive north 0.5 mile to NE 13th Street. Turn left and drive west 1 block to NE 18th Avenue. Turn left and drive south to where the road dead-ends. Parrots gather at dusk on the wires along this road or in the Australian pines to the east. Look for White-fronted, Red-crowned, Lilac-crowned, Mealy, Blue-fronted, Orange-winged, and Yellow-crowned Parrot, plus Green and White-eyed Parakeet. Another location worth checking for parrots is in Victoria Isles. To reach this area, drive south on US 1 for 1.3 miles to Las Olas Boulevard, then east 1 mile to Hendricks Isle Drive. Any of the streets north of Las Olas Boulevard from Hendricks Isle Drive east to Royal Palm Drive may have parrots. In addition to most of the species listed above, look for Blue-crowned, Red-masked, and Mitred Parakeet, numerous White-winged Parakeets, and a few Yellow-chevroned Parakeets. Gray Kingbird and Spot-breasted Oriole can be found in these or surrounding residential areas, especially in summer and fall. Also be aware that House Finch is now regular in the Ft. Lauderdale area. The origin of these birds is unknown.

Birders visiting the Fort Lauderdale area will be surprised to discover that several natural areas are just a short drive from the international airport. Northwest of the airport, **Secret Woods Nature Center** is surrounded by mangrove and maritime hammock habitat attractive to spring and fall migrants. A boardwalk and trails provide access to much of this small park along the New River. Watch for Spotted Sandpiper, Belted Kingfisher, and a variety of wading birds along the river. Eastern Screech-Owl, Great Crested Flycatcher, and Carolina Wren are resident in the hammock. Gray Kingbird is occasionally seen here during summer and Short-tailed Hawk may be spotted overhead in winter. Other wintering birds include Yellow-bellied Sapsucker, House Wren, American Robin, Cedar Waxwing, Indigo and Painted Bunting, Baltimore Oriole, and American Goldfinch. During migration look for Yellow-billed Cuckoo, Chuck-will's-widow, Eastern Kingbird, Yellow-throated Vireo, and a variety of warblers including Prothonotary, Worm-eating, Black-throated Green, Blackpoll, and Hooded. Though Smooth-billed Ani has all but disappeared from urban and suburban south Florida, the area around Greenbelt Park, directly south of the airport, has been home to at least one family of anis for several years. The birds tend to wander but often perch on a chain-link fence along the airport side of the perimeter road that separates the park from the airport. Resist the temptation to find the anis by driving the perimeter road because police and airport security heavily patrol this area. Instead, park your car in Greenbelt Park and head by foot toward the perimeter road. Walk east along the fence that separates the park from the road, scanning the fence across the road until you find the birds. The anis may also be found in weedy areas along the railroad tracks east of the airport or in undeveloped lots on Old Griffin Road, south of the park. During winter 2005 local birders were surprised to discover a Groove-billed Ani among the group. Don't be surprised to see flocks of Monk Parakeet when you visit this area.

Anne Kolb Nature Center in West Lake Park provides access to extensive mangrove forest habitat. An observation tower behind the exhibit hall provides a bird's-eye view of the forest and West Lake beyond. Two wheelchair-accessible boardwalks penetrate the forest and end at the lake edge. The Lake Observation Trail begins beyond the observation tower while the Mud Flat Trail begins south of the visitor center. Watch for Yellow-crowned Night-Heron in the mangroves along the boardwalks. Gray Kingbird is common here in summer. At low tide mudflats are exposed at the lake edge, attracting Semipalmated Plover, Ruddy Turnstone, Sanderling, Least Sandpiper, and other common shorebirds. In May 2005 a Thick-billed Vireo was found near the parking area. In addition to allowing up-close looks at the cruise ships berthed in nearby Port Everglades, **John U. Lloyd Beach State Park** provides excellent opportunities for land-based pelagic birding.

Throughout the winter months Northern Gannet can be seen feeding offshore. Magnificent Frigatebird is seen most frequently in summer. During periods of strong and persistent onshore winds, storm-petrels, shearwaters, jaegers, and other pelagic species are possible. In May 2001 Leach's Storm-Petrel, Sabine's Gull, and Arctic Tern were spotted close to shore. The park also has patches of maritime hammock that may attract migrant land birds or Caribbean vagrants. In April 2001 a Bahama Mockingbird was discovered near the nature trail that begins in the southern-most parking lot.

General information: Tradewinds Park (entrance fee on weekends and holidays) and Anne Kolb Nature Center (no entrance fee) are open daily from 8:00 A.M. to 6:00 P.M. November through April and from 8:00 A.M. to 7:30 P.M. May through October. Tradewinds Park can be very crowded on weekends. Fern Forest and Secret Woods Nature Centers (no entrance fees) are open daily from 8:00 A.M. to 6:00 P.M. Windmill Park (no entrance fee) is open daily from 7:00 A.M. until sunset. Hugh Taylor Birch and John U. Lloyd Beach State Parks (entrance fees) are open daily from 8:00 A.M. until sunset. Greenbelt Park (no entrance fee) is open daily from sunrise to sunset. Restrooms are available at all locations.

DeLorme grid: Page 115, C-2, C-3, D-2.

Hazards: Contact with poisonwood and poison ivy may result in a severe rash. As is the case when visiting any large metropolitan area, common sense is essential. Birding alone is not recommended. Lock car doors and secure all valuables out of sight.

Nearest food, gas, lodging: In Ft. Lauderdale.

Camping: Quiet Waters Park: 23 sites, 401 S. Powerline Rd., Deerfield Beach, FL 33442; (954) 360-1315. From Sample Road, drive north 2.4 miles on Powerline Road to the park entrance. Easterlin Park: 55 sites, 1000 NW 38th St., Oakland Park, FL 33309; (954) 938-0610. From I-95, exit at Oakland Park Boulevard (exit 31). Drive east 0.3 mile to Powerline Road. Turn left and drive north 0.5 mile to NW 38th Street. Turn left and drive west 0.3 mile to the park entrance. TY (Topeekeegee Yugnee) Park: 60 sites, 3300 N.

Park Rd., Hollywood, FL 33021; (954) 985-1980. From I-95, exit at Sheridan Street (exit 21). Drive west 0.6 mile to North Park Road. Turn right and drive 0.3 mile to the park entrance.

For more information: *Tradewinds Park,* 3600 W. Sample Rd., Coconut Creek, FL 33073; (954) 968-3880. *Fern Forest Nature Center,* 201 Lyons Rd. S., Coconut Creek, FL 33063; (954) 970-0150. *Hugh Taylor Birch State Park,* 3109 E. Sunrise Blvd., Ft. Lauderdale, FL 33304, (954) 564-4521, www.floridastateparks.org/hughtaylorbirch. *Secret Woods Nature Center,* 2701 W. SR 84, Dania Beach, FL 33312, (954) 791-1030. *Anne Kolb Nature Center,* 751 Sheridan St., Hollywood, FL 33019, (954) 926-2480. *John U. Lloyd Beach State Park,* 6503 N. Ocean Dr., Dania Beach, FL 33004, (954) 923-2833, www.floridastateparks.org/lloydbeach.

 # Western Broward County

Habitats: Sawgrass prairie, hardwood hammock, freshwater marsh.

Specialty birds: *Resident:* Mottled Duck, Snail Kite, Least Bittern, Wood Stork, King Rail, Purple Gallinule, Purple Swamphen, Monk Parakeet, Burrowing Owl, Spot-breasted Oriole. *Summer:* Swallow-tailed Kite, Least Tern, Gray Kingbird. *Winter:* Whip-poor-will, Painted Bunting. *Migrant:* Black Tern, Chuck-will's-widow, Yellow-throated Vireo, Black-whiskered Vireo.

Best times to bird: October through April for the greatest variety of marsh birds. April and Septem- ber to early October for migrant land birds.

Directions: *Markham Park:* From Interstate 75, exit at Royal Palm Parkway (exit 15). Drive west 0.5 mile to Weston Road and turn right. Drive north 2.8 miles to the park entrance straight ahead. From Interstate 595 exit at 136th Street (exit 1A). Drive west on SR 84 (the service road for I-595) 2 miles to the park entrance on your right. *Tree Tops Park:* From I-75 exit at Griffin Road (exit 13). Drive east 4.5 miles to Nob Hill Road (SW 100th Avenue). Turn left and drive north 0.5 mile. Turn right into the park entrance. From I-595, exit at Nob Hill Road (exit 3 if eastbound, exit 4 if westbound). Drive south 2.4 miles. Turn left into the park entrance.

The Birding

Markham Park provides the residents of western Broward County with a wide variety of recreational activities, including fishing, boating, swimming, skeet shooting, stargazing, tennis, camping, volleyball, biking, hiking, horseback riding, and picnicking. For birders, the park provides access to the adjacent Everglades Water Conservation Areas (WCA). These vast sawgrass marshes (over 860,000 acres), which make up about half of the remaining Everglades, supply water for Everglades National Park as well as metropolitan areas in southeastern Florida. The WCA also helps prevent urban flooding and provides habitat for a wide variety of wildlife. To explore just a small corner of the Everglades WCA from Markham Park, turn left at the intersection after the entrance station and drive west 0.1 mile to the nature trail parking area on the left. The nature trail itself winds through a mixture of hardwood hammock and Australian pines and can attract land birds in migration and in winter. A wide path to the left of the trailhead leads through the woods to a canal. Turn right on the dirt road along the canal and walk west toward the dike that surrounds the marsh. Beyond where the road and canal curve north, cross a bridge over the canal. You can then climb to the top of the dike. Scope the marsh from this vantage point, searching for Snail Kite year-round and Northern Harrier in the winter months. Wintering waterfowl or shorebirds may be close enough to identify but are often only distant specks.

It's possible to walk many miles along these dikes both to the west and to the north. A wide variety of wading birds, including Glossy Ibis, Wood Stork, and occasionally Limpkin, may be seen in the marsh. Along the edges, look for American Bittern in winter and Least Bittern during the summer months. King Rail and Purple Gallinule may be present year-round. Also watch for Purple Swamphen, a recently and accidentally introduced species that has spread to the Everglades and beyond. Often described as a "Purple Gallinule on steroids," this large old-world rail is frequently found in shallow open areas of the marsh. The swamphens were first discovered in artificially created wetlands to the south of Markham Park, in the Silver Lakes subdivision of the city of Pembroke Pines. To reach this area, retrace your route from I–75 by way of Weston Road and Royal Palm Parkway. Drive south 4 miles on I–75 to Sheridan Street. Drive west on Sheridan Street 1.2 miles, turning right into the parking area for the **Southwest Regional Library.** The wetland area on the east side of the parking area can be explored via a wheelchair-accessible boardwalk. Swamphens are commonly seen in shallow open areas of this marsh. Other species to look for here include Least Bittern, Wood Stork, Mottled Duck, Purple Gallinule, and Limpkin. In May 2001 at least two Masked Ducks were discovered in this wetland. In December 2001 a White-cheeked Pintail of unknown origin was found here. Two other wetland areas can be found farther west on Sheridan Street. In 0.3 mile turn left onto NW 172 Avenue, then right into Silver Lakes North Park. An artificially created marsh begins at the park and extends for 0.5 mile to the west. It was in this wetland that Purple Swamphens were first discovered. In another 2 miles is the entrance to Chapel Trail Nature Preserve. A wheelchair-accessible boardwalk provides access to this wetland area. You may also rent a canoe to explore the marsh further. Species similar to those listed for the wetlands at the Southwest Regional Library may be seen in both of these locations.

Within the 365 acres of **Tree Tops Park** are two distinct habitats: extensive live oak hammock and a man-made freshwater marsh. Both are easily accessible via a trail system that includes paved and wood-chipped walkways, boardwalks, and more than 7 miles of equestrian trails. The marsh habitat is visible on your left as you enter the park. Waterfowl, mostly Blue-winged and Green-winged Teal, join resident Mottled Duck in winter. Fulvous Whistling-Duck has also been recorded from this marsh. Park in a parking area on the right, cross the street, and double back along a paved walkway to scan the marsh. The lake on the parking-area side of the road has little suitable cover to attract waterfowl. This parking area may also be used to access the Live Oak Trail, which begins a short walk farther down the park road. This paved trail through live oak hammock should be explored for migrant and wintering land birds. An observation tower near the beginning of the trail provides canopy-level views of the hammock. Beyond the observation tower, unpaved trails lead to a series of boardwalks on the east side of the freshwater marsh. This area can also be accessed at the end of the park road. From the boardwalks, look for Sora and Wilson's Snipe in winter and Purple Gallinule year-round. Least Bittern is also present year-round but is easiest to find in summer.

The equestrian trails can be accessed from just about anywhere in the park. In November 2003 a MacGillivray's Warbler was discovered on one of these trails. Check weedy areas for Painted and Indigo Bunting. The Pine Island Ridge Trail begins behind the park headquarters, located near the parking area at the end of the park road. This paved trail leads through Pine Island Ridge Natural Area, a remnant live oak hammock north of the park boundary. At just over 29 feet above sea level, Pine Island Ridge has the highest elevation in Broward County. Look here for nesting Great Horned Owl and Yellow-billed Cuckoo, as well as a variety of migrant and wintering land birds. An equestrian trail that begins toward the end of the paved trail leads to a lake that attracts Least Tern in summer and wading birds year-round. Other sections of Pine Island Ridge can be accessed both north and west of Tree Tops Park. To reach North Pine Island Ridge, return to Nob Hill Road, turn right, and drive north 2.4 miles to SR 84, now a service road for I–595. Turn right and drive east 0.7 mile to Pine Ridge Drive. Turn right and drive 0.8 mile to a playground on the right, opposite the parking area for the Pine Island Ridge Country Club. A fitness trail through remnant live oak hammock begins behind the playground and can be excellent for migrant land birds. To reach Long Key Natural Area (formerly known as Flamingo Environmentally Sensitive Lands) from Tree Tops Park, turn left on Nob Hill Road and drive south 0.5 mile to Griffin Road. Turn right and drive west 2 miles to Flamingo Road. Turn right and drive north 0.7 mile to SW 36th Court. Turn left and drive 0.5 mile. The road curves here and becomes SW 130th Avenue. The gate to the parking area is on the left just beyond the curve. Great Horned Owl as well as migrant and wintering land birds can be found in this live oak hammock. Only the equestrian trails on this property are currently open to the public; a nature center is slated for completion in 2008.

Burrowing Owls are easy to find at **Brian Piccolo Park,** a 180-acre recreational park south of Tree Tops Park. Burrows are scattered throughout the park (including one near the entrance) and are marked with wooden stakes. Monk Parakeet is also common here. To reach this park from Tree Tops Park, drive south 2.8 miles on Nob Hill Road (which becomes Palm Avenue south of Griffin Road) to Sheridan Street. Turn left and drive east 0.5 mile to the park entrance.

General information: Markham, Tree Tops, and Brian Piccolo Parks (entrance fees on weekends and holidays) are open daily from 8:00 A.M. to 6:00 P.M. during eastern standard time and from 8:00 A.M. to 7:30 P.M. during daylight saving time. Silver Lakes North Park and Chapel Trail Nature Preserve (no entrance fee) are open daily from 8:00 A.M. until sunset. The boardwalk at Southwest Regional Library (no entrance fee) has no posted hours. Restrooms are available at all locations.

DeLorme grid: Page 115, D-1.

Hazards: Keep a safe distance from alligators. Mosquitoes are numerous in summer. Poison ivy may produce a severe rash.

Nearest food, gas, lodging: In Sunrise, Davie, and Pembroke Pines.

Camping: Markham Park: 98 sites. C. B. Smith Park: 72 sites, 900 N. Flamingo Rd., Pembroke Pines, FL 33028; (954) 437-2650. From I-75,

exit at Pines Boulevard (exit 9A). Drive east 1.7 miles to Flamingo Road. Turn left and drive north 0.4 mile to the park entrance.

For more information: Markham Park, 16001 W. State Rd. 84, Sunrise, FL 33326; (954) 389-2000. *Tree Tops Park,* 3900 SW 100th Ave., Davie, FL 33328; (954) 370-3750. *Brian Piccolo Park,* 9501 Sheridan St., Cooper City, FL 32024; (954) 437-2600.

22 Miami Area

Habitats: Maritime hammock, coastal strand, mangrove forest, estuary, sandy beach, tropical hardwood hammock, pine rockland, freshwater ponds, residential areas.

Specialty birds: *Resident:* White-crowned Pigeon, Burrowing Owl, Monk Parakeet, White-winged Parakeet, Yellow-chevroned Parakeet, Black-hooded Parakeet, Blue-crowned Parakeet, Mitred Parakeet, Red-masked Parakeet, White-eyed Parakeet, Dusky-headed Parakeet, Blue-and-yellow Macaw, Chestnut-fronted Macaw, Orange-winged Parrot, Red-crowned Parrot, Lilac-crowned Parrot, Red-whiskered Bulbul, Hill Myna, Spot-breasted Oriole. *Summer:* Magnificent Frigatebird, Swallow-tailed Kite, Least Tern, Mangrove Cuckoo, Gray

Kingbird. *Winter:* Short-tailed Hawk, Peregrine Falcon, Piping Plover, Lesser Black-backed Gull, Scissor-tailed Flycatcher, Painted Bunting. *Migrant:* Chuck-will's-widow, Yellow-throated Vireo, Black-whiskered Vireo, Swainson's Warbler, Louisiana Waterthrush, Summer Tanager, Scarlet Tanager, Rose-breasted Grosbeak.

Best times to bird: April and late August to early October for migrant land birds, late September to mid-October for raptors, November through March for wintering species, August through September and December through February for shorebirds, all year for resident exotics, early morning, late afternoon, or at dusk for parrots.

Directions: *Biscayne Gardens:* From 1-95, exit at NW 151st Street (exit 11). Drive east 0.2 mile to NW 3rd Avenue and turn right. Turn left on NW 150th Street. *Miami Shores:* From I-95, exit at NW 95th Street (exit 8A). Drive east 0.6 mile to North Miami Avenue. *Miami Springs:* From I-95, exit at the Airport Expressway (State Road 112, exit 4B). Drive west 3.5 miles, exiting on NW 36th Street. Drive 1.5 miles to Curtiss Parkway (NW 57th Avenue) and turn right. From the Palmetto Expressway (State Road 826), exit at NW 36th Street. Drive east 2 miles to Curtiss Parkway and turn left. *Key Biscayne:* From I-95 southbound, exit at Rickenbacker Causeway/Key Biscayne (exit 1), the last exit before I-95 merges with US 1. From US 1 northbound, bear right onto Brickell Avenue at the I-95 entrance ramp. Drive north 0.5 mile. Turn right onto the Rickenbacker Causeway (toll). The causeway connects the mainland to Virginia Key and then Key Biscayne, where it becomes Crandon Boulevard. *Crandon Park* is at the northern end of Key Biscayne, 4.5 miles from the Rickenbacker Causeway toll plaza. *Bill Baggs Cape Florida State Park* is at the southern end of the key, 2.5 miles farther. *A. D. Barnes Park:* From the Palmetto Expressway, exit at Bird Road (SW 40th Street). Drive east on Bird Road 0.5 mile. Turn left on SW 72nd Avenue and drive north 0.1 mile to the park entrance. From US 1, exit at Bird Road and drive west 3.6 miles. Turn right on SW 72nd Avenue and proceed as above. *South Miami:* From the Palmetto Expressway, exit at Miller Drive (SW 56th Street). Drive east 1.5 miles to SW 62nd Avenue. *Baptist Hospital:* Several highways provide access to this area. From the Florida Turnpike, exit at North Kendall Drive (SW 88th Street) and drive east 3 miles. From the Don Shula Expressway (State Road 874), exit at North Kendall Drive and drive east 1 mile. From the Palmetto Expressway (SR 826), exit at North Kendall Drive and drive west 1 mile. From US 1, drive west 1.6 miles on North Kendall Drive. *Matheson Hammock County Park:* From the intersection of US 1 and North Kendall Drive, drive east 1.4 miles on North Kendall Drive to Red Road (SW 57th Avenue). Turn left, then immediately right, continuing east 1 mile on North Kendall Drive to Old Cutler Road. Turn right and drive south 0.6 mile to the park's north entrance. The parking area for *Fairchild Tropical Garden* is at the southern end of the park, 0.2 mile farther. *Deering Estate at Cutler:* Continue south 1.3 miles, turning left where Old Cutler Road intersects with Red Road. Continue south 4.2 miles to SW 168th Street. Turn left. The parking area is on the right. *Bill Sadowski Park and Nature Center:* Return to Old Cutler Road, continue south 0.5 mile to SW 176th Street, and turn right. Drive west 0.5 mile to the park entrance.

The Birding

Southeast Florida's subtropical climate and suburban landscape of exotic vegetation provides suitable habitat for a wide variety of non-native parrots. Of the more than 75 species of parrots reported in Florida, nearly 20 are confirmed or presumed to be breeding in the state. Most of these can be found in the Miami area. The table included in this section lists parrots consistently reported from Miami-Dade County, and the neighborhoods where they are most often seen. All are found in urban or suburban areas rather than in native habitats. During the day, parrots will typically be spotted in non-native palms and other exotic trees, at backyard feeders, or on phone wires. A good strategy is to slowly drive the neighborhoods with the windows down, listening for squawking birds. Early morning or late afternoon is best. *Amazona* parrots and *Aratinga* parakeets often roost in the evening in stands of Australian pines. Almost all of these parrots are cavity nesters. Monk Parakeet is unique in that they build communal stick nests on telephone poles or other elevated structures.

The village of **Miami Shores** is an excellent place to find *Brotogeris* parakeets. One dependable location is near the intersection of NW 95th Street and North Miami Avenue. Turn right on North Miami Avenue, then left in 1 block onto NW 94th Street. Look for a canary date palm on the right. In late afternoon White-winged and Yellow-chevroned Parakeet as well as Monk Parakeet can be found in nearby trees. Other parrots often seen in Miami Shores include Red-masked and White-eyed Parakeet, Orange-winged Parrot, and Chestnut-fronted Macaw. A productive area for these species is the vicinity of the Miami Shores Country Club on NE 6th Avenue between NE 101st and NE 107th Streets. Drive

Red-whiskered Bulbul. PHOTO: LARRY MANFREDI

north 0.5 mile on North Miami Avenue. Turn right on NE 103rd Street and drive east until you reach the golf course. Also look for Hill Myna and Spot-breasted Oriole in this area. Several species of *Aratinga* parakeets can be found in neighborhoods farther north in **Biscayne Gardens.** A reliable location is on NW 150th Street between NW 2nd and NW 3rd Avenues. Regular in this area are Blue-crowned, Mitred, and White-eyed Parakeet, as well as Monk and White-winged Parakeet and Chestnut-fronted Macaw. Occasionally seen are Green and Crimson-fronted Parakeet. The parrots can be seen late in the day at feeders or in trees visible from the street. If in the area earlier in the day, two parks are worth checking, especially during migration: Enchanted Forest and Arch Creek Park are on NE 135th Street (exit 10B from I–95), near the intersection with Biscayne Boulevard (US 1). Greynolds Park is on NE 185th Street (exit 14 from I–95). The entrance is on NE 22nd Avenue. Greynolds Park once boasted a spectacular wading-bird rookery. Sadly, the rookery has been abandoned in recent years.

The city of **Miami Springs** is another good location to search for *Aratinga* parakeets. Drive north on Curtiss Parkway from its intersection with NW 36th Street. The road jogs right and bisects the Miami Springs Golf Course. The neighborhood around the Fair Haven Nursing Home (on the right in 1 mile) may have Monk, White-winged, and Yellow-chevroned Parakeet, as well as other parrots. Look for Spot-breasted Oriole here and, in summer, Gray Kingbird. The neighborhood near the intersection of Wren Avenue and Apache Street is an excellent location to see Dusky-headed Parakeet. To reach this area, continue north on Curtiss Parkway to a traffic circle. Three-quarters of the way around the circle, turn right on Westward Drive. Drive 1.4 miles to Apache Street and turn right. The intersection with Wren Avenue is in 0.2 mile. Other parrots commonly seen here include Mitred and Red-masked Parakeet and Orange-winged Parrot. In winter Painted Bunting may be seen at backyard feeders. The city of **South Miami** often has the greatest variety of *Amazona* parrots. Large mixed flocks of these raucous parrots roost in Australian pines or other non-native trees. SW 62nd Avenue between Miller Drive (SW 56th Street) and Sunset Drive (SW 72nd Street) has been the best location for these birds in recent years. The Miller Parrot Roost on SW 57th Street hasn't been the most popular roosting location in recent years but is still worth a look. From Miller Drive, go south on SW 62nd Avenue for 1 block. Turn right onto SW 57th Street and park at the tennis courts at the end of the street. Look for parrots at dawn or dusk in the Australian pines that line the canal. Search the neighborhood in the next few blocks south of SW 57th Street for Chestnut-fronted Macaw, White-crowned Pigeon, Hill Myna, and Spot-breasted Oriole. Watch overhead during the day for Swallow-tailed Kite in summer and Short-tailed Hawk in winter. The intersection of SW 62nd Avenue and SW 64th Street has been a roosting site in recent years for large numbers of *Amazona* parrots. The birds begin to assemble on phone wires just before sunset and roost in nearby trees, most often the row of Australian pines at the intersection. Commonly seen here are White-fronted, Blue-fronted, Orange-winged, Red-crowned, and Lilac-crowned Parrot.

Until 1992 **Bill Baggs Cape Florida State Park** was dominated by a forest of non-native Australian pines, for the most part only attractive to birds during migration. In August of that year, Hurricane Andrew deforested Cape Florida, providing an opportunity to restore the park's native plant communities. The ongoing restoration now provides habitat for a wide variety of migrant and wintering birds. The park lists over 230 bird species seen since 1994, including 39 species of warblers. The impressive list of rarities includes Zenaida Dove, Key West Quail-Dove, Olive-sided, La Sagra's, and Sulphur-bellied Flycatcher, Thick-billed and Bell's Vireo, Northern Wheatear, Bicknell's Thrush, Bahama Mockingbird, Townsend's, Connecticut, Mourning, and MacGillivray's Warbler, Red-legged Honeycreeper, and Western Spindalis.

If visiting the park in the winter, Turkey Vulture (and a few Black Vulture) will be conspicuous as you drive along the Rickenbacker Causeway. Watch for Great Black-backed Gull and occasionally Lesser Black-backed Gull perched on streetlights as you cross the William Powell Bridge (0.7 mile from the toll plaza) and enter Virginia Key. In summer Magnificent Frigatebird may be seen soaring over the bridge. A Purple Sandpiper was found under the bridge in December 2002. The beach on the south side of the causeway will have large numbers of Laughing Gull and a few shorebirds, mostly Ruddy Turnstone, Sanderling, and occasionally Spotted Sandpiper. Common Loon, Red-breasted Merganser, or occasionally Black Scoter may be just offshore in winter. Black-crowned Night-Heron roosts on the railings of the Bear Cut Bridge (3 miles from the toll plaza), which connects Virginia Key to Key Biscayne. Once on Key Biscayne, scan the phone wires along Crandon Boulevard in summer for Gray Kingbird, which nest near the local supermarket. In winter Short-tailed Hawk may be spotted circling over the island. Observe posted speed limits as you drive through the village of Key Biscayne.

After passing through the park entrance station, turn left 0.2 mile farther to reach the first parking area for beach access, or turn right to reach No Name Harbor. Several boardwalks pass over the dunes to reach the beach. During periods of strong onshore winds, Northern Gannet (in winter) or other seabirds may be seen feeding offshore. Common Ground-Dove is resident on the dunes and Painted Bunting winters in weedy areas between the boardwalks. During migration check snags along the dunes for Merlin or Peregrine Falcon. Chuck-will's-widow may be flushed from brushy areas in the fore dune, while a few warblers or other land birds will usually be found in the sea grapes on the back dune. Much more productive during migration are the trees along the perimeter of the parking area. Look here for Yellow-billed Cuckoo, Eastern Kingbird, Black-whiskered Vireo, Cape May Warbler, and other migrants. No Name Harbor provides access to hiking trails through several distinct habitats. A trail that begins north of the parking area leads to restored mangrove wetlands that may harbor shorebirds at low tide, migrants in the surrounding buttonwoods, or a wintering Peregrine Falcon. Least Tern, which nests on rooftops on the key, is sometimes seen here in summer. A paved bike path leads south through restored maritime forest bordering Biscayne Bay. This area can be outstanding for migrants. Most common during migration are Northern Parula, Cape May Warbler, Black-throated Blue Warbler, Prairie Warbler, Blackpoll Warbler (spring), Black-and-white Warbler, American Redstart, and Ovenbird. A trail that begins between the parking area and the main park road leads south to coastal strand habitat in the interior of the park. This area can be productive for migrants as well as wintering species. Several ponds along this trail, when not dried out, attract wading birds and occasionally waterfowl and shorebirds.

Both the bike path and the interior trail lead to the Cape Florida Lighthouse parking area at the southern end of the park. To drive to this area, return to the main park road and turn right. Lighthouse parking is in 0.6 mile. The southern entrance to the bike path is 0.2 mile farther. Scan wires along the road for Gray Kingbird in summer and Scissor-tailed Flycatcher in winter. Birders are allowed inside the fenced-in area surrounding the lighthouse only during scheduled lighthouse tours (check at the entrance station for tour times). Once inside, look for migrants along the path to the lighthouse or on a somewhat overgrown loop trail through maritime forest. This trail leads to wet areas especially attractive to Northern and Louisiana Waterthrush. The park's southern tip is also a staging area for southbound hawks in fall. Broad-winged Hawk is the most commonly seen buteo. After Hurricane Andrew, falcons would often perch on snags left standing near the lighthouse. Hurricane Wilma toppled the last of these snags in 2005. The lighthouse, built in 1825 and rebuilt in 1846, is the oldest surviving structure in Miami-Dade County. A climb to the top will provide panoramic views of Biscayne Bay. The community of houses on stilts you'll see in the bay is called Stiltsville. Many of these structures were damaged or destroyed during Hurricane Andrew. Though once privately owned, the surviving structures are now a part of Biscayne National Park.

Return to Crandon Boulevard to reach **Crandon Park,** just north of the village. The south entrance, 2.2 miles from the state park entrance (or 4.8 miles from the causeway toll plaza), provides access to the beach and to Crandon Gardens, the site of the old Crandon Zoo. Check the beach at low tide. Exposed mudflats attract plovers (occasionally including American Golden Plover) and other shorebirds, gulls, and terns. Lesser Black-backed Gull is regular here year-round. A mind-boggling assortment of exotic waterfowl and poultry has been introduced to the gardens. You also won't be able to avoid noticing the colorful iguanas that now call the gardens home. Birding in the gardens is best during migration. Another 0.3 mile north on Crandon Boulevard is the park's north entrance, which provides access to the Marjory Stoneman Douglas Biscayne Nature Center and Bear Cut Preserve. A short nature trail through maritime forest can be good for migrant land birds. The somewhat longer Osprey Trail leads to a boardwalk through mangrove forest. Look here in summer for Mangrove Cuckoo and Black-whiskered Vireo. The beach here may also have shorebirds. As you return to the mainland via the Rickenbacker Causeway, try to avoid being completely distracted by spectacular views of the Miami skyline.

A variety of habitats squeezed into a relatively small area (65 acres) has helped to make **A. D. Barnes Park** a premier migration hot spot in the Miami area. The park sightings

PARROTS OF MIAMI

Species	Field Marks	Abundance in Miami	Miami Springs	Miami Shores/ Biscayne Gardens	South Miami/ Kendall	Other Locations in Miami/Dade
Monk Parakeet *Myiopsitta monachus*	Gray face, forehead, throat, breast	Common	✓	✓	✓	Widespread
White-winged Parakeet *Brotogeris versicolurus*	Yellow and white on upper and lower wing	Common		✓	✓	
Yellow-chevroned Parakeet *Brotogeris chirriri*	Yellow on upper wing, lower wing all green	Common	✓	✓	✓	
Black-hooded Parakeet *Nandayus nenday*	Black head, gray eye ring	Uncommon		✓	✓	
Maroon-bellied Parakeet *Pyrrhura frontalis*	Maroon belly, undertail; scaly throat, breast; white eye ring	Rare	✓			
Blue-crowned Parakeet *Aratinga acuticauda*	White eye ring, blue head, red undertail	Common	✓	✓		Miami Beach, Key Biscayne
Green Parakeet *Aratinga holochlora*	Bare eye ring, undertail olive yellow	Uncommon	✓	✓		Miami Beach
Mitred Parakeet *Aratinga mitrata*	Bare eye ring; red on forehead, cheeks, lores; green underwing	Common	✓	✓	✓	
Scarlet-fronted Parakeet *Aratinga wagleri*	White eye ring;, red forehead, crown, lores; green underwing	Rare	✓			
Red-masked Parakeet *Aratinga erythrogenys*	Bare eye ring, red head, red underwing	Common	✓	✓	✓	
Crimson-fronted Parakeet *Aratinga finschi*	White eye ring; red crown, bend of wing; red and yellow underwing	Rare	✓	✓		
White-eyed Parakeet *Aratinga leucopthalmus*	White eye ring, red bend of wing, red and yellow underwing	Common	✓	✓		
Peach-fronted Parakeet *Aratinga aurea*	Orange eye ring, forehead; blue face; olive underwing	Rare	✓			
Dusky-headed Parakeet *Aratinga weddellii*	White eye ring, brownish gray head, blue flight feathers	Uncommon	✓			
Blue-and-yellow Macaw *Ara ararauna*	Blue above, yellow below	Uncommon			✓	University of Miami, Matheson Hammock
Chestnut-fronted Macaw *Ara severa*	Chestnut forehead white face	Common		✓	✓	

Species	Field Marks	Abundance in Miami	Miami Springs	Miami Shores/Biscayne Gardens	South Miami/Kendall	Other Locations in Miami/Dade
White-fronted Parrot *Amazona albifrons*	White forehead, red around eyes, red underwing coverts	Common		✓	✓	
Blue-fronted Parrot *Amazona aestiva*	Blue forehead; yellow crown, face; red wing patch; red at bend of wing	Common	✓		✓	
Orange-winged Parrot *Amazona amazonica*	Yellow forehead, cheeks; blue lore; orange wing patch	Common	✓	✓	✓	
Red-crowned Parrot *Amazona viridigenalis*	Red forehead, crown, wing patch; blue neck	Common	✓	✓	✓	
Lilac-crowned Parrot *Amazona finschi*	Maroon forehead; lilac crown, neck; red wing patch	Common			✓	
Yellow-crowned Parrot *Amazona ochrocephala*	Yellow forehead, red wing patch, red at bend of wing	Uncommon	✓		✓	
Yellow-headed Parrot *Amazona oratrix*	Yellow head, red wing patch, red at bend of wing	Uncommon			✓	
Yellow-faced Parrot *Amazona zanthops*	Yellow face, belly, under-tail; orange ear covert; brown iris (immature)	Rare			✓	
Mealy Parrot *Amazona farinosa*	White eye ring, red wing patch	Uncommon			✓	

list includes 11 flycatchers, 7 each of vireos and thrushes, 35 warblers, 4 tanagers, 2 each of grosbeaks and buntings, and 4 orioles. White-crowned Pigeon and Spot-breasted Oriole can be found here year-round, though the orioles are easiest to locate in late summer and early fall, after the young have fledged. A variety of parrots can be seen or heard in the area. Most common are Monk and Yellow-chevroned Parakeet. White-winged Parakeet is seen less frequently. Occasionally spotted are Orange-winged Parrot, Chestnut-fronted Macaw, and Blue-and-yellow Macaw. Swallow-tailed Kite and Gray Kingbird are common in spring and summer. Short-tailed Hawk is regular in winter.

After entering the park, turn right at the T intersection to reach the picnic area in oak hammock habitat. Parking is available at various locations along this road. This section of the park should be birded early in the day. By midmorning on weekends the area becomes crowded with picnickers. A freshwater pond is in the southwest corner of the park. Common species here are Anhinga, White Ibis, and other waders, Muscovy Duck, and Common Moorhen. Pied-billed Grebe, American Coot, and Belted Kingfisher join them in winter. To the right of a picnic gazebo overlooking the pond, check the brushy area for Northern Waterthrush. Solitary Sandpiper is occasionally seen working the pond edge during migration. The live oaks and ficus trees (especially those with fruit) in this picnic area attract a variety of warblers and other migrant land birds. Unusual species recorded here include Whip-poor-will, Warbling Vireo, Philadelphia Vireo, and Western Spindalis. A small tropical hardwood hammock in the southeast corner of the park provides suitable habitat for ground-feeding species such as Ovenbird, Northern Waterthrush, and occasionally Swainson's and Hooded Warbler. A La Sagra's Flycatcher was seen here in 2001. Try to avoid stepping on the diminutive spotted skunks that also can be found in this hammock.

Another small hammock worth checking is located on the north side of the entrance road. North of the T intersection, the road passes through a picnic area in pine rockland habitat, attractive to Pine Warbler during migration. At the end of this road is the entrance to the Sense of Wonder Nature Center. A series of paved trails will take you through pine rockland and tropical hardwood hammock. An elevated boardwalk at one end of the facility provides nearly canopy-level views of the hammock. Walk slowly to avoid flushing a Chuck-will's-widow during migration. Most of the migrant land birds on the park list have been seen in this section of the park. A man-made waterfall near the nature-center building tends to attract migrants for drinking and bathing. Areas with fruiting ficus or Florida trema attract a variety of warblers, vireos, thrushes, tanagers, and grosbeaks. Brushy areas are attractive to Least Flycatcher, House Wren, Indigo Bunting, and Painted Bunting, while Eastern Wood-Pewee and Yellow-throated Warbler prefer the pines. Rarities seen in this area have included Alder, Willow and Sulphur-bellied Flycatcher, Carolina Chickadee, Red-breasted Nuthatch, and Connecticut and MacGillivray's Warbler. A Tufted Titmouse, not otherwise seen in urban South Florida, has resided in the hammock for the last several years.

Undoubtedly the number-one target of birders visiting the Kendall area of South Miami-Dade County is Red-whiskered Bulbul. Released into the area in 1960, this native of southern Asia has adapted to the suburban landscape and continues to breed in small numbers in East Kendall and the village of Pinecrest. The neighborhood near **Baptist Hospital** has been most reliable for this species in recent years. Drive or walk the streets from North Kendall Drive (SW 88th Street) to SW 85th Street, between SW 89th Avenue and SW 87th Court. Bulbul often perches on phone wires but could also be spotted in trees or on rooftops. Please respect private property when birding in these residential areas. Other birds often seen in the neighborhood or on the grounds of the hospital include White-winged Dove, Monk, Yellow-chevroned, and White-winged Parakeet, Loggerhead Shrike, Hill Myna, and Spot-breasted Oriole. In summer look for Gray Kingbird on phone wires and Swallow-tailed Kite overhead. In winter watch for Yellow-bellied Sapsucker and Short-tailed Hawk. The ponds on the hospital grounds usually attract a few wading birds year-round and American Coot, Ring-billed Gull, and occasionally Ring-necked Duck in winter. Muscovy Duck is common, usually joined by a few other exotic waterfowl looking for handouts. If you fail to find Red-whiskered Bulbul around Baptist Hospital, several other locations in the Kendall area are worth a try. Locations west of US 1 include Kenwood Elementary, on SW 79th Avenue 0.2 mile south of North Kendall Drive, and Continental Park on SW 82nd Avenue and SW 100th Street. On SW 98th Street in Pinecrest, 0.4 mile east of US 1, the Royal Palm Tennis Courts and surrounding neighborhood may continue to harbor a few bulbuls, as well as Spot-breasted Oriole.

Kendall Indian Hammock Park can be productive for migrants during spring and fall. From Baptist Hospital, drive west 1.7 miles on North Kendall Drive to SW 107th Avenue and turn right. The park entrance is 0.4 mile on your right. Several trails leading through tropical hardwood hammock begin opposite the baseball diamonds (0.5 mile from the entrance). Sharp-shinned and Cooper's Hawk, Yellow-billed Cuckoo, Chuck-will's-widow, and a variety of warblers, vireos, thrushes, tanagers, and buntings can be common during migration. A few will remain for the winter. White-crowned Pigeon, Monk Parakeet, Great Crested Flycatcher, Hill Myna, and Spot-breasted Oriole may be found year-round. A stop at any of the shopping centers along North Kendall Drive may produce Common Myna. In summer these same locations may have Gray Kingbird. A good location for Burrowing Owl is **Kendall-Tamiami Regional Airport,** on SW 137th Avenue between SW 120th Street and SW 136th Street. Owls may be found in any open area along the airport roads. Burrows are often marked with orange cones. Airport residents include Loggerhead Shrike and Eastern Meadowlark.

Trails through mangrove forest and tropical hardwood hammock at **Matheson Hammock County Park** can be excellent for spring and fall migrants. Enter the park through the north entrance (at the traffic light) and look for the parking area on the left. Across the road, a small pond usually has a few wading birds or Common Moorhen at its edges. Check the surrounding trees for Hill Myna, Spot-breasted Oriole, or migrant songbirds. Smooth-billed Ani was frequently found near this pond but hasn't been seen in recent years. Scan the skies for Swallow-tailed Kite and Chimney Swift in summer, Short-tailed Hawk in winter, and Broad-winged Hawk or other raptors during migration. Also watch for parrots, including Blue-and-yellow Macaw, flying overhead. In spring or fall a walk through the adjacent picnic area usually produces a few warblers, vireos (including Black-whiskered in spring), or other migrants in the live oaks or along hammock edges. Eastern Screech-Owl can be found in thicker patches of hammock. A Sulphur-bellied Flycatcher was discovered in the picnic area in October 1995. Wintering birds have included Black-throated Gray Warbler (2000) and Brown-crested Flycatcher (2004). This area has also hosted a few Caribbean vagrants including Bahama Mockingbird and La Sagra's Flycatcher. The park road continues to an entrance station and leads to a man-made swimming lagoon. You may walk to this area by taking a path parallel to the road that winds its way through the mangrove forest. A few shorebirds such as Willet, Spotted Sandpiper, Ruddy Turnstone, and Sanderling may be feeding on the rocks that separate the swimming lagoon from Biscayne Bay. Occasionally, something out of the ordinary, such as Purple Sandpiper, will show up here.

In the western section of the park a nature trail passes through excellent tropical hardwood hammock. The trail begins directly across Old Cutler Road from the park's north entrance (cross at the traffic light). Another way to access this area is via a service road across Old Cutler Road from the park's southern entrance. The birding tends to be easier on the more open service road. Watch for White-crowned Pigeon in the treetops and Chuck-will's-widow perched on lower branches. During migration good numbers of warblers, vireos, thrushes, and tanagers can be found here. Puddles in the road may attract both Northern and Louisiana Waterthrush. Both the service road and the nature trail lead to an open area of royal palms and ficus trees. Pileated Woodpecker and Hill Myna are often seen in this area. Parrots also tend to congregate here. Possible are Monk, Yellow-chevroned, White-winged (occasional), and Mitred Parakeet, Orange-winged, Scaly-headed (rare), and White-fronted Parrot, and Blue-and-yellow Macaw. Great Horned Owl is occasionally seen in the area around the greenhouse, on your left as you approach the open area from the service road. In winter Painted and Indigo Bunting can be found in weedy areas. Blue Grosbeak is occasionally seen in these same areas during migration. Smooth-billed Ani was once commonly seen here but not in recent years.

Fairchild Tropical Garden, just south of Matheson Hammock, can have many of the same birds mentioned above but is infrequently birded due to the expensive entrance fee. Hill Myna is common and Smooth-billed Ani was resident until recently. The flowering trees in this garden attract Ruby-throated Hummingbird in winter and during migration. Buff-bellied Hummingbird was discovered here in March 2005 and again in January 2006. Several other public areas on or near Old Cutler Road can also be productive during migration. The former Parrot Jungle attraction, now a public park called Pinecrest Gardens, is on Red Road 0.3 mile north of Old Cutler Road. A series of paths crisscrosses a mixture of native tropical hardwood hammock and exotic trees and plants. The 420-acre grounds of the historic **Deering Estate at Cutler** encompass tropical hardwood hammock, pine rockland, mangrove forest, and landscaped areas. Unfortunately, access to trails is only allowed via a guided tour. **Bill Sadowski Park and Nature Center** has a short nature trail, good for Great Horned Owl and migrant land birds. Feeders at the nature center attract Painted and Indigo Bunting in winter. To reach the Black Point section of Biscayne National Park (see "Homestead Area"), continue south on Old Cutler Road 2.7 miles to SW 87th Avenue and turn left. To reach the Florida Turnpike, continue on Old Cutler Road 1.6 miles to SW 216th Street. Turn right and drive 0.6 mile to the turnpike entrance.

General information: Bill Baggs Cape Florida State Park and Crandon Park (entrance fees) are open daily from 8:00 A.M. until sunset. Restroom facilities are available in both parks. A. D. Barnes and Kendall Indian Hammock Parks (no entrance fees) are open daily from 7:00 A.M. to sunset. Matheson Hammock County Park (entrance fee for beach area only) and Bill Sadowski Park and Nature Center (no entrance fee) are open daily from sunrise to sunset. Fairchild Tropical Gardens is open daily from 9:30 A.M. to 4:30 P.M. Admission is $15 per person. Pinecrest Gardens (no entrance fee) is open daily from 8:00 A.M. to sunset. The Deering Estate (entrance fee) is open daily from 10:00 A.M. to 5:00 P.M. All locations have restroom facilities. If the gate to the parking area for the Sense of Wonder Nature Center at A. D. Barnes is locked, enter by foot via a walking path opposite the baseball diamond. When visiting Baptist Hospital, enter via the emergency-room parking area and park at the eastern end. When birding in residential neighborhoods, restroom facilities will only be found at nearby service stations and fast-food restaurants. Please respect private property when birding in these neighborhoods.

DeLorme grid: Page 118, C-3; page 119, A-2, B-1, C-1, C-2.

Hazards: Keep a safe distance from alligators (and the occasional American crocodile on Key Biscayne). Mosquitoes are numerous in summer and fall. Watch for fire-ant mounds along trails. Contact with poisonwood and poison ivy may result in a severe rash. Avoid speeding tickets, in particular in the village of Key Biscayne and on the Rickenbacker Causeway. If attempting to cross North Kendall Drive by foot in the Baptist Hospital area, use extreme caution. As is the case when visiting any large metropolitan area, common sense is essential. Birding alone is not recommended. Lock car doors and secure all valuables out of sight.

Nearest food, gas, lodging: In Miami, Coral Gables, and Kendall.

Camping: Larry and Penny Thompson Park: 240 sites, 12451 SW 184th St., Miami, FL 33177; (305) 232-1049. From the Florida Turnpike, exit at Eureka Drive (SW 184th Street, exit 13). Drive west 1.2 miles to the park entrance.

For more information: *Bill Baggs Cape Florida State Park,* 1200 S. Crandon Blvd., Key Biscayne, FL 33149; (305) 361-5811; www.floridastate

parks.org/capeflorida. *Crandon Park,* 4000 Crandon Blvd., Key Biscayne, FL 33149; (305) 361-5421; www.miamidade.gov/Parks/Parks/crandon_beach.asp. *A. D. Barnes Park,* 3401 SW 72nd Ave., Miami, FL 33155; (305) 666-5883; www.miamidade.gov/parks/parks/ad_barnes.asp. *Kendall Indian Hammock Park,* 11395 SW 79th St., Miami, FL 33173; (305) 596-9324; www.miamidade.gov/Parks/Parks/kendall_ind_hammocks.asp. *Matheson Hammock County Park,* 9610 Old Cutler Rd., Miami, FL 33156; (305) 665-5475; www.miamidade.gov/Parks/Parks/matheson_beach.asp. *Fairchild Tropical Garden,* 10901 Old Cutler Rd., Miami, FL 33156; (305) 667-1651; www.ftg.org. *Pinecrest Gardens,* 11000 Red Rd., Pinecrest, FL 33156; (305) 669-6942; www.pinecrestgardens.com. *The Deering Estate at Cutler,* 16701 SW 72nd Ave., Miami, FL 33157; (305) 235-1668; www.deeringestate.org. *Bill Sadowski County Park,* 17555 SW 79th Ave., Miami, FL 33170; (305) 255-4767; www.miamidade.gov/parks/parks/bill_sadowski.asp.

 # Homestead Area

Habitats: Mangrove forest, tropical hardwood hammock, estuary, freshwater impoundments, seasonally flooded agricultural areas, sawgrass prairie.

Specialty birds: *Resident:* Mottled Duck, Magnificent Frigatebird, Snail Kite, Purple Gallinule, Limpkin, White-crowned Pigeon, Mangrove Cuckoo, Cave Swallow (West Indian race), Common Myna, Yellow Warbler (Cuban race). *Summer:* Swallow-tailed Kite, Gray Kingbird, Black-whiskered Vireo. *Winter:* Short-tailed Hawk, Swainson's Hawk, Peregrine Falcon, Lesser Black-backed Gull, Rufous Hummingbird, Lesser Nighthawk, Western Kingbird, Scissor-tailed Flycatcher, Bell's Vireo, American Pipit, Yellow-breasted Chat, Clay-colored Sparrow, Lincoln's Sparrow, Painted Bunting, Shiny Cowbird. *Migrant:* Upland Sandpiper, White-rumped Sandpiper, Black Tern, Chuck-will's-widow, Yellow-throated Vireo, Summer Tanager, Rose-breasted Grosbeak, Blue Grosbeak, Dickcissel.

Best times to bird: Late August through May.

Directions: *Castellow Hammock Preserve and Nature Center:* From the Florida Turnpike, exit at SW 216th Street (exit 11). Turn right and drive west 5.4 miles to SW 162nd Avenue. Turn left and drive south 0.4 mile to the park entrance. *Biscayne National Park:* To access the Black Point Park section of Biscayne National Park from the Florida Turnpike in Cutler Ridge, exit at Allapattah Road (SW 112th Avenue, exit 9). Turn right on Coconut Palm Drive (SW 248th Street) and drive east 2.2 miles to the park entrance. Turn left and drive 0.5 mile to a stop sign. Turn right into the jetty/canoe-launch parking area. If coming from Old Cutler Road, turn left on SW 87th Avenue and drive south 2.6 miles to the parking area. To access Convoy Point Visitor Center from the Florida Turnpike in Homestead, exit at Speedway Boulevard (SW 137th Avenue, exit 6). Turn left and drive south 3 miles to North Canal Drive (SW 328th Street). Turn left and drive east 4 miles to the park entrance. *Southern Glades Wildlife and Environmental Area:* From the terminus of the Florida Turnpike at US 1 in Florida City, turn right on Palm Drive (SW 344th Street) and drive west 1.6 miles. Turn left on SW 197th Avenue and drive south 2 miles. Turn right on SW 392nd Street (State Road 9336) and drive west 4.5 miles to Aerojet Road.

The Birding

Castellow Hammock Preserve and Nature Center is a small (112-acre) county park nestled within the Redlands, a mostly agricultural area near Homestead. The hammock here was once the tallest in South Florida, with several champion trees, but was extensively damaged by Hurricane Andrew in 1992. Now with a much lower canopy, the hammock still attracts migrant and wintering land birds. During spring and fall, search trees around the nature center and along the hammock edge for warblers, vireos (including Black-whiskered), grosbeaks, tanagers, and other migrants. A 0.5-mile trail provides access to the hammock interior and begins behind the nature center. A butterfly garden in front of the nature center attracts migrant and wintering hummingbirds. Most are Ruby-throated, but Rufous is an almost annual winter visitor. Black-chinned Hummingbird was seen here in December 2005. Check seed feeders located within the garden, as well as at the hammock edge for wintering Painted and Indigo Bunting. Occasionally seen at these feeders are Dickcissel and Bronzed and Shiny Cowbird. White-winged Dove is common in the park and surrounding area. Watch overhead in spring and summer for Swallow-tailed Kite. Short-tailed Hawk may be seen soaring over the hammock from fall through spring.

Although 95 percent of **Biscayne National Park** is underwater, the park also protects the largest remaining tracts of mangrove forest on the Atlantic coast of Florida. This habitat can be accessed from two locations: Black Point Park, near the northern end of the national park, and Convoy Point at the southern end. The park's main visitor center is at Convoy Point. If arriving in this area by way of the Florida Turnpike, check the bridge over a canal just north of SW 216th Street for nesting Cave Swallow of the West Indian race. The swallows are most conspicuous in spring and summer but can also be seen at dawn or dusk at other times of the year. To see the swallows well, you must exit the turnpike at SW 216th Street (exit 11) and park near the canal along the northbound service road. A Bahama Swallow roosted here for several summers in the late 1980s and early 1990s before becoming a traffic fatality.

A paved trail from the Black Point Park parking lot parallels a boat channel, crossing several small bridges as it takes you onto a narrow jetty that juts into the national park. Before reaching the park boundary, a bridge on the left leads to a canoe launch that should be checked for Mangrove Cuckoo. The Cuban race of Yellow Warbler is possible anywhere along the trail. Watch for Spotted Sandpiper on rocks along the water's edge. Gulls, terns, and shorebirds frequent the tip of the jetty, which is submerged at high tide, making it off-limits to visitors. During winter, sort through the Ruddy Turnstone for a possible Purple Sandpiper. Rafts of American Coot and Lesser Scaup are often offshore. A pair of Brant spent several days in this area in winter 2000–2001, and a Glaucous Gull was found on the jetty in February 2005.

The South Dade Landfill, known to locals as Mount Trashmore, is adjacent to Black Point Park. Across SW 248th Street from the landfill, reclaimed wetland known to local birders as Dump Marsh is an excellent location in winter for American White Pelican, as well as a variety of ducks and gulls. Lesser Black-backed Gull has been found here throughout the year. Turkey Vulture will be soaring overhead, especially in winter. Scattering flocks of waterbirds usually mean a Bald Eagle or Peregrine Falcon is patrolling the area. A Black-headed Gull was discovered at the nearby water-treatment facility on a Christmas Bird Count in 2002. Black Tern sometimes passes through the area in late summer. You may occasionally see flocks of Cave Swallow of the West Indian race here as well. Greater Flamingo has been seen here on occasion, but its origin is considered suspicious. To access this area from Black Point Park, turn left immediately after leaving the jetty parking area. Drive south 0.5 mile to SW 248th Street. Turn right and drive west 1 mile to SW 97th Avenue. Turn left and double back 0.2 mile on the dirt road that parallels SW 248th Street. This will be on the opposite side of the Goulds Canal. Park along the fence just before reaching a gate, and walk the road beyond the gate to the marsh. Another area that seasonally attracts waterfowl, shorebirds, and gulls is at the intersection of SW 97th Avenue and SW 224th Street. To reach this area from Dump Marsh, return to 97th Avenue and drive north 1.5 miles to SW 224th Street. Scope this mitigation marsh, known to local birders as Cutler Wetlands, from along SW 224th Street. Rarities seen here include Hudsonian Godwit, White-rumped and Buff-breasted Sandpiper, Wilson's Phalarope, and Franklin's and Black-headed Gull.

When heading to or from the visitor center at Convoy Point, stop in late spring (May through June) or early fall (August through September) at flooded agricultural fields in the vicinity of the Homestead Motor Speedway, near the intersection of Speedway Boulevard. (SW 137th Avenue) and North Canal Drive (SW 328th Street). This has been one of the better areas in South Florida in recent years to find White-rumped Sandpiper. Black-necked Stilt nests here in summer. Numerous other shorebird species have been seen in these fields, including such rarities as American Golden-Plover, Ruff, Baird's Sandpiper, Buff-breasted Sandpiper, and Wilson's Phalarope. Convoy Point Visitor Center is at the end of North Canal Drive. There are interpretive displays and a small bookstore. Canoes may be rented for exploration of the surrounding mangrove habitat. The nearby jetty hosts gulls, terns, and shorebirds. A Common Eider was discovered here in 1999. Snorkeling and glass-bottom boat excursions to the offshore coral reefs can be arranged through the park concession. You may also be able to arrange for a boat trip to one of the park's offshore islands. Elliot Key, 7 miles east of Convoy Point, is a mangrove island with an interior tropical hardwood hammock. An old road cuts through the center of the island. Florida's first La Sagra's Flycatcher was found here in 1983, and other Caribbean vagrants, such as Key West Quail-Dove (May 2002) have been seen here as well. North America's first Red-legged Honeycreeper was discovered on nearby Boca Chita Key in March 2003. Unfortunately, the origin of this stunning tropical species is unknown.

During late summer, migrating shorebirds often congregate in puddles in fallow agricultural fields along SR 9336 in Homestead. During this time Upland Sandpiper and occasionally Buff-breasted Sandpiper can be found by searching drier areas of the fields. When reaching the residential areas beginning at SW 209th Avenue (5.7 miles from US 1), drive the side roads both north and south of SR 9336, scanning the wires for White-winged Dove among the ubiquitous Eurasian Collared-Dove. In winter Scissor-tailed Flycatcher and Western Kingbird may be seen on wires along streets just north of SR 9336, especially at dawn and dusk. Check every Western Kingbird carefully, as Cassin's Kingbird has been seen here on more than one occasion. Examine every cowbird you see in this neighborhood during winter for possible Shiny Cowbird. After crossing the C-111 canal (7.6 miles from US 1), turn left into the parking area for the South Dade Greenway. This location provides access by bicycle, horseback, or foot into **Southern Glades Wildlife and Environmental Area** via the Southern Glades Trail. A male Vermilion Flycatcher wintered in the parking area from 2003 through 2005. Check all cowbirds in winter for Shiny Cowbird. Scissor-tailed Flycatcher and Western Kingbird can occasionally be seen on wires in the vicinity during winter. Turn left to enter the Wildlife and Environmental Area at SW 232nd Avenue (Aerojet Road, 8 miles from US 1). Watch for speed bumps on this road! Drive south 0.3 mile and park beside a remnant hardwood hammock. This tiny island of tropical forest in the middle of farmland, part of **Frog Pond Wildlife Management Area,** has been dubbed **Lucky Hammock** by local birders. Almost 180 species have been seen here or in the surrounding area. Highlights include

Mississippi Kite, Black-billed Cuckoo, Brown-crested and Sulphur-bellied Flycatcher, Bell's Vireo (now regular in winter), Dickcissel, and Yellow-headed Blackbird, plus 32 species of migrant and wintering warblers, including Golden-winged, Bay-breasted, Kentucky, and Canada.

Common Ground-Dove is resident, and Gray Catbird is the most conspicuous wintering species in the area. Painted and Indigo Bunting and Yellow-breasted Chat inhabit overgrown areas on the south side of the hammock, as well as in the shrubby area across the street, especially on the back (east) side of that area. Wintering sparrows can be numerous on the east side as well, mostly Savannah and Grasshopper. Occasionally Clay-colored, Lincoln's, Chipping, Lark, Swamp, White-crowned, and White-throated Sparrow are present. Sandhill Crane, otherwise unusual in extreme southern Florida, is regularly seen feeding in the surrounding fields. Look for several species of migrating swallows, including the West Indian race of Cave Swallow, over these fields. Wintering Lesser Nighthawk is now consistently reported from this area, especially at dusk, and Antillean Nighthawk is possible in summer. The crows you see here and throughout adjacent Everglades National Park will all be American Crow. Sixteen species of raptors have been tallied in the area. Red-shouldered Hawk nests in the hammock, while Swallow-tailed Kite is seen regularly soaring over the hammock in spring and summer. Winter brings the most variety. Short-tailed, Broad-winged, and Swainson's Hawk are often seen overhead in kettles with Turkey and Black Vulture. Swainson's Hawk may also be spotted in the early morning in the surrounding fields, though Northern Harrier is much more common. As you continue south on Aerojet Road, the brushy and native planted areas on both sides of the road, dubbed "the Annex" by local birders, can be excellent for White-crowned Pigeon, plus migrant and wintering warblers, flycatchers, buntings, orioles, and many others. Bird from the roadside, and stay out of posted areas. Watch for Pileated Woodpecker, which nests in the roadside power poles. Common Myna and Shiny Cowbird can occasionally be seen perched on wires with flocks of European Starling and Brown-headed Cowbird. After 0.7 mile the road reaches a gate that is sometimes locked. Habitat beyond this gate is sawgrass prairie; Snail Kite is possible in this area, though in winter Northern Harrier is more likely. At 1 mile beyond the gate, an abandoned building on the left may have roosting Barn Owl. A permanently locked gate is 0.7 mile farther. Further access to Aerojet Road and Southern Glades Wildlife and Environmental Area is by foot only. By backtracking to SR 9336 and turning left, it is only 0.5 mile to the entrance to Everglades National Park.

General information: Castellow Hammock Preserve and Nature Center (no entrance fee) is open daily from sunrise to sunset. Restrooms are located in the nature center. The Black Point Park jetty parking area (no entrance fee) is open daily from sunrise to sunset. Restrooms are in the marina restaurant across the boat channel from the jetty. The Convoy Point entrance to Biscayne National Park (no entrance fee) is open daily from 7:00 A.M. to 5:30 P.M. Restrooms are in the visitor center. Call the park concession at (305) 230–1100 for information on access to Elliot Key or other islands in the park. Frog Pond Wildlife Management Area (470 acres, no entrance fee) and Southern Glades Wildlife and Environmental Area (30,080 acres, no entrance fee) are managed cooperatively by the South Florida Water Management District and the Florida Fish and Wildlife Conservation Commission. Frog Pond WMA consists mostly of agricultural fields and is open seasonally to dove hunting. The nearest restrooms are at the Ernest Coe Visitor Center at the entrance to Everglades National Park. Most of Southern Glades WEA may only be accessed on foot, bicycle, horseback, or canoe. The Southern Glades Trail is an unpaved, 13-mile trail following the C-111 Canal through the Southern Glades WEA.

DeLorme grid: Page 118, D-3; page 119, D-1; page 122, A-2; page 123, A-1.

Hazards: Venomous snakes (two species of rattlesnakes, cottonmouths, coral snakes) are present but rarely encountered. Mosquitoes are abundant in summer and fall. Contact with poisonwood (common on Elliot Key) or poison ivy may result in a severe rash. Watch your step on the Castellow Hammock trail.

Nearest food, gas, lodging: In Homestead and Florida City (look for Common Myna in the parking lots of fast-food franchises on US 1 just south of Palm Drive).

Camping: Larry and Penny Thompson Park: 240 sites. 12451 SW 184th St., Miami, FL 33177; (305) 232-1049. From the Florida Turnpike, exit at Eureka Drive (SW 184th St., exit 13). Drive west 1.2 miles to the park entrance. Elliot Key Campground, Biscayne National Park (accessible by boat only): 35 sites. Long Pine Key Campground, Everglades National Park: 108 sites, approximately 5.5 miles from the entrance station; no showers; (305) 272-7700. Private campgrounds are in Homestead and Florida City.

For more information: *Castellow Hammock Preserve and Nature Center*, 22301 SW 162nd Ave., Miami, FL 33170; (305) 242-7688. *Biscayne National Park*, 9700 SW 328th St., Homestead, FL 33033; (305) 230-7275; www.nps.gov/bisc. *Southern Glades Wildlife and Environmental Area*, c/o South Florida Water Management District; www.sfwmd.gov and Florida Fish and Wildlife Conservation Commission, 620 S. Meridian St., Tallahassee, FL 32399; (800) 955-8771; www.floridaconservation.org.

FLORIDA KEYS/THE EVERGLADES

24 Key Largo Area

Habitats: Mangrove forest, tropical hardwood hammock.

Specialty birds: *Resident:* Magnificent Frigatebird, "Great White" Heron, Reddish Egret, Roseate Spoonbill, White-crowned Pigeon, Mangrove Cuckoo. *Summer:* Antillean Nighthawk, Gray Kingbird, Black-whiskered Vireo, Yellow Warbler (Cuban race).

Best times to bird: Late April through August for breeding specialties.

Directions: From the terminus of the Florida Turnpike at U.S. Highway 1 in Florida City, continue south 1 mile on US 1. Turn left on Card Sound Road (County Road 905A, $1.00 toll) and drive east to access birding sites in the northern half of Key Largo. Continue south 20 miles on US 1 if driving directly to southern Key Largo and beyond.

The Birding

Card Sound Road provides access to Crocodile Lake National Wildlife Refuge as well as a reliable location for the Cuban race of Yellow Warbler. Osprey is common along the first dozen miles of this road, though Bald Eagle is also possible. At 12.5 miles, check for Yellow Warbler in the mangroves just before or just after the Card Sound Bridge tollbooth ($1.00

FLORIDA KEYS/THE EVERGLADES

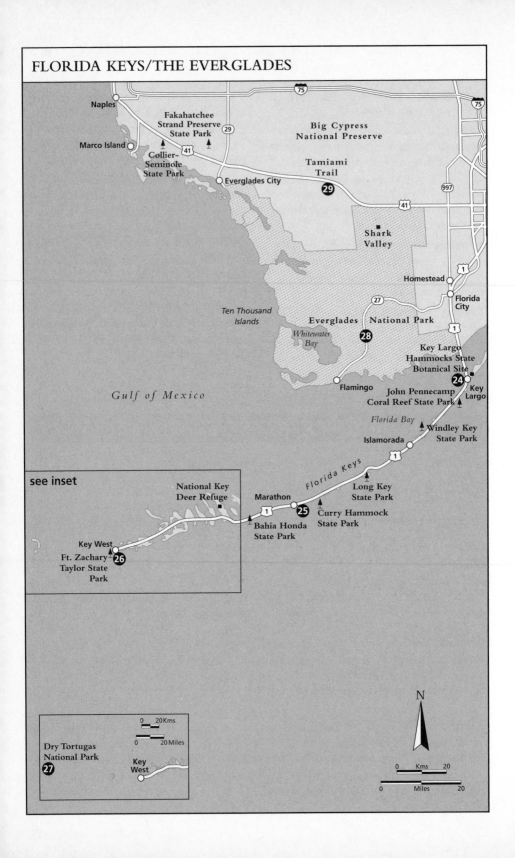

toll). Prairie Warbler also breeds here. Watch the skies for White-crowned Pigeon and the wires in spring and summer for Gray Kingbird. Magnificent Frigatebird may be seen soaring over Card Sound, especially in summer.

Crocodile Lake National Wildlife Refuge begins after the Card Sound Bridge. After 4 miles, check areas of open water for the endangered American crocodile. At low tide wading birds, including Reddish Egret and Roseate Spoonbill, often feed here. Turn right at the stop sign (4.8 miles from the bridge) onto County Road 905. The refuge, which continues on the right, as well as **Dagny Johnson Key Largo Hammock Botanical State Park,** which begins on the left, protects the largest continuous tract of tropical hardwood hammock left in the United States. The interior of the refuge can be accessed only by special-use permit for research or by organized educational groups. Most of the hammock in the state park is also accessible only by backcountry permit. You may bird along the road or explore residential areas built before the hammock was designated for protection. Please respect private property in these areas. In May 2000 a Zenaida Dove was discovered in the residential area accessed from Valois Boulevard (turn left 7 miles from the stop sign). In 1.5 miles turn left into the parking area for **Key Largo Hammocks State Botanical Site.** A self-guided nature trail (fee) provides the only public access to the state park. Spring is the best season to see hammock specialties such as White-crowned Pigeon, Mangrove Cuckoo, Gray Kingbird, and Black-whiskered Vireo. If Mangrove Cuckoo is your target bird, be aware that Yellow-billed Cuckoo also breeds here. Migrating warblers are common in spring, occasionally including Connecticut Warbler. Caribbean strays such as La Sagra's Flycatcher, Thick-billed Vireo, and Western Spindalis have also been recorded here. Commonly seen species include Great Crested Flycatcher and White-eyed Vireo. Loquat Road, just south of the parking area, should also be birded for hammock specialties. CR 905 rejoins US 1 after 0.4 mile. Look for Bobolink during migration in overgrown areas on either side of US 1.

Most locations on US 1 (also known as the Overseas Highway) in the Florida Keys can be found using the highway's mile marker (MM) system, which begins at zero in Key West. The entrance to **John Pennekamp Coral Reef State Park** (fee) is on the left at MM 102.5, 3.5 miles from where CR 905 rejoins US 1. This park provides a wide range of recreational opportunities, including glass-bottom boat tours, snorkeling and scuba trips, boating, swimming, fishing, picnicking, and camping. Canoes and kayaks may be rented for exploration of the park's extensive mangrove wilderness. Two short trails allow for hikes through mangrove as well as tropical hardwood hammock habitat. Here, Mangrove Cuckoo, Black-whiskered Vireo, and other Keys specialties are possible. A Bahama Mockingbird was seen near the entrance road in May 2004. In summer Antillean Nighthawk has been seen at dusk at the shopping center on the left at MM 100. **Florida Keys Wild Bird Center** is on the right at MM 93.6. A wildlife-rehabilitation facility for the Upper Keys, the center specializes in the care of injured waterbirds. Self-guided tours of the facility provide visitors with up-close looks at pelicans, cormorants, various waders, gulls and terns, raptors, owls, and even jaegers and other pelagic species. Large numbers of wild birds are also attracted to the mangrove and tropical hardwood hammock habitat surrounding the center, including Roseate Spoonbill, Black-necked Stilt, and migrating and wintering warblers. All can be viewed from the facility's trails, boardwalks, and observation platforms.

Several locations in the next few miles are worth a quick stop during migration for songbirds or shorebirds. Old Settler's Park is a tiny county park on the left near MM 92. The butterfly garden here may attract Ruby-throated Hummingbird. Antillean Nighthawk

Black-whiskered Vireo. PHOTO: TREY MITCHELL

has been seen near Plantation Key School at MM 90. **Windley Key Fossil Reef Geological State Park** is on the right at MM 85.3. Known more for its coral rock quarries, the park has a trail system through tropical hardwood hammock that is attractive to migrating songbirds. Caribbean strays found here include Zenaida Dove (February 1996) and Western Spindalis (January 2004). If you stop at the 1935 Hurricane Monument, just past MM 82 in Islamorada, a walk around the nearby residential area may produce migrating songbirds, as well as an occasional Scissor-tailed Flycatcher or Western Kingbird on the wires. A Fork-tailed Flycatcher was seen here in April 1996. Anne's Beach, on the left near MM 74, has a boardwalk through mangrove habitat that should be checked for migrating songbirds, Northern Waterthrush in particular. Check along the shore for feeding shorebirds or Reddish Egret. You have now entered the Middle Keys, where the Overseas Highway provides simultaneous views of the Atlantic Ocean and Florida Bay. If you are continuing your journey through the Keys, Long Key State Park is 6 miles farther.

General information: Key Largo Hammocks State Botanical Site (entrance fee) and John Pennekamp Coral Reef State Park (entrance fee) are open daily from 8:00 A.M. to sunset. Florida Keys Wild Bird Center (donations requested) is open 24 hours a day. Old Settler's Park (no entrance fee) is open daily from 7:30 A.M. to sunset. Windley Key Fossil Reef Geological State Park (entrance fee) is open Thursday through Monday from 8:00 A.M. to 5:00 P.M. Anne's Beach (no entrance fee) is open 24 hours a day. Restrooms are available at all locations with the exception of Old Settler's Park.

Backcountry permits to enter restricted areas of Dagny Johnson Key Largo Hammock Botanical State Park are available at John Pennekamp Coral Reef State Park. Call (305) 451-1202 for additional information.

DeLorme grid: Pages 122, 123.

Hazards: Keep a safe distance from alligators and crocodiles. Trespassers into Crocodile Lake NWR and Key Largo Hammock Botanical State Park are subject to arrest. These areas are regularly patrolled. At Key Largo Hammocks State Botanical Site, stay on the trails. Contact with poisonwood may result in a severe rash. Mosquitoes are abundant in summer.

Nearest food, gas, lodging: In Key Largo and Islamorada.

Camping: John Pennekamp Coral Reef State Park: 47 sites. Call (800) 326-3521 for reservations. Long Key State Park, in Layton: 60 sites; (305) 664-4815. There are private campgrounds in Key Largo.

For more information: *Crocodile Lake National Wildlife Refuge, P.O. Box 370, Key Largo, FL 33037; (305) 451-4223; http://southeast.fws .gov/crocodilelake. Dagny Johnson Key Largo Hammock Botanical State Park, P.O. Box 487, Key Largo, FL 33037; (305) 451-1202; www.florida stateparks.org/keylargohammock. John Penne-kamp Coral Reef State Park, P.O. Box 487, Key Largo, FL 33027; (305) 451-1202; www.florida stateparks.org/pennekamp. Florida Keys Wild Bird Center, 93600 Overseas Hwy., Tavernier, FL 33070; (305) 852-4486; www.fkwbc.org. Windley Key Fossil Reef Geological State Park, P.O. Box 1052, Islamorada, FL 33036; (305) 664-2540; www.floridastateparks.org/windleykey.*

25 Marathon Area

Habitats: Mangrove forest, tropical hardwood hammock, sandy beach.

Specialty birds: *Resident:* Magnificent Frigate-bird, "Great White" Heron, Reddish Egret, Roseate Spoonbill, Bald Eagle, White-crowned Pigeon, Mangrove Cuckoo, Burrowing Owl. *Summer:* Roseate Tern, Least Tern, Antillean Nighthawk,

Gray Kingbird, Black-whiskered Vireo. *Migrant:* Peregrine Falcon.

Best times to bird: Late April through August for breeding specialties; April to early May and September to early October for migrating land birds; September through October for migrating raptors.

Directions: This tour begins at *Long Key State Park,* located on US 1 (Overseas Highway) at mile marker (MM) 68. This is approximately 60 miles south of the terminus of the Florida Turnpike in Florida City.

The Birding

At MM 68.5, turn left into **Long Key State Park.** Turn left after the entrance station to access the trailhead parking area. Black-whiskered Vireo is common around the parking area in summer. A Western Spindalis was discovered here in November 2004. A boardwalk leads to an observation platform, an excellent location to observe migrating hawks in fall. The boardwalk leads through mangrove forest to the shoreline, where wintering shorebirds and Reddish Egret are possible, and to a trail that passes through hardwood hammock, good for migrant and wintering songbirds. A Key West Quail-Dove was found on this trail in June 2002.

On Grassy Key, Least Tern and Black-necked Stilt nest at Lake Edna. Other shorebirds, including White-rumped Sandpiper, may stop here during migration. To access this area, turn right onto Peachtree Road at MM 58 and walk to the lake edge. At MM 56.5 turn left into **Curry Hammock State Park.** This small park is well known to local birders as

Hawkwatch International's official site to monitor the fall passage of raptors through the Keys. During September and October large numbers of southbound hawks are tallied from this site. Most common are Osprey, Northern Harrier, Sharp-shinned, Cooper's, and Broad-winged Hawk, American Kestrel, Merlin, and Peregrine Falcon. Less frequently observed are Swallow-tailed and Mississippi Kite, Bald Eagle, and Red-shouldered, Short-tailed, Swainson's, and Red-tailed Hawk. Peeps and other shorebirds can be found feeding along the shoreline, and Magnificent Frigatebird can be seen soaring offshore.

On the right at MM 53, **Marathon Airport** is an excellent location on summer evenings to listen for feeding Antillean Nighthawk. Common Nighthawk also feeds here. The only sure way to separate these two species is to learn their distinctly different calls ("pity-pit-pit" for Antillean, "peent" for Common). Seasonally wet areas at the west end of the airport (MM 51) may attract migrating waterfowl and shorebirds. On the left at MM 50, **Crane Point Museum of Natural History** has trails through tropical hardwood hammock, good for Black-whiskered Vireo and migrating songbirds. Burrowing Owl can be found nearby at Sombrero Beach Golf Course. To reach this area from the museum, cross US 1 onto Sombrero Beach Road. Turn right (0.1 mile) onto Sombrero Boulevard, which loops around the golf course.

In summer check for nesting Roseate and Least Tern on the flat-roofed Government Center buildings on the right at MM 48.5. The terns may also be found roosting on pilings along the shoreline. Turn left onto County Road 931 (MM 48.2) to reach **Boot Key.** This is another excellent fall hawk-watch location. All of the same raptors listed for Curry Hammock can be seen here. The first mile of roadside hammock is suitable habitat for Black-whiskered Vireo and Mangrove Cuckoo. It is also attractive to migrating songbirds and the occasional Caribbean vagrant, such as Key West Quail-Dove (April 1987) and Thick-billed Vireo (October 2004). At MM 47 (just before the Seven-Mile Bridge), check the brushy area on the right for migrating Bobolink. After crossing the bridge, stop on Ohio Key (MM 39) to scope the mudflats on the left side of US 1. "Great White" Heron, Reddish Egret, and a wide variety of migrating shorebirds are possible here. Turn left at MM 37 into **Bahia Honda State Park.** The nature trail at the east end of the park can be good for White-crowned Pigeon and migrating songbirds. Shiny Cowbird has also been seen here.

Antillean Nighthawk. PHOTO: LARRY MANFREDI

National Key Deer Refuge on Big Pine Key (MM 33) is home to the smallest subspecies of white-tailed deer, as well as other threatened species. Fencing and a series of underpasses have been installed along this stretch of US 1 to protect the deer from traffic (also keep in mind that it is illegal to feed these deer). A part of the refuge can be accessed by turning right on Key Deer Boulevard (MM 30.5). After 2.8 miles, stop at the Blue Hole, an abandoned limestone quarry that has in the past hosted rarities such as Least Grebe (October 1988). A short trail encircles the quarry. Frederick Manillo Nature Trail, 0.3 mile farther, provides access to pine rockland habitat that may harbor wintering flocks of warblers. Scan the kettles of Turkey Vulture for Broad-winged and Short-tailed Hawk. From Big Pine Key, continue west on US 1 another 26 miles to Key West.

General information: Long Key, Curry Hammock, and Bahia Honda State Parks (entrance fees) are open daily from 8:00 A.M. to sunset. Crane Point Museum of Natural History (entrance fee) is open Monday through Saturday from 9:00 A.M. to 5:00 P.M., and Sunday from noon to 5:00 P.M. Restroom facilities are available at all locations. National Key Deer Refuge (no entrance fee) is open 24 hours a day.

DeLorme grid: Page 124, C-1, C-2, C-3; page 125, C-1, B-2, B-3.

Hazards: Contact with poisonwood and manchineel (rare) may result in a severe rash. Eastern diamondback rattlesnakes are present on Big Pine Key. Keep a safe distance from alligators in Blue Hole. Prepare for mosquitoes in summer.

Nearest food, gas, lodging: In Marathon.

Camping: Long Key State Park: 60 sites; (305) 664-4815. Bahia Honda State Park: 80 sites; (305) 872-2353. There are private campgrounds in Marathon.

For more information: *Long Key State Park,* P.O. Box 776, Long Key, FL 33001; (305) 664-4815; www.floridastateparks.org/longkey. *Curry Hammock State Park,* MM 57, Overseas Hwy., Crawl Key, FL 33050; (305) 664-4815. *Crane Point Museum of Natural History,* 5550 Overseas Hwy., Marathon, FL 33050; (305) 743-9100; www.cranepoint.org. *Bahia Honda State Park,* 36850 Overseas Hwy., Big Pine Key, FL 33043; (305) 872-2353; www.floridastateparks.org/bahia honda. *National Key Deer Refuge,* P.O. Box 430510, Big Pine Key, FL 33043; (305) 872-0774; http://nationalkeydeer.fws.gov.

26 Key West

Habitats: Mangrove forest, tropical hardwood hammock, sandy beach.

Specialty birds: *Resident:* Magnificent Frigatebird, "Great White" Heron, Reddish Egret, White-crowned Pigeon, Mangrove Cuckoo, Shiny Cowbird. *Summer:* Roseate Tern, Antillean Nighthawk, Gray Kingbird, Black-whiskered Vireo. *Winter:* Short-tailed Hawk, Scissor-tailed Flycatcher. *Migrant:* "Antillean" Short-eared Owl.

Best times to bird: April through August for breeding specialties; April to early May and September through October for migrating land birds.

Directions: The tour begins on Stock Island at mile marker (MM) 5 of the Overseas Highway (US 1), approximately 125 miles from the terminus of the Florida Turnpike in Florida City. Mile marker 0 is in downtown Key West.

The Birding

Key West is the end of the road, the southernmost point in the continental United States. The island has seen its share of avian mega-rarities over the years, including Scaly-naped Pigeon, Ruddy Quail-Dove, Antillean Palm Swift, and Tawny-shouldered Blackbird. It may be wise to carry a West Indies field guide when visiting this island. Before entering Key West, the Overseas Highway (US 1) crosses Stock Island. To visit the **Key West Tropical**

Antillean Short-eared Owl. PHOTO: LARRY MANFREDI

Forest and Botanical Garden, turn right onto College Road (MM 4.2). The entrance is on the right, 0.1 mile farther. As you walk the paths of this newly refurbished botanical garden, look for resident White-crowned Pigeon, Black-whiskered Vireo in summer, and migrant and wintering warblers, vireos, and other passerines. A Western Spindalis was found here in April 2005. Continue down College Road another 0.7 mile to Florida Keys Community College, where in summer Antillean Nighthawk may be seen or heard at dusk. After crossing the Cow Key Channel Bridge, turn left onto South Roosevelt Boulevard. After 0.2 mile, turn right onto Flagler Avenue. Scan the wires along the first few blocks of this road for Gray Kingbird in summer, Scissor-tailed Flycatcher in winter, Shiny Cowbird (rare) in winter and spring, and White-crowned Pigeon year-round. Return to Roosevelt Boulevard and drive south to Key West Airport (1.2 miles). In summer look for Antillean Nighthawk at dusk.

Continue on South Roosevelt Boulevard, turn right on Bertha Street (1.5 miles), then left onto Atlantic Boulevard (0.1 mile). At White Street (0.5 mile) turn right into the parking area for **McCoy Indigenous Park.** Though officially open only on weekdays, this small park can be accessed after 8:30 A.M. on weekends through the Wildlife Rescue of the Florida Keys, a bird-rehabilitation facility that shares the park grounds. Sightings at this outstanding migrant trap have included Northern Wheatear, Bahama Mockingbird, La Sagra's Flycatcher, Yellow-green Vireo, Mourning Warbler, and Western Spindalis. Smooth-billed Ani has been recorded here on occasion. Expect a wide variety of warblers and other songbirds during migration. Many of these warblers may also winter here. Check the fruiting trees around the rehabilitation center, as well as around the pond at the far end of the park. Across the street from McCoy Indigenous Park, a Bahama Mockingbird resided for several years in the early 1990s. At Higgs Beach, a short walk from the park, Florida's first Slaty-backed Gull was discovered in September 2002. The gull later relocated to a shopping center on the north side of Key West.

Ft. Zachary Taylor Historic State Park has been a reliable location for spring migrants, occasionally including the Antillean race of Short-eared Owl. Search for this owl in overgrown areas around the fort. A Red-legged Honeycreeper was found at the fort in

April 2005 and North America's first verified Loggerhead Kingbird was seen here in March 2007. To reach this site from Indigenous Park, continue west on Atlantic Boulevard, turn right on Reynolds Street (0.3 mile), left on South Street (0.3 mile), right on White-head Street (0.4 mile), and left on Southard Street (0.5 mile), following the signs to the entrance station. White-crowned Pigeon is commonly seen roosting in Australian pines along the entrance road, and Magnificent Frigatebird is often spotted just offshore. Also watch for Roseate Tern, especially on the roofs of surrounding buildings. Harris School, Monroe County's first public high school, can be reached by doubling back on Southard Street through the intersection with Whitehead Street to Margaret Street (0.4 mile). The ornamental trees surrounding the school should be checked during spring and fall for migrant land birds.

When returning to the mainland, exit at MM 10.7 on Big Coppitt Key. County Road 941 will take you to Boca Chica Key Beach, adjacent to Key West Naval Air Station. The end of CR 941 is blocked due to erosion damage, but you may continue by foot a few hundred yards to a pond on your right. A variety of shorebirds can be found here during migration. Two to three hours before or after high tide seems to be best, as the birds tend to disperse during low tide. A Curlew Sandpiper was seen here in April 2001. When birding in this area, you can avoid being interrogated by air station security by directing your binoculars toward the birds, not the fighter jets.

General information: Key West Tropical Forest and Botanical Garden (donation requested) is open daily from 10:00 A.M. to 4:00 P.M. Ft. Zachary Taylor Historic State Park (entrance fee) is open daily from 8:00 A.M. to sunset. Restroom facilities are available at both locations.

DeLorme grid: Page 127, D-1.

Hazards: Drive the streets of Key West with extreme caution. Watch for pedestrians, bicyclists, moped riders, and Conch Trains.

Nearest food, gas, lodging: In Key West.

Camping: Private campgrounds are on Stock Island and in Key West.

For more information: *Key West Tropical Forest and Botanical Garden,* 5210 College Rd., Stock Island, FL 33041; (305) 296–1504. *Wildlife Rescue of the Florida Keys,* P.O. Box 5449, Key West, FL 33045; (305) 294–1441; www.seabird sanctuary.org/KeyWest.htm. *Ft. Zachary Taylor Historic State Park,* P.O. Box 6560, Key West, FL 33041; (305) 292–6713; www.floridastateparks .org/forttaylor.

 # Dry Tortugas National Park

Habitats: Tropical islands.

Specialty birds: *Resident:* Masked Booby, Brown Booby, Magnificent Frigatebird. *Spring/Summer:* Audubon's Shearwater, Roseate Tern, Bridled Tern, Sooty Tern, Brown Noddy. *Winter:* Whimbrel. *Migrant:* White-tailed Tropicbird, Red-footed Booby, Peregrine Falcon, Upland Sandpiper, Black Noddy, "Antillean" Short-eared Owl, Antillean Nighthawk, Chuck-will's-widow, Gray Kingbird, Cave Swallow, Black-whiskered Vireo, Prothonotary Warbler, Kentucky Warbler, Hooded Warbler, Summer Tanager, Scarlet Tanager, Blue Grosbeak, Painted Bunting, Dickcissel, Orchard Oriole.

Best times to bird: April to mid-May for spring neotropical migrants, Brown and possibly Red-footed Booby, Sooty Tern, Brown and possibly Black Noddy. September through October for fall neotropical migrants.

Directions: Dry Tortugas National Park is 68 miles west of Key West. For day trips to the national park, two companies, Yankee Freedom and Sunny Days, provide high-speed ferry service to Garden Key. Travel time to Garden Key is about 2.5 hours each way, with about five hours spent on the island. The vessel used by Yankee Freedom provides greater opportunities for viewing pelagic species en route. Both ferries depart at 8:00 A.M. from Land's End Marina in Key West. From the junction of US 1 (North Roosevelt Boulevard) and State Road A1A (South Roosevelt Boulevard), drive west 2.2 miles on North Roosevelt Boulevard. Turn right on Palm Avenue and drive 1 mile to Grinnell Street. Turn right. A parking garage for the marina area is on Grinnell Street while the ferry docks are 1 block farther, at the end of Margaret Street. Your other day-trip alternative is Seaplanes of Key West, which flies four times daily to Garden Key. Though faster, this option is more expensive than the ferries, and you will spend less time (about three hours) on Garden Key. For multiday cruises to the Tortugas, Florida bird guide Larry Manfredi provides four-day/three-night tours on the M V *Playmate* from April to early May. Other bird-tour companies schedule overnight trips as well. Only multiday tours provide access to other islands in the national park. A final option is to ride a ferry and, for an additional charge, camp at the campground on Garden Key.

The Birding

Several species commonly seen in **Dry Tortugas National Park,** namely Brown and Masked Booby, Sooty Tern, and Brown Noddy, cannot reliably be found anywhere else in North America. In addition, an astounding variety of neotropical migrants use these islands as a welcome respite on their long and perilous journey over the Gulf of Mexico. Finally, almost every year rarities from the Caribbean or accidentals from Mexico or the western United States are discovered here. This all makes for an unbeatable combination, making it clear why Dry Tortugas is one of the great birding destinations in North America. If traveling to the Dry Tortugas by ferry, watch en route for pelagic species such as Northern Gannet, Audubon's Shearwater, and Bridled Tern. Multiday trips in spring may travel to areas more productive for pelagic species and in the past have produced sightings of Wilson's and Band-rumped Storm-Petrel, White-tailed Tropicbird, Parasitic and Pomarine Jaeger, and Sabine's Gull. As you enter the national park, scan each channel marker for roosting Brown Booby or Roseate Tern. Red-footed Booby has also been seen occasionally on these channel markers in spring. As Fort Jefferson on Garden Key becomes visible on the horizon, you should begin to see and hear your first Sooty Tern and Brown Noddy. If the ferry passes close to Hospital Key, you may be able to spot Masked Booby on this tiny treeless island, the only nesting location for this species in North America. As the ferry approaches the dock at Garden Key, scan the pilings of the abandoned south coaling dock. Among the loafing Brown Pelican, Double-crested Cormorant, Laughing Gull, and Royal Tern, a few shorebirds, including Whimbrel, can often be found. Other gulls and terns, including Sandwich and Roseate Tern, may also be resting on the coaling dock. Magnificent Frigatebird will be seen circling over the fort.

Adjacent to Garden Key is Bush Key, home to North America's only nesting colonies of Sooty Tern and Brown Noddy. About 50,000 Sooty Terns nest annually here, along with about 4,500 Brown Noddies. Access to this island is restricted during the breeding season, but both species can be easily seen in great swirling masses from Garden Key. Small chase boats used by multiday-tour operators will get you closer to the nesting colonies. This will provide an opportunity to scan through the tern flocks for the rare and elusive Black Noddy, an almost annual spring visitor to the area. The chase boats may also take you closer to adjoining Long Key, home to a nesting colony of Magnificent Frigatebird. Two

Red-footed Boobies also roosted here in April 2004. For several years Bush Key was connected to Garden Key by a sandbar, which filled in the original channel separating the two islands. Concerns arose that this land bridge would allow rats inhabiting Fort Jefferson to cross over to Bush Key, thus threatening the nesting terns and noddies. Hurricanes in 2004 and 2005 washed away the sandbar, though it reformed in late 2004 and may do so again. The hurricanes also caused significant damage to the vegetation

Magnificent Frigatebird. PHOTO: LARRY MANFREDI

on both Bush and Long Keys. How this will impact nesting terns, noddies, and Magnificent Frigatebirds has yet to be fully determined. Fort Jefferson sustained damage from the hurricanes as well. Large numbers of trees within the fort were knocked down; some were later cut down but others are expected to survive. How the hurricanes' damage affects the birding on Garden Key and throughout the national park remains to be seen.

Upon landing on Garden Key, the first birds you are likely to see are Ruddy Turnstone scurrying along the beach or in open areas around the campground outside the fort. A hike on the seawall around the moat that surrounds the massive brick fort may produce Spotted Sandpiper. Watch for them walking along the narrow ledges that line the fort above the moat. Swallows, mostly Barn but also including Tree, Northern Rough-winged, Bank, Cliff, Cave, and Purple Martin, may be seen soaring around the fort or over the moat. After crossing the moat and entering the fort, a water fountain, built to provide migrating birds a place to drink and bathe, will be immediately to your left. Cattle Egret will be conspicuous in open areas in the fort, searching for exhausted migrants. Upland Sandpiper is occasionally seen here during migration. In addition, migrating raptors such as Sharp-shinned Hawk, American Kestrel, Merlin, and Peregrine Falcon will often be seen swooping down on unsuspecting land birds.

During spring migration every tree within the fort parade grounds and in the campground should be carefully examined for migrant birds. Commonly seen are Mourning Dove, Yellow-billed Cuckoo, Common Nighthawk, Eastern Wood-Pewee, Eastern and Gray Kingbird, Yellow-bellied Sapsucker, White-eyed, Red-eyed, and Black-whiskered Vireo, Blue-gray Gnatcatcher, Veery, Swainson's, Gray-cheeked, and Wood Thrush, a wide assortment of warblers including Tennessee, Northern Parula, Yellow, Magnolia, Cape May, Black-throated Blue, Myrtle, Black-throated Green, Yellow-throated, Prairie, Palm (abundant), Blackpoll, Black-and-white, American Redstart, and Worm-eating, Summer and Scarlet Tanager, Rose-breasted and Blue Grosbeak, Orchard and Baltimore Oriole, Indigo Bunting, and Bobolink. Ruby-throated Hummingbird is usually found around flowering trees. Antillean Nighthawk may occasionally be seen perched on a tree limb. Use caution when attempting to separate this species from Common Nighthawk. Also search for migrants in overgrown areas such as the soldiers' barracks inside the fort parade grounds, under trees, or along foundation edges both inside and outside the fort. Migrants may also be found on top of the fort or in brick structures within the fort, such as the magazines. Avoid trespassing in posted areas near the staff residential area or in locations closed due to safety hazards. Although more sparsely vegetated than before the hurricanes, some locations outside the fort can be productive. Check the areas between the seaplane ramp and the north coaling dock and between the helipad (adjacent to the south coaling dock) and the campground restrooms. Species possible in these locations include Short-eared Owl (Antillean race), Chuck-will's-widow, Ovenbird, Northern and Louisiana Waterthrush, Prothonotary, Kentucky and Hooded Warbler, Common Yellowthroat, and Indigo and Painted Bunting. The shoreline between the seaplane ramp and the north coaling dock can be good for plovers, yellowlegs, dowitchers, peeps, and other shorebirds. The north coaling dock will provide your best chance to find a Black Noddy or two roosting on the pilings among the abundant Brown Noddy. Look for a bird noticeably smaller than Brown Noddy, with a longer, thinner bill. Also examine each Black-bellied Plover perched here or feeding along the shore, for a possible American Golden-Plover.

Multiday tours to the Tortugas usually include a visit to Loggerhead Key. The island was once as outstanding a migrant trap as Garden Key. Most of the non-native vegetation, including all the Australian pines, has been removed in recent years, thus eliminating most of the cover for migrant land birds. You'll still find a few migrants in the vegetation that remains. Scattered groups of shorebirds are usually working the beaches. Short-eared Owl (Antillean race) is occasionally flushed from the brushy interior of the island. On a really good day, usually after the passage of a front, a visit to the Tortugas may produce less commonly seen species, such as Black-billed Cuckoo, Blue-headed and Yellow-throated Vireo, Blue-winged, Golden-winged, Chestnut-sided, Blackburnian, Bay-breasted, Cerulean, Swainson's, and Connecticut Warbler, and Dickcissel. Unexpected birds are often found in unexpected places. Don't be surprised if you stumble upon a Purple Gallinule or Sora perched in a tree! Exceptional days are those that produce accidentals from the Caribbean or elsewhere. The unbelievable list of rarities seen in recent years includes White-tipped Dove, Ruddy Quail-Dove, Long-eared Owl, La Sagra's Flycatcher, Piratic Flycatcher, Fork-tailed Flycatcher, Bahama Mockingbird, Bananaquit, Red-legged Honeycreeper, and Yellow-faced Grassquit. Never knowing what will show up next is one of the reasons birders keep coming back to these magical islands.

General information: Ferry service to Dry Tortugas National Park is available year-round. Reservations are strongly recommended. An entry fee into the national park is incorporated into the ferry fee. Water is not available on the islands (hence the name "Dry" Tortugas), though bottled water is available for purchase on the ferry. Restroom facilities are in the campground, but use is restricted to campers. Ferry passengers must use the facilities onboard the ferry. Entry into Fort Jefferson is only allowed during daylight hours. Daily ranger-led tours of the fort are available. Snorkeling equipment is available at the visitor center inside the fort. Bird checklists are also available in the visitor center.

DeLorme grid: Page 126, A-2, B-1.

Hazards: The sun is unrelenting and shade is at a premium in the Dry Tortugas. Sunburn and dehydration are distinct possibilities for the unprepared visitor. Use sunscreen and drink plenty of water. If touring the top of Fort Jefferson, obey signs warning you to stay away from the edge. The walls of the fort are crumbling in many areas. If snorkeling is on your itinerary, contact with fire coral will produce a painful sting. Avoid standing on or coming into contact with any living coral. Snorkeling or swimming in the moat is prohibited.

Nearest food, gas, lodging: Breakfast and a picnic lunch are provided for all ferry passengers. There is no food or lodging available in Dry Tortugas National Park. Food, gas, and lodging are available upon your return to Key West. For multi-day tours, sleeping accommodations and meals are provided onboard the tour vessel.

Camping: On Garden Key: 10 sites (fee $3.00 per person per night). Camping is limited to 30 days per calendar year. A special-use permit is required in advance from the park superintendent for groups of more than 10 persons. Grills, picnic tables, and restrooms (primitive) are available, but there are no showers. All food and water must be packed in and all garbage must be packed out.

For more information: *Dry Tortugas National Park,* P.O. Box 6208, Key West, FL 33041; www .nps.gov/drto, www.drytortugasinfo.com. *Larry Manfredi Birding Tours,* P.O. Box 322244, Homestead, FL 33032; (305) 247–3930; birderlm @bellsouth.net.

28 Everglades National Park

Habitats: Sawgrass prairie, pine rockland, tropical hardwood hammock, dwarf cypress forest, mangrove forest, coastal prairie, estuary.

Specialty birds: *Resident:* Wood Stork, Least Bittern, "Great White" Heron, Reddish Egret, Roseate Spoonbill, Greater Flamingo, Snail Kite, White-tailed Kite, Bald Eagle, Clapper Rail, King Rail, Purple Gallinule, Limpkin, White-crowned Pigeon, Mangrove Cuckoo, Brown-headed Nuthatch, "Cape Sable" Seaside Sparrow, Shiny Cowbird. *Summer:* Swallow-tailed Kite, Least Tern, Antillean Nighthawk, Chuck-will's-widow, Gray Kingbird, Black-whiskered Vireo. *Winter:* Short-tailed Hawk, Peregrine Falcon, Lesser Nighthawk, Whip-poor-will, Brown-crested Flycatcher, Scissor-tailed Flycatcher, Western Kingbird, Nelson's Sharp-tailed Sparrow, Saltmarsh Sharp-tailed Sparrow, Painted Bunting. *Migrant:* Yellow-throated Vireo.

Best times to bird: October through April.

Directions: From the terminus of the Florida Turnpike at US 1 in Florida City, turn right on Palm Drive (SW 344th Street) and drive west 1.6 miles. Turn left on SW 197th Avenue and drive south 2 miles. Turn right on SW 392nd Street (State Road 9336) and drive west 5 miles to the park entrance.

The Birding

Covering almost 1.4 million acres at the tip of the Florida peninsula and including most of Florida Bay, **Everglades National Park** protects much of the remaining "River of Grass" made famous by conservationist Marjorie Stoneman Douglas. Designated as a national park in 1947, the park has also been declared an International Biosphere Reserve, a World Heritage Site, and a Wetland of International Importance. More than one million visitors enter the park annually. The Everglades is well known among birders and nonbirders alike for its high concentrations of wading birds. Though their numbers have decreased dramatically in the last century, a great variety of herons, egrets, and other wading birds can still be seen throughout the park. Over 300 bird species are on the park checklist, including a number of Florida specialties. Begin your exploration of the park at the Ernest Coe Visitor Center, on your right 0.5 mile beyond the park entrance sign. The visitor center has excellent interpretive displays and a short film depicting the diverse habitats within the park. Maps and checklists are available at the information desk, as is a list of the latest bird and other wildlife sightings. Be sure to submit your own list of sightings upon leaving the park. Check the native plant garden outside the visitor center for House Wren and wintering warblers. Ruby-throated and occasionally Rufous Hummingbird may be seen feeding in blooming fire-bush trees during fall and winter. Check the mahogany trees in the parking area during winter for Yellow-bellied Sapsucker. Listen year-round for Eastern Screech-Owl.

After passing through the entrance station, stop briefly at the second of two bridges over Taylor Slough (1.5 miles from the visitor center). "Great White" Heron is regular here; King Rail and Least Bittern are also possible. After 0.5 mile turn left to visit **Royal Palm Hammock.** The parking area at the end of this road (1.8 miles) can be excellent in early morning for migrant and wintering songbirds, as well as White-crowned Pigeon. Warblers especially like the ficus trees near the visitor center and at the exit of the Gumbo Limbo Trail. A male Red-legged Honeycreeper of unknown origin was seen here in February 2004. If you arrive at dawn in summer, you'll probably hear, and possibly see, Chuck-will's-widow. Swallow-tailed Kite will be soaring over the surrounding hammock in summer. In winter Short-tailed Hawk can be seen over this area, often mixed with midmorning kettles of Turkey and Black Vulture. Royal Palm Hammock features two wheelchair-accessible trails. The 0.5-mile Anhinga Trail combines a paved walkway with a boardwalk over sawgrass prairie and Taylor Slough. As water levels drop during the winter dry season, fish concentrate here, making the area very attractive to a wide variety of waders. The trail's namesake will likely be the first bird you see, and many nest here during winter and early spring. Most of the wading birds are used to the throngs of visitors and can often be approached closely. Large numbers of American alligators also concentrate here in winter; don't approach them too closely! Look for Purple Gallinule stepping gingerly on spadderdock and, in winter, American Bittern camouflaged in the sawgrass. Yellow-crowned Night-Heron roosts in pond apple trees along the boardwalk. The Gumbo Limbo Trail snakes through the tropical hardwood hammock for 0.4 mile. Look for wintering songbirds anywhere along the path, and Barred Owl in live oaks along the trail. Black-whiskered Vireo is present here in summer and Brown-crested Flycatcher is seen here almost annually in winter. The Old Ingraham Highway can also be good for migrant or wintering warblers, vireos, and other songbirds. A part of the original road through the park and now reduced to a footpath, this trail bisects the Gumbo Limbo Trail and continues about 1 mile to Hidden Lake Road.

Backtrack 0.8 mile on Royal Palm Hammock Road, turning left to access Research Road (this intersection is a good predawn spot for Whip-poor-will in winter). Turn right at the stop sign at 0.4 mile; this road will dead-end at an abandoned missile site (a vestige of the Cuban missile crisis) in 5.5 miles. Scan the wires for recently reintroduced Eastern Bluebird as you pass through the pineland section of this road. Trails accessing the pinelands can be found at 1.1 miles (Gate 2), 1.7 miles (Gate 2A), and 2.4 miles (Gate 2B). On the first hundred yards of each trail, look for Brown-headed Nuthatch, also recently reintroduced to the park. Typical pineland species are present, such as Northern Bobwhite, Pileated and Downy Woodpecker, Northern Flicker, Great Crested Flycatcher, Yellow-throated and Pine Warbler, and Eastern Towhee. Purchase a park map if you plan to hike any more of the pineland's extensive trail system. The massive Hole-in-the-Donut restoration project will become visible on your left as you approach the Bill Robertson Research Center (3.6 miles). This area was farmed even after the national park surrounded it, hence the name Hole-in-the-Donut. Non-native Brazilian pepper overran the farmland after it was absorbed into the park. A long-term effort is now underway to eradicate the Brazilian pepper and return the area to sawgrass prairie. Look for wintering warblers as well as Western Kingbird and Scissor-tailed Flycatcher around the research building. A Northern Wheatear was found here in September 2006. The restoration area itself is closed to the public, so bird this area from the road. Look for waders, migrant shorebirds, and wintering ducks in the wet areas, and sparrows and Eastern Meadowlark along the road edges. White-tailed Kite is occasionally seen over the prairie, especially toward the end of the road. Don't expect to see the Mountain Bluebird that made an appearance in this less-than-mountainous area in December 2002. Do keep an eye out for Florida panther, which prey on the white-tailed deer now attracted to this restored area.

Backtrack to the main road and turn left. After 2.2 miles turn left to reach Long Pine Key campground and picnic area. In September 2003 a Black-faced Grassquit was found along this road. At the campground and picnic area (1.5 miles), look for typical pineland species as listed for Research Road. A trail beginning at the picnic area passes through a tropical hardwood hammock that has consistently produced wintering Brown-crested Flycatcher, as well as other wintering songbirds. Antillean Nighthawk has been seen and heard over the campground during summer. Return to the main road, turn left, and drive 2 miles to the parking area for Pinelands Trail, worth a quick stop for pineland species you may have missed earlier. Continue 6 miles to the turnoff for the observation tower at Pa-hay-okee (native word for "grassy waters"). Turn right and drive 1.2 miles to the parking area. The tower is wheelchair-accessible and provides a panoramic view of the sawgrass prairie. Snail Kite is occasionally seen from the tower. Return to the main park road, turn right, and drive 7 miles to Mahogany Hammock Road. Turn right and drive 1.7 miles to the **Mahogany Hammock** parking area. Mahogany Hammock is an excellent example of

Barred Owls. PHOTO: LARRY MANFREDI

a "tree island" in the Everglades "river of grass." A 0.5-mile wheelchair-accessible, elevated boardwalk loops through the tropical hardwood hammock. Look for Barred Owl roosting in and around the champion mahogany tree. Pileated Woodpecker and Great Crested Flycatcher are common. Look for flocks of warblers, vireos, and other songbirds during migration and winter.

Return to the main road and continue south. The sawgrass prairie for the next couple of miles has nesting Seaside Sparrow of the Cape Sable race. In spring these sparrows can be heard singing from grass-top perches. By scanning the marsh, you may find one or two birds reasonably close to the road. In winter other species of sparrow may be found feeding along the road edges. Most will be Savannah Sparrow, but occasionally something unusual such as Lapland Longspur will be found. Black Rail has been heard and occasionally seen in this area. Remember, though, that tapes are not allowed in the park. In 4.4 miles turn right into a parking area at Paurotis Pond. From this point on you will notice a gradual transition from sawgrass prairie to mangrove swamp. Paurotis Pond (named after the Paurotis Palm) is a nesting and roosting location for a wide variety of wading birds, including Wood Stork and Roseate Spoonbill. The flight of wading birds at dawn as viewed from the parking area can be spectacular. Swallow-tailed Kite may be seen soaring over the pond in summer, and Snail Kite is occasionally seen here during any season. A female Vermilion Flycatcher wintered near the parking area in 2004–5 and again in 2005–6. Nine-Mile Pond, 2 miles farther, is worth a stop for Bald Eagle, White-crowned Pigeon, and Caspian Tern. Continue 4.5 miles to the turnoff for West Lake. Formerly excellent for wintering waterfowl, ducks are now only occasionally seen here. The wheelchair-accessible boardwalk loops through a flooded forest of red and black mangroves, good for warblers during migration and winter (Prairie Warbler nests here) and an occasional Mangrove Cuckoo.

Continue south 1.7 miles on the main park road to **Snake Bight Trail.** This 1.6-mile trail follows a canal through a mangrove swamp, ending at a short boardwalk overlooking Snake Bight, a broad indentation in the shoreline of Florida Bay. Mangrove Cuckoo is possible during any season, especially near the beginning of the trail. Look for White-crowned Pigeon and flocks of warblers and other wintering songbirds. You won't have to look for mosquitoes—they'll find you, often in numbers beyond belief. Be prepared! Wear plenty of repellent, a head net, or better yet, rent a bicycle at the Flamingo marina and pedal your way to Snake Bight. The view from the boardwalk will provide your best chance to see Greater Flamingo from land. Time your arrival for high tide and scope the distant shoreline, especially to the left of the end of the boardwalk. Late in the day is best, so the sun doesn't distort your scope image. Unfortunately, the growth of mangroves beyond the boardwalk has obscured a portion of the view, though it's often that portion that contains the flamingos! Hope for more than just fuzzy pink dots, and be sure to avoid confusing a flamingo with the more common Roseate Spoonbill. Great numbers of shorebirds may be feeding on the mudflats here, including Marbled Godwit and American Avocet.

Mrazak Pond is on the left, 1.5 miles past Snake Bight Trail. This small pond is relatively birdless for much of the year, but in mid- to late winter when water levels drop, large numbers of fish-eating birds, including American White Pelican, Roseate Spoonbill, Wood Stork, and other wading birds, will gorge themselves on the buffet of fish concentrated there. Blue-winged and Green-winged Teal and occasionally other species of puddle ducks can be found here throughout winter. From Mrazak Pond to Flamingo, look on winter evenings for the eye shine of Whip-poor-will on the roadsides or even in the middle of the road. The trailhead for Rowdy Bend Trail, on the left 1 mile from Mrazak Pond, passes through coastal prairie and eventually connects, after 2.5 miles, with Snake Bight Trail. Christian Point Trail, on the left 2 miles beyond Rowdy Bend, passes through coastal prairie as well; both locations can be good for Short-tailed Hawk in winter. Both species of Sharp-tailed Sparrow, as well as Swamp Sparrow, Sedge Wren, and Scissor-tailed Fly-catcher, can also be found in this habitat in winter. The Christian Point Trail reaches Florida Bay in about 2 miles; be on the lookout for Clapper Rail in this area. No board-walk is available here, so be careful that you don't sink in the mud as you search for a suit-able vantage point through the mangroves. Bear Lake Trail is reached by driving Buttonwood Canal Road (if the gate is unlocked) on the right, 0.4 mile beyond Christian Point Trail. This 2-mile trail through tropical hardwood hammock may have Mangrove Cuckoo, even in winter. White-crowned Pigeon and a variety of wintering warblers can also be found here. Flamingo is 0.4 mile beyond Buttonwood Canal Road. Another major Brazilian-pepper-eradication project has been initiated here. These open areas may be flooded in late summer or early fall, providing habitat for waders and migrating shorebirds.

Flamingo has a visitor center, restaurant, lodge, marina and boat launch, general store, campground, and picnic area. (*NOTE:* Much of this area was impacted by hurricanes in 2005. The lodge and restaurant were severely damaged and may not reopen.) Check the canal bank at the marina for American crocodile and watch the flocks of cowbirds for a possible Shiny Cowbird. Osprey nests on the water-control structure at the marina and on the tower of the visitor center. Exposed mudflats off the visitor center should be scanned at low tide for American White Pelican, Black Skimmer, and a variety of shorebirds and wading birds. "Great White" Heron, Reddish Egret, and Roseate Spoonbill are usually seen. A good vantage point is the breezeway on the second level. A Bald Eagle may be perched on one of the many mangrove islands. Wintering warblers or other songbirds may be in the trees surrounding the visitor center. Eco Pond is 0.8 mile beyond the visitor cen-ter. Prior to the hurricanes of 2005, a wheelchair-accessible observation platform provided excellent views of hundreds of wading birds, mostly White Ibis and Snowy Egret that roosted in trees in the center of the pond. Sadly, the hurricanes destroyed the observation platform, and it is unlikely to be rebuilt any time soon. Most of the trees in the center of the pond were heavily damaged; as a result, only a few wading birds now roost here. Due to saltwater intrusion, all of the cattails in this formerly freshwater pond have disappeared. Without this necessary cover, bitterns and rails, once regular here, are no longer being seen. The pond is now attractive to a variety of waterfowl and shorebirds. Watch overhead for Swallow-tailed Kite in spring or summer, Short-tailed Hawk in winter, or Bald Eagle any time of year. After sundown in winter, this is still the place to wait for Lesser Nighthawk to appear and feed over the pond. Painted Bunting and sparrows are often seen in weedy areas around the pond. In January 2001, a Yellow-faced Grassquit was found here. The surrounding coastal prairie, especially on the backside of the pond, may have both species of Sharp-tailed Sparrow, wading birds, including Roseate Spoonbill in the wet areas, and Bald Eagle, Peregrine Falcon, or Scissor-tailed Flycatcher on the snags. Smooth-billed Ani used to be regular around the pond, but this seriously declining species hasn't been seen here in several years. The campground and picnic area is at the end of the road, just beyond Eco Pond. Check the shoreline beyond the picnic area and amphitheater (0.5 mile) for shorebirds working the weed lines. Drive through the campground to search for Scissor-tailed Flycatcher, or after sunset for Barn Owl or Lesser Nighthawk. About 0.6 mile beyond the campground registration booth and at the end of loop C is the 7-mile

Coastal Prairie Trail. This is another good location in winter for Short-tailed Hawk, Sedge Wren, Swamp Sparrow, both sharp-tailed sparrows, and possibly Yellow Rail.

There are several ways to access Florida Bay from Flamingo. Tour boats are geared more to the general tourist, and are thus not very productive for birds. Canoe rentals are available at the marina. If you paddle out to Snake Bight in search of Greater Flamingo, make sure you carefully check the tides to avoid being marooned overnight on a mudflat. Small motorboats are also available for charter at the marina.

General information: The main entrance to Everglades National Park is open seven days a week, 24 hours a day. The entrance fee is $10 per vehicle, good for seven days. The Ernest Coe Visitor Center (restrooms, gift shop, interpretive displays, and theater) is open daily from 8:00 A.M. to 5:00 P.M. Restrooms are also available at Royal Palm Hammock, Long Pine Key Picnic Area, West Lake, the Flamingo marina store, and the Flamingo Visitor Center. Taped bird recordings are *not* allowed in the park. Speed limits are strictly enforced on all park roads.

DeLorme grid: Page 120, B-3, C-2, C-3; page 122, A-1, A-2.

Hazards: Keep a safe distance from alligators and crocodiles. Two species of rattlesnakes, cottonmouths, and coral snakes are present but rarely encountered. Fire ants are often found along the Anhinga Trail and can inflict a severe bite. Mosquitoes are overwhelming in summer and fall; deer flies can be a nuisance as well. Contact with manchineel (rare), poisonwood, or poison ivy may result in a severe rash.

Nearest food, gas, lodging: In Homestead and Florida City. The marina store in Flamingo is open from 6:00 A.M. to 9:00 P.M. daily.

Camping: Long Pine Key Campground: 108 sites, no showers. Flamingo Campground: 295 sites, cold showers; (305) 272-7700. There are private campgrounds in Homestead and Florida City.

For more information: *Everglades National Park,* 40001 State Rd. 9336, Homestead, FL 33034; (305) 242-7700; www.nps.gov/ever.

29 Tamiami Trail

Habitats: Sawgrass prairie, tropical hardwood hammock, cypress swamp, pine flatwoods, mangrove forest, coastal prairie, estuary.

Specialty birds: *Resident:* Mottled Duck, Magnificent Frigatebird, Least Bittern, Roseate Spoonbill, Wood Stork, Snail Kite, Bald Eagle, King Rail, Purple Gallinule, Limpkin, American Oystercatcher, Brown-headed Nuthatch. *Summer:* Swallow-tailed Kite, White-crowned Pigeon, Mangrove Cuckoo, Black-whiskered Vireo, Prothonotary Warbler. *Winter:* Short-tailed Hawk. *Migrant:* Yellow-throated Vireo, Louisiana Waterthrush.

Best times to bird: November through April.

Directions: *Shark Valley, Everglades National Park:* From the Florida Turnpike in Miami, exit at Tamiami Trail (U.S. Highway 41, exit 25). Drive west 20.5 miles to the entrance. *Big Cypress National Preserve:* Continue west 3.7 miles to the wildlife checkpoint at Forty-mile Bend, the east entrance to the preserve. *Gulf Coast Ranger Station, Everglades National Park:* From the intersection of Tamiami Trail and State Road 29, drive south 4.7 miles on SR 29 to the ranger station parking area. *Fakahatchee Strand Preserve State Park, Jane's Scenic Drive:* Return to Tamiami Trail and continue north 2.5 miles on SR 29 to Jane's Scenic Drive. Turn left, bear right in 0.3 mile, and continue 0.5 mile to park headquarters.

From Interstate 75, exit at SR 29 (exit 80). Drive south 14 miles to Jane's Scenic Drive, turn right, and proceed as above. *Fakahatchee Strand Preserve State Park, Big Cypress Bend Boardwalk:* Return to Tamiami Trail and turn right. Drive west 6.8 miles to the parking area. *Collier-Seminole State Park:* Continue west 8.5 miles on Tamiami Trail to the park entrance. If coming from Naples, from the intersection of Tamiami Trail and Collier Boulevard (County Road 951), drive east on Tamiami Trail 8.2 miles to the park entrance.

The Birding

Tamiami Trail is the original road through the Everglades, connecting Miami with Tampa. After crossing the intersection of Tamiami Trail and Krome Avenue (SW 177th Avenue, 3 miles) and passing the Miccosukee Indian bingo and resort complex, the road passes through sawgrass prairie for 21 miles before reaching Big Cypress National Preserve. Twelve miles west of the Krome Avenue intersection, turn right at water-control structure S-333, just before entering the Miccosukee Indian Reservation. This is an access point to the **Everglades and Frances S. Taylor Wildlife Management Area,** a water-conservation area for urban areas to the east. Drive north 0.4 mile on a dirt track and park near a gate. The area just beyond the gate is reliable for Marsh Wren and Swamp Sparrow in winter. Year-round, Least Bittern and King Rail are heard and occasionally seen along the marsh edge. Snail Kite and Limpkin may also be spotted here. Black-crowned Night-Heron roosts in this area.

Continue west on Tamiami Trail for 5.7 miles, turning left into the **Shark Valley** entrance to Everglades National Park. The parking area and a small visitor center are located just beyond the entrance gate. The Shark Valley tram road may only be accessed by foot, bicycle (rentals available during the day), or by taking a narrated tram tour (fee). The 15-mile paved loop road parallels a canal on the western side and travels through sawgrass prairie on the east. At the southern end of the loop, an observation tower provides breathtaking views of the endless expanse of sawgrass. Wading birds, alligators, turtles, and other wildlife can also be viewed from the tower. Spectacular numbers of wading birds roost in the vicinity of the tower at night. A walk on the canal side of the tram road can produce sightings of Purple Gallinule, Black and Yellow-crowned Night-Heron, and the secretive King Rail. In the sawgrass prairie, look for Wood Stork, Limpkin, and, in winter, American Bittern and Marsh Wren. Migrant and wintering land birds inhabit shrubby areas along the canal and patches of tropical hardwood hammock on the opposite side of the road. Two short trails, the Bobcat Boardwalk and Otter Cave Trail, access these areas. Watch overhead for Snail Kite, Bald Eagle, and Short-tailed Hawk. A walk on the tram road at dawn or dusk may yield impressive numbers of roosting wading birds, including Roseate Spoonbill.

To search for Snail Kite, return to Tamiami Trail and check in back of the Miccosukee restaurant directly across the road from the Shark Valley entrance, scanning the marsh beyond the canal. A more reliable spot in recent years for this sought-after species has been an abandoned airboat concession across from the Tower Motel, 1 mile west of the restaurant. The kites may be seen coursing over the marsh (beware of similar Northern Harrier) or may be perched on distant trees. If it's your lucky day, one may be perched on a cypress tree directly in front of your vehicle! Also check for Limpkin at this location. The east entrance of **Big Cypress National Preserve,** at the wildlife checkpoint at Forty-mile Bend, is 2.7 miles farther west. This is the intersection of Tamiami Trail (US 41) and **Loop Road** (County Road 94). Entering from this point, Loop Road is paved for the first 8

Wood Stork. PHOTO: LARRY MANFREDI

miles but unpaved (though better maintained than in past years) for the next 15.5 miles until it rejoins Tamiami Trail at Monroe Station.

Big Cypress National Preserve consists of 729,000 acres within Big Cypress Swamp. A drive on Loop Road provides a cross section of habitats within the preserve. After passing through a Miccosukee neighborhood, stop at culverts for the next few miles, listening for Limpkin and Barred Owl. Hairy Woodpecker can occasionally be seen in this area. Watch for King Rail scurrying across the road. Snail Kite is occasionally seen hunting over sawgrass prairie in this stretch. After 6 miles a dirt road on the right (opposite an abandoned gas pump) leads through excellent hardwood hammock, ending at a gate after 0.8 mile. Wintering warblers, vireos, and other songbirds, including Ruby-crowned Kinglet, can be found along this road. Bird only from the road and obey all NO TRESPASSING signs. After 1 mile Loop Road passes through pinewoods where Tufted Titmouse, Eastern Bluebird, Pine Warbler, Eastern Towhee, and other pineland species may be found. Brown-headed Nuthatch has been found here on occasion. Again, bird only from the road and respect private property. In another mile you will reach the end of the pavement and the Loop Road Environmental Education Center, operated by the National Park Service. Across from the environmental center, Tree Snail Hammock Nature Trail winds through hardwood hammock and can produce wintering warblers, vireos, and other songbirds. An interpretive sign along the trail explains how this site was once used for the production of illegal whiskey. This area, known as Pinecrest, was allegedly a hangout for gangster Al Capone. For the next 13 miles, stop at culverts to find cypress-associated species such as Pileated Woodpecker, Great Crested Flycatcher, and Tufted Titmouse. One of the more productive stops is Sweetwater Strand, 10.4 miles from the environmental center. Prothonotary Warbler nests in this beautiful setting, as does Yellow-billed Cuckoo, Eastern Kingbird, Red-eyed Vireo, Blue-Gray Gnatcatcher, and Northern Parula. Migrating Louisiana Waterthrush may be seen here in July. Also listen for Limpkin and Barred Owl here. Restrooms and a trail into sawgrass prairie can be found at Gator Hook Trailhead, 3 miles beyond Sweetwater Strand. Monroe Station and the Tamiami Trail are 2.2 miles farther.

If you skipped Loop Road and continued west on Tamiami Trail, stop at any of the culverts from Forty-mile Bend to the Miami-Dade County line. Here, cypress swamp residents such as Tufted Titmouse and occasionally Hairy Woodpecker can be found. The Oasis Visitor Center, worth a stop for an overview of the preserve, is 15 miles west of Forty-mile Bend. Monroe Station, the western entry to Loop Road, is 4.2 miles west of the visitor center. Those looking to explore the preserve on foot may want to inquire about the Florida Trail, which passes near the visitor center. Thirty-one miles of the Florida Trail pass through the preserve. The southern terminus of the trail is on Loop Road, 5.5 miles west of the Loop Road Environmental Education Center. Hiking off-trail is the only way to see the endangered Red-cockaded Woodpecker in Big Cypress. Over 50 nest clusters have been identified within the preserve, but none are accessible by road or marked trail.

To continue your tour of the preserve, from Monroe Station, drive west 3.3 miles on Tamiami Trail to Kirby Storter Boardwalk. A walk on the 0.5-mile boardwalk into a cypress swamp will produce typical cypress-associated species as well as wintering warblers, vireos, and other songbirds. Wild Turkey occasionally roosts in cypress trees at the end of the boardwalk. H. P. Williams Wayside Picnic Area is 6.8 miles farther west, at the intersection with Turner River Road (County Road 839). Driving north on this unpaved road, especially in the early morning, will provide opportunities to see large numbers of roosting herons, egrets, and other wading birds. Eastern Bluebird and occasionally Brown-headed Nuthatch can be found in pine flatwoods. Complete a loop tour of the area by driving north 7.2 miles to Wagonwheel Road (County Road 837), west 4.9 miles to Birdon Road (County Road 841), and south 4.3 miles to Tamiami Trail. Turn right and drive west 6.6 miles to the intersection with SR 29.

Everglades City is the gateway to the **Ten Thousand Islands** region of **Everglades National Park.** For access to this mangrove wilderness, stop first at the Gulf Coast Ranger Station on the Chokoloskee Causeway (SR 29). Boat tours departing from the ranger station provide opportunities to view a wide variety of wading birds, including Roseate Spoonbill. Magnificent Frigatebird, Bald Eagle, American Oystercatcher, and Mangrove Cuckoo have also been sighted on these tours. Canoe rentals are available at the ranger station. By obtaining a backcountry permit and arranging to stay at primitive camp-sites, it is possible to paddle for 99 miles through the Wilderness Waterway, all the way to Flamingo. A productive area for shorebirds can be reached by continuing south on SR 29 for 3.4 miles, following the signs to Ted Smallwood's Store. This store, opened in 1906, began as a post office and Indian trading post. The oyster bars offshore provide good habitat for American Oystercatcher and other shorebirds. American White Pelican and a variety of wading birds also can be seen here, especially at low tide.

Jane's Scenic Drive provides vehicular access to **Fakahatchee Strand Preserve State Park.** Information on guided swamp walks and canoe trips through the preserve may be obtained at park headquarters. During spring and summer, watch overhead for Swallow-tailed Kite. Jane's Scenic Drive continues for 11 miles to the western border of the preserve. Several old logging roads along the drive are available for hiking. A good map of the preserve is essential when exploring this area. **Big Cypress Bend Boardwalk,** a 2,000-foot boardwalk through a cypress swamp, is the most popular access point to the preserve. In the stretch of Tamiami Trail between SR 29 and Big Cypress Bend, watch for several marshy areas on the south side of the road. These wetlands can be good in winter for ducks, shorebirds, American White Pelican, Northern Harrier, the occasional Snail Kite, and large numbers of wading birds, including Roseate Spoonbill. Red-shouldered Hawk, Barred Owl, Pileated Woodpecker, Great Crested Flycatcher, White-eyed Vireo, Tufted Titmouse, and Carolina Wren are resident at Big Cypress Bend. Swallow-tailed Kite is usually in the vicinity during spring and summer. Wintering species include Yellow-bellied Sapsucker, Blue-headed Vireo, Blue-gray Gnatcatcher, Ruby-crowned Kinglet, and several species of warblers. A Bald Eagle nest can be viewed from the boardwalk.

Continue west 8.5 miles on Tamiami Trail to **Collier-Seminole State Park.** Expect species similar to those at Big Cypress Bend, plus White-crowned Pigeon, Mangrove Cuckoo, and Black-whiskered Vireo during summer. Boat tours on the Black Water River are available, and canoes may be rented for exploration of the river and adjacent salt marsh. The Royal Palm Hammock Nature Trail begins at the marina. This short trail with boardwalk leads to an observation platform overlooking the salt marsh. Two longer trails begin on Tamiami Trail. A 3.5-mile bicycle/hiking trail begins on the south side of Tamiami Trail 0.7 mile west of the park entrance. Part of this trail through pine flatwoods overlaps the original road to nearby Marco Island. The Adventure Trail begins on the north side of Tamiami Trail 0.7 mile east of the park entrance. This 6.5-mile trail provides access to pine flatwoods and cypress swamp. Both of these trails may be submerged in low-lying areas during the summer months.

General information: The Shark Valley entrance to Everglades National Park is open daily from 8:30 A.M. to 5:00 P.M. The entrance fee is $10 per vehicle, good for seven days. Restrooms are located in the parking area. Vehicles are not allowed to park on the entrance road or on Tamiami Trail in the immediate vicinity of the entrance road. The entrance road and/or the tram road may be flooded during the rainy season (summer/fall). Taped bird recordings are *not* allowed in the park. Speed limits are strictly enforced on the Miccosukee Indian Reservation. Big Cypress National Preserve (no entrance fee) is open year-round, 24 hours a day. The Oasis Visitor Center is open daily, except December 25, from 9:00 A.M. to 4:30 P.M. On Loop Road restrooms are located at Gator Hook Trailhead. On Tamiami Trail restrooms are located at Oasis Visitor Center, Kirby Storter Boardwalk, and the H. P. Williams Wayside Picnic Area. Hunting and off-road-vehicle use are permitted in designated areas. Refer to regulations-summary brochures, updated annually and available at check stations, for hunt dates and locations. Wear blaze orange if hiking during hunting season. The Florida Trail may be flooded during summer. The Gulf Coast Visitor Center of Everglades National Park (no entrance fee) is open daily from 7:30 A.M. to 5:00 P.M. November through April and from 9:00 A.M. to 4:30 P.M. May through October. Restrooms are located in the visitor center. Boat-tour schedules vary by season. Fakahatchee Strand Preserve State Park (no entrance fee) has neither a visitor center nor restrooms. Big Cypress Bend Boardwalk is open 24 hours. Collier-Seminole State Park (entrance fee) is open daily from 8:00 A.M. to sunset. Restrooms are located in the campground.

DeLorme grid: Page 110, C-2; page 116, A-1, A-2, A-3; page 117, B-1, B-2, B-3, C-3.

Hazards: Keep a safe distance from alligators. Cottonmouths are often seen on Loop Road. Rattlesnakes and coral snakes are present but rarely encountered. Mosquitoes are most common in summer. Use extreme caution if parking along Tamiami Trail. Vehicles often travel this road at high rates of speed. Speed limits in the Miccosukee reservation are strictly enforced.

Nearest food, gas, lodging: Miccosukee restaurant, across Tamiami Trail from the Shark Valley entrance; Dade Corners (intersection of Tamiami Trail and Krome Avenue), 17.6 miles east of the Shark Valley entrance; and Everglades City.

Camping: Collier-Seminole State Park: 137 sites. Several primitive National Park Service campgrounds are located on Tamiami Trail west of Shark Valley (Monument Lake has flush toilets and cold showers). Private campgrounds are located in Ochopee and Everglades City.

For more information: *Everglades National Park,* 40001 State Rd. 9336, Homestead, FL 33034; (305) 242-7700; www.nps.gov/ever. *Everglades National Park Boat Tours,* P.O. Box 119, Everglades City, FL 33139; (239) 695-2591. *Everglades and Frances S. Taylor Wildlife Management Area,* c/o South Florida Water Management District; www.sfwmd.gov and Florida Fish and Wildlife Conservation Commission; www.floridaconservation.org. *Big Cypress National Preserve,* HCR 61, Box 11, Ochopee, FL 33141; (941) 695-4111; www.nps.gov/bicy. *Fakahatchee Strand Preserve State Park,* P.O. Box 548, Copeland, FL 33926; (813) 695-4593; www.floridastateparks.org/fakahatcheestrand. *Collier-Seminole State Park,* 20200 E. Tamiami Trail, Naples, FL 34114; (239) 394-3397; www.floridastateparks.org/collier-seminole.

SOUTHWEST

 # Marco Island Area

Habitats: Coastal scrub, mangrove forest, maritime hammock, sandy beach, residential areas (for Burrowing Owl and Rose-ringed Parakeet), pine flatwoods, pasture, freshwater impoundments.

Specialty birds: *Resident:* Mottled Duck, Magnificent Frigatebird, Reddish Egret, Roseate Spoonbill, Wood Stork, Snail Kite, Bald Eagle, Limpkin, Sandhill Crane, Wilson's Plover, Snowy Plover, American Oystercatcher, Rose-ringed Parakeet, Burrowing Owl, Florida Scrub-Jay. *Summer:* Least Tern, Mangrove Cuckoo, Gray Kingbird, Black-whiskered Vireo. *Winter:* Peregrine Falcon, Piping Plover, Whimbrel, Lesser Nighthawk, Western Kingbird, Scissor-tailed Flycatcher, Bronzed Cowbird, Shiny Cowbird. *Migrant:* White-rumped Sandpiper, Black Tern.

Best times to bird: April through May and August through September for the greatest variety of migrant shorebirds. November through March for wintering waterfowl and shorebirds. Late afternoon for Rose-ringed Parakeet.

Directions: *Rookery Bay National Estuarine Research Reserve:* From Interstate 75 east of Naples, exit at Collier Boulevard (State Road 951, exit 101). Drive south 7 miles to Tamiami Trail (U.S. Highway 41). Continue south 0.7 mile on Collier Boulevard to reserve headquarters. Continue south 1.3 miles to Shell Island Road. *Tigertail Beach:* Return to Collier Boulevard, turn right, and drive south 5.8 miles to Tigertail Court. Turn right and drive west 0.6 mile to Hernando Drive. Turn left and drive south 0.5 mile to the parking area. *Eagle Lakes Community Park:* Return to the intersection of Tamiami Trail and Collier Boulevard. Drive west 1.4 miles on Tamiami Trail to the park entrance. *Sugden Regional Park:* Continue west 3.7 miles on Tamiami Trail to the park entrance.

The Birding

Driving south on Collier Boulevard, the headquarters and Environmental Learning Center for **Rookery Bay National Estuarine Research Reserve** is on the right 0.7 mile south of Tamiami Trail. A 1.5-mile trail system and boardwalk is planned for sometime in 2007. Shell Island Road is 1.3 miles farther. Turn right onto this graded dirt road. In 0.5 mile you

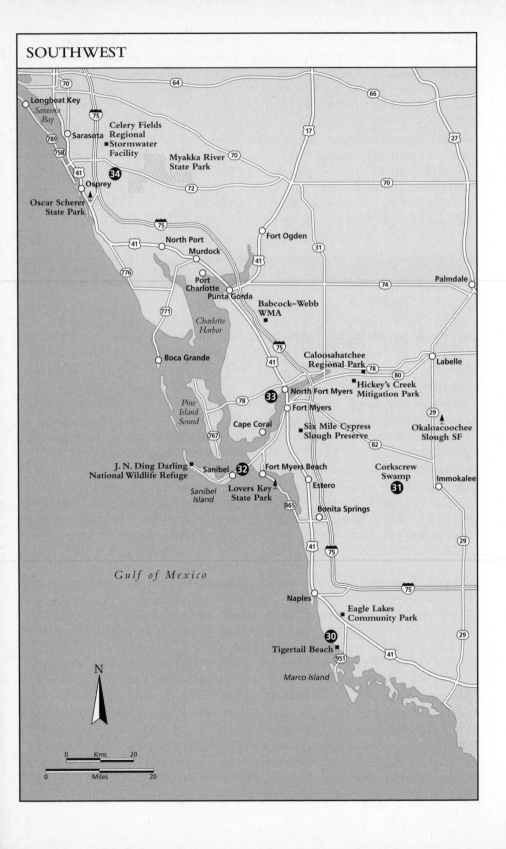

SOUTHWEST

Longboat Key
Sarasota Bay
Sarasota
Osprey
Oscar Scherer State Park
Celery Fields Regional Stormwater Facility
Myakka River State Park
North Port
Murdock
Port Charlotte
Punta Gorda
Fort Ogden
Babcock–Webb WMA
Boca Grande
Charlotte Harbor
Caloosahatchee Regional Park
Palmdale
Labelle
Pine Island Sound
North Fort Myers
Hickey's Creek Mitigation Park
Cape Coral
Fort Myers
Six Mile Cypress Slough Preserve
Okaloacoochee Slough SF
J. N. Ding Darling National Wildlife Refuge
Sanibel
Sanibel Island
Fort Myers Beach
Lovers Key State Park
Estero
Corkscrew Swamp
Immokalee
Bonita Springs
Gulf of Mexico
Naples
Eagle Lakes Community Park
Tigertail Beach
Marco Island

N

Kms 20
Miles 20

will enter scrub habitat and 0.5 mile farther, the former **Briggs Nature Center,** now a law-enforcement station for the Florida Fish and Wildlife Conservation Commission. Though the nature center, operated by the Conservancy of Southwest Florida, has been closed since 2003, birders are still allowed to access the 0.5-mile boardwalk that begins behind the main building. Florida Scrub-Jay was introduced to this area in 1989. A few remain and may be seen perched on wires along the road. Shiny Cowbird was regular here in winter when the nature center was open; the removal of feeders when the nature center closed has forced the cowbirds to go elsewhere. Access to Rookery Bay National Estuarine Research Reserve is at the end of Shell Island Road, 1.8 miles past Briggs Nature Center. The Catclaw Trail is a short trail through mangrove forest and maritime hammock. Prairie Warbler is resident, and Mangrove Cuckoo and Black-whiskered Vireo can be found in summer.

Return to Collier Boulevard and drive south to **Tigertail Beach** on Marco Island. In summer watch for Gray Kingbird perched on phone wires. Use caution when identifying crows, since both American Crow and Fish Crow are present. Check the mangroves around the beach parking area for passerines during migration and Prairie Warbler year-round. Boardwalks lead from the parking area to a tidal lagoon that separates the mainland from Sand Dollar Island, a recently formed barrier island. The best area for shorebirds is to the right. Low tide is usually best. Walk along the lagoon, watching in summer for Mangrove Cuckoo (rare) and Gray Kingbird in shoreline buttonwoods, or wade across the lagoon to reach the barrier island. Access to some of this area is restricted during the breeding season to protect nesting Snowy Plover, Least Tern, and Black Skimmer. Large numbers of shorebirds stop here to feed and rest during spring and fall migration, and many spend the winter. A few nonbreeding birds may be found in summer. American Oystercatcher as well as Wilson's and Snowy Plover are resident, while Black-bellied, Semi-palmated, and Piping Plover are here during migration and in winter. Snowy Plover is more often found on the barrier island, while American Oystercatcher is usually on mud-flats or sandbars at the northern end of the beach. Other shorebirds common in winter or migration include Willet, Spotted Sandpiper, Marbled Godwit, Ruddy Turnstone, Red Knot, Sanderling, Western and Least Sandpiper, Dunlin, and Short-billed Dowitcher. Less-common-to-occasional are Black-necked Stilt, American Avocet, Greater Yellowlegs, Whimbrel, Long-billed Curlew, and Semipalmated and Pectoral Sandpiper. Seven Red-necked Phalaropes were found after a tropical storm in September 2001. Laughing Gull is resident; winter brings Ring-billed and Herring Gull, as well as an occasional Great Black-backed or Lesser Black-backed Gull. In addition to breeding Least Tern and Black Skim-mer, Royal Tern is here most of the year, Caspian, Sandwich, and Forster's Tern in winter, and Common, Black, and Gull-billed Tern during migration. Other common beach birds are Magnificent Frigatebird (offshore), Brown Pelican, Double-crested Cormorant, Great Blue, Little Blue, and Tricolored Heron, Great, Snowy, and Reddish Egret, White Ibis, and Osprey. Roseate Spoonbill and Bald Eagle can occasionally be seen here. Winter brings Northern Gannet (offshore), Red-breasted Merganser, and Belted Kingfisher. Peregrine Falcon will occasionally be seen attacking the shorebird flocks.

To find Burrowing Owl in residential areas of Marco Island, return to Collier Boule-vard via Kendall Drive, which is 0.2 mile before Tigertail Court. A marked owl burrow is on the left side of Kendall Drive at the intersection with Hernando Drive. Other burrows can be found in the Lamplighter Road area. Turn right on Collier Boulevard and drive 0.8 mile to San Marco Drive (State Road 92). Turn left and drive 0.6 mile to Lamplighter

Road. Turn right, looking on both sides of the road for marked burrows. Other burrows can be found on San Marco Drive and adjacent side streets. Sadly, as the empty lots in which they nest are developed, the number of Burrowing Owl on Marco Island will probably continue to decrease. **Frank E. Mackle Jr. Community Park** is usually worth a stop for wintering ducks. Return to San Marco Drive, turn right, and drive 0.4 mile to Heathwood Drive. Turn right and drive 0.3 mile to Andalusia Terrace. Turn left, then immediately right into the park. A walking path encircles the lake. In addition to resident Mottled Duck and feral Mallard, winter brings Northern Shoveler, Blue-winged Teal, Ring-necked Duck, Lesser Scaup, and Ruddy Duck. Magnificent Frigatebird is occasionally seen here dipping their bills into the lake to drink.

Return to San Marco Drive and continue north for 4 miles to the Goodland Bridge. At low tide scan the mudflats for shorebirds and waders, often including Roseate Spoonbill. Continue north 2.3 miles to Tamiami Trail. The entrance to Collier-Seminole State Park (see previous section) is immediately east of this intersection. To reach an area called Fritchey Road Wetlands by local birders, turn left and drive west 5 miles on Tamiami Trail to Greenway Road. Turn right and drive north 0.6 mile to Fritchey Road. Turn right and drive east 0.7 mile to where Fritchey Road turns left. In the wet pastures just before the left turn (south side of Fritchey Road), look in winter for American White Pelican, Snail Kite, Northern Harrier, American Kestrel, Peregrine Falcon, Sandhill Crane, Limpkin, and a variety of other wading birds. Scissor-tailed Flycatcher and Western Kingbird occasionally perch on the fences. In February 2005 Yellow-headed Blackbird was seen near the farm on Greenway Road 0.5 mile beyond Fritchey Road. Other birds seen in the area include Northern Bobwhite, Common Ground-Dove, Great Horned Owl (a nest is on the right side of Greenway Road, just past Fritchey Road), Loggerhead Shrike, Eastern Bluebird, Pine Warbler, and Eastern Meadowlark.

Return to Tamiami Trail, turn right, and drive west 4.7 miles to **Eagle Lakes Community Park,** a seasonally productive location for shorebirds and waterfowl in Naples. After entering the park, turn left at the traffic circle and park near the soccer field. A series of three retention ponds are located beyond the adjacent baseball diamonds. Footpaths encircle all three ponds. The eastern pond (Pond C) usually has deeper water and lacks vegetation that's attractive to waterbirds. An observation platform is located at the central pond (Pond B). A variety of wading birds, including Glossy Ibis and Wood Stork, are conspicuous year-round. Purple Gallinule and Black-necked Stilt nest. Wood Duck once wintered here but hasn't been seen in recent years. If water levels are low during spring and fall migration, this pond can be attractive to shorebirds, which are often found on mudflats directly beyond the observation platform. Both Greater and Lesser Yellowlegs, Western and Least Sandpiper, and Short-billed Dowitcher are common. Solitary, Spotted, Pectoral, Stilt, and Semipalmated Sandpiper and Long-billed Dowitcher are less common. White-rumped Sandpiper is rare. Wilson's Snipe is occasionally flushed from the water's edge in winter. Least Tern feeds here in spring and summer, Caspian and Forster's Tern in spring and fall. The western pond (Pond A) is more attractive to ducks. Joining resident Mottled Duck in winter are Blue and Green-winged Teal, Northern Shoveler, American Wigeon, Northern Pintail, Ring-necked Duck, and Lesser Scaup. One or two Eurasian Wigeon have been seen in recent winters. Also in winter check the vegetation around the central and western ponds for cowbirds. Good numbers of Bronzed Cowbird have been seen in winter. Occasionally a Shiny Cowbird is found. Other park residents include Osprey, Red-shouldered Hawk, Fish Crow, Loggerhead Shrike, Eastern Bluebird and Pine Warbler. American Kestrel is common in winter. Watch overhead for an occasional Bald Eagle (year-round), Merlin (fall), or Peregrine Falcon (fall and winter). Lesser Nighthawk was sighted here in winter 2002–3.

Two other locations in the Naples area are worth a stop if time permits. **Sugden Regional Park** can be productive in spring and fall for warblers and other migrants. After entering the park, turn right at the stop sign and drive to the last parking area. A paved trail begins here and encircles Lake Avalon. In January 2002 a Franklin's Gull was seen on the opposite side of the lake. Rose-ringed Parakeet roosts in the Naples area. A current location to see these beautiful parakeets is the Royal Harbor subdivision. From Sugden Regional Park, drive west 2 miles on US 41. Turn left on Palm Street, then right on Marlin Drive. Enter the subdivision, bearing left in 0.2 mile onto Tarpon Drive. Arrive in late afternoon and listen for their squawking. The parakeets feed at seed feeders erected by local residents or in flowering bottlebrush trees, and roost nearby. Other parakeets, including White-eyed and Blue-headed Parakeet, may also be present.

General information: Tigertail Beach (entrance fee) is open daily from 8:00 A.M. until sunset. Parking is $6.00 per vehicle. Frank E. Mackle Jr. and Eagle Lakes Community Parks and Sugden Regional Park (no entrance fees) are open daily from 8:00 A.M. to 10:00 P.M. Restrooms are available at all locations. Please respect private property if searching for parakeets in the Royal Harbor subdivision or elsewhere in Naples.

DeLorme grid: Page 110, C-1, C-2; page 111, D-1.

Hazards: Keep a safe distance from alligators. Strong tidal currents are possible at Tigertail Beach. When wading in shallow water, shuffle your feet to avoid stepping on stingrays.

Nearest food, gas, lodging: In Marco Island and Naples.

Camping: Collier-Seminole State Park: 137 sites, 20200 E. Tamiami Trail, Naples, FL 34114; (239) 394-3397. There are private campgrounds in Naples.

For more information: *Rookery Bay National Estuarine Research Reserve,* 300 Tower Rd., Naples, FL 34113; (239) 417-6310; www .rookerybay.org. *Tigertail Beach,* 400 Hernando Dr., Marco Island, FL 34145; (239) 353-0404; www.explorenaples.com/tigertail_beach. *Frank E. Mackle Jr. Community Park,* 1361 Andalusia Terrace, Marco Island, FL 34145; (239) 642-0575. *Eagle Lakes Community Park,* 111565 Tamiami Trail E., Naples, FL 33143; www.colliergov.net/ Index.aspx?page=360.

 # Corkscrew Swamp Area

Habitats: Cypress swamp, wet prairie, freshwater marsh, pine flatwoods, hardwood hammock.

Specialty birds: *Resident:* Mottled Duck, Wood Stork, Snail Kite, Crested Caracara, King Rail, Purple Gallinule, Limpkin, Sandhill Crane. *Summer:* Swallow-tailed Kite, Chuck-will's-widow, Prothonotary Warbler. *Winter:* Short-tailed Hawk, Virginia Rail, Louisiana Waterthrush, Painted Bunting. *Migrant:* Summer Tanager, Scarlet Tanager.

Best times to bird: September through April.

Directions: *Corkscrew Swamp Sanctuary:* From I-75 east of Naples, exit at Immokalee Road (County Road 846, exit 111). Drive east 15.2 miles to Sanctuary Road. Turn left and drive 1.5 miles to the entrance. *CREW Marsh:* Return to CR 846, turn left, and drive east 13.8 miles to State Road 29. Turn left and drive north 5.5 miles to State Road 82. Turn left and drive west 5.3 miles to Corkscrew Road (County Road 850). Turn left and drive south 1.4 miles to the parking area. From I-75 in Ft. Myers, exit at SR 82 (exit 138). Drive east 20 miles to Corkscrew Road, turn right, and proceed as above. From I-75 in Estero, exit at Corkscrew Road (exit 123). Drive east, then north 18 miles to the parking area. *Okaloacoochee Slough State Forest:* Return to SR 29, turn left, and drive north 7.5 miles to Keri Road (County Road 832). Turn right and drive east 3.7 miles to the state forest kiosk on the north side of the road. From State Road 80 in Labelle, drive south 11.3 miles on SR 29 to Keri Road. Turn left and proceed as above.

The Birding

The 11,000-acre **Corkscrew Swamp Sanctuary,** maintained by National Audubon Society, contains the largest old-growth bald cypress forest remaining in North America. A 2.3-mile wheelchair-accessible boardwalk will take you through several distinct habitats found within the sanctuary. An optional route shortens the walk to 1 mile. Benches and rain shelters are available along the way. Begin your tour at Blair Center, the sanctuary's visitor center. Seed feeders at the beginning of the boardwalk attract Northern Bobwhite, Eastern Towhee, and other common species throughout the year. Chipping Sparrow, Painted and Indigo Bunting, and American Goldfinch join them in winter. On a spur trail farther down the boardwalk are additional feeders that attract most of the same species. A Pine Siskin was reported at these feeders one winter. The surrounding pine flatwoods are home to Downy Woodpecker, Eastern Bluebird, and Pine Warbler. Occasionally seen here are Hairy Woodpecker and Brown-headed Nuthatch.

As the habitat changes to wet prairie, look for Common Yellowthroat and Swamp Sparrow in the cordgrass. Wild Turkey is occasionally seen here, while the bugling of Sandhill Crane may be heard in the distance. Watch for Northern Harrier coursing over the prairie in winter. A Short-tailed Hawk may be spotted soaring above the treetops during the winter months, replaced by Swallow-tailed Kite in spring and summer. As you enter pond cypress habitat, a Red-shouldered Hawk will undoubtedly announce its presence with its distinctive call. Begin to listen for Tufted Titmouse, Carolina Wren, and White-eyed Vireo. You'll sense the slight decrease in elevation as majestic Bald Cypress begins to dominate the swampy landscape. Typically seen or heard here are Pileated Woodpecker and Great Crested Flycatcher. Sanctuary volunteers will usually be on hand to direct you to roosting Barred Owl. Winter brings Yellow-bellied Sapsucker, Eastern Phoebe, Blue-headed Vireo, House Wren, and Ruby-crowned Kinglet. Several warbler species spend the winter here, including Orange-crowned, Yellow-throated, Black-and-white, and both waterthrush. Northern Parula and Prothonotary Warbler nest in the sanctuary. Many other warblers pass through during migration, occasionally including sought-after species such as Golden-winged and Canada. An impressive 39 species of warblers are on the sanctuary checklist. Other migrants seen in the cypress swamp include Yellow-billed Cuckoo, Eastern Wood-Pewee, Veery, Gray-cheeked, and Swainson's Thrush, and Scarlet and Summer Tanager.

A spur trail leads to an observation platform overlooking wet prairie. In winter and early spring, a sanctuary volunteer is usually stationed here to direct you to Wood Stork nesting in the distant treetops. Nesting success for this endangered species varies greatly from year to year. If water levels during the breeding season are not suitable for feeding, the storks will abandon their nests. The storks are also vulnerable to cold spells, and their nests may be damaged or destroyed by windstorms. If storks are nesting when you visit, the volunteer will have a spotting scope available for closer looks. The observation platform is also a good place to watch for raptors or migrant Chimney Swift soaring over the prairie. In areas where the water is too deep for cypress to grow, water lettuce dominates. Ameri-

Limpkin. PHOTO: NANCY MORELAND

can Bittern, Purple Gallinule, Limpkin, and a variety of herons and egrets, including Yellow-crowned and Black-crowned Night-Heron, can be found here. Also look for Northern Parula and Prothonotary Warbler in summer, and Northern or Louisiana Waterthrush during winter. River otters frequent this area, occasionally climbing onto the boardwalk. Reentry into pond cypress habitat, followed by pine flatwoods, signals your return to the visitor center.

Corkscrew Marsh (also known as CREW Marsh) is north of Corkscrew Swamp Sanctuary. This 5,000-acre sawgrass marsh is part of a massive wetland system known as the Corkscrew Regional Ecosystem Watershed. Over 5 miles of trails crisscross through pine flatwoods and hardwood hammock surrounding the marsh. Brochures and trail maps are available at the trailhead parking area. It is a short 0.2-mile walk from the trailhead to an observation deck overlooking a seasonally wet pond. Continue south another 0.5 mile to an observation tower at the marsh, where an assortment of wading birds, including Wood Stork and Limpkin, may be seen. A boardwalk and trail begins at the tower and leads to an oak hammock, where migrant and wintering land birds are likely. Other side trails wind through pine flatwoods where Wild Turkey, Pileated Woodpecker, and other pineland species may be found.

In the 1930s, most of the marketable timber in the nearly 35,000 acres now known as **Okaloacoochee Slough State Forest** was harvested, with large areas of forest converted to pasture. Incredibly, eight distinct natural communities have survived, providing habitat for a wide variety of wildlife, including Florida panther and Florida black bear. The heart of the forest is the 13,382-acre Okaloacoochee Slough, through which water flows southward from the Caloosahatchee River to Big Cypress National Preserve. Keri Road (CR 832) bisects the forest; several dirt side roads provide access to the interior. If entering the forest from the west, stop first at the informational kiosk at North Loop West Road, 3.7 miles west of SR 29. Brochures, maps, and bird checklists are available here and at kiosks erected at most entry points. Much of the accessible area north of the highway is pasture or wet prairie. Watch for Crested Caracara and Sandhill Crane in these areas. Only the first mile of North Loop West Road is currently open to vehicles. Two other access roads on the north side of CR 832 are also worth a quick check. Oil Well Pad Road, which ends after 1 mile, is 1.4 miles east of North Loop West Road. Twin Mills Grade, a 4.2-mile road, is 1.4 miles farther east.

Habitat south of the road is a mixture of pine flatwoods, cypress swamp, and other wetlands. Three roads open to vehicles are worth exploring in this area. Sic Island Road, 0.1 mile east of North Loop West Road, ends after 2.6 miles at the Sic Island Loop hiking trail. Patterson Road is 1 mile east of Twin Mills Grade and ends after 1.3 miles at a primitive campground within a hardwood hammock. This area should be checked for migrant and wintering land birds. Wild Cow Grade, 1 mile farther east, becomes Mustang Grade after 4 miles and ends in another 2.2 miles at the Mustang Loop hiking trail. This road marks the eastern boundary of the state forest and passes through the widest variety of habitats. Anywhere along Wild Cow Grade, watch for Wild Turkey, Northern Bobwhite, and Common Ground-Dove. In open prairie east of the road, look for Northern Harrier in winter and Crested Caracara throughout the year. Open wetlands may have Wood Stork, Limpkin, King Rail, and other wading birds. American Bittern and Virginia Rail may be found in these areas during the winter months. Barred Owl and Pileated Woodpecker are likely in areas of cypress swamp along Mustang Grade. In summer watch overhead in this area for Swallow-tailed Kite. Snail Kite is present year-round but is most likely to be seen during spring and summer. In the pine flatwoods at the end of Mustang Grade, Great Crested Flycatcher, White-eyed Vireo, Pine Warbler, and Eastern Towhee are typically found.

General information: Corkscrew Swamp Sanctuary (entrance fee) is open daily from 7:00 A.M. to 5:30 P.M. Hours are extended to 7:30 P.M. during the spring and summer months (mid-April through September). No one is allowed on the boardwalk after dark. Restrooms, a snack bar, a theater, and a nature store are in the visitor center. Admission is discounted for National Audubon Society members. CREW Marsh (no entrance fee) is open daily from sunrise to sunset. A primitive restroom is located at the trailhead parking area. Okaloacoochee Slough State Forest (entrance fee) is open 24 hours a day. No restrooms are available. Seasonal hunting is permitted in wildlife management areas. Refer to regulations-summary brochures, updated annually and available at check stations, for hunt dates and locations. Wear blaze orange if hiking during hunting season.

DeLorme grid: Page 106, D-2; page 111, B-3.

Hazards: Keep a safe distance from alligators. Venomous snakes are present but rarely encountered. Florida black bear is occasionally seen in the vicinity of the Corkscrew Swamp boardwalk.

Nearest food, gas, lodging: In Naples and Ft. Myers. Food and gas are available in Immokalee and Labelle.

Camping: Koreshan State Historic Site: 60 sites, P.O. Box 7, Estero, FL 33928; (800) 326-3521. From I-75, exit at Corkscrew Road (exit 123). Drive west 2 miles to US 41 and the park entrance. Private campgrounds are in Naples.

For more information: Corkscrew Swamp Sanctuary, 375 Sanctuary Rd. W., Naples, FL 34120; (239) 348-9155; www.audubon.org/local/sanctuary/corkscrew. CREW Marsh, c/o Crew

Land and Water Trust, 23998 Corkscrew Rd., Estero, FL 33928; (239) 657-2253; www .crewtrust.org. *Okaloacoochee Slough State* *Forest,* P.O. Box 712, Felda, FL 33930; (863) 612-0776; www.fl-dof.com/state_forests/ okaloacoochee.html.

 # Ft. Myers Beach/Sanibel Area

Habitats: Sandy beach, mangrove forest, maritime hammock.

Specialty birds: *Resident:* Mottled Duck, Magnificent Frigatebird, Reddish Egret, Roseate Spoonbill, Clapper Rail, Wilson's Plover, Snowy Plover, American Oystercatcher, Mangrove Cuckoo. *Summer:* Least Tern, Gray Kingbird, Black-whiskered Vireo. *Winter:* Piping Plover, Whimbrel, Long-billed Curlew.

Best times to bird: August through May.

Directions: *Ft. Myers Beach:* from I-75 in Bonita Springs, exit at Bonita Beach Road (County Road 865, exit 116). Drive west 10.3 miles to Lovers Key State Park. To reach the Holiday Inn, which allows birders access through hotel grounds to Little Estero Lagoon, continue north on CR 865 (known here as Estero Boulevard) another 3 miles. *Sanibel Island:* Continue north 7.5 miles on CR 865 (at the northern end known as San Carlos Boulevard) to Summerlin Road (County Road 869). Turn left and drive west 4 miles to the Sanibel toll plaza. From I-75 east of Ft. Myers, exit at Daniels Road (exit 131). Drive west 2.5 miles to Six Mile Cypress Parkway. Turn left and drive south, then west 2.8 miles to the intersection with US 41 (Tamiami Trail). Six Mile Cypress Parkway now becomes Gladiolus Drive. Continue on Gladiolus west, then south 1.4 miles to Summerlin Road. Turn left and drive west 8 miles to the Sanibel toll plaza.

The Birding

Begin your tour at **Lovers Key State Park** on CR 865, here called the Bonita Beach Causeway. The 1,616-acre park is spread over four islands: Lovers Key, Inner Key, Long Key, and Black Island. The most accessible shorebird area in the park is conveniently located outside the fee area at Dog Beach, 0.9 mile south of the park entrance on Long Key. Parking is available on the west side of the road just past the New Pass Bridge. As the name implies, Dog Beach is an off-leash dog area. In spite of the canine commotion, shorebirds still congregate here on sandbars beyond the section used by the dogs. American Oystercatcher is resident and flocks of American Avocets are occasionally seen here in winter. All shoreline in the park east of the Bonita Beach Causeway is also outside the fee area. Waters on this side of the road are part of Estero Bay Aquatic Preserve. Shorebirds, Reddish Egret, and Roseate Spoonbill frequent this area at low tide. Osprey is commonly seen here due to the presence of several nesting platforms. To reach the Black Island Trail, pass through the park entrance station and drive to the parking area at the end of the road. This trail provides access to mangrove forest and maritime hammock on Black Island. This area may also be accessed by foot from a pedestrian entrance 1 mile north of the main park entrance. A tidal lagoon in the island's interior may have shorebirds and wading birds at low tide. Footbridges over the lagoon access beaches on the Gulf of Mexico side of the park. A tram provides round-trip transportation to the 2.5 miles of beach within the park. Expect to see Willet, Ruddy Turnstone, and Sanderling along the beach.

To reach **Little Estero Lagoon,** return to the Bonita Beach Causeway and continue north. Cross the Big Carlos Pass Bridge to the island of Ft. Myers Beach. In summer watch for Gray Kingbird on the wires or Magnificent Frigatebird soaring above the condominiums. The Holiday Inn will be on your left. Access the beach by walking around the north side of the hotel. Large numbers of gulls may be roosting here. Most will be Laughing Gull, joined in winter by Ring-billed Gull. If the beach here becomes flooded after a heavy rainstorm, terns and Black Skimmer will often join the gulls. Walk south along the beach to reach Little Estero Lagoon. Watch for Common Ground-Dove in the dunes. Common Loon and Red-breasted Merganser may be just offshore in winter. Rarities spotted off the beach have included Western Grebe and Black Scoter. The northern tip of Little Estero Lagoon can be accessed by walking around the south side of the hotel and continuing south. Good numbers of shorebirds and wading birds feed here, including Reddish Egret, Roseate Spoonbill, and American Oystercatcher. Shorebirds such as Black-bellied Plover and Whimbrel may be feeding in the grassy areas that border the east side of the lagoon. Scattering shorebirds often signal the presence of a Peregrine Falcon. Lurking in the mangroves on the opposite side of the lagoon may be Black-crowned and Yellow-crowned Night-Heron and occasionally Clapper Rail. You may wade across the lagoon at low tide to reach this area. As you walk farther south, you'll have to eventually wade across to reach the outer beach and the southern end of the lagoon.

The configuration of this beach may change dramatically from year to year with the passage of hurricanes or winter storms. Most shorebirds will be found feeding on mudflats along the edge of the lagoon. Commonly seen here most of the year will be Black-bellied, Wilson's, and Semipalmated Plover, Western and Least Sandpiper, Dunlin, and Short-billed Dowitcher. Piping Plover will join them in winter. Less common is Whimbrel and Marbled Godwit. Even more infrequent is Long-billed Curlew. Extreme rarities have included Surfbird and Curlew Sandpiper. On the outer beach look for Willet, Ruddy Turnstone, and Sanderling, joined in migration by large numbers of Red Knot or occasionally American

Avocet. Snowy Plover, which nests here, can usually be found in areas of white sand with sparse vegetation. Large flocks of Double-crested Cormorant, gulls, and terns will usually congregate on sandbars in the lagoon. In winter scan through the Laughing, Ring-billed, and Herring Gull for an occasional Great Black-backed or Lesser Black-backed Gull. Least Tern and Black Skimmer nest between the lagoon and the outer beach. This section of the beach is designated a Critical Wildlife Area, so access to these nesting areas will be restricted during the breeding season. Caspian, Royal, Sandwich, and Forster's Tern can be

Mangrove Cuckoo. PHOTO: LARRY MANFREDI

seen here most of the year. Gull-billed Tern is occasionally seen here in summer, while Common and Black Tern can be found during migration. Depending on the configuration of the beach when you visit, you may be able to walk all the way to Big Carlos Pass.

One of the most popular birding destinations in all of Florida is **J. N. "Ding" Darling National Wildlife Refuge.** To reach the refuge, cross the causeway (toll) onto Sanibel Island. At low tide shorebirds may be present along the causeway. Watch overhead for Magnificent Frigatebird, especially in summer. Gulls, terns, and Fish Crow are a constant presence. Turn right in 3.3 miles onto Periwinkle Way. In 2.5 miles bear right onto Palm Ridge Road, which in 0.3 mile (after crossing Tarpon Bay Road) becomes Sanibel-Captiva Road. In another 2 miles turn right into the refuge. Stop first in the visitor center for maps and checklists and to view the interpretive exhibits. A 4-mile, one-way auto drive (fee) begins at the visitor center and provides access to a cross section of the refuge. The 2-mile Indigo Trail also begins here. Listen for Pileated Woodpecker around the trailhead. Try to time your tour of the refuge to coincide with low tide. The mangrove-fringed tidal lagoons on both sides of the auto drive will have a variety of wading birds including Reddish Egret and Roseate Spoonbill. American White Pelican joins them in winter. Exposed mudflats will attract shorebirds such as yellowlegs, dowitchers, and peeps. A few ducks may join the resident Mottled Duck in winter, mostly Blue-winged Teal, American Wigeon, and Red-breasted Merganser. Osprey and Red-shouldered Hawk are the expected raptors year-round; Short-tailed Hawk is occasionally seen in winter.

Mangrove Cuckoo is an uncommon year-round resident of the refuge. Sightings of this species increased significantly in the months after the passage of Hurricane Charley in August 2004. Increased visibility in the mangrove canopy has apparently made this skulking species more conspicuous. Though they may be found in any suitable habitat along the auto drive, a reliable location has been the area around the Mangrove Overlook boardwalk beyond mile marker 1. A Smooth-billed Ani was reported from this area in February 2003. An observation tower near mile marker 2 is a good location to scope for ducks and shorebirds. A short trail that begins before the observation tower leads across a dike to the Indigo Trail. Sora is occasionally seen near the beginning of this cross-dike trail in winter. Gray Kingbird and Black-whiskered Vireo can be found anywhere along the auto drive in spring and summer. Prairie Warbler is a common resident throughout. The Shell Mound Trail, between mile markers 3 and 4, passes through hardwood hammock and around an Indian shell midden and is the best location along the auto drive to search for migrants. The **Bailey Tract** is a separate section of the refuge on Tarpon Bay Road. To reach this area, backtrack on Sanibel-Captiva Road to Tarpon Bay Road and turn right. The entrance is on the right in 0.7 mile. Almost 2 miles of trails wind through the tract. A series of freshwater ponds attracts ducks in winter. Yellow Rail has been recorded here occasionally in winter. Black-necked Stilt nest during summer. The surrounding thickets attract land birds during migration. Gray Kingbird and Black-whiskered Vireo breed here in summer and Eastern Towhee is resident.

Backtrack 0.2 mile to Periwinkle Drive and turn right. Return to the intersection with Sanibel Causeway Road and continue east 1.3 miles to **Lighthouse Park.** Gulls and terns, as well as Willet, Sanderling, and Ruddy Turnstone, can usually be found along the beach. In October 2001 a Surfbird was spotted here among a flock of Red Knot. A boardwalk and trails near the lighthouse pass through a mixture of mangrove forest, maritime hammock, and Australian pines that attract a variety of migrants, especially in fall. MacGillivray's and Townsend's Warbler are among the rarities discovered along the trails.

Pileated Woodpecker is common here year-round. Hurricane Charley significantly altered the composition of this hammock in 2004. Most of the Australian pines did not survive the Category 4 winds. As you return to the mainland via the Sanibel Causeway, check the beach area near the toll plaza for shorebirds at low tide. To find even more shorebirds, turn right in 2.6 miles onto John Morris Road and drive 1.2 miles to **Bunche Beach.** At low tide shorebirds may be found in either direction from the end of John Morris Road. Regularly seen here are many of the same species found at Little Estero Lagoon, including Snowy Plover. A Long-billed Curlew has been consistently seen at this location in recent years and Reddish Egret is here year-round.

General information: Lovers Key State Park (entrance fee) is open daily from 8:00 A.M. to sunset. Dog Beach (no entrance fee) is open from sunrise to sunset. Restroom facilities are available within the fee area of the park. Parking at the Holiday Inn may be seasonally restricted. Additional parking is available at the shopping center across Estero Boulevard. The toll to cross the Sanibel Causeway is $6.00 per vehicle. The wildlife drive at Ding Darling National Wildlife Refuge (entrance fee) is open every day except Friday. The refuge is open to pedestrians and cyclists from sunrise to sunset but only opens to vehicles one hour after sunrise. Restrooms are located at the visitor center (outside the fee area). Taped bird recordings are not allowed in the refuge. Parking at the Sanibel Lighthouse is $2.00 per hour. Restrooms are located near the lighthouse. There is no entrance fee, nor are there restrooms at Bunche Beach and the Bailey Tract of Ding Darling National Wildlife Refuge.

DeLorme grid: Page 110, A-2, A-3; page 111, A-1.

Hazards: No lifeguards are on duty at Lovers Key State Park or at Little Estero Lagoon. When wading in shallow water, shuffle your feet to avoid stepping on stingrays. Mosquitoes are common on the Ding Darling wildlife drive in spring and summer. Keep a safe distance from alligators.

Nearest food, gas, lodging: On Sanibel Island, Ft. Myers Beach, and Ft. Myers.

Camping: Koreshan State Historic Site: 60 sites, P.O. Box 7, Estero, FL 33928; (800) 326-3521.

From I-75, exit at Corkscrew Road (exit 123). Drive west 2 miles to US 41 and the park entrance. There are private campgrounds in Ft. Myers Beach.

For more information: Lovers Key State Park, 8700 Estero Blvd., Ft. Myers Beach, FL 33931; (941) 463-4588; www.floridastateparks.org/loverskey. Ding Darling National Wildlife Refuge, 1 Wildlife Dr., Sanibel, FL 33957; (941) 472-1100; http://dingdarling.fws.gov.

33 Ft. Myers Area

Habitats: Cypress swamp, oak/cabbage palm hammock, pine flatwoods, oak scrub, freshwater marsh, dry prairie, wet prairie.

Specialty birds: *Resident:* Mottled Duck, Least Bittern, Wood Stork, Bald Eagle, Crested Caracara, King Rail, Purple Gallinule, Limpkin, Sandhill Crane, Red-cockaded Woodpecker, Florida Scrub-Jay, Brown-headed Nuthatch, Summer Tanager, Bachman's Sparrow. *Summer:* Swallow-tailed Kite, Least Tern, Chuck-will's-widow. *Winter:* Virginia Rail, Painted Bunting. *Migrant:* Yellow-throated Vireo.

Best times to bird: September through April.

Directions: *Six Mile Cypress Slough Preserve:* From I-75 northbound east of Ft. Myers, exit at Daniels Parkway (exit 131). Drive west 2.5 miles to Six Mile Cypress Parkway. Turn right and drive north 1.8 miles to Penzance Boulevard. Turn right into the preserve parking area. From I-75 southbound, exit at Colonial Boulevard (exit 136). Drive west 0.5 mile to Six Mile Cypress Parkway. Turn left and drive south 3 miles to Penzance Boulevard. Turn left into the preserve parking area. *Hickey's Creek Mitigation Park:* From I-75 in Ft. Myers, exit at SR 80 (exit 141). Drive east 8.7 miles to the park entrance. *Caloosahatchee Regional Park:* Continue east 3.3 miles to Broadway, in the town of Alva. Turn left and drive north 0.4 mile, crossing the bridge over the Caloosahatchee River to State Road 78 (North River Road). Turn left and drive west 3 miles to the park entrance. *Babcock-Webb Wildlife Management Area:* From I-75 south of Punta Gorda, exit at Tucker Grade (exit 158). Drive east 0.5 mile to the WMA check station.

The Birding

Six Mile Cypress Slough Preserve is a 2,200-acre wetland ecosystem that drains a 57-square-mile watershed. About 80 acres of the preserve can be accessed by a 1.2-mile wheelchair-friendly boardwalk that winds through cypress swamp fringed by pine flat-woods. From the parking area, the boardwalk passes over a marshy area that often attracts wading birds, then through pine flatwoods to an observation deck beside Gator Lake. This lake was excavated to provide the base for Six Mile Cypress Parkway and has steep vertical drops on all but the side opposite the observation deck. Wading birds, occasionally including Glossy Ibis and Roseate Spoonbill, use this shallow side to feed. Double-crested Cormorant and Anhinga are present on or around the lake year-round, and ducks may be present in winter. This is a good place to watch in spring and summer for Swallow-tailed Kite soaring overhead. As habitat along the boardwalk transitions from pine flatwoods to cypress swamp, watch and listen for Red-shouldered Hawk, Barred Owl, Downy and Pileated Woodpecker, Great Crested Flycatcher, White-eyed Vireo, Tufted Titmouse, and Carolina Wren. Hairy Woodpecker has frequently been seen in the preserve. Wild Turkey has been recorded in the preserve but should not be expected from the boardwalk. In winter look for feeding flocks of Yellow-rumped Warbler. Joining them may be Yellow-bellied Sapsucker, Blue-gray Gnat-catcher, Blue-headed and occasionally Yellow-throated Vireo, Ruby-crowned Kinglet, and a variety of other warblers including Northern Parula, Yellow-throated, Prairie, Black-and-white, and American Redstart. Less common warblers such as Magnolia and Golden-winged are occasionally reported. A Western Tanager was seen here in March 2001. During some winters, flocks of American Robin, Cedar Waxwing, and American Goldfinch pass through the preserve. The boardwalk passes several ponds of deeper water, all of which may be viewed from observation platforms or photography blinds. Wading birds are attracted to the fish that concentrate here. Waders seen here include Wood Stork and both night herons. Look for Limpkin hunting along the pond edges for apple snails. Solitary Sandpiper and Northern Waterthrush may work the shallow muddy areas during winter or migration. You may also chance upon a Wood Duck if visitors ahead of you haven't already flushed it. Migration brings the possibility of spotting any number of flycatchers, warblers, tanagers, grosbeaks, buntings, or orioles. These migrants are also possible at nearby **Lakes County Park.** To reach this park from Penzance Boulevard, turn left onto Six Mile Cypress Parkway and drive 4.6 miles to US 41 (Tamiami Trail). Six Mile Cypress Parkway now becomes Gladiolus Drive. Continue 0.4 mile to the park entrance on the right. Follow the signs to the Fragrance Garden, which attracts the most migrants. In winter Ruby-throated Hum-mingbird is commonly seen around flowering trees in the garden. On the lakes in the park, resident Mottled Duck may be joined in winter by other duck species.

Two parks west of Ft. Myers along the Caloosahatchee River provide opportunities to see several birds otherwise rare in Lee County. **Hickey's Creek Mitigation Park,** on the south side of the river, was originally established to mitigate for gopher tortoise habitat in southwest Florida that has been destroyed by development. Within its 1,117 acres are a variety of habitats, including areas of oak scrub that are home to several Florida Scrub-Jays. A good area to check for scrub-jays is along the eastern border of the park, accessed from Bateman Road, 1 mile east of the park entrance. Inside the park the Hickey's Creek Trail begins at the parking area and loops 1.8 miles along the creek, crossing over at two bridges. Watch for wintering and migrant land birds along this trail. At the second bridge the 1-mile North Marsh Trail leads to a freshwater wetland area where wading birds including Wood Stork are likely. Look for Northern Bobwhite, Pileated Woodpecker, Pine Warbler, and Eastern Towhee along the 2.2-mile Palmetto Pines Trail, which splits from Hickey's Creek Trail at a power line easement south of the creek. In the town of Alva, 3 miles east of Hickey's Creek, several homes along Pearl Street have feeders that in winter attract Painted and Indigo Bunting, American Goldfinch, and occasional rarities such as Pine Siskin. White-winged Dove is common in this area. Check live oaks in the neighborhood for Barred Owl and wintering Broad-winged Hawk. Pearl Street is on the north side of the Caloosahatchee River. Turn left immediately after crossing the bridge; the feeders are on the north side of the street. Unless invited by residents into a yard, observe the feeders from your car.

Caloosahatchee Regional Park, on the north side of the river, is an excellent location for Red-headed Woodpecker. Scan snags along the park's main road, on the south side of SR 78, for this species. Within the park's 765 acres are over 12 miles of hiking, mountain-bike, and equestrian trails. Bikes and horses are restricted to trails on the north side of SR 78, accessed from a parking area 0.5 mile west of the main entrance. Several hiking trails begin at the parking area at the end of the park's main road. The Shoreline and River Hammock Trails pass through hardwood hammock, good winter habitat for Yellow-bellied Sapsucker, Blue-headed Vireo, Ruby-crowned Kinglet, and Yellow-throated and Black-and-white Warbler. Osprey and Bald Eagle are often seen along the river. Pineland species can be found along the Palmetto Path Trail. Watch overhead in spring and summer for Swallow-tailed Kite, which nests in the area. From the park, continue west 7 miles on SR 78 to State Road 31, scanning pastures along this stretch for Sandhill Crane and Crested Caracara. Florida Scrub-Jay may be found in patches of oak scrub near the intersection of SR 78 and SR 31. Turn left and drive south 3 miles to return to SR 80.

Though heavily logged beginning in the 1930s, several areas within the 65,000-acre **Babcock-Webb Wildlife Management Area** continue to provide suitable nesting habitat for the endangered Red-cockaded Woodpecker. Two nesting locations are within the recreational area of the WMA, which is open to birders year-round. To reach these locations from the WMA entrance, drive east 1.4 miles on Tucker Grade (unpaved beyond the check station) to Oil Well Grade. Turn left and drive north 0.8 mile to the small RCW sign on the left. Cavity trees are marked with white rings. Continue north 1 mile to Tram Grade, turn right, and drive east 0.3 mile to reach the second nesting location, similarly marked. Dawn and dusk are best for observing the woodpeckers in the vicinity of their nest cavities. Several other woodpecker species are possible in pine flatwoods along these roads, including Pileated, Hairy, Downy, and Northern Flicker. Also likely year-round are Northern Bobwhite, Common Ground-Dove, Brown-headed Nuthatch, Eastern Bluebird, Pine Warbler, and Eastern Towhee. Bachman's Sparrow is easiest to locate when singing in spring and summer. Listen for this sparrow in open areas of saw palmetto, where males typically sing from a low perch. Watch in summer along this route for Swallow-tailed Kite, Common Nighthawk, Chuck-will's-widow, Great Crested Flycatcher, Eastern Kingbird, Northern Parula, and Summer Tanager. An excellent location for all of these species is around Crooked Lake. To reach this area, turn right onto a dirt path that begins just north of the Red-cockaded Woodpecker nesting location on Oil Well Grade.

From Crooked Lake, return to Tucker Grade and turn left. For the next several miles, habitat along this road alternates between freshwater marsh and pine flatwoods. The marsh attracts Wood Stork, Sandhill Crane, and other wading birds throughout the year. Watch for King Rail along marsh edges. During the winter months, American Bittern, Sora, Virginia Rail, Wilson's Snipe, and Swamp Sparrow are all possible here. At 1.8 miles a gate marks the boundary of the recreation area. Sections of the WMA beyond this point are only open during hunting season, from mid-October through mid-January. Backtrack on Tucker Grade to the check station. Scan the small pond behind the check station for Least Bittern, Purple Gallinule, and Limpkin. A paved road just east of the pond leads south for 5 miles along Webb Lake, an artificial lake excavated during the construction of I-75. Waterfowl are possible on the lake during the winter months. Least Tern may be seen feeding over the lake in summer. Watch overhead for Bald Eagle year-round.

General information: Six Mile Cypress Slough Preserve is open daily from 8:00 A.M. to 5:00 P.M. October through March and from 8:00 A.M. to 8:00 P.M. April through September. Guided walks are available daily at 9:30 A.M. and 1:30 P.M. from January through March, daily at 9:30 A.M. in April, November, and December, and on Wednesdays at 9:30 A.M. from April through October. Parking at Six Mile Cypress Slough Preserve and Lakes County Park is 75 cents per hour or $3.00 for a full day. Restrooms and picnic areas are available at both locations. At Six Mile Cypress Slough Preserve, recent bird sightings are posted near the restrooms. Hickey's Creek Mitigation Park (entrance fee) is open daily from 7:00 A.M. to 6:00 P.M. Caloosahatchee Regional Park (entrance fee) is open daily from 8:00 A.M. until sunset. Restrooms at both parks are located at the parking areas. Babcock-Webb Wildlife Management Area (entrance fee) is open daily from sunrise to sunset. No restrooms are available. Seasonal hunting is permitted in designated areas. Refer to regulations-summary brochures, updated annually and available at check stations, for hunt dates and locations. Wear blaze orange if hiking during hunting season.

DeLorme grid: Page 105, C-2, D-1.

Hazards: Keep a safe distance from alligators. Eastern diamondback rattlesnakes and cottonmouths are present but rarely encountered. Mosquitoes are common in summer. Avoid fire-ant mounds. Contact with poison ivy may result in a severe rash. Use caution when driving WMA roads during rainy weather.

Nearest food, gas, lodging: In Ft. Myers.

Camping: Caloosahatchee Regional Park: 25 sites.

For more information: *Six Mile Cypress Slough Preserve,* 7751 Penzance Blvd., Fort Myers, FL 33912; (941) 432-2004. *Lee County Parks and Recreation,* 3410 Palm Beach Blvd., Ft. Myers, FL 33916; (239) 728-6240 (Hickey's Creek), (239) 693-2690 (Caloosahatchee); www.leeparks.org. *Babcock-Webb Wildlife Management Area,* c/o Florida Fish and Wildlife Conservation Commission, 620 S. Meridian St., Tallahassee, FL 32399; (800) 955-8771; www.floridaconservation.org.

Habitats: Oak/sand pine scrub, pine flatwoods, freshwater marsh, dry prairie, oak/cabbage palm hammock.

Specialty birds: *Resident:* Black-bellied Whistling-Duck, Mottled Duck, Least Bittern, Wood Stork, Bald Eagle, Crested Caracara, King Rail, Purple Gallinule, Limpkin, Sandhill Crane, Florida Scrub-Jay, Bachman's Sparrow. *Summer:* Roseate Spoonbill, Swallow-tailed Kite, Chuck-will's-widow. *Winter:* Fulvous Whistling-Duck, Whip-poor-will, Painted Bunting. *Migrant:* Black Tern, Kentucky Warbler, Hooded Warbler.

Best times to bird: October through April.

Directions: *Oscar Scherer State Park:* If northbound on I-75, exit at Laurel Road (exit 195). Drive west 3 miles to US 41. Turn right and drive north 2 miles to the park entrance. If southbound on I-75, exit at County Road 681 (exit 200). Drive west 3.3 miles to US 41. Turn right and drive north 1.5 miles to the park entrance. *Myakka River State Park:* From I-75 south of Sarasota, exit at State Road 72 (exit 205). Drive east 8.6 miles to the park entrance, on the north side of SR 72. *Crowley Museum and Nature Center:* From the north entrance to Myakka River State Park, turn left on Myakka Road, which immediately bends north. Drive 1.2 miles to the entrance. *Ackerman Park:* From I-75 in Sarasota, exit at Fruitville Road (exit 210). Drive east 0.5 mile to Corbin Road. Turn right and drive south 0.4 mile to the parking area. *Celery Fields Regional Stormwater Facility:* Continue south 0.4 mile to Palmer Boulevard (south of Ackerman Park, Corbin Road becomes Apex Road). Turn left and drive east 0.5 mile to a parking area and gazebo on the north side of the road.

The Birding

The scrubby flatwoods of 1,383-acre **Oscar Scherer State Park** comprise one of the easiest places in the state to see Florida Scrub-Jay. From the park entrance, drive 1 mile to the Lake Osprey picnic area at the end of the park road. Several trails begin at the picnic area. The 1.5-mile Blue Trail and 2-mile Red Trail pass through excellent scrub-jay habitat in the northwestern section of the park. Scrub-jays are often seen in the vicinity of the trailhead, located across from the parking area. Also watch year-round on either of these trails for Northern Bobwhite, Common Ground-Dove, and Eastern Towhee. Painted Bunting is possible during winter. The 5-mile Yellow Trail, which begins at the youth campground gate at the end of the park road, leads to pine flatwoods, patches of hammock along South Creek, and Big Lake, in the remote southeastern corner of the park. A series of shortcuts allows for 2.5- and 3.5-mile hikes through this area. Great Horned Owl, Red-headed and Pileated Woodpecker, Northern Flicker, and Pine Warbler inhabit the pine flatwoods. During summer listen at dawn and dusk for Chuck-will's-widow. Wood Duck, Mottled Duck, Sandhill Crane, and other wading birds (occasionally including Roseate Spoonbill in summer) can be found in and around Big Lake. Look for migrant and wintering land birds along the creek.

The 3-mile Green Trail begins at the nature center near Lake Osprey. The trail crosses South Creek and passes through part of the campground before entering scrubby flatwoods along the park's southwest perimeter. Several scrub-jay families can be found in this area. The South Creek Trail also begins at the nature center. This 0.5-mile trail heads west through hardwood hammock along the creek before ending at the South Creek Picnic Area. Anywhere along the creek, watch year-round for Barred Owl, White-eyed Vireo,

Tufted Titmouse, and Carolina Wren. In summer expect Swallow-tailed Kite, Yellow-billed Cuckoo, Great Crested Flycatcher, and Northern Parula. Over 20 species of warblers, including Magnolia, Chestnut-sided, Bay-breasted, Blackburnian, Tennessee, Hooded, and Kentucky have been recorded here during spring and fall migration. The 0.5-mile Lester Finley Trail begins on the opposite side of the South Creek Picnic Area and continues west along the creek through similar habitat. The observation platform at the end of this trail is a good place to scan the skies for Bald Eagle, which nests in the park. Canoes (available for rent at the ranger station) may be launched from the South Creek Picnic Area, providing opportunities to explore areas farther downstream.

Opened to the public in 1942, **Myakka River State Park** is among the oldest parks in Florida. Covering 28,875 acres, it is also one of the state's largest natural areas. Twelve miles of the Myakka River meander through the park. A 7-mile scenic drive provides access to wetlands and oak/cabbage palm hammock surrounding the river. The road crosses the river 0.7 mile north of the entrance station. This bridge provides a vantage point to scan the riverbanks for wading birds. In addition to the common herons and egrets, look for Wood Stork, Roseate Spoonbill (in summer), Limpkin, and Sandhill Crane. A variety of shorebirds, including Black-necked Stilt in summer, feed here on exposed mudflats. This section of the river can also be productive for resident Black-bellied Whistling-Duck. A short nature trail through oak/cabbage palm hammock begins 0.2 mile north of the bridge. The trail features an 85-foot canopy walkway suspended 25 feet above the ground. The adjacent observation tower provides panoramic views of the surrounding wetlands. Typical species to watch for in this habitat include Red-shouldered Hawk, Wild Turkey, Barred Owl, Pileated Woodpecker, Great Crested Flycatcher, and Carolina Wren.

Wood Duck may be found in flooded sections of the hammock. This is also a good place to look for migrant and wintering land birds.

Continue north 1.4 miles and bear left where the road forks. This road leads 0.4 mile to a boat basin on the south side of Upper Myakka Lake. Drive to the west end of the boat basin parking area and walk to a concrete dam, where the river flows south from the lake. This area also attracts storks, spoonbills, and other wading birds. Large numbers of Black Vulture often roost around the adjacent picnic area. Scan the lake for distant waterfowl or check for Purple Gallinule, Limpkin, and Sandhill Crane feeding along the shore. Watch for Osprey and

Florida Scrub-Jay. PHOTO: BRIAN RAPOZA

Bald Eagle overhead. Canoes may be rented here for exploration of the lake and river. For an ear-splitting alternative, cruise the lake on the *Myakka Maiden* or the *Gator Gal,* advertised as the world's largest airboats. Return to the scenic drive and turn left. Drive north 1.6 miles to a parking area for the Birdwalk, a boardwalk extending into Upper Myakka Lake. This can be an excellent spot to scan for wintering waterfowl. In addition to resident Mottled Duck, Blue and Green-winged Teal, American Wigeon, and Ring-necked Duck are typically common to abundant in winter. Also expect a few Northern Shoveler, Northern Pintail, Lesser Scaup and Hooded Merganser. Fulvous Whistling-Duck is occasionally seen here during winter. A Cinnamon Teal was spotted in this area in January 2001.

The park has nearly 39 miles of hiking trails winding through pine flatwoods, oak/cabbage palm hammock, and dry prairie on the eastern side of the park. The trailhead is located on the east side of the scenic drive, 0.3 mile north of the Birdwalk. Be sure to obtain a trail map at the ranger station if planning any lengthy hikes on the park's trail system. Trails are also located in the wilderness preserve on the south side of SR 72, allowing exploration of the Lower Myakka Lake area. Large numbers of wading birds and wintering waterfowl can often be found on this lake. A permit, available at the ranger station, is required to enter this area. The scenic drive ends at the north entrance to the park, on Myakka Road, 1.8 miles north of the Birdwalk. This entrance is only open on weekends and state holidays. The **Crowley Museum and Nature Center** is located north and west of the park entrance. A 2,000-foot boardwalk leads through wet hammock that attracts migrant land birds in spring and fall. Barred Owl is resident and Swallow-tailed Kite nests nearby. The boardwalk ends at an observation tower overlooking the upper Myakka River and surrounding marsh. Watch in winter for American White Pelican in the river and Sandhill Crane year-round in the marsh.

Continue north 2.4 miles on Myakka Road to Fruitville Road (County Road 780). Turn left and drive west 10.2 miles to Corbin Road, watching along the way for Crested Caracara. Turn left and drive south 0.4 mile to **Ackerman Park.** This 26-acre park includes a rectangular lake that attracts wintering waterfowl, occasionally including Black-bellied Whistling-Duck, plus an assortment of gulls and terns. Monk Parakeet nests nearby. **Celery Fields Regional Stormwater Facility** is east of the park. The impoundments here attract Mottled Duck, Wood Duck, and Black-bellied Whistling-Duck as well as a variety of wintering waterfowl and shorebirds. Other species seen here throughout the year include Least Bittern, Glossy Ibis, Wood Stork, Roseate Spoonbill, Bald Eagle, Red-tailed Hawk, King Rail, Limpkin, and Sandhill Crane. Northern Harrier is common in winter. Brushy areas may attract an impressive variety of sparrows in winter, including Field, Vesper, Savannah, Grasshopper, Song, Lincoln's, Swamp, and White-crowned. Bobolink finds these areas attractive in spring and fall. Rarities reported from this area include Snow Goose, Cinnamon Teal, and Short-eared Owl.

General information: Oscar Scherer and Myakka River State Parks (entrance fees) are open daily from 8:00 A.M. until sunset. The north entrance at Myakka River is open on weekends and state holidays from 8:00 A.M. to 5:00 P.M. Restrooms at Oscar Scherer are available at the South Creek Picnic Area, at Lake Osprey, and in the campground. Restrooms at Myakka River are available at park entrances and at picnic areas. Crowley Museum and Nature Center (entrance fee) is open Thursday through Sunday from 10:00 A.M. to 4:00 P.M. From January through April, the nature center also opens on Tuesday and Wednesday. Restrooms are available in the nature center. Ackerman Park and Celery Fields

Regional Stormwater Facility are open daily from sunrise to sunset. No restrooms are available.

DeLorme grid: Page 97, B-3, C-2.

Hazards: Keep a safe distance from alligators. Venomous snakes are present but rarely encountered. Trails may be flooded in summer.

Nearest food, gas, lodging: In Osprey and Sarasota.

Camping: Oscar Scherer State Park: 104 sites. Myakka River State Park: 94 sites in two campgrounds.

For more information: *Oscar Scherer State Park,* 1843 S. Tamiami Trail, Osprey, FL 34229; (941)

483–5956; www.floridastateparks.org/oscar scherer. *Myakka River State Park,* 13207 SR 72, Sarasota, FL 34241; (941) 361-6511; www.floridastateparks.org/myakkariver. *Crowley Museum and Nature Center,* 16405 Myakka Rd., Sarasota, FL 34240; (941) 322-1000; www .crowleymuseumnaturectr.org. *Ackerman Park,* 6481 Interstate Blvd., Sarasota, FL 34240; (941) 316-1172.

WEST-CENTRAL

35 Little Manatee River/Cockroach Bay

Habitats: Sand pine scrub, oak hammock, sod farms, mangrove forest, salt marsh.

Specialty birds: *Resident:* Mottled Duck, Reddish Egret, Roseate Spoonbill, Wood Stork, Bald Eagle, King Rail, Purple Gallinule, Sandhill Crane, Wilson's Plover, Florida Scrub-Jay, Bachman's Sparrow. *Summer:* Swallow-tailed Kite, Least Tern, Mangrove Cuckoo, Chuck-will's-widow, Gray Kingbird, Black-whiskered Vireo, Prairie Warbler, Sum-

mer Tanager. *Winter:* American Avocet, Whip-poorwill, Western Kingbird, Scissor-tailed Flycatcher, Nelson's Sharp-tailed Sparrow. *Migrant:* Upland Sandpiper, Black Tern.

Best times to bird: September through May at Little Manatee River State Park; August through September at sod farms on Cockroach Bay Road; year-round at Cockroach Bay Aquatic Preserve and E. G. Simmons Park.

Directions: *Little Manatee River State Park:* From Interstate 75 in Sun City, exit at State Road 674 (exit 240). Drive east 3 miles on SR 674 to U.S. Highway 301. Turn right and drive south 4.4 miles to Lightfoot Road. Turn right and drive west 0.1 mile to the park entrance. *Cockroach Bay Aquatic Preserve:* From I-75, drive west 3 miles on SR 674 to U.S. Highway 41. Turn left and drive south 3 miles to Cockroach Bay Road. Turn right and drive west 3 miles to the end of the road. *E. G. Simmons Park:* From the intersection of US 41 and CR 674, drive north 1.5 miles on US 41 to 19th Avenue. Turn left and drive 1 mile to the park entrance.

The Birding

Only the southern half of 2,416-acre **Little Manatee River State Park** is accessible by vehicle. From the entrance, drive 1.5 miles on the main park road and turn right to reach a canoe launch. Canoe rentals are available for exploration of the river. The Oxbow Trail, a short nature trail along the river, begins at the picnic area, 0.1 mile beyond the canoe-launch

WEST–CENTRAL

Spring Hill

Lacoochee

19

41

75

98

Crews Lake
Park

Hudson

52

Shady Hills

52

Werner-Boyce
Salt Springs
State Park

40

Port Richey

Jay B. Starkey WP

Zephyrhills

98

54

54

Holiday

54

Tarpon
Springs

19A

Brooker Creek
Preserve

Lutz

Hillsborough
River
State Park

Honeymoon
Island
State Park

John Chestnut
County Park

19

589

37

Saddle Creek Park

39

584

36

584

39

92

586

55

597

582

Thonotosassa

Lakeland

Dunedin

580

Lake Hollingsworth

4

Upper Tampa Bay
County Park

574

579

Clearwater

574

Tampa

301

75

60

37

Largo

19

275

676

Brandon

Weedon Island
Preserve

41

Seminole

693

Sawgrass
Lake Park

Boca
Ciega
Millennium
Park

699

19A

St. Petersburg

38

35

Sun City
Center

Wimauma

37

Boyd Hill
Nature
Park

Cockroach
Bay

Ruskin

674

682

41

Little Manatee River State Park

275

Ft. De Soto
Park

75

301

37

62

Bradenton

Holmes Beach

64

64

Cortez

N

Longboat Key

Sarasota
Bay

70

70

41

789

75

Sarasota

0   Kms   15

758

0   Miles   15

72

turnoff. This trail passes through an oak hammock that may attract migrant and wintering land birds. Several miles of equestrian trails through sand pine scrub offer additional hiking opportunities. A 6-mile hiking trail loops through the northern half of the park. The trail-head parking area is located on US 301, 3 miles north of Lightfoot Road. To enter this parking area, you must first obtain the lock combination at the park entrance station. The first 2 miles of this trail (if hiked clockwise) parallels the river. The trail loops back through sand pine scrub and oak hammock. Florida Scrub-Jay may be seen in scrubby areas. Other species to look for along this trail include Wild Turkey, Northern Bobwhite, Barred Owl, and Red-headed and Hairy Woodpecker. During spring and summer watch for Swallow-tailed Kite, Yellow-billed Cuckoo, Chuck-will's-widow, Summer Tanager, and Bachman's Sparrow.

From late July through September, sod farms and seasonally flooded fields on the north side of Cockroach Bay Road attract impressive numbers of migrant shorebirds and terns. Shorebirds regularly seen here during fall migration include Black-bellied and Semi-palmated Plover, Black-necked Stilt, Greater and Lesser Yellowlegs, Willet, Solitary, Spotted, Semipalmated, Western, Least, Pectoral, and Stilt Sandpiper, and both Long-billed and Short-billed Dowitcher. Terns to watch for include Black, Least, Caspian, Royal, and Forster's. Check sod fields for Upland and Buff-breasted Sandpiper, both of which prefer short-grass habitat. Rarities reported from these fields include American Golden Plover and Wilson's Phalarope. Scan marshy areas along this road for King Rail, Mottled Duck, and wintering waterfowl. Brushy areas may provide refuge for Northern Bobwhite. Check electrical wires during the winter months for Western Kingbird and Scissor-tailed Fly-catcher. Gray Kingbird is common in this area in summer. Drive to the end of the road to access **Cockroach Bay Aquatic Preserve.** A canoe trail begins here and winds through extensive mangrove habitat. During summer check mangroves along the roadside for Man-grove Cuckoo and Prairie Warbler. Black-whiskered Vireo occasionally breeds in man-groves along the bay. Scan mudflats offshore for Roseate Spoonbill and other wading birds. Several species of waterfowl winter in the bay, including Blue-winged and Green-winged Teal, American Wigeon, Northern Shoveler, Northern Pintail, Redhead, and Canvasback. Also during the winter months, Nelson's Sharp-tailed Sparrow can be found in salt marsh habitat in the preserve.

At **E. G. Simmons Park,** wading birds, shorebirds, gulls, and terns feed and rest on mudflats and sandbars exposed at low tide. Reddish Egret, Wood Stork, and Roseate Spoonbill can all be expected here. Black Skimmer and other terns congregate on sandbars or the beach. Shorebirds to watch for include American Avocet and Wilson's Plover. Bald Eagle often soars overhead. Eurasian Collared-Dove, Red-winged Blackbird, and Brown-headed Cowbird are attracted to a feeder outside the park office.

General information: Little Manatee River State Park (entrance fee) is open daily from 8:00 A.M. until sunset. Restrooms are located at the canoe launch and picnic area. Cock-roach Bay Aquatic Preserve (no entrance fee) is open daily from sunrise until sunset. No restrooms are available. E. G. Simmons Park (no entrance fee) is open daily from 8:00 A.M. to 7:00 P.M. during spring and fall. The park closes at 6:00 P.M. in winter, 8:00 P.M. in sum-mer. Restrooms are located at the beach parking area.

DeLorme grid: Page 91, C-2.

Hazards: Keep a safe distance from alligators.

Venomous snakes are present but are rarely encountered.

Nearest food, gas, lodging: In Sun City and Ruskin.

Camping: Little Manatee River State Park: 34 sites. E. G. Simmons Park: 88 sites.

For more information: *Little Manatee River State Park,* 215 Lightfoot Rd., Wimauma, FL 33598; (813) 671-5005; www.floridastateparks.org/littlemanateeriver. *E. G. Simmons Park,* 2401 19th Ave., Ruskin, FL 33570; (813) 671-7655.

36 Lakeland Area

Habitats: Hardwood swamp, cypress swamp, freshwater lakes.

Specialty birds: *Resident:* Mottled Duck, Least Bittern, Wood Stork, Roseate Spoonbill, Bald Eagle, Short-tailed Hawk, Purple Gallinule, Limpkin. *Migrant:* American Avocet, Chuck-will's-widow, Acadian Flycatcher, Yellow-throated Vireo, Blue-winged Warbler, Golden-winged Warbler, Cerulean Warbler, Prothonotary Warbler, Louisiana Waterthrush, Kentucky Warbler, Hooded Warbler.

Best times to bird: August through October.

Directions: *Tenoroc Fish Management Area:* From Interstate 4 in Lakeland, exit at County Road 33 (exit 38). Drive south 1.5 miles to County Road 659. Bear left and drive south 1.3 miles to Tenoroc Mine Road. Turn left and drive east 1 mile to the entrance. *Saddle Creek County Park:* Continue south 3.5 miles on CR 659 to U.S. Highway 92. Turn left and drive east 1.4 miles to the park entrance. *Lake Hollingsworth:* From the intersection of US 92 and CR 659, drive west 3.2 miles to Florida Avenue (U.S. Highway 98). Turn left and drive south. In 0.4 mile Florida Avenue becomes State Road 37. Continue south 2 miles to Beacon Avenue. Turn left and drive west 0.4 mile to Lake Hollingsworth Drive. Turn right and drive 0.1 mile to a parking lot on the left.

The Birding

Until the mid-1970s, the 7,300-acre tract of land now known as **Tenoroc Fish Management Area** was mined for phosphate. About 1,000 acres of "phosphate pits" remain from the mining operation. These lakes are now attractive to both anglers and waterbirds. On the north side of Tenoroc Mine Road, nesting herons and egrets may be viewed from an overlook at Picnic Lake. Look for an assortment of waterfowl here during the winter months, including Hooded Merganser. Sedge Wren and a variety of sparrows can be found in grassy and brushy areas in winter. Watch for Bald Eagle and other raptors overhead.

Adjacent **Saddle Creek County Park** was also once a phosphate mine. The nature trail at this 740-acre park is well known among Central Florida birders as a fall migration hot spot. In addition to an impressive variety of flycatchers, vireos, thrushes, tanagers, and grosbeaks, well over 30 species of warblers have been recorded here. Cerulean Warbler is regular here in August and early September. The nature trail is located at the end of Saddle Creek Park Road, 1 mile north of US 92 and just north of the intersection with Morgan Combee Road. The trail begins at an observation tower and runs along a levee for about a mile. Migrant land birds can often be viewed at eye level from atop the levee. A 1.5-mile loop trail that leads through wet hammock and cypress swamp into Tenoroc Fish Management Area also begins here. Wood Duck, Northern Bobwhite, Barred Owl, and Pileated Woodpecker are all resident in the park. Limpkin is usually easy to find around lakes on both sides of Saddle Creek Park Road. Short-tailed Hawk, which breeds nearby, can be spotted circling over the park virtually any time of year.

Lake Hollingsworth, the home of Florida Southern College, is just south of downtown Lakeland. A 2.8-mile paved walkway encircles this shallow lake. Boardwalks have been recently constructed on the north side of the lake, across from the college. Areas of emergent vegetation attract a variety of waterbirds, including Least Bittern, Glossy Ibis, Roseate Spoonbill, Wood Stork, and Purple Gallinule. In March 2002 a White-faced Ibis was found on the south side of the lake, east of the parking area. Exposed mudflats are inviting to migrant and wintering shorebirds. American Avocet, Black-necked Stilt, Stilt Sandpiper, and Long-billed Dowitcher are all recorded here on a regular basis. Large flocks of American White Pelican are sometimes seen on the lake in winter.

General information: Tenorac Fish Management Area (entrance fee) is open for birding Friday through Monday from 6:00 A.M. to 5:30 P.M. Restrooms are located at the headquarters building and at Picnic Lake. Saddle Creek County Park (no entrance fee) is open daily from 5:00 A.M. to 10:00 P.M. Restrooms are available in picnic areas. The Lake Hollingsworth parking area (no entrance fee) is open daily from sunrise to sunset. No restrooms are available.

DeLorme grid: Page 84, D-3.

Hazards: Keep a safe distance from alligators. Cottonmouths are present at Saddle Creek Park. Mosquitoes are common in summer and early fall.

Nearest food, gas, lodging: In Lakeland.

Camping: Private campgrounds are available in Lakeland.

For more information: *Tenoroc Fish Management Area,* 3829 Tenoroc Mine Rd., Lakeland, FL 33805; (863) 499-2422. *Saddle Creek County Park,* 3716 Morgan Combee Rd., Lakeland, FL 33801; (863) 534-4340.

 # Hillsborough River Parks

Habitats: Hardwood swamp, cypress swamp, pine flatwoods, hardwood hammock.

Specialty birds: *Resident:* Wood Stork, Purple Gallinule, Limpkin, Sandhill Crane, Bachman's Sparrow. *Summer:* Least Bittern, Roseate Spoon-

bill, Swallow-tailed Kite, Chuck-will's-widow, Prothonotary Warbler, Summer Tanager. *Migrant:* Yellow-throated Vireo.

Best times to bird: October through April.

Directions: *Wilderness Park, John B. Sargeant Site:* From I-4 south of Thonotosassa, exit at Thonotosassa Road (County Road 579, exit 10). Drive north 4.2 miles to U.S. Highway 301. Turn right and drive east 1.4 miles to the entrance. From I-75 in Tampa, exit at Fowler Avenue (exit 265). Drive east 1.3 miles to US 301. Turn left and drive east 3.4 miles to the entrance. *Hillsborough River State Park:* Continue east 5.6 miles on US 301 to the entrance. *Lettuce Lake Regional Park:* From I-75, exit at Fletcher Avenue (County Road 582A, exit 266). Drive west 1 mile to the entrance. *Wilderness Park, Trout Creek Site:* Return to I-75. East of the interstate, Fletcher Avenue becomes Morris Bridge Road (SR 579). Drive east 0.7 mile to the entrance. *Wilderness Park, Morris Bridge Site:* Continue east 2.8 miles on SR 579 to the entrance. *Wilderness Park, Flatwoods Site:* Continue east 1.4 miles on SR 579 to the entrance.

The Birding

The Hillsborough River flows west from Green Swamp in eastern Pasco County and winds through the city of Tampa before emptying into Hillsborough Bay. Northeast of the city, thousands of acres along the river are protected from development and provide excellent birding opportunities. **Hillsborough River State Park** includes within its 3,383 acres over 1,000 acres of pine flatwoods and oak hammock and over 2,300 acres of cypress swamp and other wetland habitat. A 1.8-mile loop road and 7.3 miles of trails provide access. From the entrance station, turn right onto the loop road and drive 0.5 mile to the parking area for the River Rapids Nature Trail. This 1.2-mile trail (with shortcuts for those with limited time) leads to an area of the river where limestone outcroppings have created rapids, an unusual sight in Florida. The trail passes through oak hammock that attracts migrant and wintering land birds. Continue on the loop road 0.3 mile to the picnic parking area. Two trails begin here: the 1.1-mile Baynard Trail and 3.4-mile Florida Trail. Both trails cross the river (via a suspension footbridge) and wind through pine flatwoods and cypress swamp on the north side of the river. In pineland areas watch for Northern Bobwhite, Common Ground-Dove, Pine Warbler, Summer Tanager, and Eastern Towhee. Residents in cypress floodplains include Red-shouldered Hawk, Barred Owl, Pileated Woodpecker, Tufted Titmouse, and Carolina Wren. Continue on the loop road 0.9 mile to a parking area for a 1.6-mile trail through a wetland restoration area. This marshy area attracts Least Bittern, Wood Stork, and other wading birds. Look for American Bittern, Sedge Wren, shorebirds, and sparrows during winter. The loop road returns to the entrance road in another 0.1 mile.

At 240-acre **Lettuce Lake Regional Park,** a 3,500-foot boardwalk meanders through cypress swamp and hardwood hammock along Lettuce Lake, a fingerlike projection of the Hillsborough River. The boardwalk may be accessed from several parking areas at the end of the main park road, 0.4 mile from the entrance. A visitor center is located near midpoint of the boardwalk, and a 35-foot observation tower is at the junction of Lettuce Lake and the river. Watch for Least Bittern, Wood Duck, Purple Gallinule, Limpkin, and other wading birds along the lakeshore. Swallow-tailed Kite, Prothonotary Warbler, and Summer Tanager can be seen here in spring and summer. A 5,000-foot nature trail circles through upland habitat where typical pineland species can be found.

Wilderness Park provides access to 16,000 acres of habitat along 20 miles of the river. The park is made up of several units, all easily accessible from US 301 and Morris Bridge Road. Watch for Sandhill Crane along both of these roads. John B. Sargeant, Trout Creek, and Morris Bridge Sites each have boardwalks along the river. All are good locations for Limpkin and migrant land birds. Canoe launches at all three sites offer opportunities for further exploration of the river. Flatwoods Site includes a 7-mile paved bike path through pine flatwoods and past seasonal wetlands. Typical species in the pinelands include Wild Turkey, Eastern Bluebird, and Bachman's Sparrow. During summer listen at dawn and dusk for Chuck-will's-widow. Wet areas attract Wood Duck, Sandhill Crane, Wood Stork, and other wading birds. A network of hiking trails connects Morris Bridge Road sites, while the Old Fork King Trail connects John B. Sargeant Site to Hillsborough River State Park.

General information: Hillsborough River State Park (entrance fee) is open daily from 8:00 A.M. until sunset. Fort Foster, a replica of a Seminole War–era military fort, is open for guided tours on weekends. Restrooms are available at the picnic area. Lettuce Lake Regional Park (donation suggested) is open daily from 8:00 A.M. to 8:00 P.M. The boardwalk and tower close at 7:30 P.M. Restrooms are available throughout the park. Wilderness Park sites (donations suggested) are open daily from sunrise to sunset. Restrooms are available at all sites.

DeLorme grid: Page 83, D-3.

Hazards: Keep a safe distance from alligators. Venomous snakes are present but rarely encountered.

Nearest food, gas, lodging: In Tampa.

Camping: Hillsborough River State Park: 106 sites.

For more information: *Hillsborough River State Park,* 15402 US 301, Thonotosassa, FL 33592; (813) 987-6771; www.floridastateparks.org/ hillsboroughriver. *Lettuce Lake Regional Park,* 6920 E. Fletcher Ave., Tampa, FL 33592; (813) 987-6204. *Wilderness Park,* 12702 US 301, Thonotosassa, FL 33592; (813) 987-6200.

38 St. Petersburg Area

Habitats: Sandy beach, maritime hammock, mangrove forest, salt marsh, hardwood hammock, hardwood swamp, pine flatwoods, oak/sand pine scrub, freshwater ponds, freshwater marsh.

Specialty birds: *Resident:* Mottled Duck, Reddish Egret, Roseate Spoonbill, Wood Stork, Bald Eagle, Clapper Rail, King Rail, Purple Gallinule, Limpkin, American Oystercatcher, Wilson's Plover, Snowy Plover, Monk Parakeet, Black-hooded Parakeet, Mangrove Cuckoo. *Summer:* Magnificent Frigatebird, Least Bittern, Swallow-tailed Kite, Short-tailed Hawk, Least Tern, Chuck-will's-widow, Gray Kingbird. *Winter:* Peregrine Falcon, Virginia Rail, Piping Plover, Whimbrel, Long-billed Curlew, American Woodcock, Whip-poor-will, Western Kingbird, Scissor-tailed Flycatcher, Nelson's Sharp-tailed Sparrow. *Migrant:* American Golden Plover, White-rumped Sandpiper, Upland Sandpiper, Buff-breasted Sandpiper, Black Tern, Acadian Flycatcher, Yellow-throated Vireo, Philadelphia Vireo, Wood Thrush, Blue-winged Warbler, Golden-winged Warbler, Bay-breasted Warbler, Cerulean Warbler, Prothonotary Warbler, Swainson's Warbler, Louisiana Waterthrush, Kentucky Warbler, Hooded Warbler, Canada Warbler, Summer Tanager, Scarlet Tanager, Rose-breasted Grosbeak, Painted Bunting, Dickcissel, Shiny Cowbird, Orchard Oriole.

Best times to bird: Late March to early May and late August to early November for trans-Gulf migrants. August through May for shorebirds.

Directions: *Ft. De Soto Park:* From Interstate 275 in St. Petersburg, exit at State Road 682 (exit 17). Drive west 2.2 miles to State Road 679 (Pinellas Bayway). Turn left and drive south 6.5 miles to park headquarters. *Boyd Hill Nature Park:* From I-275, exit at 54th Avenue South (also exit 17). Drive east 2 miles to Dr. Martin Luther King Jr. Street South (9th Street South). Turn left and drive north 0.4 mile to Country Club Way South. Turn left and drive 0.2 mile to the park entrance. *Sawgrass Lake Park:* From I-275, exit at 54th Avenue North (exit 26). Drive west 0.3 mile to Haines Road. Turn right and drive north 0.6 mile to 62nd Avenue North. Turn right and drive east 0.5 mile to 25th Street North (just before the I-275 overpass). Turn left and drive north 0.4 mile to the park entrance. From U.S. Highway 19, drive east 0.7 mile on 62nd Avenue North. Turn left on 25th Street North and drive north 0.4 mile to the park entrance. *Weedon Island Preserve:* From I-275 northbound in St. Petersburg, exit at Gandy Boulevard (State Road 694, exit 28). Drive east 2.5 miles to San Martin Boulevard. Turn right and drive south 1 mile to Weedon Drive. Turn left and drive east 1.4 miles to the main parking area. From I-275 southbound in Tampa, cross the Howard Frankland Bridge and exit at 4th Street North (State Road 687, exit 32). Drive south 2.7 miles to Gandy Boulevard. Turn left, drive east 1 mile to San Martin Boulevard, and proceed as above. *Boca Ciega Millennium Park:* Return to the intersection of Gandy

Boulevard and I-275. Drive west 1.3 miles on Gandy Boulevard to US 19, where Gandy Boulevard becomes Park Boulevard. Continue west 7.6 miles to 125th Street. Turn left and drive south 0.2 mile to 74th Avenue. Turn left and drive east 0.1 mile to the park entrance. *Walsingham Park:* Return to 125th Street, turn right, and drive north 1.8 miles to 102nd Avenue. Turn left and drive west 0.2 mile to the park's south entrance. To reach the park's north entrance from I-275, exit at Ulmerton Road (exit 31). Drive west 10.8 miles to its terminus at Walsingham Road. Turn left and drive east 0.5 mile to the entrance. *John Bonner Nature Park:* Return to Ulmerton Road, turn left, and drive west on Walsingham Road 1.3 miles to 143rd Street. Turn right and drive north 0.5 mile to the park entrance.

The Birding

Located on Mullet Key at the mouth of Tampa Bay, **Ft. De Soto Park** is considered one of the premier migrant-bird hot spots in the United States. Over 320 species of birds have been recorded in this 1,136-acre park, including 38 different shorebirds and 40 species of warblers! Birders flock to this park in April, when a dazzling array of flycatchers, vireos, thrushes, warblers, tanagers, buntings, grosbeaks, orioles, and other trans-Gulf migrants pass through. Rarities seen here just in the last few years include Purple Sandpiper, Heermann's and Thayer's Gull, Elegant Tern, Groove-billed Ani, Hammond's Flycatcher, Tropical Kingbird, Yellow-green Vireo, Black-throated Gray, Kirtland's, and Mourning Warbler, Bananaquit, Lazuli Bunting, and Shiny Cowbird.

The Pinellas Bayway connects Mullet Key to the mainland. At the intersection of the Bayway with SR 682 are several ornamental ponds visible from the road. These ponds host Mottled Duck and an assortment of wading birds, often including Wood Stork and Roseate Spoonbill. Drive south on the Bayway 3 miles to ponds on the west side of the road. During the winter months these ponds attract a variety of ducks, including impressive numbers of Redhead. Check pond edges for night-herons and other wading birds.

Reddish Egret. PHOTO: LARRY MANFREDI

Sora is sometimes seen along the edges of these ponds in winter. In summer watch for Gray Kingbird on wires along this stretch. Listen year-round for Monk and Black-hooded Parakeet. Where the shoreline becomes visible on both sides of Bunces Pass Bridge, scan the shore at low tide for Whimbrel, Willet, plovers, peeps, and other shorebirds. As you cross the bridge, watch overhead, especially in summer, for Magnificent Frigatebird. A wooded area near the boat ramp and the park campground provide good habitat for trans-Gulf migrants. Both are on the west side of the Bayway, south of the bridge. To avoid disturbing both campers and birds, it's best to park on the side of the road and explore the campground on foot. Park headquarters is at the southern end of the Bayway, where it intersects with Anderson Avenue. Stop inside to obtain a bird checklist and to check the sightings log. In spring and fall Western Kingbird and Scissor-tailed Flycatcher sometimes perch on wires in the vicinity of the headquarters building. A 0.4-mile wheelchair-accessible nature trail begins on the west side of the building and loops through a palm hammock. Look for buntings, grosbeaks, and other migrants along this trail.

From the headquarters drive east 0.1 mile on Anderson Avenue to the East Beach picnic area. Migrant warblers, tanagers, buntings, and grosbeaks can often be found in oaks in the picnic area. Scan the beach for gulls and terns, including "Herman," the Heermann's Gull first found in October 2000 and still seen in the park sporadically. East Beach Woods, on the east side of the picnic area, is a mixture of Australian pines and mangroves that can be excellent for trans-Gulf migrants. Two unmarked trails bisect the woods. Check areas around mangrove channels for ground-feeding warblers such as Prothonotary, Swainson's, Hooded, Kentucky, and both waterthrushes. From the picnic area, drive east 1.2 miles to the turnaround at the end of Anderson Avenue. Large numbers of shorebirds often congregate along the beach. White-rumped Sandpiper is regular here in May. Watch for Reddish Egret and other wading birds feeding just off the beach. Return to the intersection with the Pinellas Bayway and drive west on Anderson Avenue 0.8 mile to the Bay Pier parking area. Migrants are attracted to mulberry trees on the east side of the parking area, especially east of the ranger's residence. When fruiting in April, these trees can be swarming with birds gorging themselves on juicy berries. Look for Eastern Kingbird, Gray Catbird, Cedar Waxwing, Scarlet and Summer Tanager, Rose-breasted Grosbeak, Indigo Bunting, Orchard and Baltimore Oriole, and an assortment of wood warblers. Don't be confused by red stains on the faces and breasts of many of these birds: Those are the mulberries. A bird fountain and hummingbird feeders have been installed near these trees for the benefit of both birds and birders. Walk toward the beach, checking brushy areas for Common Ground-Dove, Painted Bunting, and Blue Grosbeak.

On the north side of Anderson Avenue, west of the Bay Pier, is an open field that in spring attracts grassland-loving shorebirds such as American Golden Plover and Upland and Buff-breasted Sandpiper. The 0.8-mile Soldier's Hole Nature Trail can be accessed from a dirt road that crosses this field. The trail provides access to mangrove habitat along Mullet Key Bayou, where at low tide Roseate Spoonbill, night-herons, and other wading birds feed. The entrance road for the fort is 0.2 mile west of the Bay Pier parking area. Check oaks and ficus trees surrounding the fort for migrant land birds. During migration this is another good spot for Western Kingbird and Scissor-tailed Flycatcher, as well as for Dickcissel. During periods of westerly winds, the nearby Gulf Pier, which extends 1,000 feet into the Gulf of Mexico, offers opportunities to scope for gannets, jaegers, and other seabirds. Beyond the fort, Mullet Key bends to the north. On the east side of Anderson Avenue is another large field that should be checked in season for grassland-loving shorebirds. On the west side you will pass several dune trails leading to the beach, followed by the North Beach parking area. The beach at the northern end of the key is separated by an inlet, with salt marsh habitat at the inlet's southern end. The salt marsh can be accessed from the southern end of the parking lot. In winter look for Nelson's Sharp-tailed Sparrow in this habitat. Clapper Rail is possible year-round. Gulls and terns usually congregate along the inlet north of this area. From the north end of the parking lot, walk through the picnic area and cross a footbridge to reach mudflats at the mouth of the inlet. This area can be excellent for wading birds and shorebirds. Long-billed Curlew has been regular here over the last several years. Also look for Reddish Egret, American Oystercatcher, Black-bellied, Wilson's, Semipalmated, Piping (in winter), and Snowy Plover, Marbled Godwit, Willet, Red Knot, Dunlin, Western and Least Sandpiper, Short-billed Dowitcher, and Black Skimmer. Watch for Peregrine Falcon patrolling the beach.

The Arrowhead Picnic Area is across the road from the North Beach parking area. A 1-mile nature trail begins 0.2 mile from the entrance and leads through oak hammock and along mangroves fringing Mullet Key Bayou. Yellow-billed Cuckoo, Great Crested Flycatcher, thrushes, vireos, and warblers can all be found here during migration. A side trail leads to a radio tower surrounded by a grassy field, good for buntings, Blue Grosbeak, and Common Ground-Dove. Great Horned Owl nests nearby. Black-hooded Parakeet has also been seen in this area. The oak hammock at the end of Anderson Avenue, between Arrowhead and North Beach, should also be checked for trans-Gulf migrants. Parking is not allowed at the turnaround at the end of the road. Park instead in the North Beach parking area.

Located on the shores of Lake Maggiore, 245-acre **Boyd Hill Nature Park** includes several distinct habitats. Enter the park via the Lake Maggiore Environmental Center, where you can obtain maps and bird checklists, as well as view interpretive displays of local flora and fauna. With 55 species of butterflies now recorded in the park, you may also want to pick up a butterfly checklist. Check flowering plants outside the center for migrant Ruby-throated Hummingbird. Behind the environmental center is an aviary that houses injured vultures, eagles, hawks, and owls. Black-hooded Parakeet nests in snags a short walk from the aviary. The park's 0.8-mile main trail parallels the shore of Lake Maggiore before returning through upland areas. Along the first half of the trail, short boardwalk spur trails provide opportunities to explore wet hammock, freshwater marsh, and the lake itself. Look for Anhinga, Least Bittern, Wood Stork, Mottled Duck, King Rail, and other waterbirds year-round. Watch overhead for Osprey and Bald Eagle, which nest in the park. American Bittern, Virginia Rail, Sora, Marsh Wren, and Swamp Sparrow are possible in the marsh during winter. Scan the lake for Ring-necked Duck, Lesser Scaup, and occasionally other waterfowl. In spring and fall you may find Acadian Flycatcher, Prothonotary and Hooded Warbler, Louisiana Waterthrush, and Orchard Oriole in the marsh. During summer watch for Least Tern and on occasion Swallow-tailed Kite over the lake. Oak hammock near the midpoint of the loop attracts migrant and wintering land birds. Residents and summer breeders here include Eastern Screech-Owl and Yellow-billed Cuckoo. This hammock continues west and can be explored via the Lakeside Loop Hiking Trail. As the main trail makes its way back to the environmental center, side trails loop around a wax myrtle pond and extend into areas of sand pine scrub and pine flatwoods. The pinelands host Northern Bobwhite, Great Horned Owl, Pileated Woodpecker, Yellow-throated and Pine Warbler, and Eastern Towhee. During winter and spring, listen for Whip-poor-will calling at dusk. In spring and summer Chuck-will's-widow can be heard. On some spring evenings, you can hear both! In winter American Woodcock has been seen at daybreak outside the park, west of the entrance along Country Club Way.

Sawgrass Lake Park provides access to one of the largest maple swamps on Florida's Gulf coast. This well-known migrant trap has attracted 35 species of warblers, including a Golden-cheeked Warbler collected in August 1964 and recorded nowhere else east of the Mississippi River. During fall migration, sought-after species such as Golden-winged and Cerulean Warbler are seen here almost annually. Also to be expected are an assortment of flycatchers, vireos, thrushes, and other trans-Gulf migrants. The park's boardwalk and trail system begins behind the Anderson Environmental Center and across a canal. The two main boardwalk trails are wheelchair-accessible but the foot trail is not. The 0.3-mile Sawgrass Trail boardwalk leads to an observation tower at Sawgrass Lake. Scan the lakeshore year-round for wading birds such as Wood Stork and Limpkin. Harder to find species include Least Bittern and King Rail. Glossy Ibis can be common here in winter, while American Bittern and Virginia Rail are seen occasionally. Blue-winged and Green-winged Teal and other duck species join resident Mottled and Wood Duck in winter. While at the tower, watch for Bald Eagle circling over the lake. Swallow-tailed Kite, Short-tailed Hawk, Least Tern, and Chimney Swift can be spotted overhead in spring and summer. The 0.6-mile Maple Trail boardwalk leads to the Oak Hammock foot trail. To reach this trail, turn left 0.3 mile from the environmental center and walk about 250 feet to the end of the boardwalk. This 0.5-mile loop trail provides access to the best location within the park to search for warblers and other migrant land birds. During fall migration species such as Tennessee, Chestnut-sided, and Blackburnian Warbler can be surprisingly common here. Several species such as Black-throated Green Warbler and Ovenbird may remain through the winter. Rarities such as Bell's Vireo and Townsend's Warbler have also been recorded in the park in winter. Return to the Maple Trail boardwalk and walk 0.2 mile to its terminus at the canal crossed earlier. A sidewalk paralleling the canal leads back to the environmental center. Watch along the canal for Anhinga, herons, egrets, and other waterbirds. Check areas of emergent vegetation for Purple Gallinule. The surrounding oaks may harbor a few migrant or wintering land birds.

Weedon Island, located on the western shore of Old Tampa Bay, has been occupied since prehistoric times. At various times in the 20th century, the island was home to a summer retreat, a speakeasy, a movie studio, and an airport. Today it is home to 3,164-acre **Weedon Island Preserve.** Two miles of wheelchair-accessible boardwalks provide access to extensive mangrove forests, while 2.7 miles of hiking trails wind through the preserve's upland habitats. Begin your tour at the Weedon Island Cultural and Natural History Center. Exhibits illustrate how Native American and early European inhabitants helped to shape the preserve we see today. A paved walkway passes by the Weedon Center and through surrounding scrubby flatwoods. The 0.3-mile walkway connects the preserve's two boardwalk loops and upland hiking trails. The Tower Boardwalk is a 0.5-mile loop leading to a 45-foot observation tower. Watch for night-herons and other wading birds in mangrove forest along the loop. The tower affords a bird's-eye view of the preserve and Tampa Bay. At low tide scan exposed mudflats in the bay for Reddish Egret, Roseate Spoonbill, Wood Stork, and American Oystercatcher. In winter look for American White Pelican and Red-breasted Merganser. Watch overhead for Osprey and Bald Eagle throughout the year. During the summer months Magnificent Frigatebird is likely to be soaring overhead. The Bay Boardwalk is a 0.7-mile loop with two observation platforms along the way in salt ponds hidden within the mangrove forest. As you walk this loop in summer, listen at dawn or dusk for the distinctive call of Mangrove Cuckoo. Also look and listen for Clapper Rail along mangrove edges. Trails through scrubby flatwoods and maritime hammock begin at the Bay Boardwalk end of the paved walkway. The north end of this trail system, known as the Boy Scout Trail, may also be accessed from a parking area on Weedon Drive, 0.2 mile north of the entrance to the main parking area. Look for Northern Bobwhite, Common Ground-Dove, Brown Thrasher, Eastern Towhee, and other resident species along these trails. Backwater areas of the preserve may be explored by canoe or kayak. The 4-mile South Paddling Trail loops through mangrove channels and between islands in the bay, offering up-close looks at a variety of wading birds. A canoe launch for this trail is located at the fishing pier, at the end of Weedon Drive, 0.3 mile south of the main parking area. In summer Gray Kingbird can be found anywhere between the fishing pier and the main parking area.

Boca Ciega Millennium Park offers the greatest diversity of habitats among parks in the mid–Pinellas County area. Several ponds along the entrance road should be checked for wintering waterfowl including American Wigeon, Blue-winged Teal, Northern Pintail, Northern Shoveler, Ring-necked Duck, Lesser Scaup, and Hooded Merganser. A bicycle/pedestrian path parallels the main park road and skirts each of these ponds. Turn into a parking area on the right side of the park road, 0.5 mile from the entrance, to access the path. A nature trail circling through pine flatwoods also begins at this parking area. Birds to be found here include Cooper's Hawk, Great Horned Owl, Pileated Woodpecker, and Eastern Towhee. Use the parking area on the opposite side of the road to reach the park's boardwalk and observation tower. This wheelchair-accessible boardwalk along Boca Ciega Bay passes through maritime hammock and mangrove forest. The hammock attracts a variety of migrant and wintering land birds. Check the tidal creek at the boardwalk's eastern end for Mottled Duck, Clapper Rail, and wading birds such as Reddish Egret, Roseate Spoonbill, and Wood Stork. From atop the 35-foot tower, scan the bay at low tide for shorebirds, gulls, and terns. American White Pelican is often offshore during the winter months. A canoe/kayak launch is available for further exploration of the bay.

Walsingham Park contains a large lake that bisects its 354 acres. A multiuse trail skirts the perimeter of the lake. A maple swamp in the northeast section of the park attracts a wide assortment of migrant and wintering land birds. To access this area, park at picnic shelter no. 6, near the Walsingham Road entrance to the park, and walk east to the swamp. Migrants recorded here include Acadian Flycatcher, Gray-cheeked Thrush, Yellow-throated Vireo, Blue-winged, Golden-winged, Cerulean, Prothonotary, Swainson's, Kentucky, Connecticut, Hooded, and Canada Warbler, Summer and Scarlet Tanager, and Blue Grosbeak. Golden-crowned Kinglet has been found here in winter. Black-hooded Parakeet is frequently seen just west of the park at a baseball field on 125th Street near Walsingham Road. **John Bonner Nature Park** is a tiny park on the Intracoastal Waterway that has attracted an astounding variety of trans-Gulf migrants, including over 30 species of warblers. Rarities found here have included Philadelphia Vireo, Black-throated Gray and Mourning Warbler, and Western Tanager. A series of trails winds through the park's oak hammock. A boardwalk leads into a salt marsh where Clapper Rail and wading birds such as Black-crowned Night-Heron and Wood Stork can be found. In summer watch over the Intracoastal Waterway for Magnificent Frigatebird. During the winter months scan the waterway for ducks, occasionally including Bufflehead.

General information: Ft. De Soto Park (toll) is open daily from 7:00 A.M. to sunset. The park receives over 2.7 million visitors annually. Birders should arrive early, especially on weekends, to avoid traffic. Restrooms are plentiful and are located in all picnic areas. Boyd Hill Nature Park (entrance fee) is open Tuesday through Thursday from 9:00 A.M. to 8:00 P.M., Friday and Saturday from 9:00 A.M. to 6:00 P.M., and Sunday from 11:00 A.M. to 6:00 P.M. The park is closed Thanksgiving, Christmas, and New Year's. Trails close half an hour before sunset. Restrooms are located in the environmental center. Drinking-water stations are located at several trail intersections. Weedon Island Preserve (no entrance fee) is open daily from sunrise to sunset. The Cultural and Natural History Center is open Wednesday through Sunday from 10:00 A.M. to 4:00 P.M. Restrooms are located in the Cultural and Natural History Center and at the fishing pier. Sawgrass Lake, Boca Ciega Millennium, Walsingham, and John Bonner Nature Parks (no entrance fees) are all open daily from 7:00 A.M. until sunset. Restrooms at Sawgrass Lake Park are located at the Anderson Environmental Center. Restrooms at all other parks are located in picnic areas.

DeLorme grid: Page 90, B-2, B-3, C-3; page 91, B-1.

Hazards: Keep a safe distance from alligators. Mosquitoes are common in summer and fall. Contact with poison ivy may produce a severe rash. As is the case when visiting any large metropolitan area, common sense is essential. Lock car doors and secure all valuables out of sight.

Nearest food, gas, lodging: In St. Petersburg.

Camping: Ft. De Soto Campground: 235 sites. Reservations can be made online at http://pubtitlet.co.pinellas.fl.us/parkspub/ParksMain.jsp.

For more information: *Ft. De Soto Park,* 3500 Pinellas Bayway S., Tierra Verde, FL 33715; (727) 582-2267; www.pinellascounty.org/park/05_Ft_ DeSoto.htm. *Boyd Hill Nature Park,* 1101 Country Club Way S., St. Petersburg, FL 33705; (727) 893-7326; www.stpete.org/fun/parks/ayboyd3 .htm. *Sawgrass Lake Park,* 7400 25th Street N., St. Petersburg, FL 33702; (727) 217-7256; www .pinellascounty.org/park/16_Sawgrass.htm. *Weedon Island Preserve,* 1800 Weedon Dr. NE, St. Petersburg, FL 33702; (727) 453-6500; www .weedonislandcenter.org. *Boca Ciega Millennium Park,* 12410 74th Ave. N., Seminole, FL 33772; (727) 588-4882; www.pinellascounty.org/park/ 03_Boca_Ciega.htm. *Walsingham Park,* 12615 102nd Ave. N., Largo, FL 33778; (727) 549- 6142; www.pinellascounty.org/park/22_Walsing ham.htm. *John Bonner Nature Park,* 14444 143rd St. N., Largo, FL 33774; (727) 586-7415.

39 Upper Tampa Bay Area

Habitats: Sandy beach, mangrove forest, salt marsh, pine flatwoods, maritime hammock, hardwood swamp, cypress swamp.

Specialty birds: *Resident:* Mottled Duck, Magnificent Frigatebird, Reddish Egret, Roseate Spoonbill, Wood Stork, Bald Eagle, Clapper Rail, King Rail, Limpkin, Sandhill Crane, Snowy Plover, Wilson's Plover, American Oystercatcher, Whimbrel, Bachman's Sparrow. *Summer:* Least Bittern, Least Tern, Mangrove Cuckoo, Chuck-will's-widow, Gray Kingbird, Black-whiskered Vireo, Summer Tanager. *Winter:* Piping Plover, American Woodcock, Whip-poor-will, Nelson's Sharp-tailed Sparrow. *Migrant:* Black Tern, Acadian Flycatcher, Yellow-throated Vireo, Bay-breasted Warbler, Prothonotary Warbler, Swainson's Warbler, Hooded Warbler, Summer Tanager, Scarlet Tanager, Rose-breasted Grosbeak, Orchard Oriole.

Best times to bird: September through April.

Directions: *Honeymoon Island State Park:* From US 19 in Dunedin, drive west 5 miles on County Road 586 (Curlew Road) to the park entrance. *Upper Tampa Bay County Park:* Return to US 19 and drive east 2.6 miles on CR 586 to County Road 584. Bear right and drive east 2 miles to the merger with County Road 580. Continue east 1.7 miles on CR 580 to Double Branch Road. Turn right and drive south 0.4 mile to the park entrance. From the Suncoast Parkway (State Road 589) in Tampa, exit at West Hillsborough Avenue (CR 580, exit 47). Drive east 6 miles to Double Branch Road. Turn left and proceed as above. *John Chesnut Sr. County Park:* Return to CR 584 and drive west 3.2 miles to East Lake Road. Turn right and drive north 2 miles to the park entrance. From US 19 in Palm Harbor, drive east 2 miles on CR 584 to East Lake Road. Turn left and proceed as above. *Brooker Creek Preserve:* Return to East Lake Road and drive north 4.2 miles to County Road 582 (Keystone Road). Turn right and drive east 2 miles to the preserve entrance. From US 19 in Tarpon Springs, drive east 5 miles on CR 582 to the preserve entrance. The environmental education center parking area is at the midpoint of the preserve's 2-mile loop road.

The Birding

Honeymoon Island State Park is located on a barrier island that is connected to the mainland by a 2-mile causeway crossing St. Joseph Sound. At low tide check beaches on both sides of the causeway for Reddish Egret, shorebirds, gulls, and terns. Common Loon, Horned Grebe, scoters, and other ducks are sometimes seen offshore. Watch overhead for Magnificent Frigatebird, which roosts on an island in the sound. To the south is undeveloped Caladesi Island, once connected to Honeymoon Island until split by a hurricane in 1921 and now only accessible by boat. **Caladesi Island State Park** consists of 650 acres of pine flatwoods and maritime hammock surrounded by 1,800 acres of beaches, coastal strand, and mangrove forest. Check the beaches for shorebirds, gulls, and terns and the hammock for trans-Gulf migrants. A concession-operated ferry service provides transportation to and from the island. To reach the ferry dock and the Pet Beach parking area, turn left 0.2 mile west of the Honeymoon Island entrance station. In October 1999 an Elegant Tern was discovered at Pet Beach, a first for Florida and one of many rarities found in the state park over the years. The list of unexpected birds includes Bar-tailed Godwit, Curlew, Baird's and Buff-breasted Sandpiper, Brant, and Green-tailed Towhee. Alcids have been recorded here on at least two occasions. A Long-billed Murrelet washed ashore in December 1986. More recently, in April 2005, a Razorbill was rescued from along the causeway but later died at a rehabilitation center.

On the main park road, 0.1 mile beyond the ferry turnoff, is a pull-off on the right for an observation area overlooking St. Joseph Sound. At low tide check inshore mudflats for waders and shorebirds and scan offshore for wintering loons, grebes, and ducks. Opposite this pull-off is another entrance for beach parking. At the north end of this parking lot is a marshy area that attracts puddle ducks, rails, shorebirds, and sparrows in winter. The park road continues west and forms a 1-mile one-way loop at its terminus. In 0.6 mile turn right to reach the Osprey Trail parking area. This 2-mile trail through pine flatwoods is named for the impressive number of Osprey that nests here. Great Horned Owl also nests along the trail. Adults and young are often conspicuous in spring. During the summer months look and listen for Gray Kingbird and Great Crested Flycatcher. This trail can be swarming with trans-Gulf migrants in spring and fall. Thirty-five species of warblers have been recorded here, regularly including Tennessee, Chestnut-sided, Blackburnian, Bay-breasted, Prothonotary, Swainson's, and Hooded. Other migrants seen in the pinelands include Yellow-billed Cuckoo, Scarlet and Summer Tanager, Rose-breasted Grosbeak, and

Indigo Bunting. Scan mudflats at the northern end of the trail for shorebirds, including Whimbrel and occasionally Long-billed Curlew. A side trail on the western side of the island skirts Pelican Cove. In spring and summer check mangroves along this trail for the occasional Mangrove Cuckoo and Black-whiskered Vireo. Nelson's Sharp-tailed Sparrow winters in the salt marsh.

Return to the park road and turn right into the next beach parking area. From here you can hike to a sand spit extending over 1 mile north. Large numbers of shorebirds, gulls, and terns congregate at the end of this spit. Shorebirds seen here most of the year include American Oystercatcher, Black-bellied, Wilson's, Semipalmated, and Snowy Plover, Marbled Godwit, Red Knot, Dunlin, and Short-billed Dowitcher. Piping Plover can be very common in winter. Terns are most numerous from spring through fall and can include Gull-billed, Caspian, Royal, Sandwich, Forster's, Common, Black, and Least. Black Skimmer is common to abundant throughout the year. If visiting Honeymoon Island in fall, you may want to take a short detour to **Dunedin Hammock Park** upon your return to the mainland. During September and October this 75-acre city park can host a remarkable assortment of trans-Gulf migrants. Several loop trails begin east of the parking area and provide access to the park's maritime hammock. To reach the park from CR 586, turn south on Alternate US 19, which is 2.5 miles west of US 19 and 2.5 miles east of the state park entrance station. Drive south 1 mile to Mira Vista Drive. Turn left and drive east 0.2 mile to San Mateo Drive. Turn left and drive north 0.2 mile to Buena Vista Drive. Turn right and drive east 0.1 mile to the park entrance.

Upper Tampa Bay County Park, as the name implies, is located at the northern end of Tampa Bay. Begin your exploration of the park at the nature center located at the end of the main park road, 1 mile from the entrance. Check the interpretive displays and pick up a park map and bird checklist. The Bobcat Trail begins behind the nature center. This short boardwalk circles through salt marsh habitat along Double Branch Creek. Clapper Rail resides in the marsh and Nelson's Sharp-tailed Sparrow can be found here in winter. A canoe launch is available for a more thorough exploration of the creek. The Otter Trail begins at the picnic area just north of the nature center. This 0.5-mile trail loops through pine flatwoods along the creek. The 0.6-mile Eagle Trail begins on the west side of the park road, 0.3 mile from the nature center. This trail winds through pine flatwoods and maritime hammock, past freshwater ponds and salt marsh, before ending along mangrove-fringed Mobbly Bay. Migrant and wintering land birds can be found in areas of maritime hammock. In the pine flatwoods look for Northern Bobwhite, Common Ground-Dove, Great Horned Owl, and Eastern Towhee. Scan mudflats at the end of the trail for wading birds such as Reddish Egret and Roseate Spoonbill and for resident and wintering shorebirds including American Oystercatcher and Wilson's Plover. Scope the bay in winter for Horned Grebe, Lesser Scaup, and Red-breasted Merganser. Look and listen in summer for Mangrove Cuckoo and Gray Kingbird.

John Chesnut Sr. County Park is at the southeastern end of Lake Tarpon. Trails in this park can be productive for migrant land birds, especially in fall. The 0.6-mile Peggy Park Trail (named for a wildlife officer killed in the line of duty in 1984) is a boardwalk and shell gravel trail through a cypress/mixed hardwood swamp along the lake and Brooker Creek. To reach this trail, turn left at a four-way intersection 0.1 mile from the park entrance. Drive south 0.3 mile to the turnaround at the end of the road. Another boardwalk begins at the boat ramp, reached by backtracking 0.2 mile from the turnaround. This trail leads to an observation tower overlooking the lake. Look for Limpkin and Least

Bittern in areas of emergent vegetation along the shore and Osprey and Bald Eagle over-head. A third boardwalk trail is located at the northern end of the park. Return to the intersection and turn left. Drive west 0.4 mile and turn right, continuing 0.1 mile to a parking area near picnic shelter no. 13. The trail begins alongside a bridge and winds for 0.6 mile through cypress/mixed hardwood swamp, ending near Lake Tarpon. This trail can be excellent for migrant land birds in fall. All of these trails are also popular with joggers.

Brooker Creek Preserve is home to a magnificent environmental education center containing ecological and historical exhibits, an auditorium, classrooms, and a nature store. The center is surrounded by over 8,000 acres of pine flatwoods and forested wetlands in the Brooker Creek watershed. A boardwalk through cypress/mixed hardwood swamp leads from the parking area to the education center complex. A short spur boardwalk takes you to an overlook of the creek. Resident species to look for here include Barred Owl, Pileated Woodpecker, Tufted Titmouse, Carolina Chickadee, and Carolina Wren. Also pause to admire the impressive sculptures along the trail. A series of interconnecting hiking trails begins south of the parking area. Currently, hikers must wade through Brooker Creek to reach these trails. Eventually the overlook near the education center will be extended over the creek and connect with the trail system. Hikers can complete a 4-mile loop or use cutoffs to shorten the walk. The trails meander through pine flatwoods, oak hammock, and bottomland hardwood forest and are often wet, especially in summer. Wild Turkey is common in drier upland areas. In pine flatwoods look for Red-headed Woodpecker, Eastern Towhee, and Bachman's Sparrow. Wading birds including Wood Stork and Sandhill Crane can be found in open wetlands. The Friends Trail is a 1.8-mile interpretive trail that can be visited during daylight hours even when the rest of the preserve is closed. To reach the trailhead, return to CR 582 and drive west 0.5 mile to Lora Lane. Turn left and drive south 1 mile to the end of the road. The trail loops through pine flatwoods and past a restored cypress swamp. An observation platform 0.2 mile from the trailhead provides an overlook of the swamp. A visit at dusk during the winter months may produce sightings of American Woodcock and Whip-poor-will in the area near the trailhead.

General information: Honeymoon Island State Park and Caladesi Island State Park (entrance fees) are open daily from 8:00 A.M. until sunset. Restrooms at Honeymoon Island are located in picnic areas and beach parking areas. The Caladesi Island shuttle ($8.00 per adult for a four-hour stay) leaves on the hour from the ferry dock on Honeymoon Island. Restrooms on Caladesi Island are located at the beach bathhouse. Dunedin Hammock Park (no entrance fee) is open daily from sunrise to sunset. Restrooms are located in the picnic area. Upper Tampa Bay County Park (donation suggested) is open daily from 8:00 A.M. to 6:00 P.M. Restrooms are located in the nature center and in picnic areas. John Chesnut Sr. County Park (no entrance fee) is open daily from 7:00 A.M. until sunset. Restrooms are located throughout the park. Brooker Creek Preserve (no entrance fee) is open Wednesday from 9:00 A.M. to 8:30 P.M. and Thursday through Sunday from 9:00 A.M. to 4:00 P.M. Restrooms are located in the environmental education center. The Lora Lane trailhead is open daily from sunrise to sunset.

DeLorme grid: Page 82, C-3, D-2, D-3; page 83, D-1.

Hazards: Keep a safe distance from alligators. Eastern diamondback rattlesnakes and cotton-mouths are present but rarely encountered. Mosquitoes are common in summer. Contact with poison ivy may result in a severe rash. Trails may be flooded in summer.

Nearest food, gas, lodging: In Dunedin and Tarpon Springs.

Camping: There are private campgrounds in Dunedin and Tarpon Springs.

For more information: *Honeymoon Island State Park,* 1 Causeway Blvd., Dunedin, FL 34698; (727) 469-5942; www.floridastateparks.org/ honeymoonisland. *Caladesi Island State Park,* 1 Causeway Blvd., Dunedin, FL 34698; (727) 469-5918; www.floridastateparks.org/caladesiisland.

Dunedin Hammock Park, 1900 San Mateo Dr., Dunedin, FL 34698; (727) 298-3278. *Upper Tampa Bay County Park,* 8001 Double Branch Rd., Tampa, FL 33635; (813) 855-1765. *John Chesnut Sr. County Park,* 2200 E. Lake Rd., Palm Harbor, FL 34685; (727) 669-1951; www.pinellas county.org/park/04_Chesnut.htm. *Brooker Creek Preserve,* 3940 Keystone Rd., Tarpon Springs, FL 34688; (727) 453-6910; www.friendsofbrooker creekpreserve.org.

 # New Port Richey Area

Habitats: Sandy beach, salt marsh, mangrove forest, pine flatwoods, sandhills, hardwood hammock, oak/sand pine scrub, freshwater marsh, cypress swamp, freshwater lake.

Specialty birds: *Resident:* Mottled Duck, Reddish Egret, Roseate Spoonbill, Wood Stork, Bald Eagle, King Rail, Clapper Rail, Black Rail, Purple Gallinule, Limpkin, Sandhill Crane, Wilson's Plover, American Oystercatcher, Monk Parakeet, Budgerigar, Brown-headed Nuthatch, Bachman's

Sparrow, Seaside Sparrow. *Summer:* Magnificent Frigatebird, Least Bittern, Swallow-tailed Kite, Short-tailed Hawk, Least Tern, Chuck-will's-widow, Gray Kingbird, Summer Tanager. *Winter:* Fulvous Whistling-Duck, Peregrine Falcon, Virginia Rail, Whimbrel, Gull-billed Tern, American Woodcock, Nelson's Sharp-tailed Sparrow. *Migrant:* American Avocet, Black Tern, Acadian Flycatcher, Prothonotary Warbler, Hooded Warbler.

Best times to bird: September through mid-May.

Directions: *Key Vista Nature Park:* From US 19 in Holiday, drive west on Moog Road 1.5 miles to Strauber Memorial Highway (County Road 518). Turn left and drive south, then west 1.2 miles to County Road 595A. Turn left and drive south 0.2 mile to the park entrance. *Robert K. Rees Memorial Park:* Return to US 19 via Moog Road. Turn left and drive north 2.8 miles to Main Street in New Port Richey. Continue north 0.2 mile to Green Key Road. Turn left and drive west 1.7 miles to the park entrance. *Werner-Boyce Salt Springs State Park:* Continue north 3.3 miles on US 19 to Scenic Drive (just north of the Gulf Ridge Mall). Turn left and drive west 0.7 mile to the trailhead parking area. *Jay P. Starkey Wilderness Park:* From US 19 in New Port Richey, drive east 4.4 miles on Trouble Creek Road (CR 518) to Little Road, where CR 518 becomes River Crossing Boulevard. Continue east 1.3 miles to Starkey Boulevard. Turn left and drive north 0.3 mile to the park entrance. From the Suncoast Parkway (SR 589), exit at State Road 54 (exit 19). Drive west 8.2 miles to Little Road. Turn right and drive north 2.2 miles to River Crossing Boulevard. Turn right and proceed as above. *Crews Lake Park:* From the Suncoast Parkway (SR 589) in Shady Hills, exit at State Road 52 (exit 27). Drive east 0.6 mile to Shady Hills Road. Turn left and drive north 2.8 miles to Lenway Road. Turn right and drive east 0.3 mile to the park entrance. From US 19 in Hudson, drive east 9.8 miles on SR 52 to Shady Hills Road. Turn left and proceed as above.

The Birding

At 101-acre **Key Vista Nature Park,** 1.5 miles of trails wind through coastal sand pine uplands along Sleepy Lagoon, Rocky Creek, and the Gulf of Mexico. Look for resident species including Pileated Woodpecker, Tufted Titmouse, Carolina Wren, and Eastern

Towhee as well as trans-Gulf migrants and wintering land birds. Both Bald Eagle and Osprey nest in the park. From the boardwalk near the beach, scan mudflats for wading birds and shorebirds and scope offshore for wintering waterfowl. Gulls, terns, and skimmers can usually be found on the park's sandy beach. **Robert K. Rees Memorial Park** is located on a narrow peninsula at the end of **Green Key Road.** During spring migration, incredible numbers of trans-Gulf migrants have been observed streaming through the park, including 26 species of warblers. At its peak in early to mid-May, double- or even triple-digit counts of Northern Parula, Cape May, Black-throated Blue, Prairie, Palm, Blackpoll, and Black-and-white Warbler, American Redstart, Ovenbird, and Common Yellowthroat are not uncommon. Migration also brings an assortment of vireos, thrushes, tanagers, buntings, grosbeaks, and orioles, plus impressive numbers of Black Tern and Bobolink. In late fall and again in early spring, amazing numbers of Yellow-rumped Warbler pass through daily. Gray Kingbird is conspicuous in the park and along Green Key Road in summer. Clapper Rail, Seaside Sparrow, and the Marian's race of Marsh Wren breed in adjacent salt marsh. Throughout the year check mudflats for Reddish Egret, Roseate Spoonbill, American Oystercatcher, and other shorebirds. Scan offshore for wintering waterfowl, including Common Loon, Horned Grebe, Redhead, Bufflehead, and Hooded Merganser. A Sabine's Gull was recorded here in October 2001 and a Pacific Loon was seen offshore in January 2003.

    Werner-Boyce Salt Springs State Park protects 4 miles of pristine shoreline and over 4,000 acres of salt marsh, mangrove forest, and pine flatwoods. Black Rail is a confirmed breeder in the salt marsh. King and Clapper Rail also reside in the park. Virginia Rail and Sora, as well as Nelson's Sharp-tailed Sparrow, can be found in the marsh in winter. Unfortunately, access is currently limited to a 0.5-mile trail through an upland area of the park. The trail begins at the parking area on Scenic Drive. In addition to resident Tufted Titmouse and Carolina Wren, a variety of migrant land birds can be seen on this trail in spring and fall. A Black-headed Grosbeak was reported here in October 2004. A 1,000-foot boardwalk and additional trails through the park are planned for the future.

    Budgerigar, an introduced parakeet native to Australia and once common along the Gulf Coast, can still be seen in small numbers in Pasco County. One roost site is in Hudson by the Perkin's Restaurant, at the intersection of US 19 and SR 52, 2.4 miles north of Scenic Drive. At dusk look for the parakeets in trees surrounding the restaurant parking lot. Large numbers of European Starling and House Sparrow also roost in these trees.

    On land once used for cattle grazing, **Jay P. Starkey Wilderness Park** has been created for use as both a well field and recreational park for coastal communities in Pasco County. Building upon the original 250 acres donated by the Starkey family in 1972, recent acquisitions have expanded the park to over 19,000 acres. Though only 65 acres are in a day-use area accessible by vehicle, 13 miles of hiking trails, 10 miles of equestrian trails, and a 6.5-mile paved bike path provide opportunities to explore the rest of the park on foot, bicycle, and horseback. From the entrance gate, drive east 0.5 mile on the main park road to an information kiosk where park maps are available. The Two Rivers Nature Center is across the road from the kiosk. A boardwalk that begins behind the nature center leads through cypress swamp to the Pithlachascotee River. This area can be productive for migrant and wintering land birds, as well as resident species such as Wood Duck, Barred Owl, and Pileated Woodpecker. A 1.6-mile interpretive nature trail winds through the eastern half of the day-use area. To reach this trail, turn right immediately after the information kiosk. Drive east 0.2 mile, where the road bends to the left. Continue 0.5 mile to the day-use-area loop road. Turn right and drive 0.5 mile to the nature trail parking area. Look for Eastern Screech-Owl, Tufted Titmouse, Carolina Chickadee, Carolina Wren, and other resident species.

The paved bike path, which begins near the information kiosk, is used by most birders to access pine flatwoods to the east of the day-use area. A variety of pineland species can be found by hiking or biking this path, including Cooper's Hawk, Wild Turkey, Northern Bobwhite, Sandhill Crane, Great Horned Owl, Red-headed and Hairy Woodpecker, Brown-headed Nuthatch, Eastern Bluebird, Yellow-throated and Pine Warbler, and Eastern Towhee. In spring and summer watch for Swallow-tailed Kite, Chuck-will's-widow, Eastern Kingbird, Chimney Swift, Yellow-throated Vireo, Summer Tanager, and Bachman's Sparrow. Check kettles of vultures overhead for Short-tailed Hawk, which nests in the area. The most productive area for many of these species is beyond the power lines that cross the bike path, at about the 2-mile marker. The area under the power lines can be excellent for sparrows in winter. Sparrows on the park list include Chipping, Field, Vesper, Savannah, Henslow's (rare), Grasshopper, Song, Lincoln's, Swamp, White-throated, and White-crowned. At dawn and dusk during winter, American Woodcock has been observed displaying and calling over the path. By following this path the entire 6.5 miles, you will reach the Suncoast Parkway Trail, a 35-mile multiple-use trail along the eastern boundary of the park.

Located in central Pasco County, 113-acre **Crews Lake Park** offers opportunities to observe an impressive array of wintering waterfowl, shorebirds and migrant and wintering land birds. From the park entrance, drive 0.5 mile on Crews Lake Road to the lakeside parking area. Walkways lead to an observation tower and fishing pier from which to scope the lake. In addition to resident Mottled and Wood Duck, look in winter for Blue and Green-winged Teal, Northern Shoveler, American Wigeon, Ring-necked Duck, and Hooded Merganser. Fulvous Whistling-Duck has been recorded here occasionally. If water levels in the lake are down, exposed mudflats may attract shorebirds including Semipalmated Plover, Black-necked Stilt, Greater and Lesser Yellowlegs, Dunlin, and Solitary, Spotted, Semipalmated, Western, and Least Sandpiper. Unexpected shorebirds seen here have included Piping Plover and White-rumped Sandpiper. Several species of tern have been recorded on and around the lake, including Least Tern in spring and summer and Black Tern during migration. Shallow areas of the lake attract wading birds such as Wood Stork, Glossy Ibis, and Roseate Spoonbill, the latter most likely in summer. Sandhill Crane is common and could be seen anywhere around the lake, including the picnic area! Also watch for Bald Eagle circling overhead. Check emergent vegetation along the lakeshore for Least Bittern, King Rail, Purple Gallinule, and Limpkin. Search here in winter for American Bittern, Virginia Rail, Sora, and Wilson's Snipe. Sedge Wren is often found during winter in grassy and brushy areas along the shore. This habitat also attracts wintering sparrows, sometimes including Clay-colored, Field, Vesper, Lark, Song, Lincoln's, and White-throated. Check these same areas during migration for Bobolink. A series of trails crisscrosses upland areas in the park and can be accessed from various points along the park road. Throughout the year look in sandhills and hardwood hammock for Wild Turkey, Northern Bobwhite, Red-headed, Hairy, Downy, and Pileated Woodpecker, Carolina Chickadee, Tufted Titmouse, and Eastern Towhee. These trails are most productive during spring and fall migration. Thirty species of warblers have been recorded here, including Blue-winged, Golden-winged, Chestnut-sided, Blackburnian, Bay-breasted, Cerulean, Prothonotary, Kentucky, and Hooded. Other migrants to watch for as you hike these trails include Yellow-billed Cuckoo, Acadian Flycatcher, Summer and Scarlet Tanager, and Rose-breasted Grosbeak.

General information: Key Vista Nature Park, Robert K. Rees Memorial Park, Jay P. Starkey Wilderness Park, and Crews Lake Park (no entrance fees) are open daily from sunrise to sunset. Restrooms are located near parking or picnic areas. The Scenic Drive trailhead at Werner-Boyce Salt Springs State Park (no entrance fee) is open daily from 8:00 A.M. until sunset. A primitive restroom is located near the parking area.

DeLorme grid: Page 82, B-3, C-3; page 83, B-1, C-1.

Hazards: Keep a safe distance from alligators. Eastern diamondback rattlesnakes are present but rarely encountered. Mosquitoes and sand flies (no-see-ums) are common in summer.

Nearest food, gas, lodging: In Holiday, New Port Richey, and Hudson.

Camping: Jay P. Starkey Wilderness Park, Crews Lake Park.

For more information: *Key Vista Nature Park,* 2700 Baillies Bluff Rd., Holiday, FL 34691; (813) 929-1260. *Robert K. Rees Memorial Park,* 4835 Green Key Rd., New Port Richey, FL 34652; (813) 929-1260. *Werner-Boyce Salt Springs State Park,* P.O. Box 490, Port Richey, FL 34673; (727) 816-1890; www.floridastateparks.org/werner-boyce. *Jay P. Starkey Wilderness Park,* 10500 Wilderness Rd., New Port Richey, FL 34655; (727) 834-3247. *Crews Lake Park,* 16739 Crews Lake Dr., Shady Hills, FL 34610; (813) 929-1260.

NORTHWEST

 ## 41 Weeki Wachee/Crystal River Area

Habitats: Sandhills, pine flatwoods, sand pine scrub, wet prairie, sawgrass marsh, cypress swamp, hardwood swamp, salt marsh, maritime hammock, sandy beach.

Specialty birds: *Resident:* Mottled Duck, Magnificent Frigatebird, Reddish Egret, Wood Stork, Bald Eagle, Clapper Rail, King Rail, Limpkin, Sandhill Crane, Whooping Crane, Snowy Plover, Wilson's Plover, American Oystercatcher, Budgerigar, Bachman's Sparrow, Seaside Sparrow. *Summer:* Least Bittern, Swallow-tailed Kite, Mississippi Kite, Least Tern, Chuck-will's-widow, Gray Kingbird, Yellow-throated Vireo, Prothonotary Warbler, Yellow-breasted Chat, Summer Tanager, Blue Grosbeak. *Winter:* Common Goldeneye, Virginia Rail, Golden-crowned Kinglet, Nelson's Sharp-tailed Sparrow. *Migrant:* Black Tern, Wood Thrush, Swainson's Warbler, Hooded Warbler.

Best times to bird: September through May.

Directions: *Alfred McKethan/Pine Island Park:* From the Suncoast Parkway (State Road 589) west of Brooksville, exit at State Road 50 (exit 46). Drive west 5.8 miles to U.S. Highway 19 in Weeki Wachee. Continue west 4.8 miles on Cortez Boulevard (County Road 550) to Pine Island Drive (County Road 495). Turn right and drive north 2.5 miles to the parking area. *Chassahowitzka Wildlife Management Area:* Return to US 19, turn left, and drive north 9.6 miles to the wildlife drive entrance. To reach the Chassahowitzka River Trail, continue north 4.2 miles on US 19 to Miss Maggie Drive, opposite the junction with U.S. Highway 98. Turn left and drive west 1.8 miles to the boat launch in the Chassahowitzka River Campground. *Crystal River Preserve State Park:* Return to US 19 and drive north 15.3 miles to

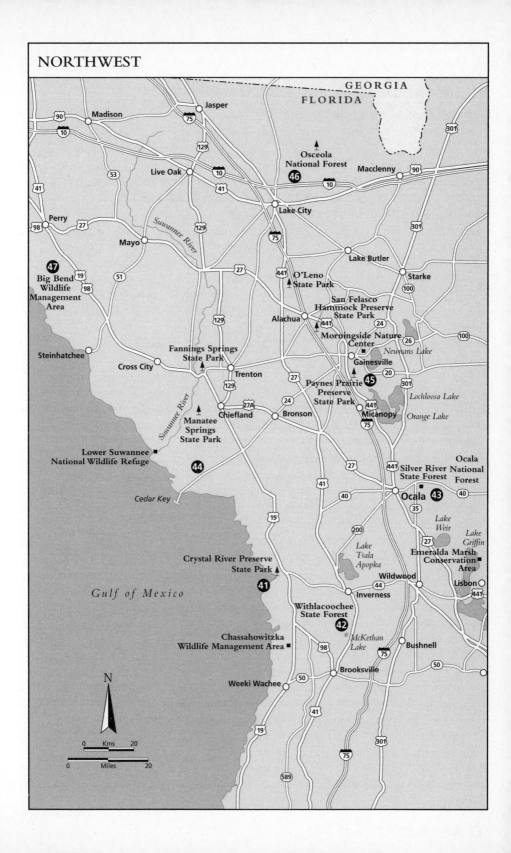

NORTHWEST

GEORGIA
FLORIDA

Madison

Jasper

Osceola
National Forest
46

Macclenny

Live Oak

Lake City

Lake Butler

Perry

Mayo

Starke

Big Bend
Wildlife
Management
Area
47

O'Leno
State Park

San Felasco
Hammock Preserve
State Park

Steinhatchee

Alachua

Morningside Nature
Center

Newnans Lake

Fannings Springs
State Park

Cross City

Gainesville

Trenton

45

Paynes Prairie
Preserve
State Park

Lochloosa Lake

Chiefland

Bronson

Micanopy

Orange Lake

Manatee
Springs
State Park

Lower Suwannee
National Wildlife Refuge

44

Silver River
State Park

Ocala
National
Forest

Cedar Key

Ocala
43

Crystal River Preserve
State Park

Lake
Weir

Lake
Griffin

Gulf of Mexico

41

Emeralda Marsh
Conservation
Area

Lake
Tsala
Apopka

Lisbon

Wildwood

Chassahowitzka
Wildlife Management Area

Withlacoochee
State Forest
42

Inverness

McKethan
Lake

Bushnell

Brooksville

Weeki Wachee

N

0   Kms   20

0   Miles   20

State Park Road. Turn left and drive west 1.5 miles to Sailboat Avenue. Turn left and drive 0.7 mile to the park's visitor center.

The Birding

Alfred McKethan/Pine Island Park provides access to areas of salt marsh and sandy beach habitat west of Weeki Wachee, in Hernando County. Walk the park's sandy beach, checking mudflats exposed at low tide for Reddish Egret, American Oystercatcher, and other wading birds, shorebirds, gulls, and terns. From the pier, scan offshore for Common Loon, Horned Grebe, and Red-breasted Merganser. Watch overhead for Bald Eagle and, occasionally, Magnificent Frigatebird. Check adjacent salt marsh for Clapper Rail, Marsh Wren, and Seaside Sparrow. Nelson's Sharp-tailed Sparrow can be found in the marsh during the winter months. Similar habitat and species can be seen by returning to CR 550, turning right, and driving south 1.5 miles to **Bayport Park.** Budgerigar may still be found in Hernando Beach, south of Weeki Wachee. To reach this area, backtrack 3 miles on CR 550 to Shoal Line Boulevard (County Road 597). Turn left and drive south 4.3 miles to Calienta Street. Turn right, then left onto Gulf Coast Drive. Residents in this community have set up nest boxes for the parakeets. Listen for their chatter as you slowly drive streets both north and south of Gulf Coast Drive. Respect private property and bird only from the road.

Chassahowitzka, from a Seminole word meaning "pumpkin hanging place," was once the largest and most pristine hardwood swamp south of the Suwannee River. Extensively logged for cypress and red cedar during the early 20th century, Chassahowitzka Swamp and surrounding flatwoods, sandhills, hammock, and salt marsh are being restored to provide habitat for the area's abundant wildlife. **Chassahowitzka Wildlife Management Area,** consisting of 33,919 acres north and west of Weeki Wachee, provides access to this vast region. Another 31,000 acres of salt marsh, estuaries, and hardwood swamp is within **Chassahowitzka National Wildlife Refuge,** extending north into Citrus County and only accessible by boat. The refuge was established in 1943 as a wintering location for ducks and other waterfowl. In recent years the refuge has become the winter home of a managed flock of Whooping Crane, whose annual migration from Necedah National Wildlife Refuge in Wisconsin is assisted by ultralight aircraft. While the pens that house the cranes are off-limits to the public, the cranes are allowed to fly outside the pens to forage and may be observed by boat. One access point is the Chassahowitzka River Trail, which begins at the boat launch in the Chassahowitzka River Campground.

A 9.7-mile driving loop traverses a cross section of habitats within the wildlife management area. A kiosk across from the hunting check station has maps and driving-tour booklets. From the kiosk, the wildlife drive heads west, then south on Indigo Lane, passing through pine flatwoods and disturbed sandhill communities. Patches of sandhill along this road are being restored through a combination of applying herbicides to invasive oaks and setting prescribed fires during the summer months to stimulate the growth of wire grass and longleaf pine. Watch in these pineland areas for Wild Turkey, Northern Bobwhite, Common Ground-Dove, Red-headed and Hairy Woodpecker, Eastern Bluebird, Yellow-throated and Pine Warbler, and Eastern Towhee. In spring and summer listen for Yellow-throated Vireo, Summer Tanager, and Bachman's Sparrow. In 1.7 miles Indigo Lane reaches a picnic area and trailhead for two interpretive trails. The wildlife drive continues south on Swamp Grade. The Wild Turkey Trace Trail begins on the west side of the picnic area and winds through sandhill habitat, good for many of the pineland species mentioned above. The Cypress Circle Trail begins on the east side and loops through sandhills that encircle a cypress dome. Red-shouldered Hawk, Barred Owl, Pileated Woodpecker, Tufted Titmouse, Carolina Chickadee, and Carolina Wren inhabit the cypress dome. In summer watch for Swallow-tailed Kite and Prothonotary Warbler. Migration brings a variety of warblers, vireos, thrushes, and other land birds. Many of these same birds can be found by hiking Pull Tree Tram or Two-mile Tram, abandoned logging roadways that head west from Swamp Grade deep into the hardwood swamp. Wood Duck can sometimes be seen on Two-mile Tram. Continue south 2.5 miles on Swamp Grade, through hardwood swamp and patches of sand pine and oak scrub, to Rattlesnake Camp Road. The wildlife drive continues east 1.6 miles to Gopher Road, leaving the swamp and returning to upland sandhills and pine flatwood habitat. These pinelands are dotted with seasonal ponds that may attract Wood Stork and other wading birds. Just to the south of the intersection of Rattlesnake Camp Road and Gopher Road are the remains of Centralia, a town whose lumber mill was once one of the largest in Florida. The town was abandoned after the swamp was logged out. Drive north 3.6 miles on Gopher Road to complete the wildlife drive and return to the entrance.

The area now known as **Crystal River Preserve State Park** was originally purchased as an upland buffer to the submerged lands of St. Martins Marsh Aquatic Preserve. The park consists of several parcels in Citrus County totaling about 30,000 acres. Much of the park is accessible via an extensive trail system, including two trails near the visitor center. The Boy Scout Trail begins at a parking area on Sailboat Avenue, 0.5 mile north of the visitor center. This short trail through wet hammock should be checked in spring and fall for migrant land birds. The 1.7-mile Crystal Cove Trail begins on the south side of Mullet Hole, a local fishing spot. To reach the trailhead, continue north 0.1 mile on Sailboat Avenue. Turn right and drive east 0.2 mile to the Mullet Hole parking area. The trail heads south through a mixture of scrub, pines, and hardwoods, past a freshwater pond, and along a tidal creek that flows into the Crystal River. Areas of hammock attract migrant land birds, especially in spring. Watch overhead in summer for Mississippi Kite. Citrus County is at the southern limit of this raptor's breeding range. Look for Least Bittern and Clapper Rail as you pass through salt marsh habitat along the tidal creek. An assortment of wading birds and shorebirds can be seen on exposed mudflats at low tide. Adjacent **Crystal River Archaeological State Park** can be good for resident and migrant land birds. From the intersection of Sailboat Avenue and State Park Road, drive east 0.4 mile to Museum Pointe Road. Turn right and drive south 0.5 mile to the visitor center parking area. A 0.5-mile paved path winds through an oak hammock and provides access to several prehistoric Indian burial and temple mounds. From the observation deck on Temple Mound "A," scan the Crystal River for wading birds and wintering waterfowl. Watch for Bald Eagle circling over the river.

The most popular birding destination in Crystal River Preserve State Park is a 2.5-mile trail known as the Eco-Walk. To reach this trail from the park's visitor center, return to US 19 and drive north 2 miles to Curtis Tool Road. Turn left and drive west less than 0.1 mile to Tallahassee Road. The entrance is almost directly opposite from Curtis Tool Road. A 9-mile bike loop also begins at the Eco-Walk trailhead. The bike trail, which skirts salt marsh habitat, can also be accessed from the end of State Park Road. The Eco-Walk passes through a variety of habitats including wet prairie, pinelands, and hardwood hammock. Resident species include Wild Turkey, Northern Bobwhite, Barred Owl, Pileated Wood-pecker, Carolina Chickadee, and Eastern Bluebird. Check ponds and marshy areas along the trail for Wood Duck and various wading birds. In summer look for Yellow-billed

Cuckoo, Great Crested Flycatcher, Summer Tanager, and Blue Grosbeak. As you walk through brushy areas of the trail in spring and summer, listen for Yellow-breasted Chat, also at the southern limit of its breeding range. Watch overhead for both Swallow-tailed and Mississippi Kite. Another good area for resident and migrant land birds is Churchhouse Hammock on the west side of US 19, across from the Crystal River Mall and 0.5 mile south of State Park Road. A 0.3-mile wheelchair-accessible boardwalk winds through pine flatwoods that in recent years, due to an absence of fire, has converted to wet hammock. The Path to the Past Trail begins near the southern entrance to the boardwalk. This 0.8-mile dirt trail passes through bottomland hardwood hammock and a sawgrass marsh before returning to the boardwalk.

Ft. Island Trail (State Road 44) is a 9-mile road that provides access to salt marsh and beachfront habitat in Citrus County. From Churchhouse Hammock, continue south 3.6 miles on US 19, turning right on Ft. Island Trail. Drive west 2.5 miles to a trail that begins at the intersection with Dixie Shores Road. This 1-mile trail passes through scrubby flatwoods and a salt marsh and loops through an island hammock. Check for migrant land birds in upland areas near the trailhead. Similar habitat attractive to migrants can be found near the trailhead for the Redfish Hole Trail. The trailhead is on the south side of Ft. Island Trail, 1.5 miles west of Dixie Shores. **Ft. Island Trail County Park** is 1 mile farther west. This small park has a pier extending into the Crystal River, worth a check for wintering waterfowl. Salt marshes line the road along the last few miles of Ft. Island Trail. Marsh Wren, Seaside Sparrow, Clapper Rail, Wood Stork, and other wading birds can be found in the marsh throughout the year, while Nelson's Sharp-tailed Sparrow is here during winter. The road ends in 4 miles at **Ft. Island Gulf Beach County Park.** Check the southern end of the beach for gulls, terns, and shorebirds, including American Oystercatcher. A Hudsonian Godwit was found at this park in January 2001. A fishing pier provides opportunities to scan the gulf during winter for Common Loon, Horned Grebe, American White Pelican, and Red-breasted Merganser. Wintering waterfowl occasionally include rarities such as Common Goldeneye and Long-tailed Duck. In spring and fall a maritime hammock at the beach's north end attracts trans-Gulf migrants. During the summer months check around the parking area for Gray Kingbird.

General information: Alfred McKethan/Pine Island Park (entrance fee) is open November through March from 8:00 A.M. to 7:00 P.M. and April through October from 8:00 A.M. to 9:30 P.M. Bayport Park is open 24 hours a day. Restrooms at both parks are located near the parking areas. Chassahowitzka Wildlife Management Area (entrance fee) is open daily from sunrise to sunset. No restrooms are available. Public boat ramps providing access to Chassahowitzka National Wildlife Refuge are in the towns of Chassahowitzka and Homosassa. Seasonal hunting is permitted in both the wildlife management area and national wildlife refuge. Refer to regulations-summary brochures, updated annually and available at check stations, for hunt dates and locations. Wear blaze orange if hiking during hunting season. Crystal River Preserve State Park (no entrance fee) and Crystal River Archaeological State Park (entrance fee) are open daily from 8:00 A.M. until sunset. Visitor centers are open daily from 9:00 A.M. to 5:00 P.M. Eco-Walk, Churchhouse Hammock, and Ft. Island Trails (no entrance fees) are open daily from sunrise to sunset. Restrooms are located in the visitor centers, at Mullet Hole, and at the Eco-Walk and Churchhouse Hammock trailheads. Ft. Island Trail and Ft. Island Gulf Beach County Parks (no entrance fees) are open daily from 6:30 A.M. until sunset. Restrooms are located near the parking areas.

DeLorme grid: Page 76, A-3; page 77, A-1, D-1.

Hazards: Keep a safe distance from alligators. Venomous snakes are present but rarely encountered. Mosquitoes are common in summer.

Nearest food, gas, lodging: In Weeki Wachee, Homosassa, and Crystal River.

Camping: Chassahowitzka River Campground: 52 sites, 8600 W. Miss Maggie Dr., Homosassa, FL 34448; (352) 382-2200; www.bocc.citrus.fl.us/parks/chass_camp/campground.htm. Private campgrounds are located in Crystal River.

For more information: *Alfred McKethan/Pine Island Park,* 10800 Pine Island Dr., Spring Hill, FL 34607; (352) 754-4027; www.co.hernando.fl.us/parks_rec/parks/parklocations/pineisland.htm. *Chassahowitzka Wildlife Management Area,* c/o Florida Fish and Wildlife Conservation Commission, 620 S. Meridian St., Tallahassee, FL 32399; (800) 955-8771; www.florida conservation.org. *Chassahowitzka National Wildlife Refuge,* 1502 SE Kings Bay Dr., Crystal River, FL 34429; (352) 563-2088; www.fws.gov/chassahowitzka. *Bayport Park,* 4140 Cortez Blvd., Spring Hill, FL 34607; (352) 754-4027; www.co.hernando.fl.us/parks_rec/parks/park locations/bayport.htm. *Crystal River Preserve State Park,* 3266 N. Sailboat Ave., Crystal River, FL 34428; (352) 563-0450; www.floridastate parks.org/crystalriverpreserve. *Crystal River Archaeological State Park,* 3400 N. Museum Point, Crystal River, FL 34428; (352) 795-3817; www.floridastateparks.org/crystalriver. *Ft. Island Trail County Park,* 12073 W. Ft. Island Trail, Crystal River, FL 34429; (352) 527-7677. *Ft. Island Gulf Beach County Park,* 15000 W. Ft. Island Trail, Crystal River, FL 34429; (352) 527-7677.

 # Withlacoochee State Forest

Habitats: Pine flatwoods, sandhills, hardwood hammock, cypress swamp, freshwater marsh.

Specialty birds: *Resident:* Wood Stork, Bald Eagle, Purple Gallinule, Limpkin, Red-cockaded Woodpecker, Bachman's Sparrow. *Summer:* Least Bittern, Swallow-tailed Kite, Chuck-will's-widow, Yellow-throated Vireo, Prothonotary Warbler, Summer Tanager. *Winter:* Virginia Rail, American Woodcock, Whip-poor-will.

Best times to bird: October through April.

Directions: From the Suncoast Parkway (SR 589) west of Brooksville, exit at SR 50 (exit 46). Drive east 4 miles to County Road 50A. Continue east 2.4 miles to U.S. Highway 41. Turn left and drive north 6.6 miles to the state forest headquarters. From Interstate 75 east of Brooksville, exit at US 98/SR 50 (exit 301). Drive west 8.2 miles to CR 50A. Continue west 1.3 miles to US 41. Turn right and drive north 6.6 miles to the state forest headquarters.

The Birding

At 157,479 acres, **Withlacoochee State Forest** is the third-largest state forest in Florida. The forest is divided into eight tracts spread over four counties. Most of the forest is long-leaf pine flatwoods, preferred habitat for Red-cockaded Woodpecker. Active nest clusters accessible by vehicle can be found in the Croom Tract, northeast of Brooksville, and the Citrus Tract, south of Inverness. To reach the Croom Tract from the state forest visitor center, drive south 5.4 miles on US 41 to Croom Road, turn left, and drive east. If coming from Brooksville, drive north 1.2 miles on US 41 and turn right. Croom Road is paved for the first 4.3 miles. An open field is on the left, 0.3 mile after the pavement ends. During the winter months American Woodcock sometimes displays here and Whip-poor-will may be heard calling at dawn and dusk. Continue east 0.6 mile to the Tucker Hill trailhead, another good spot to listen for Whip-poor-will. Over 18 miles of hiking trails (in three interconnecting loops), 44 miles of off-road bicycle trails, and 34 miles of equestrian trails wind through the forest. These trails are closed during the hunting season.

Continue east 1.2 miles on Croom Road to where power lines become visible on the south side of the road. Watch for Eastern Bluebird perched on the wires. Red-cockaded Woodpecker cavity trees, marked with red or white bands, can be found north of the road. The woodpeckers are most likely to be found in the vicinity of cavity trees at dawn and dusk. Additional nest clusters can be found 1.5 miles farther east on Trail 9. Cavity trees on this trail are located 0.3 mile north and 0.3 mile south of Croom Road. The longleaf pine flatwoods in this area is also good habitat for Yellow-throated Vireo, Northern Parula, Pine and Yellow-throated Warbler, Summer Tanager, and Bachman's Sparrow. Continue east, then south 3 miles on Croom Road (which becomes Croom-Rital Road) to Silver Lake Recreation Area. Check the lakeshore for Wood Stork, Limpkin, and other wading birds. Drive south 3.5 miles to SR 50, then turn right and drive west 1 mile to return to I–75.

To reach the Citrus Tract from the state forest visitor center, drive south 0.2 mile on US 41 to County Road 476. Turn right and drive west 1.4 miles to County Road 481. Turn right and drive north 8.7 miles (CR 481 becomes County Road 581 in Citrus County) to Trail 16. If coming from Brooksville, drive north 4.2 miles on US 41 to CR 481/581, bear left, and continue north 10.3 miles to Trail 16. Turn left into Mutual Mine Recreation Area, one of several access points to over 45 miles of hiking trails through longleaf pine flatwoods, sandhills, scrub, and hardwood hammock. The trailhead, located in the campground, leads to Loops C and D of the trail system. Species to watch for along these trails include Wild Turkey, Northern Bobwhite, Hairy Woodpecker, Yellow-throated Vireo, Pine and Yellow-throated Warbler, Summer Tanager, Eastern Towhee, and Bachman's Sparrow. Curiously, Brown-headed Nuthatch has yet to be recorded in this forest. The Citrus Tract has the largest population of Red-cockaded Woodpecker in peninsular Florida, with nearly 50 active nest clusters spread throughout the tract. Many of these nest clusters are accessible by vehicle via the tract's grid system of forest roads at 1-mile intervals. From Mutual Mine Recreation Area, return to CR 581 and drive north 2.8 miles to Trail 10. This road is paved for the first 0.7 mile. Turn left and drive west 1.7 miles to Holder Mine Recreation Area. The trailhead here leads to Loops A and B of the trail system. Continue west 2.2 miles to Trail 13. Cavity trees, marked with white bands, can be found near this intersection. Additional nest clusters can be found on Trail 13 south of the intersection with Trail 10 and on several other roads in the forest. Use caution when driving these sandy roads in two-wheel-drive vehicles.

McKethan Lake Day-use Area and **Chinsegut Wildlife and Environmental Area,** both a short drive from the state forest visitor center, are worthwhile birding stops year-round. McKethan Lake is on US 41, 0.2 mile north of the visitor center. A 2-mile hiking trail encircles the lake, passing through hardwood hammock and pine flatwoods. The trail can be productive for migrant and wintering land birds, while Wood Stork and other wading birds can be found around the lake. Chinsegut Nature Center, the headquarters of Chinsegut Wildlife and Environmental Area, is 1 mile west of US 41 on CR 476. This 480-acre property has over 6 miles of trails winding through sandhills and hardwood hammock and along May's Prairie, a basin marsh. Wading birds, including Sandhill Crane, can be found in the marsh. Hooded Merganser and other waterfowl join resident Wood Duck in winter. Wild Turkey often roost in cypress trees fringing the marsh. In summer watch for Yellow-billed Cuckoo, Common Nighthawk, Great Crested Flycatcher, Red-eyed Vireo, Northern Parula, and Summer Tanager. The hardwood hammock attracts a variety of migrant land birds in spring and fall. When the nature center is closed, this area can be accessed from a trailhead at the intersection of US 41 and CR 481. To reach this intersection from CR 476, drive south 1.6 miles on CR 481 or 2.2 miles on US 41. Another trailhead is located in the Big Pine section of the property. Continue south 1.7 miles on US 41 to Old Crystal River Road. Turn right and drive north 0.8 mile to the parking area.

General information: Withlacoochee State Forest (no entrance fee) is open daily from sunrise to sunset. State Forest Use Permits are only required for group visits. Seasonal hunting is permitted in designated areas. Refer to regulations-summary brochures, updated annually and available at check stations, for hunt dates and locations. Wear blaze orange if hiking during hunting season. The visitor center is open Monday through Saturday from 8:00 A.M. to 5:00 P.M. The day-use area of Silver Lake Recreation Area is open daily from 8:00 A.M. until sunset. Restrooms are located at the Tucker Hill trailhead and at Silver Lake, Mutual Mine, and Holder Mine Recreation Areas. McKethan Lake Day-use Area (entrance fee) is open Monday through Friday from 8:00 A.M. to 5:00 P.M. and Saturday from 8:00 A.M. to 4:30 P.M. Restrooms are located in the picnic area. Chinsegut Nature Center (no entrance fee) is open Friday and Saturday from 8:00 A.M. to 2:00 P.M. Restrooms are located at the nature center. Other trailheads at Chinsegut Wildlife and Environmental Area are open daily from sunrise to sunset.

DeLorme grid: Page 77, B-2, C-3.

Hazards: Keep a safe distance from alligators. Venomous snakes are present but rarely encountered. Trails may be flooded in summer. Mosquitoes are common in summer.

Nearest food, gas, lodging: In Brooksville.

Camping: Silver Lake Recreation Area: 92 sites in three campgrounds. From I-75, drive east 1 mile on SR 50 to Croom-Rital Road. Turn left and drive north 3.6 miles to the recreation area. There are private campgrounds in Brooksville.

For more information: *Withlacoochee State Forest,* 15003 Broad St., Brooksville, FL 34601; (352) 754-6896; www.fl-dof.com/state_forests/withlacoochee.html. *Chinsegut Nature Center,* 23212 Lake Lindsey Rd., Brooksville, FL 34601; (352) 754-6722; www.myfwc.com/chinsegut.

⑬ Ocala Area

Habitats: Freshwater marsh, freshwater lakes, pasture, cypress/hardwood swamp, oak/sand pine scrub, pine flatwoods, sandhills, hardwood hammock.

Specialty birds: *Resident:* Black-bellied Whistling-Duck, Fulvous Whistling-Duck, Mottled Duck, Wood Stork, Bald Eagle, Purple Gallinule, Limpkin, Sandhill Crane, Red-cockaded Woodpecker, Florida Scrub-Jay, Brown-headed Nuthatch, Bachman's Sparrow, Yellow-breasted Chat. *Summer:* Least Bittern, Swallow-tailed Kite, Short-tailed Hawk, Chuck-will's-widow, Acadian Flycatcher, Yellow-throated Vireo, Prothonotary Warbler, Summer Tanager, Blue Grosbeak. *Winter:* American Woodcock, Henslow's Sparrow, Painted Bunting.

Best times to bird: October through May.

Directions: *Emeralda Marsh Conservation Area:* From I-75 west of Wildwood, exit at State Road 44 (exit 329). Drive east 22.7 miles to Emeralda Avenue in the town of Lisbon. Turn left and drive north 0.7 mile to Emeralda Island Road. Turn left and drive 0.5 mile to the wildlife drive entrance. From Florida's Turnpike, exit at U.S. Highway 27 (exit 288). Drive north 13 miles to SR 44 in Leesburg. Turn right and drive east 8.7 miles to Emeralda Avenue. Turn left and proceed as above. *Silver River State Park:* From I-75 in Ocala, exit at State Road 40 (exit 352). Drive east 8.3 miles to State Road 35 in Silver Springs. Turn right and drive south 1 mile to the park entrance. *Ocala National Forest:* Return to SR 40. Turn right and drive east 4.7 miles to County Road 315. Turn left and drive north 0.1 mile to Ocklawaha Visitor Center. From Interstate 95 in Ormond Beach, exit at SR 40 (exit 268). Drive west 34 miles to State Road 19. Turn left and drive south 11 miles to Pittman Visitor Center, or turn right and drive north 16 miles to Salt Springs Visitor Center.

The Birding

Emeralda Marsh Conservation Area is a wetland treatment marsh created on more than 1,500 acres of agricultural fields along the eastern shore of Lake Griffin, southwest of Ocala National Forest. The property was originally sawgrass marsh and wet prairie, with hardwood hammock in upland areas. It was converted to agricultural fields and cattle pasture in the 1940s. Water from the lake is now cleaned as it is circulated through the restored marsh. A 4.3-mile wildlife drive provides seasonal access to the marsh and surrounding habitat. The wildlife drive begins at the Wood Duck parking area on the west side of Emeralda Island Road. During winter look for Painted Bunting in brushy areas along the road just beyond the gate. This road, known as Powerline Road, heads west along a levee and winds through several patches of hardwood swamp, with alternating areas of marsh and wet fields. The forest attracts a variety of land birds during migration and winter, including Prothonotary Warbler in spring and fall. Check for Marsh and Sedge Wren in marshy areas during the winter months. Orange-crowned Warbler and other wintering land birds can be found in willows bordering the marshy areas. Watch for Wood Duck year-round in woody areas of the marsh. Black-bellied and Fulvous Whistling-Duck are also resident in the marsh. Usually seen flying overhead, whistling-ducks, along with other duck species, can sometimes be found in pools below pumping stations. Large numbers of wading birds also concentrate in these pools. One such area is 1.8 miles from the entrance. After another 0.2 mile the wildlife drive turns north. The levee beyond this point extends west, then north along the lake, and may be explored on foot. Thickets on both sides of the levee attract a variety of migrant and wintering land birds. Yellow-breasted Chat may breed here and Yellow and Prairie Warbler are common in this area in late summer. Watch for Purple Gallinule year-round in canals with emergent vegetation. From late winter through early summer, rookeries of wading birds, including Anhinga, herons, egrets, and ibis, can be seen on willow islands on the lake side of the canals.

The next section of the wildlife drive, known as Low Levee Road, passes through fields where Bobolink can be found in spring and fall. An observation platform on the east side of the road overlooks these fields and surrounding marsh. Look for Yellow Warbler and other migrants in late summer and sparrows, including Grasshopper and Lincoln's, during winter. North of these fields are impoundments where wintering waterfowl concentrate in areas of deeper water. An assortment of wading birds, including Sandhill Crane, can be found throughout the year in areas of shallow water. Wood Stork and American White Pelican are common in fall and winter. Least Bittern and Purple Gallinule breed in sections of the impoundments with thick emergent vegetation. Scan these same areas for American

Bittern in winter. At the intersection with Airstrip Road, 0.7 mile from the observation platform, turn right and drive east. Impoundments continue on both sides of the road. If water levels are low, exposed mudflats may attract migrant and wintering shorebirds. Black-necked Stilt nests on these mudflats. In September 2004 a Purple Swamphen, origin unknown, was discovered in an impoundment on the south side of the road. On the road's north side near the end of the wildlife drive are successional fields that attract large numbers of sparrows in winter. Species to watch for include Chipping, Field, Savannah, Grasshopper, Song, Lincoln's, Swamp, White-throated, and White-crowned. Blue Grosbeak and a few Indigo Buntings breed here in summer. Check willows lining the south side of the road for Orange-crowned Warbler and other wintering land birds. The wildlife drive ends at Emeralda Island Road, 1.3 miles north of the entrance.

Several foot trails into the interior of the marsh begin at parking areas on Emeralda Island Road, both north and south of the wildlife drive exit. Birders may also hike levees bordering the Yale-Griffin Canal, which crosses the road 0.5 mile north of the wildlife drive exit. If hiking west toward Lake Griffin, check emergent vegetation in the canal for Sora, Purple Gallinule, and Limpkin. During winter scan marshes to the south for Northern Harrier. Fulvous Whistling-Duck has been reported here throughout the year. Willow thickets border the canal east of Emeralda Island Road, attracting migrant and wintering land birds, including Ash-throated Flycatcher almost annually. Large impoundments that attract wintering waterfowl are farther east. These impoundments can also be reached from a parking area on County Road 452. From the intersection of Emeralda Island Road and Emeralda Avenue, drive east 1.8 miles on Goose Prairie Road to CR 452. Turn left and drive north 1.2 miles to the parking area. In winter watch for Yellow-breasted Chat in the vicinity of the parking area. To visit **Sawgrass Island Preserve,** continue north 1.7 miles on CR 452 to South Em-En-El Grove Road. Turn right and drive east 1.2 miles to Thomas Boat Landing Road. Turn left and drive north 0.7 mile to Sawgrass Island Road. Turn right and drive east 0.2 mile to the parking area. A dirt road leads to a second parking area 0.4 mile farther north. This 1,137-acre preserve at the north end of Lake Yale consists mostly of sawgrass marsh, which is attractive to Sandhill Crane and other wading birds. Pastures and scrub border the west side of the marsh where Florida Scrub-Jay can be found. Pinelands and oak hammock on the marsh's east side provide habitat for a variety of resident, migrant, and wintering land birds. Over 8 miles of trails crisscross the property. The 1.4-mile Bent Pine Trail leads to a pond where Wood Duck often feeds.

Silver River State Park, east of Ocala, borders over 5 miles of the Silver River, which flows east into the Ocklawaha River. Only the river's headspring, the largest limestone artesian spring in the world, lies outside the park. About 550 million gallons per day flow from the spring's underground cave system. To view the spring, you must visit the Silver Springs theme park, located at the intersection of SR 40 and SR 35. The state park contains several distinct ecological communities within its 5,000 acres. Over 14 miles of trails provide access. Immediately after the entrance station, turn left into the Sandhill Trail parking area. Along this 1.6-mile trail through pine sandhills, watch for Wild Turkey, Northern Bobwhite, Red-headed Woodpecker, Yellow-throated and Pine Warbler, Summer Tanager, and Eastern Towhee. At the end of the main park road is a parking area where three additional trails begin. This is 1 mile from the Sandhill Trail parking area. Also located here are the Silver River Museum and a re-created pioneer "cracker" village. The 2.1-mile Sinkhole Trail leads through an oak hammock, good for migrant and wintering land birds. The 1.2-mile River Trail and 1.8-mile Swamp Trail loop through hardwood and cypress swamp along the river. Look here for Barred Owl, Pileated Woodpecker, Carolina Wren, and other resident species. Limpkin and other wading birds may be spotted along the river. In spring and summer watch over the river for Swallow-tailed Kite. Flocks of titmice and chickadees may be joined in winter by Ruby-crowned and, occasionally, Golden-crowned Kinglet. Lucky birders may flush an American Woodcock from forest edges.

With over 383,000 acres, **Ocala National Forest** is a vast area containing the largest concentration of sand pine scrub in the world. Florida Scrub-Jay is common in scrub habitat throughout the forest. Islands of longleaf pine sandhills support several colonies of the endangered Red-cockaded Woodpecker. Lakes along the periphery of the forest attract wintering waterfowl, while hardwood forest surrounding freshwater springs provides suitable habitat for a variety of nesting species. Stop at one of the forest's three visitor centers to obtain maps and other information. If coming from Ocala on SR 40, Ocklawaha Visitor Center is near the intersection with CR 315. A 1.5-mile trail leads from the visitor center to the Ocklawaha River, which forms the western boundary of the forest. To visit the Lake Eaton area, drive east 2.4 miles on SR 40 to County Road 314. Turn left and drive northeast 8.5 miles to unpaved Forest Road 86. Turn right and drive east 1 mile to Forest Road 79. Turn right and drive south 0.3 mile to the parking area for Lake Eaton trails. The 1-mile Sinkhole Trail winds through sand pine scrub to a large depression in the forest. A stairway leads to the bottom of the sinkhole. In the surrounding scrub, look for Florida Scrub-Jay along with Downy Woodpecker, White-eyed Vireo, Carolina Chickadee, Tufted Titmouse, Carolina Wren, Blue-gray Gnatcatcher, Eastern Towhee, and other resident species. A spur loop extends your walk by 1.2 miles. The 2.1-mile Lake Eaton Loop begins across FR 79 from the parking area. This trail first passes through an open area where damaged sand pines were harvested following the hurricanes of 2004. The trail then enters undamaged scrub and oak hammock surrounding the lake. Three observation platforms along the trail provide opportunities to scan the lake for waterbirds.

To find appropriate habitat for Red-cockaded Woodpecker, return to CR 314 and continue northeast 6.8 miles to Forest Road 88. Nest cavities can be found on FR 88 immediately south of this intersection, an area known as Salt Springs Island. Dawn and dusk are usually the best times to search for woodpeckers in the vicinity of cavity trees. Nest sites can also be found in the vicinity of Lake Delancy. To reach this area, drive north 4.5 miles on FR 88 to County Road 316. Continue north 4.4 miles on FR 88 (now unpaved) to Forest Road 75. Turn right and drive east 1.2 miles to the Lake DeLancy campgrounds, watching for cavity trees marked with white rings. Large numbers of cavity trees can be found along the next 2 miles of FR 88 north of FR 75, an area known as Riverside Island. Throughout the year search these longleaf pine sandhills for Wild Turkey, Northern Bobwhite, Red-headed, Downy, and Pileated Woodpecker, Brown-headed Nuthatch, Eastern Bluebird, and Yellow-throated and Pine Warbler. Watch for Great Crested Flycatcher and Summer Tanager and listen for Bachman's Sparrow during spring and summer. Lake Ocklawaha, at the northern end of the forest, is a reservoir created by the damming of the Ocklawaha River. To reach this area from FR 75, continue north 6 miles on FR 88 to the Rodman Dam. (*NOTE:* The last mile or so of this road, if not recently graded, can be rough and should not be driven in a low-clearance vehicle.) From the dam, scan offshore for rafts of wintering waterfowl, including American Wigeon, Mallard, Blue-winged, and Green-winged Teal, Northern Shoveler, Northern Pintail, Ring-necked Duck, Lesser Scaup, and Hooded Merganser. Bald Eagle nests along this lake in large numbers. Watch overhead in spring and summer for Swallow-tailed Kite.

From the dam continue north, then east 3.5 miles on FR 88 to SR 19. Turn right and drive south 0.6 mile to the check station for **Caravelle Ranch Wildlife Management Area.** This 26,422-acre property, located where the Ocklawaha flows into the St. Johns River, consists of pine flatwoods, cypress and hardwood swamp, and improved pastureland. Access by vehicle is only allowed during hunting season, from September through March. At other times of the year you may enter the area on foot either at the check station or through a walk-in gate 1.7 miles farther south on SR 19. Over 20 miles of multiuse trails crisscross the property. Look for Bald Eagle, Limpkin, and Wild Turkey year-round and sparrows in winter. Swallow-tailed Kite can be seen hunting over pastures in spring and summer. From the WMA check station, continue south 11 miles on SR 19 to the town of Salt Springs. A national forest visitor center is in a shopping plaza on the west side of SR 19. The entrance to Salt Springs Recreation Area is on the east side, 0.2 mile farther south. Continue south 1.2 miles to the parking area for Salt Springs Trail. This 2-mile trail leads to an observation platform along Salt Springs Run, which flows into Lake George. Watch from the platform for Bald Eagle, Limpkin, and other wading birds. Lake George, actually just a wider section of the St. Johns River, is the area's largest body of water and forms much of the eastern boundary of the forest.

Hopkins Prairie contains freshwater marsh and hardwood hammock, good for wetland species as well as resident and migrant land birds. To visit this area, continue south 7.3 miles on SR 19 to unpaved FR 86. Turn right and drive west 2.4 miles to Forest Road 86E. This road is closed to vehicular traffic but may be explored on foot. Look for Sandhill Crane and other wading birds around the wetlands. Hammock residents include Red-shouldered Hawk, Carolina Chickadee, Tufted Titmouse, and Carolina Wren. Listen for Chuck-will's-widow at dawn and dusk during summer. Return to SR 19 and drive south 1.6 miles to Silver Glen Springs Recreation Area. On the west side of SR 19, across from the recreation area entrance, is the parking area for the Yearling Trail. This 6-mile trail loops through Pat's Island, a pioneer settlement that inspired Marjorie Kinnan Rawlings to write her Pulitzer Prize–winning novel The Yearling. The "island" is actually a longleaf pine sandhill surrounded by a sea of sand pine scrub. Look for Florida Scrub-Jay, Red-headed Woodpecker, Northern Flicker, and Eastern Towhee as you hike through this historic area. The trail follows a section of the Florida Scenic Trail, which winds through the national forest for 67 miles. The Lake George Trail begins in Silver Glen Springs Recreation Area and provides access to the western side of the lake. To access the southern end of the lake, continue south 5.7 miles on SR 19 to SR 40. Turn left and drive east 3.2 miles to unpaved Blue Creek Road (Forest Road 9883). Turn left and drive north, then east 2.5 miles to Lake George Road. Turn left and drive north 1 mile to the lake. A variety of wading birds, including both night-herons, Glossy Ibis, and Limpkin, can be found here. Scan the lakeshore for nesting Osprey and Bald Eagle.

To visit **Alexander Springs Recreation Area,** return to SR 40 and turn left. Drive east 1.6 miles to County Road 445A. Turn right and drive south 0.5 mile to County Road 445. Bear left and drive south 5.7 miles to the entrance. The spring, from which 80 million gallons of water flow daily, is a popular swimming hole during the warmer months. The Timucum Nature Trail, a 1-mile loop trail through hardwood swamp, begins on the east side of the swimming hole. Barred Owl, Pileated Woodpecker, and Carolina Wren can be found here year-round. During summer look for Acadian Flycatcher, Red-eyed Vireo, Northern Parula, Prothonotary Warbler, and Summer Tanager. Watch overhead for Swallow-tailed Kite and, occasionally, Short-tailed Hawk. Anhinga, Purple Gallinule,

Limpkin, and other wading birds may be found along the creek that flows from the spring. Canoes may be rented at the adjacent campground for a thorough exploration of this area.

Return to CR 445 and turn right. Drive west 5 miles to SR 19. Turn left and drive south 1.7 miles to the Pittman Visitor Center, or turn right and drive north 9.3 miles to return to SR 40. From this intersection, drive west 23.4 miles to return to the Ocklawaha Visitor Center.

General information: Silver River State Park (entrance fee) and Sawgrass Island Preserve (no entrance fee) are open daily from 8:00 A.M. until sunset. Restrooms at Silver River are located in picnic areas. No restrooms are available at Sawgrass Island Preserve. Caravelle Ranch Wildlife Management Area (no entrance fee) is open daily from sunrise to sunset. No restrooms are available. From late February through May, Emeralda Marsh Conservation Area's wildlife drive (no entrance fee) is open to vehicular traffic Friday through Sunday from 8:00 A.M. to 5:00 P.M. The one-way drive is located on a narrow roadway with soft shoulders. Buses, trailers, and recreational vehicles are prohibited. Observe posted speed limits and stop only at designated pullovers. Hiking and biking are allowed on the wildlife drive year-round. No restrooms are available. Ocala National Forest (no entrance fee) is open 24 hours a day. Visitor centers are open daily from 9:00 A.M. to 5:00 P.M. Recreation areas (entrance fees) are open daily from 8:00 A.M. until sunset. Restrooms are located at visitor centers and recreation areas. Many state forest roads are unpaved, though usually passable by two-wheel-drive vehicles. Avoid parking along sandy road shoulders. Seasonal hunting is permitted in designated wildlife management areas at Emeralda Marsh and Ocala National Forest. Refer to regulations-summary brochures, updated annually and available at check stations, for hunt dates and locations. Wear blaze orange if hiking during hunting season.

DeLorme grid: Page 72, C-2, C-3; page 73; page 79, A-1.

Hazards: Keep a safe distance from alligators. Bears and venomous snakes are present but rarely encountered. Mosquitoes, ticks, and chiggers are present, especially in summer. Fire-ant mounds are present year-round. Use caution when driving on unpaved roads in the state forest. Four-wheel drive is recommended.

Nearest food, gas, lodging: In Silver Springs, Ocala, Leesburg, and Eustis.

Camping: Silver River State Park, 59 sites. Eleven campgrounds, with a total of 568 sites, are located throughout Ocala National Forest. Full-service campgrounds are located in Salt Springs, Alexander Springs, and Juniper Springs. Less developed campgrounds are located in Lake Eaton, Fore Lake, Hopkins Prairie, Lake Delancy, Lake Dorr, and Clearwater Lake. See www.forestcamping.com/dow/southern/ocalcmp.htm for detailed information. Call (877) 444-6777 for reservations.

For more information: *Emeralda Marsh Conservation Area,* c/o St. Johns River Water Management District, P.O. Box 1429, Palatka, FL 32178; (386) 329-4404; www.sjrwmd.com, www.stetson.edu/~pmay/emeralda/direct. *Sawgrass Island Preserve,* c/o Lake County Water Authority, 107 N. Lake Ave., Tavares, FL 32778; (352) 343-3777. *Silver River State Park,* 1425 NE 58th Ave., Ocala, FL 34470; (352) 236-7148; www.floridastateparks.org/silverriver. *Ocala National Forest,* Ocklawaha Visitor Center, 3199 CR 315, Silver Springs, FL 34488; (352) 236-0288. *Pittman Visitor Center,* 45621 SR 19, Altoona, FL 32702; (352) 669-7495. *Salt Springs Visitor Center,* 14100 SR 19, Salt Springs, FL 32134; (352) 685-3070; www.fs.fed.us/r8/florida/recreation/index_oca. *Caravelle Wildlife Management Area,* c/o Florida Fish and Wildlife Conservation Commission, 620 S. Meridian St., Tallahassee, FL 32399; (800) 955-8771; www.floridaconservation.org.

44 Lower Suwannee/Cedar Key Area

Habitats: Cypress swamp, hardwood swamp, hardwood hammock, pine flatwoods, sandhills, salt marsh.

Specialty birds: *Resident:* Magnificent Frigatebird, Bald Eagle, King Rail, Clapper Rail, Limpkin, Florida Scrub-Jay, Bachman's Sparrow, Seaside Sparrow. *Summer:* Least Bittern, Wood Stork, Roseate Spoonbill, Swallow-tailed Kite, Mississippi Kite, Black Rail, Purple Gallinule, Least Tern, Chuck-will's-widow, Acadian Flycatcher, Gray Kingbird, Yellow-throated Vireo, Prothonotary Warbler, Hooded Warbler, Yellow-breasted Chat, Summer Tanager, Blue Grosbeak, Orchard Oriole. *Winter:* Virginia Rail, American Oystercatcher, American Woodcock, Nelson's Sharp-tailed Sparrow. *Migrant:* Wood Thrush, Kentucky Warbler.

Best times to bird: October through April.

Directions: From the intersection of US 19 and County Road 347 south of Chiefland, drive west 15 miles on CR 347 to Lower Suwannee National Wildlife Refuge headquarters.

The Birding

Protecting one of the largest undeveloped river delta systems in the United States, **Lower Suwannee National Wildlife Refuge** consists of 52,935 acres of wildlife-rich habitat at the mouth of the historic Suwannee River. Forty miles of paved roads provide vehicular access to the refuge both north and south of the river. Another 50 miles of unimproved roads and trails provide access by foot and bicycle. Refuge headquarters is on the river's south side, reached via CR 347. The 0.6-mile River Trail begins near the headquarters and passes through cypress swamp to a boardwalk at the river's edge. Watch year-round for Wood Duck, Barred Owl, Pileated Woodpecker, and other swamp residents, as well as Prothonotary Warbler in spring and summer. An 8.6-mile loop drive begins 0.6 mile south of the headquarters entrance. The drive passes through mixed hardwood hammock, cypress swamp, and pine flatwoods, all good for resident, wintering, and migrant land birds. Several old logging roads provide opportunities to further explore these habitats. A Red-breasted Nuthatch was found on one of these side roads in October 2001. After returning to CR 347, continue south 6.3 miles to County Road 326. Turn right and drive west 3.4 miles to Shell Mound. The 0.3-mile Shell Mound Trail loops around and over an ancient Indian shell midden. The mound is 28 feet above sea level and offers a bird's-eye view of the Gulf of Mexico. Live oaks that cover much of the mound attract trans-Gulf migrants in spring. In September 2000 a Greater Flamingo, origin unknown, was seen offshore from this vantage point and from the end of CR 326, 0.2 mile farther. The 1-mile Dennis Creek Trail also begins at Shell Mound and winds through surrounding salt marsh habitat. A 0.1-mile wheelchair-accessible boardwalk begins 0.2 mile beyond Shell Mound. A variety of shorebirds feed here, occasionally including rarities such as Long-billed Curlew.

Return to CR 347 and continue south 1.3 miles to **Cedar Key Scrub State Reserve.** Florida Scrub-Jay, at the northern limit of its range on the Gulf coast, can be found in small numbers within this 4,988-acre preserve. The jays are sometimes seen along CR 347 from CR 326 to the reserve trailhead. Twelve miles of trails in the reserve meander through scrub habitat and along the edge of adjacent coastal marsh. In addition to scrub-jays, watch for Wild Turkey, Northern Bobwhite, and Eastern Towhee in the scrub.

Search for Clapper Rail, Marsh Wren, and Seaside Sparrow in the salt marsh. Nelson's Sharp-tailed Sparrow can be found here in winter. Osprey and Bald Eagle nest nearby. Another section of the preserve is on State Road 24. To reach the trailhead for this parcel, continue south 1 mile on CR 347 to SR 24, turn left, and drive east 2.5 miles. To reach Cedar Key, backtrack to the intersection of SR 24 and CR 347 and continue west 1 mile to the Cedar Key causeway. At low tide check mudflats on both sides of the road for gulls, terns, and shorebirds. Roseate Spoonbill is attracted to this area in summer. Also watch for Magnificent Frigatebird and Gray Kingbird during the summer months. Winter brings Common Loon, Horned Grebe, American White Pelican, and sea ducks. During spring and fall, trans-Gulf migrants may make landfall anywhere on Cedar Key. Rarities recorded on or in the vicinity of the key include Pacific Loon, Long-tailed Duck, Long-billed Murrelet, and Buff-bellied Hummingbird. Offshore is **Cedar Keys National Wildlife Refuge,** consisting of 13 islands ranging from 1 to 165 acres. The outermost island, Seahorse Key, is a sand dune rising to 52 feet above sea level, the highest elevation on Florida's west coast. Around 20,000 wading birds nest annually on these islands. The refuge is only accessible by boat, and the islands' interiors are off-limits to visitors.

From the intersection of SR 24 and CR 347, drive east 18.2 miles on SR 24 to return to US 19. In summer watch overhead for Swallow-tailed and Mississippi Kite along this route. Turn left and drive north 13 miles to County Road 320 in Chiefland. Turn left and drive west 5.7 miles to **Manatee Springs State Park.** The spring at this 2,075-acre park produces 117 million gallons of water daily. From the entrance, drive 0.5 mile to the trailhead for the 8.5-mile North End Trail. A series of loop trails meanders through hardwood hammock, sandhills, and pine flatwoods, productive throughout the year for Wild Turkey,

Swallow-tailed Kite. PHOTO: LARRY MANFREDI

Northern Bobwhite, Red-headed Woodpecker, and Carolina Chickadee. For a shorter walk, continue 0.5 mile on the main park road to the 0.6-mile Sink Trail. The parking area for the spring is 0.1 mile farther. A boardwalk leads from the spring to the Suwannee River. Look for Limpkin and other wading birds along the river. During the summer months check surrounding cypress and hardwood swamp for Yellow-billed Cuckoo, Acadian Flycatcher, Northern Parula, Prothonotary and Hooded Warbler, and Summer Tanager. Watch for migrant land birds along the river in spring and fall. During winter manatees may be spotted near the spring. To reach **Andrews Wildlife Management Area,** return to

US 19 and turn left. Drive north 4.6 miles to NW 160th Street in Fanning Springs. Turn left and drive west 1 mile to the check station. This 3,501-acre site protects the last large tract of upland hardwood forest along the Suwannee River. Six miles of roads, along with 10 miles of trails, provide access. Year-round residents include Wood Duck, Wild Turkey, Northern Bobwhite, Limpkin, Barred Owl, Red-headed and Pileated Woodpecker, Carolina Chickadee, Eastern Bluebird, and Eastern Towhee. During summer watch for Swallow-tailed and Mississippi Kite, Yellow-billed Cuckoo, Chuck-will's-widow, Chimney Swift, Acadian Flycatcher, Eastern Kingbird, Yellow-throated Vireo, Northern Parula, Prothonotary and Hooded Warbler, Yellow-breasted Chat, Summer Tanager, Blue Grosbeak, Indigo Bunting, and Orchard Oriole.

Return to US 19, turn left, and continue north 2.6 miles to **Fanning Springs State Park.** The spring in this small park produces 65 million gallons of water daily and also attracts manatees in winter. A boardwalk leads from the spring through cypress swamp to the Suwannee River. Look for Red-shouldered Hawk, Barred Owl, and Pileated Wood-pecker along the river. A 0.8-mile nature trail loops through mixed hardwoods and pinelands, attractive to migrant land birds in spring and fall. To reach birding areas in Lower Suwannee National Wildlife Refuge located north of the river, continue north 3.5 miles on US 19 to County Road 349. Turn left and drive south 21 miles to Dixie Main-line Trail, a former logging road. The 9-mile narrow lime-rock road passes through pine flatwoods, hardwood hammock, and salt marsh. Drive west 0.5 mile to the turnoff to Salt Creek. Turn left and drive south 1 mile to the parking area. A wheelchair-accessible board-walk extends into the surrounding marsh. Watch for nesting Bald Eagle. Dixie Mainline Trail ends at County Road 357. Turn left and drive south 0.8 mile to the Fishbone Creek turnoff. Turn right and drive west 0.9 mile through an oak hammock to the end of the road. An observation tower here overlooks the creek and marsh. Clapper Rail, Marsh Wren, and Seaside Sparrow all breed here. Black Rail possibly breeds here as well. Watch overhead in spring and summer for Swallow-tailed Kite, also a local breeder. Return to CR 357, turn right, and drive south 2.5 miles to Shired Island on the Gulf of Mexico. Turn right and drive 0.2 mile to the boat launch. The beach near the boat launch attracts a variety of shorebirds in winter. Scan offshore for wintering waterfowl. Trails lead through coastal hammock that may harbor a few trans-Gulf migrants. Backtrack to the intersection with Dixie Mainline Trail and continue north 7.5 miles to County Road 351. Turn right and drive east, then north 7.8 miles, to return to US 19 in Cross City.

General information: Lower Suwannee National Wildlife Refuge (no entrance fee) is open 24 hours a day. The refuge office is open Monday through Friday from 7:30 A.M. to 4:00 P.M. A restroom is located at Salt Creek. Cedar Key Scrub State Reserve (no entrance fee) is open daily from 9:00 A.M. until sunset. A primitive restroom is available at the trail-head on SR 24. Cedar Keys National Wildlife Refuge (no entrance fee) is accessible only by boat. To protect nesting birds, Seahorse Key is off-limits to visitors from March through June. Manatee Springs and Fanning Springs State Parks (entrance fees) are open daily from 8:00 A.M. until sunset. Restrooms are available at the swimming areas. Andrews Wildlife Management Area (daily-use permit required) is open daily from sunrise to sunset. No restrooms are available. At Lower Suwannee NWR, Cedar Key Scrub State Reserve, and Andrews WMA, seasonal hunting is permitted in designated areas. Refer to regulations-summary brochures, updated annually and available at check stations, for hunt dates and locations. Wear blaze orange if hiking during hunting season.

DeLorme grid: Page 64, D-1; Page 69, C-3.

Hazards: Keep a safe distance from alligators. Venomous snakes are present but rarely encountered. Mosquitoes, ticks, and chiggers are present, especially in summer.

Nearest food, gas, lodging: In Chiefland.

Camping: Manatee Springs State Park: 100 sites.

For more information: *Lower Suwannee and Cedar Keys National Wildlife Refuges,* 16450 NW 31st Place, Chiefland, FL 32626; (352) 493-0238; www.fws.gov/lowersuwannee, www.fws .gov/cedarkeys. *Cedar Key Scrub State Reserve,* P.O. Box 187, Cedar Key, FL 32625; www.florida stateparks.org/cedarkeyscrub. *Manatee Springs State Park,* 11650 NW 115th St., Chiefland, FL 32626; (352) 493-6072; www.floridastate parks.org/manateesprings. *Andrews Wildlife Management Area,* c/o Florida Fish and Wildlife Conservation Commission, 620 S. Meridian St., Tallahassee, FL 32399; (800) 955-8771; www .myfwc.com/recreation/andrews. *Fanning Springs State Park,* 18020 US 19, Fanning Springs, FL 32693; (352) 463-3420; www.floridastateparks .org/fanningsprings.

 # Gainesville Area

Habitats: Wet prairie, pastures, cypress/hardwood swamp, freshwater marsh, freshwater ponds and lakes, hardwood hammock, pine flatwoods, sandhills.

Specialty birds: *Resident:* Black-bellied Whistling-Duck, Mottled Duck, Wood Stork, Bald Eagle, King Rail, Sandhill Crane, Brown-headed Nuthatch, Bachman's Sparrow. *Summer:* Least Bittern, Roseate Spoonbill, Swallow-tailed Kite, Mississippi Kite, Purple Gallinule, Chuck-will's-widow, Acadian Flycatcher, Yellow-throated Vireo, Wood Thrush, Prothonotary Warbler, Hooded Warbler, Yellow-breasted Chat, Summer Tanager, Blue Grosbeak, Orchard Oriole. *Winter:* American Woodcock, Whip-poor-will, American Pipit, Lincoln's Sparrow, Yellow-headed Blackbird. *Migrant:* Peregrine Falcon, Rufous Hummingbird, Louisiana Waterthrush, Kentucky Warbler, Scarlet Tanager, Painted Bunting.

Best times to bird: October through May.

Directions: *Paynes Prairie Preserve State Park:* From I-75 in Micanopy, exit at County Road 234 (exit 374). Drive east 1.3 miles to U.S. Highway 441. Turn left and drive north 0.6 mile to the park entrance. *Morningside Nature Center:* From I-75 in Gainesville, exit at State Road 26 (exit 387). Drive east 8.2 miles to the entrance. *Newnans Lake:* Continue east 1 mile on SR 26 to where the road curves left. Continue straight onto County Road 329B (Lakeshore Drive). Drive south 2.3 miles to Palm Point Park, on the west side of the lake. *Chapman's Pond:* From I-75, exit at SR 24 (exit 384). Drive west 2.4 miles to SW 75th Street. Turn right and drive north 1.2 miles to SW 41st Place. Turn right and drive east 0.6 mile, past the Veteran's Memorial at Kanapaha Park and around a curve, to a parking area across from the water-treatment facility. *San Felasco Hammock Preserve State Park:* From I-75 in Gainesville, exit at County Road 222 (exit 390). Drive west 2.8 miles to County Road 241 (NW 143rd Street). Turn right and drive north 1 mile to County Road 232 (Millhopper Road). Turn right and drive east 2 miles to the trailhead parking area, just east of the I-75 overpass (no exit is located here). *O'Leno State Park:* From I-75 northbound, exit at US 441 in Alachua (exit 399). Drive north 10.6 miles to Sprite Road. Turn right and drive 0.2 mile to the park entrance. From I-75 southbound, exit at US 441 south of Lake City (exit 414). Drive south 4.8 miles to Sprite Road. Turn left and drive 0.6 mile to the park entrance.

The Birding

Of the 21,000 acres within **Paynes Prairie Preserve State Park,** 13,735 acres form a unique basin marsh, created as the underlying limestone slowly dissolved and settled. The basin is covered by wet prairie, freshwater marsh, ponds, and lakes, including Alachua Lake, and is encircled by hardwood hammock and other upland habitats. Indian artifacts found in the area indicate that the basin and surrounding habitats have been inhabited for over 12,000 years. In the late 1600s, the largest cattle ranch in Spanish-controlled Florida was located here. Legend has it that the prairie is named for King Payne, a Seminole chief. Several battles during the Seminole Wars were fought in the area. From the entrance on US 441, it is 2.4 miles to the visitor center at the end of Savannah Boulevard, the main park road. The visitor center houses displays interpreting the park's 25 distinct habitats and diverse flora and fauna. Maps and checklists are available here and at a kiosk near the visitor center parking area. Over 270 species are on the park's bird list, including 35 species of warblers. The 0.3-mile Wacahoota Trail begins at the visitor center and loops through hardwood hammock to a 50-foot observation tower at the southern rim of the prairie. Look for Barred Owl and Pileated Woodpecker in the hammock throughout the year and migrant land birds during spring and fall. From the observation tower, scan the prairie for Bald Eagle, Red-tailed Hawk, and Sandhill Crane. You may also get distant views of the park's small herd of American bison and wild horses. The bison, which disappeared from Florida in the early 1800s, were reintroduced here in 1975. The wild horses are descendants of those brought over by the Spanish in the 1500s. Several species of waterfowl and thousands of Sandhill Crane winter in the marsh. Also watch for Northern Harrier coursing over the prairie in winter.

Cone's Dike Trail begins at a trailhead near the visitor center parking area. This 8.3-mile (round-trip) trail follows an earthen dike into the center of the prairie. Look for Northern Bobwhite and Eastern Towhee along brushy sections of the trail and Sandhill Crane and King Rail in marshy areas. Watch for Least Bittern in the marsh during the summer months and Sora and Marsh Wren in winter. An assortment of sparrows can be found in winter toward the end of this trail. A Winter Wren was reported from this area in October 2000. Be prepared with proper headgear and plenty of water when hiking in this treeless landscape. From the visitor center parking area, backtrack 1.4 miles on Savannah Boulevard to the turnoff for Lake Wauberg. Turn right and drive 0.6 mile to the parking area at the lake. Look for Wild Turkey and other upland species along this road. The entrance to Puc Puggy Campground is on the left, 0.4 mile from the turnoff. Puc Puggy, which means "flower hunter," was the name given by local Seminoles to Philadelphia botanist William Bartram, who visited the prairie in 1774. He later described it as "the Great Alachua Savannah." At the lake, watch for Bald Eagle year-round and flocks of American White Pelican during winter. A boardwalk on the north side of the parking area leads to Lake Trail. This 0.9-mile trail passes between the lake and Sawgrass Pond, then returns you to Savannah Boulevard, 0.5 mile south of the visitor center parking area. Across from the Lake Wauberg turnoff on Savannah Boulevard is a parking area for Chacala Trail. This 6.5-mile series of loop trails winds though hardwood hammock, pine flatwoods, and successional fields, all good for resident, wintering, and migrant land birds. The 1.3-mile Jackson's Gap Trail also passes through hardwood hammock and pine flatwoods, connecting the Chacala Trail to Cone's Dike Trail.

Return to US 441, turn right, and drive north 3.3 miles to the parking area for Bolen Bluff Trail. This 2.8-mile (round-trip) trail passes through hardwood hammock before descending into the prairie on 0.5-mile Bolen Bluff Dike. Two alternative trails through the hammock, each 0.6 mile in length, reconnect near the dike. The hammock can be excellent in fall for migrant warblers, thrushes, and tanagers. During summer watch for

Yellow-billed Cuckoo, Great Crested Flycatcher, Northern Parula, and Summer Tanager. Acadian Flycatcher and Prothonotary Warbler breed in wetter areas of the hammock. Barred Owl, Pileated Woodpecker, Carolina Chickadee, Tufted Titmouse, and Carolina Wren may be seen throughout the year. In summer search brushy areas along Bolen Bluff Dike for Yellow-breasted Chat, Indigo Bunting, Blue Grosbeak, and Orchard Oriole. In winter check marshy areas on both sides of the dike for Sora, Sedge and Marsh Wren, and Swamp Sparrow. From the observation platform at the end of the dike, scan the prairie for Northern Harrier and Sandhill Crane. Unexpected species seen from this area have included Black Rail, Black-billed Cuckoo, and Short-eared Owl. Also prepare for other surprises when hiking out to the dike. On a sunny day several years ago, I came face-to-face with the aforementioned herd of bison on the hammock portion of the trail. They apparently were enjoying a welcomed respite from the unrelenting heat of the treeless prairie. These massive beasts may appear tame but are wild and can be unpredictable. Should a chance encounter occur, keep a safe distance. Also keep in mind that the gate to the trailhead parking area is locked at sunset, so plan your hike accordingly.

Drive north 1.2 miles on US 441 to an observation boardwalk that extends into the marsh on the east side of the road. This is a convenient location to witness dawn departure and dusk return of wintering Sandhill Crane. Also watch for Osprey, Wood Stork, and other wading birds along this section of US 441 that bisects the basin. To explore the north rim of the basin, continue north 2.8 miles to State Road 331. Turn right and drive east, then north 3.3 miles to SR 26 in Gainesville. Turn right and drive east 0.3 mile to State Road 20. Bear right, then immediately turn right at SE 15th Street. Drive south 2.4 miles to where the road curves east. Continue south 0.1 mile to the gate for LaChua Trail. If the gate is open (weekdays only), continue to the trailhead parking area. On weekends and holidays backtrack 0.5 mile to Boulware Springs Park. Park here and walk west to the Gainesville-Hawthorne State Trail at the back of the park. Turn left and walk south 0.5 mile to a gate at the state park boundary. This gate is unlocked daily at 8:00 A.M. and locked at sunset. The trail beyond the gate is known as the LaChua Connector and leads 0.4 mile to the trailhead parking area. Watch for Sandhill Crane from a prairie overlook along the connector trail. A flock of Vaux's Swift was found here in December 2005. LaChua Trail leads 3 miles (round-trip) through open fields and then along a levee through marshy areas, ending at an observation platform on Alachua Lake. From the parking area, the trail descends through an oak hammock along Little Alachua Sink. Listen for Great Horned and Barred Owl and look for Carolina Chickadee, Tufted Titmouse, Carolina Wren, and other resident and wintering land birds. Red-headed Woodpecker is occasionally seen in this area. The trail then passes through brushy fields that attract an impressive variety of sparrows in winter. Most common are Chipping, Vesper, Savannah, Song, and White-throated Sparrow. Less frequently seen are Field, Grasshopper, and White-crowned Sparrow. Also watch in winter for the occasional Western Kingbird and Scissor-tailed Flycatcher. Rarities seen in these fields include Ash-throated Flycatcher, Wilson's Warbler, Clay-colored, Lark, Henslow's, LeConte's, Fox, and Lincoln's Sparrow, and Dickcissel.

A short side trail leads to Alachua Sink, where water from the basin drains into the Floridan Aquifer. In 1881 the sink became blocked, and within two years the prairie became a lake deep enough for paddle-wheel steamers to cross from Micanopy to Gainesville. Ten years later the sink opened up, draining the lake in a matter of days! Steamships were stranded and thousands of fish were left high and dry. In recent years the basin floods only after extensive periods of heavy rain but may remain flooded for extended periods. When the basin is relatively dry, the sink reverts to a small pond attracting alligators, wading birds, and a few wintering waterfowl. Black-bellied Whistling-Duck has been recorded here year-round but are most likely in summer. When water levels drop significantly, exposed mudflats attract migrating shorebirds. Scan distant trees beyond the sink for perched Bald Eagle and Red-shouldered or Red-tailed Hawk. From Alachua Sink, the main trail follows a canal through marshes where Least Bittern, King Rail, and Purple Gallinule breed. Indigo Bunting and Blue Grosbeak nest in brushy areas along the trail. Watch overhead during summer for Mississippi Kite. Winter brings American Bittern, Northern Harrier, Sedge and Marsh Wren, and a variety of waterfowl to these marshes. The observation platform at the end of the trail offers a good vantage point from which to view the thousands of Sandhill Crane that winter in the basin.

Morningside Nature Center is a 278-acre city park on the eastern edge of Gainesville. To reach the nature center from LaChua Trail, return to SR 26, turn right, and drive west 1.5 miles to the entrance. Six miles of trails crisscross the property, most beginning near the education center, a brief walk from the parking area. A short trail leads to a bird blind where feeding stations attract titmice, chickadees, and other resident species. Painted Bunting and American Goldfinch visit the feeders in winter. Another short trail includes a boardwalk through a cypress dome. Longer trails wind through sandhills and pine flatwoods, good for Wild Turkey, Northern Bobwhite, Red-headed Woodpecker, Brown-Headed Nuthatch, Eastern Bluebird, Pine Warbler, Eastern Towhee, and Bachman's Sparrow. Newnans Lake is a short drive west of the nature center. Access is available at various points around the lake. Begin at Palm Point Park, a 16-acre city park located on a peninsula jutting from the lake's western shore. Watch for Wild Turkey along the road as you drive down Lakeshore Drive. Wood Duck, Barred Owl, and Pileated Woodpecker are resident in the hardwood swamp that fringes the lake. During summer look for Yellow-billed Cuckoo, Great Crested Flycatcher, Red-eyed Vireo, Yellow-throated and Prothonotary Warbler, and Summer Tanager. Watch over the lake for Osprey and Bald Eagle throughout the year. Swallow-tailed and Mississippi Kite are possible in spring and summer. Migration brings a wide variety of warblers, vireos, thrushes, and other land birds. The lake is also an excellent inland location to search for storm-blown seabirds. Post-hurricane sightings include Magnificent Frigatebird, Pomarine and Parasitic Jaeger, Sooty Tern, and in September 2004, Black-capped Petrel. From Palm Point Park continue south 1.4 miles on Lakeshore Drive to SR 20. Turn left and drive east 0.5 mile to Earl P. Powers Park. From the fishing pier, scan offshore for American White Pelican and wintering waterfowl. Blue and Green-winged Teal and Hooded Merganser are most common. Other species sometimes reported from the lake include Black-bellied and Fulvous Whistling-Duck, Redhead, Canvasback, and Bufflehead. When water levels in the lake are low enough to produce mudflats, migrant shorebirds may stop here to feed. A scope is usually necessary to view the shorebirds. Look for both yellowlegs, Least, Pectoral, and Stilt Sandpiper, and Long-billed Dowitcher. In 2000 30 species of shorebirds were recorded at various locations around the lake, including American Oystercatcher, Wilson's Plover, Hudsonian Godwit, Ruff, and Red-necked and Wilson's Phalarope.

Newnans Lake Conservation Area occupies 4,651 acres along the southeastern and northern shore of the lake. To reach South Tract, drive east 2.8 miles on SR 20 to County Road 234. Turn left and drive north 2.6 miles to SE 16th Avenue. Turn left and drive west 0.6 mile to the Windsor boat ramp at Owens-Illinois Park, another good spot to scan the lake for waterbirds. Trails loop through hardwood swamp on both sides of SW 16th

Avenue. Sections of the conservation area at the north end of the lake include North Tract and Hatchet Creek Tract. To reach the east trailhead of North Tract, return to CR 234, turn left, and drive north 1.8 miles. A 6.3-mile trail with two loops begins here and winds through upland areas and hardwood swamp. Continue north 2.5 miles on CR 234 to SR 26. Turn left and drive west 0.8 mile to Hatchet Creek Trailhead. Eight miles of trails offer opportunities to explore upland and floodplain habitat along the creek. Continue west 2 miles on SR 26 to the west trailhead of North Tract. This parcel (also known as Gum Root Swamp) has a 2.6-mile trail that also passes through hardwood swamp. A 0.3-mile trail connects this trail to east trailhead loops. Watch for resident, migrant, and wintering land birds along all of these trails. Local birders often go off-trail at the bridge over Hatchet Creek, hiking downstream to the lake in search of migrant shorebirds and wintering waterfowl. It was here that a Hudsonian Godwit was found in September 2000. A few Roseate Spoonbills are occasionally seen here in summer. Continue west 1 mile on SR 26 to the parking area for Gum Root Park. This small city park has trails through scrubby flatwoods and pasture, another good place to look for resident, migrant, and wintering land birds. Drive west on SR 26 another 2 miles to return to Lakeshore Drive and complete the loop around the lake.

Chapman's Pond is a water retention pond in Kanapaha Park, adjacent to Gainesville's Kanapana Water Reclamation Facility. The pond honors Frank M. Chapman, the legendary 19th-century ornithologist who briefly lived in the area. Working in cooperation with Alachua Audubon Society, Gainesville Regional Utilities constructed an observation platform that allows birders to easily view the wading birds, shorebirds, and waterfowl attracted to the pond. Trails through surrounding oak woodlands have also been constructed in Kanapaha Park. A variety of wading birds including Wood Stork and occasionally Sandhill Crane feed here throughout the year. A Reddish Egret, usually a coastal bird, was found here in June 2005. Check emergent vegetation in summer for Purple Gallinule and possibly Least Bittern. During spring and fall, migrant shorebirds are attracted to exposed mudflats along pond edges. Look for Black-necked Stilt, Greater and Lesser Yellowlegs, Solitary, Spotted, Semipalmated, Least, Pectoral, and Stilt Sandpiper, and Long-billed Dowitcher. Wilson's Snipe is common here in winter. Also look for an assortment of waterfowl in winter, when resident Black-bellied Whistling-Duck and Wood and Mottled Duck may be joined by Gadwall, American Wigeon, Blue and Green-winged Teal, Ring-necked Duck, Lesser Scaup, Hooded Merganser, and Ruddy Duck. Periodically reported here are Mallard, Northern Pintail, Redhead, Bufflehead, and Common Goldeneye. A Greater White-fronted Goose was briefly seen here in February 2001. A Eurasian form of Green-winged Teal was the subject of much discussion when it was discovered among other teal in February 2005. Osprey, Bald Eagle, and Cooper's, Red-shouldered, and Red-tailed Hawk may be spotted soaring over the area at any time of year. Mississippi Kite can be common here in spring and summer. You are most likely to see this raptor during the warmer hours of the day. Swallow-tailed Kite is also possible during the summer months. Watch in winter for Northern Harrier, Sharp-shinned Hawk, and American Kestrel. Merlin and Peregrine Falcon occasionally pass through during the winter months. Residents in park woodlands south and west of the ponds include Pileated Woodpecker, Carolina Chickadee, Tufted Titmouse, and Carolina Wren. Watch for migrant warblers and other land birds as you hike trails through these woods in spring and fall. Check open areas of the park for Loggerhead Shrike and Eastern Bluebird. Brushy areas may harbor wintering sparrows including Chipping, Savannah, Song, Swamp, White-crowned, and White-throated.

Kanapaha Botanical Gardens is on SR 24, 1 mile west of I–75. To reach the gardens from Chapman's Pond, return to SR 24, turn left, and drive east 1.4 miles to the entrance. Located on the south shore of Lake Kanapaha, the 62-acre gardens are operated by the North Florida Botanical Society. Sixteen botanical collections are accessed by 1.5 miles of paved walkways, for the most part wheelchair-accessible. The collection includes butterfly and hummingbird gardens at separate ends of the facility. Hummingbirds are seen here most often in spring and fall, though a few Ruby-throated Hummingbirds may be found during summer. Rufous Hummingbird is possible in fall. An Allen's Hummingbird was seen here from October 1996 through February 1997. Migrant and wintering land birds can also be found in the gardens.

San Felasco Hammock Preserve State Park protects almost 7,000 acres of mature hardwood hammock, sandhills, and pine flatwoods north of Gainesville. San Francisco de Potano, a 17th-century Spanish mission established to convert local Indians, was located in the southeastern section of the preserve. Both Indians and local settlers had difficulty pronouncing "San Francisco," and the area eventually became known as San Felasco. Today the preserve is popular for hiking, jogging, bicycling, and horseback riding. From the Millhopper Road trailhead parking area, a 0.9-mile loop trail winds south through the heart of the hardwood hammock. Watch for flocks of resident land birds including Downy Woodpecker, Carolina Chickadee, Tufted Titmouse, and Carolina Wren. The trail slopes down to a creek where Yellow-billed Cuckoo, Acadian Flycatcher, Red-eyed Vireo, Wood Thrush, Northern Parula, and Hooded Warbler breed. In spring and fall this trail can be excellent for migrant warblers, thrushes, and tanagers. On the north side of Millhopper Road, two trails pass through longleaf pine sandhills. One trail is 4.8 miles long, the other, 5.7 miles. Resident species include Wild Turkey, Northern Bobwhite, Eastern Bluebird, and Pine Warbler. In summer watch for Red-headed Woodpecker, Eastern Wood-Pewee, Yellow-throated Vireo, and Summer Tanager. Rarities reported from these trails include White-breasted Nuthatch, Brown Creeper, and Fox Sparrow. All of these trails are designated only for hiking.

Devil's Millhopper Geological State Park contains a sinkhole, called "Devil's Millhopper" by local farmers, that is 500 feet wide and 120 feet deep. A 236-step stairway leads to the bottom of the sink while a 0.5-mile nature trail circles the rim. Keep in mind that if you descend the 236 steps to the bottom, you must ascend all 236 steps to return to the top. The sinkhole is surrounded by 63 acres of sandhills and hardwood hammock with some swampy areas. The nature trail can be good for resident, wintering, and migrant land birds. To reach this park from the San Felasco Hammock parking area, drive east 4.2 miles on Millhopper Road to the entrance. An interpretive center, located between the parking area and the sinkhole, contains exhibits explaining the natural and geological history of the park.

Hague Dairy is an experimental farm operated by the University of Florida. The dairy and surrounding area can be excellent for blackbirds, shorebirds, and sparrows. To reach the dairy from Devil's Millhopper Geological State Park, return to Millhopper Road, turn left, and drive east 0.2 mile to NW 43rd Street. Turn left and drive north 3 miles to US 441. Turn left and drive west 2.7 miles to County Road 237. Turn right and drive north 0.5 mile to the entrance. Sign in at the office adjacent to the parking area. In winter check blackbird and cowbird flocks near cattle pens for Yellow-headed Blackbird, seen here almost annually, and Brewer's Blackbird, seen only occasionally. Eastern Bluebird and Eastern Meadowlark are common residents in surrounding pastures. Scan the pastures in winter for flocks of American Pipit. A pond beyond the cattle pens attracts migrant shorebirds in spring. White-rumped Sandpiper is possible here in May. During winter look for American Bittern, Sora, and Marsh Wren. Check surrounding brushy areas for sparrows including Chipping, Vesper, Savannah, Song, Swamp, and White-crowned. Occasionally something unexpected will appear, such as Lark, Le Conte's, or Lincoln's Sparrow, or Dickcissel. In April 2004 a Horned Lark was found here. A year earlier a pair of Southern Lapwing (apparently escaped birds) was discovered in the area. To reach the equestrian and mountain-bike trailhead at San Felasco Hammock Preserve State Park, return to US 441, turn right, and drive west 3.3 miles to Progress Boulevard. Turn left and drive south 0.6 mile to the trailhead. Eight miles of horse trails and over 18 miles of bicycle trails can also be explored on foot. During summer Black-bellied Whistling-Duck may be in Lee Sink, north of the parking area. In winter check pastures between the sink and parking area for many of the same sparrows listed for Hague Dairy. Backtrack to US 441, turn left, and drive west 2.8 miles to return to I-75 (via exit 399).

O'Leno State Park is located north of the town of High Springs, along the Santa Fe River, which flows through the park on its way to the historic Suwannee River. A 3-mile-wide natural land bridge occurs where the river flows underground. Indians, Spanish explorers, and settlers who traveled through the area used this land bridge. The 19th-century pioneer town of Keno (later changed to Leno to avoid any association with gambling) was built near where the river disappears underground. The town was at one time the southern terminus of Florida's first telegraph line. By the turn of the century, the town, bypassed by railroads crossing the state, had disappeared, but evidence of its existence can still be found in the park. The site became known as Old Leno, later shortened to O'Leno. From the entrance station, drive 1.8 miles to the parking area at the end of the main park road. The 1.4-mile River Trail begins at a wooden suspension bridge that crosses the river near the parking area. Members of the Civilian Conservation Corps built the bridge in 1938. The trail skirts the banks of the Santa Fe, leading to the sink where the river begins its subterranean journey. Around the parking area, search for resident species such as Red-headed Woodpecker, Carolina Chickadee, Tufted Titmouse, and Eastern Bluebird. Wintering land birds found here may include Golden-crowned Kinglet. Along the river, watch for Wood Duck, Barred Owl, Pileated Woodpecker, and Carolina Wren. During summer look for Yellow-billed Cuckoo, Great Crested Flycatcher, Red-eyed Vireo, Northern Parula, and Summer Tanager. From the sink, the trail passes by Ogden Pond and through pine sandhills before returning to the river. Winter Wren and Fox Sparrow are occasionally found during winter along this stretch of trail.

A series of trails leads over the natural land bridge, providing access to River Rise, the point where the river rises again to the surface. The 3.7-mile Paraner's Branch Trail begins at the River Trail near Ogden Pond and passes by several small sinkholes where river water comes to the surface. The trail winds through sandhills where Wild Turkey, Northern Bobwhite, Pine Warbler, and Eastern Towhee can be found and hardwood hammock where Acadian Flycatcher and Hooded Warbler breed. The return section of the trail follows Old Wire Road, a pioneer trail along which telegraph lines were strung. The wagon wheel ruts of early settlers can still be seen along the road. The trail reconnects with the River Trail near the suspension bridge. A spur trail from Paraner's Branch, the 1.9-mile Sweetwater Trail, leads to the 4.2-mile River Rise Trail, where you can witness the Santa Fe as it resurfaces. This area is in adjacent **River Rise Preserve State Park.** Together, both state parks total over 6,000 acres. Bellamy Road, an old stagecoach road passing over the natural land bridge, crosses US 441 just south of the O'Leno State Park entrance. Drive east on this road 1.3 miles to a parking area that provides direct access to River Rise Preserve State Park. Bellamy Road crosses the Sweetwater Trail, allowing a shorter route to River Rise. You can also reach River Rise using a trail that begins 4 miles south of Bellamy Road on US 441. This trailhead is 1 mile north of where the reemerged river crosses US 441.

General information: Paynes Prairie Preserve State Park (entrance fee for main entrance) is open daily from 8:00 A.M. until sunset. The visitor center is open daily from 9:00 A.M. to 4:00 P.M. LaChua Trail is open Monday through Friday from 8:00 A.M. to 5:00 P.M. and is closed on holidays. Restrooms are located at the picnic area near the visitor center and at Lake Wauberg and LaChua Trail parking areas. Morningside Nature Center (no entrance fee) is open daily from 9:00 A.M. to 5:00 P.M. but closed on major holidays. Restrooms are located in the education center. Newnans Lake Conservation Area, Palm Point, Earl P. Powers, Owens-Illinois, and Gum Root Parks (no entrance fees) are open daily from sunrise to sunset. Restrooms are located at Earl P. Powers Park. Chapman's Pond (no entrance fee) is open 24 hours a day. Restrooms are located in Kanapaha Park. Kanapaha Botanical Gardens (entrance fee) is open weekdays (except Thursdays) from 9:00 A.M. to 5:00 P.M. and weekends from 9:00 A.M. until sunset. San Felasco Preserve State Park (entrance fee for Millhopper Road trails) is open daily from 8:00 A.M. until sunset. Primitive restrooms are located at trailheads. Devil's Millhopper Geological State Park (entrance fee) is open Wednesday through Sunday from 9:00 A.M. to 5:00 P.M. Restrooms are located in the interpretive center. Hague Dairy has no specific visiting hours. Sign in at the office and do not trespass in fenced areas or disturb farm animals. O'Leno State Park (entrance fee) is open daily from 8:00 A.M. until sunset. Restrooms are located in the picnic area.

DeLorme grid: Page 65, A-1, C-2, C-3, D-2, D-3; page 66, C-1.

Hazards: Keep a safe distance from alligators, bison, and wild horses. Venomous snakes are present but rarely encountered. Mosquitoes, ticks, and chiggers are present, especially in summer. Trails through hardwood swamp may be wet throughout the year. Avoid obstructing working farm equipment at Hague Dairy.

Nearest food, gas, lodging: In Gainesville, Alachua, and High Springs.

Camping: Puc Puggy Campground at Paynes Prairie Preserve State Park: 50 sites. O'Leno State Park: 61 sites.

For more information: *Paynes Prairie Preserve State Park,* 100 Savannah Blvd., Micanopy, FL 32667; (352) 466-3397; www.floridastate parks.org/paynesprairie. *Morningside Nature Center, Palm Point, Earl P. Powers, Owens-Illinois, and Gum Root Parks,* c/o City of Gainesville Recreation and Parks Department, P.O. Box 490, Gainesville, FL 32602; (352) 393-8756; www .natureoperations.org. *Newnans Lake Conservation Area,* c/o St. Johns River Water Management District, P.O. Box 1429, Palatka, FL 32178; (386) 329-4500; www.sjrwmd.com. *Chapman's Pond,* c/o Gainesville Regional Utility, P.O. Box 147117, Gainesville, FL 32614; (352) 334-3400; www .gru.com. *Kanapaha Botanical Gardens,* 4700 SW 58th Dr., Gainesville, FL 32608; (352) 372- 4981; www.kanapaha.org. *San Felasco Hammock Preserve State Park,* 12720 NW 109th Lane, Alachua, FL 32615; (386) 462-7905; www .floridastateparks.org/sanfelascohammock. *Devil's Millhopper Geological State Park,* 4732 Millhopper Rd., Gainesville, FL 32656; (352) 955-2008; www.floridastateparks.org/devils millhopper. *Hague Dairy,* c/o University of Florida Department of Animal Sciences, P.O. Box 110910, Gainesville, FL 32611; (352) 392-1981; www .animal.ufl.edu/dairy/facilities.htm. *O'Leno State Park,* 410 SE O'Leno State Park Rd., High Springs, FL 32643; (386) 454-1853; www.floridastate parks.org/oleno.

46 Lake City Area

Habitats: Sandhills, pine flatwoods, hardwood/cypress swamp, hardwood hammock.

Specialty birds: *Resident:* Wood Stork, Bald Eagle, Limpkin, Red-cockaded Woodpecker, Brown-headed Nuthatch, Bachman's Sparrow. *Summer:* Least Bittern, Swallow-tailed Kite, Mississippi Kite, Purple Gallinule, Chuck-will's-widow, Acadian Flycatcher, Yellow-throated Vireo, Wood Thrush, Prothonotary Warbler, Hooded Warbler, Summer Tanager, Blue Grosbeak, Orchard Oriole. *Winter:* Whip-poor-will, Henslow's Sparrow, Le Conte's Sparrow, Rusty Blackbird. *Migrant:* Sandhill Crane.

Best times to bird: October through May.

Directions: *Osceola National Forest:* From I-75 west of Lake City, exit at U.S. Highway 90 (exit 428). Drive east 15 miles to national forest headquarters. From Interstate 10 north of Lake City, exit at US 441 (exit 303). Drive south 3.5 miles to US 90. Turn left and drive east 11.8 miles to forest headquarters. From I-10 west of Macclenny, exit at US 90 (exit 324). Drive west 9 miles to national forest headquarters. *Olustee Battlefield State Historic Site:* From forest headquarters, drive east 3 miles on US 90 to the entrance. *Alligator Lake Recreation Area:* From the intersection of US 90 and US 441 in Lake City, drive east 1.8 miles on US 90 to County Road 133 (Country Club Road). Turn right and drive south 1.4 miles to the entrance.

The Birding

Osceola National Forest contains 266,270 acres of sandhills, pine flatwoods, and hardwood swamp stretching north to the Georgia border, where it meets Okefenokee Swamp. Over 50 active nest clusters of the endangered Red-cockaded Woodpecker are located within the national forest. With continued habitat management, the Forest Service hopes to increase that number to 450. Several locations where Red-cockaded Woodpecker can be found are accessible to birders. One area is Mt. Carrie Wayside, 4 miles west of national forest headquarters on US 90. A 1-mile trail winds through longleaf pine sandhills preferred by the woodpeckers. Also watch year-round for Wild Turkey, Northern Bobwhite, Red-headed Woodpecker, Brown-headed Nuthatch, Eastern Bluebird, Pine Warbler, and Eastern Towhee. In summer look for Eastern Wood-Pewee, Great Crested Flycatcher, and Summer Tanager. During spring and early summer listen for Bachman's Sparrows singing from perches in the forest understory. Red-cockaded Woodpecker nest trees can be found along adjacent forest roads. From Mt. Carrie Wayside, drive east 0.2 mile to Forest Road 215 (Mt. Carrie Road). Turn left and drive north 0.3 mile to the first nest cluster. Cavity trees are marked with white rings. Continue north 1.7 miles to Forest Road 278. Bear left and drive west 0.3 mile to another nest cluster. During the nesting season, from April through June, use caution when in the vicinity of these trees to avoid disturbing the birds. Outside the nesting season, dawn and dusk are optimal times to see woodpeckers near their nest cavities.

To visit Ocean Pond, return to national forest headquarters and continue east 0.7 mile on US 90 to Forest Road 231. Olustee Depot Visitor Center is at this intersection. Turn left and drive north 0.5 mile to the Olustee Beach fee station. Continue north 0.2 mile to the parking area located at the south end of the lake. A fishing pier allows views of wintering waterfowl on the lake. The Trampled Track Trail begins at the north end of the parking area. This 0.1-mile wheelchair-accessible boardwalk leads through hardwood swamp along the lake. Interpretive displays describe the town and sawmill that were built here in the early 1900s. Look here for Pileated Woodpecker, Carolina Wren, and other resident species.

To reach the campground at the north end of Ocean Pond, return to US 90 and turn left. Drive east 1 mile to County Road 250A. Turn left and drive north, then east 4 miles to Forest Road 268. Turn left and drive south 0.1 mile to where the Florida Scenic Trail crosses the road. The trail on the west side of the road leads north to a boardwalk through cypress swamp. Along this boardwalk, watch year-round for Barred Owl, Carolina Chickadee, and Tufted Titmouse. In summer look for Northern Parula and Prothonotary and Hooded Warbler. Watch overhead in spring and summer for Swallow-tailed Kite. Continue south 1.2 miles on FR 268 to the campground. Big Gum Swamp, north of Ocean Pond, consists of 13,640 acres of cypress/gum swamp surrounded by pine flatwoods. Summer breeders in this habitat include Yellow-billed Cuckoo, Acadian Flycatcher, Yellow-throated and Red-eyed Vireo and Prothonotary and Hooded Warbler. To reach a loop trail through this area, return to CR 250A and turn left. Drive east, then north 3.3 miles to County Road 250. Turn left and drive east 5.7 miles to the trailhead. Prepare for wet conditions during summer on this trail.

Olustee Battlefield State Historic Site commemorates Florida's largest Civil War battle. The battle, won by Confederate troops, was fought in a longleaf pine flatwoods free of understory. A small museum displays artifacts from the era while an interpretive trail winds through the battlefield. Red-cockaded Woodpecker and Bachman's Sparrow nest in the flatwoods. At **Alligator Lake Recreation Area** in Lake City, 12 miles of trails provide access to freshwater impoundments and surrounding cypress swamp and hardwood hammock. American White Pelican and a variety of waterfowl winter in the impoundments. Marsh edges harbor wintering rails, wrens, and sparrows. Rarities found here include Greater White-fronted Goose, White-faced Ibis, and Vermilion Flycatcher. Check surrounding cypress swamp and hardwood hammock for migrant and wintering land birds, including Rusty Blackbird during winter.

General information: Osceola National Forest is open 24 hours a day, and its headquarters are open Monday through Friday from 7:30 A.M. to 4:00 P.M. Olustee Depot Visitor Center is open Wednesday through Monday from 9:00 A.M. to 4:30 P.M. Olustee Beach (entrance fee) is open daily from sunrise to sunset. Seasonal hunting is permitted in designated areas. Refer to regulations-summary brochures, updated annually and available at national forest headquarters and check stations, for hunt dates and locations. Wear blaze orange if hiking during hunting season. Olustee Battlefield State Historic Site (no entrance fee) is open daily from 8:00 A.M. until sunset. The museum is open Thursday through Monday from 9:00 A.M. to 5:00 P.M. Restrooms are located in the museum. Alligator Lake Recreation Area (no entrance fee) is open Wednesday through Friday from 11:00 A.M. to 7:00 P.M. and Saturday and Sunday from 8:00 A.M. to 7:00 P.M. The recreation area closes 30 minutes before sunset during winter. Restrooms are located in the picnic area.

DeLorme grid: Page 54, C-3; Page 55, B-2, C-2.

Hazards: Keep a safe distance from alligators. Venomous snakes (five species: eastern diamondback, dusky pygmy, and canebrake rattlesnakes, coral snake, and cottonmouth) are present but rarely encountered. Mosquitoes, ticks, and chiggers are present, especially in summer. Trails may be flooded in summer.

Nearest food, gas, lodging: In Lake City.

Camping: Ocean Pond in Osceola National Forest: 67 sites.

For more information: *Osceola National Forest*, P.O. Box 70, Olustee, FL 32072; (386) 752-2577; www.fs.fed.us/r8/florida/recreation/index_osc. *Olustee Battlefield State Historic Site*, P.O. Box 40, Olustee, FL 32072; (904) 758-0400; www.florida stateparks.org/olustee. *Alligator Lake Recreation Area*, 1498 SW Country Club Rd., Lake City, FL 32025; (386) 758-1005; www.columbiacounty fla.com/parksandrecreation.asp.

47 Big Bend Wildlife Management Area

Habitats: Salt marsh, brackish water impoundments, hardwood swamp, sandhills, pine flatwoods, hardwood hammock.

Specialty birds: *Resident:* Mottled Duck, Magnificent Frigatebird, Bald Eagle, Black Rail, Clapper Rail, King Rail, Limpkin, Wilson's Plover, American Oystercatcher, Brown-headed Nuthatch, Bachman's Sparrow, Seaside Sparrow. *Summer:* Least Bittern, Reddish Egret, Roseate Spoonbill, Wood Stork, Swallow-tailed Kite, Mississippi Kite, Purple Gallinule, Chuck-will's-widow, Gray Kingbird, Acadian Flycatcher, Yellow-throated Vireo, Wood Thrush, Prothonotary Warbler, Swainson's Warbler, Louisiana Waterthrush, Kentucky Warbler, Hooded Warbler, Yellow-breasted Chat, Summer Tanager, Blue Grosbeak, Orchard Oriole. *Winter:* Whip-poor-will, Golden-crowned Kinglet, Nelson's Sharp-tailed Sparrow. *Migrant:* Whimbrel, Black Tern.

Best times to bird: October through April.

Directions: *Jena Unit:* From US 19 in Cross City, drive north 11 miles to County Road 358. Turn left and drive west 4.6 miles to County Road 361. Turn left and drive south 11 miles to the end of the road. *Tide Swamp Unit:* Return to CR 358. Turn left and drive 1.7 miles to SW 875th Street in Steinhatchee. Turn right and drive north 0.5 mile, crossing over the Steinhatchee River Bridge, to 1st Street South. Turn left and drive west 0.6 mile to CR 361. Turn right and drive north 6 miles to Dallus Creek Road. Turn left to begin the wildlife drive. *Hickory Mound Unit:* From the intersection of US 19 and US 98 in Perry, drive west 16.2 miles on US 98 to Cow Creek Grade. Turn left and drive south 8 miles to the check station.

The Birding

Big Bend Wildlife Management Area is spread over 60 miles of sparsely populated Gulf of Mexico coastline. The wildlife management area consists of five units totaling more than 72,000 acres. Two units accessible to birders are at the southern end of this vast area. The 12,522-acre **Jena Unit** stretches between Horseshoe Beach and the fishing village of Steinhatchee. CR 361, known locally as the "Road to Nowhere," provides access to the unit but never reaches the Gulf, instead ending in expansive salt marsh. This area can be excellent for Black Rail and Seaside Sparrow. Dirt tracks lead in various directions from the end of the road, providing access to Black Rail habitat. During winter watch for Northern Harrier over the marsh.

North of Steinhatchee is the **Tide Swamp Unit** of the wildlife management area. Longleaf pine and cypress were logged extensively in this 20,298-acre tract. Upland areas were then planted in pulpwood-producing slash and sand pine that over time became wildlife deserts. These areas are slowly being restored to longleaf pine sandhills. Harvested cypress has been replaced over time by red maple, sweet gum, magnolia, and other hardwood trees. Some cypress is growing back, though slowly. These swamps may take hundreds of years to fully recover. Coastal areas continue to be dominated by salt marsh where Clapper Rail, Marsh Wren, and Seaside Sparrow breed. Nelson's Sharp-tailed Sparrow and, occasionally, Saltmarsh Sharp-tailed Sparrow, winter here. A wildlife drive (unpaved) takes you through pinelands and hardwood swamp and provides access to salt marsh habitat at Dallus Creek Landing. The drive begins and ends on CR 361 and is only open to vehicles from September through April. Enter at Dallus Creek Road and drive west 0.3 mile to Indian Island Road. To reach Dallus Creek Landing, continue west 2.5 miles on Dallus Creek Road to the picnic area at the end of the road. Check restored pinelands along this road for Wild Turkey, Brown-headed Nuthatch, and other resident species. A 1.2-mile trail begins at the picnic area and leads along Dallus Creek, then into pinelands. Backtrack 1.4 miles to Bridge Road, a shortcut to the wildlife drive. Turn left and drive north 0.3 mile to return to Indian Island Road. Look for Hooded Merganser on the small pond along the 0.5-mile section of Indian Island Road between Bridge Road and Dallus Creek Road. Backtrack to the Bridge Road intersection, turn right, and drive north 0.6 mile to Pine Island Road. Turn left and drive west 1.4 miles to Turkey Track Tram. The wildlife drive now leaves pinelands and enters hardwood swamp. Turn right and drive north 2.5 miles to Tide City Mainline. Turn left and drive west, then north 3.2 miles, to return to CR 361. If hiking this road or any of the side trams through the forest, search in summer for Yellow-billed Cuckoo, Red-eyed Vireo, Northern Parula, Prothonotary, Kentucky, and Hooded Warbler, and other breeding species. Watch overhead in summer for Swallow-tailed Kite. Check at other times of the year for migrant and wintering land birds.

Drive north 1 mile on CR 361 to the entrance road for Hagen's Cove Recreation Area. Turn left and drive west 1.3 miles to the picnic area, again looking for pineland species along the way. Hagen's Cove has one of the few sandy beaches along this stretch of coastline. Check mudflats exposed at low tide for wading birds, shorebirds, gulls, and terns. Watch year-round for Reddish Egret, Wilson's Plover, American Oystercatcher, and Willet. American Avocet, Whimbrel, Marbled Godwit, and other shorebirds pass through during migration or remain for the winter. Scan offshore during winter for American White Pelican, loons, grebes, and ducks. Gray Kingbird is common in summer along this entire coast. Magnificent Frigatebird is most likely to be seen soaring overhead during the summer months. An observation tower that once provided an excellent vantage point for scanning the Gulf unfortunately fell victim to vandals and has since been dismantled. Return to CR 361, turn left, and drive north 21.8 miles to return to US 19. Turn left and drive north 4.7 miles to US 98 in Perry.

Hickory Mound Unit is located at the northern end of Big Bend Wildlife Management Area. This 14,427-acre tract features a large brackish water impoundment, accessed via Cow Creek Grade (unpaved). The road passes through hardwood swamp before reaching the impoundment. Over 20 species of waterfowl have been recorded in the area, including Snow Goose, American Black Duck, and Common Goldeneye. An observation tower is located on the south side of the impoundment, a good place to scan for migrant and wintering shorebirds that often feed on exposed mudflats. A Hudsonian Godwit was recorded here in April 2004. Also watch for Osprey and Bald Eagle year-round, Northern Harrier in winter, and Swallow-tailed and Mississippi Kite during summer. As you get closer to the Gulf, you can't help but notice thousands of cabbage palm stumps in the surrounding marsh. Rising sea levels have slowly moved the coastline inland, over time wiping out coastal forest and replacing it with salt marsh.

West of Hickory Mound is 4,543-acre **Econfina River State Park.** To reach this park, return to US 98 and drive west 3.6 miles to County Road 14. Turn left and drive south 6 miles to the park entrance. A boat ramp provides opportunities to canoe the river and tidal creeks in search of Clapper Rail, Marsh Wren, Seaside Sparrow, and other salt marsh species. Nine miles of trails wind through surrounding flatwoods and hammocks where resident, wintering, and migrant land birds may be found. Access these trails from a trailhead near the parking area or from trailheads along CR 14, 1 and 2.3 miles north of the park entrance. The 10,600-acre Snipe Island Unit of Big Bend Wildlife Management Area may also be accessed from CR 14, via Snipe Island Grade, which begins 1.7 miles from US 98. Mostly hunters use this unit. North of US 98 is 47,532-acre **Aucilla Wildlife Management Area.** A 17-mile extension of the Florida Trail follows the Aucilla River through beautiful hardwood swamp and hardwood hammock. The river is underground along much of the trail, emerging as sinkholes with colorful names such as Chocolate Sink, Mosquito Slap Sink, Hurry-up Sink, and Kitchen Sink. To reach a section of the trail that passes several of these formations, return to US 98, turn left, and drive west 2.3 miles to Powell Hammock Road. Turn right and drive north 2.8 miles to Goose Pasture Road (unpaved). Turn left and drive west 1 mile to a cattle guard, where the trail crosses the road. On a summer hike along this trail, look for Yellow-billed Cuckoo, Acadian Flycatcher, Red-eyed Vireo, Wood Thrush, Northern Parula, Prothonotary and Hooded Warbler, and Yellow-breasted Chat. Prepare for biting insects during this season.

General information: Big Bend and Aucilla Wildlife Management Areas (no entrance fee) are open daily from sunrise to sunset. Primitive restrooms are located at Dallus Creek Landing and Hagen's Cove Recreation Area. Seasonal hunting is permitted in designated areas. Refer to regulations-summary brochures, updated annually and available at check stations, for hunt dates and locations. Wear blaze orange if hiking during hunting season. Econfina River State Park (no entrance fee) is open daily from 8:00 A.M. until sunset. A primitive restroom is located in the parking area.

DeLorme grid: Page 51, D-2; page 62, C-3, D-3.

Hazards: Keep a safe distance from alligators. Venomous snakes are present but rarely encountered. Mosquitoes are common, especially in summer. Roads in Hickory Mound Unit are often heavily washboarded.

Nearest food, gas, lodging: In Perry.

Camping: Private campgrounds are located in Steinhatchee and Perry.

For more information: *Big Bend and Aucilla Wildlife Management Areas,* c/o Florida Fish and Wildlife Conservation Commission, 620 S. Meridian St., Tallahassee, FL 32399; (800) 955-8771; www.myfwc.com/recreation/big_bend. *Econfina River State Park,* c/o 1022 Desoto Park Dr., Tallahassee, FL 32301; (850) 922-6007; www.floridastateparks.org/econfinariver.

THE PANHANDLE

 ## St. Marks Area

Habitats: Salt marsh, fresh and brackish water impoundments, sandy beach, estuary, maritime hammock, pine flatwoods, sandhills, hardwood/cypress swamp, hardwood hammock.

Specialty birds: *Resident:* Bald Eagle, Clapper Rail, King Rail, Limpkin, Wilson's Plover, Snowy Plover, American Oystercatcher, Red-cockaded Woodpecker, Brown-headed Nuthatch, Bachman's Sparrow, Seaside Sparrow. *Summer:* Least Bittern, Reddish Egret, Roseate Spoonbill, Wood Stork, Swallow-tailed Kite, Mississippi Kite, Black Rail, Purple Gallinule, Least Tern, Chuck-will's-widow, Acadian Flycatcher, Gray Kingbird, Yellow-throated Vireo, Wood Thrush, Prothonotary Warbler, Swainson's Warbler, Kentucky Warbler, Hooded Warbler, Yellow-breasted Chat, Summer Tanager, Blue Grosbeak, Orchard Oriole. *Winter:* American Black Duck, Canvasback, Greater Scaup, Surf Scoter,

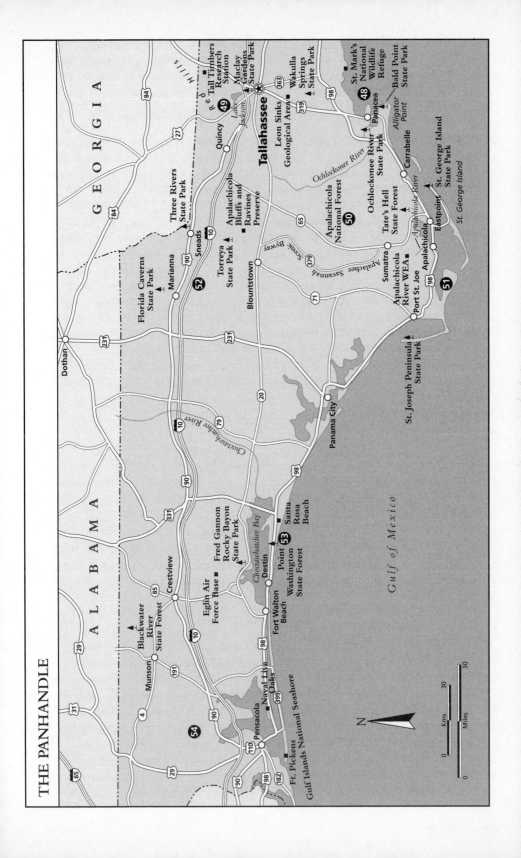

THE PANHANDLE

White-winged Scoter, Black Scoter, Common Goldeneye, Red-throated Loon, Piping Plover, American Woodcock, Short-eared Owl, Whip-poor-will, Vermilion Flycatcher, Western Kingbird, Scissor-tailed Flycatcher, Winter Wren, Golden-crowned Kinglet, American Pipit, Henslow's Sparrow, Nelson's Sharp-tailed Sparrow, Dark-eyed Junco, Rusty Blackbird, Pine Siskin. *Migrant:* Peregrine Falcon.

Best times to bird: All year.

Directions: *St. Marks National Wildlife Refuge:* From Interstate 10 westbound in Tallahassee, exit at Capital Circle Southeast (County Road 261, exit 203). Drive south, then west 11 miles to County Road 363. Turn left and drive south 10 miles to County Road 267. Turn left and drive east, then south 3.7 miles to U.S. Highway 98. Turn left and drive east 0.4 mile to County Road 59. Turn right and drive south 3.2 miles to the refuge entrance station. If not staffed, proceed 0.3 mile farther to the self-service pay station. From I-10 eastbound in Tallahassee, exit at Capital Circle Southwest (exit 196). Drive south, then east 11 miles to CR 363. Turn right and proceed as above. *Wakulla Springs State Park:* From St. Marks NWR, return to the intersection of CR 267 and CR 363. Drive west 5 miles on CR 267 to the park entrance. *Ochlockonee River State Park:* From St. Marks NWR, return to the intersection of US 98 and CR 267. Drive west 14 miles on US 98 to US 98/319. Continue west, then south 1.5 miles to US 319 north of Panacea. Turn right and drive west, then south 10.7 miles to the park entrance. From the intersection of Capital Circle and CR 363 in Tallahassee, drive west 1.3 miles to US 319/State Road 61. Turn left and drive south 2.2 miles, bearing right at US 319. Continue south 17.5 miles to US 98/319. Turn right and proceed as above. *Bald Point State Park/Alligator Point:* From the intersection of US 98 and CR 319 north of Panacea, drive south 10 miles to County Road 370. Turn left and drive east 3.7 miles to Bald Point Road. Turn left and drive north 2.8 miles to the park entrance, or continue on CR 370 to Alligator Point.

The Birding

St. Marks National Wildlife Refuge contains 68,000 acres of salt marsh, hardwood swamps, and pine flatwoods spread across three counties. An additional 31,700 acres of the refuge are submerged in Apalachee Bay. The refuge was established in 1931 to provide habitat for wintering waterfowl. Freshwater impoundments were created for that purpose in the St. Marks Unit of the refuge. Primarily hunters and anglers use the Wakulla and Panacea Units. Over 270 bird species have been recorded within the refuge, including over 30 species of waterfowl. These include Tundra Swan, Greater White-fronted, Snow, Ross's, and Canada Goose, American Black Duck, Cinnamon Teal, Eurasian Wigeon, Long-tailed Duck, and all three scoters. Wintering or vagrant species seen periodically in the refuge include White-faced Ibis, Groove-billed Ani, Vermilion Flycatcher, Tropical Kingbird, Bell's Vireo, Red-breasted Nuthatch, Brown Creeper, Winter Wren, Golden-crowned Kinglet, Dark-eyed Junco, Yellow-headed and Rusty Blackbird, Shiny and Bronzed Cowbird, Purple Finch, and Pine Siskin.

Begin your tour of the refuge at the visitor center, located 0.1 mile beyond the St. Marks Unit self-service pay station. Check the interpretive displays, obtain maps and checklists, and review the sightings list for recently seen birds. The 0.3-mile Plum Orchard Pond Trail begins behind the visitor center and winds around the pond and through adjacent woodlands. Scan the pond for Wood Duck and search surrounding forest for Wild Turkey and migrant and wintering land birds. Lighthouse Road, the main refuge road, begins beyond the visitor center and heads south 6 miles to the lighthouse along Apalachee Bay. The road first passes through hardwood swamp. Two concrete bridges are located 0.7 mile from the visitor center. During summer look here for Yellow-billed Cuckoo, Acadian Flycatcher, Red-eyed Vireo, Northern Parula, Yellow-throated, Prothonotary, Swainson's, Kentucky, and Hooded Warbler, and other breeding species. In winter watch for Yellow-bellied Sapsucker, Winter Wren, Golden-crowned Kinglet, and Rusty Blackbird. In spring and fall check for migrant land birds including both species of waterthrush. Beyond the bridges the hardwood swamp ends and a short stretch of pine flatwoods begins. A service road 0.3 mile from the second bridge is the first of many access points to over 75 miles of marked trails, including almost 50 miles of the Florida Scenic Trail. The road also leads to the refuge helipad. Park here and hike east 0.5 mile, then turn right to reach the helipad. Look in pinelands bordering the road for Red-headed, Downy, and, occasionally, Hairy Woodpecker, Northern Flicker, and Brown-headed Nuthatch. In spring and summer listen for Eastern Wood-Pewee, Summer Tanager, and Bachman's Sparrow. Check brushy areas for Chipping, Song, Field, White-throated, and other wintering sparrows. Henslow's, Swamp, and occasionally Le Conte's Sparrow can be found in wet fields surrounding the helipad. Rubber boots are highly recommended when investigating this area.

Freshwater impoundments become visible on both sides of Lighthouse Road beginning 0.8 mile from the helipad service road. East River Pool lies to the west and Stoney Bayou Pool #1 is to the east. An assortment of wading birds can be found in these pools year-round. Scan distant snags for perched Osprey, Bald Eagle, and Red-shouldered Hawk. Blue and Green-winged Teal are the most common waterfowl found here in winter. Also watch in winter for Northern Harrier coursing over the impoundments. Check emergent vegetation in summer for Purple Gallinule. Large numbers of Eastern Kingbird roosts in this area in early fall. Migrant shorebirds, sometimes including White-rumped, Baird's, and Buff-breasted Sandpiper, are attracted to exposed mudflats. In September 2005 a Lesser Sand Plover, a first for Florida, was discovered at Stoney Bayou Pool. The refuge's extensive backcountry trail system can be accessed from various points along this section of Lighthouse Road. These trails follow impoundment levees and old logging roads, allowing for exploration of remote sections of the refuge, including Stoney Bayou Pool #2 and East Stoney Bayou Pool. Vermilion Flycatcher has wintered on levees along Stoney Bayou Pool #2. As Lighthouse Road continues south, it passes a series of impoundments on the east side of the road, all good for wintering waterfowl and migrant shorebirds. Mounds Pool #1 begins in 0.5 mile and Mounds Pool #2 is 1 mile farther. Mounds Pool #3 is behind these two impoundments and can be reached by hiking a trail that begins at Gate 132, 0.8 mile farther south. An excellent variety of ducks use these ponds. Look for Mallard, Gadwall, American Wigeon, Blue and Green-winged Teal, Northern Shoveler, Northern Pintail, and occasionally American Black Duck and Snow Goose. Watch during winter for Sedge Wren in grassy areas along impoundment edges. Sora, Long-billed Dowitcher, and Wilson's Snipe may be seen in winter on exposed mudflats. White-faced Ibis has also been found here in winter.

Headquarters Pond is also on the east side of the road, 0.7 mile south of Gate 132. Several species of puddle ducks can usually be found here in winter. Search emergent vegetation along the edges of this pond for King Rail, Sora, and Purple Gallinule. Black-crowned Night-Heron often roosts on the backside of the pond. An observation platform overlooking the pond can be reached via a 0.1-mile trail that begins at the parking area 0.1 mile farther south. This parking area is also the trailhead for Mounds Pool Interpretive Trail. This 1-mile trail leads through an oak hammock to an observation platform overlooking Tower Pond, a saltwater impoundment. Look for Brown-headed Nuthatch in pines surrounding the parking area. Eastern Towhee is common in the hammock. Search here in winter for Red-breasted Nuthatch, Brown Creeper, and other vagrants from north of the Florida border. Salt marsh begins south of the levee encircling Tower Pond. Yellow-breasted Chat nests in brushy areas along this levee. Black Rail may be heard calling from the marsh in spring. South of the parking area is Picnic Pond, which attracts Lesser Scaup and other diving ducks. Long-tailed Duck and Surf Scoter have both been recorded here. Continue south 0.8 mile to Lighthouse Pool, on the west side of the road. A mixture of puddle and diving ducks can be found here in winter. Commonly seen are American Wigeon, Redhead, Ring-necked Duck, Lesser Scaup, and Hooded Merganser. Less common are Canvasback and Greater Scaup. The lighthouse parking area is at the end of the road, 0.2 mile farther. Search emergent vegetation around Lighthouse Pool for Clapper Rail year-round, Least Bittern in summer, and American Bittern during winter. Walk the 0.5-mile Levee Trail that leads between Lighthouse Pool and Apalachee Bay. Song Sparrow is abundant in winter in brushy areas along the trail. Scan offshore in winter for Common and, occasionally, Red-throated Loon, Horned Grebe, American White Pelican, Redhead, all three scoters, Bufflehead, Common Goldeneye, and Red-breasted Merganser. Check oyster bars for American Oystercatcher and exposed mudflats for Reddish Egret, Wilson's Plover, Willet, and other shorebirds. The strip of salt marsh between the trail and the bay is good habitat for Marsh and Sedge Wren and Seaside, Nelson's, and, occasionally, Saltmarsh Sharp-tailed Sparrow. You can look, but don't expect to see the Yellow-nosed Albatross that was spotted soaring around the lighthouse in July 1983.

Wakulla Springs State Park contains one of the world's largest and deepest freshwater springs. If water conditions permit, glass-bottom boat tours allow views of mastodon bones and other prehistoric creatures littering the spring basin. The Wakulla River, originating at the spring, is surrounded by 6,000 acres of cypress and hardwood swamp, hardwood hammock, and longleaf pine sandhills. Boat tours provide downriver access, while a series of trails allow for exploration of upland areas of the park. Limpkin, once a common resident spotted regularly on boat tours, is now only seen occasionally along the river. It is not yet fully understood why this species has all but disappeared from the park. A variety of waterfowl can be found in the river, including Wood Duck year-round and American Wigeon and Hooded Merganser in winter. Check emergent vegetation in winter for Sora and during summer for Least Bittern and Purple Gallinule. Throughout the year watch for Bald Eagle soaring over the river. Swallow-tailed Kite, which breeds in the area, may be seen overhead in spring and summer. Feeders near the lodge, when stocked with seed, attract Carolina Chickadee, Tufted Titmouse, House Finch, and other residents. During winter watch for American Goldfinch, joined occasionally by Dark-eyed Junco, Purple Finch, and Pine Siskin. The 0.9-mile Sally Ward Trail begins near the lodge and connects with the 1.4-mile Hammock Trail. These trails provide access to upland hardwood forest, hardwood swamp, and a cypress dome. On a summer hike, search hardwood swamp for Yellow-billed Cuckoo, Acadian Flycatcher, Red-eyed Vireo, Northern Parula, and Prothonotary and Hooded Warbler. In winter check this habitat for Winter Wren, Golden-crowned Kinglet, and Rusty Blackbird. During this season American Woodcock may lie hidden along forest edges. Check upland areas for a variety of resident, migrant, and wintering land birds. The 4.5-mile McBrides Slough Trail begins at the park entrance and winds through hardwood forest and longleaf pine sandhills. In the pinelands watch year-round for Wild Turkey, Northern Bobwhite, Red-headed Woodpecker, Brown-headed Nuthatch, and Eastern Bluebird. In summer look and listen for Chuck-will's-widow, Eastern Wood-Pewee, and Summer Tanager.

Tiger Hammock Road, located south of the state park, winds through pristine hardwood swamp along the Wakulla River. Over 160 species have been recorded in this area, including over 30 species of warblers. To reach this area, exit the park, turn left, and drive west 0.1 mile to CR 61. Turn left and drive south 3.3 miles to County Road 365. Turn left and drive west 0.3 mile to Tiger Hammock Road. Turn right and drive south 1.3 miles to the end of the pavement. Swainson's and Kentucky Warbler, Yellow-breasted Chat, Blue Grosbeak, and Indigo Bunting nest along this stretch of road. Once past the paved section, check the area under the power lines for more chats, grosbeaks, and buntings. Another 0.4 mile brings you to a small bridge, where nesting Acadian Flycatcher and Swainson's, Kentucky, and Hooded Warbler may be found in summer. Watch for Wild Turkey crossing anywhere along the road. Other breeding species found along this road include Swallow-tailed Kite, Broad-winged Hawk, Limpkin, Yellow-billed Cuckoo, Barred Owl, Chuck-will's-widow, Wood Thrush, Prothonotary Warbler, and Summer Tanager. The road ends at Lower Bridge Road, where Mississippi Kite roosts and nests nearby. Turn left and drive east 1.3 miles to return to US 98. Along both Tiger Hammock and Lower Bridge Road, American Woodcock, Whip-poor-will, and Fox Sparrow are among the possibilities in winter.

The 550-acre **Ochlockonee River State Park** is dominated by pine flatwoods, home to the endangered Red-cockaded Woodpecker. From the entrance, drive 2 miles to the picnic area at the end of the main park road. The picnic area overlooks the Dead River, which flows into the Ochlockonee River. Wading birds, including Wood Stork and Limpkin, may be found along the river. Red-cockaded Woodpecker nest trees, marked with white rings, are visible from the parking area. During the nesting season, from April through June, avoid approaching woodpecker nest cavities closely. The pinelands may be explored via a 1.5-mile wildlife drive or a 0.8-mile nature trail. Watch year-round for Wild Turkey, Northern Bobwhite, Red-headed Woodpecker, Brown-headed Nuthatch, Eastern Bluebird, Pine Warbler, Eastern Towhee, and Bachman's Sparrow. In summer look and listen for Chuck-will's-widow, Eastern Wood-Pewee, and Summer Tanager. Henslow's Sparrow may be found during winter in open, wet, grassy areas. The park is also home to white squirrels, accidentally introduced to the area and not to be confused with the larger, native Sherman's fox squirrels.

Bald Point State Park, a 4,800-acre park located at the mouth of Ochlockonee Bay, is a recent addition to the Florida state park system. From Ochlockonee River State Park, return to CR 319, turn left, and drive south 6 miles to US 98. Turn left and drive east, then north 9 miles to CR 370. Turn right and drive east 3.7 miles to Bald Point Road. Turn left and drive north 2.8 miles to the park entrance. In fall check wires along Bald Point Road for Western Kingbird and Scissor-tailed Flycatcher, then drive 0.5 mile to the parking area at the end of the road. In spring and fall search the maritime hammock surrounding the parking area for trans-Gulf migrants. A wide variety of warblers, vireos, flycatchers, thrushes, tanagers, buntings, and other land birds make landfall in the park or pause here before their return flights over the Gulf. This is also a staging area for monarch butterflies heading south to Mexico. Unexpected flycatchers recorded in the park include Olive-sided, Ash-throated, and Vermilion. A Groove-billed Ani was discovered here in October 2003. Watch overhead in fall for migrant hawks and falcons. Bald Eagle can be seen here year-round. Walk down to the beach, where an assortment of shorebirds, gulls, and terns congregate. Check oyster bars for American Oystercatcher. Scan offshore in winter for Common and Red-throated Loon, Horned Grebe, Bufflehead, Common Goldeneye, scoters, and Red-breasted Merganser. Clapper Rail, Marsh Wren, and Seaside Sparrow breed in salt marsh west of the park road. Nelson's Sharp-tailed Sparrow may be found here in winter. A wheelchair-accessible trail begins at the parking area and leads to an observation platform overlooking the marsh. On several occasions, birders have sighted Lesser Nighthawk here on winter evenings. Several dirt roads along Bald Point Road can be used to hike into pine flatwoods in the interior of the park, where Brown-headed Nuthatch, Eastern Towhee, and other pineland species may be found. Search anywhere along Bald Point Road for wintering sparrows, including Chipping, Song, and White-throated. Clay-colored, Field, and other sparrows sometimes join the mix.

Return to CR 370, turn left, and drive south, then west to **Alligator Point,** a peninsula extending into the Gulf. In summer check wires along the road for Gray Kingbird. House Finch is now resident in this area. Beach houses block your view of the Gulf for the first mile. When the Gulf becomes visible, find a place to park on any side road where space is available. Hurricane Dennis heavily damaged this section of road in 2005. Until the road is repaired, finding a place to park may prove challenging. Walk back to the beach and scan offshore for Northern Gannet, Common Loon, and all three scoters. Walk east along the beach toward Mud Cove, where in winter loons and sea ducks congregate. This is one of the better locations in the state to find Red-throated Loon. Pacific Loon has also been recorded here during recent winters. Duck flocks usually include Redhead and Lesser Scaup, with Greater Scaup occasionally joining them. Plovers, Red Knot, and other shore-birds, gulls, and terns often assemble on a sandspit toward the eastern end of this beach.

Backtrack to US 98, turn right, and drive north 6.4 miles over the Ochlockonee River Bridge to the town of Panacea. Turn left on Otter Lake Road (County Road 372A) and drive west 1.6 miles to Otter Lake picnic area and boat launch, in the Panacea Tract of St. Marks National Wildlife Refuge. Wading birds, including Wood Stork, can be seen around the boat launch. In summer check cypress trees along the lake for Prothonotary Warbler. Watch overhead in spring and summer for Swallow-tailed Kite. Trails lead into pine flatwoods where species listed for Ochlockonee River State Park, including Red-cockaded Woodpecker, may be found. Return to US 98, turn left, and drive north 1 mile to Bottoms Road (also CR 372A). Turn right and drive east 2.5 miles to the end of the road. The road passes through salt marsh teeming with Clapper Rail, Marsh Wren, and Seaside Sparrow, joined in winter by Sedge Wren and Nelson's Sharp-tailed Sparrow. Watch in winter for Northern Harrier cruising over the marsh. Short-eared Owl periodically winters in this area. From Bottoms Road, continue north 2.7 miles on US 98 to CR 319, turning left to return to Ochlockonee River State Park, or continuing north on US 98 to return to Tallahassee.

General information: St. Marks National Wildlife Refuge (entrance fee) is open daily from sunrise to sunset. The visitor center is open Monday through Friday from 8:00 A.M. to 4:00 P.M. and Saturday and Sunday from 10:00 A.M. to 5:00 P.M. The visitor center is closed on federal holidays. Restrooms are located in the visitor center and at Headquarters Pond. The Otter Lake section of St. Marks National Wildlife Refuge (no entrance fee) is open daily from sunrise to sunset. Restrooms are located in the picnic area. Seasonal hunting is permitted in the Wakulla and Panacea Units of the refuge. See the hunting-regulations brochure, available at the visitor center, for hunt dates and locations. Wear blaze orange if hiking during hunting season. Wakulla Springs, Ochlockonee River, and Bald Point State Parks (entrance fees) are open daily from 8:00 A.M. until sunset. Restrooms at Ochlockonee River and Bald Point are located in picnic areas. Restrooms at Wakulla Springs are located in Edward Ball Lodge. Boat tours at Wakulla Springs operate daily, weather permitting. Glass-bottom boat tours include a performance by "Henry, the Pole-vaulting Fish!"

Habitat surrounding Tiger Hammock and Lower Bridge Roads is private property. Bird this area only from the road.

DeLorme grid: Page 50, C-2, D-3; page 61, D-3.

Hazards: Keep a safe distance from alligators. Black bears and venomous snakes are present but rarely encountered. Mosquitoes and ticks are present, especially in summer. Trails may be seasonally wet.

Nearest food, gas, lodging: In Tallahassee and Panacea. On-site lodging, dining at Edward Ball Wakulla Springs Lodge.

Camping: Ochlockonee River State Park: 30 sites. There are private campgrounds in Tallahassee.

For more information: *St. Marks National Wildlife Refuge,* 1255 Lighthouse Rd., St. Marks, FL 32355; (850) 925-6121; www.fws.gov/saint marks. *Wakulla Springs State Park,* 550 Wakulla Park Dr., Wakulla Springs, FL 32327; (850) 224-5950; www.floridastateparks.org/wakullasprings. *Ochlockonee River State Park,* P.O. Box 5, Sopchoppy, FL 32358; (850) 962-2771; www.florida stateparks.org/ochlockoneeriver. *Bald Point State Park,* 146 Box Cut, Alligator Point, FL 32346; (850) 349-9146; www.floridastateparks.org/baldpoint.

 # Tallahassee Area

Habitats: Hardwood hammock, clayhills, sandhills, slope forest, hardwood/cypress swamp, freshwater ponds and lakes.

Specialty birds: *Resident:* Bald Eagle, White-breasted Nuthatch, Brown-headed Nuthatch, Bachman's Sparrow. *Summer:* Least Bittern, Wood Stork, Swallow-tailed Kite, Mississippi Kite, Purple Gallinule, Chuck-will's-widow, Acadian Flycatcher, Yellow-throated Vireo, Wood Thrush, Prothonotary Warbler, Swainson's Warbler, Louisiana Water-thrush, Kentucky Warbler, Hooded Warbler, Yellow-breasted Chat, Summer Tanager, Blue Grosbeak, Orchard Oriole. *Winter:* Common Goldeneye, American Woodcock, Whip-poor-will, Brown Creeper, Winter Wren, Golden-crowned Kinglet, American Pipit, Fox Sparrow, Dark-eyed Junco, Rusty Blackbird, Purple Finch, Pine Siskin. *Migrant:* Scarlet Tanager.

Best times to bird: October through April.

Directions: *Maclay Gardens State Park:* From I-10 in Tallahassee, exit at Thomasville Road (U.S. Highway 319, exit 203). Drive north 0.8 mile to Maclay Road. Turn left and drive west 0.1 mile to the park entrance. *Elinor Klapp-Phipps Park:* Drive east 2 miles on Maclay Road to Meridian Road. Turn right and drive north 0.5 mile to the park entrance. *Tall Timbers Research Station:* Continue north 10.4 miles on Meridian Road to County Road 12. Turn right and drive east 3.3 miles to the entrance. The research station may also be reached from Thomasville Road. From Maclay Road, continue north 12 miles on Thomasville Road to CR 12. Turn left and drive west 2.6 miles to the entrance. *Lake Jackson Mounds Archaeological State Park:* From I-10, exit at U.S. Highway 27 (exit 199). Drive north 2 miles to Crowder Road. Turn right and drive east 1 mile to Indian Mounds Road. Turn right and drive south 0.4 mile to the park entrance. *Faulk Drive Landing:* Return to US 27, turn right, and drive north 1 mile to Faulk Drive. Turn right and drive east 1.4 miles to the end of the road. *J. Lee Vause Park:* Return to US 27, turn right, and drive north 1.8 miles to Old Bainbridge Road (County Road 0361). Turn right and drive north 0.2 mile to the park entrance. *Thomas P. Smith Water Reclamation Facility:* From I-10, exit at Capital Circle Southwest (exit 196). Drive south 7.7 miles to Springhill Road (County Road 373). Turn right and park at the office located just south of this intersection. *Southeast Farm:* Return to Capital Circle, turn right, and drive east 5.6 miles to Tram Road. Turn right and drive east 2.5 miles to the entrance. From I-10, exit at Capital Circle Southeast (CR 263, exit 203). Drive south 8.8 miles to Tram Road. Turn left and proceed as above.

The Birding

The Red Hills, an area characterized by fertile, red clay soil and rolling hills, is located north of Tallahassee and extends into southern Georgia. Prior to colonial times, longleaf pinelands with an open wire grass understory dominated the landscape. This region was once part of a vast upland pine forest that stretched from Virginia to Texas. As the area was settled, the forests were cleared and planted in cotton and corn. While most of these distinct pinelands have disappeared from the region, several patches of quality habitat in and around Tallahassee have survived and are accessible to the public. The Red Hills is also the only location within the state where White-breasted Nuthatch can be reliably found.

Maclay Gardens State Park showcases magnificent floral gardens alongside scenic Lake Hall. Woodlands around adjacent Lake Overstreet are attractive to resident, migrant, and wintering land birds. Trails begin at a parking area 1 mile from the entrance, just beyond the gardens. A 3-mile trail encircles Lake Overstreet, the only lake in the area with a completely undeveloped shoreline. Watch along the lakeshore for wading birds, including Purple Gallinule during summer. Scan the lake for waterfowl in winter. A 0.5-mile trail connects the lake trail to a 1.5-mile trail through upland habitat. Look for White-breasted Nuthatch and other resident species in this mixed pine-hardwood forest. Mississippi Kite, which breeds nearby, can be seen overhead during spring and summer. The Lake Overstreet trail system can also be accessed from Meridian Road. The trailhead is across from **Elinor Klapp-Phipps Park.** Within this city park are over 17 miles of multiuse trails extending to the eastern shore of Lake Jackson. White-breasted Nuthatch is here year-round. Breeding species include Kentucky Warbler and Yellow-breasted Chat. Hermit Thrush, Orange-crowned Warbler, and occasionally Dark-eyed Junco can be found here during winter.

Tall Timbers Research Station is a private institute whose mission is to study and preserve natural communities in the Red Hills region. Its 4,000 acres are composed of hardwood swamps, as well as pine sandhills and flatwoods altered by agricultural practices. These "old field" pinelands contain a variety of pine species with an understory dominated by hardwood shrubs. The Stevenson Memorial Trail, honoring Florida ornithologist Henry M. Stevenson, winds through this forest. The 0.5-mile trail begins behind the research buildings and ends at a unique bird-blind cottage near Gannet Pond. Look for House Finch around the research buildings. Year-round residents to watch and listen for along the trail include Great Horned Owl, Red-headed, Downy, Hairy, and Pileated Woodpecker, Northern Flicker, White-breasted and Brown-headed Nuthatch, Eastern Bluebird, Eastern Towhee, and Bachman's and Field Sparrow. Adjacent fields harbor Wild Turkey, Northern Bobwhite, and wintering sparrows including Chipping, Song, and White-throated. Scan for Wood Duck on Gannet Pond and wintering Swamp Sparrow around its edges. Summer breeders on the property include Yellow-billed Cuckoo, Eastern Wood-Pewee, Acadian Flycatcher, Purple Martin (in gourds near the trailhead), Wood Thrush, Yellow-throated Vireo, Prothonotary, Kentucky and Hooded Warbler, Yellow-breasted Chat, Blue Grosbeak, Indigo Bunting, and Orchard Oriole.

Lake Jackson is one of several large lakes in the Tallahassee area. Easiest access is from the western side of the lake. One such access point is Crowder Landing, at the end of Crowder Road, 0.1 mile east of the entrance road to **Lake Jackson Mounds Archaeological State Park.** Scan the lake in winter for a variety of waterfowl, including Canada

Goose. A nature trail in the state park circles through a ravine forest that attracts migrant and wintering land birds. Brown Creeper, Winter Wren, and Golden-crowned Kinglet have all been recorded along this trail in winter. **J. Lee Vause Park** and **Faulk Drive Landing** also provide access to the western side of the lake. At Vause Park a trail at the end of the 0.4-mile park road leads to a boardwalk with an overlook along the lake. Faulk Drive Landing is more rustic. Drive to the unpaved boat landing at the end of the road and check surrounding brushy areas for wintering sparrows. Other species recorded here in winter include Hudsonian Godwit, Short-eared Owl, and Vermilion and Ash-throated Flycatcher. A sinkhole in the center of the lake may open on occasion, causing the lake to drain and shifting the shoreline dramatically.

Two sewage-treatment facilities located south of downtown Tallahassee attract a variety of waterfowl, shorebirds, sparrows, and other species. At **Thomas P. Smith Water Reclamation Facility,** holding ponds attract an assortment of wintering ducks and migrant shorebirds. Canada Goose is resident. Rare waterfowl recorded here include Red-throated Loon, Eared Grebe, Snow Goose, Tundra Swan, Surf Scoter, and Long-tailed Duck. Unexpected shorebirds have included American Avocet, Hudsonian Godwit, Baird's and Buff-breasted Sandpiper, Ruff, and Wilson's and Red-necked Phalarope. American Pipit is often seen in winter around the periphery of holding ponds. Eastern Meadowlark is found year-round in surrounding spray fields. Vesper and Savannah Sparrow winter in these fields. A Lapland Longspur was found here in October 2002. Check in at the office before entering the facility. Should the facility be closed, several of the holding ponds may be viewed from CR 263. **Southeast Farm,** on Tram Road, also has holding ponds and spray fields that may attract similar species. Recent rarities recorded here include Ross's Goose, Long-tailed Duck, Hudsonian Godwit, and Thayer's Gull. Western Kingbird and Scissor-tailed Flycatcher are found on occasion in spring and fall. During spring and summer, large numbers of Swallow-tailed and Mississippi Kite can be seen over the spray fields, hawking for dragonflies. Check in at the office and stay on paved roads.

Hummingbird feeders in residential areas of the Panhandle, especially in Tallahassee and Pensacola, have in recent winters attracted a wide variety of vagrant hummingbirds, including Buff-bellied, Black-chinned, Anna's, Calliope, Broad-tailed, Rufous, and Allen's. Certified hummingbird banders are often invited to visit these residential feeders, helping to identify difficult-to-distinguish immature and female birds. Many feeder owners report their sightings to local birding hot lines and welcome visitors. Always follow instructions provided by hot lines when visiting these residential feeders and respect the privacy of residents.

General information: Maclay Gardens and Lake Jackson Mounds Archaeological State Parks (entrance fees) are open daily from 8:00 A.M. until sunset. Restrooms are located in picnic areas. Tall Timbers Research Station is open Monday through Friday from 8:30 A.M. to 4:30 P.M. Check in at the research building before hiking the trail. Restrooms are located in the research building. Elinor Klapp-Phipps and J. Lee Vause Parks (no entrance fees) are open daily from sunrise to sunset. Restrooms are located throughout the parks. Thomas P. Smith Water Reclamation Facility and Southeast Farm are open only on weekdays from 8:00 A.M. to 5:00 P.M.

DeLorme grid: Page 34, D-2; page 50, B-2.

Hazards: Keep a safe distance from alligators. Venomous snakes are present but rarely encoun-

tered. Mosquitoes are present, especially in summer.

Nearest food, gas, lodging: In Tallahassee.

Camping: Private campgrounds are located in Tallahassee.

For more information: *Maclay Gardens State Park,* 3540 Thomasville Rd., Tallahassee, FL 32309; (850) 487-4556; www.floridastateparks .org/maclaygardens. E*linor Klapp-Phipps Park,* c/o Northwest Florida Water Management District, Division of Land Management and Acquisition, 81 Water Management Dr., Havana, FL 32333; (850) 539-5999. *Tall Timbers Research Station,* 13093 Henry Beadel Dr., Tallahassee, FL 32312; (850) 893-4153; www.talltimbers.org. *Lake Jackson Mounds Archaeological State Park,* 3600 Indian Mounds Rd., Tallahassee, FL 32303; (850) 922-6007; www.floridastateparks.org/lakejackson mounds. *J. Lee Vause Park,* 6024 Old Bainbridge Rd., Tallahassee, FL 32303; (850) 921-4198. *Thomas P. Smith Water Reclamation Facility, Southeast Farm,* c/o Tallahassee Water Utility, 300 S. Adams St., B-26, Tallahassee, FL 32304; (850) 891-1305; www.talgov.com/you/water/ wastewater.cfm.

50 Apalachicola National Forest

Habitats: Sandhills, pine flatwoods, hardwood hammock, pitcher plant savannahs, freshwater marsh, cypress swamp, hardwood swamp, salt marsh.

Specialty birds: *Resident:* Bald Eagle, Clapper Rail, Limpkin, Red-cockaded Woodpecker, Brown-headed Nuthatch, Bachman's Sparrow, Seaside Sparrow. *Summer:* Least Bittern, Wood Stork, Swallow-tailed Kite, Mississippi Kite, Purple Gallinule, Chuck-will's-widow, Acadian Flycatcher, Yellow-throated Vireo, Wood Thrush, Prothonotary Warbler, Swainson's Warbler, Kentucky Warbler, Hooded Warbler, Yellow-breasted Chat, Summer Tanager, Blue Grosbeak, Orchard Oriole. *Winter:* Yellow Rail, American Woodcock, Short-eared Owl, Whip-poor-will, Winter Wren, Golden-crowned Kinglet, Henslow's Sparrow, Le Conte's Sparrow, Nelson's Sharp-tailed Sparrow, Rusty Blackbird, Purple Finch, Pine Siskin. *Migrant:* Painted Bunting.

Best times to bird: October through April.

Directions: *East side of Apalachicola National Forest:* From I-10 in Tallahassee, exit at Capital Circle Southwest (exit 196). Drive south, then east 9.8 miles to State Road 61/U.S. Highway 319. Turn right and drive south 2.2 miles to US 319. Bear right and drive south 3.5 miles to Leon Sinks Geological Area. *West side of Apalachicola National Forest:* From I-10 south of Quincy, exit at CR 267 (exit 181). Drive south 12.2 miles to State Road 20. Turn right and drive west 6.8 miles to State Road 65. Turn left and drive south 30 miles to State Road 379 in the town of Sumatra. From US 98 in Eastpoint, drive north 25 miles on SR 65 to SR 379 in Sumatra.

The Birding

With 569,596 acres, **Apalachicola National Forest** is the largest of Florida's three national forests. The world's largest population of the endangered Red-cockaded Wood-pecker can be found here. The forest is divided into two districts: Wakulla, near Tallahassee, and Apalachicola, bordering the Apalachicola River. Wakulla District headquarters is located off CR 319 in Crawfordville, while headquarters for Apalachicola District is on SR 20 in Bristol, near the intersection with State Road 12. Maps and other information are available at both offices. Begin your tour of Wakulla District at **Leon Sinks Geological Area.** This part of the forest is located on a karst plain, where rain and groundwater have slowly dissolved the underlying limestone bedrock to create a landscape of sinkholes, underwater caverns, and natural bridges. Two trails provide access. The 3-mile Sinkhole Trail passes by several limestone formations and through surrounding sandhills and hardwood forest. Watch for Wild Turkey, Carolina Chickadee, and Brown-headed Nuthatch in the pinelands. Check hardwood forest surrounding sinkholes for migrant and wintering land birds. The 2.3-mile Gumswamp Trail loops through a tupelo swamp. Listen for Barred Owl year-round and look for Prothonotary Warbler in summer. Fox Sparrow has been reported from this trail in winter.

To reach Red-cockaded Woodpecker nesting areas around Lost Creek, drive south 3 miles on CR 319 to CR 267. Turn right and drive northwest 4.4 miles to Forest Road 309 (unpaved), near the Leon County line. Turn left and drive west 4.8 miles to Forest Road 350. Stop at areas of hardwood swamp along this road to look and listen for Barred Owl. Check these areas in summer for Yellow-billed Cuckoo, Acadian and Great Crested Flycatcher, Northern Parula, and Prothonotary, Swainson's, Kentucky, and Hooded Warbler. Watch overhead for Swallow-tailed Kite. Turn left on FR 350 and drive south 4.6 miles to Forest Road 352. Red-cockaded Woodpecker nest trees, marked with white rings, can be found all along FR 350. Dawn and dusk are the most likely times to see the woodpeckers near their nest cavities. Brown-headed Nuthatch and Bachman's Sparrow are also resident in these longleaf pine sandhills, though the sparrow is most likely seen in spring and early summer singing from an understory perch. Swainson's Warbler and other hardwood swamp breeders can be found in summer near a narrow bridge 0.2 mile from the intersection with FR 352. Turn right and drive north 5.5 miles on FR 352 to return to FR 309. Many Red-cockaded Woodpecker nest trees are located on FR 352. Other species to watch for along this road include Wild Turkey, Red-headed, Hairy, and Pileated Woodpecker, and Yellow-throated and Pine Warbler. Search in summer for Chuck-will's-widow, Eastern Wood-Pewee, and Summer Tanager. Turn right and drive east 0.6 mile on FR 309 to a small bridge, yet another spot to check in summer for hardwood swamp breeders. Watch overhead for Swallow-tailed Kite during spring and summer. Continue east 0.6 mile to return to the intersection with FR 350. To return to Tallahassee, continue east on FR 309 to CR 267.

Begin your exploration of the western side of the national forest at the intersection of SR 65 and SR 379 in the tiny town of Sumatra. SR 379, also known as **Apalachee Savannah Scenic Byway,** passes through longleaf pine flatwoods, pitcher plant savannahs, and cypress and titi swamps. Drive north 5 miles to a small bridge that marks an area of wet savannah. Sedge Wren and Henslow's Sparrow winter here and in similar habitat throughout this part of the forest. Le Conte's Sparrow and Yellow Rail also winter here, though the rail is notoriously difficult to find. Swallow-tailed and Mississippi Kite may be spotted hunting over these open areas during summer. Watch for Northern Harrier and Short-eared Owl (rare) in winter. Rubber boots are necessary to explore this area, though take care not to trample on sensitive plant life when walking through this habitat. A few Red-cockaded Woodpecker nest trees can be found in longleaf pine flatwoods along the stretch of road before the bridge. Continue north 0.7 mile to Forest Road 123 (unpaved). Turn right and drive east, then north 3 miles to Forest Road 180. Turn left and drive west 2.6 miles to return to SR 379. Red-cockaded Woodpecker nest clusters are found all along these forest roads. Watch for Brown-headed Nuthatch, Eastern Bluebird, Bachman's Sparrow, and other pineland species in this longleaf pine/wire grass habitat. Turn right on SR 379 and continue north 0.7 mile to Forest Road 115 (unpaved). Turn left and drive west 2.5 miles to an area of hardwood swamp. Check stream crossings in spring and summer for Acadian Flycatcher and Hooded Warbler. Continue west 1 mile to White Oak Landing.

Red-cockaded Woodpecker. PHOTO: TREY MITCHELL

Search here in summer for Swallow-tailed and Mississippi Kite, Yellow-billed Cuckoo, and Prothonotary Warbler.

Return to SR 65, turn right, and drive south 2.5 miles to Wright Lake Road (Forest Road 101). Turn right and drive west 1.7 miles to **Wright Lake Recreation Area.** Look for Red-cockaded Woodpecker nest trees along this road. Two trails begin at the lake. A 0.3-mile trail circles the lake, while a 4.3-mile trail winds through surrounding pinelands. Return to SR 65, turn right, and drive south 2 miles to Brickyard Road (Forest Road 129). Turn right and drive west 2 miles to Forest Road 129B. More Red-cockaded Woodpecker nest trees are along FR 129. Turn left on FR 129B and drive south 1 mile to **Ft. Gadsden Historical Site,** on the banks of the Apalachicola River. A small museum interprets the history of the site, a British fort during the War of 1812, and a Confederate fort during the Civil War. The Wiregrass Gentian Trail passes through remains of the fort and adjacent pine forest. Prothonotary Warbler nests in cypress trees along the river. Watch over the river in spring and summer for Swallow-tailed and Mississippi Kite. Return to SR 65, turn right, and drive south, then east 12 miles to Sand Beach Road (unpaved). Turn right and drive south 2.7 miles to Sand Beach Recreation Area, in 82,000-acre **Apalachicola River Wildlife and Environmental Area.** An observation tower overlooks Apalachicola Bay. Scan the bay in winter for loons, grebes, and ducks. Clapper Rail and Seaside Sparrow breed in adjacent salt marsh. Watch year-round for Bald Eagle, which nests nearby. Swallow-tailed and Mississippi Kite are possible here in spring and summer. A hiking trail begins at the boardwalk and circles through surrounding cabbage palm hammock. Return to SR 65, turn right, and continue east, then south 8.5 miles to US 98 and the Gulf of Mexico. This last stretch of SR 65 passes through **Tate's Hell State Forest,** a 202,414-acre wetland area named for Cebe Tate, a local farmer. Local legend has it that in the late 1800s, he chased a panther that was killing his livestock into the swamp. Tate became lost in the mosquito-infested wetland for several days and was bitten by a snake. Found in a clearing near Carrabelle, he was said to murmur before dying, "My name's Tate, and I've just been through Hell!" A boat ramp at Cash Creek, 4 miles south of Sand Beach Road on SR 65, provides access to the swamp.

General information: Apalachicola National Forest (no entrance fee) is open 24 hours a day. Leon Sinks Geological Area and Ft. Gadsden Historical Site (entrance fees) are open daily from 8:00 A.M. to 8:00 P.M. Restrooms are located at trailheads. Wright Lake Recreation Area (entrance fee) is open April through October from 8:00 A.M. to 8:00 P.M. daily and November through March from 8:00 A.M. to 6:00 P.M. daily. Restrooms are located in the campground. Apalachicola River Wildlife and Environmental Area and Tate's Hell State Forest (no entrance fees) are open daily from sunrise to sunset. No restrooms are available. Seasonal hunting is permitted in designated areas within Apalachicola National Forest, Apalachicola River Wildlife and Environmental Area, and Tate's Hell State Forest. Refer to regulations-summary brochures, updated annually and available at check stations, for hunt dates and locations. Wear blaze orange if hiking during hunting season.

DeLorme grid: Page 48, D-2; page 50, B-1; page 60, A-2.

Hazards: Keep a safe distance from alligators. Bears and venomous snakes are present but rarely encountered. Mosquitoes are present, especially during summer in Apalachicola River Wildlife and Environmental Area and Tate's Hell State Forest.

Nearest food, gas, lodging: In Tallahassee, Quincy, and Apalachicola.

Camping: National forest campgrounds are at Wright Lake, Camel Lake, Whitehead, Mack, and Hickory Recreation Areas.

For more information: *Apalachicola National Forest, Wakulla Ranger District (east side),* 57 Taff Dr., Crawfordville, FL 32327; (850) 926–3561. *Apalachicola Ranger District (west side),* P.O. Box 579, Bristol, FL 32321; (850) 643–2282; www.fs .fed.us/r8/florida/recreation/index_apa.shtml. *Apalachicola River Wildlife and Environmental Area,* c/o Florida Fish and Wildlife Conservation Commission, 620 S. Meridian St., Tallahassee, FL 32399; (800) 955–8771; www.myfwc.com/ recreation/apalachicola_river. *Tate's Hell State Forest,* c/o Florida Division of Forestry, 290 Airport Rd., Carrabelle, FL 32322; (850) 697–3734; www.fl-dof.com/state_forests/tates_hell.html.

51 Apalachicola Area

Habitats: Sandy beach, salt marsh, hardwood hammock, sand pine scrub, pine flatwoods.

Specialty birds: *Resident:* Reddish Egret, Bald Eagle, Clapper Rail, King Rail, Snowy Plover, American Oystercatcher, Brown-headed Nuthatch, Bachman's Sparrow, Seaside Sparrow. *Summer:* Magnificent Frigatebird, Least Bittern, Wood Stork, Swallow-tailed Kite, Mississippi Kite, Purple Gallinule, Wilson's Plover, Gull-billed Tern, Least Tern, Chuck-will's-widow, Gray Kingbird, Prothonotary Warbler, Hooded Warbler, Yellow-breasted Chat, Summer Tanager, Blue Grosbeak, Orchard Oriole. *Winter:* Snow Goose, Greater Scaup, Black Scoter, Common Goldeneye, Red-throated Loon, Virginia Rail, Piping Plover, American Woodcock, Western Kingbird, Scissor-tailed Flycatcher, Nelson's Sharp-tailed Sparrow, Brewer's Blackbird. *Migrant:* Peregrine Falcon, Black Tern, Chestnut-sided Warbler, Bay-breasted Warbler, Kentucky Warbler, Scarlet Tanager, Rose-breasted Grosbeak, Painted Bunting, Dickcissel.

Best times to bird: September through May.

Directions: *St. George Island State Park:* From Apalachicola, drive east 5.8 miles on US 98 to County Road 300. Turn right and drive south 4.5 miles, crossing the bridge to St. George Island. Turn left on Gulf Beach Drive and drive east 4.2 miles to the park entrance. *St. Joseph Peninsula State Park:* From

Apalachicola, drive west 7.5 miles on US 98 to County Road 30A. Bear left and drive west 12.4 miles to County Road 30E. Turn left and drive south, then west 8.7 miles to the park entrance. *St. Joseph Bay State Buffer Preserve:* Return to CR 30A. Turn right and drive north 2 miles to the main visitor access parking area. From US 98 east of Port St. Joe, turn right on CR 30A. Drive south 4.4 miles to the visitor access parking area. The Deal Tract visitor access parking area is on CR 30E, 4 miles from the intersection with CR 30A.

The Birding

St. George Island is a long, narrow barrier island located 4 miles offshore, separating Apalachicola Bay from the Gulf of Mexico. At the eastern end of the island is 1,982-acre **St. George Island State Park.** In summer check wires along the road leading to the park for Gray Kingbird. Watch these wires in winter for Western Kingbird and Scissor-tailed Flycatcher. From the entrance station, the main park road heads east, following the beach and dunes for 8 miles. Parking areas along this road provide access to the beach, where shorebirds, gulls, and terns may be found year-round. Scan offshore in winter for Northern Gannet, scoters, and other sea ducks. Florida's first Snowy Owl was discovered on the dunes here in December 1999. Other vagrants reported within the park in recent years include Groove-billed Ani, Lesser Nighthawk, Ash-throated Flycatcher, Streaked Fly-catcher (identification not confirmed), Bewick's Wren, and Shiny Cowbird. Most of these rarities have been found in or around the park's campgrounds. To reach the youth camp area, turn left 0.7 mile east of the entrance station. Drive north 0.3 mile to the parking area. The oak hammock around the youth camp attracts trans-Gulf migrants during spring and fall. Impressive fallouts are possible here after the passage of fronts. An unmarked trail begins at the restrooms and leads to Rattlesnake Cove. Check pinelands here for Brown-headed Nuthatch, Pine Warbler, Eastern Towhee, and other residents. Scan the cove for wintering loons, grebes, and sea ducks including Bufflehead and Common Goldeneye. A dirt road leads from the parking area to a boat ramp at East Cove. American Oystercatcher nests on Goose Island, visible just offshore. Along with other shorebirds, the oystercatchers can be seen feeding on oyster bars exposed at low tide. Return to the main park road, turn left, and drive east 1.6 miles to the first beach parking area. Across from the parking area, a boardwalk leads to East Slough, an arm of East Cove. Continue east 2 miles to the camp-ground entrance. Turn left and drive 0.7 mile to the far end of the campground. A 2.5-mile trail leads through pinelands and coastal scrub to Gap Point. Look along the way for resident pineland species and migrant land birds. At Gap Point scan East Cove and St. George Sound for loons, grebes, and ducks. Return to the main park road and turn left. Drive east 0.2 mile to another beach parking area. A boardwalk across from this parking area leads to St. George Sound. Continue east 3 miles to the last beach parking area, beyond which is a gate at the end of the road. A trail leading to the eastern tip of the island begins here. Snowy Plover and, occasionally, Wilson's Plover nest at this end of the park. Piping Plover and other shorebirds, gulls, and terns can be found along the beach during winter.

Located off the coast of Port St. Joe, the narrow St. Joseph Peninsula extends north from the mainland for 20 miles, separating St. Joseph Bay from the Gulf of Mexico. **St. Joseph Bay State Buffer Preserve** protects habitat at the elbow of the peninsula (Deal Tract) as well as the peninsula's connection with the mainland. Multiuse trails provide access to sand pine scrub, pine flatwood, and salt marsh communities. At the peninsula's northern end is **T. H. Stone Memorial St. Joseph Peninsula State Park.** From the entrance, drive north 0.8 mile to a parking area at Eagle Harbor. Boardwalks here provide access to Gulf-side beaches. In winter scan the harbor for Common Loon, Horned Grebe, Bufflehead, Common Goldeneye, and other sea ducks. Because the peninsula is most narrow here, this is an excellent location for fall hawk-watching. Raptors following the coast from the east move north up the peninsula before crossing St. Joseph's Bay and returning to the mainland. From late September through October, large numbers of Sharp-shinned, Cooper's, and Broad-winged Hawks and American Kestrels are observed daily, with smaller numbers of Merlins, Peregrine Falcons, and other raptors seen during the period. Monarch butterflies also stage here in large numbers during their southbound migration. A Lark Bunting was found at the north end of the parking area in December 2000. Continue north 0.7 mile to a tidal creek. Check salt marsh surrounding the creek for Clapper Rail and Seaside Sparrow. Nelson's Sharp-tailed Sparrow can be found here in winter. In another 0.2 mile, turn right into the Bayview Picnic Area. Check surrounding trees during spring for trans-Gulf migrants. Impressive fallouts can occur here and around the campground on the opposite side of the road. Search surrounding pine flatwoods for Brown-headed Nuthatch and other pineland residents. The St. Joseph Bay Trail begins at the picnic area and leads north along the bay shoreline before returning to the park road. The northernmost 7 miles of the peninsula is a designated wilderness preserve. To access the preserve, park at Bayview Picnic Area then hike 0.8 mile to the end of the park road. A service road leads north into the preserve. You may also hike this area along the beach. Snowy and Wilson's Plover nest at the northern end of the peninsula and Piping Plover winters there.

General information: St. George Island and St. Joseph Peninsula State Parks (entrance fees) are open daily from 8:00 A.M. until sunset. Restrooms are located in picnic areas. St. Joseph Bay State Buffer Preserve (no entrance fee) is open daily from sunrise to sunset. No restrooms are available.

DeLorme grid: Page 59, B-2; page 61, C-1.

Hazards: Keep a safe distance from alligators. Cottonmouths are common on barrier islands. Mosquitoes are common in summer.

Nearest food, gas, lodging: In Apalachicola and Port St. Joe.

Camping: St. George Island State Park: 60 sites. St. Joseph Peninsula State Park: 119 sites.

For more information: *St. George Island State Park,* East Gulf Beach Drive, St. George Island, FL 32328; (904) 927-2111; www.floridastateparks.org/stgeorgeisland. *St. Joseph Peninsula State Park,* 8899 Cape San Blas Rd., Port St. Joe, FL 32456; (850) 227-1327; www.floridastateparks.org/stjoseph. *St. Joseph Bay State Buffer Preserve,* c/o Apalachicola National Estuarine Research Reserve, 350 Carroll St., Eastpoint, FL 32328. (850) 670-4783. www.dep.state.fl.us/coastal/sites/apalachicola/stjoseph_buffer.htm.

52 Marianna Area

Habitats: Sandhills, slope forest, hardwood hammock, hardwood swamp, freshwater lake.

Specialty birds: *Resident:* Bald Eagle, Limpkin, Brown-headed Nuthatch, Bachman's Sparrow.

Summer: Least Bittern, Swallow-tailed Kite, Mississippi Kite, Purple Gallinule, Chuck-will's-widow, Acadian Flycatcher, Yellow-throated Vireo, Wood Thrush, Prothonotary Warbler, Swainson's Warbler,

Louisiana Waterthrush, Kentucky Warbler, Hooded Warbler, Yellow-breasted Chat, Summer Tanager, Blue Grosbeak, Orchard Oriole. *Winter:* Snow Goose, Canvasback, Red-breasted Nuthatch, Brown Creeper, Winter Wren, Golden-crowned Kinglet, Fox Sparrow, Dark-eyed Junco, Rusty Blackbird, Purple Finch. *Migrant:* Blue-winged Warbler, Golden-winged Warbler, Chestnut-sided Warbler, Blackburnian Warbler, Scarlet Tanager, Rose-breasted Grosbeak.

Best times to bird: All year.

Directions: *Torreya State Park:* From I-10 west of Quincy, exit at County Road 270A (exit 166). Drive north 1.2 miles to County Road 269. Turn left and drive west, then south 3.7 miles (over I-10) to County Road 270. Turn right and drive west, then south 5.7 miles to Torreya Park Road (County Road 271). Turn right and drive west 3 miles to the park entrance. *Apalachicola Bluffs and Ravines Preserve:* Backtrack 1 mile on CR 271 to CR 270. Turn right and drive south, then east 7.6 miles to SR 12. Turn right and drive south 2.5 miles to the entrance. *Three Rivers State Park:* From I-10 south of Sneads, exit at County Road 286 (exit 158). Drive north 5.4 miles to U.S. Highway 90. Turn left and drive west 0.4 mile to CR 271. Turn right and drive north 2 miles to the park entrance. *Sneads Park:* Return to US 90, turn left, and drive east 1.4 miles to Legion Road. Turn left and drive north 1.5 miles to the park entrance. *Florida Caverns State Park:* From I-10 westbound south of Marianna, exit at State Road 71 (exit 142). Drive north 2 miles to US 90. Turn left and drive west 3 miles to County Road 167. Turn right and drive north 2.6 miles to the park entrance. From I-10 eastbound south of Marianna, exit at CR 267 (exit 136). Drive north 2.7 miles to US 90. Turn right and drive east 1.5 miles to CR 167. Turn left and proceed as above.

The Birding

Torreya State Park offers some of the most scenic vistas in all of Florida, a state not generally revered for its awe-inspiring topography. Many of the plants found here are more typical of the southern Appalachians. The 12,000-acre park, located on bluffs overlooking the Apalachicola River, is named for a species of Torreya tree that only grows on bluffs on the river's eastern side. A specimen of this extremely endangered evergreen may be viewed near Gregory House; a plantation estate built in 1849 and originally located across the river from the park. The house was dismantled, moved, and restored in 1935 and is now located at the end of the main park road, 1.3 miles from the entrance. The park office, where maps and checklists are available, is located in the house. Beyond the house and 150 feet below, is the Apalachicola River. Watch from this vantage point for Swallow-tailed and Mississippi Kite soaring over the river during spring and summer. Bald Eagle may be seen here year-round. The Apalachicola River Bluffs Trail begins behind the house and winds down the bluff, past the remains of Confederate gun pits to the river below, then back up again to the opposite side of the house. Search along this trail in summer for breeding species including Broad-winged Hawk, Yellow-throated Vireo, Wood Thrush, Northern Parula, Louisiana Waterthrush, and Swainson's, Hooded, and Kentucky Warbler. Winter Wren, Golden-crowned Kinglet, Hermit Thrush, Dark-eyed Junco, and Purple Finch are all possible here during winter. At the base of the bluff, the trail becomes part of a 7-mile trail encircling the perimeter of the park. You can also access this trail where it intersects the park entrance road. Along the stretch of trail near the entrance, search year-round for pineland species including Wild Turkey, Northern Bobwhite, Red-headed Woodpecker, Brown-headed Nuthatch, Eastern Bluebird, Pine Warbler, Eastern Towhee, and Bachman's Sparrow. The sparrow is difficult to find, except in spring and early summer, when it sings. Chuck-will's-widow, Eastern Wood-Pewee, and Summer Tanager breed in this habitat during summer. Watch for Brown Creeper and Golden-crowned Kinglet during winter. Pinelands with

Canada Goose, Snow Geese. PHOTO: TREY MITCHELL

similar species are around the park's campground. From the park entrance, drive 0.8 mile, turn left, and drive 0.3 mile to the campground. The Weeping Ridge Trail begins here and leads to a steep ravine. **Apalachicola Bluffs and Ravines Preserve,** located south of Torreya State Park, protects 6,294 acres of sandhills and slope forest along the river. A local resident, so awestruck by the natural beauty of this site, published his theory that this must be the original home of Adam and Eve. A 3.8-mile trail now known as the Garden of Eden Trail provides access. The bird list here is similar to that of Torreya State Park.

The area along the Florida-Georgia border where the Chatahoochee and Flint Rivers meet to form the Apalachicola River was once a vast swamp. When the Jim Woodruff Dam was constructed in 1956, the swamp was flooded and Lake Seminole was born. The lake now attracts large numbers of wintering waterfowl. **Three Rivers State Park** is located along 2 miles of shoreline on the lake's western side. Sandhills and hardwood hammock occupy much of the park's 682 acres. From the entrance, drive east 1.4 miles to a picnic area overlooking the lake. Check pinelands along the entrance road for Northern Bobwhite, Red-headed and Hairy Woodpecker, Eastern Bluebird, Pine Warbler, and other resident species. Also watch for eastern fox squirrels in this area. From the picnic area, walk down the somewhat steep slope to the lake (a stairway is available). Large rafts of wintering waterfowl are usually visible in the distance. Since the Florida border bisects the north-south axis of the lake, some of the flocks may be on the Georgia side of the border. Search through the hundreds or even thousands of American Coot for Pied-billed Grebe, Canada Goose, Canvasback (often abundant), Ring-necked Duck, Lesser Scaup, and Ruddy Duck. Occasionally in the mix are Horned Grebe, Redhead, Bufflehead, and Hooded Merganser. Rarities include Tundra Swan and Snow Goose. Marshy areas along the shore may harbor puddle ducks such as American Wigeon, Blue-winged Teal, and Northern Shoveler. Least Bittern and Purple Gallinule can be found during summer in areas of emergent vegetation. Bald Eagle nests in the park and is often seen soaring over the lake. Two trails provide access to woodland areas of the park. The Half Dry Creek Trail begins at the south side of the picnic area and loops through hardwood hammock. Look for Barred Owl, Pileated Woodpecker, Carolina Chickadee, Tufted Titmouse, and other resident species. Search during summer for Yellow-billed Cuckoo, Northern Parula, Louisiana Waterthrush, and Kentucky and Hooded Warbler. Species possible in winter include Brown Creeper, Winter Wren, Golden-crowned Kinglet, and Dark-eyed Junco. The Lakeland Trail begins at the park's campground and winds along the lakeshore. A fishing pier near the campground provides opportunities to scan northern sections of the lake. **Sneads Park,** near Jim Woodruff Dam, provides access to the southern shore of the lake. Rafts of wintering waterfowl often concentrate near the shore here.

For most visitors, the main attraction at **Florida Caverns State Park** is the limestone cavern, with formations rivaling those at Carlsbad, Mammoth Cave, and other well-known locations. Surrounding the cavern are 1,300 acres of upland hardwood forest and swamp that are attractive to a wide assortment of birds throughout the year. From the entrance station, drive west 1 mile on the main park road (Hickory Drive) to the cavern and visitor center parking area. A series of trails looping through the Chipola River floodplain begins at the west end of the parking area. Look year-round for Barred Owl, Pileated Woodpecker, Carolina Chickadee, Tufted Titmouse, and Carolina Wren. On the Tunnel Cave and Floodplain Bluff sections of the trail, search in summer for Broad-winged Hawk, Yellow-billed Cuckoo, Acadian Flycatcher, Yellow-throated Vireo, Wood Thrush, Swainson's, Kentucky, and Hooded Warbler, and other breeding species. Watch overhead for Swallow-tailed and Mississippi Kite, which both breed in the park. During winter look for Yellow-bellied Sapsucker, Blue-headed Vireo, Ruby-crowned and Golden-crowned Kinglet, and Hermit Thrush. Winter Wren is sometimes seen along these trails near fallen trees. In spring and fall this area attracts an excellent variety of migrant land birds. Acadian, Least, Alder, Willow, and Yellow-bellied Flycatchers have all been reported from along the Floodplain Bluff Trail during migration. The Beech Magnolia Trail, which begins behind the visitor center, can also be good for migrants. From the visitor center parking area, backtrack 0.1 mile, bear right, and drive south 0.3 mile to Hickory Shelter Picnic Area. Check surrounding pinelands for Red-headed Woodpecker, Brown-headed Nuthatch, Eastern Bluebird, Pine Warbler, Eastern Towhee, and Bachman's Sparrow. In summer watch for Eastern Wood-Pewee and Summer Tanager. During winter Red-breasted Nuthatch is occasionally seen in the park's pineland habitat. Return to Hickory Drive, turn right, then left onto Blue Hole Drive. Drive north, then west 0.8 mile to Chipola River Sink boat ramp. Where the road turns west, watch in winter for Golden-crowned Kinglet and Rusty Blackbird. Search for Brown Creeper and Winter Wren near the boat ramp. The Chipola River flows underground near this area. Continue west 1 mile to Blue Hole Spring. Brown Creeper, Winter Wren, and Golden-crowned Kinglet can be found in winter in the area along Blue Spring Run. The Upper-Chipola trail system, offering over 6 miles of multiuse trails, begins at a trailhead across from Blue Hole Spring. Flocks of Dark-eyed Junco are sometimes seen in this area during winter. Limpkin and Prothonotary Warbler can be found along the river, though the upper reaches of the river are best accessed by canoe.

General information: Torreya, Three Rivers, and Florida Caverns State Parks (entrance fees) are open daily from 8:00 A.M. until sunset. Restrooms are located in picnic areas. At Torreya, restrooms are also located in Gregory House. Ranger-led tours of Gregory House are available daily. At Florida Caverns, restrooms are also located in the visitor center and at Blue Hole swimming area. Guided cave tours (fee) are available daily except Thanksgiving and Christmas. Apalachicola Bluffs and Ravines Preserve and Sneads Park (no entrance fees) are open daily from sunrise to sunset. No restrooms are available at Apalachicola Bluffs and Ravines Preserve. Restrooms at Sneads Park are located in the picnic area. (*NOTE:* The Apalachicola River is the dividing line here between eastern and central time. Torreya State Park and Apalachicola Bluffs and Ravines Preserve are in the eastern time zone.)

DeLorme grid: Page 32, B-1, C-3, D-3.

Hazards: Keep a safe distance from alligators. Venomous snakes (including copperheads) are present but rarely encountered. Mosquitoes are common in summer. Watch your step on steep bluff trails along the Apalachicola River. At Florida Caverns, caves other than the tour cave are closed to the public. Trails may be flooded in summer.

Nearest food, gas, lodging: In Marianna.

Camping: Torreya State Park: 30 sites. Three Rivers State Park: 30 sites. Florida Caverns State Park: 35 sites.

For more information: *Torreya State Park,* 2576 NW Torreya Park Rd., Bristol, FL 32321; (850) 643-2674; www.floridastateparks.org/torreya. *Apalachicola Bluffs and Ravines Preserve,* c/o The Nature Conservancy, Northwest Florida Program, P.O. Box 393, Bristol, FL 32321; (850) 643-2756; http://nature.org/wherewework/ northamerica/states/florida/preserves/art5521 .html. *Three Rivers State Park,* 7908 Three Rivers Park Rd., Sneads, FL 32460; (850) 482-9006; www.floridastateparks.org/threerivers. *Florida Caverns State Park, 3345 Caverns Rd., Marianna, FL 32446; (850) 482-9598;* www.floridastate parks.org/floridacaverns.

⑤③ Choctawhatchee Bay Area

Habitats: Sandy beach, coastal dunes, estuary, salt marsh, sandhills, pine flatwoods, sand pine scrub, maritime hammock.

Specialty birds: *Resident:* Bald Eagle, Clapper Rail, Snowy Plover, Red-cockaded Woodpecker, Brown-headed Nuthatch, Bachman's Sparrow, Seaside Sparrow. *Summer:* Swallow-tailed Kite, Mississippi Kite, Least Tern, Chuck-will's-widow, Acadian Flycatcher, Gray Kingbird, Prothonotary Warbler, Kentucky Warbler, Hooded Warbler, Yellow-breasted Chat, Summer Tanager, Blue Grosbeak, Orchard Oriole. *Winter:* Reddish Egret, Bald Eagle, Virginia Rail, Piping Plover, Whip-poor-will, Nelson's Sharp-tailed Sparrow. *Migrant:* Peregrine Falcon, Wood Thrush, Scarlet Tanager.

Best times to bird: October through May.

Directions: *Point Washington State Forest:* From US 98 in Santa Rosa Beach, drive south 1.2 miles on County Road 395 to the trailhead parking area. *Grayton Beach State Park:* Continue south 1.8 miles on CR 395 to CR 30A. Turn right and drive west 2 miles to the park entrance. From US 98, drive south 1.6 miles on County Road 283 to CR 30A. Turn left and drive east 0.5 mile to the park entrance. *Topsail Hill Preserve State Park:* Return to US 98. Turn left and drive west 7.2 miles to CR 30A. Turn left and drive south 0.3 mile to the park entrance. *Henderson Beach State Park:* From the intersection of US 98 and County Road 293 in Destin, drive west 1.2 miles on US 98 to the park entrance. *Fred Gannon Rocky Bayou State Park:* Return to CR 293, turn left, and drive north 6.5 miles, crossing the Mid-Bay Bridge (toll) to SR 20. Turn left and drive west 1.4 miles to the park entrance. From I-10 westbound, exit at County Road 285 (exit 70). Drive south 17.4 miles to SR 20. Turn left and drive east 3.5 miles to the park entrance. From I-10 eastbound, exit at State Road 85 (exit 56). Drive south 15.7 miles to

SR 20. Turn left and drive east 4.2 miles to the park entrance. *Eglin Air Force Base Natural Resources Office at Jackson Guard:* Return to SR 85, turn left, and drive north 0.2 mile to the entrance.

The Birding

Santa Rosa Beach is located on a long peninsula separating Choctawhatchee Bay from the Gulf of Mexico. The area is well known for its beautiful white-sand beaches. Sandhills and longleaf pine flatwoods are the predominant upland habitat. A number of coastal dune lakes are scattered throughout the area. These freshwater lakes, formed by water draining from upland areas and nestled between old dunes, are found nowhere else in the United States except along this section of coastline. The area's coastal dunes are home to the endangered Choctawhatchee beach mouse. **Point Washington State Forest** protects 15,131 acres of pinelands, with scattered wet prairie, cypress ponds, and titi swamp. The Eastern Lake Trails provide access to the eastern half of the forest, while the Longleaf Pine Greenway Trail crosses the western half. Both trails begin at a trailhead on CR 395. The Eastern Lake trail system consists of loops of 3, 5, and 10 miles. The 8-mile Longleaf Pine Greenway is part of a longer trail system that when completed will connect the forest with several state parks in the area. Watch for Wild Turkey, Northern Bobwhite, Great Horned Owl, Eastern Towhee, Bachman's Sparrow, and other pineland species. In spring look and listen for sparrows singing in areas with wire grass and saw palmetto understory. Check for migrant and wintering land birds in habitat around stream crossings.

Three coastal dune lakes lie within the boundaries of 2,200-acre **Grayton Beach State Park.** From the entrance station, drive 0.8 mile to a parking area at the end of the road. Check the beach for shorebirds, gulls, and terns, including Snowy Plover year-round, Least Tern in summer, and Bonaparte's Gull during winter. Scan offshore in winter for sea ducks and Northern Gannet. A 1-mile trail begins at the parking area and winds through dunes, coastal scrub, pine flatwoods, and salt marsh, ending at the edge of Western Lake. Search flatwoods for Red-headed Woodpecker, Brown-headed Nuthatch, and other pineland species. Wooded areas provide safe haven for trans-Gulf migrants arriving in spring. Look for Clapper Rail and Seaside Sparrow in salt marsh near the lake and along the park road. Nelson's Sharp-tailed Sparrow winters in this habitat. A 4.2-mile trail begins across from the park entrance and connects with state forest trails.

Topsail Hill Preserve State Park consists of 1,640 acres of longleaf pine forest, sand pine scrub, maritime hammock, and wetland areas. Included are 3.2 miles of white-sand beaches, two large coastal dune lakes, Morris and Campbell Lakes, as well as several small ponds. To access the beach, drive to the parking area beyond the main entrance. A tram shuttles visitors to and from the beach, though you may also hike there using the paved multiuse trail. Look for Snowy Plover and other shorebirds, gulls, and terns, especially where a stream from Morris Lake flows into the Gulf. Trails to the coastal dune lakes begin on Topsail Road. To reach this road from the beach parking area, return to US 98, turn left, and drive west 1.6 miles, then make a U-turn and backtrack east 0.3 mile. Turn right and drive south 0.5 mile to the Morris Lake trailhead. The 2.5-mile trail follows the dune line west through sand pine scrub into longleaf pine flatwoods. Look for Red-headed Woodpecker, Brown-headed Nuthatch, Eastern Bluebird, and other pineland species. Continue south 0.1 mile to the Campbell Lake trailhead. This 5.2-mile trail heads east and includes several short spur trails leading to the lake. The trail also connects with the paved multiuse beach access trail that begins at the park's main entrance. You may also access the beach from the picnic area at the end of Topsail Road, 0.1 mile south of the Campbell Lake trailhead.

Henderson Beach State Park, near the end of the peninsula separating Chocta-whatchee Bay from the Gulf of Mexico, was the first property purchased by the state as part of a land conservation program initiated to protect undeveloped coastline. The 208-acre park includes over a mile of white-sand beach. From the entrance station turn right and drive 0.2 mile to the beach parking area. Check the beach for shorebirds, gulls, and terns. Snowy Plover and Black Skimmer are resident. Least Tern can be found here during summer. Scan offshore in winter for Northern Gannet and sea ducks. A 0.8-mile trail begins at the east end of the parking lot and winds through the dunes. Migrant and wintering land birds can be found in the sparse dune vegetation.

Fred Gannon Rocky Bayou State Park is located on the north side of Chocta-whatchee Bay. The 357-acre park, dominated by sand pine scrub, pine flatwoods, and sandhills, was once an Air Force bombing range. From the entrance station, turn left and drive 0.3 mile to Red Cedar Trail, good for migrant and wintering land birds. Backtrack to the main park road, turn left, and drive 0.3 mile to the trailhead at the east end of the campground. Sand Pine Trail follows man-made Puddin Head Lake, while Rocky Bayou Trail hugs the shore of the bayou. A Brown Creeper was found on this trail in November 2002. Scan Rocky Bayou, an arm of Choctawhatchee Bay, for wintering waterfowl. Four Trumpeter Swans, origin unknown, were discovered on the bayou in December 2002.

Most of the area north and west of Choctawhatchee Bay is part of 464,000-acre **Eglin Air Force Base.** This area was originally Choctawhatchee National Forest but was con-verted to a military installation prior to World War II. Within the base is the world's largest continuous tract of longleaf pine sandhills, home to the fourth-largest population of Red-cockaded Woodpecker, as well as Brown-headed Nuthatch, Bachman's Sparrow, and other pineland species. About 280,000 acres of the base are open for hunting, fishing, and other types of recreation, including birding. An Outdoor Recreation Permit, available at the Nat-ural Resources Office at Jackson Guard, is required to enter the base. Maps, regulations summaries, and suggested birding locations are provided after purchasing the permit and viewing a safety video.

General information: Grayton Beach, Topsail Hill Preserve, Henderson Beach, and Fred Gannon Rocky Bayou State Parks (entrance fees) are open daily from 8:00 A.M. until sun-set. Restrooms are located near parking areas. Point Washington State Forest (entrance fee) is open daily from sunrise to sunset. Restrooms are located at the trailhead parking area. Seasonal hunting is permitted in designated areas. Refer to regulations-summary brochures, updated annually and available at check stations, for hunt dates and locations. Wear blaze orange if hiking during hunting season. Eglin Air Force Base (recreation per-mit) is open daily from two hours before sunrise to sunset. The Natural Resources Office at Jackson Guard is open Monday through Thursday from 7:00 A.M. to 4:30 P.M., Friday from 7:00 A.M. to 6:00 P.M., and Saturday from 7:30 A.M. to 12:30 P.M. Recreation areas are subject to closure for seasonal hunting and military training operations. Updates are available at the Natural Resources Office.

DeLorme grid: Page 28, D-3; page 45, B-2.

Hazards: Keep a safe distance from alligators. Venomous snakes are present but rarely encountered.

Nearest food, gas, lodging: In Destin, Fort Wal-ton Beach, and Niceville.

Camping: Grayton Beach State Park: 37 sites. Topsail Hill Preserve State Park: 156 sites. Henderson Beach State Park: 60 sites. Fred Gannon Rocky Bayou State Park: 42 sites.

For more information: *Point Washington State Forest,* 5865 US 98, Santa Rosa Beach, FL 32459; (850) 231-5800; www.fl-dof.com/state_ forests/point_washington. *Grayton Beach State Park,* 357 Main Park Rd., Santa Rosa Beach, FL 32459; (850) 231-4210; www.floridastateparks .org/graytonbeach. *Topsail Hill Preserve State Park,* 7525 W. 30A, Santa Rosa Beach, FL 32459; (850) 267-0299; www.floridastateparks .org/topsailhill. *Henderson Beach State Park,* 17000 Emerald Coast Pkwy., Destin, FL 32541; (850) 837-7550; www.floridastateparks.org/ hendersonbeach. *Fred Gannon Rocky Bayou State Park,* 4281 SR 20, Niceville, FL 32578; (850) 833-9144; www.floridastateparks.org/ rockybayou. *Eglin Air Force Base Natural Resources Office,* 107 SR 85, Niceville, FL 32578; (850) 882-4164.

 # Pensacola Area

Habitats: Sandy beach, maritime hammock, salt marsh, freshwater marsh, wet prairie, hardwood swamp, pine flatwoods, sandhills, hardwood hammock.

Specialty birds: *Resident:* Clapper Rail, Snowy Plover, Red-cockaded Woodpecker, Brown-headed Nuthatch, Bachman's Sparrow. *Summer:* Magnificent Frigatebird, Least Bittern, Reddish Egret, Swallow-tailed Kite, Mississippi Kite, Gull-billed Tern, Least Tern, Chuck-will's-widow, Acadian Flycatcher, Gray Kingbird, Yellow-throated Vireo, Wood Thrush, Prothonotary Warbler, Swainson's Warbler, Louisiana Waterthrush, Kentucky Warbler, Hooded Warbler, Yellow-breasted Chat, Summer Tanager, Blue Grosbeak, Orchard Oriole. *Winter:* Common Goldeneye, Virginia Rail, Piping Plover, American Woodcock, Red-breasted Nuthatch, Winter Wren, Golden-crowned Kinglet, Le Conte's Sparrow, Dark-eyed Junco, Rusty Blackbird, Brewer's Blackbird. *Migrant:* Black Tern.

Best times to bird: All year.

Directions: *Blackwater River State Park:* From I-10 west of Crestview, exit at County Road 189 (exit 45). Drive north 1 mile to US 90. Turn left and drive west 8.6 miles to Deaton Bridge Road. Turn right and drive north 3.7 miles to the park entrance. *Gulf Islands National Seashore, Naval Live Oaks Area:* From I-10 in Pensacola, exit at Interstate 110 (exit 12). Drive south 6.3 miles to its terminus at US 98. Drive east 7.3 miles on US 98 to the entrance. *Ft. Pickens:* Backtrack west 1.8 miles on US 98 to State Road 399 (toll bridge). Exit right and drive south 2.5 miles to Ft. Pickens Road. Turn right and drive west 3.2 miles to the entrance station. (*NOTE:* In 2004 and 2005 a series of hurricanes and tropical storms severely damaged Ft. Pickens Road. The road is currently open to bicyclists and pedestrians, though it is a 14-mile round-trip from the entrance station to the fort area. The fort is otherwise accessible only by private boat. Check the Gulf Islands National Seashore Web site for road repair updates.)

The Birding

With over 190,000 acres, **Blackwater River State Forest** is the largest state forest in Florida. Most of the forest consists of pine flatwoods and sandhills, with hardwood swamp and hammock found along streams and rivers, including the Blackwater River. **Blackwater River State Park** is at the southern end of the forest. The Blackwater River, one of the most pristine sandy-bottom rivers in the nation, flows through the 590-acre park. The river may be accessed from the day-use parking area 0.3 mile from the entrance or from two parking areas near Deaton Bridge, 0.5 mile south of the park entrance. Several trails provide access to surrounding habitat. The Juniper Lake Trail begins at the park's campground and leads to an oxbow lake. The Chain of Lakes Nature Trail begins at the parking area south of the bridge and winds through hardwood swamp south of the river. Look here for Mississippi Kite, Broad-winged Hawk, Yellow-billed Cuckoo, Wood Thrush, Prothonotary Warbler, and other summer breeders. Red-breasted Nuthatch, Winter Wren, Golden-crowned Kinglet, Dark-eyed Junco, and Brewer's and Rusty Blackbird are possible during winter. The Blackwater River Trail begins north of the bridge and parallels Deaton Bridge Road for 1 mile, leading to a trailhead near the park entrance. The 6.7-mile Juniper Creek Trail starts here and follows the creek north through longleaf pine sandhills and floodplain habitat within the state forest. The trail ends at Red Rock Road. This trailhead also serves as the southern terminus of the 21.5-mile Jackson Red Ground Trail, named for Andrew Jackson, whose army used this trail during the first Seminole War. Both trails are part of the Florida Scenic Trail system.

The Hutton Unit of the state forest may be accessed from a parking area on Deaton Bridge Road, 1.4 miles south of the bridge. During spring and early summer, Bachman's Sparrow can be heard singing in this pine/oak habitat. A greater variety of pine sandhill species, including Red-cockaded Woodpecker, may be found near state forest headquarters in Munson. To reach this area from the state park, drive north 3.7 miles to Morning Mist Road. Bear left and drive north 0.7 mile to Bryant Bridge Road. Bear left and drive east 1.8 miles to Sandy Landing Road. Turn right and drive north 5 miles to County Road 191. Turn left and drive south 2.3 miles to Forest Road 64. Turn right and drive west 2 miles to Three Notch Road. Turn left and drive south 2.2 miles to Forest Road 68 (Buddy Hardy Road). Red-cockaded Woodpecker nest trees, marked with white bands, can be found along FR 64 and Three Notch Road. The woodpeckers are most likely to be seen near nest cavities at dawn and dusk. Brown-headed Nuthatch and Bachman's Sparrow may also be found in this area. Turn left and drive east 0.6 mile on FR 68 to return to CR 191. Turn left and drive north 4.7 miles to state forest headquarters. Continue north 0.2 mile to State Road 4. Several state forest recreation areas with campgrounds and hiking trails are located along this road. Turn right and drive east 0.7 mile to Krul Recreation Area. The 1.3-mile Sweetwater Trail begins at a kiosk in the day-use parking area and leads to Bear Lake. The trail includes a 0.5-mile boardwalk and a suspension bridge over Sweetwater Creek. Continue east 1.3 miles to Bear Lake Recreation Area. The 4-mile Bear Lake Trail, good for migrant and wintering land birds, begins in the campground and encircles the 107-acre lake. To reach Hurricane Lake Recreation Area, continue east 0.6 mile to Forest Road 31 (Hurricane Lake Road). Turn left and drive north 8.6 miles to Bullard Church Road. Turn right and drive east 1 mile to Nichols Road. Turn right and drive north to the entrance. The 12.7-mile Wiregrass Trail can be accessed from the campground. Follow the trail north 6.4 miles to the Alabama border, or south 6.3 miles to the northern terminus of the Jackson Red Ground Trail. The Wiregrass Trail passes through extensive longleaf pine

Gray Kingbird. PHOTO: LARRY MANFREDI

sandhills, home to Wild Turkey, Northern Bobwhite, Chuck-will's-widow, and other pineland species.

Gulf Islands National Seashore consists of 12 separate units stretching 160 miles from Santa Rosa Island, south of Pensacola, to Cat Island, part of the Mississippi District. Begin your tour of the Florida District at **Naval Live Oaks Visitor Center,** located near the end of a peninsula separating Pensacola Bay from Santa Rosa Sound. Maps and checklists are available in the visitor center. In spring and fall check surrounding live oaks for trans-Gulf migrants. A 0.8-mile trail loops through this habitat. In winter scan Santa Rosa Sound for loons, grebes, and sea ducks, including Common Goldeneye. An Eared Grebe was seen here in February 2003. **Ft. Pickens** is located at the western end of Santa Rosa Island and guards the inlet to Pensacola Bay. This area is well known for spectacular spring fallouts of trans-Gulf migrants and for the many vagrants found here in fall and winter. Rarities seen in recent years include Long-tailed Duck, Pacific Loon, Groove-billed Ani, Say's Phoebe, Bell's Vireo, Bewick's Wren, Black-headed Grosbeak, American Tree Sparrow, and Shiny Cowbird. Look for gulls, terns, and shorebirds along Gulf-side beaches, accessible from parking areas along Ft. Pickens Road. Snowy Plover is resident, while Least Tern is present in spring and summer. During winter scan the Gulf for Northern Gannet. Check the bay side for loons, grebes, and sea ducks. A good vantage point is the jetty at the end of the island. Brushy and grassy areas harbor flocks of wintering sparrows, which may include Chipping, Clay-colored, Field, Lark, Savannah, Song, Lincoln's, Swamp, White-throated, and White-crowned. Watch for Scissor-tailed Flycatcher and Western Kingbird, regular around the fort in fall and winter. A few Gray Kingbirds breed in the vicinity of the fort. Search for trans-Gulf migrants in stands of trees around fort walls and batteries. Also check the Battery Worth picnic area and the 0.5-mile Blackbird Marsh Nature Trail, which begins in the campground. Sadly, many trees in these areas have fallen victim to recent storms.

General information: Gulf Islands National Seashore (entrance fee at Ft. Pickens) and Blackwater River State Park (entrance fee) are open daily from 8:00 A.M. until sunset. Naval Live Oaks Visitor Center (no entrance fee) is open daily from 8:30 A.M. to 4:30 P.M. Restrooms are available at all locations. Blackwater River State Forest (entrance fees for recreation areas) is open daily from sunrise to sunset. State forest headquarters is located on CR 191, 0.2 mile south of SR 4, in Munson. Restrooms are located at Bear Lake Recreation Area. Seasonal hunting is permitted in designated areas. Refer to regulations-summary brochures, updated annually and available at check stations, for hunt dates and locations. Wear blaze orange if hiking during hunting season.

DeLorme grid: Page 27, C-3; page 42, B-3.

Hazards: Keep a safe distance from alligators. Eastern diamondback rattlesnakes are common in the Ft. Pickens area. Mosquitoes are common in summer. Trails may be wet during periods of high water.

Nearest food, gas, lodging: In Crestview, Milton, and Pensacola.

Camping: Blackwater River State Park: 30 sites. Campgrounds are also located at the Krul, Bear Lake, and Hurricane Lake Recreation Areas of Blackwater River State Forest.

For more information: *Blackwater River State Park,* 7720 Deaton Bridge Rd., Holt, FL 32564; (850) 983-5363; www.floridastateparks.org/blackwaterriver. *Blackwater River State Forest,* 11650 Munson Hwy., Milton, FL 32570; (850) 957-6143; www.fl-dof.com/state_forests/blackwater_river.html. *Gulf Islands National Seashore,* 1801 Gulf Breeze Pkwy., Gulf Breeze, FL 32563; (850) 934-2600; www.nps.gov/guis.

CHAPTER SIX

Species Accounts for Florida's Birds

This chapter provides brief summaries, with range maps, for the 343 bird species that regularly occur in Florida. Provided separately are brief summaries for 154 vagrant species and 3 extinct (or presumed extinct) species. The occurrence of all 500 species within Florida has been verified by the Records Committee of the Florida Ornithological Society (FOSRC). Summaries describe each species' status, range, habitat preferences, seasonality, and frequency of occurrence within the state. Key locations for regularly occurring species, listed in the order in which they appear in the site descriptions, are also included. Refer to the site descriptions for specific information on finding target birds when visiting these locations. For species with widespread distribution within the state, a representative sample of locations is provided. For vagrant species with few verifiable records within the state, location and year of record are included.

Status for each species is defined as follows: *Residents* breed in Florida and are present year-round or only during their nesting season. *Visitors* are present in Florida all or part of the year (usually winter) but do not breed in the state. *Migrants* pass through Florida during spring and/or fall. Some migrants also winter in the state. Keep in mind that for some species such as shorebirds, fall migration may begin as early as July. *Vagrants* are unpredictable in occurrence and should not be expected.

Range is defined as follows: *Throughout the state* refers to any suitable habitat for that species within Florida. The *mainland* excludes the Florida Keys and Dry Tortugas. The *peninsula* excludes the Panhandle and Florida Keys and is roughly divided into *northern*, *central*, and *southern* thirds. The *Panhandle* refers to the area from Tallahassee to Pensacola and is divided into *eastern* and *western* halves at the Apalachicola River.

Frequency of occurrence is defined as follows: *Abundant* species are present in large numbers and should be easily found in the proper habitat and season. *Common* species are present in moderate numbers but should still be easy to find in the proper habitat and season. *Locally common* species are easily found but in limited geographic areas or specific habitats. *Uncommon* species are present in low numbers or are secretive in nature and may be difficult to find. *Rare* species are seen only a few times per year but may be found if persistent over the course of a season. *Occasional* species may not be seen in the state every year and should not be expected.

Range maps, shaded by season, indicate where and when each regularly occurring species is likely to be found. A range map key is located at the top of each right-hand page.

For winter visitors or species resident only during the breeding season, range during migratory periods is usually not indicated.

The following resources were used to develop the species accounts and range maps: *Florida Bird Species: An Annotated List,* William B. Robertson Jr. and Glenn E. Woolfenden, Florida Ornithological Society (1992); *The Birdlife of Florida,* Henry M. Stevenson and Bruce H. Anderson, University Press of Florida (1994); *Florida's Birds: A Field Guide and Reference,* David S. Maehr and Herbert W. Kale II, Pineapple Press, Inc. (2005); *Birds of Florida,* Bill Pranty, Kurt A. Racamaker, and Gregory Kennedy, Lone Star Publishing International (2006); *A Birder's Guide to Florida,* Bill Pranty, American Birding Association, Inc. (2005); *The Atlas of the Breeding Birds of Florida,* Herbert W. Kale, Bill Pranty, B. M. Stith, and C. W. Biggs (online at http://myfwc.com/bba/); Audubon Christmas Bird Count Data (online at www.audubon.org/bird/cbc); published reports of the Florida Ornithological Society Records Committee (online at www.fosbirds.org/RecordCommittee/FOSRCReports.htm); Florida Museum of Natural History photo archives (online at www.fosbirds.org/photoarc/uf_mat.htm); bird checklists collected from locations included in the site descriptions; sightings reports from various state online listservs, including FloridaBirds-L (http://lists.ufl.edu/archives/floridabirds-l.html), Birdbrains (http://listserv.admin.usf.edu/archives/brdbrain.html), and North Florida Birds (http://groups.yahoo.com/group/nflbirds).

Florida's Regularly Occurring Bird Species

BLACK-BELLIED WHISTLING-DUCK
Comments: Year-round resident of freshwater marshes and flooded agricultural fields. Locally common in the central peninsula but spreading throughout the peninsula.
Key Sites: Lake Apopka, Orlando Wetlands Park, Viera Wetlands, Everglades Agricultural Area, Myakka River State Park, Celery Fields Regional Stormwater Facility, Emeralda Marsh Conservation Area, Chapman's Pond.

FULVOUS WHISTLING-DUCK
Comments: Year-round resident of freshwater marshes and flooded agricultural fields, locally common throughout the peninsula.
Key Sites: Lake Apopka, Everglades Agricultural Area, Loxahatchee National Wildlife Refuge, Emeralda Marsh Conservation Area.

CANADA GOOSE
Comments: Feral resident and winter visitor, locally common in the eastern Panhandle.
Key Sites: Tallahassee area, Lake Seminole.

MUSCOVY DUCK
Comments: Feral resident of suburban ponds. Common-to-abundant throughout the peninsula, uncommon in the Panhandle.
Key Sites: A. D. Barnes Park, Kendall Area.

WOOD DUCK
Comments: Year-round resident of cypress and hardwood swamps. Common throughout the Panhandle and northern and central peninsula, uncommon in the southern peninsula.
Key Sites: Jennings State Forest, Lake Woodruff National Wildlife Refuge, Lake Apopka,

Wekiwa Springs State Park, Mead Gardens, Okeeheelee Nature Center, Avon Park Air Force Range, Hillsborough River Parks, Wakulla Springs State Park, Blackwater River State Forest.

GADWALL

Comments: Winter visitor to fresh and brackish water marshes and impoundments, uncommon throughout the mainland.
Key Sites: Lake Apopka, Merritt Island National Wildlife Refuge, St. Marks National Wildlife Refuge.

AMERICAN WIGEON

Comments: Winter visitor to fresh and brackish water marshes, ponds, and impoundments, common throughout the mainland.
Key Sites: Lake Apopka, Merritt Island National Wildlife Refuge, Viera Wetlands, Eagle Lakes Community Park, Ding Darling National Wildlife Refuge, St. Marks National Wildlife Refuge, Wakulla Springs State Park.

MALLARD

Comments: Winter visitor to freshwater marshes and impoundments, uncommon throughout the Panhandle. Locally common feral resident throughout the mainland.
Key Sites: Lake Apopka, St. Marks National Wildlife Refuge.

MOTTLED DUCK

Comments: Year-round resident of freshwater marshes, ponds, and impoundments. Common throughout the central and southern peninsula, uncommon-to-rare in the northern peninsula and Panhandle.
Key Sites: Lake Apopka, Merritt Island National Wildlife Refuge, Orlando Wetlands Park, Viera Wetlands, Indian River County Wetlands Treatment Facility, Wakodahatchee Wetlands, Everglades National Park, Myakka River State Park.

BLUE-WINGED TEAL

Comments: Winter visitor to fresh and brackish water marshes and impoundments, common-to-abundant throughout the state.
Key Sites: Lake Apopka, Merritt Island National Wildlife Refuge, Orlando Wetlands Park, Viera Wetlands, Indian River County Wetlands Treatment Facility, Wakodahatchee Wetlands, Everglades National Park, Myakka River State Park, Chapman's Pond, St. Marks National Wildlife Refuge.

NORTHERN SHOVELER

Comments: Winter visitor to freshwater ponds, lakes, and impoundments, common throughout the mainland.
Key Sites: Merritt Island National Wildlife Refuge, Viera Wetlands, Myakka River State Park, Chapman's Pond, St. Marks National Wildlife Refuge.

NORTHERN PINTAIL

Comments: Winter visitor to freshwater ponds, lakes, and impoundments, common throughout the state.
Key Sites: Merritt Island National Wildlife Refuge, Indian River County Wetlands Treatment Facility, St. Marks National Wildlife Refuge.

GREEN-WINGED TEAL

Comments: Winter visitor to freshwater ponds, lakes, and impoundments, common throughout the mainland.
Key Sites: Lake Apopka, Merritt Island National Wildlife Refuge, Orlando Wetlands Park, Viera Wetlands, Indian River County Wetlands Treatment Facility, Wakodahatchee Wetlands, Everglades National Park, Myakka River State Park, Chapman's Pond, St. Marks National Wildlife Refuge.

CANVASBACK

Comments: Winter visitor to fresh and brackish water marshes, lakes, and impoundments. Locally common throughout the Panhandle and northern peninsula, uncommon-to-rare in the southern peninsula.
Key Sites: Merritt Island National Wildlife Refuge, St. Marks National Wildlife Refuge, Lake Seminole.

REDHEAD

Comments: Winter visitor to estuaries, coastal ponds, and impoundments. Common-to-abundant throughout the Panhandle and northern and central peninsula, rare in the southern peninsula.
Key Sites: Merritt Island National Wildlife Refuge, Ft. De Soto, Big Bend Wildlife Management Area, St. Marks National Wildlife Refuge, Alligator Point.

RING-NECKED DUCK

Comments: Winter visitor to freshwater marshes, ponds, and lakes, common-to-abundant throughout the mainland.
Key Sites: Lake Woodruff National Wildlife Refuge, Lake Apopka, Viera Wetlands, Everglades Agricultural Area, Myakka River State Park.

GREATER SCAUP

Comments: Winter visitor to coastal waters, uncommon throughout the Panhandle, rare in the peninsula.
Key Sites: St. Marks National Wildlife Refuge, Alligator Point.

LESSER SCAUP

Comments: Winter visitor to coastal waters, estuaries, and lakes, common-to-abundant throughout the mainland.
Key Sites: Merritt Island National Wildlife Refuge, Orlando Wetlands Park, Pelican Island National Wildlife Refuge, Big Bend Wildlife Management Area, Wakulla Springs State Park, St. Marks National Wildlife Refuge.

SURF SCOTER

Comments: Winter visitor to coastal waters, rare throughout the Panhandle, occasional in the peninsula.
Key Sites: St. Marks National Wildlife Refuge, Alligator Point.

WHITE-WINGED SCOTER

Comments: Winter visitor to coastal waters, rare throughout the Panhandle, occasional in the peninsula.
Key Sites: St. Marks National Wildlife Refuge, Alligator Point.

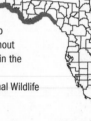

BLACK SCOTER

Comments: Winter visitor to coastal waters, uncommon-to-rare throughout the mainland.
Key Sites: Ft. Clinch State Park, St. Marks National Wildlife Refuge, Alligator Point.

LONG-TAILED DUCK

Comments: Winter visitor to coastal and inland waters, rare throughout the Panhandle and northern and central peninsula.
Key Sites: Ft. Clinch State Park, Merritt Island National Wildlife Refuge, Cedar Key, St. Marks National Wildlife Refuge, Alligator Point, St. George Island, St. Joseph Peninsula, Gulf Islands National Seashore.

BUFFLEHEAD

Comments: Winter visitor to coastal and inland waters. Common throughout the Panhandle and along the Gulf coast of the northern peninsula. Uncommon-to-rare along the Atlantic coast.
Key Sites: St. Marks National Wildlife Refuge, Alligator Point, St. George Island, St. Joseph Peninsula, Gulf Islands National Seashore.

COMMON GOLDENEYE

Comments: Winter visitor to coastal and inland waters. Uncommon throughout the Panhandle, occasional in the peninsula.
Key Sites: St. Marks National Wildlife Refuge, Alligator Point, St. George Island, St. Joseph Peninsula, Gulf Islands National Seashore.

HOODED MERGANSER

Comments: Winter visitor to freshwater lakes, ponds, and impoundments, locally common throughout the mainland. Occasionally breeds in the northern peninsula.
Key Sites: Lake Apopka, Merritt Island National Wildlife Refuge, Chapman's Pond, St. Marks National Wildlife Refuge.

RED-BREASTED MERGANSER

Comments: Winter visitor to coastal waters, common throughout the state.
Key Sites: Ft. Clinch State Park, Talbot Islands State Parks, Guana River Reserve, Merritt Island National Wildlife Refuge, Pelican Island National Wildlife Refuge, Key Biscayne, Ft. Myers Beach, Sanibel Island, Ft. De Soto, Cedar Key, St. Marks National Wildlife Refuge, St. George Island, St. Joseph Peninsula.

RUDDY DUCK

Comments: Winter visitor to lakes and ponds, locally common throughout the mainland.
Key Sites: Lake Apopka, Lake Seminole.

WILD TURKEY

Comments: Year-round resident of pinelands, oak woodlands, cypress swamp, and pastures, locally common throughout the mainland. Most common in the central peninsula.
Key Sites: Gold Head Branch State Park, Three Lakes Wildlife Management Area, Kissimmee Prairie Preserve State Park, Okaloacoochee Slough State Forest, Myakka River State Park, Avon Park Air Force Range, Wakulla Springs State Park, Blackwater River State Forest.

NORTHERN BOBWHITE

Comments: Year-round resident of pinelands and dry prairie, common throughout the mainland.
Key Sites: Three Lakes Wildlife Management Area, Kissimmee Prairie Preserve State Park, Dupuis Reserve, Everglades National Park, Babcock-Webb Wildlife Management Area, Lake Kissimmee State Park, Jay B. Starkey Wilderness Park, Osceola National Forest, Tall Timbers Research Station, Blackwater River State Forest.

RED-THROATED LOON

Comments: Winter visitor to coastal waters, rare throughout the Panhandle and northern peninsula.
Key Sites: Ft. Clinch State Park, Talbot Islands State Parks, Merritt Island National Wildlife Refuge, St. Marks National Wildlife Refuge, St. George Island, St. Joseph Peninsula, Gulf Islands National Seashore.

COMMON LOON

Comments: Winter visitor to coastal waters. Common throughout the Panhandle and northern peninsula, uncommon in the southern peninsula and Keys.
Key Sites: Ft. Clinch State Park, Talbot Islands State Parks, Merritt Island National Wildlife Refuge, St. Marks National Wildlife Refuge, Alligator Point, St. George Island, St. Joseph Peninsula, Gulf Islands National Seashore.

PIED-BILLED GREBE

Comments: Locally common year-round resident and common winter visitor to fresh and brackish water marshes, ponds, impoundments, and coastal waters statewide.
Key Sites: Lake Apopka, Merritt Island National Wildlife Refuge, Orlando Wetlands Park, Loxahatchee National Wildlife Refuge, Eagle Lakes Community Park, Myakka River State Park, Wakulla Springs State Park, St. Marks National Wildlife Refuge.

HORNED GREBE

Comments: Winter visitor to coastal waters. Common throughout the Panhandle and northern and central peninsula, uncommon-to-rare in the southern peninsula.
Key Sites: Merritt Island National Wildlife Refuge, Cedar Key, Big Bend Wildlife Management Area, St. Marks National Wildlife Refuge, Alligator Point, St. George Island, St. Joseph Peninsula, Gulf Islands National Seashore.

BLACK-CAPPED PETREL

Comments: Pelagic visitor from spring through fall. Rare to locally common off the Atlantic coast and Keys, rare in the Gulf.
Key Sites: By boat off Ponce Inlet, Islamorada.

CORY'S SHEARWATER

Comments: Pelagic visitor from spring through fall. Common off the Atlantic coast, uncommon in the Gulf.
Key Sites: By boat off Ponce Inlet, Islamorada, Destin. From shore at Canaveral National Seashore, Jetty Park, and Ponce, Sebastian, and Boynton Inlets during extended periods of strong easterly winds.

GREATER SHEARWATER

Comments: Pelagic visitor from spring through fall. Uncommon off the Atlantic coast, rare in the Gulf.
Key Sites: By boat off Ponce Inlet, Islamorada.

SOOTY SHEARWATER

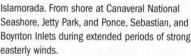

Comments: Pelagic visitor from spring through fall. Uncommon off the Atlantic coast, rare in the Gulf.
Key Sites: By boat off Ponce Inlet, Islamorada. From shore at Canaveral National Seashore, Jetty Park, and Ponce, Sebastian, and Boynton Inlets during extended periods of strong easterly winds.

AUDUBON'S SHEARWATER

Comments: Pelagic visitor from spring through fall. Common off the Atlantic coast, rare in the Gulf.
Key Sites: By boat off Islamorada, Dry Tortugas. From shore at Canaveral National Seashore, Jetty Park, and Ponce, Sebastian, and Boynton Inlets during extended periods of strong easterly winds.

WILSON'S STORM-PETREL

Comments: Pelagic visitor from spring through fall. Common off the Atlantic coast, uncommon in the Gulf.
Key Sites: By boat off Ponce Inlet, Islamorada, Destin. From shore at Canaveral National Seashore, Jetty Park, and Ponce, Sebastian, and Boynton Inlets during extended periods of strong easterly winds.

LEACH'S STORM-PETREL

Comments: Pelagic visitor from spring through fall, rare off both coasts.
Key Sites: By boat off Ponce Inlet, Islamorada. From shore at Canaveral National Seashore, Jetty Park, and Ponce, Sebastian, and Boynton Inlets during extended periods of strong easterly winds.

BAND-RUMPED STORM-PETREL

Comments: Pelagic visitor from spring through fall, uncommon and irregular off both coasts.
Key Sites: By boat off Ponce Inlet, Islamorada, Dry Tortugas, Destin. From shore at Canaveral National Seashore, Jetty Park, and Ponce, Sebastian, and Boynton Inlets during extended periods of strong easterly winds.

WHITE-TAILED TROPICBIRD

Comments: Pelagic visitor during spring and summer, rare and irregular off both coasts.
Key Sites: Dry Tortugas National Park, by boat off Ponce Inlet, Islamorada, Destin.

MASKED BOOBY

Comments: Uncommon year-round resident in the Dry Tortugas, rare off both coasts from spring through fall.
Key Sites: Dry Tortugas National Park.

BROWN BOOBY

Comments: Uncommon year-round visitor in the Dry Tortugas, uncommon-to-rare off both coasts year-round. Most often seen on buoys and channel markers.
Key Sites: Biscayne National Park, Dry Tortugas National Park.

NORTHERN GANNET

Comments: Migrant and winter visitor, common off the Atlantic and Panhandle coasts.
Key Sites: Canaveral National Seashore, Jetty Park, Ponce, Sebastian, and Boynton Inlets, Key Biscayne, Alligator Point, St. George Island, St. Joseph Peninsula, Gulf Islands National Seashore.

AMERICAN WHITE PELICAN

Comments: Winter visitor to coastal and inland waters, common throughout the mainland.
Key Sites: Guana River Reserve, Lake Apopka, Merritt Island National Wildlife Refuge, Everglades Agricultural Area, Everglades National Park, Big Bend Wildlife Management Area.

BROWN PELICAN

Comments: Year-round resident of coastal waters, common throughout the state.
Key Sites: Guana River Reserve, Canaveral National Seashore, Pelican Island National Wildlife Refuge, Biscayne National Park, Everglades National Park, Tigertail Beach, Sanibel Island, Ft. De Soto, Cedar Keys National Wildlife Refuge.

DOUBLE-CRESTED CORMORANT

Comments: Year-round resident of coastal and inland waters. Common-to-abundant throughout the peninsula and Keys and coastal waters throughout the Panhandle. Common-to-abundant winter visitor to inland waters throughout the Panhandle.
Key Sites: Ft. Clinch State Park, Guana River Preserve, Lake Apopka, Merritt Island National Wildlife Refuge, Pelican Island National Wildlife Refuge, Biscayne National Park, throughout the Florida Keys, Everglades National Park, Ding Darling National Wildlife Refuge, Myakka River State Park, Ft. De Soto, Cedar Keys National Wildlife Refuge, St. Marks National Wildlife Refuge.

ANHINGA

Comments: Year-round resident of freshwater marshes, lakes, and other inland waters, common throughout the eastern Panhandle and peninsula. Uncommon-to-rare summer visitor to the western Panhandle.
Key Sites: Lake Woodruff National Wildlife Refuge, Lake Apopka, Merritt Island National Wildlife Refuge, Orlando Wetlands Park, Viera Wetlands, Loxahatchee National Wildlife Refuge, Everglades National Park, Big Cypress National Preserve, Corkscrew Swamp Sanctuary, Myakka River State Park, Paynes Prairie Preserve State Park, St. Marks National Wildlife Refuge, Wakulla Springs State Park.

MAGNIFICENT FRIGATEBIRD

Comments: Common year-round resident in the Dry Tortugas. Common year-round visitor to the Keys and Atlantic coastal waters in the southern peninsula and Gulf coastal waters throughout the peninsula. Uncommon-to-rare visitor to coastal waters in the Panhandle and Atlantic coastal waters in the northern peninsula.
Key Sites: Key Biscayne, Biscayne National Park, throughout the Florida Keys, Dry Tortugas National Park, Marco Island, Honeymoon Island.

AMERICAN BITTERN

Comments: Winter visitor to freshwater marshes, uncommon throughout the mainland.
Key Sites: Lake Woodruff National Wildlife Refuge, Lake Apopka, Merritt Island National Wildlife Refuge, Orlando Wetlands Park, Viera Wetlands, Green Cay Wetlands, Everglades National Park.

LEAST BITTERN

Comments: Year-round resident of freshwater marshes (preferably cattail marshes), occasionally found in salt marsh and mangrove forest. Locally common in the central and southern peninsula, uncommon during summer and rare during winter in the northern peninsula and Panhandle.
Key Sites: Savannas Preserve State Park, Everglades Agricultural Area, Wakodahatchee Wetlands, Everglades National Park.

GREAT BLUE HERON

Comments: Year-round resident of coastal and inland marshes, common throughout the state. "Great White Heron," a morph of Great Blue Heron, is a common breeder in the extreme southern peninsula and Keys. "Wurdemann's Heron," a hybrid of the two morphs, is an uncommon-to-rare breeder in the extreme southern peninsula and Keys.

Key Sites: Guana River Reserve, Merritt Island National Wildlife Refuge, Orlando Wetlands Park, Viera Wetlands, Everglades Agricultural Area, Loxahatchee National Wildlife Refuge, Wakodahatchee Wetlands, Everglades National Park, throughout the Florida Keys, Big Cypress National Preserve, Ding Darling National Wildlife Refuge, Myakka River State Park, Ft. De Soto, Paynes Prairie Preserve State Park, St. Marks National Wildlife Refuge.

GREAT EGRET

Comments: Year-round resident of coastal and inland marshes. Common throughout the eastern Panhandle, peninsula, and Keys, uncommon in the western Panhandle.

Key Sites: Guana River Reserve, Merritt Island National Wildlife Refuge, Orlando Wetlands Park, Viera Wetlands, Everglades Agricultural Area, Loxahatchee National Wildlife Refuge, Wakodahatchee Wetlands, Everglades National Park, throughout the Florida Keys, Big Cypress National Preserve, Corkscrew Swamp Sanctuary, Ding Darling National Wildlife Refuge, Myakka River State Park, Ft. De Soto, St. Marks National Wildlife Refuge.

SNOWY EGRET

Comments: Year-round resident of coastal and inland marshes. Common throughout the state, except uncommon in the western Panhandle during winter.

Key Sites: Guana River Reserve, Merritt Island National Wildlife Refuge, Orlando Wetlands Park, Viera Wetlands, Wakodahatchee Wetlands, Everglades Agricultural Area, Everglades National Park, Big Cypress National Preserve, Ding Darling National Wildlife Refuge, Myakka River State Park, Ft. De Soto, St. Marks National Wildlife Refuge.

LITTLE BLUE HERON

Comments: Year-round resident of coastal and inland marshes. Common throughout the state, except uncommon in the western Panhandle during winter.

Key Sites: Merritt Island National Wildlife Refuge, Orlando Wetlands Park, Viera Wetlands, Wakodahatchee Wetlands, Everglades Agricultural Area, Everglades National Park, Big Cypress National Preserve, Corkscrew Swamp Sanctuary, Ding Darling National Wildlife Refuge, Myakka River State Park, Ft. De Soto, St. Marks National Wildlife Refuge.

TRICOLORED HERON

Comments: Year-round resident of coastal and inland marshes. Common throughout the state, except rare in the interior of the western Panhandle and northern peninsula.

Key Sites: Merritt Island National Wildlife Refuge, Orlando Wetlands Park, Viera Wetlands, Wakodahatchee Wetlands, Everglades Agricultural Area, Everglades National Park, Big Cypress National Preserve, Corkscrew Swamp Sanctuary, Ding Darling National Wildlife Refuge, Myakka River State Park, Ft. De Soto, St. Marks National Wildlife Refuge.

REDDISH EGRET

Comments: Year-round resident along sandy beaches, mudflats, and estuaries. Locally common throughout the coastal mainland and Keys, occasionally inland. Dark morph individuals predominate, though less so in the Keys and Florida Bay.

Key Sites: Merritt Island National Wildlife Refuge, Everglades National Park (Flamingo area), throughout the Florida Keys, Marco Island, Ft. Myers Beach, Sanibel Island, Ft. De Soto, Honeymoon Island.

CATTLE EGRET

Comments: Year-round resident of pastures, fields, and roadsides. Common-to-abundant throughout the mainland, except uncommon in the Panhandle and northern peninsula during winter. Migrant to the Dry Tortugas.

Key Sites: Orlando Wetlands Park, Viera Wetlands, Everglades Agricultural Area, Loxahatchee

National Wildlife Refuge, Everglades National Park, Myakka River State Park, Ft. De Soto, Paynes Prairie Preserve State Park.

De Soto, Honeymoon Island, Paynes Prairie Preserve State Park, Cedar Keys National Wildlife Refuge, St. Marks National Wildlife Refuge.

GREEN HERON

Comments: Year-round resident of freshwater marshes. Common throughout the state, except uncommon-to-rare in the Panhandle during winter.

Key Sites: Orlando Wetlands Park, Merritt Island National Wildlife Refuge, Viera Wetlands, Loxahatchee National Wildlife Refuge, Wakodahatchee Wetlands, Everglades National Park, Big Cypress National Preserve, Corkscrew Swamp Sanctuary, Myakka River State Park.

BLACK-CROWNED NIGHT-HERON

Comments: Year-round resident of coastal and inland marshes. Common throughout the mainland, except uncommon-to-rare in the Panhandle during winter.

Key Sites: Everglades Agricultural Area, Loxahatchee National Wildlife Refuge, Everglades National Park, Corkscrew Swamp Sanctuary, Myakka River State Park, Paynes Prairie Preserve State Park.

YELLOW-CROWNED NIGHT-HERON

Comments: Year-round resident of coastal and inland marshes. Common throughout the southern and central peninsula, uncommon in coastal areas of the northern peninsula and Panhandle.

Key Sites: Everglades National Park, Ding Darling National Wildlife Refuge, Myakka River State Park, Ft. De Soto, Wakulla Springs State Park.

WHITE IBIS

Comments: Year-round resident of coastal mudflats and inland marshes, common-to-abundant throughout the peninsula. Locally common in the Panhandle during summer, uncommon-to-rare during winter.

Key Sites: Orlando Wetlands Park, Merritt Island National Wildlife Refuge, Viera Wetlands, Loxahatchee National Wildlife Refuge, Everglades National Park, Big Cypress National Preserve, Marco Island, Corkscrew Swamp Sanctuary, Ding Darling National Wildlife Refuge, Myakka River State Park, Ft.

GLOSSY IBIS

Comments: Year-round resident of freshwater marshes, locally common throughout the peninsula and eastern Panhandle, rare in the western Panhandle.

Key Sites: Merritt Island National Wildlife Refuge, Viera Wetlands, Everglades Agricultural Area, Loxahatchee National Wildlife Refuge, Everglades National Park, Eagle Lakes Community Park, Myakka River State Park.

ROSEATE SPOONBILL

Comments: Locally common year-round resident of salt marsh, mangrove forest, and estuaries along the central and southern coasts and in the Keys. Post-breeding adults and juveniles are locally common during summer at inland wetlands and flooded agricultural fields and in salt marshes along the coast of the northern peninsula and eastern Panhandle.

Key Sites: Merritt Island National Wildlife Refuge, Pelican Island National Wildlife Refuge, Everglades Agricultural Area, Everglades National Park, Ding Darling National Wildlife Refuge, Ft. De Soto.

WOOD STORK

Comments: Year-round resident of coastal and inland marshes, locally common throughout the peninsula and eastern Panhandle.

Key Sites: Merritt Island National Wildlife Refuge, Everglades Agricultural Area, Loxahatchee National Wildlife Refuge, Everglades National Park, Big Cypress National Preserve, Corkscrew Swamp Sanctuary, Myakka River State Park.

BLACK VULTURE

Comments: Year-round resident, common throughout the mainland. More common at inland locations.

Key Sites: Lake Woodruff National Wildlife Refuge, Merritt Island National Wildlife Refuge, Orlando Wetlands Park, Three Lakes Wildlife Management Area, Jonathan Dickinson State Park, Loxahatchee National Wildlife Refuge, Everglades National Park, Big

Cypress National Preserve, Myakka River State Park, Wakulla Springs State Park.

TURKEY VULTURE

Comments: Year-round resident and winter visitor. Common throughout the state, most abundant around landfills during winter. **Key Sites:** Lake Woodruff National Wildlife Refuge, Merritt Island National Wildlife Refuge, Orlando Wetlands Park, Three Lakes Wildlife Management Area, Loxahatchee National Wildlife Refuge, Key Biscayne, Dump Marsh, Everglades National Park, Big Cypress National Preserve, Myakka River State Park, Paynes Prairie Preserve State Park, Wakulla Springs State Park.

GREATER FLAMINGO

Comments: One small flock of about 40 individuals seen sporadically in Florida Bay. A captive, free-flying flock resides at Hialeah Park racetrack in Miami-Dade County. Individuals seen elsewhere are usually presumed to be escapees. **Key Sites:** Snake Bight in Everglades National Park.

OSPREY

Comments: Year-round resident along coastal and inland waters. Common throughout the state, except uncommon during winter in the Panhandle and northern peninsula. **Key Sites:** Guana River Reserve, Lake Woodruff National Wildlife Refuge, Merritt Island National Wildlife Refuge, Pelican Island National Wildlife Refuge, Everglades Agricultural Area, Everglades National Park, throughout the Florida Keys, Big Cypress National Preserve, Marco Island, Sanibel Island, Myakka River State Park, Ft. De Soto, Honeymoon Island.

SWALLOW-TAILED KITE

Comments: Spring and summer resident, usually near pinelands and cypress swamp, but also seen over marshes, hammocks, and mangrove forest. Locally common throughout the eastern Panhandle, peninsula, and upper Keys, uncommon-to-rare in the western Panhandle. Abundant at midsummer post-breeding roosts.

Key Sites: Lake Woodruff National Wildlife Refuge, Orlando Wetlands Park, Everglades National Park, Fakahatchee Strand Preserve State Park, Corkscrew Swamp Sanctuary, Fisheating Creek Wildlife Management Area, Highlands Hammock State Park, Chassahowitzka Wildlife Management Area, Lower Suwannee National Wildlife Refuge, Ocala National Forest, Wakulla Springs State Park, Apalachicola National Forest.

WHITE-TAILED KITE

Comments: Year-round resident of dry prairie and brushy marshes, rare and local in the southern and central peninsula. **Key Sites:** Three Lakes Wildlife Management Area, Kissimmee Prairie Preserve State Park, Tamiami and Homestead Regional Airports in south Miami-Dade County, Research Road in Everglades National Park.

SNAIL KITE

Comments: Year-round resident of freshwater marshes, uncommon to locally common throughout the central and southern peninsula. **Key Sites:** Three Lakes Wildlife Management Area, T. M. Goodwin Waterfowl Management Area, Grassy Waters Preserve, Loxahatchee National Wildlife Refuge, Markham Park, Everglades National Park, Big Cypress National Preserve, Lake Kissimmee State Park.

MISSISSIPPI KITE

Comments: Spring and summer resident of woodlands, usually near rivers, uncommon throughout the northern peninsula and Panhandle. Coastal migrant in the Panhandle, rare migrant in the peninsula and Keys. **Key Sites:** Crystal River Preserve State Park, Lower Suwannee National Wildlife Refuge, Paynes Prairie Preserve State Park, Chapman's Pond, Wakulla River State Park, Southeast Farm in Tallahassee, Apalachicola National Forest, Torreya State Park, Florida Caverns State Park, Blackwater River State Forest.

BALD EAGLE

Comments: Common year-round resident near coastal and inland waters in undeveloped areas of the peninsula and eastern Panhandle. Uncommon in the Keys, uncommon-to-rare in the western Panhandle.

Key Sites: Merritt Island National Wildlife Refuge, Orlando Wetlands Park, Viera Wetlands, Three Lakes Wildlife Management Area, Jonathan Dickinson State Park, Everglades National Park, Oscar Scherer State Park, Myakka River State Park, Lake Kissimmee State Park, Paynes Prairie Preserve State Park, St. Marks National Wildlife Refuge.

NORTHERN HARRIER

Comments: Migrant and winter visitor to freshwater marshes, prairies, and pastures, common throughout the mainland. Migrant through the Keys.

Key Sites: Merritt Island National Wildlife Refuge, Orlando Wetlands Park, Viera Wetlands, Three Lakes Wildlife Management Area, Kissimmee Prairie Preserve State Park, Loxahatchee National Wildlife Refuge, Southern Glades Wildlife and Environmental Area, Everglades National Park, Myakka River State Park, Paynes Prairie Preserve State Park, St. Marks National Wildlife Refuge.

SHARP-SHINNED HAWK

Comments: Winter visitor to woodlands and suburban areas, uncommon throughout the state. Common migrant.

Key Sites: Jonathan Dickinson State Park, Loxahatchee National Wildlife Refuge, Kendall area, Curry Hammock State Park, Dry Tortugas National Park, Oscar Scherer State Park, St. George Island, Florida Caverns State Park, St. Joseph Peninsula State Park.

COOPER'S HAWK

Comments: Year-round resident of hammocks and hardwood swamp, uncommon throughout the state. Common migrant.

Key Sites: Curry Hammock State Park, Highlands Hammock State Park, Paynes Prairie Preserve State Park, Florida Caverns State Park, St. Joseph Peninsula State Park.

RED-SHOULDERED HAWK

Comments: Year-round resident of forest edges, common throughout the mainland.

Key Sites: Lake Woodruff National Wildlife Refuge, Orlando Wetlands Park, Loxahatchee National Wildlife Refuge, Everglades National Park, Big Cypress National Preserve, Corkscrew Swamp Sanctuary, Ding Darling National Wildlife Refuge, Myakka River State Park, St. Marks National Wildlife Refuge.

BROAD-WINGED HAWK

Comments: Uncommon summer resident of woodlands throughout the northern peninsula and Panhandle. Uncommon winter visitor to woodlands and agricultural areas in the extreme southern peninsula and Keys. Common fall migrant in coastal areas throughout the state.

Key Sites: Curry Hammock State Park, Dry Tortugas National Park, Southern Glades Wildlife and Environmental Area, Everglades National Park, Wakulla Springs State Park, Florida Caverns State Park, St. Joseph Peninsula State Park, Blackwater River State Forest.

SHORT-TAILED HAWK

Comments: Year-round resident of cypress, mangrove, and riparian forests near prairies or marshes, uncommon throughout the central and southern peninsula. Occasional summer resident in the northern peninsula, rare in the Panhandle. Locally common in the southern peninsula and Keys during winter, when frequently seen over suburban areas.

Key Sites: Three Lakes Wildlife Management Area, Loxahatchee National Wildlife Refuge, Key Biscayne, Kendall Area, Matheson Hammock Park, Southern Glades Wildlife and Environmental Area, Everglades National Park, Fisheating Creek Wildlife Management Area, Lake Wales Ridge State Forest, Saddle Creek County Park, Jay B. Starkey Wilderness Park.

SWAINSON'S HAWK

Comments: Fall migrant and winter visitor to agricultural fields. Uncommon and irregular in the southern peninsula and Keys, rare elsewhere in the state.
Key Sites: Southern Glades Wildlife and Environmental Area, Everglades National Park.

RED-TAILED HAWK

Comments: Uncommon year-round resident and common winter visitor to prairies and pastures throughout the mainland.
Key Sites: Wekiwa Springs State Park, Merritt Island National Wildlife Refuge, Okaloacoochee Slough State Forest, Myakka River State Park, Highlands Hammock State Park, Paynes Prairie Preserve State Park, St. Marks National Wildlife Refuge, Torreya State Park, Florida Caverns State Park.

CRESTED CARACARA

Comments: Year-round resident of dry prairie and pastures, local and uncommon in the central peninsula.
Key Sites: Viera Wetlands, Three Lakes Wildlife Management Area, Kissimmee Prairie Preserve State Park, Okaloacoochee Slough State Park, Lake Placid area, Avon Park Air Force Range, Lake Kissimmee State Park.

AMERICAN KESTREL

Comments: Eastern race is a common migrant and winter visitor to prairies, pastures, and agricultural areas throughout the state. Southeastern race is an uncommon year-round resident in pine flatwoods and pastures in the western Panhandle and inland areas of the northern and central peninsula. Reports of the Cuban race in the Florida Keys remain unconfirmed.
Key Sites: Jennings State Forest, Gold Head Branch State Park, Three Lakes Wildlife Management Area, Loxahatchee National Wildlife Refuge, Southern Glades Wildlife and Environmental Area, Curry Hammock State Park, Dry Tortugas National Park, Okaloacoochee Slough State Forest, Myakka River State Park, Ft. De Soto, Ocala National Forest, Blackwater River State Forest.

MERLIN

Comments: Coastal migrant and winter visitor to prairies, pastures, agricultural fields, and coastal areas, uncommon throughout the state.
Key Sites: Bill Baggs Cape Florida State Park, Curry Hammock State Park, Dry Tortugas National Park, Southern Glades Wildlife and Environmental Area, St. Joseph Peninsula State Park.

PEREGRINE FALCON

Comments: Coastal migrant and winter visitor to marshes, pastures, agricultural fields, and coastal areas, uncommon throughout the state.
Key Sites: Guana River Reserve, Anastasia State Park, Ft. Matanzas National Monument, Spanish River Park, Bill Baggs Cape Florida State Park, Curry Hammock State Park, Dry Tortugas National Park, Southern Glades Wildlife and Environmental Area, Everglades National Park, Tigertail Beach, Ft. Myers Beach.

YELLOW RAIL

Comments: Rarely seen migrant and winter visitor to wet prairie, savannah, and marshes throughout the mainland.
Key Sites: Everglades National Park, Apalachicola National Forest.

BLACK RAIL

Comments: Year-round resident of coastal and inland marshes, locally uncommon and rarely seen throughout the peninsula. Rarely seen winter visitor in the central and southern peninsula, rarely seen migrant throughout the state.
Key Sites: Lake Woodruff National Wildlife Refuge, Merritt Island National Wildlife Refuge, Everglades Agricultural Area, Everglades National Park, Werner-Boyce Salt Springs State Park, Lower Suwannee National Wildlife Refuge, Big Bend Wildlife Management Area (Jena Unit), St. Marks National Wildlife Refuge.

CLAPPER RAIL

Comments: Year-round resident of coastal marshes and mangrove forest. Common throughout the state, more often heard than seen.

Key Sites: Ft. Clinch State Park, Guana River Reserve, Merritt Island National Wildlife Refuge, Everglades National Park, Upper Tampa Bay County Park, Green Key, Crystal River Preserve State Park, Big Bend Wildlife Management Area, St. Marks National Wildlife Refuge, St. George Island, Gulf Islands National Seashore.

KING RAIL

Comments: Year-round resident of freshwater marshes, uncommon throughout the mainland.

Key Sites: Lake Woodruff National Wildlife Refuge, Orlando Wetlands Park, Indian River County Wetlands Treatment Facility, Everglades Agricultural Area, Everglades National Park, Big Cypress National Preserve, Babcock-Webb Wildlife Management Area, Myakka River State Park, Crews Lake Park, Paynes Prairie Preserve State Park.

VIRGINIA RAIL

Comments: Winter visitor to freshwater marshes, uncommon throughout the mainland.

Key Sites: Lake Woodruff National Wildlife Refuge, Orlando Wetlands Park, Wakodahatchee Wetlands, Babcock-Webb Wildlife Management Area, Boyd Hill Nature Park, Crews Lake Park.

SORA

Comments: Migrant and winter visitor to fresh and brackish water marshes, common throughout the mainland.

Key Sites: Merritt Island National Wildlife Refuge, Orlando Wetlands Park, Loxahatchee National Wildlife Refuge, Wakodahatchee Wetlands, Everglades National Park, Ding Darling National Wildlife Refuge, Paynes Prairie Preserve State Park, St. Marks National Wildlife Refuge.

PURPLE GALLINULE

Comments: Year-round resident of freshwater marshes with floating vegetation, common throughout the central and southern peninsula. Locally common spring and summer resident in the northern peninsula, uncommon spring and summer resident in the Panhandle.

Key Sites: Orlando Wetlands Park, Viera Wetlands, Everglades Agricultural Area, Loxahatchee National Wildlife Refuge, Wakodahatchee Wetlands, Everglades National Park, Corkscrew Swamp Sanctuary, Myakka River State Park, Emeralda Marsh Conservation Area, Paynes Prairie Preserve State Park, St. Marks National Wildlife Refuge, Wakulla Springs State Park.

COMMON MOORHEN

Comments: Year-round resident of fresh and brackish water marshes, common-to-abundant throughout the mainland.

Key Sites: Lake Woodruff National Wildlife Refuge, Merritt Island National Wildlife Refuge, Orlando Wetlands Park, Viera Wetlands, Loxahatchee National Wildlife Refuge, Wakodahatchee Wetlands, Everglades National Park, Corkscrew Swamp Sanctuary, Ding Darling National Wildlife Refuge, Myakka River State Park, Emeralda Marsh Conservation Area, Paynes Prairie Preserve State Park, St. Marks National Wildlife Refuge.

AMERICAN COOT

Comments: Winter visitor to coastal and inland waters, common-to-abundant throughout the mainland. Occasionally breeds.

Key Sites: Lake Woodruff National Wildlife Refuge, Merritt Island National Wildlife Refuge, Orlando Wetlands Park, Loxahatchee National Wildlife Refuge, Biscayne National Park, Everglades National Park, Myakka River State Park, St. Marks National Wildlife Refuge.

LIMPKIN

Comments: Year-round resident of freshwater marshes and cypress swamp. Locally common throughout the peninsula, rare in the Panhandle.

Key Sites: Lake Woodruff National Wildlife Refuge, Wekiwa Springs State Park, Orlando Wetlands Park, Three Lakes Wildlife Management Area, John Prince Park, Loxahatchee National Wildlife Refuge, Wakodahatchee Wetlands, Everglades National Park, Corkscrew Swamp Sanctuary, Okaloacoochee Slough State Forest, Myakka River State Park, Saddle Creek County Park, Hillsborough River State Park.

SANDHILL CRANE

Comments: Common year-round resident and abundant winter visitor to freshwater marshes, wet prairie, and pastures throughout the peninsula.
Key Sites: Viera Wetlands, Three Lakes Wildlife Management Area, Savannas Preserve State Park, Babcock-Webb Wildlife Management Area, Myakka River State Park, Lake Placid area, Avon Park Air Force Range, Lake Kissimmee State Park, Disney Wilderness Preserve, Hillsborough River State Park, Jay B. Starkey Wilderness Park, Crews Lake Park, Emeralda Marsh Conservation Area, Paynes Prairie Preserve State Park.

WHOOPING CRANE

Comments: Extirpated. Captive-bred cranes reintroduced beginning in 1993.
Key Sites: Nonmigratory flock can be seen at Three Lakes Wildlife Management Area, occasionally at Lake Kissimmee State Park. Migratory flock winters at Chassahowitzka National Wildlife Refuge.

BLACK-BELLIED PLOVER

Comments: Winter visitor to sandy beaches, common throughout the state. Common migrant to sandy beaches and flooded agricultural fields throughout the state.
Key Sites: Talbot Islands State Parks, Merritt Island National Wildlife Refuge, Everglades Agricultural Area, Key Biscayne, Biscayne National Park, Everglades National Park, Tigertail Beach, Ft. Myers Beach, Ding Darling National Wildlife Refuge, Ft. De Soto, Honeymoon Island, St. Marks National Wildlife Refuge.

SNOWY PLOVER

Comments: Year-round resident of sandy beaches, local and uncommon throughout the Gulf coast. Vagrant on the Atlantic coast and in the Keys.
Key Sites: Tigertail Beach, Ft. Myers Beach, Ft. De Soto, Honeymoon Island, St. George Island, St. Joseph Peninsula State Park, Gulf Islands National Seashore.

WILSON'S PLOVER

Comments: Year-round resident of sandy beaches with exposed mudflats. Locally common throughout the state, except rare in the western Panhandle.
Key Sites: Talbot Islands State Parks, Key Biscayne, Tigertail Beach, Ft. Myers Beach, Sanibel Island, Ft. De Soto, Honeymoon Island, St. Marks National Wildlife Refuge.

SEMIPALMATED PLOVER

Comments: Winter visitor to sandy beaches with exposed mudflats, common throughout the state. Common migrant to sandy beaches and flooded agricultural fields.
Key Sites: Talbot Islands State Parks, Merritt Island National Wildlife Refuge, Everglades Agricultural Area, Key Biscayne, Everglades National Park, Tigertail Beach, Ft. Myers Beach, Sanibel Island, Ft. De Soto, Honeymoon Island, St. Marks National Wildlife Refuge.

PIPING PLOVER

Comments: Winter visitor to sandy beaches with exposed mudflats. Uncommon throughout the mainland, more common on Gulf coast beaches.
Key Sites: Talbot Islands State Parks, Smyrna Dunes Park, Key Biscayne, Tigertail Beach, Ft. Myers Beach, Ft. De Soto, Honeymoon Island, St. George Island, St. Joseph Peninsula State Park.

KILLDEER

Comments: Year-round resident, migrant and winter visitor to lakeshores and agricultural fields, common throughout the mainland.

Key Sites: Lake Apopka, Merritt Island National Wildlife Refuge, Orlando Wetlands Park, Viera Wetlands, Three Lakes Wildlife Management Area, Kissimmee Prairie Preserve State Park, Everglades Agricultural Area, Loxahatchee National Wildlife Refuge, Myakka River State Park, Ft. De Soto, Paynes Prairie Preserve State Park, St. Marks National Wildlife Refuge.

AMERICAN OYSTERCATCHER

Comments: Year-round resident of sandy beaches and estuaries with oyster bars. Locally common along the northern Atlantic coast of the peninsula and Gulf coast of the peninsula and eastern Panhandle.

Key Sites: Talbot Islands State Parks, Pelican Island National Wildlife Refuge, Chokoloskee, Tigertail Beach, Ft. Myers Beach, Ft. De Soto, Honeymoon Island, Cedar Key, Bald Point State Park, St. George Island.

BLACK-NECKED STILT

Comments: Spring and summer resident of freshwater marshes, impoundments, and flooded agricultural fields. Common-to-abundant in the central and southern peninsula, uncommon to rare elsewhere in the state. Uncommon migrant throughout the state. Uncommon during winter in the central and southern peninsula.

Key Sites: Orlando Wetlands Park, Viera Wetlands, Everglades Agricultural Area, Loxahatchee National Wildlife Refuge, Homestead area, Eagle Lakes Community Park, Myakka River State Park, Cockroach Bay Road, Emeralda Marsh Conservation Area.

AMERICAN AVOCET

Comments: Migrant and winter visitor to coastal mudflats, brackish water impoundments, and flooded agricultural fields, locally common throughout the state.

Key Sites: Merritt Island National Wildlife Refuge, Everglades Agricultural Area, Everglades National Park, Ft. Myers Beach.

GREATER YELLOWLEGS

Comments: Migrant and winter visitor to freshwater marshes, flooded agricultural fields, and brackish water impoundments, common throughout the state.

Key Sites: Lake Apopka, Merritt Island National Wildlife Refuge, Orlando Wetlands Park, Viera Wetlands, Everglades Agricultural Area, Loxahatchee National Wildlife Refuge, Green Cay and Wakodahatchee Wetlands, Homestead area, Southern Glades Wildlife and Environmental Area, Everglades National Park, Eagle Lakes Community Park, Myakka River State Park.

LESSER YELLOWLEGS

Comments: Migrant and winter visitor to freshwater marshes, flooded agricultural fields, and brackish water impoundments, Common-to-abundant throughout the state.

Key Sites: Lake Apopka, Merritt Island National Wildlife Refuge, Orlando Wetlands Park, Viera Wetlands, Everglades Agricultural Area, Loxahatchee National Wildlife Refuge, Green Cay and Wakodahatchee Wetlands, Homestead area, Southern Glades Wildlife and Environmental Area, Everglades National Park, Eagle Lakes Community Park, Myakka River State Park.

SOLITARY SANDPIPER

Comments: Migrant and winter visitor to freshwater marshes, ponds, and flooded agricultural fields, uncommon-to-rare throughout the state.

Key Sites: Viera Wetlands, Everglades Agricultural Area, Loxahatchee National Wildlife Refuge, Homestead area, Eagle Lakes Community Park, Six Mile Cypress Slough Preserve, Okaloacoochee Slough State Forest.

WILLET

Comments: Year-round resident and winter visitor to salt marsh and sandy beaches, common throughout the state. Uncommon fall migrant in flooded agricultural fields.

Key Sites: Talbot Islands State Parks, Guana River Reserve, Merritt Island National Wildlife Refuge, Everglades National Park, Tigertail

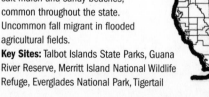

Beach, Sanibel Island, Ft. Myers Beach, Ft. De Soto, Honeymoon Island, St. Marks National Wildlife Refuge, St. George Island, Gulf Islands National Seashore.

SPOTTED SANDPIPER

Comments: Migrant and winter visitor to the shoreline of coastal and inland waters, uncommon to locally common throughout the state.
Key Sites: Key Biscayne, Biscayne National Park, Everglades National Park, Tigertail Beach, Sanibel Island, St. George Island, Gulf Islands National Seashore.

UPLAND SANDPIPER

Comments: Migrant to sod fields and dry, unplowed agricultural fields. Local and uncommon, most likely in the Panhandle during spring and in the peninsula during fall.
Key Sites: Viera Wetlands, Everglades Agricultural Area, Southern Glades Wildlife and Environmental Area, Cockroach Bay Road.

WHIMBREL

Comments: Migrant and winter visitor to coastal mudflats, uncommon throughout the state.
Key Sites: Talbot Islands State Parks, Dry Tortugas National Park, Everglades National Park, Tigertail Beach, Sanibel Island, Ft. Myers Beach, Ft. De Soto, Honeymoon Island.

MARBLED GODWIT

Comments: Migrant and winter visitor to coastal mudflats, locally common throughout the mainland.
Key Sites: Merritt Island National Wildlife Refuge, Everglades National Park, Tigertail Beach, Ft. Myers Beach, Sanibel Island, Ft. De Soto, Honeymoon Island.

RUDDY TURNSTONE

Comments: Year-round visitor to sandy beaches and rock jetties, common throughout the state. Uncommon in flooded agricultural fields during fall migration.
Key Sites: Ft. Clinch State Park, Guana River Reserve, Smyrna Dunes Park, Merritt Island

National Wildlife Refuge, Key Biscayne, Dry Tortugas National Park, Everglades National Park, Tigertail Beach, Sanibel Island, Ft. Myers Beach, Ft. De Soto, Honeymoon Island, St. Marks National Wildlife Refuge, St. George Island, Gulf Islands National Seashore.

RED KNOT

Comments: Migrant and winter visitor to sandy beaches. Locally common throughout the peninsula and eastern Panhandle, rare inland and in the western Panhandle and Keys. Seriously declining throughout its range.
Key Sites: Talbot Islands State Parks, Port Canaveral, Tigertail Beach, Ft. Myers Beach, Sanibel Island, Ft. De Soto, Honeymoon Island, Alligator Point.

SANDERLING

Comments: Migrant and winter visitor to sandy beaches, common-to-abundant throughout the state.
Key Sites: Ft. Clinch State Park, Talbot Islands State Parks, Guana River Reserve, Smyrna Dunes Park, Merritt Island National Wildlife Refuge, Port Canaveral, Key Biscayne, Tigertail Beach, Ft. Myers Beach, Sanibel Island, Ft. De Soto, Honeymoon Island, St. George Island, Gulf Islands National Seashore.

SEMIPALMATED SANDPIPER

Comments: Common migrant to coastal mudflats throughout the state, uncommon in fresh and brackish water impoundments and flooded agricultural fields. Uncommon-to-rare during winter in the extreme southern peninsula and Keys. Difficult to distinguish from Western Sandpiper.
Key Sites: Talbot Islands State Parks, Merritt Island National Wildlife Refuge, Everglades Agricultural Area, Loxahatchee National Wildlife Refuge, Everglades National Park, Tigertail Beach, Eagle Lakes Community Park, Ft. Myers Beach, Honeymoon Island, St. Marks National Wildlife Refuge.

WESTERN SANDPIPER

Comments: Migrant to coastal mudflats, fresh and brackish water impoundments, and flooded agricultural fields, common-to-abundant throughout the state. Common winter visitor to sandy beaches in the eastern Panhandle, peninsula, and Keys, uncommon inland and in the western Panhandle.

Key Sites: Talbot Islands State Parks, Merritt Island National Wildlife Refuge, Everglades Agricultural Area, Loxahatchee National Wildlife Refuge, Everglades National Park, Tigertail Beach, Eagle Lakes Community Park, Ding Darling National Wildlife Refuge, Ft. Myers Beach, Ft. De Soto, Honeymoon Island, St. Marks National Wildlife Refuge.

LEAST SANDPIPER

Comments: Migrant and winter visitor to coastal mudflats, fresh and brackish water impoundments, and flooded agricultural fields, common-to-abundant throughout the state.

Key Sites: Merritt Island National Wildlife Refuge, Viera Wetlands, Everglades Agricultural Area, Loxahatchee National Wildlife Refuge, Everglades National Park, Tigertail Beach, Eagle Lakes Community Park, Ding Darling National Wildlife Refuge, Ft. Myers Beach, Ft. De Soto, Honeymoon Island, St. Marks National Wildlife Refuge.

WHITE-RUMPED SANDPIPER

Comments: Migrant, mostly during late spring, to coastal mudflats, fresh and brackish water impoundments, and flooded agricultural fields, uncommon-to-rare throughout the state.

Key Sites: Merritt Island National Wildlife Refuge, Port Canaveral, Viera Wetlands, Homestead area, Eagle Lakes Community Park, Ft. De Soto, Honeymoon Island, Hague Dairy.

PECTORAL SANDPIPER

Comments: Migrant to fresh-water impoundments and flooded agricultural fields, common throughout the mainland.

Key Sites: Viera Wetlands, Everglades Agricultural Area, Homestead area, Southern Glades Wildlife and Environmental Area, Eagle Lakes Community Park, Cockroach Bay Road, Chapman's Pond, Ft. Walton Beach Spray Field.

DUNLIN

Comments: Migrant and winter visitor to coastal mudflats, common-to-abundant throughout the state.

Key Sites: Talbot Islands State Parks, Merritt Island National Wildlife Refuge, Everglades National Park, Tigertail Beach, Ft. Myers Beach, Ding Darling National Wildlife Refuge, Ft. De Soto, Honeymoon Island, St. Marks National Wildlife Refuge, St. George Island, Gulf Islands National Seashore.

STILT SANDPIPER

Comments: Migrant to flooded agricultural fields, uncommon to locally common throughout the state. Rare winter visitor in the southern peninsula.

Key Sites: Viera Wetlands, Everglades Agricultural Area, Loxahatchee National Wildlife Refuge, Homestead area, Eagle Lakes Community Park, Cockroach Bay Road, Chapman's Pond.

BUFF-BREASTED SANDPIPER

Comments: Migrant to grassy fields, pastures, and sod fields, rare throughout the state.

Key Sites: Lake Apopka, Everglades Agricultural Area, Homestead area, Ft. De Soto, Cockroach Bay Road.

SHORT-BILLED DOWITCHER

Comments: Common-to-abundant migrant to coastal mud-flats and scattered inland locations throughout the state. Common-to-abundant winter visitor to coastal mudflats throughout the eastern Panhandle, peninsula, and Keys.

Key Sites: Talbot Islands State Parks, Merritt Island National Wildlife Refuge, Key Biscayne, Everglades National Park, Tigertail Beach, Ft. Myers Beach, Ding Darling National Wildlife Refuge, Ft. De Soto, Honeymoon Island, St. Marks National Wildlife Refuge, St. George Island.

LONG-BILLED DOWITCHER

Comments: Migrant and winter visitor to fresh and brackish water impoundments and flooded agricultural fields, locally common throughout the mainland. Migrates later in fall and earlier in spring than Short-billed Dowitcher, best identified by call.

Key Sites: Orlando Wetlands Park, Merritt Island National Wildlife Refuge, Viera Wetlands, Everglades Agricultural Area, Loxahatchee National Wildlife Refuge, Green Cay Wetlands, Everglades National Park (Research Road), Eagle Lakes Community Park, Chapman's Pond.

WILSON'S SNIPE

Comments: Winter visitor to freshwater marshes and muddy lakeshores, common throughout the mainland.

Key Sites: Lake Apopka, Orlando Wetlands Park, Viera Wetlands, Loxahatchee National Wildlife Refuge, Wakodahatchee Wetlands, Eagle Lakes Community Park, Babcock-Webb Wildlife Management Area, Myakka River State Park, Crews Lake Park, Emeralda Marsh Conservation Area, Paynes Prairie Preserve State Park, Chapman's Pond, St. Marks National Wildlife Refuge.

AMERICAN WOODCOCK

Comments: Secretive year-round resident and winter visitor to woodland edges. Uncommon throughout the Panhandle and northern and central peninsula, rare in the southern peninsula. Usually seen at dawn and dusk.

Key Sites: Jennings State Forest, Gold Head Branch State Park, Lake Woodruff National Wildlife Refuge, Disney Wilderness Preserve, Boyd Hill Nature Park, Brooker Creek Preserve, Jay B. Starkey Wilderness Park, Crews Lake Park, Withlacoochee State Forest, St. Marks National Wildlife Refuge, Tiger Hammock Road.

WILSON'S PHALAROPE

Comments: Migrant to lakeshores and flooded agricultural fields, rare throughout the state.

Key Sites: Lake Apopka, Viera Wetlands, Everglades Agricultural Area, Homestead area.

RED-NECKED PHALAROPE

Comments: Uncommon pelagic migrant, mostly off the Atlantic coast, during spring and fall. Occasional inland after coastal storms.

Key Sites: By boat off Ponce Inlet, Islamorada.

RED PHALAROPE

Comments: Uncommon pelagic visitor, mostly off the Atlantic coast, from fall through spring. Occasional inland after coastal storms.

Key Sites: By boat off Ponce Inlet, Islamorada.

POMARINE JAEGER

Comments: Pelagic migrant and winter visitor, more common off the Atlantic coast.
Key Sites: By boat from Ponce Inlet, Islamorada. From shore at Canaveral National Seashore, Jetty Park, and Ponce, Sebastian, and Boynton Inlets and Key Biscayne during extended periods of strong easterly winds.

PARASITIC JAEGER

Comments: Pelagic migrant and winter visitor, more common off the Atlantic coast.
Key Sites: By boat from Ponce Inlet, Islamorada. From shore at Canaveral National Seashore, Jetty Park, and Ponce, Sebastian, and Boynton Inlets during extended periods of strong easterly winds.

LONG-TAILED JAEGER

Comments: Rare pelagic migrant and winter visitor.
Key Sites: By boat from Ponce Inlet, Islamorada.

LAUGHING GULL

Comments: Year-round resident along the coast and at lakes and landfills, abundant throughout the state.
Key Sites: Ft. Clinch State Park, Talbot Islands State Parks, Guana River Reserve, Merritt Island National Wildlife Refuge, Port Canaveral, Key Biscayne, Everglades National Park, Tigertail Beach, Ft. Myers Beach, Sanibel Island, Ft. De Soto, Honeymoon Island, St. Marks National Wildlife Refuge, St. George Island, Gulf Islands National Seashore.

BONAPARTE'S GULL

Comments: Winter resident along the coast and on large lakes. Locally common in the northern and central peninsula and Panhandle, uncommon-to-rare in the southern peninsula. Numbers vary from year to year.
Key Sites: Ft. Clinch State Park, Ft. Matanzas National Monument, Lake Apopka, Merritt Island National Wildlife Refuge, Port Canaveral, Viera Wetlands, Three Lakes Wildlife Management Area, Newnan's Lake, Gulf Islands National Seashore.

RING-BILLED GULL

Comments: Migrant and winter visitor along the coast and at lakes, landfills, and suburban areas, common-to-abundant throughout the state. Uncommon non-breeding resident along the coast during summer.
Key Sites: Ft. Clinch State Park, Talbot Islands State Parks, Guana River Reserve, Lake Apopka, Merritt Island National Wildlife Refuge, Port Canaveral, Three Lakes Wildlife Management Area, Key Biscayne, Biscayne National Park, Everglades National Park, Tigertail Beach, Ft. Myers Beach, Sanibel Island, Ft. De Soto, Honeymoon Island, St. Marks National Wildlife Refuge, St. George Island, Gulf Islands National Seashore.

HERRING GULL

Comments: Migrant and winter visitor along the coast and at landfills. Common throughout the northern and central peninsula and Panhandle, uncommon in the southern peninsula.
Key Sites: Ft. Clinch State Park, Talbot Islands State Parks, Smyrna Dunes Park, Merritt Island National Wildlife Refuge, Port Canaveral, Biscayne National Park, Ft. Myers Beach, Ft. De Soto, Honeymoon Island, St. Marks National Wildlife Refuge, St. George Island, Gulf Islands National Seashore.

LESSER BLACK-BACKED GULL

Comments: Locally common winter visitor, mostly along the Atlantic Coast and at landfills.
Key Sites: Talbot Islands State Parks, Merritt Island National Wildlife Refuge, Port Canaveral, Pompano Beach Landfill, Key Biscayne, Dump Marsh.

GREAT BLACK-BACKED GULL

Comments: Uncommon winter visitor along the Atlantic coast in the northern and central peninsula. Rare winter visitor along the Gulf coast and Atlantic coast of the southern peninsula.
Key Sites: Ft. Clinch State Park, Talbot Islands State Parks, Smyrna Dunes Park, Port Canaveral, Key Biscayne.

BLACK-LEGGED KITTIWAKE

Comments: Uncommon winter visitor off the Atlantic coast. Occasional winter visitor off the Gulf coast.
Key Sites: By boat off Ponce Inlet.

GULL-BILLED TERN

Comments: Spring and summer resident of coastal and inland waters, local and uncommon in the eastern Panhandle and peninsula. Uncommon winter visitor in the southern peninsula.
Key Sites: Ft. Clinch State Park, Talbot Islands State Parks, Merritt Island National Wildlife Refuge, Everglades Agricultural Area, Everglades National Park (Florida Bay), St. George Island.

CASPIAN TERN

Comments: Year-round resident of coastal and inland waters. Local and uncommon throughout the mainland, except absent from the western Panhandle during winter.
Key Sites: Talbot Islands State Parks, Merritt Island National Wildlife Refuge, Everglades Agricultural Area, Everglades National Park, Tigertail Beach, Ft. Myers Beach, Ft. De Soto, Honeymoon Island.

ROYAL TERN

Comments: Year-round resident of sandy beaches, Common-to-abundant throughout the state.
Key Sites: Ft. Clinch State Park, Talbot Islands State Parks, Guana River Reserve, Smyrna Dunes Park, Merritt Island National Wildlife Refuge, Port Canaveral, Key Biscayne, Biscayne National Park, Everglades National Park, Tigertail Beach, Ft. Myers Beach, Sanibel Island, Ft. De Soto, Honeymoon Island, St. George Island, Gulf Islands National Seashore.

SANDWICH TERN

Comments: Year-round resident of sandy beaches, locally common, mostly along the Gulf coast of the peninsula. Locally common migrant and winter visitor along sandy beaches throughout the state, except absent from the western Panhandle during winter.
Key Sites: Tigertail Beach, Ft. Myers Beach, Sanibel Island, Ft. De Soto, Honeymoon Island, St. George Island.

ROSEATE TERN

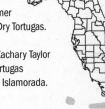

Comments: Locally common spring and summer resident in the Keys and Dry Tortugas. Often nests on rooftops.
Key Sites: Marathon, Ft. Zachary Taylor Historic State Park, Dry Tortugas National Park. By boat off Islamorada.

COMMON TERN

Comments: Common coastal migrant, especially in fall, throughout the state.
Key Sites: Ft. Clinch State Park, Tigertail Beach, Ft. De Soto, Honeymoon Island.

ARCTIC TERN

Comments: Occasional spring and summer migrant off the Atlantic coast and Keys.
Key Sites: By boat from Ponce Inlet, Islamorada. Atlantic coastal beaches during extended periods of strong easterly winds.

FORSTER'S TERN

Comments: Common migrant and winter visitor, uncommon-to-rare summer visitor to sandy beaches and inland waters throughout the mainland.
Key Sites: Ft. Clinch State Park, Lake Woodruff National Wildlife Refuge, Merritt Island National Wildlife Refuge, Three Lakes Wildlife Management Area, Everglades National Park, Tigertail Beach, Ft. Myers Beach, Sanibel Island, Myakka River State Park, Ft. De Soto, Honeymoon Island, St. Marks National Wildlife Refuge, St. George Island, Gulf Islands National Seashore.

LEAST TERN

Comments: Spring and summer resident along coastal and inland waters, common throughout the state. Often nests on rooftops.
Key Sites: Ft. Clinch State Park, Talbot Islands State Parks, Guana River Reserve, Ft. Matanzas National Monument, Merritt Island National Wildlife Refuge, Wakodahatchee Wetlands, Key Biscayne, Marathon area, Tigertail Beach, Ft. Myers Beach, Ft. De Soto, Honeymoon Island, St. George Island, Gulf Islands National Seashore.

BRIDLED TERN

Comments: Common Caribbean visitor, spring through fall, to Gulf Stream waters off the Atlantic coast, Keys, and Dry Tortugas.
Key Sites: By boat off Islamorada, Dry Tortugas National Park.

SOOTY TERN

Comments: Abundant spring and summer resident in the Dry Tortugas, rare offshore elsewhere.
Key Sites: Dry Tortugas National Park.

BLACK TERN

Comments: Migrant, especially in fall, to sandy beaches and flooded agricultural fields. Locally common throughout the mainland.
Key Sites: Ft. Clinch State Park, Guana River Reserve, Viera Wetlands, Everglades Agricultural Area, Tigertail Beach, Ft. Myers Beach, Ft. De Soto, Honeymoon Island, Green Key, St. George Island.

BROWN NODDY

Comments: Abundant spring and summer resident in the Dry Tortugas. Rare summer visitor off both coasts.
Key Sites: Dry Tortugas National Park.

BLACK SKIMMER

Comments: Year-round resident along sandy beaches and lakes and in flooded agricultural fields, common throughout the peninsula. Common resident along sandy beaches in the Panhandle from spring through fall. Common winter visitor in the Keys.

Key Sites: Ft. Clinch State Park, Talbot Islands State Parks, Anastasia State Park, Ft. Matanzas National Monument, Smyrna Dunes Park, Merritt Island National Wildlife Refuge, Port Canaveral, Three Lakes Wildlife Management Area, Pelican Island National Wildlife Refuge, Everglades Agricultural Area, Everglades National Park, Tigertail Beach, Ft. Myers Beach, Sanibel Island, Ft. De Soto, Honeymoon Island, St. George Island, Gulf Islands National Seashore.

ROCK PIGEON

Comments: Year-round resident of urban areas, abundant throughout the state.

Key Sites: All urban areas.

WHITE-CROWNED PIGEON

Comments: Year-round resident of tropical hardwood hammocks. Locally common in the southern peninsula (Miami-Dade, Monroe, Collier Counties) and Keys.

Key Sites: South Miami, A. D. Barnes Park, Kendall Indian Hammocks Park, Matheson Hammock Park, Key Largo Hammock State Botanical Site, Key West, Southern Glades Wildlife and Environmental Area, Everglades National Park, Collier-Seminole State Park.

EURASIAN COLLARED-DOVE

Comments: Native to Asia, likely reached Florida from the Bahamas, now a year-round resident in agricultural and residential areas. Locally common-to-abundant throughout the state.

Key Sites: Kendall area, Homestead area.

WHITE-WINGED DOVE

Comments: Year-round resident, origin debated, in suburban and agricultural areas. Locally common throughout the Lake Wales Ridge and southern peninsula, spreading rapidly northward. A rare winter visitor in the Panhandle, from western populations.

Key Sites: Suburban Ft. Lauderdale, Kendall area, Castellow Hammock Preserve, Homestead area, Lake Placid area.

MOURNING DOVE

Comments: Year-round resident of open woodlands, prairies, coastal strands, and agricultural and residential areas, abundant throughout the state. Greater Antillean race breeds in the Keys and Dry Tortugas.

Key Sites: Any suburban area.

COMMON GROUND-DOVE

Comments: Year-round resident in pinelands and coastal strands and around agricultural fields. Common (though declining) throughout the peninsula, uncommon in the Panhandle.

Key Sites: Ft. Clinch State Park, Guana River Reserve, Merritt Island National Wildlife Refuge, Kissimmee Prairie Preserve State Park, Jonathan Dickinson State Park, Key Biscayne, Southern Glades Environmental and Wildlife Area, Myakka River State Park, Honeymoon Island State Park, St. George Island.

BUDGERIGAR

Comments: Introduced, native to Australia. Once an abundant year-round resident in suburban areas on the Gulf coast of the central peninsula, now in severe decline.

Key Sites: Hudson, Hernando Beach.

MONK PARAKEET

Comments: Introduced, native to South America. Large, established populations in suburban areas on the Gulf coast of the central peninsula and the Atlantic coast of the southern peninsula. Smaller, unestablished populations in scattered locations throughout the peninsula.
Key Sites: Ft. Lauderdale, Miami Shores, Miami Springs, Key Biscayne, Kendall area, St. Petersburg, Tampa.

BLACK-HOODED PARAKEET

Comments: Introduced, native to South America. Large, established populations on the Gulf coast of the central peninsula. Small, unestablished populations in St. Augustine, the Palm Beach/Ft. Lauderdale/Miami area, and Key Largo.
Key Sites: Ft. De Soto, Boyd Hill Nature Park.

WHITE-WINGED PARAKEET

Comments: Introduced, native to South America. Year-round resident of residential areas in Ft. Lauderdale and the Miami area.
Key Sites: Miami Shores, Kendall area.

BLACK-BILLED CUCKOO

Comments: Rare migrant throughout the state, most likely in spring on the Gulf coast.
Key Sites: Ft. De Soto, St. Marks National Wildlife Refuge, St. George Island, Florida Caverns State Park, Gulf Islands National Seashore.

YELLOW-BILLED CUCKOO

Comments: Spring and summer resident of thickets, hammocks, and swamps, uncommon throughout the mainland and Upper Keys. Common migrant throughout the state.
Key Sites: Ft. Clinch State Park, Everglades Agricultural Area, Dry Tortugas National Park, Big Cypress National Preserve, Highlands Hammock State Park, Hillsborough River State Park, Ft. De Soto, O'Leno State Park, St. Marks National Wildlife Refuge, Wakulla Springs State Park, St. George Island, Torreya State Park, Florida Caverns State Park, Blackwater River State Forest.

MANGROVE CUCKOO

Comments: Secretive year-round resident of mangrove forest and tropical hardwood hammock, local and uncommon in the Keys, extreme southern peninsula. Local and uncommon spring and summer resident on the Gulf coast of the southern and central peninsula.
Key Sites: Key Largo Hammock Botanical State Park, Everglades National Park, Ding Darling National Wildlife Refuge, Weedon Island Preserve.

SMOOTH-BILLED ANI

Comments: Rare, local, and severely declining year-round resident of weedy and shrubby fields in the southern peninsula and Keys.
Key Sites: Everglades Agricultural Area, Loxahatchee National Wildlife Refuge, Ft. Lauderdale Airport area.

BARN OWL

Comments: Year-round resident and winter visitor in open prairies, pastures, and agricultural fields. Local and uncommon throughout the mainland and upper Keys. Roosts in hammocks and abandoned buildings.
Key Sites: Lake Apopka, Everglades Agricultural Area, Southern Glades Wildlife and Environmental Area, Everglades National Park.

EASTERN SCREECH-OWL

Comments: Year-round resident in woodlands and suburban areas, common throughout the mainland and Upper Keys.

Key Sites: Merritt Island National Wildlife Refuge, Everglades National Park, Corkscrew Swamp Sanctuary, Myakka River State Park, Highlands Hammock State Park, Wakulla Springs State Park.

GREAT HORNED OWL

Comments: Year-round resident in pinelands and hardwood hammock, uncommon throughout the mainland.

Key Sites: Loxahatchee National Wildlife Refuge, Everglades National Park, Fritchey Road Wetlands, Ft. De Soto, Honeymoon Island, Paynes Prairie Preserve State Park.

BURROWING OWL

Comments: Year-round resident of open prairies, pastures, and other cleared lands (airports, golf courses, and the like), locally common throughout the peninsula and Keys.

Key Sites: Kissimmee Prairie Preserve State Park, Brian Piccolo Park, Kendall-Tamiami Regional Airport, Sombrero Beach Golf Course (Marathon), Marco Island, Avon Park Air Force Range.

BARRED OWL

Comments: Year-round resident of cypress swamp and hardwood hammock, common throughout the mainland.

Key Sites: Lake Woodruff National Wildlife Refuge, Wekiwa Springs State Park, Kissimmee Prairie Preserve State Park, Everglades National Park, Big Cypress National Preserve, Corkscrew Swamp Sanctuary, Myakka River State Park, Highlands Hammock State Park, Lower Suwannee National Wildlife Refuge, Wakulla Springs State Park, Florida Caverns State Park.

COMMON NIGHTHAWK

Comments: Spring and summer resident in agricultural areas, pinelands, dry prairie, and scrub, common throughout the state. Abundant migrant throughout the state. Rare winter visitor (now verified) in the extreme southern peninsula.

Key Sites: Gold Head Branch State Park, Kissimmee Prairie Preserve State Park, Everglades Agricultural Area, Loxahatchee National Wildlife Refuge, Everglades National Park, Myakka River State Park, Highlands Hammock State Park, Hillsborough River State Park, St. Marks National Wildlife Refuge, St. George Island.

ANTILLEAN NIGHTHAWK

Comments: Spring and summer resident of open coastal strand, locally common in the Keys. Rare during spring in the extreme southern peninsula and Dry Tortugas. Best identified by its "pity-pit-pit" call.

Key Sites: Marathon, Stock Island, Key West, Dry Tortugas National Park.

CHUCK-WILL'S-WIDOW

Comments: Spring and summer resident of pinelands and oak hammock. Commonly heard, less commonly seen throughout the mainland. Common migrant throughout the state. Uncommon winter visitor in the southern peninsula.

Key Sites: Gold Head Branch State Park, Blue Springs State Park, Wekiwa Springs State Park, Bill Baggs Cape Florida State Park, A. D. Barnes Park, Dry Tortugas National Park, Everglades National Park, Big Cypress National Preserve, Myakka River State Park, Highlands Hammock State Park, Hillsborough River State Park, Ocala National Forest, Wakulla Springs State Park, Torreya State Park, Blackwater River State Forest.

WHIP-POOR-WILL

Comments: Winter visitor to pinelands, hammocks, and swamps, uncommon throughout the mainland. Frequently found along roadsides at dawn and dusk.
Key Sites: Everglades National Park, Brooker Creek Preserve, Withlacoochee State Forest.

CHIMNEY SWIFT

Comments: Migrant and summer resident, roosting in chimneys in residential areas. Common throughout the mainland.
Key Sites: Ft. Clinch State Park, Gold Head Branch State Park, Oscar Scherer State Park, Highlands Hammock State Park, Hillsborough River State Park, Boyd Hill Nature Park, Wakulla Springs State Park, Torreya State Park, Florida Caverns State Park.

RUBY-THROATED HUMMINGBIRD

Comments: Summer resident of woodlands, especially near water. Uncommon in the northern peninsula and Panhandle, occasional during summer in the southern peninsula. Common migrant throughout the state. Winter visitor to woodlands, botanical gardens, and residential areas. Uncommon in the southern peninsula and Keys, rare in the northern peninsula and Panhandle.
Key Sites: Fairchild Tropical Garden, Castellow Hammock Preserve, Dry Tortugas National Park, Ft. De Soto, Honeymoon Island, Kanapaha Botanical Gardens, Wakulla Springs State Park, Torreya State Park, Florida Caverns State Park.

BLACK-CHINNED HUMMINGBIRD

Comments: Winter visitor to residential feeders. Rare throughout the Panhandle and northern peninsula, occasional throughout the rest of the mainland.
Key Sites: Residential feeders in the Panhandle.

RUFOUS HUMMINGBIRD

Comments: Winter visitor, rare throughout the mainland.
Key Sites: Castellow Hammock Preserve, Kanapaha Botanical Gardens, residential feeders in the Panhandle.

BELTED KINGFISHER

Comments: Common migrant and winter visitor to coastal and inland waters throughout the state. Uncommon-to-rare year-round resident, near rivers, in the Panhandle, and scattered locations throughout the northern and central peninsula.
Key Sites: Merritt Island National Wildlife Refuge, Orlando Wetlands Park, Viera Wetlands, Loxahatchee National Wildlife Refuge, Everglades National Park, Big Cypress National Preserve, Myakka River State Park, Hillsborough River State Park, St. Marks National Wildlife Refuge.

RED-HEADED WOODPECKER

Comments: Year-round resident of pinelands, oak hammock, and pastures with dead trees. Locally common in the central and northern peninsula and Panhandle, rare in the southern peninsula.
Key Sites: Gold Head Branch State Park, Wekiwa Springs State Park, Lake Kissimmee State Park, Ocala National Forest, Morningside Nature Center, O'Leno State Park, Tall Timbers Research Station, Blackwater River State Forest.

RED-BELLIED WOODPECKER

Comments: Year-round resident of woodlands and residential areas. Common throughout the mainland, less common in the Keys.
Key Sites: Any woodland area.

YELLOW-BELLIED SAPSUCKER

Comments: Migrant and winter visitor to woodlands and residential areas, uncommon throughout the state.
Key Sites: Loxahatchee National Wildlife Refuge, Dry Tortugas National Park, Everglades National Park, Corkscrew Swamp Sanctuary, Myakka River State Park, Highlands Hammock State Park, Hillsborough River State Park, Wakulla Springs State Park, St. George Island, Torreya State Park, Florida Caverns State Park.

DOWNY WOODPECKER

Comments: Year-round resident of pinelands and other woodlands. Uncommon to locally common throughout the mainland.
Key Sites: Gold Head Branch State Park, Wekiwa Springs State Park, Turkey Creek Sanctuary, Jonathan Dickinson State Park, Everglades National Park, Big Cypress National Preserve, Corkscrew Swamp Sanctuary, Babcock-Webb Wildlife Management Area, Myakka River State Park, Highlands Hammock State Park, Hillsborough River State Park, Honeymoon Island, Wakulla Springs State Park, Torreya State Park, Florida Caverns State Park.

HAIRY WOODPECKER

Comments: Year-round resident of pinelands and hardwood swamp. Uncommon-to-rare throughout the mainland, prefers recently burned areas.
Key Sites: Big Cypress National Preserve, Six Mile Cypress Slough Preserve, Babcock-Webb Wildlife Management Area, Archbold Biological Station, Avon Park Air Force Range, Jay B. Starkey Wilderness Park, Withlacoochee State Forest, Torreya State Park, Blackwater River State Forest.

RED-COCKADED WOODPECKER

Comments: Year-round resident of mature, open pinelands, especially longleaf pine flatwoods and sandhills. Local and uncommon throughout the mainland. Easiest to find around nest cavities at dawn and dusk.
Key Sites: Three Lakes Wildlife Management Area, St. Sebastian River Preserve State Park, Babcock-Webb Wildlife Management Area, Avon Park Air Force Range, Withlacoochee State Forest, Ocala National Forest, Osceola National Forest, Apalachicola National Forest, Eglin Air Force Base, Blackwater River State Forest.

NORTHERN FLICKER

Comments: Year-round resident of pinelands and other woodlands, uncommon throughout the mainland and Upper Keys.
Key Sites: Ft. Clinch State Park, Lake Woodruff National Wildlife Refuge, Wekiwa Springs State Park, Loxahatchee National Wildlife Refuge, Everglades National Park, Big Cypress National Preserve, Babcock-Webb Wildlife Management Area, Myakka River State Park, Torreya State Park, Florida Caverns State Park.

PILEATED WOODPECKER

Comments: Year-round resident of cypress swamp, hardwood hammock, and other woodlands, uncommon to locally common throughout the mainland.
Key Sites: Wekiwa Springs State Park, Turkey Creek Sanctuary, Loxahatchee National Wildlife Refuge, Everglades National Park, Big Cypress National Preserve, Fakahatchee Strand Preserve State Park, Corkscrew Swamp Sanctuary, Sanibel Island, Myakka River State Park, Highlands Hammock State Park, Lower Suwannee National Wildlife Refuge, Wakulla Springs State Park, Torreya State Park, Florida Caverns State Park.

IVORY-BILLED WOODPECKER

Comments: Assumed to be extirpated from the United States, and possibly extinct, until rediscovered in Arkansas in 2004. Sightings in the Florida Panhandle beginning May 2005. Formerly a year-round resident of undisturbed cypress swamp, hardwood swamp, and hardwood hammock throughout much of the mainland.

Key Sites: Seen, heard, and recorded during 2005 and 2006 in hardwood swamp along the Choctawhatchee River, which forms the border between Walton and Washington Counties. Last previous report from near Highlands Hammock State Park (1967–69).

OLIVE-SIDED FLYCATCHER

Comments: Occasional migrant, more often in fall, throughout the state.
Key Sites: Ft. De Soto, St. Marks National Wildlife Refuge, Gulf Islands National Seashore.

EASTERN WOOD-PEWEE

Comments: Spring and summer resident of pinelands, uncommon in the northern peninsula and Panhandle. Common migrant throughout the state.

Key Sites: Jennings State Forest, A. D. Barnes Park, Dry Tortugas National Park, San Felasco Hammock Preserve State Park, Osceola National Forest, St. Marks National Wildlife Refuge, Wakulla Springs State Park, Ochlockonee River State Park, Tall Timbers Research Station, Apalachicola National Forest, Torreya State Park, Florida Caverns State Park, Gulf Islands National Seashore.

YELLOW-BELLIED FLYCATCHER

Comments: Rare migrant, mostly during fall in the Panhandle and on the Gulf coast of the peninsula.
Key Sites: St. George Island, Gulf Islands National Seashore.

ACADIAN FLYCATCHER

Comments: Spring and summer resident of hardwood and cypress swamps, common throughout the northern peninsula and Panhandle. Uncommon spring migrant along the Gulf coast and common fall migrant throughout the state.

Key Sites: Jennings State Forest, Gold Head Branch State Park, Ocala National Forest, Lower Suwannee National Wildlife Refuge, San Felasco Hammock Preserve State Park, O'Leno State Park, Wakulla Springs State Park, Apalachicola National Forest, Torreya State Park, Florida Caverns State Park.

ALDER FLYCATCHER

Comments: Rare migrant throughout the state, distinguished from Willow Flycatcher by call.
Key Sites: Recent reports (of birds heard calling) from Southern Glades Wildlife and Environmental Area, St. George Island.

WILLOW FLYCATCHER

Comments: Rare migrant throughout the state, distinguished from Alder Flycatcher by call.
Key Sites: Recent reports (of birds heard calling) from Amelia Island State Park, A. D. Barnes Park, Suwannee River State Park.

LEAST FLYCATCHER

Comments: Uncommon spring migrant in the Panhandle, uncommon fall migrant throughout the state. Rare winter visitor to dense thickets in the southern peninsula.

Key Sites: Lake Apopka, Loxahatchee National Wildlife Refuge, A. D. Barnes Park, Southern Glades Wildlife and Environmental Area, Everglades National Park, St. George Island.

EASTERN PHOEBE

Comments: Winter visitor to woodlands and marsh thickets, common throughout the mainland. Rare breeder in the western Panhandle.

Key Sites: Any area near water.

VERMILION FLYCATCHER

Comments: Migrant and winter visitor to freshwater marshes, prairies, and pastures, rare throughout the mainland. Individuals often return to the same location for consecutive winters.

Key Sites: Lake Apopka, Southern Glades Wildlife and Environmental Area, Everglades National Park, Alligator Lake Recreation Area, St. Marks National Wildlife Refuge, Lake Jackson.

GREAT CRESTED FLYCATCHER

Comments: Common spring and summer resident of woodlands in the central and northern peninsula and Panhandle. Common year-round resident and winter visitor to woodlands and mangrove forest in the southern peninsula.

Key Sites: Gold Head Branch State Park, Turkey Creek Sanctuary, Loxahatchee National Wildlife Refuge, Everglades National Park, Big Cypress National Preserve, Fakahatchee Strand Preserve State Park, Corkscrew Swamp Sanctuary, Oscar Scherer State Park, Myakka River State Park, Highlands Hammock State Park, Honeymoon Island, Wakulla Springs State Park, St. George Island, Torreya State Park, Florida Caverns State Park.

BROWN-CRESTED FLYCATCHER

Comments: Winter visitor to tropical hardwood hammock and mangrove forest, rare in the southern peninsula. Occasional in the northern peninsula.

Key Sites: Southern Glades Wildlife and Environmental Area, Everglades National Park.

WESTERN KINGBIRD

Comments: Migrant and winter visitor to pastures, agricultural areas, and roadsides, local and uncommon throughout the mainland.

Key Sites: Lake Apopka, Homestead area, Everglades National Park, Fritchey Road Wetlands, Ft. De Soto, Honeymoon Island, Paynes Prairie Preserve State Park, Bald Point State Park, St. George Island, St. Joseph Peninsula, Ft. Pickens.

EASTERN KINGBIRD

Comments: Spring and summer resident of woodland edges and pastures, uncommon throughout the mainland. Common to abundant migrant throughout the state.

Key Sites: Lake Apopka, Three Lakes Wildlife Management Area, Kissimmee Prairie Preserve State Park, Everglades Agricultural Area, Loxahatchee National Wildlife Refuge, Dry Tortugas National Park, Everglades National Park, Big Cypress National Preserve, Avon Park Air Force Range, Ft. De Soto, St. Marks National Wildlife Refuge, St. George Island, Torreya State Park, Florida Caverns State Park, Gulf Islands National Seashore.

GRAY KINGBIRD

Comments: Locally common spring and summer resident of coastal areas throughout the state and inland areas in the southern peninsula.

Key Sites: Ft. Matanzas National Monument, Hugh Taylor Birch State Park, Key Biscayne, Kendall area, Biscayne National Park, throughout the Florida Keys, Dry Tortugas National Park, Everglades National Park, Marco Island, Sanibel Island, Cockroach Bay Road, Ft. De Soto, Honeymoon Island, Green Key, Cedar Key, Big Bend Wildlife Management Area, Bald Point State Park, St. George Island, Ft. Pickens.

SCISSOR-TAILED FLYCATCHER

Comments: Uncommon migrant along the Gulf coast. Winter visitor to pastures, agricultural areas, and roadsides, local and uncommon in the peninsula and Keys.

Key Sites: Lake Apopka, Homestead area, Key West, Everglades National Park, Fritchey Road Wetlands, Cockroach Bay Road, Ft. De Soto, Honeymoon Island, Bald Point State Park, St. George Island, Ft. Pickens.

LOGGERHEAD SHRIKE

Comments: Year-round resident of open pinelands, prairies, pastures, and agricultural fields. Common throughout the mainland, except in the extreme southern peninsula.

Key Sites: Smyrna Dunes Park, Lake Apopka, Viera Wetlands, Three Lakes Wildlife Management Area, Kissimmee Prairie Preserve State Park, Loxahatchee National Wildlife Refuge, Kendall area, Homestead area, Eagle Lakes Community Park, Okaloacoochee Slough State Forest, Oscar Scherer State Park, Myakka River State Park, Avon Park Air Force Range, Hillsborough River State Park, Florida Caverns State Park.

WHITE-EYED VIREO

Comments: Year-round resident of thickets and forest understory, common throughout the state, except uncommon-to-rare during winter along the coast of the western Panhandle. Common migrant in coastal areas.

Key Sites: Any area with thickets or forest understory.

YELLOW-THROATED VIREO

Comments: Spring and summer resident of sandhills and hardwood hammock, common throughout the Panhandle and northern and central peninsula. Uncommon migrant throughout the state. Rare winter visitor in the extreme southern peninsula and Keys.

Key Sites: Jennings State Forest, Gold Head Branch State Park, Wekiwa Springs State Park, Loxahatchee National Wildlife Refuge, Everglades National Park, Chassahowitzka Wildlife Management Area, Lower Suwannee National Wildlife Refuge, Withlacoochee State Forest, San Felasco Hammock Preserve State Park, O'Leno State Park, St. Marks National Wildlife Refuge, Wakulla Springs State Park, Torreya State Park, Florida Caverns State Park.

BLUE-HEADED VIREO

Comments: Uncommon winter visitor to woodlands throughout the state, usually found in mixed flocks of wintering land birds.

Key Sites: Loxahatchee National Wildlife Refuge, Everglades National Park, Big Cypress National Preserve, Corkscrew Swamp Sanctuary, Myakka River State Park, Highlands Hammock State Park, Ft. De Soto, Lower Suwannee National Wildlife Refuge, Paynes Prairie Preserve State Park, St. Marks National Wildlife Refuge, Wakulla Springs State Park, Torreya State Park, Florida Caverns State Park.

WARBLING VIREO

Comments: Occasional migrant throughout the state.

Key Sites: Recent sightings from Spanish River Park, A. D. Barnes Park, Ft. De Soto, St. George Island, Ft. Pickens.

PHILADELPHIA VIREO

Comments: Rare migrant throughout the state.
Key Sites: Recent sightings from Spanish River Park, A. D. Barnes Park, Ft. De Soto, St. George Island, Ft. Pickens.

RED-EYED VIREO

Comments: Spring and summer resident of hardwood and cypress swamps. Common throughout the Panhandle and northern and central peninsula, rare and local in the southern peninsula. Uncommon-to-common spring migrant and common-to-abundant fall migrant throughout the state.
Key Sites: Gold Head Branch State Park, Highlands Hammock State Park, Hillsborough River State Park, Ft. De Soto, Paynes Prairie Preserve State Park, Wakulla Springs State Park, St. George Island, Torreya State Park, Florida Caverns State Park.

BLACK-WHISKERED VIREO

Comments: Spring and summer resident of tropical hardwood hammock and mangrove forest, common in the southern peninsula and Keys. Common spring migrant in the Dry Tortugas and the Atlantic coast of the southern peninsula, rare spring migrant along the Gulf coast.
Key Sites: Key Largo Hammock Botanical State Park, Long Key State Park, Dry Tortugas National Park, Everglades National Park, Ding Darling National Wildlife Refuge.

BLUE JAY

Comments: Year-round resident and winter visitor in woodlands and residential areas, common throughout the mainland and Upper Keys.
Key Sites: Any woodland area on the mainland.

FLORIDA SCRUB-JAY

Comments: Year-round resident of coastal and inland scrub, locally common throughout the peninsula. Florida's only endemic species.
Key Sites: Merritt Island National Wildlife Refuge, St. Sebastian River Preserve State Park, Jonathan Dickinson State Park, Oscar Scherer State Park, Archbold Biological Station, Avon Park Air Force Range, Lake Wales Ridge State Forest, Lake Kissimmee State Park, Disney Wilderness Preserve, Ocala National Forest.

AMERICAN CROW

Comments: Year-round resident of prairies, pinelands, cypress swamps, hammocks, and other rural areas. Common-to-abundant throughout the mainland interior, absent from the southeast peninsula.
Key Sites: Gold Head Branch State Park, Three Lakes Wildlife Management Area, Kissimmee Prairie Preserve State Park, Everglades National Park (including Flamingo area), Big Cypress National Preserve, Myakka River State Park, Highlands Hammock State Park, Avon Park Air Force Range, Hillsborough River State Park, Ocala National Forest, Osceola National Forest, St. Marks National Wildlife Refuge, Wakulla Springs State Park, Torreya State Park, Florida Caverns State Park.

FISH CROW

Comments: Year-round resident of both developed and undeveloped coastal areas (except along Florida Bay) and large lakes, common-to-abundant throughout the mainland. Also established in the Key West area.
Key Sites: Talbot Islands State Parks, Lake Woodruff National Wildlife Refuge, Lake Apopka, Merritt Island National Wildlife Refuge, Three Lakes Wildlife Management Area, Pelican Island National Wildlife Refuge, Greynold's Park, Sanibel Island, Ft. De Soto, Honeymoon Island, Paynes Prairie Preserve State Park, St. Marks National Wildlife Refuge, Wakulla Springs State Park, St. George Island, Torreya State Park, Florida Caverns State Park, Gulf Islands National Seashore.

PURPLE MARTIN

Comments: Uncommon to locally common spring and summer resident throughout the mainland, nesting almost exclusively in man-made structures. Common-to-abundant early migrant throughout the state.

Key Sites: Gold Head Branch State Park, Orlando Wetlands Park, Wakodahatchee Wetlands, Kendall area, Dry Tortugas National Park, Everglades National Park, St. Marks National Wildlife Refuge, Tall Timbers Research Station, St. George Island, Torreya State Park, Florida Caverns State Park, Gulf Islands National Seashore.

TREE SWALLOW

Comments: Common-to-abundant migrant, locally common-to-abundant winter visitor to freshwater marshes, prairies, and agricultural fields throughout the state.

Key Sites: Guana River Reserve, Lake Woodruff National Wildlife Refuge, Lake Apopka, Merritt Island National Wildlife Refuge, Viera Wetlands, Loxahatchee National Wildlife Refuge, Wakodahatchee/Green Key Wetlands, Everglades National Park, Big Cypress National Preserve, Myakka River State Park, Paynes Prairie Preserve State Park, St. Marks National Wildlife Refuge.

NORTHERN ROUGH-WINGED SWALLOW

Comments: Rare-to-uncommon summer resident and common migrant to freshwater marshes, prairies, and agricultural fields throughout the state. Locally common year-round resident in the southern peninsula.

Key Sites: Everglades Agricultural Area, Loxahatchee National Wildlife Refuge, Wakodahatchee/Green Key Wetlands, St. Marks National Wildlife Refuge, Florida Caverns State Park.

BANK SWALLOW

Comments: Local and uncommon migrant, more often during fall, to freshwater marshes, prairies, and agricultural fields throughout the state.

Key Sites: Everglades Agricultural Area, Loxahatchee National Wildlife Refuge, Dry Tortugas National Park.

CLIFF SWALLOW

Comments: Rare migrant throughout the state.

Key Sites: Dry Tortugas National Park, St. George Island.

CAVE SWALLOW

Comments: Caribbean race is a locally common, nearly year-round resident, nesting under highway bridges in the Cutler Ridge and Homestead areas. Southwestern race is an uncommon-to-rare migrant throughout the state.

Key Sites: Cutler Ridge, Dry Tortugas National Park, Everglades National Park.

BARN SWALLOW

Comments: Migrant to freshwater marshes, prairies, and agricultural areas, common to abundant throughout the state. Locally common summer resident in the northern peninsula and Panhandle, usually nesting under bridges or other man-made structures. Rare summer resident in the central and southern peninsula.

Key Sites: Lake Woodruff National Wildlife Refuge, Merritt Island National Wildlife Refuge, Loxahatchee National Wildlife Refuge, Dry Tortugas National Park, Everglades National Park, Big Cypress National Preserve, Ft. De Soto, Honeymoon Island, St. Marks National Wildlife Refuge, St. George Island, Gulf Islands National Seashore.

CAROLINA CHICKADEE

Comments: Year-round resident of woodlands and swamps, common throughout the Panhandle, northern peninsula, and Gulf coast of the central peninsula.

Key Sites: Jennings State Forest, Tosohatchee State Reserve, Ocala National Forest, Lower Suwannee National Wildlife Refuge, Paynes Prairie Preserve State Park, Osceola National Forest, St. Marks National Wildlife Refuge, Wakulla Springs State Park, Apalachicola National Forest, Torreya State Park, Florida Caverns State Park.

TUFTED TITMOUSE

Comments: Year-round resident of woodlands and swamps, common throughout the Panhandle and northern, central, and southwestern peninsula.

Key Sites: Ft. Clinch State Park, Gold Head Branch State Park, Guana River Reserve, Lake Woodruff National Wildlife Refuge, Big Cypress National Preserve, Corkscrew Swamp Sanctuary, Highland Hammocks State Park, Ocala National Forest, Lower Suwannee National Wildlife Refuge, Paynes Prairie Preserve State Park, Osceola National Forest, St. Marks National Wildlife Refuge, Wakulla Springs State Park, Apalachicola National Forest, Torreya State Park, Florida Caverns State Park.

RED-BREASTED NUTHATCH

Comments: Rare winter visitor to pinelands in the northern peninsula and Panhandle.

Key Sites: St. Marks National Wildlife Refuge, Florida Caverns State Park, Blackwater River State Forest.

WHITE-BREASTED NUTHATCH

Comments: Year-round resident of pinelands and mixed hardwood forests, local and uncommon in the Red Hills area around Tallahassee.

Key Sites: Elinor Klapp-Phipps Park, Tall Timbers Research Station.

BROWN-HEADED NUTHATCH

Comments: Uncommon year-round resident of pinelands throughout the Panhandle and northern, central, and southwestern peninsula.

Key Sites: Jennings State Forest, Tosohatchee State Reserve, Three Lakes Wildlife Management Area, Everglades National Park (reintroduced), Big Cypress National Preserve, Babcock-Webb Wildlife Management Area, Avon Park Air Force Range, Jay B. Starkey Wilderness Park, Withlacoochee State Forest, Ocala National Forest, Morningside Nature Center, Osceola National Forest, Big Bend Wildlife Management Area, St. Marks National Wildlife Refuge, Tall Timbers Research Station, Apalachicola National Forest.

BROWN CREEPER

Comments: Rare winter visitor to woodlands throughout the northern peninsula and Panhandle.

Key Sites: St. Marks National Wildlife Refuge, Lake Jackson, Torreya State Park, Three Rivers State Park, Florida Caverns State Park.

CAROLINA WREN

Comments: Year-round resident of woodlands and swamps, common throughout the mainland (except Miami), uncommon in northern Key Largo.

Key Sites: Any woodland or swamp.

HOUSE WREN

Comments: Common winter visitor to thickets throughout the mainland, uncommon in the Keys.

Key Sites: Gold Head Branch State Park, Merritt Island National Wildlife Refuge, Loxahatchee National Wildlife Refuge, Everglades National Park, Corkscrew Swamp Sanctuary, Oscar Scherer State Park, Myakka River State Park, Honeymoon Island, St. Marks National Wildlife Refuge, Wakulla Springs State Park, St. George Island, Florida Caverns State Park.

WINTER WREN

Comments: Winter resident of underbrush near lakes and rivers, rare in the northern peninsula and Panhandle.

Key Sites: Jennings State Forest, Gold Head Branch State Park, St. Marks National Wildlife Refuge, Wakulla Springs, Lake Jackson, Torreya State Park, Three Rivers State Park, Florida Caverns State Park, Blackwater River State Forest.

SEDGE WREN

Comments: Secretive winter resident of wet, grassy areas and salt marsh, common in the northern peninsula and Panhandle. Uncommon-to-rare during winter in the central and southern peninsula.

Key Sites: Lake Apopka, Emeralda Marsh Conservation Area, Paynes Prairie Preserve State Park, St. Marks National Wildlife Refuge, Apalachicola National Forest.

MARSH WREN

Comments: Secretive year-round resident of salt marsh, locally common on the Gulf coast of the eastern Panhandle and northern peninsula (Marion's race) and the Atlantic coast of the extreme northern peninsula (Worthington's race). Several races breeding outside Florida are uncommon winter visitors to freshwater marshes and salt marsh throughout the mainland.

Key Sites: *Worthington's race:* Ft. Clinch State Park. *Marion's race:* Green Key, Cedar Key, Big Bend Wildlife Management Area, St. Marks National Wildlife Refuge. *Wintering races:* Lake Apopka, Loxahatchee National Wildlife Refuge, Paynes Prairie Preserve State Park.

RED-WHISKERED BULBUL

Comments: Introduced, locally common year-round resident of residential areas in Kendall and Pinecrest, in Miami-Dade County.

Key Sites: Residential areas around Baptist Hospital in Kendall, Royal Palm Tennis Courts in Pinecrest.

GOLDEN-CROWNED KINGLET

Comments: Uncommon winter visitor to woodlands throughout the Panhandle and northern peninsula, rare during winter in the central peninsula.

Key Sites: St. Marks National Wildlife Refuge, Wakulla Springs State Park, Lake Jackson, Apalachicola National Forest, Torreya State Park, Three Rivers State Park, Florida Caverns State Park, Blackwater River State Forest.

RUBY-CROWNED KINGLET

Comments: Common winter visitor in woodlands throughout the Panhandle and northern peninsula. Uncommon-to-rare during winter in the central and southern peninsula, rare in the Keys. Usually found in mixed flocks of wintering land birds.

Key Sites: Jennings State Forest, Gold Head Branch State Park, Lake Woodruff National Wildlife Refuge, Wekiwa Springs State Park, Myakka River State Park, Highland Hammocks State Park, Hillsborough River State Park, Lower Suwannee National Wildlife Refuge, Paynes Prairie Preserve State Park, St. Marks National Wildlife Refuge, Wakulla Springs State Park, St. George Island, Torreya State Park, Florida Caverns State Park.

BLUE-GRAY GNATCATCHER

Comments: Spring and summer resident of pinelands, woodlands, and swamps, uncommon throughout the Panhandle and northern, central, and southwestern peninsula. Common migrant throughout the state. Winter visitor to woodlands and residential areas, common-to-abundant throughout the central and southern peninsula and Keys. Uncommon-to-rare during winter in the Panhandle and northern peninsula.

Key Sites: Any woodland or swamp.

EASTERN BLUEBIRD

Comments: Year-round resident and winter visitor to pinelands, prairies, and pastures, common throughout the mainland.

Key Sites: Jennings State Forest, Three Lakes Wildlife Management Area, Everglades National Park (reintroduced), Big Cypress National Preserve, Babcock-Webb Wildlife Management Area, Avon Park Air Force Range, Ocala National Forest, Lower Suwannee National Wildlife Refuge, Osceola National Forest, Apalachicola National Forest, Florida Caverns State Park.

VEERY

Comments: Uncommon migrant throughout the state, more common during spring along the Gulf coast.

Key Sites: Turkey Creek Sanctuary, A. D. Barnes Park, Matheson Hammock Park, Dry Tortugas National Park, Corkscrew Swamp Sanctuary, Ft. De Soto, John Bonner Nature Park, Honeymoon Island, Paynes Prairie Preserve State Park, O'Leno State Park, Wakulla Springs State Park, St. George Island, Torreya State Park, Gulf Islands National Seashore.

GRAY-CHEEKED THRUSH

Comments: Uncommon migrant throughout the state, more common during spring along the Gulf coast.

Key Sites: Loxahatchee National Wildlife Refuge, Bill Baggs Cape Florida State Park, A. D. Barnes Park, Matheson Hammock Park, Dry Tortugas National Park, Corkscrew Swamp Sanctuary, Ft. De Soto, John Bonner Nature Park, Honeymoon Island, Paynes Prairie Preserve State Park, St. George Island, Torreya State Park, Florida Caverns State Park, Gulf Islands National Seashore.

SWAINSON'S THRUSH

Comments: Common migrant throughout the state, more common during spring along the Gulf coast.

Key Sites: Loxahatchee National Wildlife Refuge, Bill Baggs Cape Florida State Park, A. D. Barnes Park, Matheson Hammock Park, Dry Tortugas National Park, Corkscrew Swamp Sanctuary, Ft. De Soto, John Bonner Nature Park, Honeymoon Island, Paynes Prairie Preserve State Park, Wakulla Springs State Park, St. George Island, Torreya State Park, Florida Caverns State Park, Gulf Islands National Seashore.

HERMIT THRUSH

Comments: Migrant and winter visitor to woodlands with dense undergrowth, common throughout the northern peninsula and Panhandle. Uncommon-to-rare during winter in the central and southern peninsula and Keys.

Key Sites: Loxahatchee National Wildlife Refuge, Lake Kissimmee State Park, Hills-borough River State Park, Paynes Prairie Preserve State Park, Wakulla Springs State Park, St. George Island, Torreya State Park, Florida Caverns State Park.

WOOD THRUSH

Comments: Spring and summer resident of hardwood swamp, uncommon throughout the northern peninsula and Panhandle. Uncommon-to-rare migrant throughout the state.

Key Sites: Ft. Clinch State Park, Gold Head Branch State Park, Dry Tortugas National Park, Ft. De Soto, San Felasco Hammock Preserve State Park, Wakulla Springs State Park, Torreya State Park, Florida Caverns State Park, Blackwater River State Forest.

AMERICAN ROBIN

Comments: Local, rare-to-uncommon spring and summer resident of woodlands and residential areas in the Panhandle. Winter visitor to woodlands and swamps, common-to-abundant throughout the northern and central peninsula and Panhandle. Irruptive winter visitor throughout the southern peninsula.

Key Sites: Gold Head Branch State Park, Lake Woodruff National Wildlife Refuge, Jonathan Dickinson State Park, Loxahatchee National Wildlife Refuge, Everglades National Park, Oscar Scherer State Park, Myakka River State Park, Highlands Hammock State Park, Hillsborough River State Park, Lower Suwannee National Wildlife Refuge, Paynes Prairie Preserve State Park, St. Marks National Wildlife Refuge, Wakulla Springs State Park, Torreya State Park, Florida Caverns State Park.

GRAY CATBIRD

Comments: Common-to-abundant migrant throughout the state. Common winter visitor to woodland thickets throughout the central and southern peninsula and Upper Keys, uncommon-to-rare during winter in the Panhandle, northern peninsula, and Lower Keys. Rare and local spring and summer resident in the Panhandle and extreme northern peninsula.

Key Sites: Gold Head Branch State Park, Loxahatchee National Wildlife Refuge, Southern Glades Wildlife and Environmental Area, Everglades National Park, Oscar Scherer State Park, Myakka River State Park, Hillsborough River State Park, Ft. De Soto, St. Marks National Wildlife Refuge, Wakulla Springs State Park, St. George Island.

NORTHERN MOCKINGBIRD

Comments: Year-round resident of residential and agricultural areas, common to abundant throughout the state.
Key Sites: Any residential or agricultural area.

BROWN THRASHER

Comments: Year-round resident of woodland thickets, common throughout the northern peninsula and Panhandle, uncommon throughout the central and southern peninsula.
Key Sites: Ft. Clinch State Park, Gold Head Branch State Park, Wekiwa Springs State Park, Oscar Scherer State Park, Myakka River State Park, Highlands Hammock State Park, Hillsborough River State Park, Lower Suwannee National Wildlife Refuge, St. Marks National Wildlife Refuge, Wakulla Springs State Park, Torreya State Park, Florida Caverns State Park, Blackwater River State Forest, Gulf Islands National Seashore.

EUROPEAN STARLING

Comments: Introduced, native to Europe. Year-round resident of residential and agricultural areas, common to abundant throughout the state.
Key Sites: Any residential or agricultural area.

AMERICAN PIPIT

Comments: Migrant and winter visitor to plowed agricultural fields, pastures, and sewage ponds. Common throughout the northern peninsula and Panhandle, uncommon-to-rare in the central and southern peninsula and Keys.
Key Sites: Lake Apopka, Viera Wetlands, Three Lakes Wildlife Management Area, Southern Glades Wildlife and Environmental Area, Hague Dairy, Thomas P. Smith Reclamation Facility in Tallahassee.

SPRAGUE'S PIPIT

Comments: Rare winter visitor to the Panhandle. Typically found in dry lakebeds as well as areas of dry, undisturbed grass, such as unmowed roadsides and between airport runways.
Key Sites: Apalachicola Airport, Florida's most reliable location for this species in recent years is no longer accessible to birders. Another formerly productive location, the causeway connecting St. George Island with the mainland, has been replaced by a bridge. The original causeway is now an inaccessible island. Several records for this species come from Lake Jackson; all are from periods of very low water levels.

CEDAR WAXWING

Comments: Irruptive winter and spring visitor to woodlands, thickets, and residential areas with fruiting trees and shrubs. Common-to-abundant throughout the Panhandle and northern peninsula, common-to-rare in the central and southern peninsula and Keys.
Key Sites: Merritt Island National Wildlife Refuge, Loxahatchee National Wildlife Refuge, Everglades National Park, Hillsborough River State Park, Ft. De Soto, Lower Suwannee National Wildlife Refuge, Paynes Prairie Preserve State Park, Wakulla Springs State Park, Alligator Point, Torreya State Park, Florida Caverns State Park, Gulf Islands National Seashore.

BLUE-WINGED WARBLER

Comments: Rare migrant throughout the state. Occasional winter visitor to the southern peninsula and Keys.
Key Sites: Dry Tortugas National Park, Saddle Creek Park, Ft. De Soto, St. George Island, Florida Caverns State Park.

GOLDEN-WINGED WARBLER

Comments: Rare migrant, mostly during fall, throughout the state.

Key Sites: Dry Tortugas National Park, Saddle Creek Park, Ft. De Soto, Sawgrass Lake Park, St. George Island, Florida Caverns State Park.

TENNESSEE WARBLER

Comments: Rare spring migrant, uncommon fall migrant throughout the state. Occasional winter visitor to the southern peninsula.

Key Sites: Mead Garden, Dry Tortugas National Park, Everglades National Park, Ft. De Soto, Sawgrass Lake Park, San Felasco Hammock Preserve State Park, Florida Caverns State Park.

ORANGE-CROWNED WARBLER

Comments: Winter visitor to thickets and woodland understory, uncommon throughout the mainland.

Key Sites: Lake Apopka, Loxahatchee National Wildlife Refuge, Corkscrew Swamp Sanctuary, Myakka River State Park, Emeralda Marsh Conservation Area, Paynes Prairie Preserve State Park, St. Marks National Wildlife Refuge, Florida Caverns State Park.

NASHVILLE WARBLER

Comments: Rare migrant, mostly during fall, throughout the state. Rare winter visitor in the southern peninsula.

Key Sites: Loxahatchee National Wildlife Refuge, Greynold's Park, Dry Tortugas National Park, Ft. De Soto.

NORTHERN PARULA

Comments: Spring and summer resident of woodlands and swamps with Spanish moss. Common throughout the Panhandle and northern and central peninsula, local and uncommon in the southern peninsula. Common-to-abundant migrant throughout the state. Uncommon winter visitor to the southern peninsula and Keys, rare in the Panhandle and northern peninsula.

Key Sites: Gold Head Branch State Park, Loxahatchee National Wildlife Refuge, Everglades National Park, Big Cypress National Preserve, Corkscrew Swamp Sanctuary, Myakka River State Park, Highlands Hammock State Park, Hillsborough River State Park, Ft. De Soto, Lower Suwannee National Wildlife Refuge, Paynes Prairie Preserve State Park, Wakulla Springs State Park, St. George Island, Torreya State Park, Florida Caverns State Park.

YELLOW WARBLER

Comments: Eastern North American race is an uncommon spring migrant and common fall migrant throughout the state. Cuban race is a year-round resident of mangrove forests, locally common in the extreme southern peninsula and Keys.

Key Sites: *Eastern North American race:* Everglades Agricultural Area, Loxahatchee National Wildlife Refuge, Dry Tortugas National Park, Honeymoon Island, Emeralda Marsh Conservation Area, Paynes Prairie Preserve State Park, St. Marks National Wildlife Refuge, St. George Island. *Cuban race:* Biscayne National Park, Card Sound Road in Key Largo, Everglades National Park (Florida Bay).

CHESTNUT-SIDED WARBLER

Comments: Rare spring migrant, rare-to-uncommon fall migrant throughout the state. Most common on the Gulf coast.

Key Sites: Dry Tortugas National Park, Ft. De Soto, Sawgrass Lake Park, Honeymoon Island, San Felasco Hammock Preserve State Park, Florida Caverns State Park.

MAGNOLIA WARBLER

Comments: Rare spring migrant, uncommon fall migrant throughout the state. Rare winter visitor to the southern peninsula and Keys.

Key Sites: Loxahatchee National Wildlife Refuge, Dry Tortugas National Park, Everglades National Park, Wakulla Springs State Park, St. George Island, Florida Caverns State Park.

CAPE MAY WARBLER

Comments: Uncommon-to-common spring migrant, mostly to coastal areas, throughout the state. Common fall migrant along the Atlantic coast of the southern peninsula, uncommon-to-rare elsewhere in the state. Rare winter visitor to the southern peninsula and Keys.

Key Sites: Loxahatchee National Wildlife Refuge, Spanish River Park, Hugh Taylor Birch State Park, Bill Baggs Cape Florida State Park, Dry Tortugas National Park, Everglades National Park, Ft. De Soto, Honeymoon Island, St. George Island.

BLACK-THROATED BLUE WARBLER

Comments: Common spring migrant, mostly to coastal areas, throughout the state. Common fall migrant along the Atlantic coast of the southern peninsula, uncommon-to-rare elsewhere in the state. Uncommon-to-rare winter visitor to the southern peninsula and Keys.

Key Sites: Turkey Creek Sanctuary, Loxahatchee National Wildlife Refuge, Spanish River Park, Hugh Taylor Birch State Park, Bill Baggs Cape Florida State Park, A. D. Barnes Park, Dry Tortugas National Park, Everglades National Park, Honeymoon Island.

YELLOW-RUMPED WARBLER

Comments: Myrtle Warbler, the eastern race, is a winter visitor to woodlands with a dense understory. Common-to-abundant throughout the state, though irruptive in the southern peninsula and Keys. Audubon's Warbler, the western race, is an occasional vagrant.

Key Sites: Any woodland area.

BLACK-THROATED GREEN WARBLER

Comments: Uncommon late-season migrant, mostly in late fall, throughout the state. Uncommon winter visitor to the southern peninsula and Keys.

Key Sites: Loxahatchee National Wildlife Refuge, Tree Tops Park, Dry Tortugas National Park, Everglades National Park, Sawgrass Lake Park, Paynes Prairie Preserve State Park, Florida Caverns State Park.

BLACKBURNIAN WARBLER

Comments: Rare to uncommon migrant, mostly in fall, throughout the state. More common on the Gulf coast.

Key Sites: Dry Tortugas National Park, Everglades National Park, Ft. De Soto, Sawgrass Lake Park, Honeymoon Island, Florida Caverns State Park.

YELLOW-THROATED WARBLER

Comments: Year-round resident of pinelands, cypress swamp, and other woodlands with Spanish moss. Uncommon throughout the Panhandle and northern and central peninsula, but withdraws from inland locations in the Panhandle and northern peninsula during winter. Common early-season migrant throughout the state. Uncommon winter visitor throughout the southern peninsula and Keys.

Key Sites: Gold Head Branch State Park, Loxahatchee National Wildlife Refuge, Big Cypress National Preserve, Corkscrew Swamp Sanctuary, Highlands Hammock State Park, Lower Suwannee National Wildlife Refuge, Wakulla Springs State Park, Torreya State Park, Florida Caverns State Park.

PINE WARBLER

Comments: Year-round resident, migrant, and winter visitor to pinelands and mixed pine/hardwood forests, common throughout the mainland. Rare during winter in the Keys.

Key Sites: Gold Head Branch State Park, Lake Woodruff National Wildlife Refuge, Everglades National Park, Big Cypress National Preserve, Corkscrew Swamp Sanctuary, Babcock-Webb Wildlife Management Area, Highlands Hammock State Park, Osceola National Forest, St. Marks National Wildlife Refuge, Wakulla Springs State Park, Apalachicola National Forest, Torreya State Park, Florida Caverns State Park.

PRAIRIE WARBLER

Comments: Florida race is a year-round resident of mangrove forest and coastal strand. Uncommon along the coast in the central peninsula, common along the coast in the southern peninsula and Keys. Northern race is a spring and summer resident of second-growth woodlands and brushy fields. Rare-to-uncommon in the Panhandle and northern peninsula. Common migrant throughout the state. Winter visitor, mostly along the coasts. Rare in the Panhandle, rare-to-uncommon in the northern and central peninsula, common in the southern peninsula and Keys.

Key Sites: Loxahatchee National Wildlife Refuge, Bill Baggs Cape Florida State Park, throughout the Florida Keys, Everglades National Park, Ding Darling National Wildlife Refuge, Ft. De Soto, Honeymoon Island, St. Marks National Wildlife Refuge, St. George Island.

PALM WARBLER

Comments: Migrant and winter visitor to open woodlands, prairies, and agricultural and residential areas. Common-to-abundant throughout the peninsula and Keys, uncommon-to-rare in the Panhandle. Western race predominates.

Key Sites: Loxahatchee National Wildlife Refuge, Bill Baggs Cape Florida State Park, Dry Tortugas National Park, Everglades National Park, Myakka River State Park, Ft. De Soto, Honeymoon Island, Paynes Prairie Preserve State Park, St. George Island.

BAY-BREASTED WARBLER

Comments: Rare-to-uncommon late-season migrant throughout the state, more common during spring along the Gulf coast.

Key Sites: Dry Tortugas National Park, Ft. De Soto, John Bonner Nature Park, Honeymoon Island, St. George Island, St. Joseph Peninsula.

BLACKPOLL WARBLER

Comments: Coastal migrant throughout the state. Common during spring in the peninsula and Keys, uncommon in the Panhandle, rare at inland locations. Rare-to-uncommon during fall throughout the state.

Key Sites: Talbot Islands State Parks, Loxahatchee National Wildlife Refuge, Bill Baggs

Cape Florida State Park, Dry Tortugas National Park, Everglades National Park, Ft. De Soto, Honeymoon Island, St. George Island.

CERULEAN WARBLER

Comments: Rare early-season migrant, mostly on the Gulf coast during spring, more widespread during fall.

Key Sites: Dry Tortugas National Park, Saddle Creek Park, Ft. De Soto, Sawgrass Lake Park, John Bonner Nature Park.

BLACK-AND-WHITE WARBLER

Comments: Uncommon migrant and winter visitor to woodlands throughout the state. Most common during winter in the southern peninsula and Keys, rare in the western Panhandle.

Key Sites: Ft. Clinch State Park, Merritt Island National Wildlife Refuge, Turkey Creek Sanctuary, Loxahatchee National Wildlife Refuge, Everglades National Park, Corkscrew Swamp Sanctuary, Oscar Scherer State Park, Hillsborough River State Park, Ft. De Soto, Wakulla Springs State Park, Torreya State Park, Florida Caverns State Park.

AMERICAN REDSTART

Comments: Common-to-abundant migrant throughout the state. Uncommon winter visitor to the southern peninsula and Keys. Rare and local spring and summer resident of woodlands in the western Panhandle.

Key Sites: Ft. Clinch State Park, Ft. Matanzas National Monument, Turkey Creek Sanctuary, Loxahatchee National Wildlife Refuge, Bill Baggs Cape Florida State Park, A. D. Barnes Park, Dry Tortugas National Park, Everglades National Park, Corkscrew Swamp Sanctuary, Oscar Scherer State Park, Ft. De Soto, Honeymoon Island, St. George Island.

PROTHONOTARY WARBLER

Comments: Spring and summer resident of cypress swamp. Locally common in the Panhandle, local and uncommon in the northern peninsula, local and uncommon-to-rare in the central and southern peninsula. Rare-to-uncommon migrant throughout the state.

Key Sites: Dry Tortugas National Park, Big Cypress National Preserve, Ft. De Soto, Chassahowitzka Wildlife Management Area, Lower Suwannee National Wildlife Refuge, Newnans Lake, Osceola National Forest, St. Marks National Wildlife Refuge, Wakulla Springs State Park, Apalachicola National Forest, St. George Island, Torreya State Park, Blackwater River State Forest, Gulf Islands National Seashore.

WORM-EATING WARBLER

Comments: Uncommon migrant, mainly near the coast, throughout the state. Rare winter visitor to the southern peninsula and Keys. Extremely rare and local summer resident of steep, wooded ravines in the Panhandle.

Key Sites: Ft. Clinch State Park, Ft. Matanzas National Monument, Turkey Creek Sanctuary, Spanish River Park, A. D. Barnes Park, Dry Tortugas National Park, Corkscrew Swamp Sanctuary, Lower Suwannee National Wildlife Refuge, Paynes Prairie Preserve State Park, Wakulla Springs State Park.

SWAINSON'S WARBLER

Comments: Spring and summer resident of titi swamp and hardwood swamp edges. Rare-to-uncommon throughout the Panhandle and northwest peninsula. Uncommon migrant throughout the state, mostly near the coast in the peninsula. Usually found foraging in leaf litter within hardwood hammocks.

Key Sites: Hugh Taylor Birch State Park, Bill Baggs Cape Florida State Park, A. D. Barnes Park, Ft. De Soto, Honeymoon Island, Tiger Hammock Road, Apalachicola National Forest, Torreya State Park, Florida Caverns State Park, Blackwater River State Forest.

OVENBIRD

Comments: Common migrant throughout the peninsula and Keys, uncommon-to-rare in the Panhandle. Uncommon winter visitor in the southern peninsula and Keys, uncommon-to-rare in the northern peninsula and Panhandle. Usually found foraging in leaf litter within hardwood hammock.

Key Sites: Ft. Clinch State Park, Turkey Creek Sanctuary, Loxahatchee National Wildlife Refuge, Hugh Taylor Birch State Park, Bill Baggs Cape Florida State Park, A. D. Barnes Park, Dry Tortugas National Park, Everglades National Park, Highlands Hammock

State Park, Ft. De Soto, Honeymoon Island, Lower Suwannee National Wildlife Refuge.

NORTHERN WATERTHRUSH

Comments: Uncommon migrant, mainly along the coast, throughout the state. Uncommon winter visitor in the southern peninsula and Keys, rare in the northern peninsula. Usually found near water.

Key Sites: Ft. Clinch State Park, Loxahatchee National Wildlife Refuge, Dry Tortugas National Park, Everglades National Park, Corkscrew Swamp Sanctuary, Ft. De Soto, Honeymoon Island, Florida Caverns State Park.

LOUISIANA WATERTHRUSH

Comments: Rare spring and summer resident, near wood-land streams, in the Panhandle and northern peninsula. Uncommon-to-rare early migrant throughout the state. Rare winter visitor in the southern peninsula and Keys.

Key Sites: Ft. Clinch State Park, Dry Tortugas National Park, Everglades National Park, Big Cypress National Preserve, Ft. De Soto, Lower Suwannee National Wildlife Refuge, Torreya State Park, Florida Caverns State Park.

KENTUCKY WARBLER

Comments: Spring and summer resident of hardwood swamps, uncommon throughout the Panhandle and northwestern peninsula. Rare-to-uncommon migrant, mostly on the Gulf coast during spring, but more widespread in fall.

Key Sites: Dry Tortugas National Park, Ft. De Soto, St. Marks National Wildlife Refuge, Apalachicola National Forest, Torreya State Park, Florida Caverns State Park.

CONNECTICUT WARBLER

Comments: Late migrant throughout the peninsula and Keys, occasionally seen on the Gulf coast during spring and on the Atlantic coast in fall. Rarely seen in the Panhandle.

Key Sites: Dry Tortugas National Park, Ft. De Soto.

COMMON YELLOWTHROAT

Comments: Year-round resident of freshwater marshes and wet prairie and pinelands, common throughout the mainland. Common migrant throughout the state. Common winter visitor throughout the peninsula, uncommon in the Panhandle and Keys.

Key Sites: Any freshwater marsh, wet prairie, or pineland.

HOODED WARBLER

Comments: Spring and summer resident of hardwood swamp, uncommon to locally common in the Panhandle and northern Peninsula.

Key Sites: Dry Tortugas National Park, Ft. De Soto, Lower Suwannee National Wildlife Refuge, San Felasco Hammock Preserve State Park, Osceola National Forest, Wakulla Springs State Park, Apalachicola National Forest, St. George Island, Torreya State Park, Florida Caverns State Park.

WILSON'S WARBLER

Comments: Rare and unpredictable migrant and winter visitor to brushy areas throughout the state.

Key Sites: Lake Apopka, Orlando Wetlands Park, Loxahatchee National Wildlife Refuge, Everglades National Park, Ft. De Soto, Emeralda Marsh Conservation Area, Lower Suwannee National Wildlife Refuge, Paynes Prairie Preserve State Park, St. Marks National Wildlife Refuge, Gulf Islands National Seashore.

CANADA WARBLER

Comments: Rare migrant throughout the state.

Key Sites: Saddle Creek Park, Ft. De Soto, St. George Island, Gulf Islands National Seashore.

YELLOW-BREASTED CHAT

Comments: Secretive spring and summer resident of brushy fields and woodlands. Uncommon to locally common throughout the Panhandle and northwestern peninsula. Rare migrant throughout the state. Local and uncommon winter resident in the southern peninsula and Keys, rare in the central peninsula.

Key Sites: Jennings State Forest, Lake Apopka, Southern Glades Wildlife and Environmental Area, Emeralda Marsh Conservation Area, Crystal River Preserve State Park, Lower Suwannee National Wildlife Refuge, Paynes Prairie Preserve State Park, St. Marks National Wildlife Refuge, Tiger Hammock Road, Tall Timbers Research Station.

SUMMER TANAGER

Comments: Spring and summer resident of oak hammock, pinelands, and hardwood swamp. Common throughout the Panhandle and northern and central peninsula. Uncommon migrant throughout the state. Rare winter visitor in the southern peninsula and Keys.

Key Sites: Gold Head Branch State Park, Wekiwa Springs State Park, Dry Tortugas National Park, Highlands Hammock State Park, Ft. De Soto, Chassahowitzka Wildlife Management Area, Ocala National Forest, Osceola National Forest, St. Marks National Wildlife Refuge, Torreya State Park, Florida Caverns State Park.

SCARLET TANAGER

Comments: Uncommon spring migrant on the Gulf coast, uncommon fall migrant throughout the state.

Key Sites: Dry Tortugas National Park, Ft. De Soto, Florida Caverns State Park.

WESTERN TANAGER

Comments: Occasional and unpredictable migrant and winter visitor throughout the state, mostly along the coasts.

Key Sites: Several recent sightings from the Tallahassee area.

EASTERN TOWHEE

Comments: Year-round resident of pinelands and hammock understory, common throughout the mainland. Two red-eyed races are resident in the western Panhandle and winter visitors to the peninsula. White-eyed race is resident throughout the peninsula and eastern Panhandle.

Key Sites: Gold Head Branch State Park, Jonathan Dickinson State Park, Everglades National Park, Babcock-Webb Wildlife Management Area, Oscar Scherer State Park, Myakka River State Park, Highlands Hammock State Park, Jay B. Starkey Wilderness Park, Honeymoon Island, St. Marks National Wildlife Refuge, Torreya State Park, Florida Caverns State Park.

BACHMAN'S SPARROW

Comments: Year-round resident of dry prairie and pinelands with saw palmetto understory. Common throughout the Panhandle and northern and central peninsula, rare in the southern peninsula. Easiest to find when singing (spring and summer).

Key Sites: Jennings State Forest, Tosohatchee State Reserve, Three Lakes Wildlife Management Area, St. Sebastian River State Buffer Preserve, Kissimmee Prairie Preserve State Park, Babcock-Webb Wildlife Management Area, Jay B. Starkey Wilderness Park, Osceola National Forest, Apalachicola National Forest, Torreya State Park, Blackwater River State Forest.

CHIPPING SPARROW

Comments: Winter visitor to pinelands, woodlands, and roadsides. Common throughout the Panhandle and northern peninsula, uncommon-to-rare in the central and southern peninsula. Rare summer resident in the Panhandle.

Key Sites: Gold Head Branch State Park, Lake Apopka, Osceola National Forest, Wakulla Springs State Park, Bald Point State Park, Tall Timbers Research Station, St. George Island, Florida Caverns State Park, Blackwater River State Forest.

CLAY-COLORED SPARROW

Comments: Rare migrant throughout the state. Rare winter visitor to weedy fields and woodlands throughout the peninsula.

Key Sites: Lake Apopka, Southern Glades Wildlife and Environmental Area.

FIELD SPARROW

Comments: Year-round resident of young pinelands, brushy fields, and thickets. Local and uncommon in the eastern Panhandle and northern peninsula. Winter visitor to fields and roadsides, uncommon throughout the Panhandle and northern peninsula, rare in the southern peninsula.

Key Sites: Jennings State Forest, Gold Head Branch State Park, Osceola National Forest, Paynes Prairie Preserve State Park, St. Marks National Wildlife Refuge, Wakulla Springs State Park, Tall Timbers Research Station, Florida Caverns State Park.

VESPER SPARROW

Comments: Winter visitor to pastures and weedy fields. Common in the Panhandle, uncommon in the northern and central peninsula, rare in the southern peninsula.

Key Sites: Gold Head Branch State Park, Lake Apopka, Paynes Prairie Preserve State Park, Osceola National Forest, Tall Timbers Research Station, St. George Island.

LARK SPARROW

Comments: Rare early migrant throughout the state. Rare winter visitor to pastures and weedy fields, mostly in the central and southern peninsula.

Key Sites: Lake Apopka, Southern Glades Wildlife and Environmental Area.

SAVANNAH SPARROW

Comments: Winter resident of weedy fields and coastal dunes, common-to-abundant throughout the state.

Key Sites: Ft. Clinch State Park, Smyrna Dunes Park, Lake Apopka, Merritt Island National Wildlife Refuge, Loxahatchee National Wildlife Refuge, Southern Glades Wildlife and Environmental Area, Everglades National Park, Honeymoon Island, Paynes Prairie Preserve State Park, St. George Island.

GRASSHOPPER SPARROW

Comments: Florida race is a year-round resident of dry prairie, rare and local in the central peninsula. Eastern race is a winter visitor to weedy fields and dry prairie, uncommon throughout the state. Races may be distinguished by song.

Key Sites: *Florida race:* Three Lakes Wildlife Management Area, Kissimmee Prairie Preserve State Park, Avon Park Air Force Range. *Eastern race:* Above locations plus Lake Apopka, Southern Glades Wildlife and Environmental Area, Emeralda Marsh Conservation Area, Paynes Prairie Preserve State Park.

HENSLOW'S SPARROW

Comments: Winter visitor to pitcher plant and pine savannas, wet prairie, and weedy fields. Local and uncommon in the Panhandle and northern and central peninsula.

Key Sites: Kissimmee Prairie Preserve State Park, St. Marks National Wildlife Refuge, Ochlockonee River State Park, Apalachicola National Forest.

LE CONTE'S SPARROW

Comments: Rare and secretive winter visitor to weedy fields in the Panhandle and northern and central peninsula.

Key Sites: Lake Apopka, St. Marks National Wildlife Refuge, Apalachicola National Forest.

NELSON'S SHARP-TAILED SPARROW

Comments: Winter visitor to coastal marshes. Locally common along the Gulf coast of the Panhandle and northern and central peninsula, rare along the Atlantic coast of the northern peninsula. Uncommon winter visitor to coastal prairie in the extreme southern peninsula.

Key Sites: Everglades National Park, Ft. De Soto, Cedar Key, Big Bend Wildlife Management Area, St. Marks National Wildlife Refuge, Bald Point State Park.

SALTMARSH SHARP-TAILED SPARROW

Comments: Winter visitor to coastal marshes. Local and uncommon along the Atlantic coast of the northern peninsula, rare along the Gulf coast of the Panhandle and northern and central peninsula. Uncommon winter visitor to coastal prairie in the extreme southern peninsula.

Key Sites: Ft. Clinch State Park, Talbot Islands State Park, Guana River Reserve, Anastasia State Park, Smyrna Dunes Park, Merritt Island National Wildlife Refuge, Everglades National Park.

SEASIDE SPARROW

Comments: Several races are year-round residents of salt marsh. Locally common in the Panhandle, along the Gulf coast of the northern and central peninsula, and the Atlantic coast of the extreme northern peninsula. Northern race is a winter visitor to salt marsh along the Atlantic coast of the northern and central peninsula. Dusky race is extinct, formerly a year-round resident of coastal marshes in Brevard County. Cape Sable race is a year-round resident of sawgrass and brackish water marshes, local and uncommon in the southern peninsula.

Key Sites: Ft. Clinch State Park, Guana River Reserve, Ft. Matanzas National Monument, Everglades National Park, Green Key, Cedar Key, Big Bend Wildlife Management Area, St. Marks National Wildlife Refuge, St. George Island.

FOX SPARROW

Comments: Winter visitor to woodlands with thick understory, usually found foraging in leaf litter. Rare throughout the Panhandle and northern peninsula.
Key Sites: San Felasco Hammock Preserve State Park, O'Leno State Park, Tiger Hammock Road, Apalachicola National Forest, Florida Caverns State Park.

SONG SPARROW

Comments: Winter visitor to weedy fields and woodlands, common throughout the Panhandle and northern peninsula, rare in the central and southern peninsula.
Key Sites: Gold Head Branch State Park, Paynes Prairie Preserve State Park, Osceola National Forest, St. Marks National Wildlife Refuge, Florida Caverns State Park.

LINCOLN'S SPARROW

Comments: Winter visitor to brushy fields and woodlands, rare throughout the peninsula, occasional in the Panhandle. Rare migrant throughout the state.
Key Sites: Lake Apopka, Southern Glades Wildlife and Environmental Area, Celery Fields Regional Stormwater Facility, Emeralda Marsh Conservation Area, Paynes Prairie Preserve State Park.

SWAMP SPARROW

Comments: Migrant and winter visitor to fresh- and salt-water marshes and wet, brushy fields and woodlands. Common throughout the mainland, rare in the Keys.
Key Sites: Jennings State Forest, Lake Woodruff National Wildlife Refuge, Lake Apopka, Merritt Island National Wildlife Refuge, Loxahatchee National Wildlife Refuge, Everglades National Park, Corkscrew Swamp Sanctuary, Myakka River State Park, Hillsborough River State Park, Paynes Prairie Preserve State Park, St. Marks National Wildlife Refuge, Tall Timbers Research Station.

WHITE-THROATED SPARROW

Comments: Winter visitor to brushy fields, woodlands, and pond and lake edges. Common throughout the Panhandle and northern peninsula, occasional-to-rare in the central and southern peninsula.
Key Sites: Jennings State Forest, Paynes Prairie Preserve State Park, Osceola National Forest, St. Marks National Wildlife Refuge, Wakulla Springs State Park, Tall Timbers Research Station, Torreya State Park, Florida Caverns State Park, Blackwater River State Forest.

WHITE-CROWNED SPARROW

Comments: Migrant and winter visitor to brushy fields, rare-to-uncommon throughout the state.
Key Sites: Lake Apopka, Paynes Prairie Preserve State Park.

DARK-EYED JUNCO

Comments: Winter visitor to brushy woodlands. Uncommon and irregular throughout the Panhandle and northern peninsula, rare in the central and southern peninsula. Most reports are of the Slate-colored race.
Key Sites: Wakulla Springs State Park, Lake Jackson, Torreya State Park, Three Rivers State Park, Florida Caverns State Park, Blackwater River State Forest.

NORTHERN CARDINAL

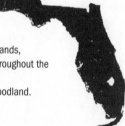

Comments: Year-round resident of brushy woodlands, common-to-abundant throughout the state.
Key Sites: Any brushy woodland.

ROSE-BREASTED GROSBEAK

Comments: Uncommon migrant and rare winter visitor throughout the state.

Key Sites: A. D. Barnes Park, Dry Tortugas National Park, Ft. De Soto, Honeymoon Island, St. George Island, Florida Caverns State Park.

BLUE GROSBEAK

Comments: Spring and summer resident of weedy fields and thickets. Locally common throughout the Panhandle and northern and central peninsula. Uncommon migrant and rare winter visitor throughout the state.

Key Sites: Jennings State Forest, Lake Apopka, Dry Tortugas National Park, Ft. De Soto, Crystal River Preserve State Park, Emeralda Marsh Conservation Area, Paynes Prairie Preserve State Park, Tiger Hammock Road, Tall Timbers Research Station, Torreya State Park.

INDIGO BUNTING

Comments: Spring and summer resident of brushy fields, common throughout the Panhandle and northern and central peninsula. Common migrant throughout the state. Local and uncommon winter resident in the central and southern peninsula, rare in the northern peninsula and Panhandle.

Key Sites: Lake Apopka, Loxahatchee National Wildlife Refuge, Dry Tortugas National Park, Ft. De Soto, Honeymoon Island, Emeralda Marsh Conservation Area, Paynes Prairie Preserve State Park, St. Marks National Wildlife Refuge, St. George Island, Torreya State Park, Florida Caverns State Park.

PAINTED BUNTING

Comments: Spring and summer resident of coastal scrub, abandoned citrus groves, and brushy woodlands. Uncommon along the Atlantic coast of the northern peninsula (though common in the extreme northern peninsula), rare in the Panhandle. Uncommon migrant along the Atlantic coast of the peninsula and in the Dry Tortugas, rare inland and on the Gulf coast. Uncommon to locally common winter visitor to brushy fields and feeders in the central and southern peninsula.

Key Sites: Ft. Clinch State Park, Talbot Islands State Parks, Okeeheelee Nature Center, Loxahatchee National Wildlife Refuge, Castellow Hammock Preserve, Dry Tortugas National Park, Southern Glades Wildlife and Environmental Area, Everglades National Park, Corkscrew Swamp Sanctuary.

DICKCISSEL

Comments: Rare migrant and winter visitor throughout the state. Rare and local summer resident of weedy fields in the central and possibly the southern peninsula.

Key Sites: Lake Apopka, Dry Tortugas National Park, Southern Glades Wildlife and Environmental Area, Ft. De Soto.

BOBOLINK

Comments: Locally common migrant throughout the state. Found in weedy fields and on roadsides.

Key Sites: Lake Apopka, Loxahatchee National Wildlife Refuge, Bill Baggs Cape Florida State Park, Dry Tortugas National Park, Everglades National Park, St. Marks National Wildlife Refuge, St. George Island.

RED-WINGED BLACKBIRD

Comments: Year-round resident of wetlands and agricultural areas, common-to-abundant throughout the state.

Key Sites: Any wetland or agricultural area.

EASTERN MEADOWLARK

Comments: Year-round resident of prairies, pine flatwoods, and weedy fields, common throughout the mainland.

Key Sites: Gold Head Branch State Park, Lake Apopka, Three Lakes Wildlife Management Area, Kissimmee Prairie Preserve State Park, Jonathan Dickinson State Park, Everglades National Park, Myakka River State Park, Hillsborough River State Park, St. Marks National Wildlife Refuge.

YELLOW-HEADED BLACKBIRD

Comments: Migrant and winter visitor to pastures and agricultural fields, usually with other blackbirds. Rare throughout the state.
Key Sites: Hague Dairy.

RUSTY BLACKBIRD

Comments: Winter visitor to hardwood swamp, uncommon-to-rare throughout the Panhandle and northern peninsula.
Key Sites: Osceola National Forest, St. Marks National Wildlife Refuge, Wakulla Springs State Park, Torreya State Park, Florida Caverns State Park, Blackwater River State Forest.

BREWER'S BLACKBIRD

Comments: Winter resident of pastures and fields, locally common in the western Panhandle, rare in the eastern Panhandle and northern peninsula.
Key Sites: Florida Caverns State Park, Blackwater River State Forest.

COMMON GRACKLE

Comments: Year-round resident of woodlands, fields, and pastures, common-to-abundant throughout the mainland. Common summer resident in the Keys. Common winter visitor to the mainland from populations north of Florida and from the Keys.
Key Sites: Gold Head Branch State Park, Lake Woodruff National Wildlife Refuge, Merritt Island National Wildlife Refuge, Loxahatchee National Wildlife Refuge, Everglades National Park, Corkscrew Swamp Sanctuary, Highlands Hammock State Park, Hillsborough River State Park, Paynes Prairie Preserve State Park, Osceola National Forest, Wakulla Springs State Park, Florida Caverns State Park, Blackwater River State Forest.

BOAT-TAILED GRACKLE

Comments: Year-round resident of wetlands and residential areas, common-to-abundant throughout the peninsula and along the coast of the eastern Panhandle, uncommon-to-rare in the western Panhandle.
Key Sites: Guana River Preserve, Lake Woodruff National Wildlife Refuge, Lake Apopka, Merritt Island National Wildlife Refuge, Loxahatchee National Wildlife Refuge, Kendall area, Everglades National Park, Ding Darling National Wildlife Refuge, Myakka River State Park, Lower Suwannee National Wildlife Refuge, Paynes Prairie Preserve State Park, St. Marks National Wildlife Refuge.

SHINY COWBIRD

Comments: Year-round visitor, likely resident, rare in the southern peninsula, Keys, and Dry Tortugas. Occasional elsewhere in the state.
Key Sites: Castellow Hammock Preserve, Key West, Dry Tortugas National Park, Southern Glades Wildlife and Environmental Area, Everglades National Park, Ft. De Soto.

BRONZED COWBIRD

Comments: Winter visitor to wetlands and pastures, rare throughout the state, though locally common and apparently breeding in the southern peninsula.
Key Sites: Castellow Hammock Preserve, Eagle Lakes Community Park.

BROWN-HEADED COWBIRD

Comments: Year-round resident of woodland edges, pastures, and fields. Common throughout the Panhandle and northern peninsula, uncommon to locally common in the central peninsula and coastal areas of the southern peninsula. Common-to-abundant winter visitor throughout the mainland and Keys.
Key Sites: Three Lakes Wildlife Management Area, Southern Glades Wildlife and Environmental Area,

Everglades National Park, Ft. De Soto, Honeymoon Island, Lower Suwannee National Wildlife Refuge, Osceola National Forest, St. Marks National Wildlife Refuge, Wakulla Springs State Park, Blackwater River State Forest, Gulf Islands National Seashore.

ORCHARD ORIOLE

Comments: Spring and summer resident of forest edges and fields with scattered trees. Common throughout the Panhandle, uncommon in the northern peninsula. Uncommon spring migrant along the Gulf coast, early-fall migrant throughout the state.
Key Sites: Gold Head Branch State Park, Dry Tortugas National Park, Ft. De Soto, Paynes Prairie Preserve State Park, Osceola National Forest, St. Marks National Wildlife Refuge, St. George Island, Florida Caverns State Park, Blackwater River State Forest, Gulf Islands National Seashore.

SPOT-BREASTED ORIOLE

Comments: Introduced from Central America, now a year-round resident of parks and residential areas with exotic landscaping, uncommon in the southeastern peninsula.
Key Sites: Miami Shores, Miami Springs, A. D. Barnes Park, South Miami, Kendall area.

BALTIMORE ORIOLE

Comments: Migrant and winter visitor to woodlands and residential areas, uncommon throughout the state.
Key Sites: Everglades National Park, Ft. De Soto, Paynes Prairie Preserve State Park, St. George Island.

PURPLE FINCH

Comments: Irruptive winter visitor to woodlands, rare-to-uncommon in the Panhandle and extreme northern peninsula.
Key Sites: St. Marks National Wildlife Refuge, Wakulla Springs State Park, Torreya State Park, Florida Caverns State Park.

HOUSE FINCH

Comments: Introduced, now a year-round resident of residential areas, uncommon to locally common in the Panhandle and northern peninsula, spreading to the central and possibly southern peninsula.
Key Sites: Residential areas in Gainesville and throughout the Panhandle, Alligator Point, Tall Timbers Research Station, Gulf Islands National Seashore.

PINE SISKIN

Comments: Irruptive winter visitor to woodlands and residential feeders, rare to uncommon throughout the Panhandle, rare in the peninsula. Usually seen with flocks of American Goldfinch.
Key Sites: Tall Timbers Research Station, Wakulla Springs State Park.

AMERICAN GOLDFINCH

Comments: Irruptive winter visitor to woodlands and residential feeders, uncommon-to-abundant throughout the state.
Key Sites: Gold Head Branch State Park, Turkey Creek Sanctuary, Jonathan Dickinson State Park, Everglades National Park, Corkscrew Swamp Sanctuary, Myakka River State Park, St. Marks National Wildlife Refuge, Torreya State Park, Florida Caverns State Park.

HOUSE SPARROW

Comments: Introduced from Europe, now a year-round resident of residential and shopping areas, common throughout the mainland.
Key Sites: Most residential and shopping areas.

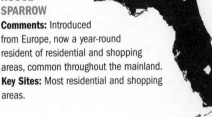

Florida's Vagrant Bird Species

Greater White-fronted Goose: Occasional during winter in lakes, impoundments, and flooded fields throughout the mainland.

Snow Goose: Uncommon during winter in lakes, impoundments, and flooded fields throughout the Panhandle, rare in the peninsula.

Ross's Goose: Occasional during winter in lakes, impoundments, and flooded fields throughout the Panhandle and northern and central peninsula.

Brant: Occasional during winter in coastal areas throughout the mainland.

Cackling Goose: Records from St. Marks National Wildlife Refuge (1957), Sebastian area (2003).

Tundra Swan: Occasional during winter in lakes and impoundments throughout the Panhandle and northern peninsula.

Eurasian Wigeon: Rare during winter in fresh and brackish water marshes, ponds, and impoundments throughout the peninsula.

American Black Duck: Rare during winter in fresh and brackish water marshes and impoundments throughout the eastern Panhandle and northern peninsula.

Cinnamon Teal: Rare during winter in freshwater marshes, ponds, and impoundments throughout the mainland.

White-cheeked Pintail: Occasional in the southern and central peninsula; many reports are likely escapees.

King Eider: Occasional during winter in coastal areas, most likely near rock jetties.

Common Eider: Occasional during winter in coastal areas, most likely near rock jetties.

Harlequin Duck: Occasional during winter in coastal areas, most likely near rock jetties.

Common Merganser: Occasional during winter in coastal areas, most likely in the Panhandle. Females are likely to be confused with Red-breasted Merganser.

Masked Duck: Occasional, formerly bred in the southern peninsula, prefers freshwater ponds and marshes with emergent vegetation.

Pacific Loon: Occasional during winter in coastal waters of the Panhandle and northern peninsula.

Least Grebe: Occasional in the southern peninsula and Keys, prefers freshwater ponds and marshes with emergent vegetation.

Red-necked Grebe: Occasional during winter in coastal waters of the Panhandle and northern peninsula.

Eared Grebe: Rare during winter in coastal and inland waters throughout the state.

Western Grebe: Occasional during winter in coastal waters.

Yellow-nosed Albatross: Records from St. Marks National Wildlife Refuge (1983), Key Largo (1992), and Tarpon Springs (2000).

Northern Fulmar: Record from Satellite Beach, Brevard County (2005).

Short-tailed Shearwater: Record from off Sanibel Island (2000).

Manx Shearwater: Rare from fall through spring off the Atlantic coast, occasional in the Gulf.

Red-billed Tropicbird: Occasional from spring through fall off both coasts.

Red-footed Booby: Occasional during spring and summer in the Dry Tortugas.

Great Cormorant: Rare during winter in coastal waters throughout the state, most likely on rock jetties.

Scarlet Ibis: Status uncertain. Some sightings may be of escapees. In 1961 Scarlet Ibis eggs were introduced to White Ibis nests at Greynold's Park in Miami. Hybridization of Scarlet with White Ibis later occurred, producing "pink" ibis. Alleged hybrids are occasionally seen in the southern peninsula.

White-faced Ibis: Occasional year-round in freshwater marshes and impoundments. Non-breeding individuals are virtually indistinguishable from Glossy Ibis and are likely overlooked.

Northern Goshawk: Occasional during winter in the Panhandle and northern peninsula.

Zone-tailed Hawk: Two records, both from the Florida Keys (2000, 2004).

Ferruginous Hawk: Records from Lake Apopka (1983–84) and Calhoun County, in the Panhandle (1986).

Rough-legged Hawk: Record from Lake Apopka (2000).

Golden Eagle: Occasional during winter in the northern peninsula and Panhandle. May be confused with immature Bald Eagle.

Eurasian Kestrel: Record from Lake Apopka (2003).

Northern Lapwing: Record from Lake Istokpoga (1997).

American Golden Plover: Rare from fall through spring in sod fields, plowed agricultural fields, short-grass prairie, and on sandy beaches with exposed mudflats throughout the state.

Lesser Sand Plover: Record from St. Marks National Wildlife Refuge (2005).

Mountain Plover: Occasional, most recent records from St. Marks National Wildlife Refuge (1977), St. George Island (1973).

Long-billed Curlew: Rare during winter on coastal mudflats throughout the peninsula.

Black-tailed Godwit: Record from Merritt Island National Wildlife Refuge (1981).

Hudsonian Godwit: Occasional during spring and fall in flooded agricultural fields and coastal mudflats throughout the state.

Bar-tailed Godwit: Occasional during winter throughout the state.

Surfbird: Occasional, recent records from Smyrna Dunes Park (2004) and Sanibel Island (2001).

Baird's Sandpiper: Rare, on coastal mudflats, fresh and brackish water impoundments, and flooded agricultural fields, mostly on the Gulf coast.

Sharp-tailed Sandpiper: Occasional, last report from near Tallahassee (1995).

Purple Sandpiper: Rare, on rock jetties, mostly along the Atlantic coast.

Curlew Sandpiper: Occasional on coastal mudflats, fresh and brackish water impoundments, and flooded agricultural fields.

Ruff: Occasional on freshwater impoundments and flooded agricultural fields.

South Polar Skua: Occasional off the Atlantic coast.

Franklin's Gull: Rare during winter at sandy beaches and landfills throughout the state. Usually found among Laughing Gulls.

Little Gull: Occasional during winter. Usually found among Bonaparte's Gulls.

Black-headed Gull: Occasional during winter.

Heermann's Gull: Record from Ft. De Soto (2000–2005), has wandered periodically along much of the state's Gulf coast.

Gray-hooded Gull: Record from Apalachicola (1998).

Belcher's Gull: Records from Pensacola (1968), Naples area (1970, 1974–76).

California Gull: Record from Apalachicola (1998).

Thayer's Gull: Occasional during winter.

Iceland Gull: Occasional during winter, mostly along the Atlantic coast.

Slaty-backed Gull: Record from Key West (2002-3).

Glaucous Gull: Occasional during winter, mostly along the Atlantic coast.

Sabine's Gull: Occasional off the Atlantic and Gulf coasts.

Elegant Tern: Records from Ft. De Soto (2001-4), Honeymoon Island (1999). May hybridize with Sandwich Terns.

Black Noddy: Occasional spring and summer vistor to the Dry Tortugas.

Dovekie: Occasional during winter off the Atlantic coast.

Thick-billed Murre: Occasional during winter off the Atlantic coast.

Razorbill: Occasional during winter off both coasts.

Long-billed Murrelet: Records from Ft. De Soto (1993), St. Petersburg (1994), Honeymoon Island (1986), Cedar Key (1994), Ft. Lauderdale (2003).

Atlantic Puffin: Occasional during winter off the Atlantic coast.

Scaly-naped Pigeon: Records from Key West (1898, 1929).

Band-tailed Pigeon: Reports from Sugarloaf Key, Monroe County (1973), Sarasota (1967), Holmes County (1967).

European Turtle Dove: Record from Lower Matecumbe Key, Monroe County (1990), possibly ship-assisted.

Zenaida Dove: Occasional in the southern peninsula and Keys.

White-tipped Dove: Records from Dry Tortugas National Park (1995, 2003).

Key West Quail-Dove: Occasional in the southern peninsula and Keys.

Ruddy Quail-Dove: Occasional in the southern peninsula and Keys.

Groove-billed Ani: Occasional during winter in weedy and shrubby fields throughout the Panhandle and northern peninsula.

Flammulated Owl: Records from Redington Beach (1978), Navarre Beach (2001).

Snowy Owl: Record from St. George Island (1999).

Long-eared Owl: Recent record from Dry Tortugas National Park (2003).

Short-eared Owl: The North American race is rare during winter in prairies, pastures, agricultural fields, and salt marsh throughout the mainland, most often seen in the Panhandle and northern peninsula. The Antillean race, presumably from Cuba, is occasional in the extreme southern peninsula, Keys, and Dry Tortugas.

Northern Saw-whet Owl: Recent record from Lighthouse Point, Broward County (2001).

Lesser Nighthawk: Rare, though locally common during some winters in the southern peninsula.

White-collared Swift: Records from Pensacola (1981), Ft Lauderdale (1994).

Vaux's Swift: Occasional during winter in the Panhandle and northern peninsula, best identified by its white throat and its call.

Antillean Palm Swift: Record (two birds) from Key West (1972).

Broad-billed Hummingbird: Record from Pensacola (2004).

Buff-bellied Hummingbird: Rare during winter throughout the mainland.

Bahama Woodstar: Last record from Homestead area (1981).

Anna's Hummingbird: Record from Tallahassee (1988).

Calliope Hummingbird: Occasional during winter throughout the Panhandle.

Broad-tailed Hummingbird: Occasional during winter throughout the Panhandle.

Allen's Hummingbird: Occasional during winter throughout the Panhandle and northern peninsula.

Golden-fronted Woodpecker: Record from Pensacola (1981–82).

Western Wood-Pewee: Records from Archbold Biological Station (1995), St. Marks National Wildlife Refuge (1986).

Cuban Pewee: Record from Spanish River Park (1995).

Black Phoebe: Record from Cocoa Beach (1954).

Say's Phoebe: Recent record from Ft. Pickens (2003).

Hammond's Flycatcher: Records from Ft. De Soto (2006) and Hal Scott Regional Preserve, Seminole County (2007).

Ash-throated Flycatcher: Rare from fall through spring in woodland and marsh thickets throughout the northern peninsula and Panhandle, occasional in the southern peninsula and Keys.

La Sagra's Flycatcher: Occasional in tropical hardwood hammock throughout the southeastern peninsula and Keys.

Sulphur-bellied Flycatcher: Occasional throughout the mainland, most records are from the southern peninsula.

Piratic Flycatcher: Record from Dry Tortugas National Park (1991).

Tropical Kingbird: Occasional during winter throughout the mainland. Reliably distinguished from the similar Couch's Kingbird by voice.

Cassin's Kingbird: Occasional during winter, usually with Western Kingbird.

Loggerhead Kingbird: Record from Ft. Zachary Taylor State Park, Key West (2007).

Fork-tailed Flycatcher: Occasional throughout the central and southern peninsula.

Thick-billed Vireo: Occasional in tropical hardwood hammocks throughout the southeastern peninsula and Keys.

Bell's Vireo: Occasional during spring and fall in the northern peninsula and Panhandle, rare from fall through spring in thickets and forest understory in the southern peninsula and Keys.

Yellow-green Vireo: Recent reports from Key West (2003), Ft. De Soto (2002).

Horned Lark: Occasional in dunes along the coast of the northern peninsula and Panhandle. Recent inland reports from Hague Dairy in Alachua County (2004) and from northern Jackson County (2007).

Cuban Martin: Record from Key West (1895). Males indistinguishable from Purple Martin.

Southern Martin: Record from Key West (1890).

Mangrove Swallow: Record from Viera Wetlands (2002).

Bahama Swallow: Most recent record from Cutler Ridge Cave Swallow roost (1988–92).

Rock Wren: Record from St. George Island (1982–83).

Bewick's Wren: Formerly an uncommon winter visitor, now occasional. Recent sightings from St. George Island (1989) and Ft. Pickens (2001).

Northern Wheatear: Occasional during fall throughout the state. Most recent records are from the southern peninsula.

Mountain Bluebird: Record from Everglades National Park (2002).

Bicknell's Thrush: Rare, most likely in spring along the Atlantic coast. In the field, nearly impossible to distinguish from Gray-cheeked Thrush if not heard singing or calling. Four records; all birds were mist-netted and measured, two from Key Largo (2002), two from Bill Baggs Cape Florida State Park (2007).

Varied Thrush: Most recent records from Honeymoon Island (1996), Panama City (2002).

Bahama Mockingbird: Occasional in tropical hardwood hammocks throughout the Keys and coastal areas of the southeastern peninsula.

Sage Thrasher: Records from Gilchrist County (1969), Ft. Pickens (1976, 1981).

Curve-billed Thrasher: Records from Pensacola (1932), St. George Island (1989).

White Wagtail: Record from Moon Lake Park, Pasco County (2007).

Black-throated Gray Warbler: Occasional throughout the state.

Golden-cheeked Warbler: Record from Sawgrass Lake Park (1964).

Townsend's Warbler: Occasional throughout the state.

Kirtland's Warbler: Occasional, records from coastal areas throughout the mainland. Winters in the Bahamas.

Mourning Warbler: Rare throughout the state.

MacGillivray's Warbler: Occasional throughout the central and southern peninsula.

Bananaquit: Occasional during winter, almost always from the Bahamas.

Western Spindalis: Occasional throughout the southern peninsula and Keys.

Yellow-faced Grassquit: Occasional, recent records from Dry Tortugas National Park (2002), Everglades National Park (2001).

Black-faced Grassquit: Occasional, recent records from Jupiter Ridge Natural Area (2004), Everglades National Park (2003).

Green-tailed Towhee: Occasional, recent record from Honeymoon Island (2003).

Spotted Towhee: Records from Franklin County (1967, 2007).

American Tree Sparrow: Occasional, recent record from Ft. Pickens (2003).

Black-throated Sparrow: Record from near Tallahassee (1976).

Lark Bunting: Occasional, recent report from St. Joseph Peninsula State Park (2000).

Harris's Sparrow: Occasional, recent record from Seminole County (2003).

Golden-crowned Sparrow: Record from Islamorada (1990).

Lapland Longspur: Occasional during winter in coastal dunes and along grassy roadsides throughout the mainland.

Chestnut-collared Longspur: Records from Tallahassee (1964, 1967), Ft. Pickens (1999).

Snow Bunting: Occasional during winter on coastal dunes along the Atlantic coast of the northern peninsula and Gulf coast of the Panhandle.

Black-headed Grosbeak: Occasional throughout the state.

Lazuli Bunting: Occasional, recent record from Ft. De Soto (2001).

Varied Bunting: Record from Siesta Key, Sarasota County (2005).

Tawny-shouldered Blackbird: Record (two birds) from Key West (1936). Difficult to distinguish from Red-winged Blackbird.

Western Meadowlark: Occasional, formerly a rare winter visitor to weedy fields in the western Panhandle.

Hooded Oriole: Record from Pensacola area (2002).

Bullock's Oriole: Occasional during winter throughout the mainland. Females often confused with Baltimore Oriole.

Red Crossbill: Occasional and irruptive in the northern peninsula.

Evening Grosbeak: Irruptive but rare during winter in the Panhandle.

Florida's Extinct (or Presumed Extinct) Bird Species

Passenger Pigeon: Once a common winter visitor in the Panhandle and northern peninsula.

Carolina Parakeet: Once common throughout most of the state.

Bachman's Warbler: Presumed extinct. Once a common migrant throughout the peninsula and Keys. Last sighting from near Melbourne (1977).

Appendix A: Birding Resources

The Internet provides access to countless Web sites related to birds and birding. Following is online contact information for various agencies and organizations that can provide additional resources for birding within Florida:

Government Agencies

- **National Park Service,** an agency of the U.S. Department of Interior, administers Florida's three national parks. Its Web site is at www.nps.gov.

- **National Forest Service,** an agency of the U.S. Department of Agriculture, administers Florida's three national forests. Its Web site is at www.fs.fed.us.

- **U.S. Fish and Wildlife Service,** an agency of the Department of Interior, administers Florida's 28 National Wildlife Refuges. Its Web site is at www.fws.gov/refuges.

- **Florida Department of Environmental Protection** administers Florida's 41 aquatic preserves and, in partnership with the National Oceanographic and Atmospheric Administration, three National Estuarine Research Reserves. The aquatic preserve Web site is at www.dep.state.fl.us/coastal.

- **Florida Division of Recreation and Parks,** an agency of the Florida Department of Environmental Protection, administers Florida's 154 state parks. Its Web site is at www.floridastateparks.org.

- **Florida Division of Forestry** manages Florida's 33 state forests. Its Web site is at www.fl-dof.com.

- **Florida Fish and Wildlife Conservation Commission** (www.florida conservation.org) administers the state's 152 Wildlife Management Areas and Wildlife and Environmental Areas. This agency also oversees the **Great Florida Birding Trail,** a 2,000-mile trail connecting 446 birding sites, many of which are included in this guide. The birding-trail Web site is at http://floridabirdingtrail.com.

- Five regional water management districts are responsible for preserving and managing the state's water resources. Management programs include recreational opportunities in conservation areas managed by the water management districts. Site descriptions for several water management district conservation areas are included in this guide. The five water management districts in Florida are: **St. Johns River Water Management District,** (www.sjrwmd.com), **South Florida Water Management District** (www.sfwmd.gov), **Southwest Florida Water Management District** (www.swfwmd.state.fl.us), **Suwannee River Water Management District** (www.srwmd.state.fl.us), and **Northwest Florida Water Management District** (www.nwfwmd.state.fl.us).

Birding Organizations

The **Florida Ornithological Society,** the state's birding organization, is open to professional ornithologists as well as beginning birders. Its Web site is at www.fosbirds.org. Publications include *Florida Field Naturalist,* a peer-reviewed quarterly journal featuring original research papers on birds and other wildlife as well as field reports of rare and unusual bird sightings. The FOS Records Committee reviews and evaluates documentation of the occurrence of birds rare or not previously observed in the wild in Florida and regularly updates the state's official bird checklist. All rare bird sightings should be submitted to the

Records Committee Managing Secretary using the online documentation form available at www.fosbirds.org/forms/FOSReportForm.htm. The Florida Ornithological Society also collaborated with the Florida Fish and Wildlife Conservation Commission and Audubon of Florida to create the *Atlas of the Breeding Birds of Florida,* a record of the distribution of all breeding birds in the state. The results of this project are available at www.fosbirds .org/atlasdata/BBAFrameset.html or http://myfwc.com/bba.

Audubon of Florida, an affiliate of the National Audubon Society, is the state's conservation advocacy organization, focusing primarily on protecting birds and their habitats. Its Web site is at www.audubonofflorida.org. The organization has established several nature centers and sanctuaries, including Corkscrew Swamp Sanctuary. Audubon of Florida has also developed the **Important Bird Areas Program** to identify areas in the state considered critical for birds. The resulting IBA Program manuscript is available at www.audubon.org/bird/iba/florida. The National Audubon Society coordinates annual **Christmas Bird Counts** in Florida and elsewhere. Archived CBC data is available at www.audubon.org/bird/cbc. Local Audubon chapters affiliated with Audubon of Florida, 43 in all throughout the state, offer a variety of field trips and environmental education programs for members and nonmembers alike. A Web page providing links to Florida's local Audubon chapters is at www.audubonofflorida.org/who_chapters.html.

Rare-bird Alerts and Listservs

Currently, the Internet provides the only access to Florida's Rare Bird Alert Listserv (the telephone-based Rare Bird Alert was discontinued several years ago), available at listserv .admin.usf.edu/archives/flrba.html. To post a sighting, you must subscribe to the listserv, but subscription is not necessary to view archived postings. Birders without e-mail access may call (407) 925–5900 to report rare bird sightings.

Several birding listservs in Florida provide opportunities to post bird sightings, trip lists, photographs, and requests for information. With the exception of the Tropical Audubon Bird Board, subscription is necessary to post sightings. You do not need to subscribe to view archived postings. Keep in mind that because these listservs are not moderated, questionable sightings are sometimes posted. Most of the following listservs may also be accessed via the Regional Mail page of www.birdingonthe.net, Jack Siler's comprehensive birding Web site.

FloridaBirds-L: www.lists.ufl.edu/archives/floridabirds-l.html
Florida/Bahamas: http://groups.yahoo.com/group/flabirding
BirdBrains: http://listserv.admin.usf.edu/archives/brdbrain.html
FloridaSW: http://groups.yahoo.com/group/swflbirdline
North Florida: http://groups.yahoo.com/group/nfbirds
Tropical Audubon Society Bird Board: www.tropicalaudubon.org/tasboard/index.html

Appendix B: References

American Birding Association. *ABA Checklist: Birds of the Continental United States and Canada*, Sixth Edition (2002).

American Birding Association. *Birdfinding in Forty National Forests and Grasslands* (1994).

Austin, Dr. Daniel F. *Pine Rockland Plant Guide: A Field Guide to the Plants of South Florida's Pine Rockland Community*, Dade County Department of Environmental Resources Management (1998).

Bowman, Reed. Secretary's Reports of the Florida Ornithological Society Records Committee (1996–2004). Available online at www.fosbirds.org/RecordCommittee/FOSRCReports.htm.

Brand, Stijn, Casey A. Lott, and M. Brennan Mulrooney. "Two Bicknell's Thrushes Banded during Spring Migration on Key Largo: First Accepted Records for Florida," *Florida Field Naturalist, Vol. 33, No. 3* (2005).

Epps, Susan Allene. *Parrots of South Florida*, Ft. Lauderdale, Fla., Dunlap Design Associates, 2002.

Florida Fish and Wildlife Conservation Commission. *The Great Florida Birding Trail: East, West, Panhandle, South Sections.*

George, Jean Craighead. *Everglades Wildguide*. National Park Service Division of Publications, 1988.

Greenlaw, Jon S. Secretary's Reports of the Florida Ornithological Society Records Committee (2005). Available online at www.fosbirds.org/RecordCommittee/FOSRCReports.htm.

Hammer, Roger L. *A FalconGuide to Everglades National Park and the Surrounding Area.* Guilford, Conn.: The Globe Pequot Press, 2005

Hernando Audubon Society. *Birding Sites in Hernando County.* 1995.

Juniper, Tony, and Mike Parr. *Parrots: A Guide to Parrots of the World.* New Haven, Conn.: Yale University Press, 1998.

Kale, Herbert W., Bill Pranty, B. M. Stith, and C. W. Biggs. *The Atlas of the Breeding Birds of Florida.* Florida Fish and Wildlife Conservation Commission, 1992. Available online at http://myfwc.com/bba/.

Maehr, David S., and Herbert W. Kale II. *Florida's Birds: A Field Guide and Reference.* Sarasota: Pineapple Press, Inc., 2005.

Myers, Ronald L., and John J. Ewel. *Ecosystems of Florida.* Orlando: University of Central Florida Press, 1990.

National Audubon Society. The Christmas Bird Count database, 2005. Available online at www.audubon.org/bird/cbc.

National Geographic Society. *Field Guide to the Birds of North America, Third Edition.* 1999.

Nelson, Gil. *The Shrubs and Woody Vines of Florida.* Sarasota: Pineapple Press, Inc., 1996.

O'Keefe, M. Timothy. *Hiking Florida.* Guilford, Conn.: The Globe Pequot Press, 2007.

Pearlstine, Elise V., Frank J. Mazzotti, Kenneth G. Rice, and Anna Liner. "Bird Observations in Five Agricultural Field Types of the Everglades Agricultural Area in Summer and Fall," *Florida Field Naturalist, Vol. 32, No. 3* (2004).

Pranty, Bill. *A Birder's Guide to Florida.* Colorado Springs: American Birding Association, Inc., 2005.

Pranty, Bill. Field Observations spring report, March–May 2005, *Florida Field Naturalist, Vol. 33, No. 4,* Florida Ornithological Society (2005).

Pranty, Bill, Andrew Kratter, and Reed Bowman. Records of the Bullock's Oriole in Florida, *Florida Field Naturalist, Vol. 33, No. 2* (2005).

Pranty, Bill, and Helen W. Lovell. "Population Increase and Range Expansion of Black-hooded Parakeets in Florida," *Florida Field Naturalist, Vol. 32, No. 4* (2004).

Pranty, Bill, Donald J. Robinson, Mary Barnwell, Clay Black, and Ken Tracey. "Discovery and Habitat Use of Black Rails along the Central Florida Gulf Coast," *Florida Field Naturalist, Vol. 32, No. 2* (2004).

Pranty, Bill, Kirt A. Radamaker, and Gregory Kennedy. *Birds of Florida.* Lone Pine Publishing International, 2006.

Radamaker, Kurt, and Cindy Radamaker. "A Recent Record of the Kirtland's Warbler in Florida," *Florida Field Naturalist, Vol. 30, No. 3* (2002).

Raffaele, Herbert, James Wiley, Orlando Garrido, Allan Keith, and Janis Raffaele. *A Guide to the Birds of the West Indies.* Princeton, N.J.: Princeton University Press, 1998.

Riley, Laura, and William Riley. *Guide to the National Wildlife Refuges.* New York: Collier Books, 1992.

Robertson, William B. Jr., and Glen E. Woolfenden. *Florida Bird Species: An Annotated List.* Orlando: Florida Ornithological Society, 1992.

Sarasota Audubon Society, Manatee County Audubon Society, Venice Area Audubon Society. *Birding Hotspots in Sarasota and Manatee Counties.* 1998.

Sibley, David Allen. *The Sibley Guide to Birds.* New York: Alfred A. Knopf, Inc., 2000.

Stevenson, Henry M., and Bruce H. Anderson. *The Birdlife of Florida.* Gainesville: University Press of Florida, 1994.

Tennant, Alan. *Snakes of Florida.* Boulder, Colo.: Taylor Trade Publishing, 2003.

Wilmers, Thomas J. "First Record of the Zone-tailed Hawk in Florida," *Florida Field Naturalist, Vol. 33, No. 2* (2005).

Woolfenden, Glen E., and Richard C. Banks. "A Specimen of the Varied Thrush from Florida," *Florida Field Naturalist, Vol. 32, No. 2* (2004).

Woolfenden, Glen E., and Jon S. Greenlaw. "Specimen Evidence for the Occurrence of Both Gray-cheeked and Bicknell's Thrushes in Florida," *Florida Field Naturalist, Vol. 33, No. 3* (2005).

Woolfenden, Glen E., and Michelle van Deventer. "First Record of the Varied Bunting from Florida," *Florida Field Naturalist, Vol. 34, No. 1* (2006).

Index

All bird species included in the text are listed below. With few exceptions, only site locations highlighted in bold in the text are listed below.

Dovekie, 9, 271
Dowitcher
    Long-billed, 6, 46, 50, 86, 88, 136, 153, 155,
        189, 190, 201, 241
    Short-billed, 6, 11, 26, 43, 46, 48, 50, 86, 88,
        135, 136, 142, 153, 160, 165, 241
Dry Tortugas National Park, 119–23
Duck
    American Black, 6, 39, 197, 200, 201, 270
    Harlequin, 270
    Long-tailed, 25, 43, 174, 184, 200, 202, 207,
        222, 226
    Masked, 8, 46, 49, 87, 95, 270
    Mottled, 4, 12, 39, 40, 43, 46, 49, 52, 57, 73,
        74, 86, 88, 91, 95, 96, 136, 143, 145, 148,
        150, 153, 158, 160, 161, 162, 169, 190, 225
    Muscovy, 8, 14, 103, 104, 224
    Ring-necked, 6, 39, 43, 46, 49, 55, 86, 88,
        91, 104, 136, 150, 160, 162, 169, 180, 190,
        202, 215, 226
    Ruddy, 6, 39, 43, 46, 49, 91, 136, 190, 215,
        227
    Wood, 4, 12, 29, 39, 40, 46, 51, 53, 55, 57,
        58, 61, 68, 80, 83, 86, 88, 136, 145, 148,
        149, 150, 154, 156, 161, 168, 169, 173,
        176, 178, 179, 183, 185, 189, 190, 192,
        200, 202, 206, 224
Dunedin Hammock Park, 165, 166, 167
Dunlin, 6, 11, 26, 43, 50, 135, 142, 160, 165, 169,
    240
Dupuis Management Area, 77–78, 79

E

E. G. Simmons Park, 153, 154
Eagle
    Bald, 4, 11, 27, 29, 30, 33, 36, 39, 40, 43, 46,
        47, 49, 52, 53, 55, 56, 57, 58, 59, 61, 66,
        69, 70, 73, 74, 77, 78, 108, 116, 126, 127,
        129, 131, 132, 135, 137, 146, 147, 149–50,
        153, 154, 160, 161, 166, 168, 169, 172,
        173, 180, 181, 184, 185, 187, 189, 190,
        197, 201, 202, 203, 210, 214, 216, 234
    Golden, 271
Eagle Lakes Community Park, 136–37
Econfina State Park, 197–98
Egan's Creek Greenway, 25
Eglin Air Force Base, 219, 220
Egret
    Cattle, 5, 14, 49, 121, 231
    Great, 5, 11, 49, 135, 231
    Reddish, 4, 11, 25, 31, 32, 33, 36, 43, 44, 45,
        48, 71, 73, 80, 113, 114, 115, 116, 127,
        135, 141, 142, 143, 144, 153, 159, 160,
        161, 162, 164, 165, 168, 172, 190, 197,
        202, 231
    Snowy, 5, 11, 49, 127, 135, 231
Eider
    Common, 48, 109, 270
    King, 270
Elinor Klapp-Phipps Park, 206, 207, 208

Emeralda Marsh Conservation Area, 178, 182
Everglades Agricultural Area, 84
Everglades and Frances S. Taylor Wildlife Man-
    agement Area, 129, 133
Everglades National Park, 123–28, 131, 132, 133

F

Fairchild Tropical Garden, 106, 107
Fakahatchee Strand Preserve State Park, 131–32,
    133
Falcon, Peregrine, 7, 26, 31, 33, 46, 50, 89, 100,
    101, 108, 116, 121, 127, 135, 136, 137, 142,
    160, 190, 213, 235
Fanning Springs State Park, 185, 186
Faulk Drive Landing, 207
Faver-Dykes State Park, 34
Fern Forest Nature Center, 91, 94
Finch
    House, 8, 93, 202, 204, 206, 269
    Purple, 6, 200, 202, 214, 269
Fisheating Creek Wildlife Management Area,
    65–66, 67
Flamingo, Greater, 5, 108, 126, 128, 183, 233
Flamingo (town), 127
Flicker, Northern, 5, 13, 46, 59, 69, 77, 124, 146,
    148, 181, 201, 206, 249
Florida Caverns State Park, 216, 217
Florida Keys Wild Bird Center, 113, 114, 115
Flycatcher
    Acadian, 5, 7, 13, 17, 28, 29, 46–47, 160,
        162, 170, 181, 184, 185, 188, 191, 192,
        195, 198, 200, 202, 203, 204, 209, 216, 250
    Alder, 104, 216, 250
    Ash-throated, 8, 52, 89, 179, 188, 203, 207,
        212, 272
    Brown-crested, 8, 52, 105, 110, 124, 125, 251
    Fork-tailed, 49, 51, 52, 87, 114, 122, 273
    Great Crested, 5, 12, 13, 14, 29, 38, 40, 46,
        59, 69, 86, 91, 93, 105, 113, 124, 126, 130,
        132, 138, 140, 145, 147, 149, 160, 164,
        174, 177, 180, 188, 189, 192, 194, 251
    Hammond's, 158, 272
    La Sagra's, 8, 16, 80, 87, 92, 100, 104, 105,
        109, 113, 118, 122, 272
    Least, 7, 52, 104, 216, 251
    Olive-sided, 100, 203, 250
    Piratic, 122, 273
    Scissor-tailed, 6, 52, 101, 109, 114, 118, 125,
        127, 136, 153, 159, 188, 203, 207, 212,
        222, 252
    Streaked, 212
    Sulphur-bellied, 44, 100, 104, 105, 110, 272
    Vermillion, 8, 52, 83, 109, 126, 195, 200,
        201, 203, 207, 251
    Willow, 104, 216, 250
    Yellow-bellied, 216, 250
Frank E. Mackle Jr. Community Park, 136, 137
Fred Gannon Rocky Bayou State Bayou,
    219, 220
Frenchman's Forest Natural Area, 80, 81

About the Author

Brian Rapoza is Field Trip Coordinator for Tropical Audubon Society in Miami and has led birding field trips throughout Florida. His Birding Recaps for the South Florida area are published regularly on the Tropical Audubon website and in its newsletter. He is compiler for the Miami and Coot Bay/Everglades National Park Christmas Bird Counts and for North American Migration Counts for Miami-Dade and Monroe Counties. He has traveled extensively throughout the state, tallying more than 400 bird species. As a science teacher for Miami-Dade County Public Schools since 1988, he has led thousands of school children on bird watching expeditions through Everglades National Park and other Miami-area birding destinations. He is a returned Peace Corps Volunteer, having served in the Philippines from 1983 to 1985 and is past president of the Returned Peace Corps Volunteers of South Florida. Brian is originally from New Bedford, Massachusetts and graduated from the University of Massachusetts in 1980 with a Bachelor of Science degree in marine biology.